13/01/2003

To Neil with all our love
Mum & Lynn   xxxx

TO THE ENDS OF THE EARTH

TO THE ENDS OF THE EARTH

THE HISTORY OF POLAR EXLORATION   RICHARD SALE

Dedication

To Susan
For consistently tolerating my absence in the Arctic on her birthday, and allowing the Antarctic to routinely jeopardise Christmas.

Acknowledgements

I would like to thank the staff of libraries and museums, archives and galleries all over the world for their kind assistance in providing information and illustrations for this book.

I would like to thank Maria Gavrilo and Roald Potapov in St Petersburg for their kind hospitality and assistance, and Eugene Potapov in the UK for his help with my very poor Russian. Thanks are also due to library, gallery and museum staffs too numerous to mention individually in cities throughout Austria, Australia, Canada, Denmark, Holland, Iceland, New Zealand, Norway, Russia, Sweden, the UK and the USA. Particular thanks are also due to Alyson and Ian Morris and Chris Bartle in the UK for their continuous assistance.

Equally importantly I would like to thank those who have made journeys to the Arctic and Antarctic so rewarding over the years: Harriet Backer, Susan Barr, Roger Francis, Chris Hamm and Nathan Sale. And most particularly Per Michelsen and Tony Oliver for their consistent companionship.

Finally I would like to thank Quark Expeditions (and Debra Taylor in particular) for their help in getting me to a few of the more remote sites in the southern hemisphere and the North-West Passage.

HarperCollinsPublishers
77-85 Fulham Palace Road
London
W6 8JB

The Harper Collins website address is:
www.fireandwater.com

10 9 8 7 6 5 4 3 2 1

08 07 06 05 04 03 02

First published 2002

© 2002 Richard Sale

ISBN 0 00 711124 X

Edited and designed by Blackingstone Books
Colour origination by Colourscan, Singapore
Printed and bound by Printing Express Ltd. Hong Kong

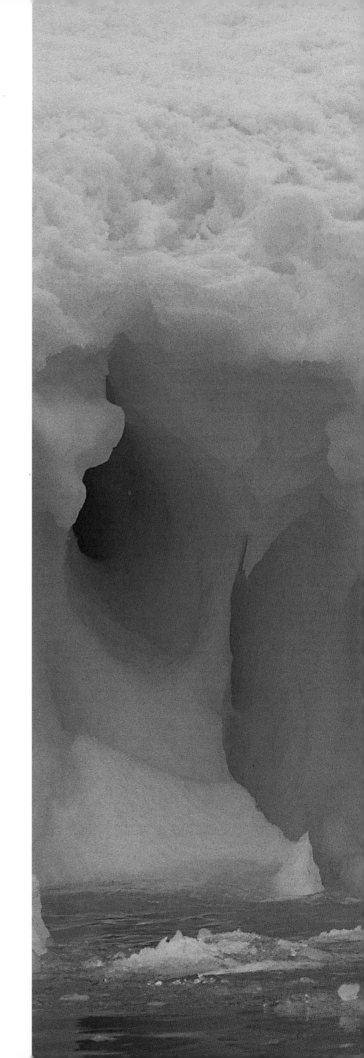

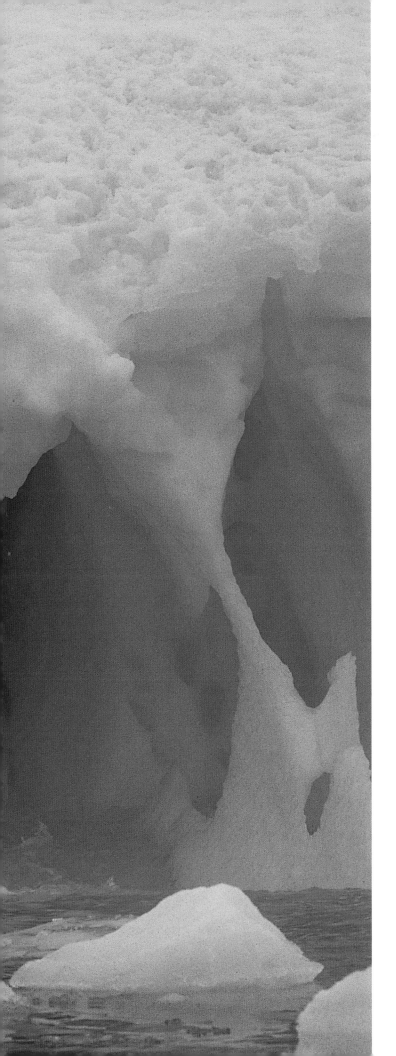

CONTENTS

Introduction   6

The Arctic   12

Before the heroes came   12

Passages to Cathay   19

Explorers in the west   75

Explorers in the east   100

Striving for the pole   106

Antarctica   146

Before the heroes came   146

Hunters in the south   152

Science heads south   157

Striving for the pole   169

Selected bibliography   220

Index   223

Half title page top **Iceberg, Antarctica**
Half title page below **Midnight sun, Barrow Strait and Cornwallis Island**
Title page **Paradise Bay, Antarctica**
Left **Iceberg detail, Antarctica**
Richard Sale

Introduction

'People, perhaps, still exist who believe that it is of no importance to explore the unknown polar regions. This, of course, shows ignorance. It is hardly necessary to mention here of what scientific importance it is that these regions should be thoroughly explored. The history of the human race is a continual struggle from darkness towards light. It is, therefore, to no purpose to discuss the use of knowledge: man wants to know, and when he ceases to do so, he is no longer man.'

Fridtjof Nansen

The men who sailed the tiny wooden ships that explored the oceans of the medieval world faced cruelties almost beyond imagining. From harbour mouth to home again the ships were rarely still, their decks frequently washed by the waves. The sailors were constantly exposed to the elements, trimming sails and minding the wheel, tasks that could not wait for an improvement in conditions. Their clothes, usually inadequate rags, were invariably sodden. When they could retreat below decks they added their dampness to cramped living quarters that could be oven-hot in the tropics, perishing cold in high latitudes, and always squalid.

If they survived the storms (and many did not), or the ever-present risk of the tarred wood of the ship being rapidly consumed by flames from the cooking fire, they could succumb to starvation, thirst, disease or injury. Food could only be preserved by salting, a process that delayed, but could not eliminate, putrefaction. Anywhere a man could survive, fungus, mildew, cockroaches and rats could too, and usually much better. Four hundred years after the first ocean explorations those searching for John Franklin noted their provisions were 'discoloured, stinking and unfit' and had to be destroyed. One man wrote of the crossing of the Pacific on Magellan's round-the-world trip that 'we ate only old biscuit turned to powder, all full of worms and stinking of rat urine'. In the dark crevices of the ship the rats fed and bred, their populations reaching prodigious numbers. On Ellsworth's 1934 voyage home from Antarctica the rats killed and ate the ship's cat. Elisha Kent Kane, the American Arctic explorer, wrote that if he were asked 'the three besetting curses of our Arctic sojourn, I should say RATS, RATS, RATS'. The rats carried leptospirosis and Weil's disease, salmonella, even plague.

And even without rats to infect the food and weaken the men through ill health, there was scurvy, which required no infestation or degradation of the food, but merely the absence of vitamin C. The disease's name derives from the Old English word for gnawing or shredding, a word which also meant contemptible or disgusting. All are descriptions which apply well to a disease which causes the gums to grow black and shrink until the teeth fall out, the skin to become covered with livid blotches, limbs to swell and joints to hurt. Scurvy caused old wounds to open and new areas to fail to heal, and there were few sailors who did not have an old wound, or several, for these were belligerent times and naval discipline was harsh. Without vitamin C scurvy is remorseless, and the bloated patient becomes covered in ulcers which ooze pus and blood. Gnawing and shredding, contemptible and disgusting. Secondary infections are likely, death inevitable.

Scurvy afflicted mariners for centuries. Long before the cause was established (memorably Edward Wilson on Scott's Discovery Expedition claimed that the clear symptoms of scurvy in the men were actually caused not by the disease, but by tobacco and the constant use of foul language) remedies were available: lime juice, fresh meat and vegetables. But the effectiveness of the former decreased with storage time (a fact not

Above **The *Endurance* in the Weddell Sea during Shackleton's most famous expedition. This shot, by Frank Hurley, was taken on a Paget plate, an early form of colour photography (see page 199).**
Mitchell Library, State Library of New South Wales, Australia

Below **The *Hecla* and *Fury* in winter quarters at Igloolik. The engraving illustrates that the British made considerable efforts to keep their sailors exercised and happy during the winter. During** Barents' expedition to Arctic Russia his men played golf, rather than the cricket the British clearly preferred. The line joining the ships across the snow bollards was to prevent men crossing between them becoming lost in winter's darkness, and was a feature of most expeditions. Illustrations from Nordenskiöld's book on his first transit of the North-East Passage show a similar arrangement linking the ship to the shore camp.
From William Edward Parry *Journal of a Second Voyage.*
Richard Sale Collection

Left **Sno-Cat A for Able crossing a crevasse on aluminium bridging during the TransAntarctic crossing of Sir Vivian Fuchs.**
Canterbury Museum, New Zealand

Below **The critical position of HMS *Investigator* on the north coast of Baring Island. This is one of a series of sketches by S. Gurney Cresswell, an officer on Robert McClure's ship, one of the Franklin search vessels. Baring Island is now known as Banks Island.**
Richard Sale Collection

understood at first), while supplies of the latter two could not be guaranteed. Ironically, as food ran short men were often forced to eat the rats that caused the shortage, so acquiring fresh meat. With the modern understanding of diet it is often assumed that scurvy was beaten centuries ago, but it probably contributed to the loss of Scott's South Pole team.

Water, too, was a problem, as a man dies quickly of thirst, only slowly of starvation. If a ship were becalmed water could run short and supplies often became brackish or stagnant. On Magellan's Pacific crossing the same informant noted that the water was 'impure and yellow'; it is not hard to imagine the source of the impurities and colour, and the likely effect on debilitated men.

Added to this list of known objective dangers were the subjective ones of loneliness and homesickness and, more importantly because it represented a collective dread, the fear of the unknown. It is fact, not myth, that the outer edges of ancient maps were inscribed 'here be monsters'. Hugeness is terrifying, ugliness is evil incarnate, so it is no surprise that unknown waters and lands were thought to be the home of monsters. And, often, what the mariners did find – whales, sharks, even turtles and sea snakes – were vast beyond their knowledge or understanding, and anything so monstrous could hardly be a portent of good: around the next cape, over the next wave, lurked Leviathan.

So why did they come, these brave frail men? It is usually said that the driving force was greed, a desire to find new lands to exploit, but a glance at history shows that to be too glib an answer. Before Europeans set out on their journeys of exploration the Chinese had reached India, Persia and east Africa, and the Arabs had sailed their dhows the opposite way. Yet neither contemplated the possibility of exploring further. It is true that developments in Europe – the stern rudder instead of the side-oar, lateen and square sails, better navigational instruments – allowed ships to sail ocean rather than coastal waters, but these inventions were driven by a need to innovate.

Geographically the Portuguese were the best placed of the Europeans for ocean voyages, their kingdom having a long Atlantic coast. In Dom Enrique (Henry the Navigator) they also had a prince who was interested in exploration, for a variety of reasons. One was undoubtedly economic: the fall of Byzantium to the Ottoman Turks had made trade with the east more difficult and so more expensive. But there was also the possibility of reducing the size and influence of the Muslim world.

The Christians had finally expelled the Muslims from Iberia, and the Portuguese were certainly interested in the possibility of outflanking the Turks. They were also intent on making contact with the legendary Christian Kingdom of Prester John so that the Muslim world might be encircled. The development of ships and the need and desire for exploration coincided with the invention of the printing press and the Renaissance. The former allowed mass communication, which further stimulated minds made fertile by the latter. The Portuguese, and later the other European nations, explored because they wanted to know.

This desire to know led to the discovery of Antarctica, the exploration of the North-West Passage and the journeys to the poles. In each case many of the pioneering voyages were made by the British. Though the search for the North-West Passage started with the Elizabethan privateer Martin Frobisher, the Golden Age of the search was the first half of the 19th century. This coincided with the end of the Napoleonic Wars, during which the society folk of Britain had been unable to travel to the Continent and had contented themselves with home-grown attractions such as the Tour of the River Wye where they sought the Picturesque, views of the natural world which could be admired and sketched. Gentle scenery was favoured, the wilder country of the English Lake District being seen as 'too horrid' to contemplate: it is claimed that some travellers drew the blinds of their carriages as they posted through the mountains, so fearful were they of the prospect. These notions passed easily to the Arctic: John Franklin's books on his land expeditions to the Mackenzie and Coppermine Rivers are full of romantic descriptions of the landscape and the horrors of the journey; it is no surprise that when Mary Shelley needed to exile to his doom the monster created by Baron Frankenstein she took him to the Arctic and its dreadful icy wastes. Romanticism and dread were also to condition later British expeditions.

The voyages in search of the North-West Passage, and then in search of Franklin's last expedition, also established the fact that the polar winter could be survived. Though scurvy was an issue and the problems of condensation and, therefore, ice in the ships made the winter a trial, the British proved that the polar winter could be tolerated rather than endured at some risk, the position which had prevailed during earlier attempts. This owed a great deal to the lessons learned earlier in the Royal Navy (who supplied the crews for the passage and pole attempts), lessons which were contemptuously dismissed or humorously reported (depending on the speaker) as 'rum, bum and concertina'. Given enough drink and entertainment, and a willingness to turn a blind eye to below-decks activity, a peaceful, if not necessarily wholly contented, atmosphere prevailed.

Franklin's expeditions were made before the Golden Age of polar exploration, the time when the North-West Passage was finally traversed and the South and North Poles reached ('perhaps reached' in the case of the North). By then the British Empire had expanded to include a significant proportion of the earth, and the British attitude towards polar travel reflected the national mood (or, at least, that of those who ran the country). Britain was then the world's most powerful nation and reacted petulantly when its view of the way things should be was challenged. When other nations began to take an interest in Antarctica the Marquis of Lothian spoke for the establishment élite as a whole when he said 'I should not like to see foreign names upon that hemisphere where all civilised points are inhabited by our countrymen and belong to this country', relegating at a stroke all the non-British countries of the southern half of the world to the league of uncivilised nations.

Yet for all the pomposity and arrogance of the British establishment the men at the sharp end exhibited a tenacity and spirit that was admirable. They sought to do great things, to establish British indomitability. Shackled by the amateurism of their leaders they were doomed to suffer and, often, fail, but there was something noble about their efforts. Scott's decision to use ponies and his failure to learn how to use dogs or skis was ludicrous, but reflected his superiors' view that 'derring-do will see us through' and that the British way – whatever it was – was innately superior. After Amundsen had beaten Scott to the South Pole, Helmer Hanssen, one of Amundsen's team, said of Scott that no one would ever do it that way (by manhauling) again. Ironically, anyone using a method other than manhauling (perhaps with sail assistance) to reach either pole today would be considered to be operating outside the unwritten laws of modern polar trekking.

The Americans were latecomers to polar exploration. Their early expeditions included dramatic and agonising failures that mirrored the reckless enthusiasm of youth. Later, a nation whose ethos was (and is) based on rewards and glory being heaped on winners might almost be expected to have generated a debate such as that between Peary and Cook, the fact that neither might have actually reached the pole in 1909 reinforcing the point. That is unfair, as the debate (which went beyond normal argument into the realms of vindictiveness) and the rival claims seem to have been fuelled as much by personal animosity as by the facts; but the probable deception involved in Byrd's North Pole flight in 1933 makes the point again.

By contrast to the British and the Americans, the Norwegians, the third nation associated with the Golden Age of polar exploration, went about their expedition business in a methodical, professional way. Though their greatest men, Nansen and Amundsen, were not free of personal ambition, their expeditions were smaller and more democratic. When the *Terra Nova* met the *Fram* in the Bay of Whales the men of Scott's expedition were astonished to discover that the latter had individual cabins rather then separate quarters for officers and men. The Norwegians, on the verge of independence on Nansen's trips, newly independent on Amundsen's, were expressing that freedom by acting as a tightly knit group of friends.

But even as expeditions reflected national identities or moods, individual explorers can be glimpsed through society's veneer. What were these men like? Shackleton said that a polar explorer needed optimism, patience and physical strength. The great explorers had these three qualities in abundance, but it is neither a prerequisite nor a logical outcome of them that an explorer should be any less ambitious or greedy, or should not possess any other vices of ordinary men. Interestingly Shackleton's list does not include courage, which would seem, to ordinary mortals, to be a fundamental requirement. He did mention it, but thought it less important. Neither did he mention luck, which would also seem to have played a part in some of the most famous expeditions where men trod a thin line between success and failure. Shackleton almost died getting to within 160km (100 miles) of the South Pole, and probably would have done if the weather had been just a little worse. Nansen survived bear and walrus attacks on his trip from the *Fram*, but only just; and might not have survived at all had it not been for the chance meeting with Jackson. Many of the great stories of polar exploration involve survival against the odds, making heroes only of those that return.

It was the method of that survival that was the fascination because it explored the disputed borderline between life and death. Valerian Albanov, one of just two who survived the *Saint Anna* disaster in the Kara

Sea, spoke of how, with their ship frozen in the ice, the crew wrote letters to those who lived in the present while they, the writers, lived only in the past – before the ship was entombed – or the future, when life would start again. Only survivors have that future in which to tell their stories. At a bleak moment Albanov regrets that no one will know how he died. Perhaps some of the greatest polar stories are those untold and beyond telling, the heroism of men who did not survive, but died experiencing unimaginable horrors and terrors in a lonely, remorseless land.

Many of the men who went to the polar regions would have done so even if they had known the details of those desperate deaths, because they were driven by some inner demons. Their exploits were a vicarious thrill for the newspaper readers at the turn of the 20th century. In the main those people led static, humdrum lives, while the explorers pushed the boundaries of existance at the edge of the known world. Small wonder their exploits could fill the front pages for days on end. Today's reader is better travelled, and film and television have made the exotic commonplace. There are more diversions and so the exploits of the modern polar traveller – driven by the same demons – have been relegated to a few paragraphs on an inside page. Modern man – an adventurer rather than explorer as invariably he/she knows what to expect, geographically – has much warmer, lighter clothing, better equipment, a global positioning system that requires no knowledge of navigation, and a radio to summon instant rescue or transport. He is flown to the start, flown back from the endpoint. It is a more sanitised adventure and, since it can be tried by anyone who has both the inclination and, more importantly, the money, it is more commonplace.

That is why the old explorers still command the greater coverage. Then if a man wanted to reach a pole he first sailed his ship across treacherous waters – a journey which took weeks, not the few hours of a plane ride. He had to overwinter as he could not reach his start point in time to trek the same year. He had to lay depots because his food was heavy and cumbersome, and he had to come back – no pole pick-up by ski plane. He was out of contact with his base for weeks at a time, giving his trip an imperative which is now largely lacking. The explorer can still die, but whereas safe return was once doubtful it is now highly probable.

Yet for all that, those pushing back the frontiers of the possible – Ousland, Gjeldnes, Larsen, Kagge, Dupre, Hoeschler – are from the some mould as Nansen, Amundsen and Shackleton, and it is likely that the polar regions will continue to attract such men.

The air tractor used during Mawson's Australasian Antarctic Expedition of 1911–14. The plane had crashed on its trial flight in Australia and, with its wings removed, was to be used to haul loads. It was not a startling success.
University of Adelaide, South Australia

The Arctic

Before the heroes came

From the first time man began to consider the night sky of the northern hemisphere, he probably realised that the stars circled one fixed star, and that while some stars rose and set others were visible at all times. This fact was first set down by the Chaldeans, who inhabited the south-eastern part of Babylonia – now southern Iraq – over 5,000 years ago. The Greeks realised that the further north the observer travelled the greater was the number of stars that were always visible. For observers in Greece itself, the circle in the heavens which defined the boundary between stars which were always visible, and those that rose and set, passed through the constellation of Arktos, the Great Bear. The Greeks therefore referred to this circle as the Bear's Circle, the Arctic Circle. The fact that the circle enclosing always-visible stars grew bigger as the observer went north meant that the earth was a sphere, that it rotated and that there was a northern pole to its axis of rotation. The Greeks understood this (in principal) but the information was lost in Dark Age Europe and took many centuries to retrieve. What was not lost was the name Arctic.

In the last third of the 4th century BC, perhaps about 330BC, when Aristotle was teaching at his school in Athens and his former pupil Alexander the Great was campaigning in India, a Greek named Pytheas set sail from Massalia (now Marseille), a trading port on the Mediterranean coast to the west of Italy. Pytheas was a gifted astronomer who had worked out the method of calculating latitude by measuring the shadow cast by a vertical pillar at a solstice. He probably wanted to travel north to confirm his method, perhaps even to reach the pole, which would have given him an exact fix. He may also have been an adventurer who wanted to visit Ultima Thule, the land where the sun neither set in summer nor rose in winter, word of which had reached Greece through traders. But it is likely that those who financed Pytheas' voyage were merchants who wanted more direct access to the tin and amber of northern Europe, goods which then reached the Mediterranean by land and river, and whose trade was controlled by others.

Pytheas sailed through the Gibraltar Straits and turned north. As far as Brittany he was probably following a known, if not well known, route, as it is thought that as early as 500BC the Carthaginian Himilco had reached the tin-mining area around Quiberon. Beyond that Pytheas was crossing waters unknown to the Greeks. He was away six years and exactly where he went has been the subject of debate ever since. Later Greeks and Romans who had access to his account dismissed Pytheas as a fraud, but modern experts are more sympathetic. It is likely that he followed the coast to the western tip of Brittany, then crossed to Britain; Cornwall, due north of Brittany, being another tin-producing area. Pytheas continued north, sailing around Britain to reach Orcas (probably the Orkneys, but some have suggested the Shetland Isles), then continued north again, sailing for six days to reach 'Thule' where the summer day was 21 or 22 hours long (too long for the Shetlands, thought by some to be the location of Thule). In Thule Pytheas heard that north again the sea stiffened or congealed. Some have suggested that he reached Iceland, but his Thule was inhabited and Iceland certainly was not at that time: Iceland is also further than six days' sail from Scotland. It is likely that Pytheas had actually reached Norway, a remarkable achievement, but one that so outpaced the understanding of the day that it was dismissed for almost 1,000 years.

Early Arctic dwellers

Of course, whether Pytheas' journey was real or fable, whether his Thule was Norway or the Shetlands, it was a voyage to a world which was already inhabited. Norway had been settled by Germanic tribes moving north, folk who eventually met and pushed north a people who were already living there. These were the Saami (the now-preferred name for an ethnic group formerly called Lapps) who herded their reindeer across the vast taiga (coniferous forest) and tundra of northern Scandinavia and western Russia. Like the Finns, the Saami had originated beyond the Urals, in the steppes of central Asia. As the ice sheets of the last Ice Age retreated the dwellers on the steppes had moved north behind them. At first the populations of the Arctic coast and the steppe could maintain contact, but ultimately the spread of the larch forests which now dominate Siberia isolated the tribes of the north, forcing them to take a different evolutionary path. The isolation created by the forest also allowed the gyr falcon, the world's largest falcon and the avian symbol

Above **Summer tents at Ammassalik in east Greenland. Photograph by Th N. Krabbe in September 1908.**
Courtesy of the National Museum of Denmark, Department of Ethnography

Above **A reconstructed Inuit winter house at Resolute, Cornwallis Island, northern Canada. Animal skins were stretched over the bone framework as for the summer house. The houses were partially subterranean, the entrance crawl being lower than the house floor level to create a cold-air trap. The Inuit slept on the raised platform beneath which their few possessions would be stored.**
Richard Sale

Above **Ancient tent ring on Ellesmere Island. Summer tents used skins stretched over a framework and held down with a ring of stones.**
Richard Sale

of the high Arctic, to develop differences from its genetically almost identical cousin, the saker falcon of the Mongolian steppes. As with the humans of the Arctic and those of the temperate zone, the gyr and saker falcons can still cross-breed.

In 1947, while inspecting a mammoth graveyard at 71°N near the headwaters of the Berelekh River (on the Siberian mainland due south of the New Siberian Islands) Russian scientists found evidence of human habitation dating to perhaps 10,000 years BC, the oldest remains so far discovered north of the Arctic Circle. Sporadic finds from later periods indicate that these early Arctic dwellers were flint-using hunters who preyed on the mammoths and other animals which had migrated north as the climate warmed. Little is known of these folk, man emerging from the frosty mists of northern time only about 4,500 years ago. By then people with the generic name Palaeo-Eskimo were found all around the Arctic rim. They had crossed the land bridge which then existed between Asia and Alaska – though even without this the Bering Straits represented little barrier to a sea-hunting people – and the Nares Strait between Canada and Greenland which regularly froze in winter. Evidence of the earliest cultures – called Arctic Small Tool tradition from the size of the stone implements used – comes from sites as remote as Wrangel Island off eastern Siberia and Independence Fjord in Greenland's Peary Land. Depending on where these nomadic peoples lived they hunted sea mammals – seals, walrus, perhaps even whales – or land mammals, reindeer/caribou and musk oxen. They also hunted birds and polar bears.

About 2,500 years ago the Arctic became colder. The distribution of animals altered, necessitating changes in the peoples dependent on them. In the eastern Arctic a new tradition arose, known as Dorset Culture from its first identification near Cape Dorset on Baffin Island. The Dorset people hunted sea mammals, certainly whales as large as narwhal and beluga, almost exclusively. For this they used kayaks (from the Inuit *qajaq*) made by stretching animal skins over a simple wooden framework, a vessel which was light enough to carry and could be rolled if it capsized. They used tents made of animal skins stretched over driftwood or bone frames – the skins held down by a circle of stones – in summer, capable of rapid erection and packing. In winter the Dorset folk had fixed houses of stone and turf, again with roofs of frames and skins, heated and lit by burning blubber oil in soapstone heaters/lamps. They also cooked over blubber, the use of oil an indication of their efficiency in killing whales, seals and walrus. The Dorset folk could also build houses of snow (the word 'igloo' simply means house, its use to solely describe a hemispherical building of snow blocks being a modern, romantic idea). They had knives to cut snow blocks, harpoons, and crampons for moving on ice. They made carvings in ivory and soapstone. They also had an animalistic belief system which revolved around a shaman, a witch doctor/holy man who could bridge the gap to the spirit world. The Dorset Culture lasted 2,000 years before being replaced by a new tradition, the Thule People.

The origins of the Thule People are still debated. The conventional wisdom is that they developed on the east Siberian/west Alaskan coast and spread west in about the 11th century AD, though perhaps two centuries later, replacing or subsuming a people they called the Tunit (now thought to have been the Dorset Culture folk). It is conjectured that their westward expansion was driven by the search for the origins of the iron technology which the Norsemen had brought to Greenland, iron weapons and tools having been traded eastwards across the Arctic. The alternative view (strongly held by its proponents, but dismissed by mainstream historians) is that the Thule People originated in Greenland and were, in fact, the result of interbreeding between Norsemen left behind when the Greenland settlements were abandoned, and Dorset folk. That Norsemen who expanded into the Arctic possessed iron technology is indisputable. It is also true that the present-day Inuit (a short, stocky people) have legends of the Tunit that speak of their height and physical strength, a description which fits the Norsemen well.

Whatever the origins of the Thule People – and absorption of a limited number of Norse settlers would mean that their size would be lost over generations, only their technology prevailing – they, or their culture, spread rapidly across the Arctic to become the forerunners of the modern Inuit. Inuit, meaning simply 'the people', is now the preferred term for the indigenous Arctic people, Eskimo – which derives from the Athabascan 'eater of raw meat' – now being considered derogatory. Inuit is plural, a single person being an Inuk.

The Inuit still used tents for summer expeditions and stone and turf winter houses, with windows made of seal gut. They wore skin clothing and used skin bedding. The sealskin for their clothes and *kamiks* (waterproof boots that were ideal for use in kayaks) was prepared by scraping off the blubber, then sealing the skin in old urine until it became pliable enough to be stretched. This preparation, and the manufacture of clothes and kamiks, was women's work. From their kayaks the Inuit hunted sea mammals using a harpoon with a barbed point that detached from the throwing handle, but remained attached by rope – usually walrus leather, the strength of which amazed early Europeans by being greater than that of their ropes – to a sealbladder float. The float prevented the animal diving: it was then overtaken by the kayaker and dispatched at short range with a spear. Interestingly, the introduction of the rifle to the Inuit was not wholly successful. A dead animal might sink out of sight, a wounded animal escape: by contrast the harpoon and float took hold of the prey. The Inuit also hunted whales, perhaps initially by harpooning those which had been trapped by sea ice during the early winter. The term *savssak* refers to this entrapment. The animals, forced to breath through a hole of diminishing size, were an easy target. Later the Inuit also hunted bowhead whales – vast, but slow-moving – a hunt which, controversially in view of bowhead numbers, still continues. On land they used sledges drawn by dogs (originally domesticated wolves) to hunt polar bear and other animals with bow and arrow. In addition to kayaks the Inuit also had the

Above **Umiak and kayaks at Ammassalik in east Greenland. Photograph by Th N. Krabbe in September 1904.**
Courtesy of the National Museum of Denmark,
Department of Ethnography

Right and below **Whale Alley originally consisted of about 60 bowhead whale skulls, mostly in groups of two and four, set upright, nose down, along the edge of the beach. There were also 'arches' of whale jawbones and curious structures of stone – stone rings and enclosures and well-formed meat stores. The skulls and jawbones were obviously brought to the site as no other bones have been found here. This remarkably impressive site is thought to be around 700 years old.**
Richard Sale

umiak or women's boat, a flat-bottomed boat, also made of skins over a wooden frame, rowed by two to six oars, depending on size. This was used to move the family between hunting grounds.

The Inuit cooked in soapstone, later iron, pots over a blubber-oil stove. But despite the apparent integration of the Inuit to the Arctic theirs was a precarious life. Failure of the caribou or whales to migrate along a normal route could mean starvation, as could a bad run of luck for a hunter. The Inuit were subsistence hunters, a fact which led to misunderstandings and appalling accusations at the time of Franklin's disappearance. The insecure nature of their lives coloured the rest of the world's perception of them. Shamanism envisaged all living creatures as having both human and animal, and spiritual and physical, qualities, a view reflected in their art in which humans and animals frequently transpose. The *angakok*, or shaman, was the man most able or most in tune with nature, a bridge between the real and spirit worlds, frequently taking the falcon or polar bear as his 'familiar'; the former because it was thought to be able to fly to heaven, the latter because it was feared and admired for its strength and hunting skills. The shaman would communicate with the spirit world, usually during a trance, in an attempt to promote successful hunting. This practice did not require fixed 'temples', though a remarkable find was made on Yttygran Island off the Bering Sea shore of Siberia's Chukotka Peninsula where about 60 bowhead skulls had been arranged in groups, together with stone pits which held mummified whale and walrus meat, and a stone shrine.

Norsemen move west

It was the Inuit that the first Europeans met when they reached Greenland and northern Canada, but it must be remembered that the Inuit are not circumpolar. In Europe the original Arctic dwellers were the reindeer-herding Saami, while in Russia there are several groups, similar to the Saami, including the Nganasans of the Taimyr Peninsula and the Chukchi of the Chukotka Peninsula whose lifestyles also depended on hunting and herding reindeer. The Inuit are also themselves divided into sub-groups.

The first Europeans to meet the Inuit were Norsemen from Iceland. Norse Vikings settled on Iceland in about AD870, fleeing – it is said – from the tyranny of King Harald. But Iceland was not uninhabited, the southern coast being home to Irish monks who had probably arrived in *currachs* (cowhide boats) via the Faeroes a century or so earlier. These Irish monks have never been given the credit they deserve; many books on Iceland fail to note their pre-Viking settlement of the island, and other books on Arctic history ignore early journeys to the north. Abbot Brendon journeyed north of Iceland, meeting a 'floating crystal column' (an iceberg?) and seeing a 'smoking mountain rising from the sea' (Beerenberg on Jan Mayen?). On another journey north of Iceland a monk reached a place where the sea was frozen and, at midnight in summer, there was enough light 'to pick the lice off one's shirt'.

The Norse Vikings made journeys both north and west from Iceland. To the north they discovered Svalbard, meaning cold edge. For political reasons the Norwegians have claimed that this was the Svalbard archipelago, but most experts believe it was north-east Greenland. To the west they certainly saw the east coast of Greenland, Norsemen being blown off route and discovering a land of mountains at the end of the 9th century. The first landing on Greenland was by Eirik the Red in AD982 following his banishment from Iceland for murder. Eirik spent three years in exile in the land to the west, unable to return to Norway from where he had already also been banished for murder. He returned with tales of the lush, green land (a truism for the coastal plain, though it is now usually stated that Eirik's name – Greenland – was a propaganda exercise) and persuaded many to return with him in 986. Of the 35 ships which set out, 21 turned back or were wrecked, 14 reaching the safety of the fjords near Julianhåb (Qaqortoq). More Icelanders arrived in 987, two settlements being established: Østerbygd – eastern settlement – at Qaqortoq, and Vesterbygd – western settlement – at Godthåb (Good Hope, now Nuuk). The ruins of Eirik's own settlement of Brattahlid – across the Tunulliarfik (Eiriksfjord) from Narsarsuaq – can still be seen.

In AD986 Bjarni Herjolfsson was blown off route while returning to Iceland from the Greenland settlements and saw land to the west. However, it was another 15 years before Liefur Eiriksson, son of Eirik the Red and the man who brought Christianity to Greenland, set out to explore this new land, having bought Bjarni's boat. This was the first of at least three (perhaps as many as six) 'Vinland' voyages. The Icelandic sagas suggest that the Vikings explored southern Baffin Island, the Labrador coast and Newfoundland (where the ruins of a winter camp at

Above **The ruins of Eirik the Red's settlement of Brattahlid across the fjord from Narsarsuaq, south-west Greenland.**
Richard Sale

Right **The page of Eirik the Red's *Saga* which deals with the settlement of Brattahlid.**
Stofnun Árna Magnússonar á Íslandi,
Reykjavik, Iceland

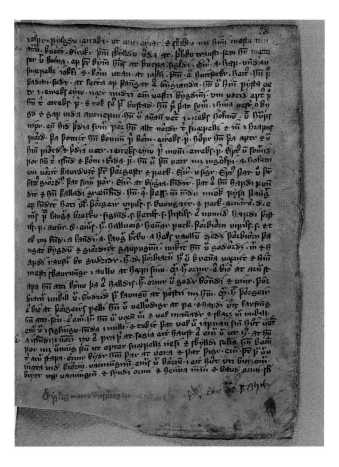

L'Anse aux Meadows is the only indisputable site so far discovered), and perhaps even the Cape Cod area of New England (if the vines of 'Vine-land' were really vines and not just berries). In the winter of 1002/3 Snorri Thorfinnsson was born in a Vinland winter camp, the first non-native American to have been born in the New World.

The Norsemen of Greenland certainly reached 73°N on the west coast, three cairns discovered north of Upernavik suggesting an overwintering. Inside one cairn a stone had been hidden: inscribed in runic it recorded the building of the cairns and the names of the builders. It is thought that the cairns date from the 14th century. Early in the next century the western settlement (which had a maximum population of 1,000 living in 90 farms, and four churches) disappeared. It is less clear when the eastern settlement (maximum population 2,000; 12 churches, a cathedral, a monastery and a nunnery) disappeared. The last known Bishop of Greenland died in 1377, and the last known ship to have sailed from Greenland left in 1410.

What happened to the Norse settlers is a mystery. The Norse certainly had contact with the Greenlandic Inuit: they called them *skrællinger*, possibly deriving from *skral*, small or weak, or from Karelia, a district of northern Finland/Russia whose native inhabitants were similarly short, stocky and dark. There were undoubtedly conflicts – Inuit legends recall skirmishes – but there was also trade and it is unlikely that the Inuit killed off the Norse. A change to a colder climate which made farming more difficult and animal husbandry marginal because of the lack of hay for winter fodder is more likely to have been the cause. The Greenlandic Norse supported 17 churches and two monastic houses, presumably with tithes. As agriculture failed life became untenable: those who could leave did, those who stayed probably died or were integrated into Inuit society. With the departure of the Norse the western Arctic was forgotten for a century or so, though a trade in the prized white gyr falcons continued and curiosities such as polar bears occasionally arrived in Europe. The other Arctic curio, the narwhal tusk, came a little later: a tusk was found on the shore of the Kara Sea in the mid-16th century. It was immediately thought to be from a unicorn and added impetus to the search for northern passages to

Above **Norse hood excavated at Herjolfsnœs, west Greenland.**
Courtesy of the National Museum of Denmark, Department of Ethnography

Right **This small soapstone statue was bought by the author from a Greenlandic carver who called it a 'Thuleman' and claimed it was an ancient design, a folk memory of the meeting of the Norsemen with the Inuit of north-west Greenland. The excitement this generated was somewhat tempered by other locals who claimed that the curious triangular head was modelled not on a Norse hood, but the parka hoods of US airmen who were stationed in north-west Greenland during the 1939–45 war!**
Richard Sale

the east, the merchants that sponsored them 'knowing that Unycorns are bredde in the landes of Cathaye, Chynayne and other Oriental Regions'.

But before the merchants sent vessels north another reason for heading that way arrived from a most unlikely source. The decree of the Catholic church that only 'cold' food could be eaten on Fridays had made fishermen wealthy, fish being considered cold as they lived in the cold sea. Cod, which when salted lasted a long time, was particularly prized. The Basques of the northern border country of Spain and France and the fishermen of Bristol, England, grew wealthy on cod. At first the Bristolians fished close to Iceland, but the Basque grounds were unknown, the Basques themselves too shrewd to reveal their secret. Eventually the Bristolians too found a new cod fishery. From it they returned with cod already salted, a procedure which required a land base. There is a legend in Bristol that

before his westward journey Columbus visited the city and spoke to fishermen who, unlike the Basques, did not keep quiet about their finds. It is also said that Bristolian merchants wrote to Columbus after his voyage, complaining that he was taking credit for discovering what was already known.

Following Columbus' discovery, under the terms of the Treaty of Tordesillas in 1494 the Pope granted the Spanish the western hemisphere and Portugal the eastern, a situation intolerable to the English, French and Dutch, as it made them the buyers of the spices and other treasures of the east rather than the merchants. Shortly after the signing of the treaty a man arrived in Bristol offering to lead an expedition to Cathay. The man was Giovanni Caboto. Can it be entirely a coincidence that Caboto, who, like Columbus, was born in Genoa and at about the same time, chose Bristol to approach?

Passages to Cathay

Early voyages

Giovanni Caboto, now the honorary Englishman John Cabot, was given Letters Patent by Henry VII to explore for new lands and a passage to Cathay. Cabot's licence stipulated that he was to give 20 per cent of all profits from the voyage to the king and that no one was to disembark on any land discovered without Crown permission. Cabot left Bristol on 20 May 1497 in the *Mathew* (more likely named for Mathye, his wife, then the disciple) with a crew of 18. On 24 June he landed in Newfoundland, just a short distance from L'Anse aux Meadows. Finding evidence of inhabitants and fearing confrontation because of his limited numbers, Cabot took on water and left, exploring the local coast before returning to Bristol. On the next voyage Cabot (now the Grand Admiral Cabot, England's answer to Admiral of the Ocean Columbus) sailed with five ships, one of which soon returned after being damaged in a gale. The fate of the rest is a mystery. Sebastian Cabot, John's son, claims to have been on this trip and gives a plausible account of crossing the Arctic Circle, encountering 'monstrous heaps of ice swimming in the sea', days 18 hours long, and the entrance to a gulf heading west where many men died of cold. Kind historians wonder if he had sailed into Davis Strait and found Hudson Strait. Less generous folk claim that as Sebastian was a known storyteller he may not even have been on the expedition. Certainly he sheds no light on the fate of his father.

True or false, Sebastian Cabot's hint that he knew the secret of the North-West Passage kept him comfortable for the rest of his life, firstly in the pay of the Spanish (despite a disastrous trip to South America when he should have been heading north), and then the English. The latter gave him the title Grand Pilot of England and a fat salary. Trading on his title Cabot, now an old man and not fit to travel, persuaded London merchants to back a venture to find the North-East Passage (a curious decision if he knew the secret of the north-western route) and organised the first expedition to head that way. In 1553 three ships set out, following in the wake of the Norseman Ottar who, legend has it, sailed as far as the White Sea in the 9th century. Separated by a storm off northern Norway one, the *Edward Bonaventure* under Richard Chancellor (who carried, as did the other captains, a letter signed by Edward VI beginning 'Kings, Princes and Potentates

Above **The Letters Patent to discover new lands granted to John Cabot by Henry VII. The Letters were the authorisation warrant for Cabot's first voyage.**
UK Public Records Office

inhabiting the North-east partes of the worlde...'), made it to Archangelsk (Archangel). Chancellor discovered to his amazement that this was not in Cathay but Muscovy (Russia). He was warmly welcomed by officials of Czar Ivan IV (the Terrible) and taken the 2,400km (1,500 miles) to Moscow by sledge. At the capital he was equally well received and negotiated an Anglo-Russian trade treaty that made the London merchants (who formed the Muscovy Company) rich. Sadly on the return trip to England his ship, now carrying a Russian ambassador (Ossip Nepeja, the first such ambassador to England) was wrecked off Scotland. Chancellor died saving Nepeja's life.

The other two ships of the expedition reached the

Kola Peninsula where they decided to overwinter. Ill-prepared for the Arctic winter and with scout parties failing to find locals to help, all 66 men of the two crews died, probably from a combination of cold and scurvy: their bodies were found by Russian fishermen the following spring. A legend soon sprang up that the English sailors had been frozen to death as they worked, the commander at his desk, pen in hand, others carrying plates or cups, or in the act of eating. This seems absurd now, but the Arctic was an unknown, fearful land in the early 16th century and such things seemed all too likely: this version of the death of the crews formed the basis of the tale of *The Flying Dutchman*. After the Russian discovery the two ships were sailed back to England: to complete the disaster they were both wrecked en route.

In 1556 the Muscovy Company, emboldened by their trade agreement, put the miseries of 1553 behind them and tried again, Stephen Burrough sailing the *Searchthrift* to the Kara Sea where his progress was blocked by ice. Burrough overwintered at Kholmogory and returned safely, his gloomy pronouncements stopping further attempts until 1580 when, shortly after Frobisher's attempt to go west, the company tried one more time, this time with two ships, Arthur Pet commanding the *George* and Charles Jackman the *William*. The ships carried a vast inventory of tradable goods and 'a large Mappe of London to make show of your Citie' in order to impress the natives of Cathay. The expedition reached the Kara Sea where Pet, faced with a dispiriting mix of ice and fog, turned back. The *William* was never seen again.

Frobisher and Davis sail west

When the English (properly the British after the Act of Union between England and Wales) next tried to reach Cathay they headed north-west again. The expedition's leader was Sir Martin Frobisher, a Yorkshire-born pirate and slave-trader who had won his knighthood (as had his contemporary Sir Francis Drake) by presenting Queen Elizabeth I with the looted treasure of Spanish galleons. Unfortunately Frobisher had followed up the raid which won him his knighthood with one on a French ship carrying wine for an English merchant. Had it been a Frenchman's wine the capture would have brought him loud applause, but as it was he was thrown

Left **Sir Martin Frobisher by Cornelis Ketel.**
Bodleian Library, University of Oxford, UK

in jail and lost his fortune. Needing to restore his position he persuaded Michael Lok (brother of a slaving captain Frobisher had sailed with) to finance a trip to Cathay. Frobisher left London in June 1576 with the queen's blessing, with three tiny ships on a journey 'for finding of the passage to Cataya beyng a matter in oure age above all other, noteable' (as George Best, Frobisher's lieutenant, noted in his book on the trip). One ship, so small it was manned by just four sailors, sank off Greenland's southern tip, a second turning for home (where the captain reported the loss of Frobisher and his ship, the *Gabriel*, a premature obituary). Frobisher continued, finding Baffin Island and entering the bay which now bears his name. He sailed along it, convinced that to his right was Asia, to his left America.

In the bay Frobisher recorded two firsts: the first encounter with the Inuit (since the Vikings), and the first account of that merciless tyrant of the Arctic, the mosquito. The Inuit have an expression for these insects which swarm each summer and make life a misery for animals and man alike – *sordlo pujok*, like smoke. Frobisher noted that the insect was like 'a small fly or gnat that stingeth and offendeth so fiercely that the place where they bite shortly after swelleth and itcheth very sore', as good, and still valid, a description as could be conjured. Frobisher's meetings with the Inuit were, at first, less aggravating, with an exchange of gifts and attempts at an exchange of language; but then five of his men went missing. This reduced him to a crew of just 13 and enraged him – had they mutinied or been captured? If the latter, would they be eaten by these natives who had been seen eating raw fish and raw seal? In the end the worried Frobisher took a hostage (and his kayak) and sailed for home. There, in damp, chilly, autumnal London, the Inuk died, probably of pneumonia.

Above **The battle with the Inuit on Frobisher's expedition, by John White. Little is known of Elizabethan artist White, but it is conjectured that he accompanied Frobisher on his second voyage. Circumstantial evidence is supported by the authenticity of the painting – the uniforms, the setting and the incident itself.**
The British Museum

Right **John White's is one of the first paintings of Inuit. In 1654 a superior painting by an unknown artist was made of four Inuit who were taken to Norway and Denmark by Captain David Dannel. The painting is now in the Danish National Museum.**
Photograph by John Lee. The National Museum of Denmark, Department of Ethnography

Frobisher had brought back a lump of black rock, so like coal that Michael Lok's wife threw it on her fire. To her amazement it glistened. Retrieved and tested, it was, said Lok, gold ore of astonishing concentration. Three official assayers dismissed it as pyrite – fool's gold – but a glib-tongued Venetian alchemist resident in London convinced Lok's business associates that it was the real thing. In 1577, carrying the hopes of the 'Company of Cathay', famed to exploit the source, Frobisher was back in Frobisher Bay. This time the meeting with the Inuit was less cordial. Frobisher found some items of clothing from the five missing men in an Inuit tent, rekindling his fears of abduction. In trying to grab a hostage he was shot in the backside with an arrow, the incident precipitating a battle in which five Inuit were killed and one sailor badly wounded. Ironically, in view of Frobisher's fear of Inuit cannibalism, wounded Inuit threw themselves into the sea as they were convinced the English sailors would eat them. Frobisher captured a man, woman and child, loaded 200 tons of ore into his ship and sailed for home. Back in London the male Inuk entertained the queen by killing swans from his kayak, but all three Inuit soon died of pneumonia.

Despite expert misgivings over the gold ore Queen Elizabeth was convinced and underwrote a huge expedition of 15 ships which sailed under Frobisher in May 1578. By error the fleet reached Hudson Strait where ice destroyed one ship (and another fled home), but eventually worked its way back to Frobisher Bay. There on an island still called Koblunarn (White Man's Island) Frobisher built a stone hut and began mining the 'gold' ore. He took back almost 2,000 tons, but all attempts by the London alchemists failed to turn it into anything valuable. Michael Lok's backers turned on him and he ended up in Fleet's debtors' jail. Frobisher joined his old colleague Drake in raids on the Spanish West Indies: he died in 1594 from wounds received in the taking of the Spanish fort at Brest in France.

The next to try his luck was John Davis, who in June 1585 sailed with the *Sunshine* and the *Moonshine*. It could be argued that the latter was aptly named as the Elizabethan mathematician/alchemist Dr John Dee had been involved in the early discussions on the voyage. Born in Beguildy, Radnorshire, the Welshman Ieuan Ddu had been a famous local wizard before his brilliance as a scholar took him to Cambridge University and made him tutor to Elizabeth I. His fame as an astrologer and necromancer are said to have made him the model for Shakespeare's Prospero. Dee's spirit-world contacts had told him of a river that split America, leading directly to Cathay, and this had been one of the principal reasons for Sir Humphrey Gilbert's disastrous attempts to create a settlement in Newfoundland. The spirits also

Above **'A wonder in the heavens and how we caught a bear'** by Levinus Hulsius in Gerrit de Veer's **The Three Voyages of Willem Barents. The wonder is a parhelion or sun dog caused by ice crystals in the atmosphere. The poor bear looks completely outnumbered.**
Richard Sale Collection

Left **At the western end of Frobisher Bay, near Iqaluit.**
Richard Sale

guided Dee to form an alliance with John Davis and Adrian Gilbert, Humphrey's brother, but Davis, a shrewd, sea-hardened man, may have seen through Dee's occult posturings because the astrologer seems to have departed the scene before the expedition set out. Perhaps he foresaw failure...

Davis reached the east coast of Greenland, but could not land because of glaciers and icebergs (where was he?), then rounded Kapp Farvel (Cape Farewell) and reached the less desolate fjords the Vikings had settled. Here he met Inuit, the meeting being a joy of trade and mutual kindness. Pushing on, Davis explored the strait which now bears his name as far north as the Arctic Circle, then explored Baffin Island's eastern coast, discovering Cumberland Sound. He returned to Britain convinced that a North-West Passage was a reality – it was just a question of locating the right channel.

Davis returned north in May 1586, this time with four ships, two of which explored Greenland's east coast while Davis took the other pair to the west coast where the sailors took on the locals at long jump (victory for Britain, but only because of persistent foul play). Relations turned sour when the Inuit began to steal anything of iron they could find, including the

ship's anchor. Davis took a hostage against the return of the anchor, but when good weather arrived sailed with the Inuk still aboard; the man died before Britain was reached. Davis again explored the coast of Baffin Island, finding, as Frobisher had, that the 'muskyto... sting grievously' before heading home.

Davis sailed again in 1587 in the *Ellen*, a 20-ton ship that leaked so badly the crew almost lost heart. Despite this the *Ellen* reached 73°N, on the west Greenland coast, a new northing record, then crossed Baffin Bay, but was forced south by sea ice. Davis explored more of Baffin Island's east coast, then headed into Cumberland Sound again, reaching Pangnirtung where, in hot July sunshine, the crew went ashore and organised a foxhunt with the dogs they had taken with them as company. Further south Davis also reached the eastern end of Hudson Strait, but did not explore it.

Barents sails east

When Europeans next headed north for Cathay they were Dutch rather than British and sailed for the North-East Passage. Having recently thrown out the Spanish, the Dutch were keen to establish themselves on the world stage and, ignoring the English failures along the Russian coast (and that of Oliver Brunel, financed by a Belgian merchant, in 1584), sent two expeditions in May 1594. Willem Barents, born on the North Sea island of Terschelling, commanded the *Mercurius*, while Cornelius Nai commanded *De Swane* and, confusingly, another *Mercurius*. The plan was for Barents to attempt to round the northern tip of Novaya Zemlya (New Land), while Nai would attempt to penetrate the Kara Sea, either by sailing between Novaya Zemlya and Vaygach Island, or between the latter and the mainland. Barents pushed to about 77°N – a northing record – at the northern end of Novaya Zemlya, but from there all that could be seen was ice, with no glimpse or hope of open water. For several weeks he probed the ice but eventually had to admit defeat. When he rendezvoused with Nai he found him jubilant. Sailing through the Yugor Strait, Nai had negotiated the ice of the Kara Sea and found open water. Deciding that 'there is absolutely no further doubt that the passage to China is free and open' he turned around.

Back in Holland the delighted House of Orange and the Dutch merchants sent a fleet of seven ships out in 1595. Barents went again, but was not the leader of the expedition, merely master of the *Greyhound*. This time the strait to the Kara Sea, reached in late August, was blocked with ice. After several weeks of trying to break through, during which time two men were killed by a bear, the fleet sailed home. The Dutch, their fingers burned, decided not to organise another official expedition, but offered a substantial reward to anyone discovering the passage. A group of Amsterdam merchants took up the challenge, financing two ships which sailed in May 1596. The ships were commanded by Jacob van Heemskerk and Jan Cornelius Riip, much to Barents' aggravation. He was, however, offered a place on a ship and chose to go with Heemskerk. In what is now called the Barents Sea the Dutch chased a polar bear in a row boat, slaughtering it with muskets and axe.

Sailing north from Bear Island the Dutch passed icebergs (which, delightfully, a sailor new to the Arctic initially thought were huge swans) and a dead whale which 'stank monstrously' before reaching another island with an array of pointed mountains. These gave the island its name – Spitsbergen (though on their charts they called their discovery *Het Nieuwe Land* – The New Land). The Dutch had discovered – or, perhaps, rediscovered – Svalbard. Exploring the island's west coast they named Amsterdam Island and wondered at the plantlife, birds and warm days so far north. When the sun allowed a latitude calculation the Dutch had reached 79°49'N, the north-western tip of Spitsbergen.

Ice now blocked further progress and the Dutch returned to Bear Island where, after an argument with Barents, Riip decided to head home. Barents persuaded Van Heemskerk to head east and, dodging icebergs and floes, was able to go around the northern tip of Novaya Zemlya. But it was now early September and the sea ice soon blocked the entrance of the bay in which the Dutch had sheltered and named Ice Haven. The name was inappropriate, the ice soon tumbling in to crush the ship: the crew of 17 would be 'forced, in great poverty, misery and grief, to stay all that winter', while the noise of the ice 'made all the hair of our heads to rise upright with fear'. The Dutch built a hut of driftwood: when they put nails in their mouths before use they noticed that icicles formed on them before they could begin hammering them in.

Inside the hut were bunks and a bath, and a huge central fire over which they cooked food from the ship supplemented by the meat of local wildlife of which polar bears were particularly abundant. When the weather permitted they played a form of golf on a course between the hut and the ship about 3km (2 miles) away.

Above **The interior of the Barents' team hut on Novaya Zemlya. The engraving (by Levinus Hulsius in Gerrit de Veer's *The Three Voyages of Willem Barents*) makes the hut look quite inviting, a fact belied by the description of the dreadful winter the team actually spent.**
Richard Sale Collection

Below **Willem Barents. Barents' journey even inspired Shakespeare. In *Twelfth Night* Fabian, a servant of Olivia, tells Sir Toby Belch '...and you are now sailed into the north of my lady's opinion; where you will hang like an icicle on a Dutchman's beard...'**
Rijksmuseum, Amsterdam, Holland

The cold of the Arctic winter was so intense that all cracks in the hut were sealed, almost poisoning the men with fumes from the unventilated fire. To escape the cold the men huddled close to the fire, but often found that they smelled burning socks before their cold feet had registered they were too close to the flames. They also suffered from scurvy, despite the fresh meat. In all five of the 17 were to die from the disease, including Barents, whose death occurred during the homeward journey. The Dutch ship had been so battered by the ice it was unseaworthy, so two rowing boats were converted to sailing skiffs and used to sail south along the Novaya Zemlya coast as soon as the summer sun of 1597 had cleared the way of ice. Barents died on 20 June: five weeks later van Heemskerk and the other survivors met a group of Russian fishermen at the island's southern tip. Almost dead from scurvy, their gums so deteriorated that their teeth were falling out, and unable to eat solid food, the Dutch were nursed to health and taken to the mainland where they were met by Riip who had come to look for them.

Back in Holland the Dutch, still wearing caps of Arctic fox fur, each complete with a foxtail, were greeted as heroes. In Heemskerk's case it was a true reflection of the man: years later during a battle between the Dutch and Spanish, having lost a leg to a cannon shot, he held onto his sword and urged his men forward until he died of bloodloss. His monument in Amsterdam notes that he 'steered his way through ice and iron'. But Heemskerk returned from the ice empty-handed, while another expedition, which had gone around the Cape of Good Hope, was laden with cargo. The Dutch stared wide-eyed at these riches and forgot about the North-East Passage.

Whalers in the north

On 1 May 1607 Henry Hudson and his crew (of 11, one being John, Hudson's 14-year-old son) sailed the *Hopewell* out of Gravesend. The Muscovy Company was losing profits on its Russian trade to Dutch companies and had decided to try for Cathay again. Hudson's plan was simple: the north-east and north-west routes were ice-bound, but near the pole the sun was 'a manufacturer of salt rather than ice' and the sea should be clear, so Hudson was sailing due north, over the pole. Hudson reached the east coast of Greenland and headed north as far as Hold-with-Hope (73°N). From there he headed north-west, eventually reaching Barents' New Land and sailing north to a point where it became clear that the theory of salt rather than ice was wrong.

Heading south Hudson was pushed west where he saw a volcanic island which lay north of Iceland. He called it Hudson's Touches. Back in London he was able to tell his merchant-masters that while the route to Cathay had eluded him, the bays of Svalbard were home to vast numbers of huge whales.

The British merchants waited two years before following up Hudson's discovery, then sent Jonas Poole to check its accuracy. With Poole's confirmation the British decided to exploit the Svalbard whale stock. In this they were not alone. The Dutch remembered Barents' stinking whale carcass, and the Danes and French rapidly heard tales of whaling riches. The key to the successful plundering of the Svalbard stock were the Basques who had been hunting whales since at least the 12th century. Much of the terminology of whaling, for instance harpoon, was Basque, developed over the centuries of hunting the Right Whale in the Bay of Biscay. The British killed walrus on Bear Island (though not very expertly at first) but had to engage Basques – who were already whaling off the Labrador coast – to teach them how to kill Svalbard whales. The Basque technique was to establish a land station where the whale carcass was stripped and the blubber rendered to oil, and from which small boats took the catchers out to the whale. This was an especially good technique in Svalbard where millennia of trouble-free life had both increased the whale population and encouraged them to use sheltered bays close to shore. There was considerable ill-feeling between the British and Dutch over the whaling particularly after the Dutch took possession of Hudson's Touches, renaming it Jan Mayen after Jan Jacobsz May, a Dutch whaling captain. Jan Mayen (the name was retained by the Norwegians, who claimed sovereignty in 1929, as it had by then been in common usage for 300 years) was a particularly useful base as the whales migrated past it en route for Svalbard. On Svalbard the Dutch also had the best land station: Smeerenburg (Blubber Town) on Amsterdam Island. It is still common to see descriptions of Smeerenburg stating that it had a church, a bakery and a brothel, serving a population of several thousand, but the archaeological evidence does not support this delightful view of the Arctic Klondike town, suggesting a population of 200 at most housed in barrack-like rooms, and an absence of clergy and women.

The whale that the Dutch, British, French and Danes sought was the bowhead. As the trade increased the numbers of whales fell dramatically. It is estimated that the North Atlantic bowhead stack was

Above **Smeerenburg, a contemporary painting by Cornelius de Man.**
Rijksmuseum, Amsterdam, Holland

20,000–25,000 when whaling began, giving a sustainable annual yield of perhaps 500. The number actually taken exceeded this many times. By 1650 the Dutch had abandoned Jan Mayen: within another half-century Svalbard had been all but abandoned too, though ships continued to visit throughout the 18th century. By then whaling had also changed: the whales were not only less numerous, but more wary of the sheltered bays, and the Basque and American whalers were hunting different species in the open ocean. Land stations had always been cumbersome. They had to be set up each year, and hauling huge dead whales back to them was time- – and manpower- – consuming. The stations could be plundered when vacated, a fact which led to deliberate overwinterings. These were often disastrous: on Jan Mayen the seven men left in 1633 were found dead of scurvy in June 1634, and a similar fate befell a Smeerenburg party in 1634/5. Ironically, all eight Britons survived an accidental wintering in 1630/1.

The North-West Passage

Though the Muscovy Company checked Henry Hudson's account of the Svalbard whales they were obviously impressed enough with his journey to back him again, this time to try for the North-East Passage, again in the *Hopewell*. The journey was unsuccessful, the ship being stopped by the ice of the Kara Sea, but was significant for two reasons. Firstly the crew spotted a mermaid: 'From the navel upwards her back and breasts were like a woman's... Her body was as big as one of us, her skin very white... long hair hanging down behind, of colour black. In her going down they saw her tail which was like the tail of a porpoise and speckled like a mackerel'. An illusion created by a harp seal and months at sea in all-male company? Secondly, Hudson made a curious entry in his log to the effect that the return of the *Hopewell* was 'my free and willing return, without persuasion or force of any one of (my company)'. Many have speculated that this entry implies problems between Hudson and Robert Juet, his first mate. Hudson was an old man, already a grandfather. He was moody and capricious, his indecisiveness a burden to his crew. Juet was also elderly, an irritable trouble-maker whom many captains would have rejected, but who Hudson took on each of his journeys. They appear to have behaved like an old, grumpy married couple.

The Muscovy Company was less pleased with Hudson than they had been previously and declined to back a third voyage. So Hudson approached the merchants of Amsterdam who financed, in 1609, another trip to the Kara Sea, this time in *De Halve Maan* (The Half Moon). At the ice edge there was a mutiny (perhaps instigated by Robert Juet) as a result of which Hudson turned around and sailed across the Atlantic, discovering the Hudson River, Coney Island and Manhattan (the future site of New Amsterdam, later New York). The crew shot half-a-dozen native Americans for fun and fed alcohol to many more for the amusement of getting them drunk, behaviour which reflects badly on both Juet, who seems to have been the ringleader, and Hudson who not only allowed, but assisted, the folly.

Back in Britain Hudson's discoveries lit up the faces of the London merchants (while the activities of his crew barely raised an eyebrow) and in April 1610, with a crew of 22, he sailed the *Discovery* back to America. One of the crew was Henry Greene who seems to have usurped Robert Juet's place as Hudson's favourite. Juet's response was to become drunk and angry. Hudson calmed him, but the mood of the whole crew was then depressed by the journey through the violent waters of the Hudson Strait. Hugging the northern Quebec shore Hudson sailed between it and Digges Island to reach the vast, calm waters of what he was convinced was the Pacific Ocean. Turning south Hudson watched the Quebec shore waiting for the cities of Japan that would soon come into view; instead the bleak Arctic tundra held his eye all the way to the entrance to James Bay. There, at about 51°N, in Rupert Bay, the *Discovery* was frozen in as a distinctly un-Cathay-like winter took hold. In the dismay of not finding Java (where Hudson had told his crew they would spend Candlemas), Hudson replaced Juet, now openly sneering at his captain's hopes, with Robert Bylot. Juet nursed his grievance during a hard winter which saw several men succumb to scurvy, one dying of it. As the winter toyed with the men's minds Hudson picked a fight with Greene, his one-time favourite, then demoted Bylot. The pair joined Juet and others in plotting the takeover of the ship, reasoning that with so little food and so many sick with scurvy no one would escape alive without positive action. In June

1611 after the ship had been freed from the ice, Hudson was seized, and together with his son, four sick men and three others, was placed in an open boat. The ship's carpenter, whom the mutineers needed, chose to go with Hudson. The nine in the boat had only the clothing they wore, no water or food, no means of making fire and one gun. They stood little chance of surviving – and were never heard of again. The 13 mutineers sailed to Digges Island which they knew was rich in wildfowl. There, in a fight with the local Inuit, four men, including Henry Greene, were killed. Later Robert Juet died of scurvy leaving Robert Bylot, eventually the only man still capable of standing, to steer the boat into Berehaven in Ireland's Bantry Bay.

Back in London the eight survivors might have expected to be tried and hanged, their 'excuse' for mutiny hardly holding water, as in addition to the sick

Below **The documented verdict passed on the Hudson mutineers.**
UK Public Records Office

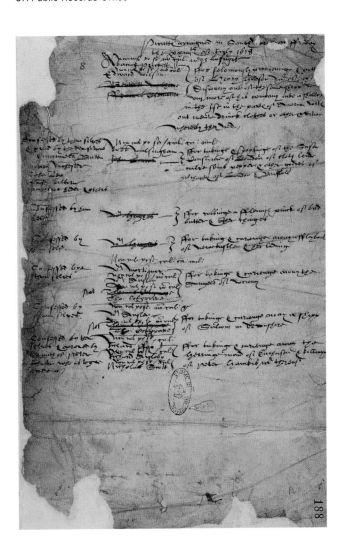

men they had also cast adrift healthy ones and the captain for no better reason than that they did not like them. But Bylot's claim to have found the North-West Passage allowed economics to triumph over the law of the land (and justice). Bylot, Prickett (a servant of Sir Dudley Digger, co-sponsor of the expedition – whose account of the mutiny is the fullest and, hardly surprisingly, exonerates him completely), and Edward Wilson, ship's surgeon, were soon heading back to Hudson Bay. When, eventually, four of the mutineers were tried for mutiny they were found not guilty.

The expedition of 1612 was commanded by Sir Thomas Button. Not only did it include some of the Hudson mutineers, it also used Hudson's ship *Discovery*. Bylot navigated it to Hudson Bay which Button then crossed, wintering at the mouth of the Nelson River (named for Francis Nelson, who died there, as did several others, of scurvy: five men were also killed by Inuit). He then headed north to reach Southampton Island and the Roes Welcome Sound (though the sound was not actually given that name until Foxe's expedition of 1631). Button thought the sound was the channel that would finally lead to the Pacific, but returned to England having done little more than nose the *Discovery* into it. In 1615 Bylot sailed again, now as master of the *Discovery*, with William Baffin as pilot. This time the northern coast of Southampton Island was reached, but Bylot and Baffin concluded that the Roes Welcome Sound was not the way to Cathay. On this journey Baffin calculated the longitude of the *Discovery* by taking a complete lunar observation on 21 June, a feat which earned him the admiration of all that followed him and that has led many of today's experts to consider him the greatest of the early Arctic explorers. It was in recognition of this that Sir William Parry named Baffin Island (close to which the observation was made) in his honour.

Baffin, lowly born and self-taught, had been on an expedition to West Greenland and two whaling trips to Svalbard before accompanying Bylot. He was clearly a better seaman and when the *Discovery* sailed again in 1616, though Bylot was still nominally master, Baffin was the real commander. Convinced that Hudson Bay was not the way to go, Baffin headed north through Davis Strait, discovering Baffin Bay, then Lancaster Sound, Jones Sound and Smith Sound, each named for an expedition backer. It was a masterful journey, one of the greatest of all in terms of discoveries, but ironically Baffin's maps were not published, and the details were soon forgotten. The man charged with publishing Baffin's data decided that the maps, and some tables, were too expensive to produce and so left them out. With the first phase of exploration of the Canadian Arctic coming to an end, it was 200 years before Baffin Bay was entered again. By then it was thought to be a new discovery.

The Danes and the race to Cathay

In the 17th century Denmark controlled what is now Norway, giving the Danes not only an Arctic seaboard, but also a perceived right to the legacy of the Vikings. It also gave them a duty to see if there were still survivors of the Viking settlements of Greenland, to which end Christian IV organised three expeditions (under the Scot John Cunningham and Englishmen John Knight and James Hall, all of whom were officers in the Danish navy) in the early years of the century. They found no Vikings, but did kidnap some Inuit. Next a Dane, Jans Munk, was dispatched to look for a North-East Passage in 1610. The voyage failed in the Kara Sea ice as had so many others before it. In May 1619 Munk set out again with two ships, the *Enhiorningen* (Unicorn) and *Lamprenen* (Lamprey). Munk reached and crossed Hudson Bay, wintering at the mouth of the Churchill River, now famous for its annual congregation of polar bears and bear-watchers. Sixty-five men overwintered, the illustration in Munk's book on the expedition – the first for a general readership, and one of the more charming examples – suggesting that conditions were not too bad. In reality they were grim: by early June all but three men were dead from scurvy and Munk, one of those remaining, wrote in his journal, 'Herewith, goodnight to all the world and my soul into the hand of God'. In fact he survived, and with his two companions sailed the *Lamprey* back to Denmark where Christian IV ordered him to go back and retrieve the *Unicorn*. Not surprisingly Munk failed to raise a crew and the second trip was abandoned.

The next attempt on the North-West Passage was in 1631 when two almost identical ships left London and Bristol, the most celebrated ports of 17th-century England. Each ship was 70 tons, square-rigged and manned by a crew of 22. They were named for Charles, the king of England, and his queen, Henrietta Maria. The master of the *Charles* was Luke Foxe, a self-taught Yorkshireman, a career seaman with an arrogant (but largely justified) opinion of his worth who called himself 'North-West' Foxe and had been trying for years to gain sponsorship for a voyage to discover the passage. Finally he had persuaded London merchants to fund

Above **Jens Munk's winter camp in Hudson Bay.**
From *Navigatio Septentrionalis.*
The Royal Library, Copenhagen, Denmark

the trip. Sir Thomas Roe, an ambassador of the king, agreed to act as patron and a renamed ex-Royal Navy ship was made available. Foxe boasted that his was the best ship in the world, though in reality it was a pensioned-off tub, barely seaworthy.

When the merchants of Bristol heard about Foxe's voyage they hastily gathered the money to mount a rival search. Whichever port controlled the trade with Cathay, with its priceless merchandise of silk and spices, would be the richest in England, and Bristol was not about to be second in that particular race. To captain their ship the Bristolians chose Thomas James, a Welsh-born barrister, a gentleman, but one of limited

experience of the sea and sailing, though he had once taken charge of a small fleet which sailed to clear the English Channel of pirates.

To avoid a charge of favouritism King Charles gave each man an identical letter. The winner of the race for the passage was to deliver it to the Emperor of Japan. The letters were in English as it was reasoned that the emperor, being both a king and a cultured man, would obviously speak the language. On the afternoon of 3 May 1631 James took the *Henrietta Maria* out of Bristol's harbour, to be followed two days later by Foxe and the *Charles*. Foxe caught and passed his rival at Resolution Island at the entrance to the Hudson Strait.

In Hudson Bay the two ships met by chance in late August, the two captains and their officers sharing a meal on the *Henrietta Maria*. It was not a happy occasion, Foxe writing that the time spent with James was 'the worst spent of any time of my discovery'. James, he noted, was a gentleman who 'could discourse of Art, but he was no seaman', recalling Macaulay's famous suggestion that the navy of King Charles comprised gentlemen and seamen, but the gentlemen were not seamen and the seamen were not gentlemen. James was no more impressed with Foxe, but he did try to persuade him that they should winter together. Foxe declined and sailed north, exploring the eastern coast of the bay as far as Southampton Island, and then exploring the vast bay, which now bears his name, between the island and Baffin Island. But before winter could take hold of his ship he turned west and sailed home to be greeted not by the congratulations of his sponsors as he had imagined, but their communal spleen-venting. James was overwintering and might discover the passage in the spring: where was the glory in returning empty-handed?

For his part James headed south, discovering James Bay and building huts on Charlton Island – which he named for the king – for overwintering. On nearby Danby Island he found a row of stakes driven into the shore, the only evidence ever discovered of the fate of Henry Hudson after the mutiny on the *Discovery* in 1610. James' crew spent an appalling winter. It was so cold frost formed on their beds, adding to the miseries of scurvy. When, finally, spring arrived so did the mosquitoes which plagued the men further. James, anxious to contact (hopefully friendly) Indians on the shore, climbed a tree to watch for a signal as his men set fire to brushwood. The fire spread rampantly through the tinder-dry island woodland, James being lucky to escape from his look-out and his long-suffering men escaping death only by fleeing to the ship. After months during which they had all but frozen to death, the closeness of death by burning must have seemed an ironic twist of fate. The survivors then sailed home without further incident.

Both Foxe and James wrote books. Foxe's is less polished but probably more honest. It begins with a plea (and a side-swipe at James' effort) 'Gentle Reader, expect not heere any flourishing Phrases or Eloquent termes, for this Child of mine begot in the North-West cold Clime, (where they breed no Schollers,) is not able to digest the sweet milke of Rethorick, that's food for them...', and goes on to note that Foxe had done his best 'with such Tackling, Cordage and Raftage as I had, to Rigge and Tackle this ship myself' which, if stretching the nautical simile to breaking point at least leaves the reader in no doubt about his view of himself as a master mariner. It must have been a great disappointment that James' *The Strange and Dangerous Voyage of*

Above **Captain Thomas James. whose account of his Arctic journey may have inspired the *Rime of the Ancient Mariner*.**
Richard Sale Collection

Captain Thomas James became a classic: it is said to have inspired Coleridge to write the *Rime of the Ancient Mariner*.

The Hudson's Bay Company

In Britain the failure of Foxe and James ended thoughts of a North-West Passage, while the upheaval of the Civil War and the execution of Charles I banished thoughts of the New World for two decades. But with the Restoration the country turned its eyes outwards again.

French fishermen from St Malo had followed the Basques and Bristolians to the great cod-fishing grounds off Newfoundland, so it is no surprise that a Malouin also followed in the wake of Cabot's ship. Jacques Cartier made three journeys (1534, 1525 and 1541), discovering the St Lawrence River and naming

the country Canada. It is said that he got the name from a Huron Indian, asking him what the place was called and not realising the Huron had given him the name of his village. It is a plausible tale. Samuel de Champlain, who followed Cartier, named Quebec from the Huron *kebek*, 'a narrowing of the waters'. French enthusiasm for their new colony was based on cod-fishing and the trapping of beaver on the rivers that threaded the forests of Quebec. Beaver fur was waterproof, easily shaped and very durable, ideal material for hats, the Canadian animals being a lucky replacement for the European species which had been hunted almost to extinction to satisfy the trade. For half a century the French controlled the beaver trade, then in 1666 the restored English king, Charles II, was visited by two French trappers who enquired whether the king was interested in making himself (and them, of course)

Above **A north-west view of Prince of Wales Fort, Hudson Bay. The engraving is by J. Saunders from a drawing by Samuel Hearne. The Hudson's Bay Company set up many such forts across northern Canada. They offered protection from rival fur-trading companies and infuriated native Americans. The protection was needed: the company's initials, HBC, were later said to mean 'Here Before Canada', which is certainly how its early managers behaved. The company motto *Pro Pelle Curem* is difficult to translate accurately. It was claimed to mean 'a skin for its equivalent', suggesting the trading nature of the company. Later those on the management side suggested it meant 'we skin you before you try to skin us', while those on the trapping side preferred 'we risk our skins for your pelts'. More tragically, when alcohol had become a major trade item, the motto was translated as 'a skin for a skinful'.**

Hudson's Bay Company Archives, Provincial Archives of Manitoba, Canada

rich. Indeed he was, and an expedition was sent to Hudson Bay to see if the Frenchmen's tales were accurate. When the ship, the *Nonsuch*, returned loaded with furs the king granted his nephew Prince Rupert, son of the exiled king of Bohemia, jurisdiction over the fur-trapping lands. A group of merchants was assembled, the combination of prince and merchants being termed the Governor and Company of Adventurers of England Trading into Hudson's Bay, a title soon shortened to the Hudson's Bay Company. The company was granted 'sole trade... of all those Seas Streightes Bayes Rivers Lakes Creekes and Soundes... that lye within the entrance of... Hudson's Streightes...'

In his monarchical way King Charles dismissed both the claims of the native peoples and the French to the land he had given away. The French were eventually ousted by force while the Huron, Cree and other native tribes were just ignored. The Hudson's Bay Company established a series of forts around the southern shores of Hudson Bay, employees rarely venturing out of them to explore the local area. The lack of initiative in aiding the search for a North-West Passage was criticised in

Much more significant than the Hudson's Bay Company's explorations of western Hudson Bay was James Cook's voyage in the *Discovery* and *Resolution* (1776–80) to the northern Pacific to investigate the western end of the North-West Passage. Cook arrived late and was unable to travel very far north because of the ice of the Beaufort Sea, though he did satisfy himself that Asia and America were not joined north of the Bering Strait, following the Alaskan shore as far as Icy Cape. He found a safe anchorage on the Alaskan shore at the end of an inlet he explored – now the town of Anchorage on Cook Inlet – and sailed up an eastward heading arm that he discovered was just another blind alley. His almost tangible weariness is reflected in the name he gave it – Turnagain Arm. Cook then turned south, landing in Hawaii in December 1778. Two months later he was murdered in a confrontation with the locals over a stolen boat. It was a sad end for one of the greatest explorers of any age.

UK National Maritime Museum

Above **The sea ice of the Beaufort Sea. Driven chiefly by wind, the ice in the Beaufort circulates clockwise, the motion – the Beaufort Gyre – being the main ice movement of the Canadian Arctic.**
Richard Sale

Britain, but with profits from fur-trading being so high the criticism at first fell on deaf ears. Eventually in 1719 the company provisioned an expedition of two ships commanded by John Knight to explore the inlets of western Hudson Bay. The expedition of 40 men disappeared. Later explorers found their wintering quarters on Marble Island, near Rankin Inlet, and there were Inuit stories that men had survived until at least 1721 before succumbing to hunger and disease. In 1741 the company, responding reluctantly to suggestions that it was deliberately avoiding finding, perhaps even covering up the existence of, the passage – the first accusation was undoubtedly true, though the second was not – allowed one of its captains, Christopher Middleton, to lead another expedition. Middleton discovered Wager Bay but was accused of having actually discovered a channel not an inlet, an accusation which ruined him and resulted in a second expedition, in 1746, under William Moore, which confirmed Middleton's findings and also discovered Chesterfield Inlet.

But although they had been involved in these seaborne expeditions, not until 1769 did a company man set out to explore the wilderness that lay west of Hudson Bay. The man was Samuel Hearne, and though the company's main aim was to see if there was any truth in the Indian rumour that a river flowed between banks of solid copper, the London-born Hearne was also travelling for its own sake. He was a keen naturalist, a good artist, and loved to camp out in the wilds beyond the walls of Fort Prince of Wales, set at the mouth of the Churchill River where he was employed. Hearne's first two attempts to find and follow the legendary river failed due to incompetent guides and poor equipment, but when he set out for a third time in December 1770 he was guided by a group of Chippewyan Indians led by a brilliantly resourceful man named Matonabbee.

Despite occasional severe hardship – the explorers lived off the land and on one occasion when hunting failed to provide food for the seventh day in succession an old pair of boots were boiled and chewed – the group eventually reached and followed the river to its

Above **Samuel Hearne carved his name into a rock at Sloop Cove near Churchill.**
Richard Sale

Left **Samuel Hearne. An engraving from 1796 by an unknown artist.**
Hudson's Bay Company Archives, Provincial Archives of Manitoba, Canada

mouth. There to Hearne's horror the Chippewyans massacred a group of Inuit. One badly wounded Inuit girl clung to Hearne's knees begging for help, but when he pleaded for her life the Chippewyans ignored him and speared her to death as she lay at his feet.

Hearne found one piece of copper ore and visited an Indian mine from which limited metal was extracted. At the mouth of the river, the imaginatively named Coppermine, Hearne erected a cairn and claimed all the local land for the Hudson's Bay Company. He was the first European to have seen the ocean between Hudson Bay and the Siberian coast, though there are still some who doubt if he actually reached the coast, believing much of his account was concocted from Indian tales. Hearne's woefully wrong positioning, in latitude and longitude, of the river mouth, does not help his cause.

Back at Fort Prince of Wales Hearne, now its commander, was eventually forced to surrender it to a French gunboat: Hearne was captured and the fort destroyed. Matonabbee, believing Hearne and the other Englishmen killed, hanged himself as his own position among the Chippewyan had depended on the company's existence. In fact Hearne survived captivity, was released and regained the governorship. Eventually he went back to England where he died, aged 47, virtually penniless. He died awaiting the cheque for £200 from a publisher for his classic book *A Voyage from Prince of Wales' Fort... to the Northern Ocean...*: for comparison, 20 or so years later Jane Austen was being offered £10 for her first novels.

Three years before Hearne's death another man set out westward. Alexander Mackenzie was born on the Hebridean island of Lewis, his burning ambition to succeed likely emanating from the poverty of his childhood. Orphaned by the age of 16, Mackenzie joined the North-West Fur Trading Company (a rival to the Hudson's Bay Company, though later the two merged) and rapidly rose through its ranks. In the North-West Mackenzie met Peter Pond, a tough Connecticut-born American who had explored west of Hudson Bay and discovered Lake Athabasca. Pond told Mackenzie of native stories of a river which flowed west from the Great Slave Lake (discovered by Samuel Hearne) to the sea. Hoping that the river might be navigable and the sea the Pacific Ocean, Mackenzie left Fort Chippewyan on the southern shore of Lake Athabasca on 3 June 1789. With him were four French-Canadian *voyageurs* (expert paddlers), an Indian guide called English Chief (named because he was a chief and spoke English!), a German and an assorted bunch of women and Indians. The group travelled in three canoes which were paddled and portaged north to the Great Slave Lake. Here ice made progress difficult and mosquitoes made life virtually intolerable, but the team pressed on, reaching, and then descending, the legendary river. Travelling at a remarkable rate (an average daily progress of 40km/25 miles) the party headed west, then north-west.

Mackenzie's account of the journey is a curious mix of styles. He is sometimes eloquent about the sheer beauty of the landscape through which they passed. He is also interesting when talking about the native peoples they met (though often disapproving of their habits and lifestyle). But on his companions he is almost silent. Mackenzie was clearly driven by his ambition to reach the Pacific, his men merely the means of achieving that end – hardly worth mentioning except to occasionally complain about them. As the expedition moved further north the Indian fear of Inuit (a strange, and mutual, loathing with no apparent historical cause: the two peoples, and the various tribes within them, regarded each other as enemies just because they existed, almost as though there was a natural order) meant that local guides were difficult to obtain. Mackenzie got around this by kidnapping – nothing was allowed to prejudice his great exercise.

Eventually Mackenzie reached the river's huge delta, a complex of narrow channels, swamp, taiga

Above **Sir Alexander Mackenzie by Sir Thomas Lawrence.**
National Gallery of Canada, Ottawa

Left **Three days after sighting the Pacific Ocean, in a mixture of vermilion face-paint and bear grease, Alexander Mackenzie wrote an inscription on a rock beside the Dean Channel. The North-West Company had yet to merge with the Hudson's Bay Company and as a good North-West Company man Mackenzie wrote that he had arrived from Canada, not Hudson's Bay.**
Archives of British Columbia, Canada

islands and pingos. He resolutely tried to force a way through this chaos and on 12 July he camped on what most experts now believe to be Garry Island (at 69°29'N, 135°35'W). That night the team had to move because the water lapping the shore rose into their camp. Mackenzie thought this was due to the wind, but two days later realised it was a tide: he had reached the sea. Mackenzie hurriedly climbed to the high point of the island and looked north. All he could see was ice – this was not the Pacific Ocean.

Mackenzie called the river he had explored Disappointment. He returned along it, regaining Fort Chippewyan on 12 September. Today the river is called the Mackenzie. It is North America's second longest (after the Mississippi/Missouri complex, though it is longer than either, draining 20 per cent of Canada). Though his employers were unimpressed – he had returned with neither furs nor a route to the Pacific – Mackenzie's journey is now seen as one of the greatest in Canadian history. It was not his last. Sharing his employer's frustration he headed west again in 1793, following the Peace and Parsnip Rivers, then the Bella Coola to the sea. On 19 July Mackenzie notes, 'I could perceive the termination of the river and its discharge into a narrow arm of the sea'. He had reached the Pacific Ocean. He was the first European to gaze at the ocean from the American shore; the first to have crossed the continent.

The Royal Navy tries for the North-West Passage

The Napoleonic Wars removed all thoughts of exploration from European minds in the late 18th/early 19th centuries, but their legacy provided the new impetus for British searches for a North-West Passage. Britain was now the major world power, its pre-eminence based on naval might. But such status brings fears as well as benefits and these were, in part, exploited to persuade the British Admiralty to use naval ships to search for an Arctic seaway. Russia, a likely competitor on the world stage, lay at the other end of such a passage and seemed intent on expanding into America. The Russians had taken the Aleutian Islands and Alaska; Otto von Kotzebue had discovered Kotzebue Sound; and one reason for Bellingshausen's Antarctic journey had been to look for naval bases, a point hardly likely to have been lost on the British. But it is too simplistic to say that the maintenance of their superpower status was the only reason for the search. John Barrow, Second Secretary to the Admiralty (and the senior civil servant, as opposed to politician or

Above **William Scoresby was not only a man of courage and intellect, but also possessed a withering stare, capable of turning the strongest man to jelly. It is claimed that he once stared at a ship's ferocious guard dog and that the dog, in panic, jumped overboard and drowned.**
Richard Sale Collection

naval officer, there) is usually, and rightly, identified as the major influence on the decision to use naval ships. Though he undoubtedly understood the need to maintain an active navy and a complement of experienced officers, Barrow was also a geographer and historian with a number of published articles. He was interested in exploration for its own sake, and the naval expeditions of which he was the architect went not only to the Arctic but to Africa and Antarctica.

Barrow's enthusiasm for exploration coincided with a sudden break-up of the Arctic ice, icebergs spilling down into the Atlantic – and cooling Europe – as the Arctic Ocean unfroze. This change (due to one of the earth's periodic temperature shifts) was noted by William Scoresby, a Whitby-based whaler. Whitby, on the Yorkshire coast of England, had a fleet of Arctic whalers which made a good living during the late 18th/early 19th centuries and Scoresby was one of the most successful whaling captains. But he was much

Above **The first communication with the Inuit of Prince Regent Bay, as drawn by John Sacheuse. The wholly incongruous scene was to be mirrored over and again as the British failed to learn the lessons of Inuit survival in the Arctic and, later, the Antarctic.**
From John Ross *A Voyage of Discovery... in HM Ships* Isabella *and* Alexander.
Richard Sale Collection

more than a sea captain: he was also a scientist and surveyor and, later, a social worker and clergyman. His observational science in the Arctic has led many to call him the Father of Arctic Science, and his book *An Account of the Arctic Regions* has been called 'one of the most remarkable books in the English language'.

Noting the melt of Arctic waters Scoresby sailed beyond 82°N (probably a record northing at the time) and wrote to Sir Joseph Banks, President of the Royal Society, suggesting that the lack of ice made it an ideal time for a renewal of the quest for a northern sea route to the Orient. Scoresby was hoping that he might lead a British expedition, but when Barrow heard of his suggestion he chose naval men. Barrow organised two expeditions in 1818: John Ross and William Edward Parry were to search for the North-West Passage, David Buchan and John Franklin were to sail over the North Pole. The two expeditions were then to meet off the Siberian coast. That it was still thought possible that a

route over the pole might exist despite the evidence to the contrary seems ridiculous now, but at the time there were many scientists, some of them eminent, who believed in a temperate polar ocean (the perpetual sunlight of summer melting the ice) whose currents forced a ring of ice southwards: if the ring was breaking up, the ocean might be reached.

Buchan in the *Dorothea*, and Franklin in the *Trent*, fared badly. A violent storm forced them to shelter in Spitsbergen's Magdalenafjord, then pack ice, probably pushed south by the storm, imprisoned and threatened to crush their ships. Once extricated (by another storm which broke up the ice), Buchan abandoned the expedition and sailed home. Ross and Parry, in the *Isabella* and *Alexander*, had a more interesting time. They were heading north to seek the passage, as the land expedition of Hearne (see below) had shown that the sea at the mouth of the Coppermine River was still frozen in July. Northwards, of course, if the science was correct, the sea would be open. The crew included James Clark Ross, John's nephew, Edward Sabine, a Royal Artillery officer, and a south Greenlander John Sacheuse (who had reached Britain as a stowaway on a whaler) who would interpret during the first encounter between the Inuit of north-west Greenland and Europeans since the Vikings.

That meeting, in Prince Regent Bay, was remarkable for two reasons. The Inuit had been isolated from

Above **After his retreat in Lancaster Sound John Ross wrote, 'The land which I saw was a high ridge of mountains extending directly across the bottom of the inlet. The chain appeared extremely high in the centre.' John Barrow, supported by Parry, effectively dismissed Ross' actions as cowardice, but in the Arctic mirages can give the impression of distant peaks. This shot was taken in Larsen Sound on the western side of the Boothia Peninsula.**
Richard Sale

their fellow Greenlanders to the south for generations by a minor ice age. They had come to believe they were the only people on earth, and what Ross seems to have thought were friendly greetings, Sacheuse was able to interpret as shouts of 'Go away'. But more importantly the meeting resulted in an image which, behind its amusing depiction of the event, was to be a mirror of later British polar expeditions. On the right are fur-clad Inuit, on the left British naval officers in dress uniform – tailed coats, buckled shoes, cocked hats – a bizarre scene.

Apart from making contact with the Inuit, Ross discovered red snow, a phenomenon caused by growth of the unicellular plant *protococcus nivalis*. He also rediscovered Baffin Bay (which at the time was believed mythical) and the entrance to Smith, Jones and Lancaster Sounds. He ignored the first two, but sailed a short distance into Lancaster Sound. Then he stopped, sighting a mountain range which, he said, clearly showed the sound was a bay. Parry could not see these mountains (as he was several miles behind Ross this is not surprising) and urged him to continue, but Ross declined and returned to Britain where he was damned for his timidity both privately and publicly. That red snow was the only discovery of the expedition, and the fact that the men pulling their noses violently (supposedly an Inuit greeting) provided fodder for newspaper cartoons, did not endear Ross to Barrow. When Ross offered his services for future expeditions, he was declined, though his naval superiors obviously did not entirely share the view of the civil service as they promoted him.

The man who ate his boots

When Barrow tried again in 1819 it was Parry who commanded, in the *Hecla*, accompanied by Matthew Liddon in the *Griper*. Parry had been unmerciful in his condemnation of Ross' decision to turn back in Lancaster Sound. Parry was 29; most of his crew, which included Sabine, were younger. This youthful, energetic team were intent on pushing forward: it is said that the crew cheered when Parry decided to enter the sound despite heavy pack ice and numerous icebergs. Parry pushed west through what is now called the Parry Channel (comprising Barrow Strait and Melville Sound), discovering and naming Devon, Somerset, Cornwallis, Bathurst and Prince of Wales Islands. As they sailed Sabine noted that the compass needle pointed south – the expedition was north of the North Magnetic Pole.

Parry headed south into Prince Regent Inlet, but was stopped by ice, then continued west to Melville Island. From there he could see (and name) Victoria and Banks Islands, but further progress into what is now called McClure Sound (but was then Banks Strait)

Above **Cutting into Winter Harbour. The engraver has given the impression of the cut channel being a sinuous British stream, but it is more likely that the exhausted sailors took a direct route.**
From William Edward Parry *Journal of a Voyage for the Discovery of a North-West Passage.*
Richard Sale Collection

Below **Surgical tools from Parry's first expedition found at Winter Harbour.**
Vancouver Maritime Museum, Canada

Below **Parry's ships *Hecla* and *Griper* in Winter Harbour, Melville Island, 1819–20. The starry night, camp fire and snug-looking ships – and Parry's description of the winter – are almost certainly at odds with the hardships the men faced.**
From William Edward Parry *Journal of a Voyage for the Discovery of a North-West Passage.*
Richard Sale Collection

was impassable because of ice. Parry had reached 110°W and was therefore able to claim a prize of £5,000 offered to anyone who could reach that longitude north of the Arctic Circle: he shared the reward among his crew. He may have guessed that beyond the McClure Sound was open sea: if he was correct, he was within 160km (100 miles) of open water and had found the northern North-West Passage (not that traversed by Amundsen) though it would be many years before that would be proved. On Melville Island Parry sought shelter in Winter Harbour. There he overwintered, his ships de-rigged and covered with wagon cloth to form an exercise yard. Bread was baked, beer brewed and a reasonable, scurvy-free winter was passed. In June 1820 Parry explored Melville Island while waiting for the ice

Below **One winter journey from Fort Providence, all the way to Fort Chippewyan, on Franklin's land expedition, was led by George Back, sent by Franklin to avoid a possibly murderous conflict that had arisen between Back and Hood over a beautiful Indian girl named Greenstockings by the British after a particularly striking part of her costume. The two men had actually fought a duel over the girl, another officer having the foresight to remove the powder from their pistols to avoid bloodshed. After the incident Franklin was left with no choice but to separate the men. Hood, a gifted artist, painted this portrait of Greenstockings and her father, from which it appears that they might have been the models for Garry Trudeau's *Doonesbury* characters. Greenstockings bore Hood's child, so it would seem that he was the winner in the midshipman escort competition.**
National Archives of Canada

to free his ships, adding musk ox, caribou, hare and birds to the menu. In August the ships were finally freed and the expedition returned to Britain where Parry became the most famous man in the country (until Franklin arrived). His expedition had been an undoubted success. John Barrow thought that success in finding the passage was now just one journey away, a view which Parry endorsed publicly, though privately he was much less certain.

Parry's seaborne journey had been supported by a land expedition led by John Franklin which was intended to survey the north American coast east and west of the river mouths reached by Hearne and Mackenzie. Franklin had no experience which fitted him to command such an expedition, but then neither did any of the other candidates available to Barrow. With Franklin were John Richardson, surgeon and naturalist, George Back, Robert Hood and John Hepburn. Accompanied by four Orkney islanders collected on the way to Canada, Franklin headed west in late August. The expedition landed at the Hudson's Bay Company's York Factory on the south-western shore of the bay, then moved inland to Cumberland House, a company post, where the Orcadians turned back. Richardson and Hood overwintered at the house, but Franklin, Back and Hepburn continued to Fort Chippewyan on Lake Athabasca. The cold was intense, temperatures so low that their tea, left to brew in best English tradition, froze before they could drink it.

At Fort Chippewyan Franklin found he had walked into a bloody feud between the rival Hudson's Bay and North-West fur-trading companies. He could avoid the conflict, but it prevented him from buying the supplies he had banked on. So when his team, escorted by guides, voyageurs and assorted camp-followers headed north in 1820 it was poorly provisioned and too big to service easily by hunting. Starting in July and going by way of Fort Providence on the Great Slave Lake, Franklin was forced to overwinter in the Fort Enterprise which he built close to the source of the Coppermine River. From this log-built camp Franklin's team were forced to shuttle supplies from Providence and Chippewyan through the winter.

In June 1821 Franklin finally started down the Coppermine, but problems continued: at Bloody Falls (named for the massacre of the Inuit on Hearne's journey: skulls and bone were still visible when Franklin arrived) the Indian guides/hunters deserted, fearful of reprisals. Then the voyageurs expressed fears about using their fragile, birch-bark canoes on the sea. But

Above **The expedition encamped at Point Turnagain,
21 August 1821.**
From John Franklin *Narrative of a Journey to the Shores of the
Polar Sea.*
Richard Sale Collection

Franklin persevered, becoming the first European to reach the river's mouth since Hearne. From the mouth, with a depleted party, he set out east along the coast. The plan had been to reach Repulse Bay, but by late August, with both supplies and men almost exhausted, Franklin was forced to admit defeat. He named his furthest east Point Turnagain; then, after wasting time wondering whether to overwinter, headed back towards the river. The weather was atrocious, the sea threatening to destroy the canoes; in desperation the team landed and started to trek across the tundra. The country was devoid of life and almost barren of vegetation and as their food ran out, despite abandoning their canoes to save weight, progress slowed to a crawl. Surviving on *tripe de roche*, a lichen scraped from rocks, and the leather of their boots and jackets, the party finally reached the Coppermine River. There Richardson almost died trying to swim across with a line, and precious days were lost in building a canoe to replace those they had abandoned.

Once over the river Back and the three strongest voyageurs headed off for Fort Enterprise: one man died before it was reached. The Indians who had fled from Bloody Falls were supposed to have stocked the fort with food hunted and gathered locally, and to have waited for Franklin, but they had done neither. Finding Enterprise empty Back started out after the Indians. In the main party Franklin was forced to abandon Hood who was too weak to move: Richardson and Hepburn stayed with him while Franklin continued slowly behind Back. Two men died and four tried to return to the river camp. Only one arrived, a half-Iroquois, half-European called Michel Teroahauté. He brought meat he claimed to have been cut from the body of a wolf, but his curiously healthy appearance and odd behaviour convinced Richardson the meat was human flesh. His fears that Teroahauté had killed the other three men were, he felt, confirmed when Hood died of a single gunshot wound. Teroahauté, the only one present at the time, declared it had been suicide – but the wound was in the back of Hood's head. When the three men set off for Fort Enterprise, Richardson and Hepburn feared for their own lives when Teroahauté claimed to have stopped to gather *tripe de roche* but returned without any. To Richardson it was clear that he 'had halted for the purpose of putting his gun in order with the intention of attacking us'. To forestall this Richardson shot the heavily armed Teroahauté.

At the fort Franklin and his team were in the last stages of starvation. More men died, and the rest were only days from death when the Indians found by George Back arrived with food. The hint of cannibalism, the murders and the general horror of the trip made Franklin a hero in Britain, where he was known as the 'man who ate his boots'. His book on the trip sold out and second-hand copies were said to have changed hands for much more than the cover price. It is no surprise: the book is a fine one, the copy at the British Library being inscribed, in an unknown hand, 'this is one of the most affecting narratives ever written.'

Franklin and Parry again

Despite his misgivings Parry agreed to lead another expedition in 1821, the *Fury* replacing the worn-out *Griper*. This time Parry went to Hudson Bay, a decision which seems curious in the light of the string of early failures there, but reasonable when considered against his opinion that the ice at the western end of the Parry Channel would prove a consistent bar to progress. Parry hoped that the ice would be less severe in the south and intended to find a westerly route out of the bay to the north of Southampton Island.

Parry confirmed Middleton's discovery that Repulse Bay was not the way west. Parry overwintered on Winter Island at the mouth of Lyon Inlet. His choice of names indicates a lack of romance – if he was not honouring a nobleman who might return the favour at a later date he was stating the obvious: on Melville Island he had wintered at Winter Harbour, this time it was on Winter Island. Here the British made friends with a group of local Inuit, one of whom, a woman called Iligliuk, drew a map which led Parry to a strait which he named Fury and Hecla after his ships. During the summer of 1822 Parry navigated the strait to its western end, but was unable to break out into what he called the Polar Sea (the Gulf of Boothia). This was a remarkable feat: not until 1948 was the strait navigated from the gulf to Foxe Basin, and not until 1956 the other way – the way Parry attempted it – both journeys requiring an ice-breaker. Parry then wintered on Igloolik, an island close to the mouth of the strait. He tried to get through the strait again in 1823, but failed, and returned to Britain.

Parry went north again in 1824, this time trying to find a route by way of Lancaster Sound and Prince Regent Inlet, avoiding both Fury and Hecla Strait and the exit from Parry Channel, but hoping to forge a route from the western end of the strait. The attempt was doomed: the British had not discovered just how far north the Boothia Peninsula reached. That year there was also heavy ice in Baffin Bay and it took Parry all summer to reach Lancaster Sound, much of the time spent in hauling the ships (*Hecla* and *Fury* again) through the thick ice by the back-breaking work of anchoring a hawser to a floe far ahead and heaving on it. The sound itself was almost free of ice, allowing Parry to reach Port Bowen on the eastern shore of Prince Regent Inlet where he wintered. In July 1825 when ice freed the ships Parry went south along the inlet's western coast, but a sudden storm pushed ice against the ships pinning them against the shore. *Fury* was damaged beyond repair and abandoned (at Fury Beach), Parry retreating for home with everyone on board the *Hecla*.

There had been a second expedition in 1824, and another in 1825 linked to Parry's third voyage and a second land expedition of John Franklin. In 1824 George Lyon sailed the *Griper* northwards with the intention of reaching Repulse Bay and then sledging across the narrow peninsula (the Rae Isthmus) at its back, which Iligliuk had shown on her map, to reach the sea beyond (Committee Bay), perhaps linking up with Parry. It was a good plan, but heavy ice and appalling weather in Roes Welcome Sound so badly damaged the *Griper* that Lyon did well to get the ship back to Britain at all: he had not even reached Repulse Bay. The next year Frederick Beechey, who had been Franklin's lieutenant on the *Trent* in 1818, took the *Blossom* to the Bering Strait in the expectation of meeting Parry when he exited the passage, or Franklin when he reached the strait overland. Beechey waited in vain: Franklin reached Foggy Island, just 250km (156 miles) away, but Parry was half a continent away, battling the ice of Prince Regent Inlet.

Given the horror of the earlier land journey it is intriguing why Franklin was willing to lead another in

1825 and why Richardson and Back were prepared to go with him. But go they did. This expedition was better equipped, supplies being easier to obtain now the fur-trade war was over. The men followed the Mackenzie River, easier to navigate than the Coppermine, and with fur-trade forts spaced at intervals along its length so that the journey was hardly similar to that of Alexander Mackenzie. The expedition did descend into horror as the previous one had, but was remarkably successful. At the river's delta mouth Franklin led one team west in two boats, *Lion* and *Reliance*, passing Herschel Island, which he named for the Herschels, father and son, famous British astronomers. Had his team not been halted by thick fog, they would have reached Point Barrow and met Beechey's expedition: Franklin stopped just 250km (156 miles) short. At the same time Richardson led a team eastwards in *Union* and *Dolphin*. Richardson named Franklin Bay for the expedition leader as a mark of the 'respect and regard' he had for him, and the strait between the mainland and Victoria Island for his two boats on his way to the Coppermine River. When Franklin returned to England in 1827 the North American coast from near Point Barrow to Point Turnagain had been mapped.

The North Magnetic Pole

The failures drained the Admiralty's resolve, and with the public's enthusiasm turning to apathy there was no incentive for the government to invest more money, particularly as it had been clear since the outset that even if a passage existed it would not be useful. In the latter stages of the American moon-landing programme in the 1970s public apathy followed such a series of successes that it had become routine. Interest was only rekindled by the near-catastrophe of Apollo 13. For the British of the first third of the 19th century apathy followed a series of failures, many of which did not even have the benefit of a horror story. What was needed to

Above **The Smoking Hills of Franklin Bay. The cliffs of the western side of the bay are of bituminous shale which ignited (probably as a result of a lightning strike) several thousand years ago and have been smouldering ever since.**

Richard Sale

revitalise public interest was a major success – or a major tragedy.

The North-West Passage was to supply the latter. But first a private individual, Felix Booth, Sheriff of London and gin bottler, stepped forward to finance another attempt. Booth's commander was John Ross, ignored since 1818 for his timidity, but a man with an interest in steam navigation who had tried, unsuccessfully, to persuade the Admiralty to let him take a steamship to the Arctic. So keen on the idea was he that Ross part-financed the trip from his own pocket. Ross' nephew, James Clark Ross, who had been on all of Parry's voyages as well as John Ross' first Arctic voyage, was to go with him. Booth's plan was for the ship to make for Prince Regent Inlet, following its western shore to find a channel that opened westward. Ross' ship was the *Victory*, a paddle steamer: when the expedition set out, in 1829, *Victory* was the first steam-driven ship to head north-west. The engine and fuel store were so vast that another ship was needed to carry the expedition's supplies. Worse still the steam engine gave the ship a speed barely above walking pace, the boilers leaked (despite dung and potatoes being put in them on the manufacturer's instructions) and the boiler room was so hot the stokers could only work for short periods before becoming exhausted and fainting. Fortunately when the paddles were lifted out

of the water the *Victory* sailed well and Prince Regent Inlet was eventually reached.

Ross sailed south of Parry's Fury Beach – the beached *Fury* had gone – naming the Gulf of Boothia and Boothia Felix (now the Boothia Peninsula) for his patron. Ross overwintered in Felix Harbour in Lord Mayor's Bay (also named in Booth's honour: he was also remembered in Sheriff Harbour, to round off a fine bag of dedications), the steam engine which had so enthralled him being dismantled and manhandled on to the shore as so much rubbish. During the winter of 1829/30 *Victory* was visited by Inuit who told Ross that there was no westward channel to the south. This influenced Ross' later explorations, though it was not finally confirmed that Boothia Felix was a peninsula until Rae's trip of 1846.

The spring of 1830 did not release the *Victory* and James Ross decided to trek – with dog- and manhauled sledges, and with Inuit guides – across Boothia Felix to see what lay to the west. He discovered King William's Land (now King William Island), reaching its northern tip which he called Cape Felix, naturally. At the cape James Ross noted 'the pack ice... that had... been pressed against that shore, consisted of the heaviest masses that I had ever seen in such a situation... the lighter floes had been thrown up, on some parts of the coast... having travelled as much as half a mile beyond the limits of the highest tide-mark'. It was this ice pressure that was to trap and destroy Franklin.

Ross now turned south-west and continued to Cape Victory: he was only about 350km (220 miles) from Point Turnagain, but was out of food and had to return to Felix Harbour. It had been a significant journey, but the most significant discovery was missed: Ross did not explore southwards on the west side of King William. Had he done so he would have found that his Poctes Bay was not a bay and that King William was an island, not a peninsula. Many have argued that this lack of knowledge contributed to the loss of Franklin. He chose to go down King William Island's west edge because he believed – as Ross did – that the eastern side was a bay. It is an easy excuse for the failure of Franklin's final expedition, particularly as Amundsen did go to the east of King William Island on his successful transit. But even had Franklin known King William was an island he would still have failed, as his ships had too deep a draft to negotiate the shallow waters of the eastern coast and of Simpson Strait to the south of King William. There is evidence that Franklin did indeed try the eastern side before trying, fatefully, the western side.

During the summer of 1830 the *Victory* could be moved only 6.5km (4 miles) to Sheriff Harbour where the following winter was spent. When summer 1831 came the ship remained entombed and James Ross set out on another sledge trip. He recrossed Boothia Felix and headed north along the Boothia Felix coast. At 8am on 1 June at 70°5'17"N, 96°46'45"N magnetic measurements showed that Ross had reached the North Magnetic Pole. His team raised a cairn and a jackstaff, since 'nature had erected no monument', from which fluttered the Union Flag as Ross solemnly claimed the territory for the British Crown.

Later, back at the ship, this act of possession took on a surreal aspect when the British attempted to explain to the Inuit that the local area no longer belonged to them. Since the nomadic Inuit did not understand the concept of land ownership their baffled response dealt with the lack of seals that year and the need to acquire more fish-hooks. It would have made just as much sense to them if Ross had told them that Britain owned the sky.

The *Victory* was finally freed from the ice in late summer, but managed to gain just a few miles northward before being entombed again. During the winter

Above **James Clark Ross at the North Magnetic Pole. A charming engraving from Robert Huish's book *The Last Voyage of Capt John Ross*. It almost certainly caught the imagination of the public despite its errors. The Aurora Borealis can only be seen at night and Ross travelled during the continuous daylight of the Arctic summer; the telescope is highly fanciful as the magnetic pole is discovered with a dip circle and does not require the 'conquering' of a mountain. In fact the pole was discovered at sea level (more or less).**
Richard Sale Collection

of 1831/2 the crew began to show signs of scurvy, despite John Ross' intelligent use of fresh meat to keep it at bay. Ross therefore decided to abandon the ship, hauling boats and supplies north to Fury Beach where there were still supplies from Parry's last voyage. Fury Beach was reached in July and a hut (Somerset House) built. But before the boats could be rigged for a voyage to Lancaster Sound winter set in again. During this fourth winter one man died of scurvy. With most of the crew now ill, many weeks in 1833 were spent transporting supplies to the ice edge. Finally, on 15 August, the boats were launched. To the men's joy

Lancaster Sound was open water. On 25 August, to even greater delight, a sail was sighted. The ship lowered a boat and rowed towards the expedition. When Ross asked what ship it was he was told it was 'the *Isabella* of Hull, once commanded by Captain Ross'. The ship had been John Ross' first Arctic command in 1818 and was now a whaler. Ross noted that when he told the *Isabella*'s mate (who had brought the boat across to them) that he was the same Captain Ross, 'with the usual blunderheadedness of men on such occasions, he assured me I had been dead two years'.

Back in Britain John Ross was knighted, James Ross promoted. The only sour note was Sir John Barrow's unfair review of John Ross' book; he had still not forgiven what he saw as the cowardice of 1818. But now, as then, Barrow's article was published anonymously. Not that there was much need for secrecy, as John Ross was at war with just about everyone, including his nephew James. Ludicrously, John was claiming to have discovered the North Magnetic Pole while James was claiming to have commanded the *Victory*.

In 1832, nothing having been heard from John Ross for nearly three years, people in Britain began to clamour for a search expedition. Ross' having been a private venture the government and Admiralty were not keen to finance a search, but eventually some private money was also raised and George Back, veteran of the two Franklin overland expeditions, returned to Canada with instructions to follow the Great Fish (now Back) River to the sea and then to head north to Fury Beach where, it was assumed, Ross would head if he ran low on food. The assumption was correct, though the search was far too late, few having much hope that Ross could have survived four winters. That he had is likely to have influenced the Admiralty when there was an equal clamour to search for the missing Franklin expedition.

Back established a base on the shores of the Great Slave Lake and overwintered. During the winter he met Greenstockings (see page 40) again, immediately recognising her because she had retained her beauty. She now had a number of children, one of whom, presumably, was Robert Hood's though, not surprisingly, Back makes no such comment. In April 1834 news arrived that Ross had

Despite the failure of John Ross to find the passage, the expedition had aroused sufficient interest to persuade the Admiralty to send George Back northwards again in 1836, though his instructions were to survey the last section of uncharted coast, southwards from the Fury and Hecla Strait to Point Turnagain. To do this Back sailed the *Terror* to Repulse Bay with the intention of crossing Melville Peninsula on foot. But the *Terror* was trapped in the ice, squeezed and battered for ten months. When she was eventually released she was almost unseaworthy and Back sailed for home immediately. He just made it to Ireland's west coast, beaching the ship to prevent her sinking.

UK National Maritime Museum

returned safely to England, but Back continued with his trip, though on a reduced scale, following the Great Fish River to Chantry Inlet. Ice and lack of time prevented more than just a survey of part of the bay's shoreline, marking another point on the map of the mainland.

Dease and Simpson, and Rae

Following the overland expeditions of Franklin the missing sections of the North American coast were filled in by men from the Hudson's Bay Company. Between 1836 and 1839 Peter Dease, a senior company official, and Thomas Simpson, cousin of company governor George Simpson, made a series of journeys. Though Dease was nominally in charge it was Simpson, a young man of burning ambition and amazing stamina, who was the driving force. Simpson's abilities were remarkable: he could travel up to 80km (50 miles) daily on foot, sometimes in winter, for day after day, and shrug off conditions which would have repelled ordinary men. On the pair's first expedition, to fill in the gap between Franklin's Foggy Island and Point Barrow, Simpson and five others left Dease and the rest of the

Above **Thomas Simpson – date and artist unknown.**
Hudson's Bay Company Archives, Provincial Archives of Manitoba, Canada

team and pushed west across dreadful country, wading freezing cold rivers up to their waists and being cold day and night. Borrowing an Inuit umiak for the last stage of the trek they finally reached Point Barrow.

Next Dease and Simpson made for the coast east of Point Turnagain. In 1838 Simpson descended the Coppermine River and pushed east over ice, passing Turnagain and discovering an island he named for the young British queen: Victoria Island. Halted by the conditions he returned in 1839 and sailed two boats, *Castor* and *Pollux*, all the way to Back's Chantry Inlet, discovering en route that King William was an island, not a peninsula: the channel separating King William Island and the Adelaide Peninsula is now called Simpson Strait.

Now Simpson's ambition seems to have overcome him. He wrote, 'Fame I must have, but it must be alone.' Fed up with Dease, his senior, Simpson walked to the Red River settlement (Fort Garry, now the site of Winnipeg), a journey of almost 3,200km (nearly 2,000 miles) which he completed in 61 days, on foot, in winter. He was happy there would be a message at the fort telling him to continue his explorations by linking Chantry Inlet to Fury and Hecla Strait. There was no message. Certainly disillusioned, probably furious, he headed south, intending to reach a US port and a ship for Britain. Just after he left the instructions he craved arrived. But it was too late: Simpson was dead. He had started his journey with four other men. The survivors told how Simpson, enraged by the injustices of life, shot dead two of them, the other two fleeing in terror. When they returned to camp Simpson had shot himself. Perhaps that tale is true – but why go back to a camp occupied by a murderous companion? The events surrounding Simpson's death are still debated. What is clear is that a major explorer had died without fulfilling his potential. He was 31 years old.

The last big piece of the jigsaw was finally fitted in 1847 when Dr John Rae, later to discover Sir John Franklin's fate, crossed the isthmus from Repulse Bay to Committee Bay (which he had already crossed in 1846) and headed north along the bay's western shore. Rounding what is now called the Simpson Peninsula Rae headed north, looking for a channel that separated Ross' Boothia Felix from the mainland. When he reached Lord Major's Bay he realised there wasn't one. Boothia Felix was the Boothia Peninsula, and the coast of Canada had been mapped.

Franklin's last expedition

In 1845 Sir John Barrow was in his 81st year. He had occupied the same post for 41 years, and felt the time had come to retire. James, now Sir James, Ross had returned from Antarctica with the news that there was little to encourage the British to go there again, a fact which may have encouraged Barrow to remember the unfinished business in the north. He wrote to the Admiralty pointing out Britain would be a laughing stock if, having found the eastern and western ends of the North-West Passage, she did not explore the part in the middle. The Admiralty agreed, making *Erebus* and *Terror*, Ross' Antarctic ships, available.

But who should command? James Ross declined: he was, he said, too old at 44. John Ross was, of course, still beyond the pale. Parry could not be tempted out of retirement and Back's health had not recovered from the excesses of 1836/7, while Sir John Franklin was not only old but had just been dismissed from his position as governor of Van Dieman's Land (Tasmania).

Nominally the dismissal followed an unseemly row with a junior, though it was actually engineered by a vested interest on the island who feared Franklin's humanitarian view of prisoner treatment might affect the profits they made from prison labour.

Franklin had had a distinguished service career. He had fought at the Battle of Copenhagen when he was just 15. He had been a signal officer on the *Bellerophon* at Trafalgar: the ship was the most heavily engaged in the battle. Franklin emerged unscathed, but was later wounded at the Battle of New Orleans where Packenham's army was routed by Andrew Jackson. But despite all this he was not promoted. He was, it seems, amiable and competent, but dull, and the governorship of a prison colony was his only reward. After his dismissal Franklin returned to Britain looking for both justice and a job. He was almost 60 and overweight, clearly not suited to what might be an exhausting command. But his second wife, Lady Jane Franklin, campaigned relentlessly on his behalf, seeing the expedition as a way of allowing her husband to regain the prestige cruelly robbed by the unfair dismissal from Tasmania. Eventually the Admiralty succumbed to her pressure.

Franklin was given two ships for the expedition, *Erebus* and *Terror*, the pair James Clark Ross had taken south. They were strengthened to withstand pressure from the ice and fitted with railway locomotive steam engines which turned screw propellers, a radically new idea. Sir John Barrow reasoned that the ships, reinforced at the bow and powered from the stern, would plough through the Arctic ice. John Ross had his doubts and also worried about the crew size. The compliment was 133 men and Ross noted how hard it had been to feed one-sixth that number when the *Victory* had been lost. But Barrow was hardly likely to listen to John Ross. The ships were being stocked with tinned food, a revolutionary new idea which promised to eliminate both hunger and scurvy. The canned meat and vegetables were supplied by Stephen Goldner, the man with the lowest tender, but a production line that left much to be desired in terms of the quality of the food and the cleanliness of his production methods. It was said that the only part of the pigs that did not go into Goldner's cans was the squeal, and that with slaughtering of pigs, sheep and cows being carried out on the premises and within sight of other animals the filth that also reached the cans was indescribable. Goldner's cans arrived only hours before the ships sailed, too late for samples to be checked for quality, or the can seals examined.

Above **A daguerreotype of Sir John Franklin.**
UK National Maritime Museum

Below **Goldner cans from Franklin's expedition on Beechey Island.**
Richard Sale

On 19 May 1845 the *Erebus* and *Terror* were made ready to depart the River Thames. Just before sailing a dove flew down and perched on a mast. The commander and crew were cheered by this obvious happy omen. On 26 July the two ships were seen by a whaler, moored to an iceberg on Baffin Bay, close to the entrance to Lancaster Sound. After an exchange of greetings the whaler sailed away. It was the last time that either ship or any of the crew – reduced to 129 after four men had been sent home from Greenland – were seen by European eyes.

History had taught the British not to be too concerned if nothing was heard of Arctic expeditions for several years, but by 1848 James Ross (now Sir James after his southern success) was demanding a rescue mission. That year Ross took two ships to Somerset Island where he was forced to overwinter before retreating in the face of heavy ice. At the same time two more ships were dispatched to the Bering Strait. Despite sledge journeys eastwards (ironically following one of Franklin's land routes) no trace was found of Franklin. During his trip Ross tried the ingenious idea of trapping Arctic foxes and fitting them with collars that carried a message of hope to Franklin, then releasing them. It was the first of many ideas for contacting the beleaguered crew, one of the more entertaining being that of releasing thousands of message-bearing balloons.

During the decade that followed the first rescue attempts more than three dozen expeditions set out in search of Franklin or clues to his disappearance. Many of these were official expeditions from Britain, but some were private. Of the latter, most were at the instigation of Lady Jane Franklin. Jane Griffin had met Franklin when he married her friend Eleanor Porden, marrying him after Eleanor's death and after several chaste dalliances of her own, most notably with Peter Roget, author of the famous thesaurus. Lady Jane was a formidable woman who campaigned relentlessly on behalf of her lost husband, badgering the Admiralty into further searches and spending a fortune on her own. She also wrote to Zachary Taylor, president of the United States, asking for help. That request failed to elicit an official response, being defeated by procrastination in the government, but it did result in a semi-official one when congress backed and part-funded an expedition set up by Henry Grinnell, a New York shipping magnate. The 'First Grinnell Expedition' was also the first American expedition to the Arctic, igniting a public enthusiasm which was to lead, ultimately, to the tragedies and successes of Greely, Cook and Peary.

Charles Francis Hall, another American, also went north on a Franklin search. Hall was a curious man whose later death is the subject of one of the Arctic's most enduring mysteries. Hall believed he had been chosen by God to lead Franklin survivors (who had sought refuge with the Inuit) back to civilisation. Hall actually murdered one travelling companion whom he thought was inciting mutiny, so intent was he on his crusade and so deep was his paranoia that mankind was seeking to stop him. Yet Hall's notes of his interviews with the many Inuit he met form the basis of a coherent story of what exactly did happen to Franklin and his crew. Hall also retrieved the skeleton of one of Franklin's men, and took it back to the US: the skeleton, believed to be that of Henry Le Vesconte, an officer on the *Erebus*, was eventually taken back to Britain and buried at Greenwich. Another skeleton, thought to be that of John Irving, an officer on the *Terror*, was also repatriated and buried in Edinburgh. Le Vesconte and Irving were the only two of Franklin's men to return to Britain.

The Franklin search filled in almost all the gaps in the map of the Arctic coast and the islands close to it. The numerous expeditions also gathered such evidence as existed on the fate of Franklin and his men. There were too many searches to cover them all adequately, but several were too important to exclude.

In 1850 Richard Collinson in the *Enterprise* was given command of an expedition of two ships – Collinson in the *Enterprise*, Robert McClure commanding the *Investigator* – which sailed to the Bering Strait to

Opposite above **Noon, midwinter at Port Leopold on James Clark Ross' expedition in search of Franklin. The original painting was by W.H. Browne who accompanied the expedition.**
Richard Sale Collection

Opposite below **The Arctic Council by Stephen Pearce. The council was a group of the great and the good of British Arctic exploration, formed to offer advice to the Admiralty on the conduct of the Franklin search. They probably did not meet as a group, as depicted here, but the painting does illustrate all the main players in the Royal Navy's quest for both the North-West Passage and Franklin. On the wall are (left to right) portraits of John Franklin, James Fitzjames and Sir John Barrow. The others are (left to right) George Back, William Edward Parry, Edward Bird, James Clark Ross, Francis Beaufort, John Barrow Jnr, Edward Sabine, William Hamilton, John Richardson and Frederick Beechey.**
By courtesy of the UK National Portrait Gallery, London

Above **The sledge party leaving HMS *Investigator* under the command of Lt Cresswell. This is one of a series of sketches by S. Gurney Cresswell, an officer on McClure's ship *Investigator*. Cresswell was involved in sledge trips in Prince of Wales Strait as well as leading one retreating party from the *Investigator* to Melville Island.**

Richard Sale Collection

search eastwards. Probably by design, the ambitious McClure found himself ahead of his commander, and instead of waiting headed east. He reached the mouth of the Mackenzie River and sailed eastward towards the Coppermine. On hearing from local Inuit that they had not seen a ship like his before he reasoned that Franklin had not followed the mainland coast, and headed northeast. McClure entered a waterway (which he named for the Prince of Wales) between Victoria and Banks Islands and, to his growing excitement, realised that he was heading directly for Parry's Barrow Strait and Winter Harbour. When he was finally stopped by heavy ice McClure was only 50km (30 miles) from Barrow Strait and sent out a sledge party which found that the Prince of Wales was a strait, not a sound: McClure had discovered the North-West Passage, a fact which he promptly noted in a cairn he built. *Investigator* spent the winter in the ice of Prince of Wales Strait, then sailed south around Banks Island, McClure intending to reach Barrow Strait by going north along the island's west coast. He rounded the northern tip of Banks, but was forced by heavy ice to overwinter in Mercy Bay, so called because the finding of such a comfortable harbour seemed an act of providence. But though providential as a winter quarters, the bay was a trap from which *Investigator* was never to escape.

McClure sledged to Winter Harbour, proving that a passage existed north of Banks Island as well, then waited for the ice to free his ship or rescue to arrive.

When neither happened, and with his crew dying of scurvy and starvation, he decided that in the spring of 1853 two parties would set out by sledge, one east towards Port Leopold on the north-eastern tip of Somerset Island where James Ross had left supplies in 1848, the other south-west to, and up, the Mackenzie River. These teams were to comprise the sickest men and carry few supplies. McClure and the fitter men would overwinter again in the hope that *Investigator* would be freed and could sail east to complete the passage. That McClure was intending to send men to their deaths is obvious from the comment of Johann Miertsching, a Moravian missionary who accompanied the ship as interpreter. Miertsching, who was to go with the Mackenzie team noted, 'How many of us will in this way see Europe? The answer is "No One"'.

But before McClure could carry out his ridiculous plan Lt Pim arrived at the ship from the *Resolute*, one of the ships of Belcher's 'Arctic Squadron' which had sailed west along Lancaster Sound looking for both Franklin and McClure. The *Resolute* had wintered on Dealy Island (off Melville Island), finding a note McClure had left at Winter Harbour which gave the position of Mercy Bay. McClure returned with Pim to the *Resolute* where its commander, Henry Kellett, a senior officer, effectively ordered him to abandon his plan and the *Investigator* and to bring his men to the *Resolute*. In doing so McClure's crew completed a transit of the passage from west to east, but in two ships and by sledge between them. Back in Britain McClure received a knighthood and claimed – and was given – the government reward for discovering the passage: he had actually found two passages, completing both by sledge. But McClure declined to share the reward with Kellett on the grounds that he had ordered the abandonment of the *Investigator* which, McClure complained, could have been freed and so completed the journey. Kellett, presumably amazed and appalled, gave money for the relief of McClure's still sick crew who also got nothing from McClure, receiving only the Arctic pay that was due to them.

Trailing his second-in-command, Collinson, in the *Enterprise*, unwittingly followed McClure up Prince of Wales Strait, finding his note on the discovery of the passage, and then up the west coast of Banks Island, though ice prevented him from reaching Mercy Bay. Collinson then sailed south again before turning east. He sailed between Victoria Island and the mainland, overwintering in Cambridge Bay. Had it not been for his timidity it is possible Collinson would have reached Victoria Strait, perhaps discovered the remains of Franklin's expedition (if Inuit reports on the movement of the *Erebus* are correct Collinson might even have found the ship), perhaps even – though more doubtfully – sailed north and reached Lancaster Sound. But Collinson did not push too hard into doubtful country, so much so that one of his officers noted, 'Poor Sir John. God help you – you'll get none from us.' However, sledge parties from the *Enterprise* explored the east coast of Victoria Island proving that there was another North-West Passage to the south of McClure's. Collinson then returned to Britain. Interestingly, during this sledge journey along the Victoria coast Collinson's men found a cairn erected by John Rae and, beyond it, three further cairns. Exactly who had built these has never been satisfactorily explained, but Collinson chose to ignore them. They also found a piece of washed-up door frame which almost certainly came from one of Franklin's ships. Again the find was ignored. It is true that his expedition's only interpreter was with McClure and so he could not properly question the local Inuit who may well have had information on Franklin's fate (they actually drew a picture of a ship trapped in ice, but Collinson did not realise its significance: he did attempt to sledge across the ice of Victoria Strait to King William Island – had he succeeded he would have discovered what happened to Franklin – but did not complete the journey). Collinson's journey to Cambridge Bay was a masterpiece of navigation in such a large ship – a fact acknowledged by Amundsen – but his decision not to follow up clues probably relating to the main objective of his trip delayed discovering the fate of Franklin for several years.

The first trace of where Franklin had gone after the whaler had left *Erebus* and *Terror* in Baffin Bay was found in 1850 when a whole fleet of ships had gathered at Beechey Island prior to searching from the Arctic's eastern end. The Americans De Haven and Kane from Grinnell's first expedition were present, as were several Royal Navy ships and John Ross on a private search mission. While many of the commanders were conferring on the island men from the *Assistance*, a Royal Navy ship commanded by Horatio Austin, who had already found some naval stores and meat cans at Cape Riley on nearby Devon Island, found three graves. They were of William Braine and John Hartnell of the *Erebus*, and John Torrington of the *Terror*. All three had died in early 1846, Torrington the first on 1 January. Clearly Franklin had spent the winter of 1845/6 on Beechey Island. But though the discovery was welcomed, it offered no clue.

In Britain Lady Jane Franklin, dismayed at the lack of positive news, was financing her own expeditions. One of these, in 1851 in the *Prince Albert*, led by William Kennedy, included Joseph René Bellot, a handsome Frenchman who captured the hearts of every lady in England, not least by offering to work for nothing in such a noble cause. The trip discovered nothing about the fate of Franklin, but did find the narrow strait separating the Boothia Peninsula from Somerset Island. This – Bellot Strait – was sledged, but at its far side the party crossed Peel Sound rather than exploring southwards. On a later expedition Bellot disappeared when a crack opened in an ice floe.

Left **The graves of the three Franklin expedition sailors at Beechey Island. The headstones are replicas of the originals which have been removed to the museum in Yellowknife. A narrow causeway links the 'island' of Beechey with Devon Island, in the background.**
Richard Sale

Below '**The Departure of the South-West Division', an engraving in** Edward Belcher's *The Last of the Arctic Voyages.* **During his expedition Belcher sent sledge parties out in many directions to search for Franklin, but apart from the graves on Beechey Island had little to show for his efforts.**
Richard Sale Collection

The *Resolute* which rescued McClure and his crew was part of the 'Arctic Squadron' of five ships commanded by Sir Edward Belcher which sailed in 1852 to search from Lancaster Sound. Belcher was a tyrannical man, intensely disliked by his junior officers, and with dissension causing his expedition to disintegrate, he ordered all the ships that were sealed in ice to be abandoned, transferring all the crews to the one free ship (and two supply ships which had fortuitously arrived). To comply with the order to desert the *Resolute* Kellett, though appalled by the decision, closed up his ship, his and McClure's men sledging to Beechey Island. In a curious sequel, in 1855 an American whaler discovered the *Resolute* drifting undamaged in the ice of Davis Strait, having travelled 1,600km (1,000 miles) eastwards through the Parry Channel. It is claimed that when they boarded the Americans found unspilled wine glasses still on the messroom table. The ship was towed back to the US where it was refitted (even pictures and books being carefully restored or replaced) and returned to Britain as a gift to Queen Victoria. It was a fine gesture, but the Admiralty failed to live up to it: in 1880 the *Resolute* was broken up. From her timber a writing table was made and presented to the American president. The table later languished in the White House basement for many years until it was rescued and used by John F. Kennedy. Later still the table achieved a moment of notoriety when it became an important prop in a 'meeting' between President Bill Clinton and Monica Lewinski. Belcher had abandoned five ships and was court-martialled for the offence by a furious Admiralty. Though his reputation was shredded he was found not guilty because he was able to show that his orders had been sufficiently vague to allow the interpretation he had chosen to find in them.

The next news of Franklin's fate came from Dr John Rae, a Hudson's Bay Company surgeon. Rae was an Orkney islander who rapidly learned that the adoption of Inuit methods made survival much easier than it was for those naval officers who insisted on maintaining naval method in an environment for which it was entirely unsuitable. This idea – 'going native' as the British establishment contemptuously called it – almost certainly added to the venom with which Rae's news was greeted. In 1853, on a second overland journey in search of Franklin (and with a secondary purpose of surveying small sections of unexplored coast to confirm that Boothia was a peninsula) Rae met Inuit who told him of their meeting with a large group of (perhaps 40) white men who were dragging a boat along the western shore

Above **Dr John Rae, an engraving from a portrait by Stephen Pearce. Rae was a consummate Arctic traveller, learning from the Inuit and putting what he had learned to good use. Not only did he complete the map of Canada's Arctic shore but he has a strong claim to being the discoverer (if not the traveller) of the North-West Passage. Rae also discovered the fate of Franklin, telling a story for which the British establishment never forgave him.**
Hudson's Bay Company Archives,
Provincial Archives of Manitoba, Canada

of King William Island. By sign and pidgeon Inuit they learned that the white men had abandoned ships crushed in the ice and were looking for caribou and birds to hunt. Later the Inuit had found the remains of many men close to the Great Fish River. Some were in a tent, others under an overturned boat and, as Rae reported, 'from the mutilated state of many of the bodies, and the contents of the kettles, it is evident that our wretched countrymen had been driven to the last dread alternative – cannibalism – as a means of sustaining life'.

Rae brought back relics which he had traded from the Inuit. These proved beyond doubt that the men were Franklin's; and, given the size of the party, they could not really have been anyone else's. But these

Above **The inhospitable terrain of King William Island. With its frost-shattered rocks, minimal shelter and limited vegetation and animal life, King William was a desperate place for the Franklin survivors.**

Richard Sale

positive finds were all but washed away by the wave of public indignation that followed the publication of Rae's account of cannibalism, particularly as the account was based on Inuit testimony; Rae had not visited the campsite and seen the kettles for himself. *The Times* thundered that no one could take this seriously as the Inuit 'like all savages are liars'. Charles Dickens was equally outraged. Egged on by Jane Franklin, who orchestrated a campaign against Rae and his account, Dickens published articles in his magazine *Household Words*. Speaking for much of the country he claimed that the story was bound to be false as it was based on the word of 'the savage' and 'we believe every savage to be in his heart covetous, treacherous and cruel'. Dickens went on to hint that it was more likely that the Inuit had murdered Franklin's men and that if there was indeed human flesh to be found in kettles it was an

offering by the Inuit 'to their barbarous, wide-mouthed, goggle-eyed gods.' Having demolished the Inuit testimony Dickens went on to note that 'it is in the highest degree improbable that such men [Franklin's] would, or could, in any extremity of hunger, alleviate the pains of starvation by this horrible means'. Dickens also noted that as Franklin's men had no fuel and so could not light fires they could not have practised cannibalism, not being able to cook the meat: the Inuit ate raw meat, but they were savages of course, not civilised Englishmen.

The reaction to Rae's news is a lesson in Victorian values. The belief in the innate superiority of the Briton to any native, and even to anybody from a civilised country, is manifest (the upper classes in Britain also put the working class in much the same category as the 'savages' they so despised). The logical extension of this xenophobia (perhaps racism would be a better word) was that the British officer class had nothing to learn from natives and everything to teach them. It was an attitude that had sent men in dress uniforms to the Arctic and would, in not so many years, send others equally unprepared to Antarctica.

The controversy hurt Rae immensely. He felt humiliated, a feeling heightened when the government did not honour him with the knighthood they had bestowed on much less deserving individuals, and quibbled over the payment of the reward for finding the fate of Franklin, Lady Jane Franklin consistently lobbying against him.

Lady Jane Franklin chose not to believe his story and pressed for another search expedition. The Admiralty and government were reluctant: too many ships and lives had been lost already; it was now ten years since Franklin had sailed away, and the Crimean War had begun. The Admiralty's publication of Rae's story – it was they, not he, that had told *The Times* – was an effort to call a halt to further expeditions. Despite public pressure and Lady Franklin's moral blackmail they stood firm, forcing Lady Jane to finance the final search herself.

In 1857 Francis McClintock, already a veteran of several search missions and a sledging expert, took command of the *Fox*, a small, but highly manoeuvrable ship, and headed north. The *Fox* almost failed to make a search at all, heavy ice sealing her in. The ship drifted south for eight months before being released and did not make Lancaster Sound until July 1858. McClintock found Peel Sound closed by ice and in desperation went down Prince Regent Inlet in the hope

The McClintock note is actually made up of two, written one year apart on an official form that requested, in six languages, its return to the Admiralty or local British consul. The first note, signed by Lt Graham Gore and Charles Frederick Des Voeux, mate, was written in May 1847 and states:

HMS Ships Erebus *and* Terror *28 May 1847 wintered in the Ice in Lat 70°5'N, Long 98°23'W. Having wintered in 1846–7 at Beechey Island in Lat 74°43'28''N Long 91·39'15''W after having ascended Wellington Channel to Lat 77° and returned by the west side of Cornwallis Island. Sir John Franklin commanding the Expedition. All well. Party consisting of 2 officers and 6 men left ship on Monday 24th May 1847.*

The date of the wintering on Beechey is wrong – it was 1845/6 – but the remarkable information is that Franklin had sailed around Cornwallis Island finding open water in Wellington Channel but presumably being stopped by ice at about 77°N. What was the condition of the ice in the Parry Channel? Could he have sailed west from Cornwallis and gone beyond Melville and Banks islands towards Alaska?

The second message reads:

(25th April) 1848 HM Ships Terror *and* Erebus *were deserted on the 22nd April 5 leagues NNW of this (hav)ing been beset since 12th Sept 1846. The officers and crews consisting of 105 souls under the command (of Cap)tain FRM Crozier landed here – in Lat 69°37'42'' Long 98°41' (This) paper was found by Lt Irving under the cairn supposed to have been built by Sir James Ross in 1831 – where it had been deposited (4 miles to the northward) – by the late commander Gore in June 1847. Sir James Ross' pillar has not however been found and the paper has been transferred to this position which is that in which Sir J Ross pillar was erected – Sir John Franklin died on the 11th June 1847 and the total loss by deaths to this date 9 officers and 15 men.*

Right **'The Franklin Message'.**
From Francis McClintock's *The Voyage of the Fox in the Arctic Seas.*
Richard Sale Collection

This note was signed by 'James Fitzjames, Captain HMS *Erebus*'. It was also signed 'FRM Crozier, Captain and Senior Offr', Crozier adding a postscript 'and start on tomorrow, 26th, for Backs Fish River'.

Despite its brevity the note reveals a great deal. The two ships had left Beechey in summer 1846 and headed south, presumably through Peel Sound, becoming beset off King William Island in September and being abandoned two years later. Lt Gore (who left the first message) was dead, as were 23 others (three on Beechey, 20 later, including Franklin), a much higher death rate than on any previous expedition. A later discovery of the likely grave of Lt Irving at Victory Point suggests that if he was the man who went to Ross' cairn he was fit enough to have survived for some time after the suggested journey south towards the Great Fish (Back) River.

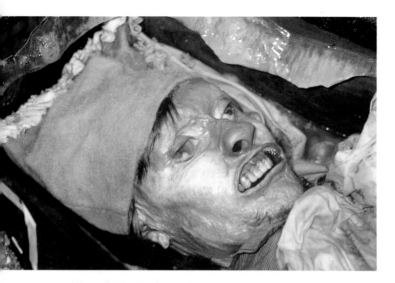

Above **The almost perfectly preserved bodies of John Hartnell, top, and John Torrington, are revealed after the Beechey Island exhumations.**
Richard Sale Collection

McClintock almost reached Starvation Cove on the Adelaide Peninsula before turning north along King William Island's west coast. Along the shore he found remnants of the expedition including an almost intact skeleton. Ahead of him Hobson was finding the only note ever discovered from the Franklin expedition as well as a boat (pointing north) holding two skeletons and many other items, and the vast pile of supplies at Victory Point. The fate of the Franklin expedition had been discovered, though the manner in which it came about was, and still is, a matter of conjecture.

The conventional scenario, established 30 to 40 years later, is that with *Erebus* and *Terror* beset and food and fuel running low, the men abandoned the ships and started south, intending to use boats to follow the Great Fish (Back) River to a Hudson's Bay Company outpost. Overcome by hunger and (perhaps) scurvy they died one by one, the last groups perishing at Starvation Cove on the Adelaide Peninsula and Montreal Island in Chantry Inlet. This story is now challenged, in part by analysis carried out on bones from King William Island and autopsies on the three corpses at Beechey Island, and also by close examination of Inuit testimony gathered by Charles Hall. The bone analysis shows high levels of lead as well as distinct signs of scurvy. High lead levels are also present in the Beechey corpses, though their deaths were from natural causes.

The finding of significant levels of lead has led to Professor Owen Beattie, the leader of the teams which carried out the analyses, to suggest that lead poisoning from the solder used to seal the food tins carried by the expedition was a factor in crew deaths. Canning was a new technique in the 1840s and the lethal potential of lead was not understood. A more recent suggestion has been that the food within the cans was contaminated on account of poor hygiene at Goldner's canning factory. One writer has even suggested botulism as a cause of death. Certainly the death rate was very high and the preponderance of officer deaths also suggests a can-based mechanism: as a rule officers fed better than crew, and the cans might have been considered the better fare. Roald Amundsen relates a story told to him by Inuit he met at Gjøahaven during his journey through the passage. This maintains that Inuit retrieving cans of food from the Franklin trip died after consuming the contents. It is also the case that hundreds of empty cans were left on Beechey Island, seemingly more than could have been consumed in a single winter. Were many found to be bad and abandoned? However, against this hypothesis is

that Bellot Strait was navigable. He pushed through the strait but was unable to exit its western end and retreated to overwinter close to the eastern end, spending the dark months laying down supply depots for sledge journeys in the spring.

In April 1859 three teams set out. One headed north-west, while McClintock and Lt William Hobson headed south to explore King William Island.

the fact that without modern medicines botulism has a very high mortality rate, perhaps 75 per cent. The cans were large and many men would have eaten from each one opened. How can so many men have survived so long if many cans were contaminated?

An alternative scenario, one supported by Inuit stories and now gaining credibility, suggests that with men dying, perhaps from a combination of contaminated food and scurvy, Crozier (in command after Franklin's death) decided to abandon the ships. He brought as much as possible ashore, then set out south. At first his crew managed to shoot a lot of game (after Franklin the Inuit abandoned King William Island because its animal life had been exterminated) but eventually food runs out. One group of men now try to regain the ships, some dying along the way – this scenario would explain why the discovered boat was pointing north not south – while others continue south, driven eventually to cannibalism. One ship appears to have broken free of the ice and was probably sailed to Kirkwall Island off Adelaide Peninsula's western coast where it was beset again. This ship sank when Inuit cut into it to plunder its contents.

This latter account seems much more plausible. But there are certainly some mysteries in the Franklin story: why did Crozier go south when Fury Beach, where there were still supplies, was closer? Why were so many luxury items hauled by a sick, starving crew? Who was the giant with long teeth the Inuit claimed to have found on the ship near Kirkwall Island? Why did the survivors, if they were heading for the Great Fish River, choose to cross Simpson Strait at its widest point rather than at its narrowest? The latter offers the intriguing possibility that the very last survivors may have been heading for Repulse Bay, and there are tantalising Inuit tales of white men surviving for many years and even that some almost made it to Hudson's Bay Company forts. Quite whether the still-unsolved (and probably unsolvable) mysteries warrant the suggestion of extra-terrestrial intervention of a recent theory seems unlikely.

When McClintock returned Lady Jane Franklin used her formidable powers of persuasion on his behalf, using him as a final weapon against Rae. She lobbied for McClintock to receive a knighthood, which he did, and for his name to be placed on her husband's memorial in Westminster Abbey, which it was. She also ensured that the memorial, and another in Waterloo Place, bore inscriptions which stated that Sir John Franklin was the discoverer of the North-West Passage. If the discovery requires only the identification of a waterway then it was John Rae who did that, in 1846. Franklin's expedition did not discover a complete waterway until after his death (and may not even have done so then – though if a ship really was sailed to Kirkwall Island then they may have, without realising it). McClure's discovery post-dated both. If the requirement is to have completed a navigable route rather than merely identifying it, then Amundsen wins the race.

Right **The Franklin Monument on Beechey Island. The monument was erected by Edward Belcher. Beside it are the ruins of Northumberland House, a timber depot built during the Belcher expedition.**
Richard Sale

The passage completed

After the disastrous loss of the Franklin expedition and the costly and exhausting searches, the British gave up the idea of a North-West Passage. It was clearly of no commercial value, the need to keep naval officers and ships occupied had slackened, and given a choice between national honour and the national exchequer pragmatism won. Not until 1902 did an expedition return to the Canadian Arctic when Otto Sverdrup sailed in the second *Fram* expedition. A few years later the North-West Passage was finally completed by ship.

The Norwegian Roald Engebreth Gravning Amundsen was born on 16 July 1872 and grew up, a pugnacious boy, on the outskirts of Oslo (then Christiania), acquiring early the skills of skiing and seamanship. Having obtained his master's certificate, chiefly by working on sealing boats, Amundsen served his polar apprenticeship on the *Belgica*. By 1901 he felt ready to take command of his first expedition. As a teenager Amundsen had been inspired by the books of John Franklin: not the tragic events surrounding his disappearance, but the accounts of the overland journeys to the shores of the Arctic ocean. Most of all Amundsen wanted to be the first to complete a transit of the North-West Passage.

Amundsen had learned much from the early accounts of the British in the Arctic. He realised that safety lay in small ships which were highly manoeuvrable and had shallow drafts; that it lay in fewer men as the land could only support a limited number; and

that it lay in adopting Inuit methods of dress. In 1901 he bought *Gjøa* (pronounced 'you-ah'), a tiny (47-ton) herring-fishing boat. The ship was refitted, the hull sheathed against ice and a small engine installed. At midnight on 16 June 1903 Amundsen and his crew of six (including Adolf Lindström, who had been with Sverdrup on *Fram*'s second voyage, and Helmer Hanssen, who would later accompany Amundsen to the South Pole) took *Gjøa* out of Oslo fjord. On 25 July Amundsen stopped at Nuuk in west Greenland to add ten dogs to those he already had. In Greenland he met the Danes Rasmussen and Mylius-Erichsen, men whose names are prominent in the history of Greenland exploration.

Leaving Greenland *Gjøa* made good progress, going through Lancaster Sound to reach Beechey Island on 22 August. Now, faced with a choice of routes, Amundsen headed south-west, then south through Peel Strait. This choice, rather than west towards Banks Island, was probably due to Amundsen's wish to reach the North Magnetic Pole (or at least to study magnetic variations close to it) as he had been concerned that without some scientific purpose his trip would be dismissed as a mere adventure. Making amazing progress through open water *Gjøa* reached the entrance to Sir James Ross Strait (between Boothia and King William Island) on 30 August.

As Amundsen soon found – and Franklin had, perhaps, already found – Sir James Ross Strait is shallow and shoal-filled. *Gjøa*, despite her limited draft, ran

aground early on 31 August, damaging her keel. After getting the ship afloat again, fire broke out in the engine room and threatened to engulf the fuel tanks. The fire was put out quickly, but Amundsen was left in no doubt about what could have ensued. Soon after *Gjøa* grounded again on a reef, this time much more seriously as it happened at high tide. The next high tide failed to refloat the ship which was then battered by a storm which threatened to haul her along the reef, tearing her bottom out. Amundsen decided to abandon ship, but Anton Lund, ship's mate, suggested jettisoning cargo to reduce the draft. This worked, the ship floating free: *Gjøa* and the expedition were saved.

Continuing south, *Gjøa* rounded the southern tip of King William Island. Amundsen could see that Simpson Strait was ice-free, but it was now mid-September and he preferred to overwinter in a natural harbour where the ship would be protected and could be anchored just metres from shore. There was, too, the need to stay close to the North Magnetic Pole – the passage could wait a little. The chosen anchorage was named Gjøahavn, now Gjøahaven, a Canadian historic park.

At Gjøahavn the crew were visited by the local Inuit and Amundsen learned all he could from them on dog-driving, sledging (particularly how to coat sledge runners with ice so they slid more easily), clothing, igloo building and survival techniques, lessons that proved invaluable later in Antarctica. He set out on a sledge journey to find the magnetic pole on 1 March, but it was too cold for both men and dogs. Forced to retreat, the men had to help haul the sledges, showing Amundsen that manhauling was 'futile toil' (something the Royal Navy had failed to learn despite dozens of lessons). But Amundsen failed to appreciate the lesson of starting too early and made the same mistake again in Antarctica. When he did finally go again he took just one companion, Peder Ristvedt. The two reached Sir James Ross' cairn and found that the pole had moved, the first proof that it migrated. The two men circled the area, but though in his book on the passage journey Amundsen claims to have passed over the 'new' pole he did not in fact approach closer than 50km (30 miles) of the new site. It is not clear why Amundsen did not reach the pole, and the miss rankled with him for the rest of his life.

The sledging took most of the summer; winter came early and the expedition stayed at Gjøahavn. The next summer Ristvedt and Helmer Hanssen explored the east coast of Victoria Island by sledge. Then, on 13 August 1905, *Gjøa* left her harbour and became the first ship to navigate Simpson Strait. After four days the ship had reached Collinson's most easterly point: a North-West Passage had now been fully explored. On 26 August *Gjøa* met the US whaler *Charles Hansson* off Nelson Head, the southernmost point of Banks Island. Further east, at King Point near Herschel Island (west of the mouth of the Mackenzie River) ice stopped *Gjøa*, forcing the crew to overwinter for a third time. In

Above **The crew of *Gjøa* photographed when the ship arrived in Nome, Alaska.**
USA Library of Congress

Below **Dawn, Herschel Island. The island was named by John Franklin for the British father-and-son astronomers.**
Richard Sale

Right **On 6 March 1897 men from whalers moored at Herschel Island were playing baseball on the ice in a temperature of 20°C beneath a blue sky. Within seconds a storm arrived, dropping the temperature to –20°C and creating a white-out. The men scrambled to find cover, any cover, but the next day five bodies, all frozen to death, were found. Eight years later Amundsen arrived at the island. It was from Herschel that Amundsen headed south with the news that he had completed the North-West Passage.**
Richard Sale

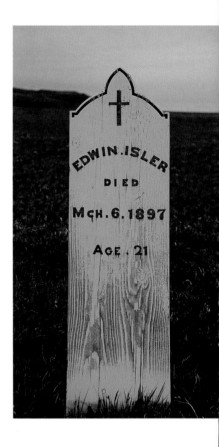

Above **The eastern end of the Bellot Strait. At its narrowest the strait is barely 300m (1,000ft) wide, but over 600m (2,000ft) deep. On its southern side is Zenith Point, the most northerly point of the American mainland. Though discovered and sledged in the winter of 1851/2 by Joseph René Bellot, the strait was not navigated until 1942.**
Richard Sale

Above **The SS *Manhattan* nears Point Barrow during the first commercial transit of the North-West Passage.**
US Navy Historical Centre

October, using dog-sledges, Amundsen, two Inuit and William Moys, captain of a shipwrecked US whaler, travelled south to Eagle City where Amundsen formally announced his completion of the passage. Technically, of course, that was not completed until 1926 when, with Amundsen back on board but one crewman, Gustav Wiik, having died, *Gjøa* was sailed around Point Barrow and through the Bering Strait. The ship reached San Francisco on 19 October 1906 where it stayed until 1972 when it was returned to Norway to stand close to *Fram* on Oslo's Bygdøy museum's site.

Not until 1940 was Amundsen's traverse repeated, and then in the opposite direction, the Canadian Henry Larsen skippering the *St Roch* from west to east, overwintering at Cambridge Bay and Sir James Ross Strait. In 1942 *St Roch* went through Bellot Strait (the first transit by ship) to reach Lancaster Sound rather than following *Gjøa*'s route. In 1944 Larsen took the *St Roch* west again, following the northern passage – west from Lancaster Sound, then south-west along the Prince of Wales Strait. The journey was completed in 86 days, *St Roch* becoming the first vessel to complete the passage in both directions and the first to complete it in one season. In 1962 the USS *Skate* made the first submarine transit, travelling east–west, then in 1969 the 155,000-ton US tanker *Manhattan* made the first commercial transit, using the northern route, escorted by the Canadian icebreaker

John A. Macdonald. Eight years later, in 1977, Dutchman Willy de Roos piloted the 13m (42¹/₂ft) ketch *Williwaw* east–west, the first singled-handed transit.

Knud Rasmussen had followed the passage over land (with dog-sledges) as early as the 1920s, a feat which was repeated by the Japanese Naomi Uemura in 1974/6. In 1991/3 the young Spaniard Ramón Hernando de Larramendi followed in their dog tracks, but actually went further. Starting at Narsarsuaq – and travelling with three colleagues, though none of them completed the full journey, joining Larramendi for certain stages – he kayaked Greenland's west coast to Ukkuisissat, then used a dog-sledge to reach Siorpaluk, crossing Smith Sound and Ellesmere Island (to Eureka) before turning south to follow the passage down the Boothia Peninsula's east coast, then along the mainland coast to Inuvik. The team kayaked to Kotzebue and then used dog-sledges to reach Anchorage. A similar, but shortened, journey from Prudhoe Bay to the Gulf of Boothia was made solo by kayak and dog-sledge by Jonathan Waterman in 1997/9.

In 1984 and 1985 the first commercial passenger transits were made east–west, then west–east. Today there are regular passenger trips and, with the possibility of the Arctic ice reducing due to global warming, there are again whispers that a commercial route might become a reality.

The North-East Passage

The conquest of Siberia

In 1533 the three-year-old Ivan IV inherited the title of Grand Prince of Muscovy from his father. Ivan's grandfather, Ivan III, had freed Muscovy from the rule of the Mongol Golden Horde and had expanded the princedom as far as the Urals. In 1547 Ivan was crowned Czar, the first Russian to hold the title. Six years later he established a relationship with western Europe by signing his trade agreement with Richard Chancellor. Ivan IV has become known as Ivan the Terrible, his cruelties being considered gross even during a period of history not noted for the benign treatment of those considered enemies of the state. Ivan's reign of terror, aided by disease, ill-considered military campaigns and, most particularly, a drying up in the supply of furs, had brought Russia to the edge of disaster. The sable, a member of the marten family with a much-prized thick coat, had been all but exterminated in northern Muscovy: without new sources of supply Ivan faced economic ruin. He therefore encouraged (or, at least, failed to discourage: Ivan's support was vague and ambiguous) the Stroganovs, one of Muscovy's most powerful mercantile families (and claimed as the source of the original beef stroganoff), to probe eastwards beyond the Urals where it was known that there was a seemingly limitless supply of furs.

Across the Urals, traditionally the boundary of Europe and Asia, lay Siberia, named from the Mongolian *siber* meaning beautiful and pure or, perhaps, from the Tartar *sibir*, which translates as 'sleeping land'. The sheer scale of Siberia is breathtaking. Trains on the Trans-Siberian Railway take eight days to chug their way from Moscow to Vladivostock, six of those days spent east of the Urals. East of the Europe/Asia obelisk the train crosses five time zones. East of Vladivostock, a traveller would cross three more as he edged around the Sea of Okhotsk and continued to Bering Strait. Siberia stretches from the Arctic Ocean to the Mongolian Steppes: it covers almost 8 per cent of the world's land area. The whole of the United States of America, including Alaska, together with all the countries of Europe (apart from European Russia) could be fitted into Siberia; an area three times the size of Italy would remain uncovered. Lake Baikal, Siberia's largest lake is, by volume, the largest freshwater lake on earth, holding one-fifth of the world's fresh water. Each of its three great rivers – the Lena, the Ob and the Yenisey –

drains a basin bigger than western Europe. But the size of Siberia is modern knowledge: when Ivan took an interest in the area the Russians knew only that it extended as far as Lake Baikal.

It is usually written that it was to this majestic wilderness that the Stroganovs sent Vasily Timofeyevich, a notorious cossack and Volga pirate known as Ermak. In reality Ermak crossed the Urals – hauling boats over the mountains so he could make use of the rivers beyond – to attack the Mongolian khanate of Siberia, which at that time comprised only what is now the south-western corner of modern Siberia. Ermak was a leader in the Ivan the Terrible style, anyone foolish enough to question his authority being tied in a sack along with a bag of sand and dumped in the nearest river. He seems to have been driven by the chance of plunder rather than only expansionist zeal, but the vast wealth in furs he 'liberated' from the control of avaricious middlemen led to a massive Russian expansion eastwards. In that sense Ermak can be seen as having led the Russians into Siberia. Ironically, in view of his preferred method of disposing of his enemies, Ermak died by drowning during a river crossing, weighed down by his massive armour.

At first, despite his tacit support for the Stroganov initiative, Ivan was appalled by the reprisal raids Ermak's incursions generated on Russia's southern border. His mood soon changed when the first batch of furs, thousands of sable, arrived. Within a century the Russians had reached Kamchatka, leaving only the extremities of Taimyr and Chukotka beyond the Czar's grasp. In Moscow the arm of government which administered Ermak's first conquest was called Sibirskiy Prikaz, the Siberia Department, which had administered the khanate during the Mongolian rule of Russia. As Russia expanded eastwards the department took over the administration of all the land east of the Urals, but the name remained the same and so the modern Siberia came into being. In view of the source of the name it was a fortunate accident, for Siberia really is the most beautiful land.

The fur trappers and, to a lesser extent, the religious dissidents who followed them, explored Siberia by water rather than land. In this they were not only applying common sense in so vast a land, but following a tradition which was centuries old. The aboriginal peoples of northern Russia close to the White Sea were land-dwellers herding reindeer in much the same way as their Saami cousins to the west. These folk were displaced, in part at least, by migrants from central

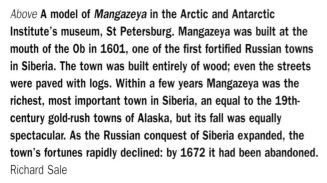

Above **A model of *Mangazeya* in the Arctic and Antarctic Institute's museum, St Petersburg. Mangazeya was built at the mouth of the Ob in 1601, one of the first fortified Russian towns in Siberia. The town was built entirely of wood; even the streets were paved with logs. Within a few years Mangazeya was the richest, most important town in Siberia, an equal to the 19th-century gold-rush towns of Alaska, but its fall was equally spectacular. As the Russian conquest of Siberia expanded, the town's fortunes rapidly declined: by 1672 it had been abandoned.**
Richard Sale

Above **The ancient peoples of the White Sea coast were once known as Samoyed. The name is now considered a term of abuse, akin to Eskimo. Originally the word was thought to mean 'self-eater' and Samoyeds were widely believed to be cannibals. It is probable that the word actually derives from Saami, the now-preferred term for Lapps as the folk were closely related to the Saami of the Kola Peninsula. Today the people call themselves Nentsy. During his journey through the area in 1893 Frederick Jackson, whom Nansen met on Franz Josef Land, drew this picture of a now long-gone Nentsy ritual site on Vaygach Island. The site consisted of one large and many small carved wooden effigies and a vast heap of reindeer antlers and polar bear skulls. This illustration of the site is from Frederick Jackson's *The Great Frozen Land*.**
Richard Sale Collection

Russia. Documentary evidence shows that as early as the 12th century the newcomers were using the river systems which feed the White Sea in order to trade.

By the 15th century the area around the White Sea was being called Pomary (from *po mor* – by the sea) and its inhabitants were famous as hunters who travelled the ice and seas of the local Arctic in search of seals, walrus and bears. There is a tradition that the Starostin family hunted in Svalbard prior to the founding of the Solovetsk monastery (on an island in the White Sea) in 1425, and documents suggesting the Russian Czar had taken possession of 'Grumant' in the mid-16th century. Grumant is Greenland, but it was at first thought that Svalbard was part of Greenland.

Russian scholars believe the anecdotal/documentary evidence is strong proof of Pomore activity in Svalbard prior to the Barents expedition and have even claimed dendrochronological evidence dating from the mid-16th century to support this. Western sources are more sceptical, pointing out that wood could have been carried to Svalbard by currents, or by the hunters

themselves. The debate has a political overtone, Norway being consistently nervous about the strength of its sovereignty claim over Svalbard, particularly with a Russian presence on the islands and the oddity of Svalbard's position after the implementation of the Schengen Agreement on 1 January 2001. Since it is certain that the Pomores reached Novaya Zemlya it seems likely that they did indeed reach Svalbard before Barents, though whether this was as early as the 14th or 15th centuries is questionable. The Pomores used the *koch*, a superbly adapted vessel for exploring Arctic waters. The koch was small with curved sides and a rounded bottom so that it would ride up under ice pressure. It had a single mast and sail, but was light enough to be rowed. This, and its shallow draft, made it highly manoeuvrable in ice, its rounded bottom

Above **The ruins of a Russian cross on Kvitøya, one of the islands of the Svalbard archipelago. Although the cross is almost certainly later than the Pomores, it is indicative of the long Russian history of this area of the Arctic.**

Per Michelsen

allowing it to be readily freed if pack ice threatened to trap it. The koch looked somewhat like *Gjøa*, Amundsen's North-West Passage ship. The same design, now known as a *karbas*, is still in use today in the White Sea, a wooden ship usually still held together in the traditional way with nails of juniper. Juniper does not rust or split the wood if ice pressure moves the timbers, as metal nails would.

The Pomores could survive for several weeks in the boats and almost indefinitely off the land. In 1743 four men were accidentally marooned on Edgeøya (off Spitsbergen's eastern coast) when the ice-bound ship they had left for a night ashore had disappeared by the next morning. For six years they survived by hunting, drinking blood to ward off scurvy (the one man who objected to drinking blood died) and were in good health when rescued in 1749. Though this was at least 200 years after the supposed first Svalbard journeys survival technology had altered little over that time, implying an integration with the environment almost to Inuit standards.

Over the years that followed the Russian expansion into Siberia, Pomore skills at navigating rivers and the icy seas off the northern Siberian shore were critical. The term 'cossack' derives from the Chinese for 'a man who has no king', men who lived beyond the emperor's rule. In Russia cossacks were those who avoided or bought their way out of serfdom when it was instigated at the time of Ivan III. Cossacks lived on the edge of

society: they were frontiersman, a tough breed who were Russia's first line of defence against Mongol and Tartar incursions, and who led the settlement of Siberia. Ermak was a cossack, and it was cossacks who led the groups of *promyshlenniki* (hunters and trappers) that pushed ever eastwards. By 1620 they had reached Taimyr, rounding Cape Chelyuskin, the northernmost point of the Eurasian mainland. By 1630 they had reached the Lena River. In 1633 the cossack Ivan Rebrov sailed down the Lena to the sea, turned east and reached the Yana River and, later, the Indigirka. In 1642 Mikhail Stadukhin reached the Kolyma River, though by then another cossack, Dimitri Kopylov, had already seen the Pacific. In 1639 Kopylov had led a band of promyshlenniki along the Okhota (hunter) River to a foggy bay crammed with driftwood. The sea that brought the wood ashore was called Okhotsk after the trapping party.

Dezhnev sails east

One of the most significant of all expeditions to the Arctic took place in the north in 1648. Despite the vast wealth of Siberia, new sources of sable and other fur-bearing animals were always being sought. It is estimated that during the last half of the 17th century over 100,000 sable were trapped annually. By 1648 rumours were spreading that the country of the Anadyr River, which reached the Sea of Okhotsk in southern Chukotka, was rich in fur. That way, too, lay mammoth and walrus ivory, and an expedition set out to discover a sea route to both treasuries. The nominal leader of the expedition was a trader, Fedot Alekseyev, an agent for a wealthy Moscow merchant. Moscow appointed the cossack Semen Ivanovich Dezhnev to protect Alekseyev and his promyshlenniki. Little is known of Dezhnev. He was probably a Pomore born in about 1605, and had seen service with Stadukhin. The expedition which now bears his name consisted of seven kochs, his own, those of Alekseyev, and others filled with unattached but eager promyshlenniki, 90 men in total.

The expedition left in June 1648. In ice conditions which must have been remarkably favourable, but weather which was not, the expedition had lost four ships before Chukotka was reached, and another was wrecked on the Chukotka coast. The remaining two, commanded by Alekseyev and Dezhnev, rounded Cape Dezhnev, Chukotka's north-eastern tip, and sighted the Diomede Islands. The men landed on the Chukotka shore where there was a skirmish with the native folk: back at sea the two ships were separated in a storm.

Alekseyev and his men were never seen again, though Alekseyev's Yakut mistress did survive. (Alekseyev's mistress was likely to have been a hostage, it being standard practice among the promyshlenniki to take local hostages which were then ransomed, usually for pelts: it is unlikely that the relationship between Alekseyev and the woman was a love match.) Dezhnev's koch was driven south of the Anadyr River and then ashore. The ship had travelled over 3,000km (2,000 miles) in 100 days and passed through the Bering Strait.

Dezhnev still had 25 men with him. They crossed the mountains to reach the Anadyr but discovered that its valley had neither sable nor game animals (it had, possibly, already been exhausted by local hunters). A group of 12 men went upriver looking for food, but found none, nine men disappearing as they trekked back to the river mouth. The survivors overwintered, then built boats of driftwood and went upriver again. They overwintered once more and then, amazingly, met a group of men from a team commanded by Mikhail Stadukhin who, unaware of the sea expedition, had walked to the Anadyr.

Several more men were killed in fights with locals, but Dezhnev, emboldened by the relative ease with which Stadukhin had reached the Anadyr overland, was determined to explore the area. At the river's mouth he found a huge walrus colony, collecting a load of ivory. He also met Alekseyev's mistress. She told him that Alekseyev's koch had been driven ashore, that all but a handful of the men had been killed in a battle with natives, and that the survivors had died. (There was a persistent rumour that they had reached Kamchatka and lived there for several years, but no firm evidence has ever been discovered to substantiate this.) Finally Dezhnev returned home. Over subsequent years he returned to the Anadyr, collecting over 2 tons of walrus ivory. Later he successfully petitioned for a reward for his discoveries and eventually retired to Moscow.

Bering and Russian America

Strangely, despite both its significance and its value as an epic tale of adventure and survival, Dezhnev's journey was forgotten for almost a century. Before its rediscovery Peter the Great had sponsored an expedition which, though achieving much less than Dezhnev's, has become much better known. Czar Peter was an enthusiastic amateur geographer, but his interest in Russia's Arctic coast had to take second place to foreign wars and the feuding of St Petersburg. In late

Above **A koch, as would have been used by Semen Dezhnev.**
This drawing is from Mikhail Belov *Arctic voyages and the design of Russian ships in the 17th century.*
Richard Sale Collection

Above **The lighthouse/memorial to Semen Dezhnev at Cape Dezhnev, the easternmost point of Asia.**
Richard Sale

1724 Peter helped rescue sailors from a capsized boat in the Gulf of Finland. The icy waters chilled him and he developed pneumonia. As he lay dying he finally gave orders for an expedition to see if Asia and America were joined at the Chukotka Peninsula. Interestingly he noted that he had seen a map which indicated 'a passage through the Arctic Sea'. Did a misty knowledge of Dezhnev's journey exist?

On 26 January 1725 Peter signed the papers that finalised the expedition. Two days later he died. The man appointed to lead the expedition was Vitus Jonassen Bering, a 44-year-old Dane recently retired from Russia's Imperial Navy. To make the voyage the Russians decided to take the expedition overland to the Sea of Okhotsk, then to cross it in ships built at the shore. They would then cross Kamchatka and build a ship for the northern journey on the peninsula's eastern shore. This epic journey took three-and-a-half years. On the journey across Siberia one section of the expedition, separated from the forward party, had to eat their horses, then their leather harnesses, and finally their clothing and boots to fend off starvation. Ill-clad and bootless they survived the winter in holes dug in the snow, a curiously amateur scenario given the abundance of food Siberia offered any man with a gun. At the Sea of Okhotsk the expedition discovered that the local timber was so poor nails were useless and built a craft (the *Fortuna*, probably named in hope rather than expectation) that was held together with leather straps, more raft than ship. In this they successfully crossed to Kamchatka twice (a crossing of 1000km/600 miles each way, a remarkable achievement), ferrying all their supplies and men.

On Kamchatka, Bering had to cross the rugged mountain chain that runs down the spine of the peninsula, an epic journey through blizzards that 'rolled like a dark smoke over moors' with nights spent in snow holes. Living off the land now, his supplies having dwindled away, Bering built his ship, the *Svyatoy Gavriil* (St Gabriel). On 14 July 1728 the ship sailed from the Kamchatka River. Bering had spent three-and-a-half years getting to this point: his ship was stacked with food for another year. His voyage lasted just 51 days. Sailing north-east he hit the southern Chukotka coast, following it east to discover St Lawrence Island (named for the saint's feast day, on which it was first sighted). He then sailed north, bad weather preventing him from seeing the Alaskan coast to the east. During a friendly meeting with some Chukchi natives Bering was told that the Asian coast soon turned west, not east towards America. With this information he discussed options with his two deputy commanders. Alexei Chirikov, a Russian assigned to the expedition as a navigator, felt they should press on to the Kolyma River and so prove the absence of a land bridge. Martin Spanberg, a Dane like Bering, disagreed, believing their mission was accomplished. Bering sided with Spanberg and after a couple of days' sailing, reaching 67°19'N, the ship turned south again.

History has been kind to Bering: James Cook, who surveyed the area 50 years later, named the strait and the sea beyond it (where Bering turned) for him. Cook did not know of Dezhnev's journey; neither did the Russians in St Petersburg, but they were far less impressed by Bering's incautious uninspiring voyage than Cook, despite the leadership he had shown during the crossing of Siberia. He had explored neither the Chukotka nor American shores, he had not proven beyond doubt that no land bridge existed, and he had returned along his outward route when an eastern deviation might (and almost certainly would) have brought new discoveries.

Yet despite official displeasure, when Bering submitted plans for a second expedition they were approved. During this second Kamchatka Expedition (1741/2) Bering discovered some of the Aleutian Islands and Kayak Islands, while his deputy – Alexei Chirikov again – discovered Prince of Wales Island. Chirikov's attempted landing in southern Alaska was disastrous: he sent his first mate, Abraham Dementiev, ashore with ten armed men, but they did not return, forcing Chirikov to depart. A local legend maintains that the native Indians killed the Russians, but some experts believe it is more likely they were drowned when their boats were caught in the now-notorious rip tides of the Lisyansky Strait.

The expedition also included Georg W. Steller, the German naturalist becoming the first European to land on Alaska when, sensing history in the moment, he leapt ashore first at Kayak Island. Steller's name is associated with several Alaskan species, most notably Steller's (or Northern) sea lion and Steller's sea cow. These animals kept some of the members of the expedition alive when Bering's ship (the *St Peter*) was wrecked on one of the Commander Islands. Bering and many other members of his crew died of scurvy on the island, now called Bering Island in his honour. Steller's sea cow was a huge manatee, up to 8m (26ft) long and weighing 6 tons. Its size, slowness, docility and taste were a lethal combination and it was hunted mercilessly by early travellers. It was discovered in 1741: by 1768 it was extinct.

Part of the cargo which the survivors of Bering's second expedition brought back to Russia were sea-otter pelts. The pelts generated a new rush of exploration, the sea otter being pursued eastwards, along the Aleutian chain and through southern Alaska as numbers in each of its strongholds were drastically reduced. It is estimated that in the first 20 years of the 19th century Russia took over 70,000 sea otters, as well

Above and right **Bering, dreadfully ill and clearly dying, had been taken ashore and placed in a shallow pit beneath a tent, probably to offer him some protection from both the elements and the foxes that were regularly attacking the dying men and corpses. The pit sides collapsed, half burying him, but Bering refused to be excavated as the sand was warm. As a consequence when he finally died he had to be partially exhumed before he could be buried. What is thought (with good supporting evidence) to be his body was exhumed again in 1991 when a Russo-Danish expedition excavated the Bering Island site. Bering's head was reconstructed from his skull by the Russian forensic expert Professor V.N. Zvyagin. The head is clearly not that of the 'standard' face of Bering which has been seen until now. That appears to be of Bering's mother's uncle, Vitus Pedersen Bering (1617–75), a poet and historian.**
Institute of Forensic Medicine, Moscow, Russia/Svend Albrethsen

Above **The Russian settlement of New Arkhangelsk as seen during the Litke expedition of 1822/9. The site is now occupied by the town of Sitka. The engraving is by Frederich Heinrich von Kittlitz.**
Anchorage Museum of History and Art, Alaska, USA

as 1,250,000 fur seals, 60,000 beaver and other fur-bearing animals. By the middle of the century the animals were all but extinct and the Arctic fox colonies set up on the Aleutian Islands had almost exterminated many local species. Russia was also economically crippled by the Crimean War and nervous about the vulnerability of its American colonies to the British who were active in the Yukon and whose navy patrolled the Pacific: James Cook had already sought the entrance to the North-West Passage and explored Russian America. Nikolai Muraviev, governor-general of Irkutsk, noted that as the USA was 'bound to spread over the whole of North America' (a view which later concerned both Britain and Canada) Russia must come to terms with the

'surrender of our North American possession'. Russia also hoped that the USA might provide protection from the British for Siberia's vulnerable east coast. What followed is usually termed 'the sale' of Alaska to the USA (for $7.2millon, the Russians having beaten the Americans up from $5,000,000). Despite the price being less than 2 cents per acre, there were many in the US who thought it high, and it took a long while for Russia to extract any cash. But the 'sale' was not all it seemed. It was, rather, a 100-year lease agreement, explaining why it was not until 1969 that Alaska became a State of the Union. There were also oddities over the lease payments which were suspended in 1917 after the Russian revolution, and may have been the basis of the US arms deal with Stalin during the 1939–45 war. The whole subject is shrouded in mystery and even now is largely classified information.

The Great Northern Expedition

Bering's Second Kamchatka Expedition was one detachment of what became known as the Great Northern Expedition, an enterprise which, building on Bering's suggestion, surveyed the entire north coast of Russia from the White Sea to Chukotka (and also the east coast as far as Japan), a monumental exercise. In part the work was carried out to explore the feasibility of a

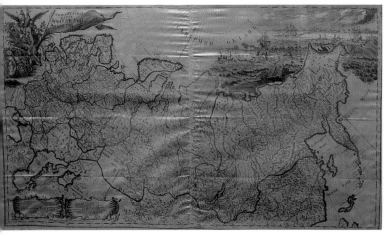

Top **An aerial view of Cape Chelyuskin, the most northerly point of Eurasia. It was first reached on 9 May 1742 by Semen Chelyuskin of the Great Northern Expedition who built a cairn.**
Susan Barr

Above **In 1745 this silk map of Russia was sewn for the Czar. The achievement of the Great Northern Expedition which charted the northern shore was monumental: it was another hundred years before the British had achieved a comparable survey of the Canadian shore.**
Richard Sale

sea route to China – another search for the North-East Passage that had eluded the British and Dutch. The Arctic coast work was completed by five separate teams, their timescales indicating the capricious nature of the Arctic ice. The team charged with surveying from the White Sea to the Ob River failed to complete the task in 1735, driven back by ice and scurvy. The team leaders were court-martialled for failing to carry out their orders, the harshness of that official view being shown when the new leaders did no better in 1736, being forced to overwinter and finally reaching the Ob

Gulf in 1737. The return journey proved no easier, the team finally arriving back in Arkhangelsk in 1739. It had taken six summers to complete the survey.

The team surveying from the Ob to the Yenisey River fared even worse. In the three years 1734–6 they failed to exit the Ob Gulf. Only in 1737 after a sledge party (using reindeer rather than dogs) had been sent out in desperation to complete the task, were ships finally able to make the journey. The teams that were surveying from the Yenisey to the Khatanga River had by far the hardest task, having to round the vast Taimyr Peninsula, Siberia's northernmost landmass. Consequently two teams were used, travelling east from the Yenisey and west from the Lena. The Yenisey team used a ship (the *Ob Pochtalyon* – Ob Postman!) which had reached the Yenisey in 1737. Its commander was Fedor Minin: in five summers he failed to travel more than 450km (280 miles), was court-martialled and reduced in rank to the lowest grade of seaman. Minin did, however, send out a sledge team in 1740. Battling atrocious weather this team managed little more than Minin himself. Heading westward was a team under the cartographer Vasily Pronchishchev which included his wife, who could not bear to be separated from him, and Semen Chelyuskin. In 1736 the team, in the Yakutsk, reached Cape Chelyuskin (then North-East Cape, but subsequently renamed) but were forced to turn back by ice and scurvy. Pronchishchev died of the disease, and within a week his heartbroken wife had died too. Not until 1739 did the Yakutsk, now under Khariton Laptev, try again. Laptev reached Cape Faddeya but was forced to overwinter. In 1740, trying again to reach Cape Chelyuskin, the ship became trapped in the ice and sank; the crew, riddled with scurvy, only just reached safety in time. Laptev gave up the idea of a sea survey, sending out sledging teams which explored all but the most northern Taimyr in 1741. In 1742 Semen Chelyuskin completed the survey, journeying 4,000km (2,500 miles) by sledge, mostly on sea ice.

The final section of coast, from the Lena to Chukotka and on to Kamchatka, occupied the years 1735–41. In 1735 Peter Lasinius in the *Irkutsk* managed no more than ten days sailing from the Lena before the ice trapped him. During the subsequent winter Lasinius and many of his crew died of scurvy. In 1736 Dimitri Laptuv, a cousin of Khariton Laptev, took the Irkutsk as far as Cape Svyatoy Nos. Not until 1740 was the Indigirka River reached. From there a sledge party set out for the Anadyr River, leaving one small part of the Chukotka coast unsurveyed.

The passage completed

Following the success of the Great Northern Expedition in mapping the Russian Arctic coast the idea of a North-East Passage was revived by Mikhail Lomonosov (a Russian academician: Lomonsov was a Pomore and, rumour had it, an illegitimate son of Peter the Great) who suggested that while a coastal passage had been found to be impracticable, a more northerly route might exist. Lomonosov died just before his expedition to explore this possibility set out, Vasili Chichagov taking command. The expedition travelled beyond 80°N between Svalbard and Greenland, aiming for the Bering Strait, but were then stopped by ice. Exploration stalled too, and it was 100 years before another effort was made.

Adolf Erik Nordenskiöld was born in Finland of Swedish parents and studied geology at university. Moving to Sweden at the age of 25 he took part in a number of Arctic expeditions, primarily to Spitsbergen – in 1868 he was on the *Sofia* which reached 81°42'N, then a northing record – but also to the Russian Arctic, particularly to the Kara Sea and as far east as the Yenisey River. These latter journeys taught him a great deal about the area and its ice conditions, and by 1878 he was convinced that with appropriate timing a transit of the North-East Passage was possible. In 1878 Nordenskiöld acquired the *Vega*, a 300-ton, three-masted whaler with a steam engine and, with a crew totalling 30 (including Louis Palander, the ship's captain), set out from Karlskrona in southern Sweden on 22 June. Though Nordenskiöld's journey is often portrayed as a private venture it is worth remembering that it was commissioned and financed by the Russian Czar.

On the first stage of the journey the *Vega* was accompanied by the *Lena*, a much smaller ship with a crew of nine. By early August the ships had reached the Kara Sea, finding it ice-free – Nordenskiöld's earlier voyages had shown him that in late summer the sea had much less ice, though it was frequently ice-filled in early summer.

Nordenskiöld crossed the Kara Sea without incident, reaching Dickson Island (named for Baron Oscar Dickson, patron of many early Arctic voyages) at the northern end of the Yenisey estuary on 6 August. The *Vega* and *Lena* took on fuel from the *Express* and the *Fraser*, two supply ships which had accompanied them, then headed east again, the *Lena* often leading as she drew less water and the coastal waters off Taimyr are shallow. On 19 August the two ships reached Cape Chelyuskin, Nordenskiöld noting that 'the landscape was the dullest

Above **Adolf Erik Nordenskiöld by Georg von Rosem. In the background of the painting the *Vega* is trapped in ice.**
The National Museum of Art, Stockholm, Sweden

Above **Two Chukchi sealskin boats approaching the *Vega*.**
From A.E. Nordenskiöld *Vegas färd kring Asien och Europa*.
Courtesy of the Swedish Polar Research Secretariat

Above **The *Vega* and *Lena* at Cape Chelyuskin.**
From A.E. Nordenskiöld *Vegas färd kring Asien och Europa.*
Courtesy of the Swedish Polar Research Secretariat

and most desolate I have seen in the high north', a sad picture for Eurasia's most northerly point.

Nordenskiöld now attempted to head directly for the New Siberian Islands, but ice forced him south, back to the coast. The Lena delta was reached on 27 August, the *Lena* then leaving to follow the river to Yakutsk. The *Vega* continued through open water, detouring to the southernmost of the New Siberian Islands but being unable to land because of shallow water. By 5 September Nordenskiöld had reached the huge bay of Chaunskaya Guba. The next day they met their first Chukchis. Interestingly, the Chukchis could speak no Russian, but did have a smattering of English, presumably picked up from American whalers. Continuing along the coast Nordenskiöld met the first serious ice of the voyage at Cape Schmidta. This held the ship up for four days: it was to prove a crucial delay as they were stopped again on 28 September, just two days' sailing from Cape Dezhnev. This time the ice did not disperse: winter had arrived and it held the ship until the summer of 1879.

The winter was spent comfortably, a credit to Nordenskiöld's thorough preparations. Scurvy was eliminated by stocks of cloudberries and cranberry juice, and good clothing kept the crew warm in temperatures down to –46°C. The ship's food was good and plentiful, and often traded with the Chukchis for fresh meat. A hole was kept open in the ice in case water was needed to douse a fire (the *Vega* being heated by four cast-iron stoves) and to measure the tides, one of a series of scientific studies which included the building out of snow-blocks a geomagnetic observatory.

On 18 July 1879 the *Vega* became free. Two days later she passed Cape Dezhnev and reached the Bering Strait. The completion of the North-East Passage had been a masterpiece of good organisation and seamanship, and is one of the greatest of all polar voyages. But Nordenskiöld had not yet finished. The *Vega* sailed on to Japan, then around China to the Indian Ocean and across it to reach the Suez Canal. She sailed across the Mediterranean to the Straits of Gibraltar, then around Portugal, Spain and France to the English Channel and the North Sea, finally reaching Sweden in April 1880. At every stop on the way Nordenskiöld was fêted. On 24 April (still Vega Day in Sweden) the ship reached Stockholm. As the ship sailed into the city the sun broke through the clouds and a double rainbow formed above her, entrancing the thousands who had turned out to see the travellers return. Nordenskiöld was made a baron and he continued his travels to the Arctic, making important journeys to the Greenland ice cap. He died in 1901 aged 68.

Above **An aerial view of the remnants of *Baymaud* in Cambridge Bay.**
Susan Barr

Above **By 1920 Amundsen was newsworthy in the USA as this newspaper cutting shows.**
Richard Sale Collection

Amundsen and the *Maud*

The second west-to-east transit, and the third overall, was made by Roald Amundsen in the *Maud*. Amundsen's plan was to repeat Nansen's drift in *Fram*, but the ship was in too poor a condition. Amundsen therefore had *Maud* (named for the Norwegian queen) built, modelling her on *Fram*. At her launch Amundsen smashed a block of ice rather than the customary bottle of champagne across her bow, saying 'You are for ice. You shall spend your best years in ice and you shall do your work in ice'. *Maud* left Oslo in June 1918 with a crew that included Helmer Hanssen, veteran of *Gjøa* and the South Pole, and Oscar Wisting who had also been to the pole.

Amundsen went north, passing Cape Chelyuskin the first summer, but being forced to overwinter soon after. During the winter he fell, breaking his shoulder, was mauled by a polar bear and almost died of carbon-monoxide poisoning. Two sailors (Tessem and Knutsen) also left the ship and headed for Dickson on skis. Both died on the way. Later authors have suggested that Amundsen's known lack of sympathy for sick crew members was the reason behind Tessem leaving the ship, and that Amundsen must therefore bear responsibility for his death. The evidence is less persuasive: Tessem was certainly suffering from headaches (migraine attacks?) but there does not seem to have been undue pressure on him to go. Knutsen volunteered to accompany him: although the journey to Dickson was straightforward it was obviously foolhardy to go alone. What exactly happened is a mystery, but Russian historians believe Knutsen died, probably in an accident, though his body has never been discovered. A body, believed to be that of Tessem, was found: it is thought that as he was crossing a frozen river close to Dickson he slipped, hit his head and died. A memorial to him has been raised above his grave at Dickson.

Maud was not released from the ice until September 1919, but could only sail for 11 days before being frozen in again near Ayon Island. In 1920 *Maud* was released in early July and rounded Cape Dezhnev. By now Amundsen had given up the idea of immediately repeating the *Fram* drift and headed for Nome, Alaska where he arrived on 27 July. After resupplying the ship he sailed north again. Only three of the original crew were willing to sail this time – one was Oscar Wisting, but this time Helmer Hanssen did not go – and Amundsen intended to recruit Chukchis for the voyage. *Maud* was forced to overwinter at Cape Sverdzekamen (Cape Stoneheart). During the winter her propeller was damaged, and in July 1921 she sailed back to Nome and then on to Seattle. By now Amundsen had lost interest in the expedition, his enthusiasm fired by the thought of flying to the pole. Oscar Wisting tried to take *Maud* north once more, but failed to reach 77° at the New Siberian Islands. *Maud* returned to Seattle where she was seized by Amundsen's creditors. She was bought by the Hudson's Bay Company, renamed *Baymaud* and intended for use as a supply vessel. She was unsuitable, drawing too much water, and was abandoned at Cambridge Bay where she sank at her mooring in August 1930. Today the sad remnants of the ship, just breaking the surface, are a visitor curio.

Развертываются и укрепляются на льду первые палатки.

The *Chelyuskin* rescue

Despite the obvious difficulties involved in transits of the North-East Passage Russian (by now Soviet) enthusiasm for a northern sea route was undiminished. In July 1932 Vladimir Voronin took the sealer *Aledsandr Sibiryakov* eastwards, going around the northern tip of Severnaya Zemlya, the first vessel to make that trip. Heavy ice off Chukotka smashed the ship's propeller, but using a makeshift sail the *Sibiryakov* reached the Bering Strait, the first one-season transit. Encouraged, the Soviets sent a fleet of 11 ships eastwards in 1933. One was the 4,000-ton *Chelyuskin*, not an ice-breaker, but sufficiently large to nose through significant ice. Entering a narrow lead off Chukotka the *Chelyuskin* became ice-bound, drifting into Bering Strait, then north-west towards Wrangel Island. After wintering in the ice, on 13 February 1934 the ship was crushed and sank. The quartermaster, who had stayed on board until the end, was knocked over by a shifting barrel as he attempted to jump to safety and was drowned. The 104 survivors – including a baby girl born in 31 August 1932 in the Kara Sea and named, of course, Karina – set up a camp on the ice, the expedition leader Professor Otto Schmidt citing Albanov's journey as the reason for not attempting a crossing of the ice to Chukotka or Wrangel.

Ample supplies were removed from the *Chelyuskin* before she sank and the campers had a reasonably

comfortable time awaiting rescue by air, their stay enlivened (or perhaps not!) by a non-stop series of lectures by Schmidt, a devout Communist. Starting on 5 March and continuing until 13 April, seven pilots made repeated flights to a makeshift ice runway and safely rescued all the survivors. The pilots (Lyapidevski, Levanevski, Molokov, Kamanin, Slepnev, Vodopyanov and Doronin) were the first people to be awarded the Hero of the Soviet Union, Anatoli Lyapidevski being the very first recipient.

Following the loss of the *Chelyuskin* there were further transits of the passage in the 1930s, but it has never become a regular route either for Soviet/Russian or other shipping. The passage has also had commercial tourist transits by ex-Soviet Academy ice-breakers, though these too have been limited in number. It is likely that even if global warming reduced the ice cover north of Siberia, Russian nervousness about foreign vessels near its northern shore will mean that the passage will not become a popular route.

Explorers in the west

Canada: *Fram* II

In 1880 the British ceded their rights to the islands discovered by its North-West Passage expeditions to Canada. The move formally ended British interest in the passage and would also, it was hoped, encourage the recently established Canadian Confederation to take control of the area which was by then being seen as 'open land' to whalers and explorers. But the young Canada had more pressing problems – expanding and consolidating its confederacy south of the treeline.

In 1902 Otto Sverdrup, captain of the *Fram* on Nansen's expedition, led his own expedition, the second in *Fram*. This was a masterpiece of organisation and execution. During 1898–1902 Sverdrup and his 15-man crew (one of whom was Sverre Hassel, later to go with Amundsen to the South Pole) charted over 250,000 sq km (100,000 sq miles) of the Arctic using *Fram* and sledges. Ellesmere Island's west coast was explored, Axel Heiberg and the Ringnes Islands discovered. The 'new' lands were named for the expedition's sponsors (Heiberg was a Norwegian consul, the Ringnes brothers owned an Oslo brewery) and at first claimed for Norway. This claim eventually awakened concerns in Canada over the ownership of all the Arctic islands off the mainland coast. With the US making noises that were interpreted as suggesting it might be willing to dispute ownership with both Canada and Norway, Canada eventually claimed all lands north to the pole and compensated Sverdrup for taking possession of his charts as a means of substantiating the claim. The amount to be paid was argued over and eventually settled at $67,000, paid on

Below **Memorial cross on Ellesmere Island. Beyond is the frozen sea of Slidre Fjord and Axel Heiberg Island. Was this cross set up by Sverdrup's crew? Two men died on the trip but both were apparently buried at sea. One of those who died was the ship's doctor who committed suicide. The history of Arctic exploration is littered with the suicides of doctors, probably because of their easy access to drugs. Close to the cross scurvy grass grows. The** site seems too small to be a grave site, which might explain the grass as having sprung from the stomach or pocket of the interred corpse. Did it fall from the pocket of one of the men erecting the cross? If so, that is evidence for it having been erected by Sverdrup as later explorers would not have carried such a basic antiscorbutant.**

Richard Sale

11 November 1930. Sverdrup died on 26 November aged 76. He had worked until he was 72 when the Norwegian government belatedly awarded him a pension: he was grateful for the Canadian cash as it offered his wife security.

Canada: the *Karluk* disaster

In the wake of the Sverdrup voyage, and following disturbing news that whalers who had established a base on Herschel Island were 'debauching' the local Inuit, the Canadian government finally acted on the Arctic islands. In 1904 the government bought the *Gauss* (which had taken Drygalski's German expedition to Antarctica), renamed it *Arctic* and placed it under the command of the Quebecois Joseph-Elzéar Bernier. In a series of expeditions from 1904 to 1911 Bernier visited many of the islands of Arctic Canada, retrieving historically important documents left by the British, rebuilding cairns and adding his own cairns and plaques to establish Canadian sovereignty. He also made several unsuccessful attempts to navigate the North-West Passage.

Following Bernier's expeditions Canada underwrote the Canadian Arctic Expedition of Vilhjalmur Stefansson, which sailed in 1913. The voyage, in the *Karluk*, was an Arctic contemporary of Shackleton's *Endurance* and followed the same pattern: ship beset in the ice, ship sinks, crew faces difficult journey to land. However, there was to be no joyful ending; the *Karluk* crew's retreat was a harrowing tale of death and misery. Nor was their journey behind the guiding light of a great leader, the tale – largely ignored for decades, but recently revived – adding another chapter to the story of a controversial explorer.

Stefansson was Canadian-born of Icelandic parents and attracted early attention with his claims that British failure in the Arctic had been the result of a mindset that it was a hostile, barren wasteland where man could not survive unless he took his civilisation with him. In reality, Stefansson claimed, the Arctic was a friendly place, its tundra a vegetation-rich prairie, its sea a wildlife paradise, its abundance able to support any party willing to exploit it. His argument was compelling, but failed to acknowledge that the Inuit rarely travelled in groups of more than ten or so and, despite his description of them as 'fat and healthy', were frequently the victims of hunger. His view that Franklin's men had died through ignorance also made the valid point (condoned by others) that had they split into smaller groups and gone in different directions they

might have survived. Stefansson's pseudo-science convinced the Canadian government and the Hudson's Bay Company who funded the introduction of reindeer (for herding) to south Baffin. Despite Stefansson's 'Arctic Prairie' the project failed. Stefansson had some training as an ethnologist and, based on very flimsy evidence, also suggested that there was a race of blond Inuit on Victoria Island who were the descendants of the Norse Greenland settlers. The tribe proved to be a myth.

Knud Rasmussen savaged Stefansson for his poor ethnography, while Roald Amundsen criticised his claims as an explorer, though some have suggested that Amundsen's criticisms derived as much from self-interest as fact. But despite the criticisms, Stefansson's gift for self-publicity and the apparent plausibility of his arguments to a government willing to be convinced led to his appointment as leader of the Canadian Arctic Expedition. Stefansson's aim was to search for new land in the Beaufort Sea. Some scientists claimed that currents and ice-drift rates meant that there must be land there, perhaps even a vast amount, and Stefansson relished being its discoverer. He had talked several organisations into funding a search, but when the Canadian government offered to provide more money he immediately changed allegiances.

To captain the *Karluk* Stefansson employed Bob Bartlett, the captain of Peary's North Pole ship and arguably the finest ice captain on the planet. Bartlett had serious reservations about the ship and the lack of organisation of the expedition, but nevertheless took *Karluk* northwards from British Columbia in June 1913, heading for the Bering Strait, Point Barrow and Herschel Island, the expedition's winter base.

Karluk's limited speed made for a long trip. Stefansson told Bartlett to hug the Alaska/Yukon coast so that the expedition could go ashore and continue by sledge if need be, but as they neared Herschel Bartlett chose to head north, following open water leads which, he hoped, would eventually allow him to travel east again. But by September the ship was stuck in the ice. The *Karluk* was carrying a curious band of travellers. There were, as would be expected, scientists and sailors, but there were also Inuit hunters Stefansson had recruited in Alaska, one of whom had brought his wife and two children, girls aged eight and three. On 19 September Stefansson announced that he was heading for the shore to hunt caribou and would be gone for ten days. It was a surprising decision as he had already told the party that caribou were virtually extinct on this section of coast. The team he took – his personal

assistant, the expedition photographer (Hubert, later Sir Hubert, Wilkins, the pioneering polar aviator), the anthropologist and two Inuit hunters – looked more suited to finding blond Inuit or new lands than game animals. Stefansson also took the best dogs.

Soon after Stefansson's departure a violent storm battered the area. Stefansson claimed to have seen the ship, stuck fast in its ice floe, being driven westwards by the wind and that open water between his team and the ship prevented him from returning to her. It is probable that he did – he can hardly have fortuitously invented the correct story. He claims to have headed west to see if *Karluk* had reached shore. What is certain is that he linked up with two ships which had also headed for Herschel carrying other scientists and supplies for the expedition. He reported the situation to Ottawa, noting that the ship might, or might not, sink and that those on board would probably survive. Then he headed north to seek his continent.

The *Karluk* and its 25 passengers and crew drifted west to the Bering Strait, then on towards Siberia. Bartlett knew that the ship's design meant she would likely suffer the fate of the *Jeanette* rather than that of the *Fram* and organised his inexperienced team – Alastair Mackay had been the doctor on Shackleton's *Nimrod* expedition (indeed, he had reached the South Magnetic Pole with Mawson and David) and James Murray had also been on *Nimrod*, but the remainder were mostly polar newcomers – to build igloos on, and transfer supplies onto, the ice. He also built sledges for

the evacuation he knew would be necessary. On 10 January 1914 the ice pressure that had often threatened the ship finally succeeded in rupturing the hull. Bartlett was the last to leave, hoisting the ship's flag and putting Chopin's *Funeral March* on his gramophone. It was still playing when the ship sank.

Bartlett now organised the setting up of supply dumps southwards along a route to Wrangel Island. He also sent a party of six to try to reach Herald Island, a small island north-east of Wrangel. Two of this team returned, reporting that the other four had reached open water short of the island and were searching for a route to it. Mackay and Murray, together with Henri Beauchat, an anthropologist, and sailor Stanley Morris, now decided to strike out on their own. Bartlett tried to dissuade them, but when he failed he gave them the supplies they asked for in exchange for a letter absolving him of responsibility for their future welfare, and wished them well. Several days later a returning supply party told Bartlett that there was no sign of the men sent to Herald Island, or any apparent hope of reaching it, and that Mackay's party had been spotted, utterly exhausted. Bartlett swore them to secrecy so as to avoid alarming the rest: so well did they obey that, writing years later, one survivor was still unaware of the conversation.

Finally Bartlett felt ready to leave 'Shipwreck Camp'. Harnessing all of the dogs and manhauling as well, the survivors moved between supply dumps, at each of which an igloo had been built. The team was

Above **William Laird McKinlay using eiderdown to clean his mug before enjoying a meal of blood soup. The *Karluk* survivors on Wrangel survived on a diet of eggs and the roots of the sparse vegetation and the occasional seal they were able to catch. The seals brought abundant food, but not for long, the survivors often facing periods of near starvation when their only meals were soup created from rotting meat scraps and other unappetising morsels.**
Richard Sale Collection

Siberian coast. With spring fast approaching the sea-ice bridge to the mainland would soon be gone, so on 18 March Bartlett and one of the Inuit crossed Wrangel and headed south. Their journey took 45 days through some of the most dangerous ice Bartlett could remember. Finally they reached Siberia and a Chukchi village. From it, with replenished supplies they travelled 650km (400 miles) to the shore of the Bering Strait and found a ship bound for Alaska. On 28 May they landed and raised the alarm.

Back on Wrangel three of the remaining members of the *Karluk* team tried to reach Herald Island and the four-man team that had headed there. Slowed by breaking ice they failed, then in a blizzard on the return route they became lost and were stopped by open water. They used a small ice floe as a raft but it capsized, dumping the three into the water. Sodden and freezing they camped, but the ice broke up, again separating them. One man, Chafe, frost-bitten and exhausted, but still with the last of the dogs, tied himself to one and released the rest. He reasoned the loose dogs would find the Wrangel camp and that his would follow them, dragging his stumbling body. He was right and, to his joy, he discovered the other two men had also made it. Chafe had six minor operations to stop the spread of gangrene, carried out with a pocket knife: one of the other two had a frost-bitten toe amputated with a hacksaw blade.

To comply with Bartlett's instructions the three men walked to Rodger's Harbour on Wrangel's southern shore, Bartlett believing it was the easiest place a relief ship could reach. Two of them died there, possibly from protein poisoning as a result of their diet, exacerbated by frostbite and exhaustion. Later another member of the team, back at the main camp, died of a bullet wound to the head. It is still debated whether the death was murder, suicide or an accident as the man was cleaning a gun.

In Alaska Bartlett hired the *Bear* to rescue his team. On 20 August 1914, five months after he had left, he brought the ship to within 30km (20 miles) of Wrangel, but was stopped by heavy ice. Forced to return to Alaska for more coal he returned in September to discover that a schooner, the *King and Winge*, alerted by a Russian trader he had met in Siberia, had rescued the survivors on 7 September.

Three men had died on Wrangel. Mackay's team of four were never seen again and in September 1924 an American ship intending to claim Herald Island for the USA found a tent and the bodies of four men: the team

eventually stopped by perpendicular ice ridges almost 20m (66ft) high stretching away in both directions. Here Bartlett proved a brilliant leader by encouraging his team to carve through the ridges, using the debris then created to fill in the troughs between them, rather than trying to find a way around and, perhaps, failing. Ignoring Herald Island, Bartlett pushed for Wrangel which was finally reached on 12 March after a gruelling 20-day trek.

But land brought only relative safety. Wrangel was (and is) uninhabited and barren, a home to walrus and polar bear. It was still 320km (200 miles) to the

Bartlett had sent had reached the island after all, and had died there. The survivors included all four members of the Inuit family.

While war raged in Europe nothing was heard of Stefansson and it was assumed that he, too, had died. Then in 1918, after five years out of contact, living off the land as he claimed man could, he returned. He had found the last three islands of Canada's Arctic archipelago – Borden, Brock and Mackenzie – but had not discovered the continent he craved. By then *Karluk* had faded from men's minds and Stefansson was greeted as a hero. He wrote a book called *The Friendly Arctic* – an ironic title in view of the death toll on his expedition – in which he gave a biased account of the disaster, blaming Bob Bartlett. Bartlett, who along with other members of *Karluk* believed Stefansson had abandoned the ship rather than going hunting and had already published his own book on the trip, maintained a dignified silence. In 1921 Stefansson organised an expedition to colonise Wrangel Island, an astonishing decision, but not as astonishing as the decision of one of the *Karluk* survivors, Fred Maurer, to join it: perhaps Maurer was trying to exorcise ghosts. Strangely, or perhaps not, Stefansson did not accompany his team of four men and an Inuk woman: one man died and Maurer and the other two men tried to escape by following Bob Bartlett's route to Siberia: they were never seen again. The Inuk was the lone survivor.

William Laird McKinlay, a 25-year-old Scot, survived the *Karluk* disaster then, after a period in hospital, went to war, adding the horrors of the Western Front to those of Wrangel Island. McKinley was wounded and discharged in 1917. For decades he brooded over the injustice of Stefansson's claims about Bartlett. Finally, after 60 years, he published his own account because, he said, he wanted 'to destroy the Stefansson myth, for the man was a consummate liar and cheat'. He also wanted people to understand that despite Stefansson's claims it was Bob Bartlett who was the true hero. The latter wish was granted, Bartlett now being seen as a great explorer in the Shackleton mould. The book was probably too late to secure the first wish. Stefansson was long dead, his latter years spent in honour, though the Canadian government turned down all his subsequent requests for the funding of another expedition.

It has been suggested that Canada's refusal of Stefansson's request was not entirely due to disapproval of his leadership of the 1913 expedition but because he had moved to the USA and it was feared he might betray their flimsy case for sovereignty of the Arctic islands. Following their purchase of the Sverdrup charts the Canadian government sent officers of the Royal Canadian Mounted Police to the Arctic, the presence of a police force underwriting their territorial claims. Larsen's voyages in the *St Roch* can be seen as a further sovereignty statement, though the outrage over the *Manhattan*'s voyage – undertaken without prior consent from Canada – suggests that even in the latter half of the 20th century the Canadians were still nervous about their ownership claims for the archipelago.

Greenland: Egede seeks the Norse settlers

After the failure of the Norse settlements in Greenland there was no contact between Europeans and the Greenlandic Inuit for several centuries. Englishman John Davis met Inuit in 1585 during his voyage in search of the North-West Passage, and there was spasmodic contact and bartered trade during the 17th century. Then in 1703 the Danish king was approached by an Icelander who suggested a more formal trading arrangement and a re-establishment of contact between the Danish Crown (whose territories then included both Iceland and Norway) and Greenland. A few years later the king was petitioned again, this time by Hans Povelsen Egede, a young pastor who wished to find the Norse settlements.

The king accepted both proposals. Egede's search for Norsemen was unsuccessful, but he was charmed by the Inuit and stayed for almost 15 years converting them to Christianity. His attempt to create a new Danish colony failed, however, the settlers abandoning Greenland in the face of their inability to grow sufficient food. During Egede's stay an Inuit child who had been taken to Copenhagen returned carrying smallpox. Around 25 per cent of the Inuit population of Greenland died of the disease, Egede distinguishing himself by his work with the sick and with orphaned children.

But there is a disturbing undercurrent in Egede's evangelism, an inability to comprehend how the Inuit could be so (relatively) good and peaceful, an apparent belief that Christian behaviour in a pagan community was itself shameful. Later scholars (for instance Nansen) have questioned Egede's replacement of shamanism with Christianity and the consequent loss of social cohesion. It is also ironic that the Dane's work during the smallpox epidemic was in relieving the victims of a disease imported from Denmark.

Egede travelled the south-western coast of Greenland from Godthåb – now Nuuk (the settlement he established), searching for a mythical channel said to give access to the east coast. Greenland's west coast was always the more accessible of its vast coastlines: it had the larger number of Inuit settlements and remained (relatively) ice-free so that North-West Passage seekers and Franklin searchers had sailed almost its entire length by the 1880s. The east coast was more forbidding, and settlements there were not only fewer in number but much poorer than those on the west coast, their inhabitants constantly on the verge of starvation. Whalers who headed north along the deeply indented east-coast shore risked confrontation with ice that seemed almost malevolent in its relentless pursuit of their ships. In 1777 a dozen ships were trapped there, then smashed and sunk in turn, their crews transferring to those that remained beset but above water. When the last went down, over 300 men were lost. Later the Scoresbys, father and son, mapped sections of the east coast while carrying out one of the most successful of whaling operations. William Scoresby Snr explored Scoresby Sound, which he believed, wrongly, was the elusive channel that Egede had sought which cut across Greenland, while William Jnr sailed to 72°N, noting the reduction in ice that led him to call for renewed attempts to find the North-West Passage.

Following Scoresby Jnr's voyage the British naval officers Clavering and Sabine went even further north along the coast. South of the Scoresby-mapped coast the German Ludwig Giesecke (reputedly the librettist of Mozart's *The Magic Flute*) and Danish naval officer Wilhelm Graah filled in the gaps to Cape Farewell (Kapp Farvel), though it was not until 1883 that other Danish naval officers, Holm and Garde, discovered Ammassalik, the main Inuit settlement on the east coast. Also active was the German Polar Expedition of 1869/70 under Karl Koldeway and Julius von Payer (later the co-discoverer

Above '**Dangers of the Whale Fishery**' from William Scoresby's ***An Account of the Arctic Regions.*** This somewhat fanciful illustration was supposed to convey the dangers of whaling to the book's readers. Though hunting whales, particularly sperm whales, was indeed dangerous for the whalers it was, as noted earlier, lethal for the whale.
Richard Sale Collection

of Franz Josef Land). The expedition comprised two ships, the steam-driven *Germania* and the sailing ship *Hansa* and was intended to reach the North Pole by way of Greenland's east coast, an ambitious, and foolhardy, idea even with the limited knowledge of the day. When the pack ice threatened, the *Germania* steamed away, an apparently misunderstood message not warning her that the *Hansa* was trapped. The *Hansa*'s 14-man crew built a house of coal on the ice and watched the ship sink, 'groups of feeble rats struggling with death and trembling with cold' and the weather batter their floe almost out of existence. With death apparently inevitable the crew finally escaped the ice and reached southern Greenland. Meanwhile the *Germania*, all hopes of the pole gone, surveyed the east coast.

Greenland: Nordenskiöld, Peary and Nansen

With those sections of the Greenlandic coast amenable to exploration by ship surveyed, attention naturally turned to the vast inland icefield covering more than 1.8 million sq km (around 750,000 sq miles). The first steps on this ice sheet were made in 1751 when the Danish trader Lars Dalager and five Inuit penetrated about 15km (10 miles) from near Paamiut (Frederikshåb). Dalager did as well as other early attempts and rather better than the English mountaineer Edward Whymper, conqueror of the Matterhorn, who in two attempts in the 1860s barely got out of

Above **An illustration of ice travel from Robert Peary's *Northward over the Great Ice* which deals with his Greenland trips of 1886 and the 1890s. The illustration is captioned 'coasting' and shows that Peary had already absorbed some good ideas on polar travel: skis (though he is using the 'old-fashioned' long, single stick), lightweight sledges and Inuit clothing. He also seems to have decided that conservation of energy was no bad thing either.**
Richard Sale Collection

sight of the ice edge near Ilulissat (Jakobshavn). The next journeys on to the inland ice were made by the three giants of polar exploration in the late 19th century – Nordenskiöld, Peary and Nansen.

First was Nordenskiöld. In 1870 he made a tentative exploration with a Swedish colleague and two Inuit from a base camp in Auleitsivik Fjord, south of Disco Bay, reaching about 57km (just over 35 miles). He did not return until 1883. By then Nordenskiöld was over 50 and his great journeys were behind him. Starting from the same place as in 1870 his team penetrated about 116km (72$^{1}/_{2}$ miles). From a camp there the expedition's two Saami members Pava Lars Tuorda and Anders Rossa skied on, returning two-and-a-half days later. They claimed to have reached 42°51'W, a distance of 230km (almost 144 miles), though as they had no means of measuring distances modern opinion favours a turning point of 46°W (about 100km/60 miles from Nordenskiöld's camp). The two men reported seeing no exposed land during their whole journey, which surprised Nordenskiöld who believed that Greenland had an ice-free, perhaps even wooded, heart.

The next of the great three to visit the inland ice was Robert Edwin Peary. Peary was born on 6 May 1856 at Cresson, Pennsylvania. When he was three his father died and his mother moved back to Maine, her own state. Peary grew up as an only child, a strangely preoccupied boy made more silent by a lisp that bothered him throughout his life. By 1886 Peary was an engineer in the US navy. That year he requested, and was granted, three months leave and with the Dane Christian Maigaard (assistant governor of the now-defunct settlement of Ritenbank) set off for the inland ice, pushing 160km (100 miles) inland and bivouacking on the ice.

Two years after Peary's first expedition, Nansen arrived on Greenland's east coast. Fridtjof Nansen was born on 10 October 1861 at Christiania (now Oslo) to middle-aged parents whose previous marriages had already provided them with six children. He was very bright and also a good sportsman, excelling at skiing (where he was brave enough to compete in ski jumping, then an infant, and dangerous, sport). He spent a season on a sealer in Arctic waters while at university, then took the curatorship of the zoology department at Bergen Museum. His work on zoology earned him a doctorate; his later work as a Norwegian statesman and with the League of Nations gained him the Nobel Peace Prize in 1922. As a man Nansen was handsome, and very attractive to women; one of his many lovers was Kathleen Scott, Robert Scott's wife. They had conducted the affair while Scott was returning from the pole (and dying in the process). When news came of Amundsen's success he wrote to Kathleen telling her how much he wished her husband had been first. At the same time he wrote to tell another, Norwegian, that he was glad that Amundsen had succeeded. As a man Nansen was vain and arrogant, and by contrast to his success with women, made few male friends. As a scientist and statesman he was a man of immense accomplishments, and as an Arctic explorer a near genius in his imagination of what might be achieved, his arrogance being transformed into a single-mindedness that carried all before it.

Nansen had dreamed of crossing Greenland by ski since the early 1880s, Peary's 1886 trip giving him the incentive to try immediately. Peary's plan was to return and complete the crossing in 1887, but his navy work took him to Nicaragua where after a survey expedition he advocated a canal across that country rather than across Panama: many thought his idea had the greater merit, but Panama was the eventual choice. Peary's absence gave Nansen his chance. His preparations were meticulous. Many of the Franklin searchers had used dogs, particularly the Americans Kane and Hall, but Nansen had no experience with them. The Saami used reindeer, but they eat only lichen and there might be none on Greenland. Nansen therefore decided to use skis and to manhaul his sledges, though he did take a pony.

Until Nansen's journey no one considered manhauling practical: the sledges were either too heavy, or the runners too thin, and so sank into the snow. But Nansen constructed sledges based on the wide-runnered type favoured by Norwegian farmers. He made the first skis to have metal edges, and created sleeping bags and clothing of new designs. He went to Sweden and questioned Nordenskiöld, then the world's foremost polar expert, who was amazed that the Norwegian was planning to ski east-to-west, the opposite way to all previous expeditions. The logical reason for Nansen's choice might have been that Greenland's west coast had more settlements and so it would be easier to reach a satisfactory end point. But that was not Nansen's stated view – he saw a start from the east as a cutting off of the possibility of retreat. It would be, as he later sensationally remarked, 'Death or the west coast'.

For his trip Nansen chose five companions, all of them expert skiers. They were Otto Sverdrup (later captain of the *Fram*), Olaf Dietrichsen, a surgeon, Kristian Kristiansen Trana, and two Saami, Ole Nielsen Ravna and Samuel Johannesen Balto. Nansen had arranged for

the sealer *Jason* to take the men to Greenland's east coast, but the deal was that their drop-off should not interfere with sealing. So despite sailing from Iceland in mid-May it was not until 17 July that the ship was close enough to the coast – off Sermilik Fjord – for Nansen to feel able to leave her. The team still had 20km (12½ miles) to go – the *Jason* dare not risk the coastal ice – and this proved to be a very long way. Soon the scattered pack coalesced, and the two boats were trapped. They were now at the mercy of the drifting ice, attempts to reach the shore being defeated by violent storms. With pony feed dwindling and their own rations being depleted, the pony took its place on the menu. That improved the food supply, but not the spirit of the party: all the men feared a possible drift into the Atlantic, but the Saami, no seafarers, feared it most. Then a visiting bear so terrified Balto that he swore that if he survived he would never drink again. When questioned about this strange remark he confessed that he had only volunteered for the trip because he had been drunk at the time.

The team finally reached the coast on 29 July, but were by then almost 400km (250 miles) south of Sermilik. Determined to approach (if not to regain) the fjord Nansen rowed north, keeping the boats close to the shore. On the journey they met an Inuit group which acted as a guide, and by 10 August the team had reached Umivik, an excellent harbour. Here Nansen decided that, though still 160km (100 miles) short of Sermilik, it would have to do as a start point. For five days the weather kept them in camp, then, on 15 August, after safeguarding the boats and leaving some supplies (in case 'death or the west coast' proved a questionable slogan) they started. The steep climb on to the ice cap was hard going – on the first day they managed just 5km (3 miles) and a climb of 200m (660ft), all of it in *finnesko* (reindeer-skin boats) as the gradient was too much for skis. Two more days of hard labour were followed by a storm that kept them pinned in their tents, in which they slept three to a reindeer-skin sleeping bag to share warmth.

The relentlessly hard climb caused Trana to ask, 'How can people wish so much suffering on themselves that they do this?' but still they continued. By 27 August they were over 2,000m (6,600ft) above sea level, but progress was so slow Nansen was forced to change objectives. He had planned to cross from Sermilik to Qasigiannquit (Christianshåb). The change of start point had been forced by the ice drift; the time lost now forcing a change to the finish point. The team would, he decided, head for Nuuk (Godthåb) which was 150km (about 95 miles) closer. On 29 August they reached ice which sloped gently upwards and so they could walk in showshoes, but not until 2 September at over 2,500m (8,200ft) above sea level were they finally able to use skis.

Even with skis the effort was considerable, and almost every day the men were hungry and thirsty. They were also skiing across a polar desert, with nothing to break the white monotony: as the first men to do this the psychological burden must have been considerable. The weather was also trying, with temperatures falling to –40°C and occasional gale-force winds creating whiteouts and forcing snow through every tiny opening in the tents. On the move the chill factor of the wind was appalling. On 4 September Nansen noticed that first his nose hardened and had to be massaged, then his throat went numb and stiff and he had to wrap 'some mittens and other things' around it. Then, worst of all, 'the wind found its way in through my clothes to the region of my stomach and gave rise to horrid pains'. That is from his book. His diary is more explicit, noting 'p [penis] was in the process of freezing'. He solved the problem by stuffing a felt hat down his trousers.

On 19 September the wind blew from behind the team and they rigged sails on their sledges. After several unsuccessful attempts, a steering system was evolved and soon they were speeding along. So much ground was being covered – 70km (about 44 miles) during the day – that Nansen decided to keep going as night fell: it was an almost fatal decision as a huge crevasse was only spotted at the last second. During the day they also saw land ahead: the next day they found pools of water on the glacier and for the first time in weeks could drink their fill. As the ice dropped sharply Nansen was able to identify that below them was a fjord which ran inland from Nuuk. By 24 September they were off the ice, the first time for 40 days: they had crossed 560km (350 miles) of ice.

By 26 September they had almost reached the head of the fjord. The men built a boat, stretching tarpaulin over a scrub-wood frame. In this Nansen and Sverdrup, after a trying time following a river to the fjord, set off for Nuuk. They arrived on 3 October, though it was the 12th before the rest of the team were brought in.

Though Nansen managed to get mail on to the last ship leaving for Denmark that summer he and his men spent the winter in Nuuk. When the team returned to Norway an estimated one-third of the population of

Above **Resting on the inland ice. These engraved illustrations are from Nansen's book on the crossing.**
Richard Sale Collection

Above **Though it was common in Norway to cross-country ski with a single stick Nansen's men invariably used two on the Greenland crossing. However, the sticks were still very long and had no basket to spread the thrust.**
Richard Sale Collection

Above **During the crossing Nansen also realised the value of harnessing the wind. Sails were used by most later explorers, and are a feature of almost all modern expeditions.**
Richard Sale Collection

Oslo was there to welcome them, and they were fêted for ten days. Nansen, in particular, was greeted as a hero, not only in Norway but all over Europe. His reputation as a polar traveller was made: the *Fram* expedition would further it and it would never diminish. In that respect, the difference between Nansen and Amundsen, whose polar achievements were greater, deserves a book in itself.

Nansen's crossing was a bitter blow to Peary whose desire for fame became the chief purpose of his life. He believed that his reconnaissance of 1886 gave him proprietorial rights over the ice cap (much as he later felt over the pole) and resented Nansen's intrusion which he saw as cheating. But he determined to make his own journey, choosing a part of Greenland that was still unexplored: his would be not only a journey of danger, but also of discovery – altogether a better effort. Peary's team was a curious one, comprising his wife, Jo; Matthew Henson, his valet from Nicaragua; the Norwegian Eivind Astrup, an expert skier; Langdon Gibson, a hunter; meteorologist John Verhoeff; and Dr Frederick Cook 'surgeon and ethnologist'. Cook was ten years younger than Peary and had no previous experience of exploration. Later Peary was to note that he felt 'much confidence' in Cook. Later still he was to fear and despise him as a rival, and to loathe him as the attempted usurper of a prize he felt was rightfully (if not, perhaps, actually) his own.

The expedition also included nine fare-paying passengers sent by the Philadelphia Academy of Natural Sciences who were to conduct experiments while the ship was in Greenland. The team sailed from New York in June 1891 in the *Kite*. On 11 July in the pack ice of Melville Bay, north-west Greenland, the ship's rudder struck ice: the tiller swung violently and broke both of Peary's lower leg bones just above the ankle. He had Cook to thank for not only setting the leg so expertly his recovery time was minimised and the leg healed completely, but also for placating the paying passengers when it looked as though the expedition might be called off.

The team established a winter camp in Red Cliff House, McCormick Bay. There Peary and Cook took the first of the series of photographs, some of which appear in Peary's books, more of which appear in their respective collections. Some of those of naked Inuit women would grace the pages of *Playboy*, but most are formal poses – and include men as well. That Peary's interest was not entirely anthropological is supported by his fathering children by an Inuit woman, as did Matthew

Above **Peary's team for his 1891/2 expedition. The very young-looking Henson was to stay with Peary throughout his Arctic career, but Cook became an implacable opponent, in part because of the death of Verhoeff and, later, that of Astrup.**
Richard Sale Collection

Henson. Their half-Inuit grandchildren still live in north-west Greenland.

On 3 May 1892 Peary, with Astrup, Cook and Gibson, each with a four-dog team, set off for the 'White March' on the inland ice. In using dogs Peary logically extended Nansen's advances in polar equipment, adding Inuit lore – he also built snow igloos for camps – to Nansen's Saami-based ideas. The route to the ice was difficult and Peary's leg was hurting. Once on the ice two dogs died and another escaped. Peary now sent Cook and Gibson, with two dogs, back, continuing with Astrup and 14 dogs (one of which soon died). Both men and dogs ate pemmican; later in the trip the dogs' diet was supplemented by being fed their weakest remaining member after it had been killed and cut up.

On 5 June Peary and Astrup crossed the high point of the ice (at 1,740m/5,700ft) and sledged on, the days merging in monotonous similarity until finally on 1 July they reached land again. In bright, warm sunshine they found purple, white and yellow flowers, and twittering snow buntings instead of ice. There were also muskoxen, which supplemented Peary's wholly inadequate food rations: without the meat from the oxen the two men would probably have died.

What Peary believed he saw to the east was the Arctic Ocean running through a channel – Peary Channel – separating Greenland from a neighbouring island. To the south he saw only frozen ocean. Seeing land where there was only ocean, and (more rarely) ocean where there was land, were mistakes others had and would continue to make, but this one by Peary would have serious implications for others later.

After three idyllic days – warm and sunny, with bees buzzing, butterflies flitting between the flowers, delightful birdlife (including a gyr falcon) and musk-ox steaks – the two men set off for Red Cliff House. Taking a more southerly route which rose to 2,440m (8,000ft) they arrived on 6 August. It had been a remarkable journey even if its successful outcome had owed more to the good fortune of finding muskoxen than meticulous planning similar to Nansen's.

In the little time they had before the *Kite* sailed the team now explored Inglefield Gulf. Verhoeff and Peary had developed a mutual dislike early in the expedition – one reason why Verhoeff did not go on the inland ice trip. This may be why he decided that he would prefer a walk back to Red Cliff House rather than a return by boat. He did not arrive, and despite searches no trace of him was ever found.

Back in the US, Peary's journey – he had sledged some 2,200km (1,400 miles) – was well received. He even had a congratulatory letter from Nansen signed 'Your Admirer'. He lectured extensively, Matthew Henson bringing the five dogs that had survived the inland ice trip on stage at the start of the talk: the dogs lay at Peary's feet as he spoke and, so it is said, stood and howled, in unison and on cue, when he finished. The lecture usually brought the house down. Peary enjoyed the adulation, but knew that he must keep travelling to ensure a constant supply. In 1893, with the approval of the US president (but most definitely not of his overruled navy superiors) he went north again. Astrup and Henson ('my coloured man') were with him, but Cook was not. Cook had asked permission to publish a short report in a medical journal and had been refused: Peary would tolerate no competition. Annoyed, Cook resigned from the expedition.

A new winter hut – Anniversary Lodge – was built and there on 12 September Jo Peary gave birth to a daughter, the Pearys first child: despite her genteel upbringing, Jo was a formidable, courageous woman. Apart from the birth the expedition achieved little, an attempt on the inland ice failing in bad weather. Eivind Astrup surveyed Melville Bay while Peary was away on the attempt – a significant survey, much to Peary's great annoyance – and most of the team went home in 1894. Peary, Henson and Hugh Lee stayed on, and in 1895 Peary repeated his sledge journey to the northeast coast. He took a different route, but again survived only because of the muskoxen there. He then found three meteorites, two of which he transported back to the US. The meteorites – the source of Inuit iron – were very well received and turned the indifferent expedition into an apparent success. His powerful Washington friends persuaded a reluctant navy to allow Peary to return in 1896 for the third, and largest, meteorite. He failed to reach it.

In 1897 the navy, exasperated with his trips, posted him to the west coast, far away from the Arctic, but Peary's friends again intervened and, against official desires, he was granted five years' leave of absence. That year he brought home the largest meteorite and six live Inuit. The acquisition of both meteorites and Inuit is now viewed suspiciously. Peary often spoke of 'my Eskimo' seemingly believing he owned the Inuit around his Greenland bases, just as he later felt that he owned the pole. He once asked of the Inuit 'of what use are they?' and answered himself that they existed only to help him discover the pole. Peary felt that taking the meteorites was acceptable; the Inuit no longer needed a source of iron as he gave them all the iron goods they required (true, though is that the only point?), and he felt justified in surrendering six of their number to the cause of science as he was their saviour. In reality the Inuit did not feel any unreserved adoration of Peary such as many (including Peary) have claimed. They were impressed by the size of his ships and by his gifts, but much less so by him.

It is doubtful whether the six Inuit he brought back to the US thought very highly of him. They were displayed as circus freaks and five died quickly in an unfamiliar New York climate among unfamiliar

Above left **Peary handing out gifts to the Inuit.**
USA Library of Congress

Above right **Inuit obtaining iron from a meteorite. The drawing is by Albert Operti who accompanied Peary on the 1896 trip.**
Richard Sale Collection

The photograph, *above left*, **(taken by Peary's wife) and drawing,** *above*, **show controversial aspects of Peary's dealings with the Inuit which further fuelled Dr Frederick Cook's animosity towards him. Peary's consistent use of the expression 'my Eskimo' and his insistence that he knew what was best for them (even better than they did themselves) have become an embarrassment even to his supporters.**

American illnesses. The only survivor, Minik, an eight-year-old boy, lived on for another 20 years. It was hardly a happy life – as a boy he had not only watched his father and relatives die, but attended a fake burial for his father, only later discovering that his skeleton was exhibited in a museum glass case. The story of the six Inuit is an unpleasant tale of racist abuse and Peary's involvement in it, and his silence during it, does him no credit.

Peary returned to Greenland in 1898, intending both to explore further north and to reach the pole. Henson was with him again but not Astrup who died in January 1896. Frederick Cook later accused Peary of responsibility for the death, claiming his rage at Astrup over the Melville Bay survey had unhinged the young Norwegian and that he had committed suicide as a result. Cook extended the argument to include Verhoeff, whom he also maintained had committed suicide because of Peary's dreadful behaviour. The true cause of Astrup's death is still debated, while Verhoeff's death also remains a mystery.

Consistently paranoic, Peary was now concerned

that Otto Sverdrup, leading the second *Fram* expedition, would steal his ideas, just as Nansen had, and decided to push to Adolphus Greely's Fort Conger base on Ellesmere Island with Henson, the Inuk Ahngmalokto, 16 dogs and three sledges in midwinter and so ensure that Sverdrup could not use it the following spring. Peary and Sverdrup actually met – Sverdrup invited Peary for a coffee, but Peary snootily declined: Henson claims that it was this meeting which made Peary decide on the winter trip to Fort Conger, so convinced was he that Sverdrup had designs on the pole. In fact Sverdrup had no interest in either the pole or Fort Conger and the hasty decision was to cost Peary his toes. Though his report of the incident to Morris K. Jesup, president of the American Museum of Natural History and sponsor of the trip, is laconic and dispassionate ('I found, to my annoyance, that both feet were frosted', '...it was evident I should lose parts or all of several toes' and '...the final amputation was performed') the reality was horrific. When Peary removed his boots, frost-bitten skin fell from his toes, leaving bones emerging from festering flesh. Yet after losing

Above **Peary's ships *Windward* and *Erik* at Nuuk. This fascinating shot is one of a pair of stereo images taken to add to the enjoyment of the US public. The exploits of Peary and other Arctic explorers were hot news in the USA (and in Europe) even before the Cook–Peary controversy gripped nations.**

US Navy Historical Centre

Greenland: the Danes complete the coastal map

Peary's exploration left only the north-eastern coast of Greenland unexplored. The 1906 Danish expedition led by Ludvig Mylius-Erichsen was intended to fill that gap. The expedition sailed in the *Denmark* in 1906, establishing a base at Danmarkshavn at about 75°N. After overwintering, a series of supply depots was established northwards, including one in a cave near Lambert Land (which already lay north of Peary's supposed coastline). Eventually two teams set off northward. At North-East Foreland (well to the east of Peary's supposed coastline) the teams separated. Mylius-Erichsen, with Höeg Hagen and the Greenlander Jorgen Brönlund, headed west to find the Peary Channel. Johan Peter Koch, Tobias Gabrielson and Aage Bertelsen headed north to find the cairn Peary had erected at Cape Bridgman. Koch was successful and had, during his journey, peered into Independence Fjord. On his return he met Mylius-Erichsen whose team had spent a wearying time exploring Danmark Fjord: Peary's Channel had not been found. Koch was convinced it did not exist at the end of Independence Fjord either, but Mylius-Erichsen felt duty-bound to check. The two teams parted. Koch reached the ship after 84 days' sledging: his team had covered almost 2,000km (1,200 miles).

When Mylius-Erichsen had not arrived by September search parties went out, but found nothing. The search was resumed in spring 1908. At the cave on Lambert Land they found the huddled body of Brönlund and a note he had written explaining that Hagen had died on 15 November, and Mylius-Erichsen on the 25th after they had tried to return to the ship over the inland ice. In an act of selfless bravery Brönlund had struggled on, with frost-bitten feet, carrying the notes of the trip to where he knew his body would be found. His own poignant last message began, 'Succumbed at 79 Fjord after attempting return across inland ice in November. I arrived here in fading moonlight and could go no further because of frost-bitten feet and the dark...' The three had followed Independence Fjord to Peary's viewpoint. Forced on to the inland ice by open water as the sea ice melted in late summer their dogs had died and, as winter folded its cold, dark arms around them, so had they.

Koch's search for the bodies of Mylius-Erichsen and Hagen failed. In 1910 the Danes tried again to find them, sending Ejnar Mikkelsen (who had been on the Ziegler-Baldwin expedition) and six others in the 40-ton *Alabama*. One of the crew was Iver Iversen, a mechanic

his toes by 15 March 1899, he was back on the ice by 19 April. Whatever the merits of his North Pole claim and no matter how dubious his treatment of his team members (particularly in this instance, of Henson who undoubtedly saved his life at Conger) and the Inuit, Peary could be eye-wideningly brave.

In 1900, after a winter on north-west Greenland, Peary followed Lockwood's route along the north coast, then pushed on, reaching, and naming, Cape Morris Jesup (Greenland's most northerly point at 83°39'N). The team continued past Cape Bridgman until their supplies finally ran out at Cape Wyckoff on Clarence Wyckoff Island, off the eastern tip of Peary Land, the island that lay beyond the 'Peary Channel'. This trip was the most significant of all Peary's expeditions on Greenland, though he spent two more winters in Greenland. In both 1901 and 1902 he tentatively pushed towards the pole from Ellesmere Island, reaching 84°17'N in April 1902.

Above **Mylius-Erichsen's expedition unloading from the *Danmark*. The performance of the motor car was not much more impressive than it had been for Shackleton.**
Richard Sale Collection

Above **Brönlund's grave site in north-east Greenland.**
Leif Vangaard, Danish Polar Centre, Copenhagen

collected in Iceland from another ship when the *Alabama*'s mechanic turned out to be incompetent. Landing near Cape Bismarck, Mikkelsen relocated Brönlund's body that year and erected a cairn over it. But the autumn journey was at the cost of five toes from one man's foot, amputated without a doctor or antiseptic, and with half a bottle of whisky as anaesthetic.

After wintering on the ship two teams set out in the spring of 1911. Mikkelsen and Iversen went north hoping to find the bodies of Mylius-Erichsen and Hagen, and then to follow the Peary Channel to the west coast. There should have been three men, but Jørgenson, who had survived the amputation of his toes, was not fit to travel. A second team of three men went inland to explore a *nunatak* (rock 'islands' which project above the surrounding 'sea' of ice) discovered by Alfred Wegener during the *Danmark* expedition.

Two men were left at the ship. When the sea ice near the *Alabama* melted she sank, but the two men escaped in time and, together with the returned nunatak team built a hut and then erected a series of cairns to the north as a warning to Mikkelsen should he be forced to return that way. One of these cairns was found by a sealer who sailed to their rescue. To the north and, of course, unaware of the *Alabama*'s fate, Mikkelsen and Iversen had crossed the inland ice and descended, with difficulty, to the head of Danmark Fjord. They found no bodies, but did locate a note in a cairn raised by Mylius-Erichsen. It said that the Peary Channel did not exist, that Peary Land was not an island but part of the mainland. A second note detailed the desperate journey in the heavy snow of late summer with the dogs dying of exhaustion, a prelude to the terrible journey across the inland ice and Brönlund's heroic struggle.

That struggle was about to be repeated by Mikkelsen and Iversen. By the time the two men had reached Lambert Land, battling through the same wet snow, and unable to find any wildlife, all but two of their dogs had died of exhaustion and starvation, and Mikkelsen was so debilitated by scurvy he could no longer walk. Had they not found depots laid down by Koch for Mylius-Erichsen the two would have died. As it was their journey was a fight against appalling weather and starvation punctuated by short periods of eating at the depots. They also ate their last two dogs, even consuming the livers though they knew they were poisonous. At one point Iversen was so desperate for food that he asked Mikkelsen to carry their rifle as he feared he might shoot and eat him. Interestingly, during a discussion on cannibalism (and whether one could eat the other if he died) Iversen said that first he would have to cut off the hands as they are what make a person human: several of the skeletons found by the Franklin search teams had had their hands removed.

Eventually, 30km (20 miles) from Danmarkshavn and its hut, they had to leave everything behind as they no longer had the strength to carry anything except their own weight – and barely that. As they approached the hut they had to rest less than 50m from it as they were too exhausted to go on. After resting at the hut they tried to go back to recover their records, but could make no progress through vile weather. In desperation they turned towards the *Alabama*. Utterly exhausted they reached the site: the ship was gone and a note in the hut they found there said their colleagues had gone too.

The two men survived the winter by hunting and eating the supplies left at the hut. During one hunting trip Iversen claims that he saw his grandfather sitting on a rock wearing his familiar red cap: when he returned to Denmark he found that the old man had died at precisely the time he had the vision. In the spring the two returned for their records, recovering everything except Mikkelsen's diary which had been eaten by a bear. Too weak to attempt the journey south to the Inuit settlement at Scoresbysund they waited all summer for rescue. It did not come. After another winter things were looking grim: they were short of food, suffering from scurvy and Mikkelsen had a threatening

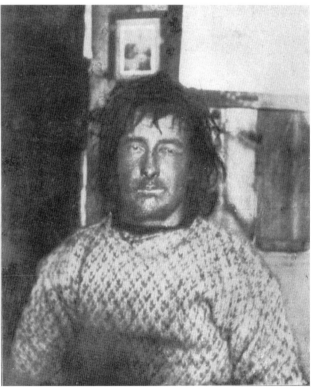

Top and above **Ejnar Mikkelsen and Iver Iversen after their two-year ordeal. The suffering they endured is etched into their faces, while their staring eyes reflect the isolation of their stay in north-east Greenland.**
Danish Polar Centre, Copenhagen

boil-like tumour on his neck. Using the knife with which he ate and skinned carcasses, suitably sharpened, and a pool of water as a mirror as Iversen could not bear to do it, Mikkelsen lanced the tumour, the pain causing him to faint. Soon after this operation the two fell out for the first time in the more than two years they had spent together – a mutual silence over an ill-chosen song by Iversen. They had just made up when a rescue ship arrived.

Mikkelsen and Iversen's survival against almost overwhelming odds is arguably the greatest in polar history. Others have endured similar, perhaps worse, conditions, but never for as long. And the pair had also found the records which completed the mapping of Greenland.

Mylius-Erichsen's discovery of Peary's errors was confirmed in 1912 by the first expedition in a series which was to become legendary, the Thule Expeditions. It was led by the Greenland-born, part-Inuit/part-Dane Knud Rasmussen who was accompanied by Peter Freuchen (who had been on the *Danmark* expedition). In part the journey was a search for Mikkelsen, but as it started from the west coast it linked the journeys of Peary and Mylius-Erichsen. Rasmussen, a brilliant anthropologist, went on to lead most of the seven Thule expeditions which did much to bring the culture of the Inuit to the western world. On the Fifth Expedition Rasmussen sledged all the way to the Bering

Strait, becoming the first man to traverse the North-West Passage by land (ie ice). During the traverse, in 1923/4, Rasmussen heard Inuit stories about British sailors as far back as John Ross, showing that the oral tradition of the Inuit was almost as good as the written word. Their tales confirmed some of the more surprising (and disbelieved) stories that 19th-century Western travellers had been told about expeditions dating back to the time of Frobisher. Rasmussen also discovered further relics of Franklin's last expedition.

After the delineation of Greenland's coast the island became a scientific study area. In 1912 J.P. Koch and Alfred Wegener (both of whom had been on the *Danmark*) and two others crossed the inland ice westwards from Danmarkshavn to Laxefjord, a distance of 1,100km (700 miles), about twice as far as Nansen's transit and 300km (186 miles) more than Peary and Rasmussen. They overwintered on the ice before starting out, the first men to do so. The team used horses rather than dogs, eating them in turn as they became exhausted: they had taken 16 animals, but six died in a stampede when they first went ashore.

Wegener was later to die in another overwintering (1930/1) on the ice, exhaustion overtaking him as he struggled to get off the plateau. At the same time the British Arctic Air-Route Expedition set up a base on the inland ice to study weather conditions and so determine if trans-Atlantic flights across Greenland were feasible. The expedition, led by the 23-year-old Henry George (Gino) Watkins, established their base in August 1930. On 3 December Augustine Courtauld was left alone there when it was realised there were insufficient supplies for the planned two-man team. Not until 5 May 1931 was he relieved, a total of 153 days of solitude, far more than Byrd experienced in the Antarctica. A search party on 18 April failed to find the buried station and Courtauld was feared dead, but he survived, with none of the mental scars that might have been expected given that he had lived in fear of his tent collapsing under the weight of snow or his air becoming exhausted. He had not changed his clothes for five months; had run out of lighting oil and so lived in darkness; had taken no exercise; had little food, and been forced to suck snow for water to conserve fuel. His pressure cooker failed the morning of his rescue.

Below **Pelts of Arctic fox and Arctic wolf drying at a trapper's hut in Muskoxhavn, north-east Greenland.**
Richard Sale Collection

share of Greenland until 1933. In that year four men raised the Norwegian flag at the Myggbukta trapping station on east Greenland, and Norway claimed Eirik Raudes (Eirik the Red's) Land, encompassing east Greenland north of the Inuit settlement of Illoqqortoormiut (Scoresbysund). That settlement was established only in 1924/5 when the Danes moved – some would claim, with justification, though deported would be a better word – a number of Inuit from Ammassalik. The ownership of Eirik Raudes Land went to the International Court at The Hague. The Danish claim was supported by Greenland (a campaign led by Knud Rasmussen) and by the USA whose foreign policy was still dominated by the Monroe doctrine: the US had no wish to add a third country to Canada and Denmark in the American Arctic sector. The court found in favour of Denmark. Today, although Greenland has been granted home rule, the Danes still maintain a military presence at Daneborg on the north-east coast and annually patrol the east and north coasts by dog sledge (the Sirius patrol) in order to reinforce its sovereignty.

Greenland: adventurer's paradise

In 1978 the Japanese Naomi Uemura, the first from his country to have climbed Everest, used a dog-sledge to travel to the North Pole (5 March–28 April), the first solo journey there. Evacuated by aircraft because of poor weather, Uemura began a second journey on 10 May from Cape Morris Jesup. Resupplied during his trip he sledged the length of the inland ice, completing his journey on 22 August, the first 'long axis' crossing of the ice cap.

Today, crossings of the inland ice are virtually a rite of passage for polar explorers and mountaineers, east–west or west–east traverses being completed regularly. Special mention must, however, be made of two journeys. In 1996 two 25-year-old Norwegians, Rune Gjeldnes and Torry Larsen, parachuted on to the south-

Greenland: Eirik Raudes Land

About the same time as these first winterings on the inland ice Greenland was the centre of an international court case. Norwegian fur trappers had been overwintering on Greenland's east coast since the early years of the 20th century, their presence fuelling a dispute that had rumbled on since Norway had transferred from the Danish to the Swedish crown in 1814. Since Eirik the Red had been Norwegian, Norway had protested about the continuing Danish possession of West Greenland. Norway gained its independence in 1905, but the upheavals in Europe during the next two decades meant that it did not make moves to acquire a

Svalbard

With a few relatively minor exceptions the coastline of the Svalbard archipelago had been delineated by the early 18th century, the discoveries of whalers being allied to the more scientific work of such expeditions as that of the Russians in the 1760s and the British navy under John Phipps in 1773. Later, Swedish expeditions in particular carried scientific studies inland as well as along the coast. Otto Torell in the *Magdalena* visited the fjord now named for his ship, while Nordenskiöld sailed to 81°42'N in 1868. Soon after, scientific parties were overwintering on Spitsbergen (Nordenskiöld leading the first party to do so in 1872/3: that expedition also sledged across and around Nordaustlandet – North-East Land). In 1896 and 1897 the British explorer Sir Martin Conway surveyed a large area of central Spitsbergen and climbed many of the main peaks.

Though Conway's expedition was an exploration/adventure, the scientific studies had a purpose: to see if Svalbard had exploitable resources.

It had. It is known that early sealers and whalers had exploited Svalbard's readily accessible coal, but the first commercial mining venture was in 1899 when Soren Zachariassen hauled coal from Isfjorden to Norway. By the first decade of the 20th century several companies had been formed with money not only from Norway, but Britain, Holland, Russia and the USA. The major name was that of the American capitalist John Munroe Longyear. He first visited Svalbard as a tourist in 1901 (a 'hotel' was set up in Adventfjorden in 1898: it was to this that Zachariassen sold some of the first coal he mined), then bought one of the original mining companies to form, with Frederick Ayer, the Arctic Coal Company. The company mined in Adventfjorden, finding a seam so rich that 200 miners were employed. The village built to accommodate them was called Longyear City. As Longyearbyen it is now Svalbard's administrative centre. Other major mining centres were Sveagruva and Pyramiden (Swedish companies, though the

latter was sold to the Russians), Barentsburg (Dutch, but sold to the Russians) and King's Bay (Norwegian: now the site of the Ny Ålesund research centre).

After gaining its independence Norway was granted sovereignty over Svalbard in 1920 at a conference to which, significantly, the Russians were not invited. Signatories of the Svalbard Treaty recognise Norway's position, but are granted equal rights regarding mineral exploitation. During the 1939–45 war the Germans set up a base near Longyearbyen, Svalbard being important as a meteorological station because of the Arctic convoys to Russia. The Norwegians landed troops and the Germans retreated. Later *Tirpitz* and *Scharnhorst* bombarded the Norwegian bases. Following the war the Russians sought to modify the Svalbard Treaty, fearing NATO occupation of the archipelago. Their attempt was rejected, though Svalbard became, and remains, demilitarised. Russian suspicions meant that they continued to mine coal at Barentsburg and Pyramiden even though it was uneconomic to do so. The Norwegians did the same at Longyearbyen, the faintly ridiculous situation being reached of the two nations spending money for no better reason than that the other one was. The rise of tourism has, however, compensated Norway for its decision to stay at Longyearbyen. The airport there allows tourists to arrive in just a couple of hours from Tromsø (itself easily reached from anywhere in the world). From Longyearbyen tourist ships explore the historically interesting sites and scenically magnificent fjords of Spitsbergen, though lately new regulations have taken certain sites off-limits as tourists were looting them, even to the extent of digging in old whaler graveyards for bones.

As the polar bear is totally protected and Kong Karls Land and Edgeøya off the east Spitsbergen coast – both off-limits to tourists – are important bear denning areas, such tourist ships offer excellent chances of seeing bears in their natural habitat. Again, though, there has been a need to restrict tourist traffic, though this time by winter visitors using snow scooters. Incidents in which bears and Svalbard reindeer were harassed – potentially lethal for the animals, the bears overheating if forced to run long distances, the reindeer using energy which may not be replaceable in the harsh Svalbard winter – have led to the introduction of specific routes from which visitors are not allowed to deviate.

Left **Longyearbyen today.**
Richard Sale

Above **Longyeardalen before the city was built.**
From Fries and Nystrom *Svenska polarexpeditionen 1868 med kronoångfartyget Sofia.*
Courtesy of the Swedish Polar Research Secretariat

Right **Barents named Spitsbergen for the pointed mountains he saw there. It is not clear which ones he first spotted as there are many examples on the island. These peaks are at Haitanna, Hornsund, at the southern end of the island.**
Per Michelsen

Left top **Lonnie Dupre, in front, and John Hoeschler kayaking in Melville Bay, north-west Greenland.**
Lonnie Dupre/John Hoeschler

Left below **Sledging in northern Greenland during the Dupre/Hoeschler circuit of the island.**
Lonnie Dupre/John Hoeschler

Above **Dupre and Hoeschler's camp at Cape Raven in east Greenland. In the foreground is a lake, the sea ice of the fjord being visible beyond the ridge.**
Lonnie Dupre/John Hoeschler

ern inland ice on 19 March determined to make the first complete north–south traverse of Greenland. Abseiling down the ice front they used kayaks in an attempt to paddle to, and around, Kapp Farvel (Cape Farewell), Greenland's southernmost point. This attempt was defeated by weather which made the crossing dangerous, though the two did come within sight of the cape. Having paddled back to the mainland they regained the ice cap and, using sails (wings) to aid the towing of 175kg (386lb) pulks, they skied north, reaching Cape Morris Jesup where they were collected

by air on 13 June. Their trek of 2,928km (1,830 miles) was the longest unsupported ski journey at that time, but has lately been bettered by others in Antarctica.

Then in 1997, American Lonnie Dupre (who in 1991 had completed the first west-to-east dog-sledge transit of the North-West Passage) and Australian John Hoelscher planned an 18-month clockwise circumnavigation of Greenland by kayak and dog-sledge. Their plan called for a 2,400km (1,500-mile) kayak trip along the west coast from Paamiut to Qaanaaq during the summer of 1997, then a 4,160km (2,600-mile) dog-sledge trip from Qaanaaq around the northern tip of the island and along the east coast to Ammassalik during the spring of 1998. Finally there would be a 1,488km (930-mile) kayak journey around Greenland's southern tip to complete the 15-month venture. The men's kayaks could be tied together to form a catamaran, a safer option on the open sea, and one which also allowed the possibility of a sail to aid progress. The trip did not go according to plan. Fierce headwinds made the first leg much more difficult than had been imagined and it was not completed before the men had to move to Qaanaaq in late August. After training runs during the winter Dupre and Hoelscher set out on 14 February, but were forced to abandon the trek in late

Jan Mayen

One of the most spectacular of Arctic islands is Jan Mayen. Only 54km (34 miles) long and 2.5km (1½ miles) wide at its narrowest point it is dominated by Beerenburg, an active volcano which rises to 2,277m (7,470ft). Fumaroles add a sense of other-worldliness when viewed against the glaciers which flow down the peak into the sea. The island is composed of black lava sand and jagged red-brown lava cliffs, the sombre colours a complete contrast to the vivid green of mosses and lichens. After the whalers had deserted the island, it was for decades rarely visited. In the First International Polar Year (1882–3) it was the base for the Austro-Hungarian expedition: later it was visited by fur trappers who exterminated the Arctic fox population. In 1922 the Norwegians (who have sovereignty) set up a meteorological station. In 1960 a LORAN (radar) station was added for both civilian and military trans-Atlantic aircraft. Both stations are still in operation. Today the island is occasionally on the itinerary of tourist ships, landings by air being largely restricted to station personnel.

Right **The volcano of Beerenberg, which dominates the remote island of Jan Mayen, is rarely seen, its height and position attracting clouds.**
Richard Sale

March by relentless cold, bad weather and appalling ice conditions. They had reached Cape Jefferson at the northern end of the Kane Basin. The pair then transferred to Ammassalik and kayaked 1,200km (750 miles) to Qaqortoq. They were forced to stop there by the fast approaching winter. Since that first attempt, Dupre and Hoelscher have completed the circumnavigation.

From February to May 2000 they sledged 2,900km (1,800 miles) between Constable Point, near Scoresbysund and Qaanaaq. The trip, rivalling Uemura's as one of the longest ever accomplished by dog-sledge, involved both pressure-ridged sea ice and glacier travelling, the latter at one point requiring the belaying of the dog-sledges because of crevasse danger. Their camp was also invaded one night by a pack of hungry wolves. The weather was unkind too, the team at one stage being tent-bound during a five-day storm. During the trek Dupre and Hoelscher rediscovered the world's northernmost piece of land, Oodaaq Island which lies just 379.5 nautical miles from the North Pole. The island, which measures only 28m by 14m (92 by 46ft) and is 1m (3¼ft) high, is a gravel bar consisting of quartz and slate and has proved elusive in the past as it is frequently hidden by the pack ice and its position was not accurately fixed. Dupre and Hoelscher give its position (by GPS) as 83°40.5'N, 30°39.5'W.

Returning in 2001 the pair kayaked the short sections of the west coast that they had not been able to complete in 1997 (Paamiut to Qaqortoq and a section south of Savissivik), then completed the journey from Constable Point to Ammassalik, a distance of 1,100km (690 miles) between late July and early September. This section of the east Greenland coast is among the most inhospitable on the island, with mountains falling directly into the sea, the kayak trip being extremely hazardous, involving long sections of open sea.

In all, Dupre and Hoelscher travelled over 8,000km (more than 5,000 miles) around Greenland and an additional 2,300km (1,450 miles) of 'cultural' journeys around the Kane Basin, Nares Strait and Inuit villages, a truly remarkable feat and one unlikely to be repeated in the foreseeable future.

Right '**Nie zurück' (No Return) by Julius Payer. Payer was a gifted artist as well as a fine Arctic explorer and painted this picture of the heartbreaking incident where the crew of the *Tegetthoff* had to be persuaded that though the ship offered an apparent end to their misery they had no choice but to ignore it, heading for Novaya Zemlya instead.** Heeresgeschichtliche Museum, Wien, Austria

Explorers in the east

Russia's Arctic islands

The Czar's silk map (see page 70) shows Novaya Zemlya (which had been discovered as early as 1032), but none of the other four archipelagos of the Russian Arctic. Novosibirskiye Ostrova (the New Siberian Islands) were first recorded in 1770 when Ivan Lyakhov, who was trapping furs near Cape Svyatoy Nos, noticed a herd of reindeer heading south towards him across the sea ice. Following their tracks northwards he discovered two islands, and tracks coming from further north. In 1773 Lyakhov took a boat north and discovered a larger island. On it he found a copper kettle, indicating that more discreet trappers had come this way before: the island is still called Kettle Island.

In 1848 Henry Kellett, captain of the *Herald*, sailed through the Bering Strait as part of a Franklin search expedition and discovered Herald Island, naming it for his ship. He climbed to the top and saw land to the west. This was called Kellett's Land on early British maps. Though it is likely that this was the first time Wrangel Island had been seen, it may have been spotted previously by whalers. The American Thomas Roys in the *Superior* made the first whaling trip through the Bering Strait in the same year (1848), and was rapidly followed by others. By 1852 there were over 200 whalers working the waters near the strait. The whalers were by then already searching for new grounds so decimated was the bowhead population. By 1858 the strait was fished out and the whalers transferred to the sea of Okhotsk, exhausting that by 1860. The whalers then turned to hunting walrus and also to the Chukotka Sea. In 1867 Thomas Long in the *Nile* saw Wrangel, naming it for Baron Ferdinand von Wrangel, who had explored the Siberian coast by land in the 1820s (writing a superb description of the Chukchi tribes) and may have sighted the island. It is Wrangel – Long's name – rather than Kellett's which is now the accepted name for the island. Wrangel had never been inhabited and was rarely visited, and was largely ignored. Finally, Vilhjalmur Stefansson's abortive attempt at settlement in 1921 seems to have stirred the Soviets into action and in 1924 the armed ice-breaker *Krasny Oktyobr* (Red October) landed a party who formally claimed sovereignty for the USSR. A two-man wintering party (Ushakov and Urvantsev: see below) was left on the island.

Franz Josef Land was the next island group to be discovered, though the formal discovery of 1873 was almost certainly preceded by a sighting in 1865 by Nils Fredrik Rønnbeck in the sealer *Spidsbergen*. Rønnbeck sighted what he modestly called Rønnbeck Land while sailing north-eastwards from Svalbard, and there are no candidates other than Franz Josef. The now-official name of the islands derives from the undisputed discovery by an Austro-Hungarian expedition. The 24-man expedition left Bremerhaven in June 1872 in the *Tegetthoff* (named for Admiral Wilhelm Tegetthoff) under the command of Karl Weyprecht and Julius van Payer. Weyprecht, a naval lieutenant, commanded at sea, while Payer, an army lieutenant, was in charge on land. The object of the expedition was to reach Asia, but to do so by way of the open polar sea rather than the North-East Passage, belief in the existence of the sea having not finally died. The *Tegetthoff* met the *Isbjørn*,

which had made a preparatory journey the previous year on 12 August, the two celebrating the birthday of Emperor Franz Josef on the 18th, then going separate ways. In 1871 the *Isbjørn* had reached 79°N.

On 21 August, at 76°22'N, the *Tegetthoff* was trapped in the ice (see below). All winter the ship drifted, but the hoped-for release in 1873 failed to materialise. By 30 August 1873, now fogbound as well as trapped, the ship had drifted to 79°43'N. When the fog lifted the crew were astonished to see land; Cape Tegetthoff on Hall Island. Not until November had the ice around the ship consolidated sufficiently for the Austrians to cross the 40km (25 miles) or so and set foot on the new land for the first time. They headed east, reaching an island named Wilczek (after the Isbjørn's commander) where they formally claimed all

the land of the archipelago for Austro-Hungary, naming it Franz Josef Land for their emperor.

With the ship sealed in for another winter, and it becoming clear that she might not survive a second period of intense ice pressure, the decision was made to abandon her in the summer of 1874. Payer therefore decided to explore Franz Josef. He made three trips, on the second of which, lasting 28 days, he sledged north to Cape Fligely on Rudolf Island (named for the emperor's son), the most northerly point of the archipelago. There Payer erected a cairn and left a note (which was found in 1899 by the Duke of the Abruzzi). With summer now approaching Payer's team made a nervous journey back to Wilczek Island wondering if the *Tegetthoff* would still be there. She was, and the entire crew – now 23 as one man had died of tuberculosis – abandoned her, hauling everything they could carry in the ship's boats. Their journey southward started on 20 May and rapidly became a fight for survival against cold, hunger and scurvy. Then on 15 July the men were appalled to see the *Tegetthoff* in the distance. Despite eight weeks of body- and mind-shattering effort the northward drift of the ice had returned them to within 14km (9 miles) of the ship. Many wanted to re-board, but Weyprecht and Payer persuaded them that the ship was doomed and that their only chance of survival lay in heading south again. With the wind shifting in their favour they now made real progress and in mid-August finally reached open water. They had hauled their boats over 550km (340 miles), but were only 240km (150 miles) from the *Tegetthoff*.

But the men's ordeal was not yet over. They were running very short of food and when they finally reached Novaya Zemlya were unable to land near supply depots that the *Isbjørn* had laid down because of rough seas. With the boats being driven away from the coast and things looking distinctly bleak the men were fortunately spotted by the Russian ship *Nikolai*. They were rescued, fed and given the news that peace had descended on Europe and that Napoleon had died.

The final Russian Arctic archipelago, Severnaya Zemlya, was not discovered until the Arctic Ocean Hydrographic Expedition of 1910–15. Anxious to establish an easily navigated North-East Passage in the wake of its defeat by Japan in the war of 1904–5 Russia built two ice-breakers, *Taymyr* and *Vaygach*, to more thoroughly explore the Siberian coast. The series of voyages by the two ships culminated in the first transit of the passage from east to west. The leaders of this historically important expedition were Boris Viltiski and Alexander Kolchak, both of whom were anti-Communist. Viltiski escaped to London after the transit, but Kolchak led the White Russian forces in Siberia. He was captured and executed by firing squad in 1920. During the 1913 voyage of the two ice-breakers the southern island of Severnaya Zemlya – initially called Nicholas II Land, but changed to Northern Land after the Revolution – was discovered. The archipelago was thoroughly explored by George Ushakov, one of the greatest of all Russian Arctic travellers. Ushakov had lived on Wrangel for three years (1926–9) to bolster Russia's sovereignty claim and was made leader of the Northern Land Expedition in 1930. Accompanied by Sergei Zhuravlev, a hunter/trapper, and Nikolai Urvantsev, Ushakov set out by dog-sledge on a journey of 3,000km (almost 2,000 miles) that took two years. Ushakov was proudly Communist – his names on the archipelago include Cape Hammer and Sickle and October Revolution Island – but Urvantsev was not. Following the expedition Ushakov was awarded the Order of Lenin. Urvantsev, an Arctic explorer with a pedigree almost the equal of Ushakov's, vanished in Stalin's purges, but not before he had established Irkutsk University. Urvantsev was written out of the official book on the expedition but today, thankfully, his name has been reinstated, his contribution recognised.

In 1947 the skeletal remains of a human, together with traces of a camp, were discovered on Severnaya Zemlya. Though never formally identified they are believed to be of a member of a team lead by Russian geologist V.A. Rusanov. Rusanov, accompanied by his French fiancée Juliette Jean and a small crew, disappeared in 1912 during an attempt to take a ship west–east through the North-East Passage. This sad discovery implies that Rusanov had perhaps made it to the archipelago before the official discovery, but the evidence is by no means conclusive. Other items obviously from Rusanov's trip were found hundreds of miles to the west and these imply that the expedition failed to escape the Kara Sea. The skeletal remains are, therefore, another enduring Arctic mystery.

Above **Ermak, the world's first ice-breaker, named for the cossack who led the Russian annexation of Siberia. Though the ship's concept was Soviet she was actually built in Newcastle-upon-Tyne, England, in 1898.**

Arctic and Antarctic Institute, St Petersburg, Russia

Voyages in the eastern Arctic

Russian interest in northern sea routes was rekindled by Nordenskiöld's voyage. In the 1890s Vice-Admiral Makarov had the *Ermak* built, the world's first ice-breaker, and attempted to reach the North Pole with her in 1899. He failed, reaching 81°28'N close to Svalbard, but he had laid the groundwork for the voyages of the *Taimyr* and *Vaygach* which, as noted earlier, completed the second transit of the North-East

Passage. Russia's continuing enthusiasm for a northern sea route led to a near disaster in 1933, but before that, in 1914, a Russian ship was involved in a trip every bit as harrowing as the more famous voyages of the *Jeanette* and the *Karluk*.

The *Saint Anna*, with Georgi Brusilov commanding, left Arkhangelsk on 4 September 1912, much too late in the year for Arctic travel. Brusilov had been delayed in Alexandrovsk (now Murmansk) and had also failed to sign on the crew he needed. His second-in-command had not arrived and he could find only five experienced sailors. As he left the White Sea Brusilov had an unknown deputy, Valerian Albanov, and his crew of 23 included a woman, Yerminiya Zhdenko, who was to act as nurse. The objective of the trip was to discover new whaling and sealing grounds, though there was also a vague suggestion of making the second transit of the North-East Passage.

Brusilov may have been seduced by Nordenskiöld's (correct) suggestion that the Kara Sea was ice-free in the late summer – if so he was abruptly brought back to reality when, after traversing the Yugorski Strait, the *Saint Anna* became ice-bound close to the Yamal Peninsula on 15 October. The crew walked to the peninsula and saw the tracks of local reindeer herders. These locals offered salvation, but the crew decided to stay with the ship: it was an understandable, but incorrect decision – during the next 17 months the *Saint Anna* drifted slowly north, finally reaching 82°58'N off the northern tip of Franz Josef Land. There a simmering conflict between Brusilov and Albanov finally boiled over. The problem seems to have been Albanov's exasperation with Brusilov's incompetent leadership; Albanov demanded to be relieved of his duties and requested permission to leave the ship. Food and fuel were running low (the samovar, that ubiquitous Russian feature, was by now fuelled only by bear fat and seal blubber) but Brusilov had no plan other than to hope the ship would break free. Brusilov gave his permission for Albanov to leave. To his surprise, but also to his delight, 13 men decided to go as well.

Albanov supervised the construction of sledges and kayaks and loaded them with supplies which Brusilov itemised and made him sign for, increasing Albanov's antagonism. For a map Albanov had only the one in his copy of Nansen's book *Furthest North*. Using this he hoped to reach the base camp of the Russian Georgi Sedov who was using Franz Josef as the starting point for his expedition to the North Pole (though he did not know which island Sedov had decided to use) or Frederick Jackson's Elmwood Camp.

Albanov seems glad to have been away from the ship. It was only 120km (75 miles) to land and the second winter had been appalling, the bear-grease lamps creating an evil smoke and condensation which caused mildew to form on all surfaces: everyone on board was soon covered in a layer of greasy smoke residue. Yet the ice turned out to be little better. The 14 men left on 10 April and dragged their sledges just 5km (3 miles). They were then kept in their tents for three days by a blizzard, an inauspicious start. In the absence of sleeping bags the men slept in *malitsas* – smocks of reindeer hide, fur on the inside – two men huddling together, their legs inside one malitsa, their head and torso in another. After the blizzard Albanov sent one clearly ailing man back to the ship: another man volunteered to take his place, a remarkably brave offer given that these on the *Saint Anna* thought the ice party were, at least, misguided.

Albanov calculated their position as the weather improved: they had walked 5 km (3 miles) south but had drifted 35km (22 miles) north. Despite this discouraging news the men pressed on. By 16 April daily visits from their shipmates stopped as they had travelled too far from, and also now lost sight of, the ship. By day 11 of the trek their fuel was exhausted and they were forced to suck icicles or to drink small quantities of seawater to survive. On that day three men gave up and returned to the ship.

The trek of the remaining 11 men became a nightmare. If they arrived at a *polynya* (an area of open water: such pools are often found in the frozen ocean, kept open by currents or consistent winds) they could shoot seals and so obtain blubber to heat water, but if they did not hunger, cold and thirst were almost overwhelming. On 3 May one man went off in search of flat ice he claimed to have seen – was he brave or had he gone mad? – and disappeared. The rate of progress was about 3km (2 miles) daily despite the use of the kayaks in leads and the slow progress and monotony began to sap the men's mental strength. To Albanov's horror they became listless and childlike; one fell into the sea when he attempted to climb an iceberg from his kayak, just for the fun of it. To add to Albanov's worries the symptoms of scurvy began to appear and the south-westerly drift of the ice (the wind had changed) meant he became unsure as to the direction in which Franz Josef Land lay. Even when they shot a polar bear the men's health did not improve as they ate the liver and so overdosed on vitamin A. Albanov realised that the liver was the cause of their illness and forbade its future appearance on the menu, probably saving them from the fate of Andrée's team.

Albanov was increasingly frustrated by the men's attitude. Some had become fed up with hauling the kayaks and wanted to abandon them despite the fact that when the pack ice broke up they would be crucial to their survival. Their failure to realise this, coupled with their lack of interest in where they were, a problem which exercised their leader constantly, exasperated Albanov. He was aware that they had drifted west, but that they were now drifting south – would they miss Franz Josef altogether and reach the Barents Sea? It meant almost certain death if they did. Finally on 9 June he spotted land to the east, though it took another 17 days of exhausting trekking over unruly ice to reach it. During that time two men made off with the best of the equipment, clearly intent on saving themselves at the expense of their comrades. Albanov swore that if he ever saw them again he would kill them. Ironically he did see them when they finally made landfall at Cape Mary Harmsworth on Alexandra Land. Mellowed by the flowers blooming on the island, by the thought of feasting on gull eggs and by their remorse, Albanov relented.

Albanov fixed his position when he found a note left by Frederick Jackson, and decided to push east for Cape Flora. Again he was frustrated by his men who seemed willing only to sleep. One man declined to move at all and was left behind. When, overcome by conscience, the men returned for him, he was dead. The apathy is strange given the imperative of reaching Cape Flora; one suggested explanation is that the periods of malnutrition had led to vitamin deficiencies which can create such a condition. Whatever the cause another man soon died, leaving eight to struggle on. During the crossing of Prince George Land four men, including Albanov, had used the remaining two kayaks, the others having been abandoned at various times when exhaustion was overwhelming, to take all the

equipment by sea while four men skied cross-country. The expected rendezvous failed, the four kayakers pushing on alone. These survivors reached Bell Island, a base used by Englishman Benjamin Leigh Smith during his expeditions on 1880–2. Leigh Smith's trips were for exploration, scientific study and hunting and he built a substantial hut at what he named Eira Harbour after his ship: it is still there and in remarkably good condition. The *Eira* suffered the same fate as her predecessor the *Tegetthoff*, being holed and sunk by ice pressure. As a result Leigh Smith and his crew were marooned on Cape Flora, unable to reach the Eira Harbour hut. The misery of their enforced winter was doubtless relieved by the fact that they managed to offload 320 litres (70 gallons) of rum and a huge quantity of champagne, whisky, gin, sherry and beer before the ship went down.

Had Albanov found Leigh Smith's hut he might have been able to rest and eat well, and to make use of a rowing boat Leigh Smith had left. But despite, as he later discovered, walking within 100m of it, he missed it and so decided to press on for Cape Flora. On the sea crossing between Bell and Northbrook Islands a violent storm forced Albanov and his companion Alexander Konrad on to an ice floe. To escape the savagery of the weather the two got into their malitsas. When the floe broke up in the violent seas they fell into the sea 'like two unwanted kittens thrown together in a sack to be drowned'. But they survived, and managed to reach Cape Flora on 9 July, 90 days after leaving the *Saint Anna*. Of the second kayak there was no sign. At Cape Flora Albanov and Konrad found huts and supplies in plenty, remnants not only of Jackson's expedition, but those of Abruzzi, Ziegler and Sedov. Exhausted, filthy and dressed in lice-infested rags the two men were finally able to relax. They expected to overwinter, but were discovered just 11 days later by the *Saint Foka*, a supply ship looking for Sedov.

Albanov and Konrad were the only survivors of the *Saint Anna*. Of the four skiers, the other two kayakers, the Saint Anna and those who remained with her, no trace was ever found.

Striving for the pole

The first attempts

It is an arguable point which expedition has the right to be termed the first to attempt to reach the North Pole as many of the early travellers, for instance Henry Hudson, assumed that to reach Cathay it was necessary merely to sail north over the pole, the pole itself being an incidental along the way. Arguably the first to sail north with the specific intent of reaching the pole was the Englishman Constantine Phipps who, in 1773, sailed the *Racehorse* and the *Carcass* (the latter commanded by Skeffington Lutwidge) past Svalbard. He failed of course, but the trip was a valuable experience for a 14-year-old midshipman called Horatio Nelson. It was also almost Nelson's last trip as he only narrowly avoided being killed by a polar bear. It is said that only the firing of a gun from the ship, which frightened the bear away, saved Nelson's life. The young man's excuse

for the encounter was that he wished to take a bear skin back for his father.

After Buchan and Franklin came William Edward Parry, hero of attempts at the North-West Passage. In 1827 Parry took the *Hecla* (and his new wife's pet dog Fido) to Spitsbergen's north coast. Having pocketed the £5,000 prize for reaching 110°W he was now intent, at the very least, on collecting another £1,000 for reaching 83°N. It was not to be: Parry had realised that his best hope lay in dragging sledges across the ice, but hedged his bet on finding open water by fixing steel runners to the two boats he took on the trek. This allowed his men to use the boats to cross leads, but the boats were heavy and exhausting to drag. With Parry in charge of one boat and James Clark Ross the other the expedition set out. The weather was awful, almost constant rain making the snow soft, so increasing the friction on the runners. The men were soaked, often falling into pools on the ice surface to add to their misery, and so perpetually cold. Parry also discovered,

Above Walruses attack a boat from the *Trent (top)*; the expedition driven into the ice (below). Both illustrations are taken from Frederick Beechey's book *A Voyage of Discovery towards the North Pole*, which detailed the Buchan/Franklin expedition of 1818. Beechey was one of Franklin's officers.
USA Library of Congress

Left The *Racehorse* and the *Carcass* on 31 July 1773. It is not clear that the clergy would approve of the game being played on the ice: leap-frog has always had a curious reputation. The next to try for the North Pole after the Phipps expedition were David Buchan, in the *Dorothea*, and John Franklin, in the *Trent*. They followed the same route along Spitsbergen's western shore, but after a violent storm had threatened to crush their ships and another storm had freed them from the ice, the expedition was abandoned.
Richard Sale Collection

as others were to find later, some with disastrous consequences, that as his team went north – painfully, and painfully slowly, often reduced to a speed of only 250m (273yd) per hour – the ice was drifting south at almost the same speed. Finally he was forced to admit defeat. He had established a record (82°45'N) but not won the prize: he was 220km (170 miles) north of the *Hecla*, but had walked several times that distance.

Above The boats hauled up for the night. The apparent domesticity of this illustration from Parry's book *Narrative of an Attempt to reach the North Pole* is at odds with the realities of the trip.
Richard Sale Collection

After Parry's attempt British naval expeditions returned to the quest for the North-West Passage, but during the search for Franklin further voyages were made northward. The graves on Beechey Island opened up the possibility that Franklin had headed north and in 1852 Edward Belcher had explored Wellington Channel, his men sledging across northern Cornwallis, Bathurst and Melville Islands. In the same year Lady Jane Franklin provided a ship, the *Isabel*, and the Admiralty a crew under Edward Inglefield, to try another route northward. Inglefield followed Baffin's route, passing Cape Isabella and naming Cape Sabine (soon to become infamous) as he traversed Smith Sound and looked into what he thought was the polar sea. Inglefield also named Ellesmere Island which forms the west side of Kane Basin and Smith Sound.

The Americans head north

Inglefield's route north attracted the attention of Americans who were keen not only to help find Franklin but also to pursue their own ambitions of reaching the North Pole. Exploration of the route was to prove that the British did not have a monopoly on disaster in the Canadian Arctic. The first American to follow Inglefield was Elisha Kent Kane, a man whose courage and perseverance outweighed poor health: he suffered from rheumatism and a bad heart, and died of a stroke when only 37. Kane had already been on one search expedition, the first to have been sponsored by the New York businessman Henry Grinnell in response to Lady

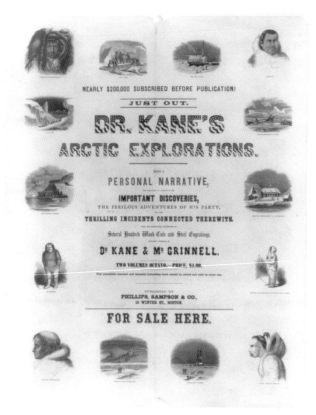

Top **The Second Grinnell Expedition to the Arctic. The image has a convoluted ancestry, being an engraving by John Sartain from a painting by Jas Hamilton which was itself based on an Elisha Kent Kane sketch.**
USA Library of Congress

Above **Kane's two books on the Grinnell expeditions sold phenomenally well: over 60,000 copies in the first year of publication and reviewed, almost always favourably, over 1,000 times. It was said that only the Bible was seen on more American tables. The books remain classics of Arctic literature, both well written and beautifully illustrated.**
USA Library of Congress

Top **Isaac Hayes' team rounding Cape Alexander.**
Richard Sale Collection

Above **A lithograph of Charles Francis Hall from the only known photograph of him.**
Permission of Chauncey Loomis

Franklin's request to the US. Kane had been surgeon on the First Grinnell Expedition (two ships, the *Advance* and the *Rescue*, commanded by Edwin De Haven) which had been one of the several at Beechey Island when the first traces of Franklin's men had been found. Now, three years later, Kane was commanding his own expedition. In the *Advance* – which was little bigger than Frobisher's ship – with a crew of 17, Kane sailed beyond Inglefield's northernmost point, reaching the Kane Basin. His hope that this was the open polar sea – which was still claimed to exist by some scientists and whalers – were now dashed: the ice advanced and Kane was forced to overwinter at Rensselaer Harbour on the Greenland coast. He had come equipped with dogs and sledges to pursue the journey north, but the dogs died of a mysterious illness.

Despite this setback much was achieved. Isaac Israel Hayes, Kane's surgeon, sledged along Ellesmere Island as far as Cape Frazer, and another team reached the Humboldt Glacier on Greenland ('a plastic, moving, semi-solid mess, obliterating life, swallowing rocks and islands and ploughing its way with irresistible march [to] … the sea', as Kane noted in his book of the expedition). The *Advance* failed to escape the ice when summer came, forcing a second overwintering. With little fuel or fresh food, and scurvy beginning to take its toll, Hayes took half the men and headed south, hoping to reach a Danish settlement. They managed 480km (300 miles) but were forced to retreat after spending three months held captive by a savage winter. The return trip was an epic involving the rounding of Cape Alexander on a ledge which narrowed to 40cm (15in) above a drop into the sea and certain death. On the *Advance* Kane and the others survived only because local Inuit gave them food. Finally in the summer of 1855, with the *Advance* still locked into the ice, all the men headed south. Using sledges and boats they made it to Upernavik in August.

Kane's surgeon Isaac Hayes returned with his own expedition in 1860. Sailing in the *United States* with a young astronomer, August Sonntag, Hayes overwintered near the entrance to Smith Sound. He and Sonntag made trips on to glaciers flowing from Greenland's inland ice, but on one Sonntag fell through the sea ice. Though he was quickly dragged clear he died during the night and Hayes abandoned the trip.

As he neared the US on his return journey Hayes passed the *Rescue* which was taking Charles Francis Hall north for the first time. Hall was on another Franklin search expedition, one which was to form the basis of most subsequent attempts to piece together Franklin's fate from Inuit testimony. Hall's was the last American expedition for a decade, the Civil War calling a halt to such frivolous adventures. When peace returned, so did Hall, heading north again in 1871, this time in the *Polaris* and intent on reaching the North Pole.

Hall believed that he 'was born to discover the North Pole. That is my purpose. Once I have set my right foot on the Pole, I shall be perfectly willing to die.' It was a partially prophetic comment. With him were Sidney Budington as captain, the German Emil Bessels – a surgeon with previous Arctic experience – and two Inuit families (including several children). One of these families Hall had befriended on his Franklin searches, the other was that of Suersaq, also known as Hans Hendrik, who had already proved invaluable to Kane and Hayes and would later accompany Nares. The *Polaris* sailed to 82°11'N, the furthest north reached so far in the Kane Basin, then overwintered on Greenland's coast at 81°37'N, the furthest north anyone had done so to date. Though Hall called the winter base Thank God Harbour it was not really a harbour, the ship lying in the lee of a vast iceberg called Providence Berg, clearly a heartfelt name. At the harbour, on 8 November 1871, Hall died.

The expedition now broke up in confusion. Budington and Bessels were the senior expedition members, but Budington thought Bessels arrogant, and Bessels thought Budington an ignoramus. When summer came Budington tried to take the ship south, but it was soon beset again. The ice was now drifting south and had soon cleared Smith Sound. There might have been optimism among the crew, but it was soon shattered when on 15 October gale-driven ice threatened to sink the ship. Anxious to save what they could the team began to unload boats and stores on to an ice floe. This job had not been completed before the gale separated the floe and the ship, and to the horror of those on each the two drifted apart and were soon lost to each other's view. As the ship drifted away, above the screaming wind a voice could be heard calling forlornly from the ice floe, 'Goodbye *Polaris*'.

Those on the ship were driven north to the Greenland coast near the Inuit settlement of Etah whose hunters had earlier kept Kane's team alive. The crew, now numbering 14, built a house with wood from the *Polaris*, survived a reasonably comfortable winter and then, in boats made from more *Polaris* timber, went south in June 1873, soon being picked up by a whaler.

On the ice floe the other members of Hall's team –

Above **Emile Bessel's sketch of Hall's funeral. In the background can be seen the observatory built for the expedition's scientists. It had a coal-burning stove to warm them as they studied astronomy and local geology, meteorology, and so on.**
Permission of Chauncey Loomis

one was a baby born on 12 August 1872 to Hans Hendrik and his wife, an addition to the three children they already had – had a more dramatic winter. The Inuit were all on the floe. Though they included a nursing baby, they could also build snow igloos and hunt seals from the kayaks that had been offloaded. That kept the party alive when the stores from the ship had run out. The 19 men, women and children spent the winter on the ice floe, which was roughly 150m (165yd) square. They were often hungry and, when the sun returned, also fearful that the ice floe would suddenly break up and hurl them into the sea. Eventually, on 1 April 1873, they crowded into the two salvaged boats – built to accommodate a maximum of 12 men – and prayed for a ship to spot them as they had to abandon a lot of food and clothing. Two ships passed without seeing them but on 30 April, close to the Labrador coast after having drifted about 2,400km (1,500 miles), they were taken on board the *Tigress*. Two days after their rescue there was a violent storm: it would almost certainly have overwhelmed the two boats.

Hall's expedition had been an official US venture, sanctioned by President Grant and underwritten by the navy, so there was a board of inquiry into its conduct and the death of the leader. It heard that the expedition had been far from happy. Budington had been a secret – and not-so-secret drinker – which brought him into conflict with the god-fearing Hall; Hall and Bessels had disagreed repeatedly, Bessels once threatening to leave the ship and to take the German crewmen, of whom there were several, with him; some members of the crew were upset with Hall's strange and occasionally autocratic methods, and fearful of continuing the northern journey. It also learned that Hall had experienced strange symptoms for two weeks before his death, bouts of violent sickness interspersed with periods of recovery. The problems had started with what Dr Bessels called an 'apoplectical insult' – a stroke – which he verified by noting paralysis, testing it with a needle. The board decided that Hall had indeed, died of apoplexy. Suspicious of the board's finding, in 1968 Chauncey Loomis, a Dartmouth professor who was writing a biography of Hall, persuaded the Danes to allow an autopsy. This proved difficult as Hall's internal organs had fused with, and become indistinguishable from, his flesh. But hair and fingernail samples showed large amounts of arsenic, almost certainly administered during the last two weeks of his life. Hall had exhibited classic symptoms of arsenic poisoning and had also been convinced he was being poisoned by Budington or Bessels, but, as Loomis rightly notes, at this remove from the event nothing definite could be determined. Perhaps Hall did indeed have a stroke – he noted on one sledge trip that he could no longer run in front of the dogs: clearly he was unwell – and, perhaps fearful of Bessels, had self-administered patent medicines. In the 1860s many of these contained arsenic. Yet Bessels' treatment of Hall – when it was allowed – was curious. He declined, when requested, to administer an emetic which would have cleared Hall's stomach of any poison and continued to inject him – nominally with quinine, but quinine crystals and arsenic powder would have been indistinguishable to those crew members who saw the injections prepared – long after the 'fever' he said he was treating had subsided. When Bessels was not allowed to treat Hall his condition improved. Yet what, if he was guilty, was Bessels' motive for murder? He was clearly at odds with Hall, but could that really have led a civilised man to murder? Of course, the harshness of, and fear induced by, the Arctic has done strange things to men's minds. Hall's death was obviously suspicious, but must remain a mystery.

The British try one last time

Having stayed away from the Arctic since Belcher's near-farcical expedition, the British navy, inspired by Hall's voyage, decided to try again for the North Pole. In 1875, with the blessing of Queen Victoria and Prime Minister Disraeli (just as Hall had received a blessing from President Grant) George Nares set out with the *Alert* and the *Discovery*. Despite the lessons of the Franklin disaster and the myriad search expeditions, the British Admiralty had learned nothing. Both ships were huge rather than small and manoeuvrable, the crew numbered 120, too many to live off the land; the sledges which had already proved too heavy and cumbersome were again taken; the food was much the same as that which had probably contributed to Franklin's downfall.

Yet despite their size Nares brilliantly took his ships through the Kane Basin ice. The *Discovery* wintered in Lady Franklin Bay, the *Alert* continuing to winter near Cape Sheridan where the Alert meteorologist station is now placed. It was a new record northing, both for a ship and for a wintering station. In 1876 Albert Markham took a sledge team north from the *Alert* establishing a new furthest north record of 83°20'26"N on 12 May. By then all hope of the pole was gone and survival was in the balance. The men were exhausted by boat-hauling – they had reached a point only 117km (73 miles) from the ship but had walked over 800km (500 miles) as they had to return for the second of two boats each time as they were so heavy – boats had been taken in case open water was reached. The men were also crippled by scurvy. Finally the one reasonably fit man was sent alone to cover the last 50km (30 miles) to get help. Nares, concerned by the state of Markham's men – one of whom died – immediately sent a rescue party out for his second land party. This team had traced Ellesmere Island's north coast as far as Alert Point, but would all have died of scurvy without the rescue team.

Two sledge parties also set out from the *Discovery*. That ship's crew had enjoyed better health due largely to Hans Hendrik (Suersaq) supplying them with fresh meat. One sledge party surveyed the Ellesmere coast south of the ship and returned in reasonable health, but the other, under Lewis Beaumont, which had surveyed Greenland's north coast, found itself returning in deep, soft snow. Exhausted and with two men dead from scurvy Beaumont found open water between him and the *Discovery*. At that stage a rescue party arrived and the remaining men were saved.

Nares now had less than one-fifth of his men free of scurvy and wisely decided to abandon a second over-

Above **The exhumation of Charles Francis Hall. Hall lay in a plain pine coffin in a shallow grave. When the lid was removed the body was found to be wrapped in the US flag, its colours staining his flesh. In a morbidly humorous touch, Hall's last resting place had been made by the *Polaris* carpenter – Nathaniel Coffin.**
Permission of Chauncey Loomis

wintering and to head for home. In the inquiry which followed the expedition the evidence of two doctors that the sledge party's scurvy had been caused by a lack of lime juice was rejected. John Rae's view that fresh meat, fish and vegetables were effective anti-scorbutants, and evidence that lime juice itself aged significantly and so became less effective with time, were quietly ignored. One of the committee who decided that everything possible had been done and nothing could be improved, either on the matter of anti-scorbutants or equipment, was Clements Markham, cousin of Albert Markham who had almost died returning from the furthest north, and the man instrumental in appointing Robert Falcon Scott to lead the expeditions to Antarctica.

Above **A sledge party from the *Alert* making a push for the pole.**
UK National Maritime Museum

The Americans try again:
Greely and the *Jeanette*

In 1875 Karl Weyprecht, co-leader of the expedition that discovered Franz Josef Land, proposed that rather than the piecemeal approach to Arctic exploration that had, up to that time, been the norm, a co-ordinated international effort should be made to carry out scientific studies in the area. This was agreed, and during the International Polar Year of 1882/3 a dozen stations were set up and manned through the winter. A Dutch expedition in the *Varna* was trapped by ice in the Kara Sea before reaching the proposed station, but the crew and scientists escaped to the mainland unharmed. All except one of the other stations were manned successfully and uneventfully. The exception was the US expedition under the command of Adolphus Washington Greely: its story is one of the most horrific for which there are the first-hand accounts of survivors.

Greely took his expedition of 25 men (including himself and two Inuit hunters) north in the *Proteus* in the early summer of 1881, eventually reaching the point where Nares's *Discovery* had overwintered. Here a base – Fort Conger, named for a US senator who had been a principal supporter of the expedition – was built, and the scientific studies of the Polar Year began. But Greely's trip had a dual purpose: he had also been told to try to reach the pole or, at least, to better Nares' record. To that end James Lockwood, one of Greely's two officers, laid down depots along a route towards the north Greenland coast.

The summer of 1882 seems to have been idyllic. Insects and butterflies flitted among the flowers, and muskoxen provided a ready source of fresh meat. There was internal dissension within the team – Greely had alienated his other officer, Frederick Kislingsbury, the team doctor Octave Parry and some of his men with his stubbornness and poor decision-making – but they were not to have an instrumental effect on the course of the expedition. In early April Lockwood headed north with one dog-sledge and three manhauled sledges. After four weeks of travelling most of the party was sent back, Lockwood continuing with Sgt David Brainard, the Inuk Frederick (Thorlip Frederick Christiansen) and the dog-sledge. Finding and using depots left by Beaumont's party from the Nares expedition Lockwood pushed on, eventually reaching the northern end of Lockwood Island at 83°24'N. They had extended Beaumont's survey by 240km (150 miles) and Markham's furthest north by 6.5km (4 miles). After 60 days they were back at Fort Conger. It had not, strictly, been an attempt at the pole, but it was a notable achievement and established a new northing record.

During the same summer Greely explored Ellesmere Island, surveying a good deal of country and discovering Lake Hazen (named for General William Hazen, chief signal officer of the US, Greely's commanding officer). The expected supply ship did not arrive, but with supplies and game still (relatively) abundant there was no need for concern. Another winter passed and in the summer of 1883 Lockwood tried to go north from Ellesmere. Unfortunately open water stopped him (though it is doubtful if he would have managed to break his own record by more than 1° or so). Instead Lockwood headed west, discovering and tracing Greely Fjord.

Back at Fort Conger the length of separation from civilisation and continuing uncertainty over the absence of a relief ship was taking its toll. As Greely's dispute with Parry intensified the commander tried to have the doctor arrested for insubordination. Eventually, with the situation at Fort Conger deteriorating, Greely decided to head south to where supply dumps should have been laid down even if the relief ships had been unable to reach the expedition. Of two possibilities, Cape Sabine on Ellesmere or Littleton Island on the Greenland coast, he chose the former.

Greely's choices have been debated ever since. Should he have stayed at Fort Conger where game was plentiful? He did not know he had been abandoned, and without a relief ship Conger meant starving slowly rather than starving quickly. Should he have gone to the

Greenland side where the Inuit of Etah had a history of helping expeditions? Again, how was he to know that the Cape Sabine cupboard was bare?

The team loaded everything including all the scientific data into two boats, and headed south through difficult ice and bad weather. It took 16 days to cover the 320km (200 miles) to Cape Sabine but just as they approached it the wind dropped, the pack ice came together and the boats were trapped. It took a further 19 days for the men to cross the last 21km (13 miles) of ice to Ellesmere, most of that time being buffeted by blizzards. They reached land on Pym Island off Cape Sabine. It took two men a further eight days to reach the cape and return with a note that told Greely he and his men were in for a long, hungry winter.

General Hazen had attempted to get a relief ship north in the first summer, but had at first been thwarted by Robert Lincoln, son of Abraham Lincoln and now US secretary of war. Lincoln responded to requests for a ship with queries on the spending related to the expedition. Eventually a ship, the *Neptune*, sailed. Despite several attempts to get through the ice it got no further than the mouth of Kane Basin. Minimal supplies were left at Cape Sabine and Littleton Island and the ship retreated. The next year the command of the relief operation was given to Ernest Garlington. He was a cavalry officer, promoted when many of the officers on his unit, the 7th cavalry, were killed with Custer at the battle of Little Big Horn. As an army man he was an odd choice for a naval expedition, but Hazen was army too, as was Greely and his expedition.

The relief party had two ships, the *Proteus* (which had taken Greely north) and the *Yantic*, a much slower ship which soon lost contact with the faster vessel. The *Proteus* reached Cape Sabine on 22 July, but Garlington did not unload any supplies, preferring to head north. The ship's captain, Richard Pike, favoured waiting one or two days as there was considerable ice in Kane Basin, but eventually agreed to steam north again. Soon, in sight of clear water, the *Proteus* was caught by ice floes and very quickly began to sink. Garlington threw as much material overboard as possible, but the majority of the supplies for Greely were lost, and much of what he did salvage drifted away on the ice. Garlington now left enough at Cape Sabine to last Greely three weeks then took the rest and headed south. He left a note on Littleton Island which was picked up by the *Yantic* when she arrived. Faced with deciding whether to go north towards Greely or south after Garlington, Frank Wildes, the

Top '**The Farthest North of All Time', engraving by Albert Operti (who later accompanied Peary to Greenland), of Lt Lockwood, Sgt Brainard and the Inuk Frederick at 83°24'N on 13 May 1882.**
USA National Archives and Records Administration

Above **Hauling ice at Fort Conger. Left to right are the Inuk Jens, Greely, Cross and Kislingbury.**
USA Library of Congress

Above **The *Proteus* sinking.**
USA National Archives and Records Administration

Yantic's captain, headed south, leaving no supplies at Littleton. The *Yantic* and Garlington's men were eventually united at Upernavik. There it was decided that it was too late in the year to go north again and the *Yantic* sailed back to St John's on Newfoundland. A flurry of telegrams now sought advice. But though pressed by General Hazen and, especially, by Greely's wife, Robert Lincoln vetoed a further attempt to go north. Greely had been abandoned.

On Pym Island Greely's men built a rough hut of stone around an upturned boat. They collected what Garlington had left at Cape Sabine and, as there was little meat, Greely sent a team of four, including two Inuit, to collect such supplies as Nares had left at Cape Isabella, 65km (40 miles) away. It took five days to get there, but the cache contained only about 65kg (140lb) of meat. On the way back with this one man, Joseph Elison, became so cold that two others had to stay with him, attempting to warm him in a four-man sleeping bag, while the last man went for help. All four were saved, but only for a greater nightmare. The two Inuit hunters tried desperately to find game but apart from the odd seal there was nothing: Cape Sabine was no Fort Conger. Eventually one Inuk died of scurvy aggra-vated by exhaustion, the other drowning when his kayak was ripped by ice.

The death of the Inuit and the coming of winter meant an end to fresh food. With supplies dwindling Greely cut the food ration – mouldy bread and soup heated by burning rope and bootsoles – to about 160g (6oz) daily. Eventually even the buffalo-hide or sheep-skin sleeping bags were being boiled and eaten, and by May men were dying daily. One day Charles Henry was discovered to be stealing food. Greely convened a court martial and Henry was sentenced to death in his absence. Too weak to carry out the sentence himself Greely allowed three NCOs to organise it. The facts of the death were never published, but it seems that fearful of Henry's strength – he was bigger than most in the crew, and now better fed – the men lured him away on a pretext and shot him in the head without warning. On the day of the execution the doctor died, his end perhaps aided by self-administered drugs.

When spring came the diet of old leather and tallow was supplemented by seaweed, lichen, flowers, sand fleas and shrimps. These 'supplements' became the only 'food' when everything else edible ran out on 12 May. It took all the survivors' energy to bury their dead comrades in the shallow graves of a makeshift cemetery. Then they were forced to move from the hut to a tent on a drier site because meltwater was making it unbearable. Many of the men could now hardly stand, and death seemed to be both inevitable and welcome. Greely wrote what he thought might be his last note, a curious mixture of pathos and bathos that prefigured Scott: 'Seven of us left – here we are – dying, like men. Did what I came to do – beat the old record.'

In Washington the government had finally realised that Greely might be in trouble, though funding was stalled while a relief bill was debated (at length) and passed. Finally the *Thetis* and *Bear* sailed north. To his considerable aggravation Garlington was not given command, that going to Winfield Schley. On 22 June after following notes left by Greely's men at Cape Sabine and Cape Isabella the ships arrived at Pym Island and discovered the horrors of the camp. Only seven of the 25 men were alive, and of those Joseph Elison was in a pitiful state. Frost-bitten on the trip to Cape Isabella he had seen all the flesh rot from one foot leaving the bones exposed. The skin had sloughed from his hands and his comrades had tied his spoon to his stump so he could eat what little was still available. Dr Parry had amputated both feet and some of his fingers: on the *Thetis* he lost his remaining fingers, then half his legs. His condition worsened and his leg stumps were amputated: it was all to no avail, Elison dying two weeks after rescue.

Schley not only brought back the survivors but also those bodies he could retrieve. The cemetery was a gruesome sight, with heads and feet sticking out of the earth, a testimony to the exhaustion of the burial parties. The exhumed bodies displayed unmistakable signs of cannibalism, much of the flesh having been cut from the bones. The survivors denied all knowledge of this, and an official inquiry decided that any flesh which had been removed had been 'with a view no doubt to use as shrimp bait'.

The aftermath of the expedition was sordid. Some of the survivors exhibited themselves in a freak show for $1,000 per week until ordered to desist. Hazen accused Garlington and Wildes of cowardice, and Lincoln of incompetence. The government closed ranks to defend Lincoln, and Hazen was tried for 'conduct prejudicial to good order'. He was found guilty, but merely censured and allowed to retire quietly: he died two years later. Garlington's career suffered, but having been party to one infamous act he was later involved in another, the massacre of native Americans at Wounded Knee. For that he received the Congressional Medal of Honour, the United States of America's highest award. Greely did well on the lecture circuit and

Above **Greely's camp, photographed by the expedition's rescuers.**
US Navy Historical Centre

Below **The remains of Greely's hut on Pym Island.**
Robert Wallace

Above **The *Jeanette* sinking.**
US Navy Historical Centre

wrote a book on the expedition which blasted Lincoln, Garlington and Wildes. It sold in large numbers, especially to the British. Some of the truths of the terrible winter on Pym Island were, not surprisingly, left out of Greely's book, but are now available in print: they make harrowing reading.

Two years before Greely set out another American expedition had headed north. It too was a disaster – though unknown to Greely at the time – but led to one of the most audacious attempts ever on the North Pole. The purpose of the US navy expedition led by George Washington De Long in the *Jeanette* – the renamed *Pandora* bought from Sir Allen Young, a veteran of the British navy Franklin search – was to discover if Wrangel Island was part of a continent that reached as far as Greenland and to explore its coastline northward. Hopefully De Long would find the open polar sea and so be able to reach the North Pole. In case ice intervened his team of 33 had sledges and dogs. The *Jeanette* sailed in July 1879, reaching pack ice close to Herald Island where she was soon beset. De Long hoped he might now drift north to open water, but instead he went north-west, passing close enough to Wrangel to realise it was a small island rather than part of a larger land mass.

For two years the *Jeanette* drifted. In May 1881 the islands of Jeanette and Henrietta were discovered. Soon after the ice started to pressurise the ship and she began to take on water. Boats, equipment and food were offloaded on to the ice. Tents were erected, but in the middle of the night the ice beneath the camp split. The men moved the tents, the midnight call allowing them to watch as the *Jeanette* sank into the lead the crack created. De Long now started for the New Siberian Islands, a difficult journey that involved hauling three heavy boats. It took 47 days to reach Bennett Island, the most northerly of the New Siberians, and after a ten-day rest the men set out for mainland Russia. They were now rowing their boats, picking a route through the drifting pack ice. Though De Long was anxious to keep the boats together a storm blew up separating the three: no trace of the smallest boat or its crew of eight was ever found.

The other two boats reached the coast near the Lena Delta. One of them with 11 men led by George Melville and John Danenhower had the good fortune to land at the delta's south-eastern corner and so rapidly found the main stream. They soon met local Tungus

Above **George Melville discovers the bodies of De Long and his team.**
US Navy Historical Centre

who provided food and shelter and took them to a village. Melville decided he must now reach Bulun, the largest local settlement where he might find Russian officials who would help organise a search for the other boats and also help his own men reach Yakutsk and safety. But first he rested his men, an understandable decision, but one which would later be criticised.

De Long's boat, with 13 men aboard, together with Snoozer, *Jeanette*'s mascot dog – all the other dogs had been killed as they took up room and ate precious food – landed in the maze of streams of the delta. Forced to wade ashore through new-forming ice to reach marshy ground, the men were soon chilled and exhausted. On 6 October the first men died from the effects of frostbite. The remainder struggled on, occasionally finding huts erected by local hunters – tantalising glimpses of security. With their food running out De Long made the painful decision to kill Snoozer for his meat. Then, when that ran out, De Long decided to send the two strongest men ahead while he remained with the others. Soon after they departed the native hunter Alexei, who had joined the *Jeanette* in Alaska, died of exhaustion after hunting every day with no luck. On 17 October the men ate the last of their leather: four days later two men died. On 29 October the ship's doctor James Ambler wrote a poignant last letter to his brother.

By then only he, De Long and the Chinese steward Ah Sam remained alive. De Long made a last diary entry on 30 October, the 140th day since leaving the *Jeanette*. It is thought that Ambler was the last to die: he was found holding a gun, presumably to ward off animals or birds which had been attracted by the corpses.

Nindemann and Noros, the two men sent forward by De Long, survived by eating discarded fish-heads they found in a hut. Near starvation, they finally met locals, but were unable to make them understand that men were dying nearby. The two were taken south, but a message they wrote quickly found its way to Melville. He immediately joined them in Bulun, discovered where De Long was and set out to find them. But it was now 5 November and Melville was still suffering from frostbite. By 11 November he was in the vicinity of De Long's camp but running short of food, a curiosity he maintained was due to locals having deceived him. By now certain that De Long was dead (and probably correct) he spent his last day searching for, and finding, the expedition records, then abandoned his search. The following spring (March 1882) Melville again set out. After a two-week search the bodies of the first to die were uncovered from the snow. As he walked nearby Melville tripped over something – it was the frozen hand of De Long protruding from the snow.

Twenty men had died, eight in the lost boat, 12 in De Long's party, with little to show for the loss except the discovery of two small islands. Of the survivors, Danenhower later shot himself, another went insane. Melville, who took the brunt of the criticism for his delay in reaching Bulun, was in the *Thetis* when the remnants of Greely's expedition were found at Cape Sabine.

Nansen and the *Fram*

Two years after the discovery of De Long's body the 23-year-old Fridtjof Nansen read an article about relics of the *Jeanette* being found on an ice floe off Qaqortoq (Julienhåb) on the south-west coast of Greenland. The author of the article, Professor Henrik Mohn, conjectured that the discovery implied a current flowing across the Arctic Ocean from Siberia: Nansen realised that such a current might take a ship over, or very close to, the North Pole. If the ship could survive being trapped in the ice it would be released near the coast of Greenland. What was needed was a vessel strong enough to resist ice pressure and a team of men willing to spend perhaps five years on board her.

For the ship Nansen turned to Colin Archer, son of a Scottish immigrant to Norway and a boat-design genius. The ship Nansen and Archer built was the *Fram* – Forward – her cost borne by the Norwegian government as an expression of national pride: later Nansen was influential in the gaining of Norwegian independence. *Fram*'s hull was a half-egg in cross-section with a minimal keel (on some ships the keel had been gripped by ice and then pulled downwards) and a removable rudder (for a similar reason). The cross-beams and stern were huge and of well-seasoned oak to withstand ice pressure. The ship had both a steam engine and sail capability. She also had a windmill which generated electricity for lighting. *Fram* was large, 34.5m (183ft) lay on the waterline and grossing over 400 tons. Visitors to Oslo who take a trip to the Fram Museum at Bygdøy, across the harbour from the city, can compare *Fram* and *Gjøa* which are both preserved there. The latter is tiny by comparison, but *Fram* did not need the manoeuvrability of *Gjøa*: her task was merely to be imprisoned in, resist the pressure of, and drift with, the ice.

Besides Nansen *Fram* had a crew of 12, including Otto Sverdrup, who had crossed Greenland with Nansen, as captain, and Hjalmar Johansen, the son of a townhall caretaker. Johansen had gained a place at university to study law but had to leave when his father died as he could no longer afford to stay. So keen was he to go with Nansen that he not only applied in writing but visited Nansen unannounced. Johansen agreed to do any job and was taken on as a stoker.

When the ship arrived in Vardø, the final Norwegian port before departing for Siberia, the crew celebrated their last night ashore in the time-honoured way – by getting drunk. To their shock Nansen berated them, telling them that if it were not for the fact they were leaving that day he would dismiss them all. It was the first hint of the occasionally difficult times to come. Nansen was a strange leader: he was domineering and arrogant, his undoubted intelligence producing, as one man noted 'a mania for interfering in everything'. Nansen believed he was an authority on all subjects and could do everyone's allotted job better than they could. Yet he was also, and often, cheerful, humorous and good company.

The *Fram* sailed through the Kara Sea, around Cape Chelyuskin and north along the New Siberian Islands to enter the pack. On 5 October 1893 the rudder was raised: *Fram* was frozen in. At first, to Nansen's confusion, the ship drifted south, but soon began his expected steady drift north. Though the ship was cramped, life was tolerable. By luck Nansen had loaded food – canned vegetables and preserved cloudberries, a Norwegian delicacy – which kept the crew free of scurvy. The winter was brutally cold at first as Nansen, fearful of fire and wishing to preserve fuel, refused to allow any heating: he was persuaded to relent when the inside temperature dropped to −30°C. There were excursions on the ice enlivened by occasional polar-bear visits, and regular feast days. And the *Fram* behaved just as Nansen and Archer thought she would: on the open sea she rolled and pitched dreadfully, but when the ice closed around her she rose on it and drifted serenely.

Fram drifted through the winter, the summer of 1894 and into a second winter. But it was clear that her direction was north-west rather than north. On 12 December 1894 she passed the record northing for a ship (set by Nares' *Alert*), but by then Nansen had realised she would never reach the pole and announced his intention of heading north with one companion and all the dogs. His chosen partner was Hjalmar Johansen. During the winter sledges and kayaks were built ready for the trip. On 6

January 1895 *Fram* broke the record for furthest north (held by Lockwood), but almost succumbed to ice pressure, the most frightening time of the whole journey. But neither the new record nor the careful preparations for the voyage stopped Nansen's mood swings. When he and Johansen finally departed on 26 February 1895 almost everyone left on the *Fram* was glad to see the back of him. But those who cheered did so too soon: only 500m from the ship a sledge broke. It had to be repaired and Nansen did not finally depart until 28 February: that day the *Fram* was at 83°50'N and still heading north.

With them Nansen and Johansen had six sledges, 28 dogs and 1,100kg (2,426lb) of equipment. Accompanied by other members of the crew the procession made just 6km (3½ miles) despite shedding some load. After two further days of agonising progress Nansen had to admit that they had started too early (the sun only reappeared on 3 March) and with too much weight. He returned to *Fram*, leaving Johansen on the ice (though two men skied out to join him). *Fram* was now beyond 84°N. The loads were reorganised and on 14 March they set off again, with just three sledges and 760kg (1,676lb) of equipment.

Nansen had secretly thought that with just 6° of latitude to cross the pole would be easily reached. But the pressure ridges of the ice soon proved him wrong. Progress was slow and it was also bitingly cold, with daytime temperatures down to −40°C and reaching −47°C at night. For days neither man had any respite; even at night in their double reindeer-skin sleeping bag they were cold. Fixing latitude from the sun Nansen found that they were travelling much more slowly than he had anticipated; at their rate of progress they would not reach the pole until at least two weeks after his calculated date. Unless things improved they would have to turn back before reaching it.

Progress did not improve. Their clothes, the sweat of effort freezing them into suits of armour, chafed their bodies causing sores; Johansen fell through the ice and almost froze; and the dogs had to be killed one by one. On 4 April Nansen calculated they were at 86°2.8'N when he had hoped they were much further. They continued for three more days then Nansen went ahead on skis. Before him lay a sea of hummocky ice. Later he wrote of his thoughts: 'There seems little sense in carrying on any longer; we are sacrificing valuable time and doing little.' And so, at 86°14'N, a new record by almost 3°, they turned for Franz Josef Land.

At first the going was comparatively easy, a fact which led them to travel too long without camping.

Above **Nansen and Johansen about to set off from the *Fram*. Nansen is second from the left, Johansen fourth from the right.**
From Fridtjof Nansen *Furthest North*.
Richard Sale Collection

That in turn led them to forget to wind their watches. The watches stopped, but as they had little idea how long they had stopped they could no longer be sure of their longitude. To compensate they steered an easterly course as, like Albanov before them, the pair could not afford to miss Franz Josef on its west side and finish in open ocean. The weather continued to hold, though the routine killing of dogs darkened their mood, and latitude checks showed they were still a long way from Franz Josef.

Then the weather changed: the wind shifted bringing blizzards and, worse, altering the ice drift unfavourably. Johansen was becoming tired, the strain of managing two sledges to Nansen's one wearing him down. When the third sledge was finally abandoned on 13 May Johansen was joyful. Summer having arrived the temperature rose, but this also meant more open water slowing their progress. Nansen was also increasingly concerned about their position. Julius von Payer had claimed to have seen Petermann Land lying north of Cape Fligely: he had been fooled by ice and atmospherics, but Nansen did not know that Petermann was a myth.

As May progressed the melting ice proved more difficult and food was also running low and had to be rationed. June brought the first sight of seals and gulls: Nansen shot two gulls, giving the men their first fresh meat for months. But the temperature also rose above freezing making the going, through slush, even worse.

Despite the gulls both dogs and men were now starving. Slaughtered dogs provided blood soup for Nansen and Johansen, but meagre meat for the remaining dogs. When the slush would no longer support a man on skis the two kayaks were bound into a catamaran and paddled. It was almost as hard as walking. On 21 June, 100 days from the *Fram*, Johansen shot a seal, the first of several. It was the first sign that things were getting better, and they improved still further when a polar bear and her two cubs were shot.

No longer hungry, Nansen and Johansen waited in the camp they had established on 21 June until 19 July. By then rain and high temperatures meant that kayaking was easy. Four days later they recognised that the cloud bank they had been staring at for a month was actually a glacier. Currents and wind made sure that reaching land was not easy, and Johansen was lucky to survive an attack by a polar bear (he shouted for Nansen to get the gun and then told him 'you must look sharp', remembering to use the formal Norwegian form of 'you'; the two men maintained that formality, despite four months together on the ice: not until New Year's Day 1896 did they agree to exchange the formal 'de' for the familiar 'du'). On 7 August they reached the ice edge. It was a joyous moment but meant the end for the last two of the 28 dogs that started out from *Fram*.

What the two men had seen was Eva-Liv Island (named later by Nansen for his wife and daughter) in north-eastern Franz Josef. What they first landed on was Adelaide's Island, a little way south, on 10 August. Thinking he was on the west side of the archipelago Nansen decided to kayak west to Gilles Land and then on to Svalbard. Gilles Land had been seen by Dutchman Cornelis Gilles in 1707, but it was not where he claimed it was: he had actually seen Kvitøya. Had Nansen been where he thought he was and headed west he and Johansen would have found 400km (250 miles) of open sea. It is doubtful whether the men would have survived.

As it was, when they headed west, the two kayaks strapped together as a catamaran again, the two men had to endure a walrus attack before finally landing at Helland's Point on north-west Jackson Island (as Nansen later named it). Now, in late August, it was clear winter was coming. Desperate to avoid another winter, but trapped by ice and weather, the pair eventually landed on the southern coast of Jackson Island.

There they built a hut of low walls of stones and turf, digging out the floor and draping walrus skins over a huge log laid between the end walls. Inside it was remarkably snug. With plenty of fresh bear and walrus meat cooked over a blubber fire, a comfortable enough winter was passed. Nansen actually gained weight, though he also had a bout of chronic lumbago and had to be nursed by Johansen.

On 19 May 1896 they refloated their catamaran and headed west again, still unsure of their exact whereabouts. Disaster almost struck in June when the poorly moored catamaran floated away. Nansen took off his top clothes, and dived into the chilling water to retrieve it. With his limbs becoming numb he barely reached the shore again. A few days later a walrus almost sank them. They beat the walrus off, but one kayak was holed and by the time they got ashore much of their equipment was wet. For two days they stayed in their camp to dry things out. On the second day Nansen thought he heard a dog barking and, leaving Johansen behind, set out on skis to investigate.

At his Elmwood base Frederick Jackson was told that there was a man approaching and wandered out to meet him. Jackson recalls in his book on his own trip, 'I saw a tall man on skis with roughly made clothes and an old felt hat on his head. He was covered with oil and grease, and black from head to foot... His hair was very long and dirty, his complexion appeared to be fair, but dirt prevented me from being sure on this point, and his beard was straggly and dirty also... I inquired if he had a ship? "No," he replied "my ship is not here" – rather sadly I thought.'

Jackson thought he recognised a man he had met when he lectured in London in 1892. After discovering he was right he said, 'I am damned glad to see you.' The relief Nansen and Johansen must have felt can only be imagined, yet within days Johansen was noting that his once sociable, agreeable companion had returned to his normal arrogant self. The two sailed in Jackson's ship *Windward* on 7 August and were in Vardø on the 13th. On the 20th they heard that *Fram* was also safely home. The ship had reached 85°56'N in November 1895, but had then drifted south again. She was released from the ice in August 1896. After calling at Svalbard to see if there was any news, Sverdrup took the ship on to Norway, arriving on 20 August just a week after Nansen and Johansen.

Nansen returned to Oslo a hero, the raptures his courageous trek had engendered echoing not only across the country but the world. The dissenting

voices – those who thought that for a leader to abandon his expedition was a monstrous and unjustifiable act; those who felt the trek had been foolhardy; Peary's acerbic comment that Nansen should at least have tried to return to *Fram* – were drowned out by the cheering. *Fram* was the second and last great expedition of Nansen's life, but such was the success of it and his Greenland crossing, and the manner of the accomplishment of both, that they were to maintain his reputation as an explorer throughout his life.

Andrée and the *Eagle*

Otto Sverdrup had two reasons for stopping at Svalbard on his way home with *Fram*. The prime reason was, of course, to hear of any news of Nansen and Johansen. The other was to check on the progress of the Swede Salomon August Andrée who was planning a balloon flight to the North Pole. Andrée had become interested in balloons in 1876 at the age of 22, but it was not until 1893 that the interest had developed into a passion with practical results. From 1893 to 1895 he undertook nine flights in his balloon *Svea*,

Top left **Nansen's photograph of the winter hut on Jackson island.**
Richard Sale Collection

Above left **The remains of the winter hut. In this recent photograph of the camp site on Jackson Island the same rocky profile dominates the background to the shot.**
Susan Barr

Top right **The two kayaks strapped together to form a catamaran. This shot, as with several others in Nansen's book *Furthest North*, had to be staged after Nansen and Johansen had returned to civilisation.**
Richard Sale Collection

Above right **Jackson greets Nansen at Elmwood. There was no camera present when the actual meeting took place so it was recreated the following day. Nansen dressed as he had been the previous day, but by then he had washed, and trimmed his beard and hair. A lock of his hair is still preserved in the Fram Museum, Oslo. Jackson was overwhelmed by meeting Nansen: of Johansen he said only that he 'seems a splendid little fellow'.**
Richard Sale Collection

including one of 400km (250 miles) which took 16½ hours, and one of 284km (177 miles) that crossed the Baltic Sea from Stockholm to Eskörn Island. The latter was particularly interesting as Andrée used a guide rope trailing on the sea to slow the balloon, and sails on it to alter the direction of travel. He found he could vary the direction by up to 27° from the wind. By 1894 Andrée was considering the use of a balloon in the Arctic. He believed that he had a balloon which was gas-tight for 30 days, more than enough time judging from his earlier flights, and thought he had solved the potential problem of icing on the fabric – the guide ropes, three of them, each 350m (382yd) long and made of coconut fibre, would not only allow

manoeuvrability, but would keep the balloon low enough for ice not to form. The endpoint of the flight could not, of course, be fixed: Andrée assumed that given enough time in the air the balloon was bound to reach somewhere.

In June 1896 the *Virgo* took Andrée's balloon, the *Örnen* (Eagle), to Danskøya, an island off Spitsbergen's north-western corner. The site is now called Virgohamna, Virgo Harbour. The crew of three – Andrée, Nils Ekholm and Nils Strindberg – waited until 21 August (Sverdrup visiting them on the 14th) but the wind was consistently wrong. On that day the *Virgo* had to leave for Sweden and the three men went with her. In 1897 Andrée returned. Nils Ekholm, concerned

Above **A superb cartoon published in Sweden during the 'race' for the North Pole between the Salomon Andrée and the Norwegian Fridtjof Nansen. Nansen in his boat is left behind as Andrée is reeled into the pole by a smiling Inuk. The people of Sweden applaud while the Norwegians can barely conceal their sorrow and fury. Quite how the Inuk – or anyone or anything – was actually supposed to haul Andrée down to the pole is another matter.**
Richard Sale Collection

Right **Just before the launch of the *Eagle* the three crewmen compose themselves in the gondola.**
Richard Sale Collection

Below right **The launch of the *Eagle*. The guide ropes, whose loss put a risky venture even more in peril, can be seen still dragging on the beach.**
Richard Sale Collection

with the hydrogen leakage rate he had measured in 1896, had pulled out, his place taken by Knut Frœnkel. The *Eagle* was launched on 11 July, but immediately there was a problem. Andrée had changed his guide ropes, attaching the coconut-fibre ropes to hemp ropes with a simple screw, the idea being that if the lower section of the rope hooked firmly on to any projection on the ice the screw could be used to detach it, saving the top section of rope. But the wind rotated the

Above **This shot by Nils Strindberg of the stricken *Eagle* is one of the ghostly images of the expedition which emerged when the discovered film was developed.**
Courtesy of the Swedish Polar Research Secretariat

balloon and the coconut ropes unscrewed themselves. Without their ballast the *Eagle* rose to 600m (2,000ft): within seconds of the launch Andrée had lost not only his steering potential but his perceived protection against icing. The balloon headed north-east and, an hour later, disappeared from view.

In those days before radio Andrée's only available means of communication were carrier pigeons (fast, but not too reliable) and buoys which, rather like messages in bottles, were unpredictable. Five buoys were eventually picked up, but by then all hope for the team was gone. Only one pigeon was recovered when it was shot four days later: its message read 'July 13 at 12.30pm. Lat 82°2'N, Long 15°E, good speed towards east 10° south. All well. This is the third pigeon post. Andrée'. Despite many searches, continued until 1899, nothing

else was heard of, or from, the balloon. The shot pigeon was stuffed and presented to the inconsolable fiancée of Nils Strindberg.

On 6 August 1930 the Norwegian sealer *Bratvaag* anchored off the south-western tip of Kvitøya, the rarely visited island to the north-east of Svalbard's Nordaustlandet. The scientists brought by the ship disembarked and, 200m (218yd) inland, discovered a snow-covered camp and the remains of the three balloonists. A more extensive search in September revealed the diaries of the crew and, most remarkably, about 20 photographic negatives that could still be printed. The images, when developed, must have given the darkroom staff a start, reaching across 30 years to record the sad end to the *Eagle*.

The flight had been uneventful at first, *Eagle* heading north-east to about 82°30'N. Then, at about 2am on 12 July, the wind backed to east. The balloon headed west, then north-east again. Rain now caused the balloon to fall and the gondola struck the ice. It banged across the ice for several hours, then one of the shortened guide ropes became trapped. For 13 hours it stayed trapped, then broke free. Ice began to form on the balloon and soon it was dragging the gondola across the ice again. By 7am on 14 July the flight was over. The balloon had travelled 830km (520 miles) in 65½ hours and had landed at 82°56'N.

The three men were forced to head south across the ice hauling three sledges, on one of which was a boat. At first they decided to head for Cape Flora on Franz Josef Land, but soon revised the plan when they realised how slowly they were moving. By early September they were sick with stomach cramps and severe diarrhoea. They were also exhausted and set up camp on an ice floe, allowing its drift to carry them south. On 5 October they reached Kvitøya but now, inevitably, faced an Arctic winter with little chance of relief and none of escape. The diary entries became shorter, more fragmented and enigmatic, and finally stopped in mid-October.

From the position of the bodies it was clear that Strindberg had died first, as his body was buried beneath rocks in a gap between two boulders, though his death must have occurred after the diaries of Andrée and Frœnkel stopped as it is not mentioned. The cause of death has been the subject of speculation ever since the discovery. From the photos and diaries it is clear that polar bears were shot for food. Analysis of meat samples discovered at the camp showed the presence of trichinae (a parasitic nematode). If the meat had been eaten raw or poorly cooked the men could have developed trichinosis (which would explain the severe diarrhoea) and died. That is still the opinion of many experts, though cold, exhaustion and even suicide, induced by their hopeless position, cannot be ruled out.

The Italians head north from Franz Josef

After Leigh-Smith, Jackson and Nansen had better established the geography of Franz Josef Land, many explorers with designs on the pole believed it would make an ideal starting point for expeditions northward. The first of these was Walter Wellman, an American journalist, who arrived in 1898. Wellman had already tried once from Svalbard, reaching 81°N in 1894. In 1898, accompanied by three other Americans (one of whom was Evelyn Baldwin) and five Norwegians, Wellman (in the *Frithjof*) took one of Jackson's huts and a great deal of supplies from Elmwood and, prevented by ice from heading far north, set up a base at Cape Tegetthoff and a northern camp on Wilczek Island. The main expedition spent a comfortable winter at Cape

Above **Andrée's camp site on Kvitøya, a rarely visited site due to the remoteness of the island and the difficulties of approaching it because of sea ice. The last acts of the Andrée expedition were immensely moving. The bodies were brought home from Kvitøya by a ship accompanied, as it neared port, by a flotilla of smaller craft. There was a state funeral attended by the Swedish king. But most touching of all was the gesture by Gilbert Hawtrey, an English schoolmaster living in New Hampshire. Anna Charlier, Strindberg's fiancée, had married Hawtrey when, after a dozen years, all hope of Nils' return was gone. She had accompanied Hawtrey to the US and taught piano at his school, the stuffed pigeon from Andrée's balloon flying above the instrument. She died before the discovery on Kvitøya, but Hawtrey did not, and on hearing the news had Anna's body exhumed and her heart sent to Sweden to be buried beside her first love.**
Per Michelsen

Tegetthoff, but two Norwegians, Bjørvik and Bentsen, had a rougher time at the northern camp. Bentsen sickened and eventually died, leaving Bjørvik alone and miserable. In February Bjørvik was relieved by Wellman as he moved north. Already disheartened by the death, Wellman and his team of four and 42 dogs were enveloped in a storm which disrupted the ice causing the loss of most of their equipment and eight dogs, and they abandoned the attempt short of 82°N: the expedition sailed for home in the *Capella*, a Norwegian sealer.

The next to try his luck from Franz Josef was Luigi Amedeo, Duke of the Abruzzi, who arrived in 1899 with a large team of Italians and Norwegians. The duke's plan was to sail his ship, the *Stella Polare*, north along the coast, sledging on when ice prevented further progress. On 6 August the Italians were visited by Wellman and the *Capella*'s captain. Captain Støkken's son was part of the duke's team. The *Stella Polare* sailed north of Rudolf Island. The duke hoped that Petermann Island did exist, despite Nansen's claim, but he was disappointed and as wintering in the open sea was a recipe for disaster the ship returned to Teplitz Bay on the west coast of Rudolf. The journey to the pole started in the spring of 1900. In charge was the duke's deputy, Umberto Cagni, who led a team of four (himself, Simone Canepa, Alessio Fenoillet and Giuseppe Petigax) supported by three teams who returned at intervals after carrying supplies. All the teams used dog-sledges. Sadly the second support team failed to reach Teplitz Bay: one of the three lost was Henrik Støkken, son of the captain of the *Capella* – their meeting on the *Stella Polare* was their last. In 1901 Captain Støkken returned, looking for his son: he failed to find any trace of him or his two Italian colleagues and erected a memorial to them at Cape Flora.

Cagni's team spent 104 days on the ice travelling 1,200km (750 miles) and reaching 86°34'N, a new record. On his return, Cagni claimed that the journey over the sea ice was too difficult and that future attempts should be made from Greenland. When Captain Støkken returned in search of his son, another expedition, the first of two financed by New Yorker William Zeigler, also arrived in Franz Josef, intent on disproving Cagni's pessimistic assertion. The first expedition, in 1901/2, was led by Evelyn Baldwin who had been with Wellman in 1898/9, and also with Peary in Greenland in 1893. With 15 Siberian ponies, over 400 dogs and a total of 42 men, the expedition was massive. Its ship, the *America*, was elegantly described by one observer as being like a floating haystack. Baldwin set up base (Camp Ziegler) on Alger Island, well south of what he had hoped, but ice prevented the *America* going further north. In the summer of 1902 Baldwin started laying depots towards the north. His teams worked under a considerable handicap as the leader refused to allow them to take sleeping bags as these took up space which could be better used. Despite the misery this involved, by June a series of depots had been laid to Rudolf Island. At that point, and for no very good reason, Baldwin took the expedition home. It had been, as someone noted, a complete waste of effort.

In 1903 Zeigler financed a new attempt. Not sur-prisingly he did not appoint Baldwin as leader, preferring Anthony Fiala, who had been with, and unimpressed by, Baldwin in 1901/2. Again the expedition was large (though only half the size of Baldwin's). Its base was in Teplitz Bay where supplies from Abruzzi's expedition were found to be usable. The *America*, which again transported the team, was frozen in, but ice pressure in December wrecked her and she disappeared in a storm in January 1904. Fiala's first attempt at the pole was thwarted by bad weather and equipment failures after just two days. Now, faced with a lack of enthusiasm for continuing, Fiala returned to Cape Flora with most of the team. Jackson's Elmwood was occupied and coal was found locally, securing fuel in case of a second winter. A supply ship (Wellman's *Frithjof*) failed to reach the base and a second overwinter was indeed required. In March 1905 Fiala finally attempted the pole again. His team reached 82°N but open water then stopped progress. Again Fiala's men lost heart and a retreat was ordered. This time a relief ship managed to reach Cape Flora. It was the *Terra Nova* which, five years later, took Scott to Antarctica.

As Fiala's team was being evacuated from Franz Josef, Robert Peary was heading north again. His furthest north in 1902 (84°17'N) was still a record in the western Arctic, but over 2° less than Cagni's attempt from Franz Josef Land. Peary's efforts in 1901/2 seem curiously tentative, at odds with his obsession with fame and the pole. Arguably the most experienced polar traveller of the time, with an enviable record of exploration in northern Greenland, he had actually achieved very little in his quest for the pole. His 1901 journey seems lacking in conviction. His backers thought so too and sent Dr Frederick Cook to examine him. Cook suspected pernicious anaemia and recommended eating liver, to which Peary replied, 'I would rather die'. Cook also looked at his feet and told him, 'you are through as a traveller on snow on foot'. Peary was then 46. The news would have been unwelcome, the messenger, a rival and a younger one at that, unpopular. A relationship which had started with mutual respect was turning sour.

During the years after his 1902 furthest north achievement – another journey where the result failed to justify the preparation – Peary had recharged his mental batteries, refitted his expedition coffers and now, in 1905, approaching 50, was ready for another (probably his last) try. He had a new ship (the *Roosevelt*: Peary had not lost his touch in keeping real power on his side) and had taken her to a point just beyond that reached by the *Alert*: it was only 3km (2 miles) beyond, but it satisfied Peary's lust for records. Early the following year supply depots were established ready for the pole attempt. That began on 6 March. The journey was troubled by a huge lead, by ice drift and bad weather, and by early April it was clear the pole was unattainable. Even a new record northing was doubtful. But Peary decided on a last dash and, achieving daily travel rates which were, if true, remarkable, reached 87°6'N on 21 April, bettering Cagni's record by 32'. There are many who doubt Peary's claim (particularly as he was still troubled by his amputated toe stubs and also had a hernia) though most experts believe he probably got very close to Cagni's latitude, perhaps even going a little further. But the doubts generated by his unlikely account of the last dash colour judgements over his later claims.

At his northern point, whatever it was, Peary turned and headed, not for his ship, but for the Greenland coast which, because of ice drift, was now due south. Feeding killed dog to remaining dogs and burning sledges for fuel, the team made it – but only just. Then on the route west to the ship Peary's team overtook one of their supply teams. It was fortunate they did: though Peary was almost out of food and fuel, the supply team was in a far more desperate position and would likely have died had he not arrived.

The last miles to the ship were desperate. Had Peary not known the coast so well and been so experienced it would have ended tragically. As it was he brought 12 men (his eight and the supply team's four) to safety.

Cook and Peary

In September 1909 an astonished world was informed that the North Pole had finally been reached. Not once, but twice. On 2 September Dr Frederick Cook announced via a telegram office in the Shetland Isles (where the Danish supply ship taking him from Greenland to Denmark stopped briefly) that he had stood at the pole on 21 April 1908. Then, on 6 September Robert Peary used a similar office in Indian Harbour, Labrador, to say he had reached the pole on 6 April 1909. Each had friends in high places and within days the *New York Herald*, which had backed Cook, and the *New York Times* and National Geographic Society, behind Peary's, had begun a war. It was a dirty war in which the reputations of both men were tarnished beyond redemption, and one which, 90 years on, shows no signs – nor has much chance – of ending in a truce, honourable or otherwise.

Above **Cagni's Furthest North Camp at 86°18'20". The next day the team marched to 86°31'.**
From Luigi Amedeo di Savoia, Duke of the Abruzzi *On the Polar Star in the Arctic Seas.*
Richard Sale Collection

Below **Peary at his furthest north, 87°6'N, on 21 April 1906.**
From Robert Peary *Nearest the Pole.*
Richard Sale Collection

Returning from his claimed furthest north in 1906 Peary found that his ship, the *Roosevelt*, needed a refit. The work was not completed in time to sail in 1907, so Peary did not head north again until 1908. Now 52, he must have known that if he failed in 1909 he would be unlikely to have another chance. His expedition was huge: in addition to the 22 who started out on the *Roosevelt* there were 49 Inuit from Etah and 246 dogs. The *Roosevelt*'s captain, Bob Bartlett (captain, too, in 1905/6, later captain of the *Karluk* and a great Arctic explorer in his own right) again took the ship to Cape Sheridan on Ellesmere's north coast. From there a wintering base was established at Cape Colombia. On 28 February 1909, 24 men, 19 sledges and 133 dogs set out north.

At one stage they were held up by a huge open lead for six days (of good weather). When the lead closed the caravan moved on. One by one the support teams departed south. Sadly, during the return of one of these support teams Ross Marvin, Peary's 'secretary', drowned in a lead. Finally, on 1 April, Peary sent Bartlett and the last support team back. Bartlett had wanted to go all the

Above **Cook's camp at Svartevoeg on the northern coast of Axel Heiberg Island.**
From Frederek Cook *My Attainment of the Pole.*
Richard Sale Collection

Below **Crossing the ice on Peary's trip to the pole. The original black-and-white print was hand-coloured to add dramatic effect.**
USA Library of Congress

way, and had certainly wanted to reach 88°: he took one last latitude observation – 87°46'49"N. Peary and his team were 246km (154 miles) from the pole. With him Peary now had Matthew Henson, the Inuit Egingwah, Ooqueah, Ootah and Seegloo, five sledges and 40 dogs. This team reached the pole at about 1pm on 6 April. On those last five days they had averaged almost 50km/31 miles per day (straight-line distance). On the first 31 days they had averaged about 17km/10½ miles per day (straight-line distance again). Peary remained at the pole for about 30 hours, then raced back to the *Roosevelt*, arriving on 27 April, just three days after Bartlett, who had travelled at least 490km (310 miles) less. At Etah on 17 August Peary heard that Cook was claiming to have beaten him to the pole, but on Labrador went ahead with his announcement.

Cook's claim was even more remarkable than Peary's as the latter had retraced his own earlier journeys. Cook was sponsored by John R. Bradley, gambling club owner and big game hunter, and sailed, in 1907, in a ship bought by and renamed after him. The *John R. Bradley* was captained by Moses Bartlett, cousin of the *Roosevelt's* Bob. Cook and Rudolph Francke were dropped off at the Inuit village of Annoatok close to Etah. Francke had been employed by Bradley as a cook and was somewhat taken aback to discover he was now to accompany Cook on a journey towards the pole. After overwintering at Annoatok the two set out in February 1908 with nine Inuit. Instead of going north, the 'normal' (and Peary) route to the pole, they headed west, crossing to Cape Sabine, then traversing Ellesmere Island to reach Cape Thomas Hubbard at the northern tip of Axel Heiberg Island, a journey of over 800km (more than 500 miles). At the cape Cook left a large supply dump, then on 18 March headed north across the sea ice with just two Inuit companions, Ahwelah and Etukishook, two sledges and 26 dogs. He reached the pole on 21 April, having travelled about 800km (500 miles) in 34 days.

On the return ice drift pushed them west and persistent fog and poor weather prevented them from calculating their position. With food running very short they at last had clear weather and were able to pinpoint their position. They were in the Prince Gustav Adolf Sea, with land to the south and west, and Axel Heiberg off to the east. Cook now continued to head south, taking Hassel Sound between the Ringnes Islands and reaching the Grinnell Peninsula on the north-western tip of Devon Island. They had by now run out of ammunition and had to fashion harpoons,

Above **On his journey Cook built igloos as camp sites, so there was no need to carry tents.**
Byrd Polar Research Centre, Ohio State University, USA

bows and arrows from muskox horn and whalebone. The three men headed east along Jones Sound, then overwintered in an old Inuit winter house, continuing towards Greenland in February 1909. Once more low on food they existed for a short time on candles and hot water until a bear was killed. By the time they reached Annoatok they were hungry again, so much so that they were barely able to stand and had eaten all their leather straps. They had been away 14 months, having taken food for just two.

Cook was fêted on his arrival in Copenhagen, but things rapidly turned sour for him. On his journey south Peary spoke with the two Inuit who had accompanied Cook and claimed they told him that they had never been out of sight of land. In the US Peary's vitriolic attacks on Cook, in telegrams and to the press, had the opposite affect to that intended, rapidly drawing sympathy for Cook. In several polls public opinion was 80 per cent in Cook's favour, often higher. Outside the US the less heated atmosphere allowed more sober judgements, and these tended to back Peary. Cook's position was made much worse by an independent, but coincidental, charge that his claim to have climbed Mount McKinley, North America's highest peak, was a fraud. In the end Peary won over the majority, often grudgingly, as Cook was a far more amiable man, a complete contrast to the blustering Peary who lacked Cook's social skills. In the early 1920s Cook became involved with an oil company and was tried, convicted and imprisoned for fraudulently claiming that land owned by his company was oil-bearing. There seems little doubt that the perceived frauds over McKinley and the pole contributed to his downfall. Cook served seven years of a 14-year term: it was during his time in Fort Leavenworth (where he rapidly became the most popular prisoner, both with inmates and staff) that he was visited by Amundsen. In the end it was shown that the land was oil-bearing, just as Cook had claimed. He was released in 1930. On 5 May 1940 he suffered a cerebral haemorrhage; he was given an unconditional pardon by President Roosevelt on 16 May, and died on 5 August. To the end he maintained the validity of his claim to the pole, recording a tape for posterity. Its final words were 'I state emphatically that I, Frederick A. Cook, discovered the North Pole.'

By contrast to Cook, who suffered public humiliation with forbearance and good grace, Robert Peary railed against the injustice of not being given full credit for his discovery for the rest of his life. He had sacrificed his best years to the search for fame and the pursuit of the pole. He had been away for most of his eldest daughter's formative years, and had never seen a second daughter who had died aged seven months. The honours he received could not assuage his bitterness, which, his wife claimed, hastened his death on 20 February 1920. Ironically the stated cause was pernicious anaemia, the illness Cook had diagnosed all those years before. It is of course possible that the bitterness was not solely due to the fact that what he felt was his just reward for his life's work – the pole – had become soured by dispute. If he had not actually reached the pole, and had known he had not, then the bitter taste could have been that of defeat. Peary managed to convince most of the world of the validity of his claim. A dishonest man might convince himself that he deserves a prize, but unless he is especially deluded he will not be able to convince himself that he has actually secured it.

Millions of words have been written on Cook and Peary. At the time the dispute was simple – was it Cook or Peary who first reached the pole? Now the question is different – did either of them? This is not the forum to review the evidence, but certain observations can be made. Peary's claim is based on extraordinary rates of travel. Most of those who have sledged to the pole consider them too high: some ludicrously so. In a carefully considered book Wally Herbert judged that Peary did not reach it, his claim being immediately rebuffed by a 'scientific study' commissioned by the National Geographic Society, still Peary's staunchest supporter.

There is also the fact that Peary took only Henson and Inuit to the pole. Was this because he wanted to be the only white man there, or was it to hedge his bets, as in those non-politically correct days no one would take the word of a black man or a native against that of a white man? Amundsen, a friend of Cook, agreed Peary's claim (indeed, he changed his own plans and headed south as a result) but noted that Peary's word had to be taken as he was alone: 'Of course, the Negro Henson was too ignorant to know whether they reached it or not.' Today that seems a shocking comment, but it was the general opinion of the time. It also accords with Peary's own view of Henson: despite occasional admissions that Henson was his right-hand man and an essential part of the team, Peary also famously upbraided him for not calling him 'sir' at all times – 'You will pay attention when I am talking to you and show that you hear directions I give you by saying "yes, sir", or "all right, sir".'

But much more importantly, and a fact which gave even his staunchest supporters of the time something to think about – particularly those who, like Peary, had experience on ice – was that by his own admission Peary took no measurements of his longitude, nor magnetic variation, and made no allowance for ice drift. His claim to have gone north along the 70°W meridian is at odds with all experience of ice movements and, unsupported by longitude readings, stretches credibility. If he really did travel by dead reckoning as he claims, then at his final camp he had no idea where he was. This would explain his poor humour there when approached by Henson: his sun shot might have told him that he was still some way from the pole. The strange omissions from his diary are certainly consistent with that view.

But if Peary's claim lacks credibility the situation is no less problematic for Cook supporters. There is the curiosity of cropped photographs. There is the contradictory testimony of his Inuit companions: when interviewed by others they at first backed up his claim to have reached the 'Great Navel' as they call the pole (the Inuit name is usually given as Great Nail, the

explanation being that the place the white explorers sought must be something tangible, and iron was the most valuable commodity to an Inuk, but the true translation of the Inuit is navel, now nail), but are later claimed to have stated that they had never been out of sight of land. Cook's supporters make much of the earliest statements, claiming that the later ones were made under duress; the Inuit were often accused of telling the white man what he wanted to hear. The charge was made at the time of Rae's discovery of Franklin's fate, and there was some truth in it, but Cook's two Inuit seem to have told a consistent tale of not reaching the pole throughout the rest of their lives.

There is the issue of whether enough supplies could be carried by the three men to last the described trip, as Cook makes no mention of hunting. But, as noted above, Cook had set out with food for eight weeks and survived 14 months, so his team were clearly capable of looking after themselves well. There is the fact that Hassel Sound, 'narrow' according to Cook, is actually wide. In claiming it to be narrow Cook was following Sverdrup who also stated it was narrow (from observation only). In reality it is 24km (15 miles) wide at its narrowest point. Cook was a remarkably good observer of natural phenomena, yet it has to be said that it is occasionally very difficult to be sure where sea ice ends and a low coast begins, and he did accurately place a small island at the sound's northern end. His supporters note that whether he did or did not traverse Hassel Sound has no bearing on the validity of his pole claim, but it does: if he was not telling the truth about that, relatively trivial, aspect of his trip, why believe his pole claim? All the doubts raised by the sceptical about Cook's journey are rebutted by his supporters, usually by cogent arguments, though occasionally the logic of the rebuttals is clamorous and suspect. But Cook's opponents are often equally hysterical.

One interesting consideration is the fact that Cook, a humane man, was appalled by Peary's treatment of both members of his expeditions and the Inuit. Cook claimed that both Verhoeff and Astrup had been driven to suicide by Peary, and felt that Peary's constant reference to 'my Eskimo', implying ownership, was distasteful. He also disliked Peary's assumed 'ownership' of the pole. Did Cook conspire to teach Peary a lesson for his arrogance?

Finally there is the mystery of the phantom and actual land of Cook's journey. In 1906 Peary claimed to have seen land, Crocker Land, to the north-west of Axel Heiberg. Cook claimed to have seen Bradley Land, as he

called it, to the south of Peary's. Many have suggested that Cook's Bradley was based on Peary's Crocker and is evidence of his fraud. When Donald McMillan went to explore Crocker Land in 1913/17 he too saw it from Ellesmere Island. When he reached it had disappeared. Yet when he returned to Ellesmere McMillan saw it clearly again and would have sworn to its existence had he not known with certainty it did not exist: Crocker/Bradley was phantom. But there are those who believe that Cook may have seen ice islands now known to exist at about the same position as he claimed for Bradley Land. And if he did see those ice islands then he must have been in a position to do so.

Meighen Island, to the west of Axel Heiberg, is fact. When Cook had his first clear day after fog on his return from the pole he claimed to have seen land to the west and south, and Axel Heiberg to the east. As has been pointed out, from where he was Meighen Island would have been clearly visible: it rises to about 150m (500ft). Some of the anti-Cook faction claim it would have obscured his view of Axel Heiberg, but that is not so if his position was calculated accurately. However, he claims there was land to the west which is only possible if he was further south than he thought. In that case Meighen would have been even further north. But these are minor issues in comparison to a real mystery. Cook's Inuit companions plotted the journey they said they had actually made on a map based on Sverdrup's discoveries, and they accurately plotted the position and size of an island they claimed to have seen to the north-west of Axel Heiberg. It was clearly Meighen Island, at that time undiscovered (it was not officially discovered until 1916 when Stefansson came this way). Why then, if Cook had discovered Meighen, did he not mention it to lend greater credence to his supposed fraudulent story?

At this remove in time the truth of the two claims can no longer be ascertained. While in general the polar environment does a remarkable job of preserving objects left either deliberately or casually, the nature of the Arctic Ocean precludes such survivals. No new evidence is likely either from the north or from the diaries and logs of the two men and their expeditions. No one will ever know for certain which, if either, was telling the truth. Overall it is probable that Peary got close to the pole, but did not reach it, defeated by his own navigational naïveté and incompetence. The Cook claim is more intriguing. There are seemingly compelling reasons for discounting it, not least the fact that by his own admission Cook was no navigator: how could someone incapable of plotting longitude and having difficulty with latitude possibly know where he was on the shifting ice of the Arctic Ocean? Yet equally compelling ones suggest he did indeed travel a long way out across the ocean towards the pole and so, perhaps, might have reached it. It is also the case that whichever journey Cook actually made – the one he defended or the one told by his companions – it was both more interesting and tougher than Peary's.

The Cook/Peary tale is a manifestation of an age in which mysteries are seen as either evidence of a conspiracy or nuisances which get in the way of a precise interpretation of the world. In another age the tale, which has elements of both, might also be seen as having a 'whodunit' beauty of its own, for while it is likely that neither Cook nor Peary reached the pole, it is possible that one or both of them did.

Balloons and aeroplanes

Andrée's flight had failed, but it had always been a risky venture. Balloon technology was at its limit and Andrée's steering method was, at best, haphazard. Ten years later airships had replaced balloons, offering acceptable steering in all but the worst weather. Gas leakage had also been reduced, and with a higher speed and better steering, flight times were also lower. The first to try the new technology was Walter Wellman, the man who had already tried his luck with a dog-sledge.

This time Wellman chose Spitsbergen for his base. In 1906 he brought the first airship to Danskøya (where Andrée had launched) but abandoned the attempt when it became apparent that his engines were useless. He returned in June of the following year. It took until August to reconstruct the 1907 hanger, but in that month the weather was continuously awful. Only on 2 September could the airship (the *America*) finally be pulled from the hanger. Initially towed by a small steamer, she flew 24km (15 miles) northwards, but was then hit by a storm. As Wellman noted, 'there ensued a hard fight between the storm and the motor. The latter triumphed'. It was just as well, as the storm threatened to crash the *America* into jagged mountains.

Wellman was back on Danskøya in 1909, and the *America* was launched on 15 August. Wellman had this

Top **Cook's Inuit at the North Pole.**
Byrd Polar Research Centre, Ohio State University, USA

Right **Hand-coloured print of Peary's North Pole shot.**
USA Library of Congress

time fitted two guide ropes, just as Andrée had, believing that if the airship was kept close to the ground hydrogen leakage would be minimised. But in a re-run of Andrée's launch one of the guide ropes fell off and the *America* climbed rapidly. Fortunately this incident was observed by the Norwegian coastal steamer *Farm* which, sensing trouble, gave chase, and rescued the *America*'s four-men team.

For a few years, despite the debate over the validity of Cook and Peary's pole claims, interest in reaching the pole died. Then the 1914–18 war intervened and not until the 1920s was another attempt made to reach the North Pole. The development of air travel, in both airships and aeroplanes, had moved on and, as always, man was enthusiastic to apply the latest technology to tackle problems in remote and hostile areas. The main enthusiast was Roald Amundsen whose *Maud* expedition had completed the North-East Passage, but entirely failed to emulate *Fram*'s ice drift. Amundsen left *Maud* in 1921 to buy an aircraft, but his first attempted flight from Alaska to Spitsbergen failed due to bad weather. He tried again in 1923, using a plane with an insufficient fuel capacity; his plan was to carry a sledge and kayak, and to complete the journey with these after he had made a forced landing. He was perhaps fortunate that his plane crashed on its first trial flight.

In 1925 Amundsen renewed his acquaintanceship with Lincoln Ellsworth whom he had declined to take on *Maud*. Ellsworth was the son of a wealthy American financier who agreed, after some soul-searching, to underwrite an expedition of two seaplanes. The two Dornier-Wal planes (N–24 and N–25) were to take off from King's Bay (Ny Ålesund) on Spitsbergen, each carrying three men and enough food for three weeks. The plan was to land at the pole, transferring all fuel and men into one plane for a continuing flight to Alaska. The planes took off on 21 May 1925 and flew for eight hours. Then, assuming they were close to the pole, they landed. Once down they discovered that a headwind had reduced their speed: they were only at 88°N. The N–25, piloted by Hjalmar Riiser-Larsen, with German mechanic Ludwig Feucht and Amundsen on board, had engine trouble on the descent. They were forced on to a narrow lead and come to rest against an iceberg. The N–24, piloted by Leif Dietrichsen, with mechanic Oskar Omsdal and Ellsworth, landed in a large pool, but col-

lided with an ice floe, and the cabin filled up with water. The two crews could not at first see each other, but after 24 hours had made visual contact and exchanged messages by semaphore: they were 5km (3 miles) apart. Over the next few days ice drift took the doomed N–24 crew closer to the N–25. Eventually the entire team was back together again, but only after Omsdal had fallen into the sea, knocking out seven teeth on the ice edge as he did so.

The six men managed to get N–25 safely on to the ice floe. Then Amundsen spelled out the reality of their situation. They could try and build a runway for N–25; going on half rations gave them until 15 June to do so. At that time each man could choose to try to get to Greenland (across several hundred kilometres of sea ice) or to stay with the plane, trying to get it off the ice until food ran out. The stark choice galvanised the men, but several attempts to construct runways failed. Finally, desperately, the N–25 was hauled on to another floe and a channel was cut in a pressure ridge, allowing access to an area of level snow. This was stamped down, the nightly drop in temperature freezing it. On the morning of 15 June Riiser-Larsen fired the engines. The plane lifted off just metres from the runway's end, missed an iceberg by centimetres and flew on. Using dead reckoning they reached Hinloppen Strait, off northern Spitsbergen, where they were forced to land as fuel was running out. The next day a sealing ship was spotted and, using the remaining fuel, the six men drove the N–25 towards it. They had been away 26 days and the sealing captain looked at them as though they were ghosts. Sadly the joy of reaching King's Bay was tempered by the news that Ellsworth's father had died on 2 June.

The following year Amundsen and Ellsworth were back at King's Bay ready to try for the pole again, but this time in an airship, a dirigible designed by the Italian Umberto Nobile who was to accompany the expedition. Despite Amundsen's attempts to reduce his role, Nobile was intent on maximising his share of the glory of the trip and Benito Mussolini, Italy's Fascist dictator, was equally intent on maximising the propaganda benefit for his own ends. Amundsen and Ellsworth arrived on Spitsbergen in early April and were joined on 29 April by Richard Byrd of the US navy, his plane a Fokker tri-motor named the *Josephine Ford*, and his pilot Floyd Bennett. Byrd had asked permission to use King's Bay for a proposed flight to Greenland, but now announced that he intended to fly to the pole. Amundsen, perhaps conscious of his switch from North to South Pole and the

Above **Byrd's plane *Josephine Ford* being taken ashore at King's Bay, Spitsbergen.**
USA Library of Congress

Below **Byrd and Bennett take off from King's Bay, Spitsbergen.**
USA Library of Congress

subsequent furore, did not object. Perhaps, too, Amundsen reasoned that the main prize was already lost: at that time it was assumed the pole had already been reached (by Peary, Cook's claim having been dismissed, Peary's not yet questioned). Amundsen offered Byrd every assistance, including a stack of survival gear none of which, despite his plan, Byrd possessed.

On 7 May 1926 Amundsen's airship, the *Norge* (originally designated the N–1 – Nobile 1 – its name changed by Amundsen) arrived, having been flown from Italy. During the flight Riiser-Larsen had been horrified by Nobile's dismal efforts as pilot. Nobile was now equally aghast at Amundsen's refusal to race Byrd for the privilege of first flight to the pole: the loss of this chance for glory must have been a very hard blow to the Italian. At 00.37 GMT on 10 May Bennett and Byrd took off. At 16.07 the plane was back, and they claimed to have reached the pole. Byrd announced that just as they began their return trip he had dropped and broken his sextant, the flight to King's Bay being by dead reckoning, a fantastic feat. Byrd was welcomed as a hero, his and Bennett's achievement being soon heralded across the world. Then, in 1960, the Swedish meteorologist professor Gösta Liljequist analysed the capabilities of the plane, its flight timings and local weather charts, and concluded that Byrd was unlikely to have flown beyond 88°N. By then Byrd had completed an illustrious naval and polar career and had died. It was assumed that he was unaware of his failure, but more recently it has been noted that many computed positions were added to his charts after the flight. There was also the curiosity that Byrd had taken a huge number of small flags to drop at the pole and not one of them was seen by the *Norge* three days later. It has also emerged that Floyd Bennett confided in a friend that he and Byrd had made no attempt at the pole: the *Josephine Ford* having developed an oil leak, they had merely flown about for the requisite number of hours beyond view of King's Bay and then returned. The idea that Richard Byrd died unaware that he had not reached the pole, and that he had performed a near-miraculous feat of navigation on the return route, must therefore be re-evaluated. There are also persistent rumours that Byrd's South Pole flight was not quite as it seemed.

Blissfully unaware of any problems with Byrd's flight, at 1am on 11 May the crew of 16 – including Amundsen, Ellsworth, Nobile, Riiser-Larsen, the Swede Finn Malmgren and Oscar Wisting, Amundsen's faithful companion – lifted the *Norge* off from Ny Ålesund. At

1.30am on 12 May the *Norge* circled over the pole, flags of the USA, Norway and Italy being dropped on to the ice, attached to sharpened aluminium stakes so they stood upright and flapped in the wind. (Nobile defied Amundsen and Ellsworth by making the Italian flag much bigger than those of Norway and the USA, so large that it fouled on the airship and momentarily threatened a propeller.) Amundsen and Wisting, the first two men to see both poles (and, arguably, in the teams that were first to reach each pole) shook hands.

So far the flight had been uneventful, but beyond the pole the *Norge* ran into fog and began to ice up. Icing on the radio aerials prevented communication, and chunks of ice thrown from the propellers threatened the gas bag. By adjusting altitude the icing was minimised, allowing the airship to continue. At 7.30am on 13 May the Alaskan coast near Point Barrow was seen, but low cloud forced the *Norge* to fly high and to go along the coast to reach the Bering Strait avoiding Alaska's inland mountains. One of the two engines began to fail, and the spare would not start. After a flight of over 50 hours the crew were exhausted (not least because there were only two seats). The intended landing at Nome was abandoned and at 8am on 14 May the *Norge* touched down at Teller 90km (56 miles) to the north-west.

The flight had been a major success, but its aftermath was ugly. To their annoyance Amundsen and Ellsworth discovered that Nobile had, in secret, persuaded the Norwegian backers of the expedition to add his name as co-leader. In Italy Mussolini promoted Nobile to general and ordered him to lecture to the 'Italian colonies' in the US. A large crowd of Italian-Americans were gathered at Seattle when the expedition arrived: Nobile, in military uniform, made the Fascist salute and was fêted while Amundsen and Ellsworth were virtually ignored. Nobile's lecture tour – in which he claimed to have both masterminded the expedition and piloted the airship, neither of which was correct – creamed off much of the available audience (and their entrance

Above right **Amundsen, Byrd, Bennett and Ellsworth after Byrd and Bennett's flight.**
USA Library of Congress

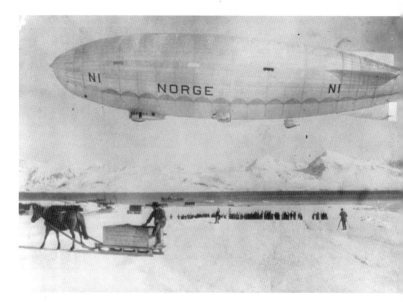

Above centre **The launch of the *Norge*.**
USA Library of Congress

Right **The airship mast at Ny Ålesund, King's Bay, Spitsbergen.**
Per Michelsen

money) leaving both Amundsen and Ellsworth short of cash. Ironically, Nobile eventually believed his own propaganda about being a major explorer, a delusion that led to tragedy.

For his own expedition Nobile decided to use an airship similar to the *Norge* (but called *Italia* to reinforce the nationalistic identity of the expedition) to make a series of three flights, two exploring Severnaya Zemlya and the area north of Greenland, one to the pole. The latter was to include the setting down of a party of six scientists during an extended stay. Despite Nobile's attempts to drum up enthusiasm for the venture even Mussolini seems to have been lukewarm, as nothing very new was being proposed.

After one aborted attempt, a 60-hour flight from King's Bay to Franz Josef Land, Severnaya Zemlya and Novaya Zemlya were made in mid-May 1928. Then, on 23 May, the *Italia* with a crew of 16 (14 Italians, the Swede Finn Malmgren who had been on the *Norge* flight, and a Czech) took off for the pole, flying via Cape Bridgman on Greenland's north coast. On the eastern leg to the pole the wind was favourable, boosting the average speed to 105kmph (66mph). But the same wind slowed the return, while cloud hampered navigation. Although the airship was in radio contact with the *Citta di Milano*, her support ship, the fixing of position by radio was a young science. The cloud caused heavy icing of the *Italia* and at 10.33am on 25 May, after 55 hours flying, she began to descend rapidly. The gondola smashed into the ice, ripping it from the ship which, freed of the load, rose even more rapidly, taking six men to their doom. No sign of the ship or men was found, though the survivors reported seeing a column of smoke later, implying a hydrogen fire.

Of the ten men who lay on the ice, one was dead, Nobile had a broken arm and leg, and Natal Cecioni (who had also been on *Norge*) had a compound leg fracture. The survivors had little equipment and their radio did not, at first, work. With no polar experience there was fear and dissension, and eventually three men, Adalberto Mariano, Filippo Zappi and Finn Malmgren set off in an attempt to reach Spitsbergen and get help. With the gondola on the ice north of Nordaustlandet this was probably a forlorn hope, but with no radio and few supplies, waiting for rescue was none too enticing either.

The radio operator Giuseppe Biagi repaired the radio and began to transmit their position, but all that was heard from *Citta di Milano* was an endless string of telegrams and press statements. In fact a radio operator on the ship had picked up the SOS, but his superior, convinced everyone was dead, dismissed the report. Only when a radio ham near Arkhangelsk heard the SOS and informed Moscow was the position of the survivors fixed.

The loss of the *Italia* was a blow to national pride, especially when of the 18 ships, 22 planes and 1,500 men of six nations deployed to search only one seaplane was Italian. After the position of the survivors' camp – which included a red tent which was to become famous as a symbol of the failed expedition – was fixed it was overflown on 18 June, 23 days after the crash. On 23 June the Swedes Einar Lundborg and Birger Schyberg landed at the camp. The plan was to evacuate one man (as the Swedes' Fokker CVD could accommodate only three), then to return with a single pilot to rescue two men at a time. Nobile wanted Cecioni taken as he was the most seriously injured, but Lundborg thought Nobile himself should go to co-ordinate rescue operations. That was a strange, misguided idea, but Nobile agreed and, accompanied by his dog Titina which was his constant companion (and had been on *Norge*), flew out. The news spread around the world rapidly – a Fascist general had saved himself and his dog before his companions. A furious Mussolini demoted Nobile, and the expedition leader's attempts to influence the rescue were quietly ignored. In his own version of the *Italia* disaster Nobile claims that it took more courage for him to go than to stay as he understood the possible consequences. He did not, perhaps, understand them clearly.

On 24 June Lundborg returned alone, but his plane's skis dug in on landing turning it over, and Lundborg became a member of the Red Tent camp. Further flights were cancelled due to fog until 6 July when Schyberg flew in to pick up Lundborg. Before further flights could be made the Russian ice-breaker *Krassin*, the world's most powerful, developing 10,500hp, crashed through ice up to 3m (10ft) thick and reached the Red Tent on 12 July. Two days earlier a look-out plane from the ice-breaker had spotted men on the ice: Mariano and Zappi. Mariano was exhausted and frost-bitten, but Zappi was in much better shape and told a remarkable story. The three-man team had made slow progress, then Malmgren (who had been in pain since the crash) had collapsed and asked to be left to die. Not only had the Italians done so, but they had taken his food portion. When found Zappi, who claimed not to have eaten for 12 days, was wearing some of Malmgren's clothes. The Russians, appalled by Zappi's demeanour, were also suspicious of his healthy appearance. Later Zappi

contradicted himself and claimed Malmgren had died before they left him, and even admitted cannibalism, though this was later officially denied. The suspicion that Malmgren might have been murdered further tainted the expedition. By contrast to Zappi, Mariano's condition was wretched: he lost a foot to amputation and died a few months later. The crew of three of the only Italian rescue plane also died when they crashed on their way home.

Most tragically of all, the *Italia* disaster also resulted in Amundsen's death. He had been at a celebration dinner for Hubert Wilkins and Carl Eielson, who had flown a Lockheed Vega plane from Point Barrow to Spitsbergen via the pole, when news of the *Italia* came through. He immediately offered his services, claiming past disagreements meant nothing when lives were at stake. Mussolini did not agree and told the Norwegian government their assistance was not required. Realising the stupidity of not helping when Svalbard was Norwegian territory, the government was forced to drop Amundsen, putting Hjalmar Riiser-Larsen in command.

Amundsen was nearing his 56th birthday, but looked much older. He had recently published his autobiography which had stunned everyone, including his friends, with its paranoia and bitterness. In common with most great achievers Amundsen was an almost demonically driven man, perpetually striving to the limit, yet lonely and fearful. One third of his book was taken up with his pursuit of Nobile over the *Norge* aftermath. He was relentless, just as he had been in his pursuit of Hjalmar Johansen. Did he now feel guilt over Johansen's death and Nobile's need to prove himself?

Top **The Red Tent from the air. The photograph has a curiously superimposed look suggesting the image may have been manipulated in some way.**
Richard Sale Collection

Above **Nobile and Titina after their rescue.**
Richard Sale Collection

The chapter on the South Pole was short and mentioned the incident at the Royal Geographical Society's dinner in London where Curzon had proposed 'three cheers for the dogs' after Amundsen's speech (making matters worse by urging the Norwegian to stay calm and not respond), and the attitude of the Americans to Frederick Cook. In the US on a lecture tour after the *Norge* expedition Amundsen had visited Cook in Fort Leavenworth jail, a kind gesture for an old friend fallen on hard times, but the American press, egged on by the National Geographic Society, Peary's champion, saw it as support for Cook against Peary. As the press pictured the former as liar, the latter as hero, Amundsen was pilloried. The Curzon incident betrayed a guilt Amundsen felt over Scott's death; the Cook incident merely heightened his bitterness and alienation.

The autobiography clouded his reputation at home. Norway had always been ambivalent about him; the country had loved Nansen, yet for all his accomplishments, the strange, brooding Amundsen had never been taken to their hearts. Nansen had a wife and children, and a reputation as a lady's man. Amundsen was known for pursuing married women by letter with pleadings of overwhelming love which disappeared the moment they left, or were tempted to leave, their husbands. These weird, platonic relationships contrasted with rumours of sordid deeds in seedy brothels. The curious incident of Kakonita and Camilla did not help. These two young girls had been rescued from poverty in Chukotka during the *Maud* expedition – Kakonita motherless, dirty and lice-infested, Camilla an unwanted half-breed. They had been taken to Oslo as foster children, to be given a home, security and an education. It was a laudable act until Amundsen, apparently tiring of them or the responsibility, packed them off to Seattle for return to Chukotka. The two settled in America and lived contented lives there, but it was no thanks to him.

So when Norway declined his offer to help with the *Italia* search Amundsen was embittered once again. But his honour was now at stake: he had said he would go, and he must. So when the French offered him a Latham 47 seaplane for a private mission he accepted immediately. He met pilot René Guilbaud and his crew of three in Bergen, together with his own chosen companion Lief Dietrichson. By the time they reached Tromsø it was clear the Latham was unsuitable. But Amundsen had given his word, and the six men took off on 18 June. When they were overdue in Spitsbergen the rescue effort was so directed towards *Italia* that nothing was done: Amundsen was the great survivor. Searches were made some days later, but not until 31 August was anything found, when fishermen hauled in a float and fuel tank from the plane. It seemed they had been removed in an attempt to construct a raft. It is hard to know if the idea of the indomitable explorer striving to the last and dying a lingering death is more, or less, painful than a tired old man's life ending quickly via a plunge into the sea.

Drift stations and submarines

The general acceptance of Peary's claim to have reached the North Pole not only forestalled Amundsen's attempt, and persuaded him to head south, but also all ground-based attempts for almost 60 years, with the exception of that by the Russian Georgi Sedov who made an attempt from Franz Josef Land in 1912. After two winters and summers largely involving science and survey, Sedov set off with two others. Scurvy had already killed one man; Sedov was sick; it was mid-February, the polar night; and the trio had insufficient equipment and supplies for the proposed six-month trek to the pole and back (or on to Canada). Other expedition members tried to stop the men, but they continued. Sedov died on Rudolf Island in early March: the other two managed to return safely. It was during the retreat of the remainder of Sedov's expedition that Albanov and Konrad (the survivors of the *Saint Anna*) were met. The fact that Sedov did not have a radio also resulted in the first Arctic flight by an aeroplane (as opposed to balloon or dirigible), made in 1914 by the Russian pilot Jan Nagursky. He flew a French-built Maurice Farman seaplane from Krestovaya Bay, Novaya Zemlya. The plane had been shipped there in pieces and assembled by Nagursky and his mechanic Kuznetsov in the open in appalling weather. The two then made a total of five flights across the Barents Sea, but failed to find any trace of Sedov.

In the Soviet Union the *Chelyuskin* affair had demonstrated that camping for long periods on sea ice was feasible, even comfortable if supplies were adequate. It could be argued that Nansen, Cook, Peary and others had already shown this, but *Chelyuskin* showed the viability of a fixed camp and team. The logical extension was a deliberate floe camp, the Arctic drift allowing science to be pursued across the Arctic Ocean. Specifically such drift stations would contribute to an understanding of the drift itself and to the opening of a sea route along Russia's northern coast. The first drift station was set up in June 1937. In charge was Ivan Papanin, accompanied by two scientists, Yevgeni Fedorov and Petr Shirshov, and radio operator Ernst Krenkel. Shirshov and Krenkel were veterans of the *Chelyuskin* camp. There was also a dog (Vesydy – Happy), the polar bear guard. The team were landed 25km (15 miles) from the pole and drifted until February 1938 when they were rescued from a melting floe close to Scoresbysund in east Greenland.

The team lived well in an insulated, but cramped, tent, electricity for the radio generated by an 'exercise

Above **The last photograph of Roald Amundsen, taken as he was about to board the Latham for his last flight on 18 June 1928.**
From F. Behounek *Männen på isflaket*, courtesy of the Swedish Polar Research Secretariat

cycle' which powered a generator. The drift station was entirely successful, the men remaining well throughout, and excellent data were obtained. It is also a memorable trip for one claimed incident (based on truth, but probably apocryphal) which has gone down in the annals of Russian polar science. Papanin was a devoted Communist. The two scientists were also party members, but Krenkel was not. Regular party broadcasts were received but Krenkel, who took them down, was not allowed either to hear them read by Papanin or to discuss them. He was therefore required to walk around the tent while the party members held their meeting. Papanin was not a scientist and so had no allotted task (other than as leader, which was hardly taxing as there were few decisions to be made). He apparently spent most of his time dismantling and reassembling his pistol. Krenkel, aggravated by his enforced retirements to the cold Arctic wastes and driven to distraction by Papanin's constant activity with the pistol (Papanin would work blindfolded and

Top **The cycle mechanism which powered the generator at Papanin's tent. The generator chiefly provided electricity for the team's radio.**
Arctic and Antarctic Institute, St Petersburg, Russia

Above **The Papanin team's tent and the plane which landed them on the ice close to the pole.**
Arctic and Antarctic Institute, St Petersburg, Russia

Above right **The interior of Papanin's tent.**
Maria Gavrilo

behind his back to vary the work) took revenge on the ship home. After Papanin had again dismantled his gun, Krenkel added a likely looking item to the pieces and retired. It is said that two days later Papanin had to be rescued from his cabin after he was heard beating his head on the wall in frustration at not being able to reassemble the gun.

The 1939–45 war ended the projected Soviet drift-station programme, but it began again in 1950, a series of stations being set up and manned through to the 1980s. As a prelude to the 1950 stations the Soviets also landed an aircraft at the pole on 23 April 1948. The pole team comprised scientists led by Mikhail Somov – the others were Pavel Sen'ko, Mikhail Ostrekin and Pavel Gordienko – and they became the first men to be confirmed as having stood there. On 4 August 1958 the US navy submarine USS *Nautilus*, commanded by W.R. Anderson, reached the pole on a sub-surface crossing of the Arctic Ocean. The submarine's name recalled that of Sir Hubert Wilkins' craft in which he had also tried to reach the pole underwater in 1931, failing to do more than descend beneath a single ice floe: it is believed his *Nautilus* had been damaged by sabotage, perhaps understandably as the technology of the time made the projected trip dangerous if not fool-hardy. On 12 August 1958 James Calvert, commander of the submarine USS *Skate*, surfaced at the pole. Not until 18 August 1977 did a surface ship reach the pole, the nuclear-powered Russian ice-breaker *Arktika*.

Over the ice to the pole

The first overground expedition to reach the pole was in April 1968 when a Canadian/US team led by Ralph Plaisted used snowmobiles to travel from Ward Hunt Island, off Ellesmere Island's northern coast. Four men reached the pole on 19 April and were then taken out by aircraft. The same year a team of four set out to cross the Arctic by way of the pole. The British TransArctic Expedition, comprising leader Wally Herbert, Allan Gill, Kenneth Hedges and Fritz Koerner, set out from Barrow on Alaska's north coast on 21 February 1963 with 40 dogs and four sledges. Despite the winter start they were forced to retreat early in the trip when a pressure ridge of ice heading south threatened to overwhelm them. Sustained by air drops of supplies the team pushed on, sometimes making lengthy detours because of leads. By the time Plaisted reached the pole Herbert's team were about 500km (300 miles) from Barrow. By the beginning of July, Herbert noted, they had sledged 1,900km (1,180 miles), but were still only at 81°33'N.

On 14 July the four established a summer camp and waited for autumn to bring easier sledging conditions. Polar bear and seal meat were added to the menu during their summer 'holiday', by which time ice drift had moved them 1°30' closer to the pole. On the 8th Allan Gill stumbled and injured his back. They returned to their summer camp intending to have Gill evacuated, but the weather and ice conditions would not allow an aircraft to approach or land. They therefore had to remain at the camp site throughout the winter, though the statements on local ice conditions being too difficult for a landing – made by Herbert – caused dissension with the expedition's organising committee in London who wanted the injured man taken off the ice as soon as possible. Gill remaining with the team was seen as Herbert's preferred option and a not-altogether sensible one.

In the event Gill recovered and was able to start with the team on 24 February 1969. Winter drift had taken them north, but also east, and it was still a long way to the pole. The winter cold was intense (below –50°C) but progress was steady and the pole was reached on 5 April, 407 days after leaving Barrow. The remainder of the journey was rather less fraught, though one of their two-man tents caught fire on the first day south of the pole. A new tent dropped to them had a 'No Smoking' sign fixed inside it. On 23 May the team sighted land. They reached it ('Little Blackboard Island' off Nordaustlandet, Svalbard) on 29 May and after a further 13 days of difficult travel over broken ice were picked up by a relief ship.

Later trips to the pole filled in the perceived gaps in human endeavour. In 1978 the Japanese Naomi Uemura set off from Ellesmere Island on 5 March solo, but with a dog team, and reached the pole on 29 April. He was then taken by air to Cape Morris Jesup on Greenland's north coast and sledged the island's length between 10 May and 22 August. In 1986 the Frenchman Jean-Louis Etienne made a solo ski journey to the pole, with air resupply every ten days. The first unsupported journey was made in 1986 when a team of eight (one of whom was evacuated when his ribs were broken by a sledge) led by Will Steger and Paul Schurke used dog teams hauling 3 tons of equipment. Steger's team included Anne Bancroft, the first woman to reach the pole. On day 32 of the 47-day journey the team met Etienne on his solo ski trek. It was this chance meeting that led to Steger and Etienne (and others) organising the TransAntarctic Expedition.

Right **On 1 April 1959 the USS *Skate*, the first submarine to have surfaced at the pole, repeated the trip so that the ashes of Sir Hubert Wilkins could be scattered there. Wilkins had not only attempted the first submarine crossing of the Arctic Ocean but was a pioneer polar airman.**
US Navy Historical Centre

In 1990 the Norwegians Erling Kagge and Børge Ousland made an unsupported ski trek from Ward Hunt Island. They had started as a threesome, but on the ninth day Geir Randby had injured his back and had to be evacuated. Despite all his equipment and food being taken out with him the purists maintained this invalidated the journey. The discussion was rendered academic when Børge Ousland made a solo, unsupported journey from Cape Arktichesky at the northern end of Severnaya Zemlya in 1994. Ousland had chosen a Russian start because although it was 200km (125 miles) further to the pole the ice was usually less disrupted. Ousland pulled a sledge constructed of inner and outer shells which could be locked together with skis to form a catamaran which he used to cross leads. Starting on 2 March 1994 Ousland covered an area of very broken ice, but then maintained a steady average of 15km (10 miles) daily. This increased as he neared the pole, which he reached on 22 April.

Steger's intention when he set out in 1986 was to journey to the pole and back unsupported, but he had been unable to complete the return trip. The out-and-back, unsupported journey was not completed until 1995 when it was achieved by Canadian Richard Weber, who had been part of Steger's team in 1986, and the Russian Mikhail Malakhov. Weber rightly noted that the early pioneers had not had the advantage of air evacuation from the pole and that the pair's journey would therefore be closer in spirit to them. The two had already tried the trip once before in 1992 when they started from Ward Hunt with a team of three on 13 March. But on 22 April (day 39) Bob Mantell realised he would not make the trip and returned to Ward Hunt alone, reaching it on 7 May. Weber and Malakhov were eventually forced to accept defeat in June at 89°38'N. During the trek they saw whales at 89°N, the furthest north ever. In 1995 Weber and Malakhov started on 14 February, hauling one sledge at a time because of their weight (each man had two sledges, each weighing more than 50kg/110lb, as well as a heavy backpack) and so covering double distances. On 28 February they established a depot at 83°50'N, returning to Ward Hunt for more supplies. Starting out again they experienced temperatures down to −58°C. They reached their depot on 17 March and, now with sledges weighing 140kg (309lb) and 20kg (44lb) backpacks, they started for the pole. They reached it on 12 May and, with lightened loads, returned to Ward Hunt, reaching it on 14 June 107 days after setting out. They had covered 1,500km (almost 1,000 miles).

The next landmark was the unsupported crossing of the Arctic Ocean, achieved by the Norwegians Rune Gjeldnes and Torry Larsen who had already completed the unsupported south–north traverse of Greenland. The pair set out from Cape Arktichesky on 16 February 2000, starting in the Arctic twilight as the sun did not appear until the 29th. They crossed ice so thin that they had to keep moving as to stop might mean to fall through it: with survival time measured in minutes and no chance of rescue by his team-mate this concentrated their minds wonderfully. They reached the pole on 29 April after 74 days of travel. Progress towards Canada was slow and on 13 May, at 88°N with 550km (344 miles) to go, they made the bold decision to leave their pulks behind, continuing on ski with everything in backpacks. Their packs weighed 45kg (99lb), so heavy that a fall meant waiting for assistance, and the possibility of a broken leg. With time, food and fuel running out their crossings of leads became increasingly audacious (or foolhardy). Inevitably Gjeldnes fell through the ice of one lead and was lucky to be wedged by his pack rather than pulled down by it; he was rescued by Larsen after several minutes' partial immersion. The pair ran out of food and fuel 45km (28 miles) from Ellesmere Island's Cape Discovery and were then stopped by an open lead. Had this been continuous around the coast it would have been disastrous, but they forced a way across, landing on 3 June after a trek of 109 days.

Gjeldnes' fall through the ice clearly demonstrated the hazards facing any solo trekker, but Børge Ousland was back on the ice in 2001 intent on repeating the Gjeldnes/Larsen crossing of 2000, but solo and unsupported. He also started from Cape Arktichesky, on 3 March. After one week his sledge cracked. Despite efforts to repair it a new sledge had to be brought to him by helicopter. Continuing against a headwind and across extremely broken ice Ousland reached the pole on 23 April, where he found a collection of people, including an Arab in full national costume. Ousland accepted a meal from Weber and Malakhov (see above) who were on a commercial pole trip. He then continued alone. The wind was occasionally favourable and he was able to use a sail (wing) to assist him, on one day covering a record 72km (45 miles) and several times covering more than 50km (30 miles). Ousland also used a drysuit to swim across leads and so reduce the time to bypass them, towing his sledge behind him. In all he used the suit 23 times. Ousland reached Ward Hunt Island on 23 May after covering 1,996km (1,250 miles)

in 82 days. Purists will argue that the replacement sledge and chilli con carne at the pole invalidates Ousland's claim of a first solo, unsupported traverse of the Arctic Ocean, but the fabled man-in-the-street will likely have little sympathy for such arguments and will view the journey as a success.

Today the North Pole is regularly reached by commercial trips on Russian ice-breakers. Each year the Russians construct ice runways at 89°N to fly in adventure seekers who ski the 'last degree' and are then taken back to 89° base by smaller planes. The pole has been reached by motorcycle, hot-air balloon and relay teams. Yet despite this commercialism journeys to it from Canada or Siberia (or any other starting point) are extremely hazardous. The broken nature of the ice, the open water (a Japanese explorer drowned in a lead during Ousland's solo crossing) and the risk from polar bears (stealthy hunters whose approach can go unnoticed and which represent a particular hazard to the tent-bound, sleeping trekker) are added to the problems of cold and bad weather, making the Arctic a more daunting challenge than Antarctica. The substantial thinning of the sea ice noted by Ousland in 2001 – he carried out thickness measurements as he had in 1994 – makes matters worse. For man the effect of global warming on the fragile ecology of the Arctic is a tragedy. For a man the effect could be lethal.

Top right **Børge Ousland, the outst nding polar traveller of the present generation.**

Above right **A self-portrait taken during Ousland's solo, unsupported North Pole Trek.**

Right **During his unsupported Arctic traverse, Ousland used a drysuit to swim across leads.**
Børge Ousland

Antarctica

Before the heroes came

The Ice Ages of the Quaternary era of geological time squeezed the ancestors of modern man into a narrowing belt of the earth. Paradoxically, the quantity of water locked into the glaciers and ice sheets of the polar regions lowered the levels of oceans by as much as 100m, opening land bridges that meltwaters later covered, closing the door to further migration. The Aborigines walked across the Torres Strait that now separates New Guinea from Australia, but further exploration of the islands of the south Pacific required ocean-going boats. About 2,500 years ago the peoples of New Guinea began a slow advance eastwards across the islands of Melanesia. They settled Vanuatu, Fiji, Tonga and Samoa, then crossed the vast and empty Pacific, reaching the Marquesas Islands by about AD300. From there the settlers headed north and south across the islands of Polynesia, reaching Hawaii in about AD800, New Zealand a century or so later. A stepping stone to New Zealand were the Cook Islands. In about AD650 Ui-Te-Rangiora pointed his canoe *Te-Ivi-O-Atea* southwards from Rarotonga, one of the southerly islands of the group. After days at sea Ui-Te-Rangiora and his crew discovered either sea ice or an island covered in ice.

Though often dismissed as pure legend the remarkable feats of seamanship required by the colonisation of Polynesia make the journey feasible, at least theoretically. Exactly what Ui-Te-Rangiora discovered is the subject of a debate that is unlikely to be satisfactorily resolved. As with the story of Pytheas' journey to the Arctic, Ui-Te-Rangiora's voyage implies achievements by early travellers which are at odds with the accepted wisdom that exploration of the polar wildernesses awaited the rise of Western civilisation, an assertion which owes as much to an arrogant view of history as it does to lack of evidence. That said, it has to be accepted that while the existence of the Arctic could well have been known from quite early times, it is unlikely that Ptolemy included *Terra Incognito* on his map because rumours of the Cook Islander's voyage had reached Greek ears.

The Greeks reasoned the earth was spherical. To Pythagoras, the 6th-century BC mathematician and philosopher, only a sphere would satisfy the purity he believed underwrote the cosmos. More pragmatically, Eratosthenes, who died in 194BC, had during his time as head of the great library of Alexandria calculated the circumference of the earth by measuring the length of the shadow of a stick at noon at two different places (Aswan and Alexandria) and pacing the distances between them. This simple, beautiful method gave him an answer of staggering accuracy. To the Greeks it was obvious that to balance this spherical earth, the lands of the north, those defined by Arktos, the constellation of the bear, must be balanced by lands to the south, the Antarktos. Not only did a southern land mass obviously exist but, as the Greeks assumed the balance of the earth extended to climate as well, it must also be inhabited.

By the early years of the 16th century the assumed southern continent was taking shape as discoveries by Portuguese and Spanish sailors, driven by the need to find trade routes to Asia free from the control of the city states of Italy and hostile Muslims, extended the frontiers of the known world. It had been assumed that Terra Australis, as it had become known, might be an extension of Africa, but Bartolomeo Diaz and Vasco de Gama showed that it was not. Ferdinand Magellan and Sebastian del Cano negotiated the straits between the South American mainland and Tierra del Fuego, then crossed the Pacific to reveal that the land of the south was not connected – as had also been considered likely – to Asia. Magellan named Tierra del Fuego – the Land of Fire – not from volcanic activity as is still commonly believed (and occasionally written) but from the camp fires of the indigenous people. Magellan believed Tierra del Fuego was an island, though back in Europe most believed it to be the tip of the southern continent. Not for another century would the Dutch explorers Willem Schouten and Jacob Le Maire in the ships *Hoorn* and *Eendracht* show that Tierra del Fuego was indeed an island, though Drake's observations of the passage which bears his name had hinted as much 40 years before. To add to the excitement of discovering Cape Horn, the Dutch also collided with a creature of unknown species which they confidently recorded as a sea monster.

In 1642 Abel Tasman sailed around Australia, proving it was not part of a southern continent, and in the years that followed expeditions beyond latitude 50°S showed that the Southern Ocean was an empty place, pushing back the possible shores of the expected land mass. It is an intriguing aspect of the search for the southern continent that it ran the normal reel of discovery backwards. The Americas were unknown, unsuspected by everyone except those with an intimate knowledge of the Norse sagas, their discovery leading to expeditions which investigated and mapped their extent. The southern continent was suspected. It was pencilled in on maps, however tentatively or imaginatively, expeditions progressively shrinking its projected extent until it was finally discovered.

Furthest south

The record for man's 'furthest south' probably starts with Englishman Francis Drake, though there are still references to the claim of the Florentine-born merchant Amerigo Vespucci who, in 1502, sailed southwards along the western shore of South America, discovering the Rio de la Plata and continuing to a point where, he claimed, the night was 15 hours long. It was 7 April when Vespucci measured the night hours: on that date a night of that length would mean he had sailed to 72°S, placing him south of the Antarctic Circle. He would have sailed along the Antarctic Peninsula, reaching either the Weddell or Bellingshausen Seas. No credible historian believes that Vespucci had actually gone south of 54°S.

More credibly, in 1578, during his circumnavigation of the world, Francis Drake sailed through the Magellan Strait and headed north-west across the Pacific. On 9 September a strong north-easterly wind pushed his flotilla of three ships southwards to about 57°S. After the loss of the *Marigold* the wind eased, allowing the two remaining ships to regain Tierra del Fuego. Here the master of the *Elizabeth* declined to follow Drake any further and returned through the Magellan Strait leaving Drake to continue alone in the *Pelican* (later renamed *Golden Hind*). On 24 October he again reached 57°S before continuing across the Pacific.

It is unclear how long Drake's record stood. In September 1599 the Dutchman Dirck Gherritz claims his ship was blown to 64°S and that he spotted what are now the South Shetland Islands. Four years later the islands were again spotted, also by a Dutch ship, the *Blijde Bootschap*, the Good News, a wholly inappropriate name as it had been commandeered by pirates and then driven south by a storm. However, both these southerly claims date not from the early 17th century but from 1819, just after the American War of Independence. They were made by Edmund Fanning, a Connecticut sealer who had worked out of South Georgia and was about to embark on an expedition to find the southern continent when the war intervened.

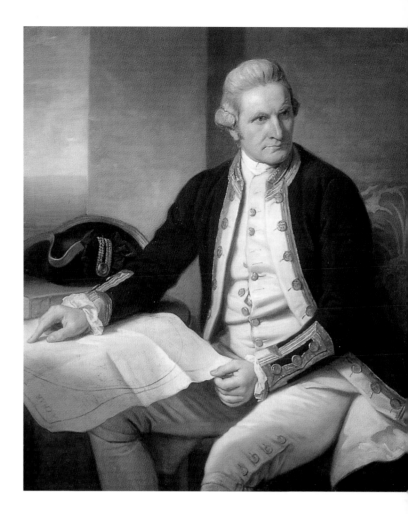

Above **Nathaniel Dance's portrait of James Cook, the Yorkshireman who has a claim to being the greatest seaborne explorer of all.**
UK National Maritime Museum

Fanning was presumably far from enchanted by the British or by their claim on the rich sealing grounds of the South Shetlands, and wished to see William Smith's claim to have discovered the islands nullified. Fanning not only put forward the earlier claims of the Dutch ships, but also another by the possibly fictitious Captain Frazer who, Fanning claimed, had not only seen the islands in 1712 but named them South Iceland. There were also claims by several pirates that they had passed 60°S while in the grip of the Southern Ocean's notorious weather. Jacob l'Hermite declared he had passed 60°S in 1624, while much later, in 1687, the delightfully named Lionel Wafer, a surgeon turned pirate, claimed to have spent Christmas Day at 62°45'S. Though all of these claims have their doubters, it is generally agreed that George Shelvocke, a British Royal Navy captain turned privateer, reached 61°30'S in the *Speedwell* during the austral summer of 1719–20.

Shelvocke's expedition was also notable for two other events. Firstly, on 1 October 1719, William Camell fell overboard and drowned. Camell was probably the first man to drown south of 60°S, a fact which was doubtless of no comfort as the chilly waters of the Southern Ocean closed over his head for the last time. Secondly, after passing through the Le Maire Strait (between Tierra del Fuego's eastern tip and Staten Island) the *Speedwell* was followed for several days by a solitary black albatross 'hovering above us as if he had lost himself'. Thinking this was a sinister omen Simon Hatley, Shelvocke's second captain, killed the bird with a shotgun after several attempts in the hope that its death would bring an end to the 'contrary tempestuous winds, which had oppressed us ever since we got into this sea'. In 1728 Shelvocke published *A Voyage round the World by way of the Great South Sea*. In 1797 the book was read by William Wordsworth who suggested to his friend Samuel Taylor Coleridge that he use the incident in the epic poem he was writing (and that the 'tutelary spirits of these regions take upon them to avenge the crime'). Coleridge substituted a more romantic crossbow for the shotgun and used the killing as the central theme of the *Rime of the Ancient Mariner*. Interestingly, the Arctic has a claim to be the basis of the poem, an indication of the hold the polar regions had on the 19th-century English mind.

James Cook

Not until 1773 was the Antarctic Circle crossed, during the second of the momentous voyages of James Cook, the Yorkshireman who has a claim to being the greatest seaborne explorer of all time. In 1768 Cook explored the southern Pacific at modest latitudes, charting the east coasts of New Zealand and Australia. In terms of defining the extent of the elusive southern continent that voyage is of limited interest, but Joseph Banks, the botanist who accompanied Cook, set down the first known expression of enthusiasm for reaching the South Pole merely for the sake, the fun, of doing so. It would, Banks said, be 'Glorious… to set my heel upon the Pole and turn myself 360° in a second!'

In 1771 Cook proposed searching for land at higher latitudes and set sail with two ships, *Resolution* and *Adventure*, and orders from the British Navy Board for 'prosecuting your discoveries as near to the South Pole as possible'. Cook crossed the Antarctic Circle at about 1.15pm on 17 January 1723, eventually reaching 67°14'S (at 40°46'E, about 145km/90 miles off Kronprins Olav Kyst) before being stopped by ice which stretched to the horizon. In February Cook and the *Resolution* were separated from the *Adventure*, commanded by Tobias Furneaux. The two ships did not meet while wintering on New Zealand and so Cook was alone when he headed south again. He crossed the circle again on 20 December 1773, reaching 67°31'S (at 142°30'W between the Amundsen and Ross Seas, about 720km/450 miles from land) on the 22nd. Christmas Day was 'spent in jollity', though on 26 December two men were 'put in irons for being drunk, and threatening the second lieutenant'. When the two had sobered up they expressed their sorrow and were released.

Encouraged by warmer weather and fewer icebergs (or 'ice islands or hills' as the crew called them) Cook headed south again. On 30 January he noted in his journal that at 'a little after 4am we perceived the clouds to the South near the horizon to be an unusual Snow White brightness which denounced our approach to field ice.' What Cook was seeing is now called ice blink, the reflection of unseen ice in the sky. The ship reached the edge of the sea ice at 8pm. It 'extended East and West in a straight line far beyond our sight; as appeared by the brightness of the horizon; in the Situation we were now just in, the Southern half of the horizon was enlightened by the Reflected rays of the Ice to a considerable height.' Because of this bright ice blink 'the clouds near the horizon… were difficult to distinguish from the Ice hills… The outer or Northern edge of this immense Ice field was composed of loose or broken ice so close packed together that nothing could enter it; about a Mile in began the firm ice, in one compact solid body and seemed to increase in height as you traced it to the south.' The crew counted 97 ice hills rising from the sea ice, but saw no evidence of land.

The *Resolution* had reached 71°10'S at about 107°W. The difficulty of fixing the ship's exact longitude – Cook and Charles Clarke, second lieutenant and a gifted navigator, differed by 4° in their best estimates – means it is not easy to say exactly how close Cook came to land. At worst he was some 160km (100 miles) from Thurston Island, at best he was only about half that distance and so was tantalisingly close to seeing Mount Coldwell at the western end of Thurston's Walker Mountains.

While Cook was making his furthest south Tobias Furneaux was sailing the *Adventure* east from New Zealand, staying below 60°S all the way to Cape Horn and beyond to avoid the notorious cape waters. Because of fog and haze he missed seeing Elephant Island, though he was probably within 37km (20 nautical

miles) of it. He also narrowly avoided seeing the South Orkneys (just beyond his range of vision, though again there was fog) and South Georgia (within range, but obscured by haze). On his own return journey Cook landed on South Georgia, naming it for King George III in whose name he claimed it for Great Britain. It was, he said, 'a land doomed by nature to perpetual frigidity, a terrain savage and horrible... not a tree nor a shrub to be seen, no not even big enough to make a toothpick'. Though this was the first landing on the island it had been seen before, the London merchant Antoine de la Roche probably sighting it in 1675 when his ship was blown off course after rounding Cape Horn, and the Spaniard Gregorio Jerez seeing it again in 1756 (when he named it San Pedro, but did not land).

Cook had sailed all the way around Antarctica. He had not proved conclusively that the southern continent existed (though he conjectured, correctly, that the presence of icebergs implied land) but he had established that if it did it was unlikely to be either inhabited or habitable. He wrote, 'The disappointment I now met with did not affect me much; for to judge of the bulk by the sample it would not be worth the discovery'. And, 'should anyone possess the resolution and the fortitude to elucidate this point by pushing yet

Top In this watercolour by William Hodges, Cook's ships *Resolution* and *Adventure* are taking on ice from an 'ice hill' for water.
Mitchell Library, State Library of New South Wales, Australia

Above The waters of the Southern Ocean are notorious for their storms, nowhere more so than off Cape Horn. Here a ship battles with a force 8 wind and sea close to the cape.
Richard Sale

Above **Thaddens von Bellingshausen, probably the first man to sight Antarctica.**
Scott Polar Research Institute, University of Cambridge, UK

further south than I have done, I shall not envy him the fame of his discovery, but I make bold that the world will derive no benefit from it.' Despite the denials Cook was an ambitious man and it is possible to detect disappointment in this apparently sanguine acceptance.

Not for almost half a century would Antarctica, the true southern continent, be seen, and then, as is occasionally the case for things which take an age to arrive, it was sighted from two different ships in the space of three days.

The continent sighted

Faddey Faddeyevich Bellingshauzen was born in 1778 in Ösel, now called Saaremaa or Sarema, an Estonian island in the southern Gulf of Riga. At the time of his birth Estonia was a recent acquisition of the Russian Empire. In the west Bellingshauzen – itself an approximation to the Cyrillic original – has been given the Germanic name Thaddens von Bellingshausen, following the translation of his account of his southern voyage into German in 1902, the noble 'von' presumably added as a mark of respect. In 1819 Czar Alexander I appointed Bellingshausen commander of an expedi-

tion of two ships, *Vostock* and *Mirnyi*, both considerably larger than Cook's *Resolution* and *Adventure*. The expedition was to discover the South Pole (and hence, by inference, the southern continent) and a southern base for the Russian Pacific fleet.

Bellingshausen sailed in July 1819. He visited South Georgia, meeting a pair of British sealing ships and charting the southern coast, and then sailed to the South Sandwich Islands which had been seen, but not visited, by Cook. Bellingshausen confirmed that South Sandwich was an island group and not part of a larger land mass. He next crossed the Antarctic Circle, becoming the first man to do so since Cook, although the event does not seem to have mattered much to him as he did not record it. The exact date is also not helped by the fact that Russia still maintained the Julian calendar (not changing until 1918) whereas the other nations active in the Southern Ocean used the Gregorian. A further complication is Bellingshausen's use of three different times ('ordinary' time, ship time – in which the day changed at noon – and 'astronomical' time) and made no allowance for time zones as he journeyed across the ocean. Exact dates are therefore likely to be wrong by half or one day. However, by general agreement Bellingshausen crossed the circle on 26 January and on 27 January was at 69°21'28"S, 2°14'50"W when he observed 'a solid stretch of ice running from east to west'. Lt Lazarev on the *Mirnyi* wrote that the ships had encountered 'continental ice', a phrase Bellingshausen himself used in a later letter. It is very probable that the Russians were seeing the ice shelf (the western edge of the Fimbul Ice Shelf) extending from the Princess Martha and Princess Astrid coasts. It is, however, a moot point whether Bellingshausen actually knew what he was looking at. His description implies that he knew he was not observing pack ice, but ice shelves were unknown at the time so his use of the word 'continental' may have been fortuitous. What can be said is that he obviously knew he was seeing something unknown. If the ice shelf is considered to be part of Antarctica then Bellingshausen had become the first man to see the southern continent. If the definition of a continent requires that a man sees land, then the true discovery had to wait a little longer.

Unlike the Russian admiral, the Englishman William Smith was a working sailor, probably starting in the coastal coal trade before serving on Greenland whalers. In 1811 he was master of a colliery vessel, the following year becoming master of the *Williams*, an ocean-going

ship in which Smith made several journeys to South America. In January 1819 Smith took the *Williams* out of Buenos Aires bound for Valparaiso, but the wind would not allow him to round Cape Horn, forcing him southwards where he sighted the South Shetlands (naming them New South Britain). The rest of the journey was uneventful: he arrived at Valparaiso in March and left again for Montevideo in May. Smith had been careful to keep news of his discovery secret as he had seen a lot of whales near the South Shetlands. But when he reached Uruguay he was shocked to discover that news of his find had already arrived; the careless words of his crew in Valparaiso had quickly carried across the Andes. Smith returned around the Horn in June 1819, returning in October, this voyage allowing him to survey the northern coasts of the South Shetlands and to land. He planted the Union Jack and claimed the islands for King George. The acquisition seemed important as Smith believed he saw pine trees growing on one island implying (as a British newspaper formally announced in August when the news finally reached London) a temperate climate, though this unlikely 'discovery' was soon shown to be false.

When he arrived in Valparaiso Smith's ship was chartered by Captain William Shirreff, the senior British naval officer in the Pacific, who wished to continue the survey of the new lands and to formalise the British claim. In an effort to prevent further news of the discovery leaking out Shirreff ordered the *Williams* anchored offshore, though it is likely that sealers had by then already landed on the islands, making a nonsense of both the secrecy and the British claim. When the *Williams* sailed in early December 1819 Smith had been joined by Captain Edward Bransfield, a Royal Navy officer, installed by Shirreff to give the expedition legitimacy.

The ship reached Livingston Island in the South Shetlands on 19 December, the first landfall being named Cape Shirreff by the dutiful Smith and Bransfield. The pair resurveyed the northern coastlines, then headed south, proving the new lands were islands and discovering Deception Island, the flooded volcanic caldera now popular with tourists to Antarctica. One day later, on 30 January 1820, having sailed south from Deception, Smith and Bransfield saw

Tower Island and, rising beyond it, the peaks of what they called Trinity Land. Today this is the Trinity Peninsula, the northernmost part of Graham Land on the Antarctic Peninsula. If land is the criterion for identifying the true Antarctic continent then Smith and Bransfield are the discoverers, just three days after Bellingshausen had observed the continental ice shelf. Smith and Bransfield then sailed eastwards through what is now the Bransfield Strait, seeing Trinity Land again before heading north where they discovered Elephant Island (named the following year by American sealers because of the abundance of elephant seals) before returning to Valparaiso.

One last name must be mentioned when considering who can be attributed as the discoverer of Antarctica, that of National Palmer. Palmer was born in Stonington, Connecticut, in 1799. At the age of 12 he was sailing as a blockade runner during the American War of Independence and was master of his own ship by the age of 19. In 1819/20 Palmer was part of a sealing expedition to the South Shetlands and in 1820/1 was master of the *Hero* on a similar trip. During this voyage he met Bellingshausen in an extraordinary incident on 6 February 1821 during which the two Russian ships *Vostock* and *Mirnyi* were separated in thick fog in the Bransfield Strait. When the fog lifted, to the Russians' astonishment the *Hero* lay between them. Bellingshausen invited Palmer aboard and was later escorted by the American ship to the safe anchorage of Deception Island (which Palmer had almost certainly been the first to discover: he was probably also first to land on Deception). There are several accounts of the meeting and the American version of these have formed the basis of the claim that Palmer was the first to see Antarctica. In fact he had first seen what is now called Graham Land (part of the Antarctica Peninsula: in deference to the American the southern section of the peninsula is now called Palmer Land) on 17 November 1820, ten months after Smith and Bransfield. Palmer was, however, the first to discover the South Orkney Islands when, as master of the *James Monroe*, he accompanied the British ship *Dove*, under George Powell, on a sealing trip. The discovery was on 6 December 1821, but finding no seals Palmer sailed away leaving Powell to claim the islands for Britain. Powell went ashore on an island he named Coronation in honour of the recently enthralled George IV.

After the chance meeting with Palmer, Bellingshausen completed his voyage. In all he sailed over 240° of longitude (two-thirds of the way around the world)

south of 60° and crossed the Antarctic Circle half-a-dozen times. It was a masterful enterprise, but Bellingshausen had found no southern continent, no useful bases, and sealing grounds that were already overrun by British and Americans. The Czar was not impressed and declined to authorise the cash needed to publish Bellingshausen's maps.

Finally the southern continent had been discovered, though its shores had still to be mapped, an exercise that occupied sealers and scientists for decades, and its true nature was unknown. As late as 1895, just 15 years before Amundsen's polar trek, Nansen was suggesting that Antarctica might comprise a group of islands rather a single land mass.

Hunters in the south

Sealers

The killing of fur seals on a commercial basis began on the Falkland Islands in 1766 and would, as the seal population collapsed, inevitably have led the sealers to seek out new breeding grounds even if the early explorers had not, unwittingly, done it for them. When James Cook took possession of South Georgia for the British Crown he noted that fur seals were 'pretty numerous', his comment being enough to trigger the arrival of British and American sealers once the Falkland Islands' population had been decimated. In 1800/01 there were at least 17 sealing ships at the island, their catch totalling over 100,000 animals. By 1822 James Weddell was calculating that well over a million animals had been taken. By then the South Georgia population had been hunted to the edge of extinction: indeed, it was actually believed that not only were the fur seals commercially extinct but that they had been entirely wiped out on the island. It is thought that a few – perhaps no more than ten animals – survived, probably on Bird Island off South Georgia's north-western tip.

The extinction of the seals on South Georgia led to the sealers exploiting the South Shetlands. The rapid spread of the news of William Smith's discovery is an indication of the sealers' enthusiasm for new stock. It is also possible that those sealers shrewd enough to have foreseen the collapse of the South Georgian seal population had already sought new land. If sealers discovered the South Shetlands before Smith they would certainly have kept quiet about it, a fact which has led many to wonder whether not only the South Shetlands but also the Antarctic Peninsula were known before (though probably not long before) the official discoveries. It is estimated that the sealers took over 300,000 seals from the South Shetlands in the period 1820–2. By the 1822/3 season the catch was so poor that visiting the islands was no longer commercially viable: new lands had to be sought.

Smith's crew had little incentive to stay quiet about what they had seen around the South Shetlands as the *Williams* was a freighter. For the sealers the incentive was huge. In the early years of the 19th century a top-quality fur-seal pelt fetched $5 in the USA and even a tiny ship could hold 10–20,000 skins. In the 1820/1 season – a season which lasted from late November until mid-January, a total of just seven weeks – the Fanning–Pendleton expedition from Stonington, Connecticut, operated on the South Shetlands. The five ships of the expedition – one of which was Nathaniel Palmer's *Hero* – took back 51,000 skins, netting perhaps $250,000 for the 70 men who crewed them. One ship, the *Hersilia*, carried 18,000 skins and this was merely the number of top-quality pelts. It is possible that as many again were rejected. The five ships of Fanning–Pendleton were joined on the islands by a further 25 American ships and an equal number of British. There may also have been smaller numbers of ships from Australia, South Africa and France. Although it was not until 1822/3 that the seal population of the South Shetlands was deemed commercially extinct, even during the 1821/2 season ships of the second Fanning–Pendleton expedition had found a reduction in numbers. That was the reason Nathaniel Palmer and George Powell sailed east and discovered the South Orkneys. Though Palmer was not impressed, there were seals on the islands. The population was small and was rapidly annihilated, the South Orkneys having no seals for over 100 years until a single animal was spotted on Signy Island (an island named for his daughter by the Norwegian whaler Petter Sørlle, a later visitor) in 1947. The population has now increased to several thousand.

Though greed was the driving force for the slaughter, the behaviour of the seals contributed to their downfall. Devoid of fear because of the absence of a land predator in Antarctica the seals were curious about these new creatures and happily waddled up to them, only to be clubbed or shot. The numbers killed were so great that clubbing was the preferred means of dispatch, the sealers walking along the crowded beaches swinging without pause, stopping only as a result of exhaustion or complete annihilation. The sealers

Above **Since they have been protected elephant-seal numbers have increased, creating ironic images as they recolonise areas of South Georgia such as Grytviken.**
Richard Sale

preferentially took breeding females and young males as their skins were of better quality, leaving the breeding bulls, whose skins also took more salt to cure, alone. The effect of this targeting, together with the sheer numbers killed, ensured that the stock would collapse. Late in the season, when there were fewer seals and those that were found rapidly fled into the sea, the sealers would often pursue them in boats and shoot them. Dead seals sank quickly, so the success rate in gathering them was unlikely to exceed one in five, while wounded animals might escape only to die later.

Often the sealers were left on shore while their ship went off to drop men at other sites, the men living in poor-quality tents, crude huts or in rock shelters, with little protection from wind and cold. It would seem that only the exceptional pay made the job bearable. After the seals had been skinned, the carcasses were left on the beaches to rot or to feed the petrels and skuas. Very young pups would not be killed as their skins were valueless, but without mothers they starved to death. The salted skins were packed for transport, though even here the stupidity of the exercise is apparent. It is reported that on one large ship returning to London with 100,000 skins on board, the poorly preserved skins became so overheated during the equatorial part of the voyage that they started to rot. By the time London was reached the whole cargo had degenerated into a stinking heap that had to be dug out of the hold and was fit only for spreading as fertiliser.

After the virtual destruction of the fur seals commercial interests turned to elephant seals whose hides made an excellent leather and whose rendered blubber was as good as whale oil for lighting lamps and lubricating machinery. The huge bulls, too dangerous to club (they are surprisingly quick at turning a ferociously-toothed mouth to anyone approaching, and have a neck whose flexibility and extension is equally surprising) were lanced with a long spear or shot. Bulls yielded 150–300 litres (33–66 gallons) of top-quality oil, enough to fill one or two barrels. Some idea of the seasonal slaughter is gained by noting that a single ship could carry 15,000 or more barrels away from South Georgia. The story of the exploitation of the southern elephant seal follows that of the fur seals, with massive over-killing resulting in commercial extinction.

Whereas catches of elephant seals were still reasonable at the end of the 1870s, in the 1885/6 season only two animals were taken, and they yielded just a few tens of barrels of oil. Ironically the populations of fur seals on some islands had by then recovered sufficiently for sealing to begin again, on the Falklands and certain sites on the Antarctic Peninsula. But the same greed and lack of foresight prevailed, and fur-seal populations again fell disastrously, leading to regulations being introduced by the British to control the numbers taken. The elephant-seal population on South Georgia also recovered sufficiently for sealing to begin again in the early 20th century, over 250,000 bulls being slaughtered in the 50 years to 1960. The elephant seal is now protected.

The return of the fur seal to South Georgia is one of the great recovery stories of the animal world. From the handful left after exploitation there were still probably less than 100 in the early 20th century, this growing to several thousand by the 1950s and, perhaps, a million today. Ironically, this satisfying recovery of an endearing species is largely the result of an excess of krill, on which the seals feed, as a result of the slaughter of the krill-feeding baleen whales by commercial whalers.

Whalers

The first phase of Antarctic whaling coincided with the seal hunts, many of the companies involved operating both whalers and sealers. The whalers sought the right whale, southern cousin of the Arctic species, and brought it to the edge of extinction just as they had the northern species. The right was so-named because it was the right one to kill. It was slow, swimming at a maximum of 6 knots, and so vulnerable to the rowed whaling boats, and it was so heavy with blubber that it floated when killed. The latter was both convenient, for obvious reasons, and a commercial boon: more blubber meant a higher oil yield. By contrast rorquals (blue, fin, sei, humpback, Bryde's and minke whales) are fast, occasionally reaching speeds of over 15 knots (sei whales have been recorded at speeds of over 25 knots), too quick for a rowed boat to catch. If chance allowed a rorqual to be harpooned it was not a forgone conclusion that it could be taken. There are numerous stories of harpooned rorquals dragging boats, and even ships, for up to a day. In many such elongated hunts the line parted before the whale died.

In the early years of whaling, with men hand-throwing harpoons from rowing boats launched from sailing ships, the catches were not huge. The hunt was also dangerous. Boats could be overturned and men drowned, either during the occasionally lengthy period when a stricken whale towed the whalers – the infamous 'Nantucket sleigh ride', named for America's principle whaling port – or when a wounded whale attacked. Ships were also rammed and sunk by whales. The whale 'hero' of Herman Melville's *Moby Dick* is said to have been based on Mocha Dick, a white sperm whale which wrecked two boats, killing two men, from a Bristol whaler operating close to the Falkland Islands in May 1841. The sperm whale was a favoured species of early whalers because of the spermaceti wax found in its head and the ambergris found in the intestine. Ambergris was used in perfume manufacture and was, literally, worth its weight in gold. The production of ambergris is not well understood: it is believed that it is produced by the whale as a means of coating the non-digestible beaks of giant squid so as to prevent them from damaging the whale's gut. It is often expelled by the whale and is found floating on the surface. Ironically in view of its use in perfume, the substance is probably excreted by the whale, and some scientists have even suggested it is a by-product of sperm whale constipation. In about 1860 the population of sperm whales crashed because of over-exploitation for spermaceti and ambergris.

The contract the whalers sailed under held almost as many dangers as the whaling itself, though these were less obviously life-threatening. Many (almost all when the whales were plentiful) sailed for a percentage of the profit, emphasising the need to kill more whales, but meaning that there was no pay in the event of a man surviving a disaster. The share was known as a lay and was expressed as a fraction, for example 1/100 (1 per cent). First-time sailors were given a long lay, that is a big number. As many first-timers did not understand the system (or, probably, fractions) they attempted to get a bigger number, unscrupulous ship owners being only too willing to accommodate them. Many sailors, needing to buy clothes and so on for a voyage, were given an advance on their lay which had to be repaid from their share. Some owners – particularly the Nantucket Quakers, a singularly rapacious and whale-bloodthirsty lot for being Christian pacifists – charged hefty interest on the lay advances, and since some whaling trips lasted two or three years, this could seriously reduce a sailor's pay. For those few who were allowed, or opted for, a wage, the situation was hardly better: their pay usually ceased in the event of a shipwreck, and if they survived they were required to make their own way home, and pay their own fare.

The killing rate of the great whales was probably, in terms of the population, manageable at first, but the prize for capture of these huge rorquals was considerable. Baleen (whalebone) was needed for women's corsets and umbrella stays, and fetched prices of up to £10,000 per ton when whales were scarce in the late 19th century. With such rewards it was inevitable that the technology to hunt the great whales would not be long in arriving. The problem was solved in the 1860s by the Norwegian Svend Foyn who designed the first steam-powered whale boat, and also invented the explosive harpoon.

Foyn's new technology also allowed more whales to be killed, small killing ships hauling their catches quickly to larger factory ships on which the carcass was

Above **Grytviken. The name means Pot Cove, the pot being the three-legged tri-pot in which blubber was rendered to oil, though the pots in question were discovered there, having been left behind by elephant sealers.**
Richard Sale

rendered to oil, or to shore stations. The boom time of Antarctic whaling was the 20th century. In 1906 a Norwegian–Chilean enterprise anchored a factory ship in the Deception Island caldera. Then in 1908 the British formally claimed the island and leased it to a Norwegian whaling company, a move aimed at cleansing the caldera of the 3,000 or so whale carcasses that had accumulated there. Contrary to the belief that only the blubber can be rendered into oil, as much as 50 per

Above **A blue whale being measured at a South Georgia whaling station. A flensing hook can be seen leaning against the whale.**
Southampton Oceanographic Centre, UK

cent of the total yield comes from the whale's flesh and bone. The ruins of the caldera's whaling station are now a target for tourist cruise ships. A story tells of two drunken Norwegian whalers climbing on to a long-dead, but unprocessed and therefore overripe, whale and attacking it with their flensing hooks (the hockey-stick-like knives used to cut blubber into strips prior to its being ripped off). The released decomposition genes tore the whale apart, hurling the two whalers into the bay. The tale is probably apocryphal, but hopefully true. A factory ship was stationed at the South Orkneys in 1912 – the first whale to be processed was taken by Petter Sørlle – whaling continuing until the 1930s.

But the story of Antarctic whaling is the story of South Georgia. Whaling began here in 1904 when the Norwegians built the first shore-based station at Grytviken, the first of six such shore stations on South Georgia, and the longest to operate, closing only in 1965. Stromness closed in 1931, but continued as a ship-repair station until 1961. During the period of station operations, 1904–65, the whalers of South Georgia took almost 90,000 fin whales, over 40,000 blues, about 27,000 humpbacks, some 15,000 sei whales and almost 4,000 sperm whales. These figures are in addition to the catches of right whales that had brought the species to the edge of extinction in the first phase of Antarctic whaling. The figures are also for the South Georgia shore stations. In 1937/8, the catch – the

highest in any Antarctic season – was 46,000 whales, and figures around 40,000 were caught annually for ten years or so on each side of this peak. Today the Antarctic whales are protected, perhaps too late for the right and blue whales whose numbers are not recovering as might be expected, though other species' numbers are slowly improving. Ironically, the rusting stations of Grytviken and Stromness, now in part taken over by belligerent bull and shy young elephant seals, are a target for tourists.

Though the early phase of Antarctic whaling and sealing ranks high on the list of human infamy, it was also the spur to the partial discovery of the new continent. Many of the exploratory trips were purely commercial, but some ship owners did encourage their masters to explore for its own sake. Of these particular mention must be made of Enderby Brothers, a Scottish firm which was one of the leading British (and therefore Antarctic) sealing and whaling companies of the 1820s and 1830s. One of their masters was James Weddell, of Scottish ancestry but born in Ostend in 1787. After becoming a master in the Royal Navy, Weddell joined Enderby and made three voyages to Antarctica in the *Jane*. During the first he independently discovered the South Orkneys: it was Weddell who named them. During his third voyage he identified a new species of seal, now named for him on the South Orkneys, then sailed south. The weather, at first atrocious, improved and the *Jane*, accompanied by the *Beaufoy*, passed 70°S on 16 February 1823. The amazed Weddell, seeing no ice in any direction, recognised a rare opportunity and continued south. Eventually, on 20 February he reached 74°15'S, a point 344km (215 miles) south of that reached by Cook almost 50 years earlier. There was still open water ahead of him and Weddell conjectured – reasonably, but wrongly – that it went all the way to the pole. Weddell's crew were keen to continue, but he was more cautious. It was almost March, the start of the southern autumn; Weddell knew how unusual the conditions were and that the sea ice would eventually form well to the north of him: if the *Jane* and *Beaufoy* became trapped there was no hope of rescue. He therefore turned north, but not before naming the sea for King George IV and firing a cannon in salute. In 1900 the name was changed to Weddell Sea in honour of its 'discoverer', a controversial decision as there were some who believed that the American Ben Morrell in the *Wasp* had an earlier claim. It is known that Morrell sailed the edge of the sea in early 1823, but did not go much below 65°S until March, eventually reaching 70°S on 14 March.

Another Enderby master, Englishman John Biscoe, became the third man to circumnavigate Antarctica during an expedition which left Britain in 1830 with two ships, *Tula* and *Lively*. During the trip Biscoe discovered more continental land than any previous expedition, including more of the Antarctic Peninsula, and Enderby Land, the first part of the continent to have been discovered in the Indian Ocean sector: Biscoe named it for his employer. Biscoe returned with neither whales nor seals, the enlightened view of his employers made clear by their not dismissing him, but encouraging the Royal Geographical Society to award him with an honour. John Balleny, after whom the islands off Cape Adare are named, was also an Enderby man.

Science heads south

The French

Expeditions such as those of the Enderby captains became increasingly rare as the seal population was depleted. But just as the sealers departed, the scientists moved in, driven by an upsurge of interest following James Clark Ross' expedition to the North Magnetic Pole in 1831, stimulated by recent discoveries in the field of magnetism. The German scientist Carl Gauss had discovered the existence of the earth's magnetic field, and when he predicted the position of the South Magnetic Pole three expeditions were soon dispatched to reach it. The French sent Jules-Sébastien-César Dumont d'Urville, born in 1790 in the Calvados region of Normandy and most famous for having brought the Venus de Milo to Paris from the Greek island of Milos. Dumont d'Urville left Toulon in September 1837 with two ships, *Astrolabe* and *Zélée*. The expedition failed to reach the magnetic pole, but discovered Terre Adélie, which Dumont d'Urville named for his wife. The Adélie penguin was first identified by the expedition's naturalist.

The Americans

Arriving in Antarctica at about the same time as the French was an American expedition under the command of a New Yorker, Lt Charles Wilkes. Wilkes had been chosen to lead an Antarctic expedition in 1828 – for which he bought a lot of equipment with money from his own pocket, money that was not reimbursed when the expedition was cancelled – but was given command of the 1838 trip only when several other officers had declined. Events were to prove that they had been more sensible

Above **'A View of the Antarctic Continent'.**
From Charles Wilkes' *Narrative of US Exploring Expeditions 1838–42.*
USA Library of Congress

than Wilkes, the expedition later being described as the most ill-prepared ever to venture to Antarctica, and also the unhappiest. Wilkes was a tyrannical commander: 62 of the crew of his six ships were discharged as unsuitable or incompetent, and a further 42 deserted. Six men were killed in a battle with the Polynesians of the island of Malolo, and several more died of disease. Of the six ships, one sank and one was sold, another having been sent back early in the trip when she could not keep up with the rest. The expedition was also involved in a controversial incident when one of its ships sailed past those of Dumont d'Urville's. Each side blamed the other though the incident seems to have been the result of a misunderstanding rather than a snub. After four years visiting not only Antarctica, but the Philippines and Hawaii, Wilkes and his remaining three ships arrived back in the USA. In France Dumont d'Urville was fêted, and he and his crews given large rewards. In the US Wilkes was court-martialled, charged with inaccurate surveying and the harsh treatment of his crew. The former charge was based on inconsistencies discovered by James Ross and seem to have been founded on mirages rather than incompetence. On the latter, Wilkes was found guilty of a single charge relating to the punishment of one sailor: he was reprimanded. In reality, despite the obvious problems, the Wilkes' expedition was a success: around 2,500km (over 1,500 miles) of coastline, from the Balleny Islands to the Shackleton Ice Shelf, was surveyed. In addition, Wilkes was the first to describe Antarctica as a continent.

Left **Sir James Clark Ross by John R. Wildman.**
The Ross Ice Shelf, named for Sir James, is one of the wonders of the natural world. Though by its nature variable in size it generally occupies an area from 76°–86°S, 155°W–160°E, the largest body of ice in the world. It reaches almost 1,000km (600 miles) inland, an average of about 300km (200 miles) across the sea. It is up to 700m (2,400ft) thick and its 60m (200ft) frontal ice cliff is 650km (400 miles) long. The ice shelf covers an area of over 600,00 sq km (about 230,000 sq miles), roughly the area of France. The Ross shelf advances into the sea at a rate of about 670m (2,200ft) annually.

It is from such ice shelves – others are the Ronne and Filchner in the Weddell Sea, the Larsen on the eastern side of the Antarctic Peninsula, and the Amery, West and Shackleton on the Kerguélen side of Antarctica – that the great tabular icebergs, such a feature of Antarctica, break free. In an average year over 700 cu km (about 140 cu miles) of icebergs are created from the continent. In 1956 one was seen which measured 333km (208 miles) by 100km (60 miles), making it a bit bigger than Belgium.
UK National Maritime Museum

Below **Mount Erebus, which James Clark Ross named for one of his ships.**
P.S. Kristensen, courtesy of Quark Expeditions

The British

The contrast between the Wilkes' expedition and that of James Clark Ross could hardly be more extreme. Ross was already a veteran of polar travel having spent many years in the Arctic, searching for the North-West Passage with Parry, then reaching the North Magnetic Pole with his uncle, Sir John Ross. His expedition was also well funded and prepared, and his two ships, *Erebus* and *Terror*, were shallow-draughted and strengthened so as to be able to navigate ice. Ross sailed in September 1839, exploring the Kerguélen Islands before reaching Hobart. At the time Sir John Franklin was governor of Van Diemen's Land (as Tasmania was then called). Ross later named an island he discovered for Franklin, but the true irony of their meeting was that when Franklin disappeared in the Arctic on what is arguably the most famous of all polar voyages, he was in command of *Erebus* and *Terror*, the same two ships. In Hobart Ross heard about the Dumont d'Urville and Wilkes expeditions and was annoyed at their impudence in invading 'his' territory. Wilkes had left charts for him, and Ross' disparaging remarks about them led to the American's court-martial (though it didn't stop the Englishman from making use of the data).

Ross sailed south in November 1840 pushing through the pack ice to discover the sea which bears his name. Ross saw and claimed Victoria Land (named for the queen), then continued south to discover the volcanoes which he named for his ships. Mounts Erebus and Terror are on Ross Island, though at the time Ross believed the island to be part of the mainland (it was Robert Falcon Scott in 1902 who found it was an island). On 22 January 1841 Ross set a new furthest south record, reaching 78°9'S. Ross also discovered what he called the Victoria Barrier, 'a mighty and wonderful object far beyond anything we could have thought or conceived'. Later the Victoria Barrier was called the Great Ice Barrier and, eventually, the Ross Ice Shelf. Ross sailed over 550km (350 miles) along the ice shelf, marvelling at its unyielding 60m (200ft) ice cliffs which offered neither a passage through nor any glimpse of what lay beyond.

After Ross' expedition the world lost interest in Antarctica: clearly there was no habitable land; the animal life had been exploited to exhaustion if not extinction; and any mineral wealth was locked beyond or beneath impenetrable ice. Besides, Franklin's loss in the Arctic was much more interesting to both governments and the public. One exception was the scientific expedition aboard the *Challenger* sponsored in part by Britain's leading scientific institution, the Royal Society, and with Sir Charles Wyville Thomson as chief scientist, which explored the area in 1872–6. When *Challenger* crossed the Antarctic Circle on 16 February 1874 it was the first steam ship to do so, and the first since Ross 33 years before. The expedition was extraordinary: it covered over 110,000km (nearly 70,000 miles) and its report ran to 50 volumes.

The first landing

Twenty years later the first official landing on the continent was made. Svend Foyn's invention had, not surprisingly, made him rich and he organised and funded an Antarctica whaling expedition in 1893. The *Antarctic* (originally the *Kap Nor* but renamed by Foyn) left Norway in September, captained by Leonard Kristensen, but with Henryk Bull as Foyn's agent, a co-leadership that led to antagonism and ill-feeling which seems to have affected the entire crew and, consequently, the trip. The ship visited the Kerguélen Islands where an entire population of about 16,000 fur seals were slaughtered. Bull, who had never seen a seal hunt, was horrified and later called for international control of sealing. In Melbourne the seal pelts were sold and the *Antarctic* spent the southern winter unsuccessfully hunting whales around Campbell Island. They also took on new crew to replace two who jumped ship and several who were dismissed for refusing to sail to Antarctica. One of the newcomers was Carsten Borchgrevink, born in 1864, probably in Oslo, to a Norwegian father and English mother. Borchgrevink studied and travelled in Europe then, after the death of his father, emigrated to Australia in 1888, eventually becoming a teacher. He attempted to join the *Antarctic* as a scientist, but was accepted as a deck hand. The ship sailed south in September (but was forced to land in New Zealand after it collided with an iceberg), eventually crossing the Antarctic Circle on 25 December 1894, the first to do so since the *Challenger* 20 years before.

On 18 January 1895 the crew landed on Possession Island where Borchgrevink found lichen growing in sheltered areas, the first discovery of vegetation in Antarctica and one which dumbfounded many leading botanists who had claimed that the climate was too hostile to sustain plantlife. Six days later, on 24 January 1895, the expedition landed at Cape Adare, on the mainland itself. Who was first ashore, and whether they were, in fact, the first to land on the continent, remains a mystery – but an appealing one, so bizarre was the landing.

Above **Carsten Borchgrevink claimed the first landing on Antarctica though his claim is disputed. Later Borchgrevink led the first expedition to overwinter on the continent.**
Canterbury Museum, New Zealand

There had been persistent rumours of landings on the mainland for years, the absence of documented trips being easily accounted for, without any need to dismiss them as nonsense. In the period from Cook's voyage to the *Antarctic*'s arrival at Cape Adare well over a thousand sealing and whaling ships had sailed Antarctica's water, probably 50 times as many as had visited purely for exploration. It seems inevitable that some of those ships would have seen the continent (though almost certainly none before the sightings of Bellingshausen, Smith and Bransfield). If land was spotted sealers invariably went ashore in the hope of finding breeding grounds. If they found nothing they might not bother to tell anyone, if they found seals they had an interest in not telling. On 7 February 1821 John Davis, an American sealer from New Haven, Connecticut, and master of the *Cecilia*, put men ashore near Hughes Bay, an inlet of the Antarctic Peninsula near Trinity Island. His men searched the coast for about an hour. Davis himself did not go ashore. Opinions differ over whether the landing was on the mainland or on an offshore island, but many believe it was actually on the peninsula. It is also possible that Davis' men were not the first; John McFarlane, a British sealer, master of the *Dragon*, was in the South Shetlands in November 1820 and sailed south at some stage, landing men at an unknown destination. There are a handful of later claims too, so the exact status of the *Antarctic*'s shore party is unclear: it represents only the first authenticated landing.

As the ship's boat neared the mainland the *Antarctic*'s captain, Leonard Kristensen, was at the prow, Borchgrevink at the stern. As the boat beached Kristensen stepped ashore, while Borchgrevink leaped into the water and rushed forward to beach the craft. At the same time, Alexander Van Tunzelman, a Campbell Island youth who had joined the ship in New Zealand, jumped ashore to hold the boat for his captain. Later, all three would claim to have been first man ashore and the argument would reach the correspondence column of *The Times* of London.

The *Antarctic*'s party collected more lichen and some penguins from a nearby rookery and returned to the ship. Despite the landing the crew felt the voyage had been a disaster; no catch to speak of and having to endure the constant bickering of Bull and Kristensen. To make matters worse, when the ship docked in Melbourne they heard Svend Foyn was dead. Almost the entire crew jumped ship and found other vessels for the journey home.

Winter in the south: *Belgica*

In the wake of the Antarctic voyage Borchgrevink and Bull teamed up to try to launch another expedition, a short-lived venture. Bull soon left in disgust at Borchgrevink's continuous claims to have been a leader of the 1894–5 trip and to have been first man ashore, and Borchgrevink's disgust at Bull's excessive drinking. Borchgrevink therefore organised his own trip and sought finance and sponsorship. He planned an over-wintering at Cape Adare, suggesting the use of skis, dogs and a tethered balloon for observation (in all of which, events were to prove him right). Borchgrevink secured backing from a commercial company (one with the remarkably honest name of Commercial Company) who agreed to drop his team at the cape, to go whaling, and to return the next year. Initially Britain's Royal Geographical Society were keen to be involved, but became nervous about the commercial aspects and pulled out, deciding instead to back a national expedi-tion. Undeterred, Borchgrevink continued with his plan.

At the same time, the American Dr Frederick Cook began to seek backing for his own trip, but when this fell through he applied for the job of medical officer on another expedition, and was accepted. The expedition was organised by Adrian de Gerlache, a Belgian naval officer. While the British were still trying to raise £100,000 to finance their own expedition, de Gerlache raised about one-tenth of that. He bought a Norwegian steam whaler (*Patria*, renamed the *Belgica*) for 60,000 Belgian francs. The ship was three-masted and steam-sail powered, 33m (about 110ft) in overall length, 8m (26ft) wide and 4.5m (15ft) draught. She was built of oak, the bow and stern sheathed in greenheart, an American tree of the laurel family renowned for its hardness – special tools were needed to work it – and also for its elasticity, a combination which offered excellent protection against ice rubbing. Under sail, but with the addition of the 150hp engine, she could manage 7 knots. The boat was crewed by Belgian and Norwegian sailors under a Belgian captain, Georges Lecointe.

De Gerlache invited a number of scientists, his final selection creating an international expedition. Emile Danco was Belgian, Henryk Arctowski was Polish (the Polish base on King George Island is named for him), Antoine Dobrowolski was Russian, while Emile Racovitza was a Romanian. Most interesting of the initial appointments was Roald Amundsen, who at 25 was on his first polar expedition. Then, after the first-appointed medical officer pulled out, another was selected without interview, and joined the ship in Rio de Janeiro. He was Frederick Albert Cook MD, already a veteran of Arctic expeditions and the man who had failed to put together his own trip south. So when the *Belgica* finally reached Antarctic waters she had on board Amundsen, later to be the first man to set foot on the South Pole and, arguably, the first to see the North Pole, and Cook, whose claim to have reached the North Pole would become infamous, but has never been discredited.

In Rio, Cook noted, the locals were more interested in the ship's absence of luxuries than in what the expedition was hoping to find or do. This, and the view of one visiting cabinet minister – 'well on in the winter of life,' as Cook delicately put it – that if there were no women on board he wouldn't want to go, led Cook to conclude that 'so long as beautiful women, good wine, fine cigars and delicate foods are not found at the south pole, Latin Americans will probably not aspire to reach it'. Equally indiscreet was Cook's comment on the seasickness which afflicted everyone when the rough southern waters were entered. It seemed, he noted, 'to

Above **Henryk Arctowski, Dr Frederick Cook and Roald Amundsen photographed in a Patagonian studio before the *Belgica* trip. Clearly the photographer asked them to strike as natural a pose as they could manage.**
USA Library of Congress

be in evidence in direct proportion to the mental development of the personnel'. The captain was the first to succumb, and the seaman 'of lowest mental development' the last 'to loosen the gastric bonds'.

After exploring Tierra del Fuego – Cook's book on the expedition contains extremely interesting passages on the native Fuegans – the ship headed south. It was now mid-January 1898, late to be setting out for Antarctica, a fact that has led many to speculate that it had been de Gerlache's intention all along to have *Belgica* locked into the polar ice for the winter. The ship had supplies for three years, more than normal prudence would require, and many of those on board suspected the plan. It must have been even more apparent after time was spent surveying the Hughes Bay area: not until 15 February was the Antarctic Circle crossed. It was not an auspicious day: ice encased the ropes, cutting one man's hands, and plated the deck causing several, including the cook, to slip, losing the day's soup. Steering towards the narrow, dark bands whose appearance, like spectral lines on the ice blink, indicates the presence of open water, the *Belgica* continued south. Finally, on 23 February de Gerlache asked the crew how they felt about overwintering. To a man they opposed the idea. At this point in his account Cook claims that the officers and scientists were also against the plan, but that they had become resigned to

de Gerlache's unspoken intention despite their misgivings. In his book on the expedition Cook notes that to attempt to overwinter with only one ship would be foolhardy, particularly as no one knew where they were or that they were staying. If the *Belgica* were crushed by the ice the crew would have little hope of rescue, and 'death by freezing or starvation would be our lot'. Apparently swayed by the arguments de Gerlache agreed to head north for the winter and to return south the following spring. The way north was blocked by pack ice, so *Belgica* headed west, but as soon as she was clear of the pack de Gerlache changed his mind again.

Despite the austral winter beckoning, he decided to try for a new furthest south record, an ambition which the scientists opposed, but not vociferously enough to halt the ship's progress. Forced to seek shelter from a ferocious storm by going into the pack ice, the *Belgica* found leads heading south, but by 3 March the ship was surrounded by ice. After a futile week attempting to free the ship, it became clear that the expedition was trapped, at 70°20'S, 85°W in the Bellingshausen Sea. Man's first experience of the Antarctic winter had begun.

By Cook's account the *Belgica*'s crew rapidly became

not only resigned, but excited by the prospect of overwintering, though the fact that the ice was drifting (westward through 7° of longitude in the first two months) caused consternation – where would they be next spring? Was it possible the ship could be dragged over shallow rocks and have her bottom ripped out? Later a new fear arose: movement of water beneath the ice, caused by a storm, created ridges on either side of the ship, which seemed to threaten her survival.

Eventually the crew settled down to a reasonably ordered life. The scientists pursued their studies and there were regular trips out to observe ice and icebergs – the expedition had already become the first to ski on Antarctica, and now did so regularly – and to kill penguins and seals. At first the killing was chiefly for

scientific purposes, though later the men would be glad they had been so diligent. King Leopold of Belgium's birthday was celebrated in style on 9 April, a liberal supply of wine adding to the enthusiasm for a 'Grand Concourse of Beautiful Women' in which points were allocated for the best attributes of pictures of women from a Parisian magazine someone had brought along.

On 16 May the men realised – by fixing their position from the stars – that the sun had disappeared the previous day. At noon that day the northern sky brightened, but the sun had truly gone. With the long Antarctic night came a 'curtain of blackness' which seems to have entered the souls of many of the officers and men, the brief reappearance of the sun due to refraction the next day merely heightening its loss. The melancholy even affected Nansen; the ship's cat, who became lethargic and aggressive when roused, eventually died. The men might have too, as besides suffering from deep depression they were all becoming ill with scurvy. Cook, as medical officer, persuaded them to eat seal and penguin as from studying the reports of Arctic expeditions he knew this was a cure for the disease. It was a difficult task: by Cook's own admission penguin 'seems to be made up of an equal proportion of mam-

mal, fish and fowl. If it is possible to imagine a piece of beef, an odiferous codfish, and a canvas-back duck, roasted in a pot, with blood and cod-liver oil for sauce, the illustration will be complete.' Danco, there to study the earth's magnetic field, did not heed the advice. He would, he said, rather die than eat penguin, a prophetic comment as on 5 June he did die (though as much due to an existing heart complaint as the debilitation of scurvy). His was the second death on the expedition, Carl Wiencke, one of the sailors having fallen overboard on the journey south. Cook describes this in a very affecting passage. Cook threw Wiencke the log line and hauled him to the ship, but those on board were unable to complete the rescue before Wiencke, exhausted in the freezing sea, lost his grip.

One advantage of the fresh-meat diet was that the food was plentiful. When there was open water near the ship there was always an abundance of penguins and seals, and Cook had also lain in stocks prior to winter's arrival. Cook notes that a cornet blown to tell men on the ice that meals were ready also brought penguins waddling right up to the ship and seals out on to the ice, their curiosity being their downfall.

To the diet, Cook added a 'light' cure, making sure

that the men had a dose of heat and light from the fire each day. This was enough to dispel the gloom of perpetual night though it could do little for the permanent sense of isolation. Two sailors went insane, Engebret Knudsen (whose condition was temporary, though he died shortly after the expedition was over) and Adam Tollefsen. Ironically, Tollefsen's insanity occurred later in the year, his mind finally unbalanced, according to Cook, as much by the permanent daylight of the Antarctic summer as by the isolation.

On 22 July (after ten weeks of night) the sun came back. By 28 July they could feel the sun's warmth, but it was some time before they could expect the ice to melt and free the ship. At first they hoped to be free by late October, then late November, but it soon became clear that the *Belgica* could be held for a second winter. Eventually, in early January 1898, Cook suggested hacking a channel to open water. The attempt to use tonit (an explosive: the *Belgica* carried almost a ton of it, Cook having noted in Rio its potential usefulness in freeing the ship if it became 'embraced by the Frost King') was unsuccessful, but several weeks of labouring with picks and saws was. On 14 February the *Belgica* broke free and sailed for Punta Arenas, arriving on 28 March. There Cook discovered that in the time they had been away from the world the Spanish–American war had been fought. The scientists left the *Belgica* and made their way home, as did Amundsen. Aggravated by what he saw as de Gerlache's pro-Belgian attitude, he escorted the insane Tollefsen home independently.

The expedition had proved that man could survive the Antarctic winter, though the lowest recorded temperature, −43°C, was no lower than the Inuit had been coping with for centuries. It had also provided Roald Amundsen with his first polar experience and laid the groundwork for his later trips. Cook was impressed by Amundsen 'who was the biggest, the strongest, the bravest, and generally the best dressed man for sudden emergencies', particularly by his ability to ski and his willingness to be involved in everything. But Cook's admiration for Amundsen was nothing in comparison to Amundsen's for Cook. Amundsen later wrote, 'I came to know Dr Cook intimately and to form an affection for him and gratitude to him which nothing in his later career could ever cause me to alter. He, of all the ship's company, was the one man of unfaltering courage, unfailing hope, endless cheerfulness, and unwearied kindness. When anyone was sick, he was at his bedside to comfort him; when any was disheartened, he was there to encourage and inspire. And not

only was his faith undaunted, but his ingenuity and enterprise were boundless.' And as the pair, roped together, explore a crevassed landscape '...the experienced polar explorer walks in front, I follow... It is interesting to see the practical and calm manner in which this man works.' It was Cook who kept the men healthy, Cook who suggested the way of extricating the *Belgica* from the ice (though the idea of cutting channels in the ice had been practised by the British navy in their search for the North-West Passage for almost 100 years, though usually to reach rather than leave a harbour). Cook improved clothing, sleeping-bag and tent design: Amundsen's tent, which Scott found at the South Pole, was sewn to Cook's design, and Amundsen had used Cook's snow goggles on his trek. Cook was also the pioneering polar photographer, Amundsen recognising the value of photography in providing a record of achievement that disarmed sceptics (a true irony, given the use of Cook's own photographs to challenge his later claims).

Cook was not only a remarkable leader and polar pioneer, but was also an excellent writer. His account of the *Belgica* expedition is a superb read, his boyish enthusiasm jumping from every page. He is also lyrical, poetic even, in his description of a land he clearly loved. Given his sense of place and his real achievements it is deeply sad that his reputation has been so soiled.

Winter in the south: *Southern Cross*

As the *Belgica* sailed south, Carsten Borchgrevink was still trying to organise his own expedition back in Britain. Having lost official support, in part because of his dealings with a commercial company, he had now lost the commercial backing as well. He therefore approached George Newnes, a self-made man whose fortune was based on *Tit-Bits*, a magazine which had captured the fancy of the British public from its first edition in October 1881 by offering fun and entertainment at a time when the majority of popular reading was worthy, but dull. Much taken with Borchgrevink's enthusiasm and experience Newnes gave him £40,000. At one go the Anglo-Norwegian had obtained double the money the Royal Geographical Society had raised for a national expedition over several years of trying.

To transport his expedition Borchgrevink bought *Pollux* from Norway, a ship built by Colin Archer, the genius designer who had built the *Fram* for Nansen. The ship was of oak with a greenheart sheathing, the total over 3m (almost 11ft) thick at the bow and a metre (3ft) thick along the sides. Borchgrevink re-registered the ship as the *Southern Cross* and installed Bernhard Jensen (of whom Borchgrevink noted 'a man he looked and a man he was') as captain. Most of the officers and crew were also Norwegian. As scientists Borchgrevink chose the young physicist Louis Bernacchi, Belgian-born, of Italian descent but now Australian; William Colbeck, an English navigator and surveyor; and Nicolai Hanson, a Norwegian zoologist. Another Norwegian, Herlof Klövstad, was the medical officer. The ship's complement was completed by Norwegian Anton Fougner, Hugh Evans, born in England, but resident in northern Canada, and two Lapps. All the men except Bernacchi had polar experience, most were expert skiers and the Lapps were expert with dogs, brought specifically to handle Borchgrevink's Siberian and Greenlandic dog teams. Borchgrevink also took kayaks, but not the observation balloon he had originally intended. Despite criticisms at the time and later, the expedition was well thought out and organised.

During the journey south many of the crew were ill, probably from drinking contaminated water on the Cape Verde Islands, accentuated by the stench of the dogs as the equator was approached. Hanson was the sickest, and never fully recovered. The ship was late reaching Tasmania (where pigeons were taken on board, in part to satisfy the enthusiasm of local racing enthusiasts, in part to act as message carriers: the former was of little success, the latter none), and lost more time when Borchgrevink attempted to clear the pack ice too far to the east, despite Colbeck's warning. *Southern Cross* spent six weeks getting nowhere before Borchgrevink agreed to move further west. When he did the ship pushed through the pack into open water in just six hours. As a result of the delays it was 1 March by the time stores had been unloaded at Cape Adare. The *Southern Cross* headed north immediately. The next day Robertson Bay (enclosed to the west by Cape Adare) froze over: the ship had been just one day from being frozen in. The unloading had taken 12 days: when the dogs had been landed they had immediately slaughtered the local penguin colony. Later, when a storm forced the two Lapps to remain onshore for a night, the dogs crawled into their tent and curled up with them.

Borchgrevink had chosen Cape Adare simply because he had been there and he knew it was possible to land, but it proved to be an unfortunate choice. The expedition's site was windy and the cape was difficult to climb, making access to the 'true' continent difficult. This made life awkward for the scientists and probably exacerbated the animosity between them and Borchgrevink which

Top **The *Southern Cross*, in which the first team to overwinter on Antarctica headed south.**
Canterbury Museum, New Zealand

Above **Cape Adare.**
P.S. Kristensen, courtesy of Quark Expeditions

had arisen during the journey south. Borchgrevink was a short-tempered man and, occasionally, an arbitrary leader. On the journey he had refused to let the men write letters home in case any information reached the newspapers and compromised Newnes' intended scoop. The ructions this caused led him to reluctantly reverse the decision, but left a bitter taste. Now the windswept site was another cause for complaint – perhaps the men realised that without the leader's senseless loss of six weeks messing around in the pack ice the *Southern Cross* could have gone further south and found a better site. When the ship returned and they explored McMurdo Sound they found this to be true.

Camp Ridley (as Borchgrevink called it in honour of his English mother: he claimed Ridley ancestry which

Above **Herlof Klövstad, William Colbeck, Hugh Evans, Anton Fougner and Nicolai Hanson standing in front of Camp Ridley. The flag was presented to the team by the Duke of York, the expedition's patron. The photograph was taken by Louis Bernacchi.**

Canterbury Museum, New Zealand

Below **During the austral autumn of 1899 the *Southern Cross* team made the first tentative sledge journeys onto the sea ice off Cape Adare. Carsten Borchgrevink is photographed heading out towards Possession Island.**

Courtesy of Nicolai Vogt

included Nicholas Ridley, the Protestant bishop burnt as a heretic in Mary Tudor's reign) consisted of two huts linked by a canvas-covered storage area, home to its ten occupants for the next 11 months. The huts were anchored to the ground – literally, with anchors from the *Southern Cross* from which ropes were attached to the huts – and were adequate for the winter-long campaign. The only problem occurred when a lighted candle set fire to a mattress and threatened the entire hut; fortunately the fire was quickly put out. Because of the difficulty of moving inland, the intended sledge journeys were much curtailed, though explorations did prove the advantages of dogs.

But the journeys also provided further evidence of Borchgrevink's unsuitability as a leader. On an early trip the sledge party was caught by a storm which broke up the sea ice, resulting in waves crashing into the camp. Borchgrevink's behaviour in the ensuing chaos was, according to Bernacchi, disgraceful: he saved himself, leaving the rest to rescue the supplies. Bernacchi thought him 'thoroughly incompetent and a miserable coward'. In his account of the incident Bernacchi refers to Borchgrevink throughout as a 'booby': later he refined his ideas and changed the reference to 'disreputable beggar'. Part of the problem lay in Borchgrevink's frequent claims to be a scientist: he professed to be a practised surveyor, but couldn't use

a theodolite; he often claimed to be a naturalist, but on one occasion identified a range medusa (jellyfish) as an octopus. Borchgrevink said he had discovered gold on Duke of York Island (which he named for the expedition's patron, who had presented the expedition with a Union Flag which was flown at Camp Ridley). The scientists believed (rightly) that his find was iron pyrites, but Borchgrevink ignored them and continued to talk of the importance of his find and the commercial exploration he and Newnes would undertake. Later, in an attempt to bring the scientists to heel (having realised their opinion of him) he claimed he had a contract which prevented all expedition staff from criticising him: if they did it was mutiny, punishable by 15 years' imprisonment when they returned to civilisation. At this point Bernacchi confided in his diary his view that Borchgrevink was insane, confirming an opinion he had probably come to a little earlier when the leader had informed him, quite seriously, that he could read people's minds.

These actions, together with frequent long-term disagreements with individual men in which he tried to get others to take his side (one row, with Colbeck, lasted most of the trip and was at times both bad tempered and irrational) led to tensions. But these may well have alleviated some of the depressive problems that afflicted the *Belgica*'s crew by providing a focus for fears and frustrations. It is also true, of course, that while the men may have been nervous that the *Southern Cross* might not return, leaving them to face another Antarctic winter, they did not suffer the constant worry of their ship being broken up by ice and so leaving them completely helpless.

Several on the expedition had near misses, but the only death was that of Hanson whose condition worsened steadily. Some have suggested he had scurvy, but none of the others showed any sign of the disease and Hanson's symptoms were not characteristic. He died on 14 October after bidding farewell to the other nine and saying that 'it is not so hard to die in a strange land, it is just like saying goodbye to one's friends when starting on a long journey'. Hanson had been looking forward to the arrival of the Adélie penguins which nested at the cape: two days after his death over 250,000 of them arrived, a continuous stream of birds that took two weeks to come ashore. At his own request Hanson was buried in the shadow of a huge rock on top of Cape Adare, the first man to die on the continent, and the first to be buried there.

By January 1900 the men were anxious to leave, but the *Southern Cross* did not arrive until the 28th. Ironically, all but one of them, who had taken to scanning the horizon for any sign of the ship, were asleep in the huts when she finally turned up, and were woken by Captain Jensen hurling a sack of mail on to the table and shouting 'post'. Back on the ship, the expedition explored the Ross Sea and then sailed along the ice shelf, finding the harbour that would later be called the Bay of Whales (the starting point for Amundsen's journey to the pole). Here two teams of men landed, one using sledges, the other skis. Borchgrevink led the sledge team and claimed to have established a new furthest south record of 78°50'.

The British claim Antarctica

Back home in Britain, the expedition was heralded for having established the position of the South Magnetic Pole by careful measurement of the earth's magnetic field and for the first discovery of insect life on Antarctica. A dispute arose over Hanson's notebooks: many said the zoologist had given Borchgrevink personal charge of these, but he claimed never to have seen them. The argument, never fully resolved, reached the letters page of *The Times* and the staff of the British Museum's National History Department. The staff, which included Edward Wilson, later one of Scott's team, took the side of Hanson, who had been a staff member before the trip: they were particularly vehement in his support after Borchgrevink's outrageous reference to the dead zoologist as 'my late taxidermist'.

As a consequence of the ructions over Hanson's notes and the latent hostility of the Royal Geographical Society, Borchgrevink did not receive the honour and glory to which he believed he was entitled and which he craved. He turned his back on an ungrateful (as he saw it) nation and spent the rest of his life in Norway. Thirty years later, when he was in failing health and suffering from the illness that would kill him – though it would take four more years – Borchgrevink was belatedly awarded the Patron's Medal of the Royal Geographical Society.

The main reason for the society's antagonism was Sir Clements Markham, the president. Markham was born in 1830, just 25 years after Trafalgar. He joined the Royal Navy at 14 and while still a young man was on Horatio Austin's Franklin search expedition of 1850/1. This taste of the Arctic appears to have given him a lifelong enthusiasm for polar exploration, one he was able to indulge when he became president of the society in 1893. His lack of enthusiasm for Borchgrevink's offer to lead a

Right **Borchgrevink's claim to have reached 78°50' is viewed with suspicion by some experts. Two days later a second team headed south. They reached 78°45', but later corrected this to 78°50', a suspiciously convenient correction. Unlike Borchgrevink's team which took no photograph the second team recorded their 'furthest south'. From left to right are Hugh Evans, Louis Bernacchi and Anton Fougner photographed by Julius Johansen.**
Canterbury Museum, New Zealand

British Antarctic expedition was not straightforward. One stated view was that Borchgrevink was not a scientist and a leader should be one (a view which was altered later, Scott being appointed leader of the *Discovery* expedition because he was a navy man and *not* a scientist). It was also true that Borchgrevink came with baggage which the British found unseemly: he had sought commercial sponsorship and there was the public mud-slinging over who had been first to set foot on the continent. In reality, though, the reasons were more fundamental: Borchgrevink was a foreigner, one whose English was poor and heavily accented. When Markham discovered that Borchgrevink had obtained sponsorship from Newnes (and that it amounted to double the cash he had managed to scrape together in two years) he was incensed, and raged against him in a way that today would bring a rapid response from a libel lawyer. Markham claimed that Borchgrevink had falsified accounts over the purchase of the *Southern Cross* (and, by implication, had pocketed the difference); that he had forged the seaworthiness certificate for the ship; that he had bought poor-quality dogs; and, for good measure, that he was stupid and unprincipled. But Markham had no evidence to support either claim, or the one that Borchgrevink had embezzled Newnes' cash. The fact that Borchgrevink proved to be a poor leader and an

egotistical man cannot be used to bolster Markham's appalling outburst: that evidence only came to light two years later. However, it is likely that Markham used the information to bolster his own prejudices, which were Britain's every bit as much as they were this own.

In 1899, at the 7th International Geographical Congress, held in Berlin, Markham's speech on Antarctica ignored the contributions of all non-British explorers and proposed that to aid future exploration the continent should be divided into four quadrants, Victoria, Enderby, Ross and Weddell: three named for British explorers, the fourth for the British queen. When the British newspapers talked of the need for Antarctic exploration (one talked of it being 'feeble' that men did not know everything there was to know about his world) they spoke of it as Britain's destiny. One member of the queen's inner circle claimed that the exploration 'should be done by Englishmen... almost every name in the south has been given by this country... I should not like to see foreign names upon that hemisphere where all civilised points are inhabited by our countrymen and belong to this country.' The arrogant assumption that only Britain had the right to explore Antarctica was backed by the equally arrogant proposition that only the British knew how to do it. The latter would lead, eventually, but inevitably, to disaster.

Striving for the pole

Scott: the *Discovery*

When Markham, who had been pressing for a national expedition, finally received government assent and finance he chose Robert Falcon Scott as its leader, a strange appointment for several reasons. It could be argued that the logical candidate was the Scot William Bruce who had been the doctor and naturalist on the *Balaena*, one of the four ships of the Dundee Whaling Expedition of 1892/3 which had made important observations of seals and penguins. Bruce was to have been on the *Antarctic* expedition, but failed to reach Melbourne in time. His place was taken by Carsten Borchgrevink; how different the history of the continent might have been had the immensely competent Bruce made the trip. Bruce's application for the proposed British expedition was held in limbo for almost a year and, in frustration, finally he decided to launch his own expedition. Markham immediately forgot that this situation had been prompted by his own prevarication and wrote to Bruce in annoyance, calling the proposed Scottish expedition 'mischievous rivalry'. Markham, the old navy man, wanted a navy man in charge. He was fearful that, as with other expeditions, it might be decided to appoint a scientist to lead, with a sailor to captain the ship. That would not do; Scott was to be captain and leader. But why Scott?

Robert Falcon Scott was born on 6 June 1868 in Devonport near Plymouth, the son of a brewer. He joined the Royal Navy at the age of 13 as a cadet and, showing a reasonable intelligence, rose relatively quickly, achieving the rank of lieutenant. Markham's stated reason for appointing him is that he recognised his potential when they first met when Scott was an 18-year-old midshipman, and that chance meetings had kept them in touch. However, there is evidence that the ambitious Scott realised the promotion potential of leading the expedition and visited Markham several times to plead his cause. Whatever the reason, Scott – recently promoted to commander in the navy – was to be leader of the British national expedition. His team was to include Edward Wilson as naturalist and assistant doctor, Frank Wild (one of whose distant ancestors was James Cook), Louis Bernacchi from the *Southern Cross* expedition, and a young Irish merchant marine officer, Ernest Shackleton.

Markham attempted to impose his will on his young leader and though he did not wholly succeed he was sufficiently influential to decide upon the way in which not only this first expedition but, more crucially, Scott's fateful second trip would be conducted. Although accepting that an existing whaling ship would be adequate, Markham insisted on a new ship being built. But he ignored all the lessons learned by the Norwegians, and particularly the innovations of Colin Archer, the designer of the *Fram*. Scott visited Archer at Nansen's suggestion but was unimpressed: it was, he wrote, 'rather wasted time'. The expedition's ship, the *Discovery*, was designed by a naval architect and looked much like the Arctic ships of Markham's youth. It had their design flaws too, with poor insulation and ventilation so that the men suffered from both condensation and cold, a dreadful combination. The hull design was not rounded, so the ice had a better chance to grip the ship, a flaw that led to its being trapped for two winters. She was jerry-built and leaked badly, necessitating significant repairs in New Zealand: the seawater in the hold also spoiled some supplies. Markham wanted the ship to overwinter, for no better reason than it was romantic. The navy objected on grounds of the economic madness of allowing a research vessel to be out of action for so long, and the safety issue. Borchgrevink had demonstrated the correct method for overwintering parties: sadly, pointing this out to Markham probably hardened his opinion.

Markham was against the use of dogs on xenophobic sentimental and aesthetic grounds. He acknowledged that they had proved to be of some value to Eskimos, but in a way which implied that nothing better could be expected of savages. He was appalled that Peary's Greenland trips had resulted in the death of dogs, through both overwork and the expedient of feeding the weakest dog to the remainder, and considered that such cruelty could not be justified. Even Nansen is on record as stating that while he agreed it was cruel to the dogs the alternative was to be cruel to men. The discussion raises a moral issue: is it right for men to make animals suffer in pursuit of their own ends? Had he taken such a stance Markham's position would be more understandable, and might even have done him credit. But that is not why he dismissed Nansen's view as being of 'no value'. Occupation of the moral high ground was something the upper echelons of Victorian Britain took for granted, and was not the point. Markham's view of dogs was based on the British hunting and shooting tradition: a man who would exhaust a dog or, worse still, kill one to feed others was the sort who might shoot a fox, and not to be countenanced.

Markham was against skis too. He had neither used or seen them, nor, apparently, spoken to anyone who had, but he was not a man willing to let facts get in the way of a well-held prejudice. Markham was a Victorian and Victorian Britain not only ruled the civilised world but knew how to. The nation had just witnessed sailors manhauling the carriage bearing the coffin of Queen Victoria across London: a beautiful vision, and one which could be easily transferred to the Antarctic. The use of dogs would ruin that romantic image of strong men hauling sledges through deep snow. Men being manly, men performing astonishing deeds in spite of appalling conditions and odds, men behaving heroically and gloriously – men being Englishmen.

Scott visited Nansen and was persuaded of the merits of both dogs and skis, but failed to understand that to learn to handle both required training. He thought that the techniques could be picked up easily in a week or two and so dispensed with dog handlers (Borchgrevink had taken two Lapps) or formal ski lessons. One outcome of the latter was that a member of the *Discovery*'s crew became the first man to sustain a significant injury on Antarctica (if Hanson's death is overlooked) when he broke a leg skiing. Another was a diary entry for 6 January 1903 when Scott notes, 'On the whole our skis have been of little value... dropped all the dogs out of the traces and pulled steadily ourselves for seven hours, covering ten good miles...' So, despite Nansen's advice on the advantages of dogs and skis we now have a picture of Scott's men hauling a heavy sledge across the ice at about 2kmph (1¼mph), their skis on the sledge and their dogs wandering along beside it. If the eventual consequences of this lack of understanding were not so tragic the image would be laughable.

The *Discovery* left Britain in August 1901, Scott's leadership style – harsh and aloof: he insisted on daily deck scrubbing even when the temperature was sub-zero – being typically naval and causing some resentment among the men. The ship called at New Zealand for repair and to load the dogs (which had been shipped out separately). Sheep were also loaded – twice as many as dogs – to provide fresh meat later. In January 1902 the expedition discovered Edward VII Land which defines the eastern end of the Ross Ice Shelf. Scott then rose to 240m (550ft) in a hydrogen-filled balloon to gain man's first aerial view of the continent. Wilson was extremely caustic, noting that Scott 'knowing nothing whatever about the business, insisted on going up first and through no fault of his own came back safely'. On the second balloon ride Shackleton took the first aerial photograph of Antarctica.

Scott now announced that the ship would indeed overwinter, despite naval misgivings, causing further resentment in the crew. The *Discovery* was sailed into McMurdo Sound (named by James Clark Ross for Archibald McMurdo, a lieutenant on the *Terror*: it was thought to be a bay until Scott discovered that what Ross had thought to be part of the continent was an island) and a hut was erected nearby. Scott's plan for his men to learn sledging and skiing now got underway. The results were mixed, the dogs proving unmanageable, the men being divided into pro- and anti-ski factions. The main problem, apart from the fact that cross-country skiing takes a long time to master, was that Scott had taken Nansen's advice and brought the

old-fashioned single long stick rather than the twin sticks that were now becoming standard in the Nordic countries. Scott had also failed to bring 'skins' for the ski bases. Consequently, unless the snow was just right, men hauling sledges found their skis sliding backwards, a tiring and frustrating experience which led many to abandon skis altogether.

When summer came Scott selected Wilson and Shackleton to join him on a trek south, a trip which he obviously hoped might actually reach the pole itself. They set out on 11 November 1901 with five sledges, but their dogs pulled them in a single line, an inefficient arrangement. They also took skis, but did not use them at all times. Because of the lack of supply dumps and the large weight of food the trio had to backtrack frequently so that for every mile route they made, they effectively travelled three. By 25 November they had passed the 80th parallel, the first men to do so, but by now it was clear they would not make the pole: their supplies were running low, the first of the dogs had died, and the flat ice shelf ahead was leading to a range of substantial mountains, not all the way south as Scott had hoped. There was also friction between the trekkers. One day Scott shouted 'Come here, you bloody fools' to Wilson and Shackleton. Quietly Wilson asked if Scott was speaking to him. When Scott said no, Shackleton said it must then have been him. Scott declined to answer and Shackleton told him that he 'was the worst bloody fool of the lot' and that 'every time you dare to speak to me like that, you'll get it back'. Perhaps this marked the start of the future rivalry between the pair.

Above **The first-ever balloon launch on Antarctica. Robert Falcon Scott was taken aloft, to the disgust of Edward Wilson.**
Scott Polar Research Institute, University of Cambridge, UK

Right **The hut at Hut Point at the southern end of Ross Island, with, beyond it, the *Discovery* in McMurdo Sound.**
Scott Polar Research Institute, University of Cambridge, UK

Left **Edward Wilson, who accompanied Scott on both his expeditions and died with him returning from the pole, was a gifted artist. This painting shows the *Discovery* close to an iceberg.**
Scott Polar Research Institute, University of Cambridge, UK

Above **The return of the southern party. Scott and Wilson are greeted by Reginald Koettlitz (the expedition's surgeon/doctor who was known as Cutlets to his colleagues) while, some way behind (see figures far right), the sick Shackleton is helped in.**
Scott Polar Research Institute, University of Cambridge, UK

But despite the friction the trek continued, the men now forced to feed their dogs with dog meat. Wilson was the unhappiest about this: no means of killing the dogs had been brought and so he had to use a scalpel. Both men and dogs were also hungry, their inexperience in polar travel allowing the British to unwittingly put their heads into a noose. By 24 December Scott and Shackleton, both weak with hunger, were exhibiting symptoms of scurvy. Wilson wanted the trek to end, but Scott insisted on them pushing on reach 82°S, which they reached on 28 December. Scott and Wilson continued to 82°17'S, by definition a new furthest south record, while Shackleton was left at camp at 82°15'S, nominally to look after the dogs.

The weather, which had been remarkably good up until then, turned and the three were very lucky in finding their first food dump on the return journey. They killed the last of the dogs and began a slow and difficult journey manhauling back to the ship. Weakened by hunger and plagued by bad weather the noose now tightened. Had they missed any of their dumps they would almost certainly have died, and

given the occasional limited visibility they were fortunate not to; even so they were still lucky to make it to the ship. Shackleton became very ill on 18 January, and Wilson thought he would die. A lesser man probably would have, but Shackleton's ferocious will kept him going. On 3 February, after 93 days on the ice, the exhausted trio reached the *Discovery*.

At the ship Scott found that a relief ship (the *Morning*, captained by the William Colbeck who had had so many problems with Borchgrevink on the *Southern Cross*) had arrived. Scott also heard that Albert Armitage, his deputy on the expedition, had led a sledge trip on to the Antarctic ice cap. Armitage was therefore the first man to have set foot on the ice cap, reaching an altitude of 2,740m (9,000ft). His team had travelled 385km (240 miles) and reached 78°S. But Scott also found that the *Discovery* was firmly iced in and that a second overwintering was inevitable. Many of his crew went home on the *Morning*, as did Shackleton, Scott clearly deciding that Antarctica was not big enough for both of them.

After an uneventful winter Scott used the second summer to retrace Armitage's route across Victoria Land (but, pointedly, without taking Armitage). Sending some of his men back when they could not keep up with his punishing manhauling schedule Scott travelled about 1,100km (680 miles) achieving a 'furthest west' mark. The two seamen who accompanied him to this point were William Lashly and one who was later to achieve immortality on the continent, Edgar Evans. The *Discovery* was finally released from the ice on 14 February 1904, Scott returning home to the hostility of his navy superiors but the adulation of a nation. He wrote a best-selling book, but in it showed that he had learned little from his near-disastrous trip south and his equally fraught westward push with Lashly and Evans. Each journey had teetered on the brink of oblivion because of the use of manhauling and the narrow safety margins against poor weather and conditions. Yet Scott wrote that the use of dogs 'does rob sledge-travelling of much of its glory... no journey ever made with dogs can approach the height of that fine conception which is realised when a party of men go forth to face hardships, dangers, and difficulties with their own unaided efforts, and by days and weeks of hard physical labour succeed in solving some problem of the great unknown. Surely in this case the conquest is more nobly and splendidly won.' Markham, his benefactor, agreed: 'The sledge journeys without dogs are quite unequalled.' Markham was right

of course, the journeys *were* unequalled; and given the limited experience of Scott and his men they were remarkable, Scott also showed astonishing powers of endurance and great courage. But his failure to heed the lessons of both his own and others' experience were to prove fatal.

Drygalski

Nine days after the *Discovery* departed from England the *Gauss* left the Elbe estuary, carrying the German Antarctic Expedition, led by von Drygalski. Though the Germans had been active in the Arctic in a relatively minor way, this was their first foray south. It rankled that despite the fact that Karl Gauss had made the most important contribution to the study of terrestrial magnetism it had been other nations that had followed up the work with practical science. Now with other nations again heading south after the brief lull in activities it would be, as von Drygalski notes in his book on it, 'a matter of national honour and duty not to lag behind'. Even so, little was actually done until de Gerlache sailed south in the *Belgica*. For Germany to be upstaged by Belgium, a much smaller country with a short coastline, limited seafaring tradition and equally limited resources, was a shock. The response was an upsurge of nationalist fervour: 'Germany too should become actively involved, unless she were once again prepared to stand humbly by, leaving the glory to other nations' and '...it is important to show the flag, to demonstrate Germany's might and power... and bring honour to the fatherland'.

Despite the patriotic drive for an early expedition, the Germans, as would be expected, planned well. Erich von Drygalski, a 36-year old physicist with a particular interest in glaciology, had led a successful expedition to west Greenland in the early 1890s. The ship which carried the expedition was specially built, and named for Karl Gauss. The *Gauss* was captained by Hans Ruser, the total complement of 32 men (in Antarctica, others were left en route) including four other scientists. The

Germans therefore followed the model of previous successful expeditions, splitting leadership of the expedition from captaincy of the ship, that had been rejected by the British. The ship sailed to the Kerguélen islands to collect 40 dogs, then headed south, discovering Wilhelm II Land on 21 February 1902. However, late that day the ship became trapped in the ice and despite attempts over the next week to break free – including the use of explosives – it was apparent by early March that the *Gauss* was imprisoned for the winter at a position just north of the Antarctic Circle.

From its winter position the scientists did what work they could. The extinct volcano Gaussberg was observed and named – and later climbed – and von Drygalski went up to about 500m (1,640ft) in a captive balloon to observe it, finding the air at that height so warm he could remove his gloves.

The expedition zoologist, Ernst Vanhöffen, had a dredge line fitted below the ship to collect fish. When the line snapped, another was rigged by attaching it to the foot of an Emperor penguin. Two holes, one at the bow, one at the stern, were drilled through the ice and the bird was forced into one. The penguin made valiant efforts to get out, but eventually swam to the second hole. After a couple of abortive attempts when the line came free, the method succeeded. The penguins were also used in less scientific ways, their skinned bodies being used to feed the ship's boilers, the high oil content making them a good substitute for coal. In the context of the expeditions of the time, which overwintered almost exclusively on seal and penguin meat, and fed dog meat to dogs, it was a straightforwardly pragmatic solution to a fuel crisis. There were also several sledge journeys south, one reaching about 71°S, a slightly risky idea as the ship was moving in the ice currents.

The following spring it seemed that the *Gauss* was so firmly held that a second winter was likely, but von Drygalski noticed that the ice was melting more quickly where it was covered by the fall-out from the ship's funnel smoke. As a physicist he rapidly realised why heat from the sun is absorbed by dark objects, and laid out a channel – the 'dirt road' – which was made from boiler ash and any other dark rubbish to hand, causing the underlying ice to thaw. Saws and explosives were also used, but it was the dirt road that formed the escape channel, the ship finally being freed in late February.

It had been an interesting and, scientifically, successful expedition. From the collected data the meteorologist Wilhelm Meinardus was able to infer the existence of the Antarctic Convergence (the narrow confluence – 30–50km/20–30 miles wide – where the warm waters of the Atlantic, Indian and Pacific Oceans meet the cold waters of the Antarctic), though its existence was not confirmed for another 20 years. In all the scientific data filled 20 volumes, and took von Drygalski 30 years to write up. But the Kaiser and the German public were not impressed: little land had been discovered and the furthest south the team had reached was north of the *Discovery*'s winter base. When von Drygalski asked the Kaiser's permission to return to Antarctica his request was refused.

Nordenskjöld

The summer of 1901 saw yet another expedition preparing to leave Europe, led by the Swede Otto Nordenskjöld, nephew of Adolf Erik Nordenskiöld, the first man to sail the North-East Passage. The difference in spelling of the men's surname ('j' rather than 'i',) is modern and follows the currently preferred Swedish forms of the two names. Otto was a 32-year-old geologist who had organised the expedition privately, the Royal Swedish Academy of Sciences having objected when he sought government backing. Though he managed to raise the cash to get the expedition underway, Nordenskjöld was debt-ridden for years after and much of the proposed scientific work had to be abandoned while the scientists hunted for seals when food ran short. Nordenskjöld's ship, the *Antarctic*, was captained by a Norwegian, Carl Anton Larsen, a man with plenty of polar experience: he had been on the *Jason* which took Nansen to Greenland for his crossing of the ice cap, and had also been to Antarctica twice before, firstly in 1892/3 to search for whales, then again in 1893/4 when he explored the northern end of the Antarctic Peninsula. Larsen is credited with the first use of skis on Antarctica and with discovering petrified wood on Seymour Island. He also sailed along the edge of the ice shelf which now bears his name.

The *Antarctic* sailed late, in October 1901, and did not leave Buenos Aires until late December, so the plan of establishing a winter base at the southern end of the Antarctic Peninsula was soon abandoned: there was too much sea ice for the ship to penetrate far enough south, and the Larsen Ice Shelf lay between the expedition and the peninsula. Nordenskjöld therefore set up camp on Snow Hill Island which lies south of Seymour Island (and east of James Ross Island and the peninsula). As soon as the wintering hut had been erected, the ship departed leaving six men (Nordenskjöld and five others) behind.

The winter was a hard one, with frequent storms and low temperatures. When summer came Nordenskjöld and two men set out southwards by dog-sledge, hoping to meet the *Antarctica* at Robertson Island, but had to return when the ship did not arrive. It also failed to rendezvous at Snow Hill, forcing the six men to prepare for a second winter. The ship had attempted to sail the Antarctic Sound (between the peninsula and Joinville Island) but had been stopped by the ice. Realising it could not hope to reach the Snow Hill men, three men went ashore at Hope Bay (in late December 1902) intending to sledge to the camp and return with the winter party. The ship retreated north to escape the ice, then went east around Joinville Island and tried to go south again, but she soon became trapped in the pack. On 11 January 1903 a large ice floe was driven into the ship. With no hope of repairing the damage the crew salvaged what they could, but stayed with the ship until she sank on 12 February. The crew then trekked across the sea ice to Paulet Island.

The Swedes were now in three groups, none of them knowing the state of the other two. At Hope Bay the sledging trio headed for Snow Hill, but were unable to cross the dangerously part-thawed sea ice separating the winter camp from James Ross Island. They returned to Hope Bay and, when the ship failed to return, built a makeshift hut in which they overwintered. The windowless hut, sealed against the bitter polar winter, was heated by burning seal blubber. They also used blubber for cooking so by winter's end the hut walls, the men and their clothing were caked in black soot and grease. When summer 1903 came they sledged off towards Snow Hill again, and by an extraordinary coincidence met Nordenskjöld and Ole Jonassen who had sledged to James Ross Island. Approached by three black-faced men dressed in greasy rags Nordenskjöld was convinced he had found continental natives, his delight at meeting fellow expedition members being tempered by the loss of a momentous discovery. Jonassen was less thrilled at the prospect and took out his revolver just in case: the point where the two groups met, on Vega Island, named by Nordenskjöld for his uncle's ship, was named Cape Well-Met.

On Paulet Island the remnant *Antarctic* crew killed over 1,000 Adélie penguins and overwintered, one man dying after a prolonged illness. When spring arrived Larsen set out with five others in an open boat salvaged from the ship, going first to Hope Bay where a grimy

Top **The stone hut at Hope Bay. This was built by Andersson, Duse and Grunden after they had failed to make it to Snow Hill Island. The three men spent the winter of 1903 here.**
From O. Nordenskjöld *Antarctic II*.
Courtesy of the Swedish Polar Research Secretariat

Above **The three sledgers who, dirty and dressed in greasy, ragged clothing convinced Otto Nordenskjöld he had discovered Antarctic natives. From left to right the men are Duse, Andersson and Grunden.**
From J.G. Andersson *Antarctic*.
Courtesy of the Swedish Polar Research Secretariat

note directed him to Snow Hill. At the same time, concerned because the *Antarctic* was well overdue, the Swedes sent a relief ship, as did the Argentineans. The Argentinean navy gunboat *Uruguay* arrived first, reaching Snow Hill Island where two of Nordenskjöld's men were spotted. The relieved pair and two Argentineans arrived at the camp just hours before Larsen arrived. Incredibly all three Swedish groups had met up, the remaining men on Paulet Island being taken off as the *Uruguay* headed north.

It might be assumed that the drama of the expedition detracted from the science, but Nordenskjöld's was arguably the best scientific trip of the time; the science report ran to six volumes and 4,000 pages. The Swedes had found numerous fossils, including that of a giant penguin, and made important discoveries on plantlife, oceanography and geology.

Charcot

The Argentineans had rescued the Swedes, getting south ahead of the Swedish relief ship and also ahead of the *Français*, which carried the French Antarctic Expedition under the leadership of Dr Jean-Baptiste Charcot, son of Jean-Martin Charcot, a world-famous neurologist who is said to have influenced Freud. On his father's death Jean-Baptiste inherited a small fortune in cash and art and used it to buy a ship with the intention of exploring the Arctic (an idea which, judged by later events, was not greeted with loud enthusiasm by his wife, a granddaughter of Victor Hugo). When Charcot heard that Nordenskjöld was missing he decided to sail south instead, and when government and public money was donated in response to this humanitarian decision, it meant that he led a national expedition. It did not start well. The *Français* with its crew of 21 (Charcot, Captain Ernest Cholet and 19 others) and pet pig Toby left Le Havre on 15 August 1903, but the expedition was less than two minutes old when a hawser snapped, one flying end killing a seaman named Maignan. The funeral and enquiry delayed the new departure for 12 days. When the *Français* finally left Adrian de Gerlache, leader of the *Belgica* expedition, had joined the party (though he left in Buenos Aires, unable to stand the separation from his new fiancée).

Finding that the *Uruguay* had rescued Nordenskjöld, Charcot sailed for the western side of the Antarctic Peninsula, wintering on Booth Island, which forms the western side of the famous Lemaire Channel. Charcot's decision not to venture into the Ross Sea was to avoid any problems over British claims, a fact that Scott noted, calling Charcot 'the gentleman of the Pole'. The French team seem to have enjoyed a pleasant winter – there were early trials of a motorised sledge – apart from losing Toby, who ate a quantity of fish still attached to fish-hooks, and died a miserable death. The ship was moored in Port Charcot, a narrow inlet across the mouth of which a rope was slung to keep the pack ice out. The *Français* broke out easily in late December 1904, though then hit a rock and needed rapid repairs before limping back to South America where she was sold. When the French eventually reached home, Charcot's wife divorced him on the grounds of desertion.

Charcot remarried, insisting on a prenuptial agreement with his new wife which allowed him to go on expeditions. In 1908 he headed south again, in the *Pourquoi Pas?* naming Marguerite Bay for his accommodating wife and overwintering on Petermann Island: he also discovered and named Charcot Land – now known to be an island, Charcot Island – for his father. In 1937 he sailed the *Pourquoi Pas?* to Iceland where she was lost, with all but one crewman drowned.

Shackleton: the *Nimrod*

Back in Britain after his return from the *Discovery* Ernest Shackleton nursed a burning desire to return. He writes in *Heart of Antarctica*, his account of the *Nimrod* expedition, 'I had been invalided home…', but must

There was one other team in the south during this time, that of William Bruce, the Scot who many believe should have led the *Discovery* expedition and who so infuriated Sir Clements Markham by organising a 'rival' trip. Refused government money, Bruce then sought the backing of Andrew Coats, the London-born, but Glasgow-based, clothing magnate. Bruce was a proud Scot, which appealed to Coats'

"Music hath Charms."
This Photo was taken off Coats Land, Lat. 74°01'S Long 22°W discovered by the Scottish National Antarctic Expedition

Scott Polar Research Centre, University of Cambridge, UK

nationalism. He backed the trip, allowing Bruce to buy the *Scotia*, a Norwegian whaler, in which the Scottish National Antarctic Expedition set sail in November 1902. The team wintered on Laurie Island in the South Orkneys, then carried out a remarkable amount of hydrographic and zoological research in the Weddell Sea during the summer of 1902/3 before overwintering on the ice-bound ship in 1903. When freed the ship returned to South America, leaving six men on Laurie Island where they made an impressive study of the local penguins. The *Scotia* returned with three Argentineans who joined two of the six men on the island, the others rejoining the ship which headed south to 74°S, discovering Coats Land. The Argentineans eventually took over the Laurie Island base, changing its name from Osmond House to Orcadas. The Bruce expedition may have made limited discoveries in terms of new land – though Coats Land was a significant find – but from a scientific point of view, and from consideration of Bruce's leadership, it has never received the credit it deserves. It is also rarely mentioned that it was on this expedition that bagpipes were first played on the Antarctic continent. The photograph of the piper serenading an apparently entranced penguin was made into a postcard. It is enchanting, but in order to keep the penguin close to the skirling pipes it had to have one foot tied to the ice.

have known – or been suspicious at the very least – that his health had not been the entire reason for his departure. He had already said when still on the *Discovery* that one day he would return and show himself a better man than Scott. This resentment was sharpened by the heroic reception Scott received and by the account of the southern journey in Scott's *Voyage of the Discovery* in which he referred to Shackleton as 'our invalid' and in other derogatory ways, and implied that the trek had failed because of Shackleton's 'sudden break-down'. The situation was probably not helped by the fact that Shackleton not only had a head start on the lecture circuit, having reached Britain first, but was a better speaker (which many suggest was due to his Anglo-Irish heritage: he was born in Kilkea in 1874), Scott's jealousy further fuelling Shackleton's resentment.

Almost certainly aware that there was little chance of his being invited on another Scott expedition, Shackleton decided to launch his own, working quickly to ensure a return to the south before any second Scott trip could be organised. The problem, as always, was finance, but this was solved in February 1907 when William Beardmore, a rich industrialist and shipbuilder based in Glasgow, for whom Shackleton was working as an early form of public relations officer, agreed to fund the trip.

Shackleton bought a 41-year-old Dundee-built sealing ship called the *Nimrod*. He intended to change her name to *Endurance*, a short form of his family motto *Fortitudue Vincimus* (By Fortitude – or Endurance – We Conquer) but in the end did not. He attempted to sign up several members of the *Discovery*'s crew, but many turned down the invitation. Of these the one that caused Shackleton's greatest pain was Edward Wilson: Wilson had taken on work and would not give it up. Worse was to follow when Wilson took Scott's side after a row broke out over the use of the Discovery base. Scott had decided to return to Antarctica – but not yet – and claimed 'squatter's rights' on the site. Indeed, he tried to claim rights to the whole Ross Sea. Shackleton was aghast, but under pressure from Wilson, who saw the dispute as an issue of morals, agreed to stay east of 170°W.

Shackleton visited Nansen who was now the ambassador in London for newly independent Norway. Though only in his mid-40s Nansen had acquired a (deserved) status as the Great Man of polar exploration. To the younger explorers of the time – Amundsen, Scott and Shackleton amongst others – he was a mentor, a polar guru, and God-speed from him had almost taken on the aura of a papal blessing. Nansen was amazed that Shackleton had learned so little from the *Discovery* trip. He was intending to walk not ski, and instead of taking dogs he was taking ponies. If the former, given Shackleton's own experience of skis on his journey with Scott and Wilson (when they had arguably saved his life on the return trip), was beyond comprehension, the latter was beyond reason. Ironically, after Nansen had met Frederick Jackson on Franz Josef Land following the *Fram* expedition they had discussed the use of horses in Antarctica. The incredulous Nansen had advised against it: now here, despite all the evidence in support of dogs, was another Briton with the same idea. An even greater irony is that Shackleton got his idea for horses from Jackson, who had tried both animals on his expedition to Franz Josef Land. The dogs were a complete success, the horses a constant problem: nevertheless Jackson had come down in favour of horses. History does not record Nansen's view, if any, of Shackleton's decision to take a motor car as well.

The *Nimrod* left London in July 1907, stopping in Australia where the geologist Douglas Mawson was added to the crew, and New Zealand where shortage of space meant that five of the Manchurian ponies which had already arrived there had to be left behind. Shackleton also now realised that to conserve coal he would need to be towed to the ice edge. He appealed for help and the Union Steamship Company of New Zealand offered a tramp steamer (the *Koonya*, six times the size of *Nimrod*), its cost defrayed by the company and the New Zealand government. The tow was a nightmare journey through the mountainous seas of a ferocious storm during which one pony was injured so badly it had to be destroyed: another injured animal was also put down later. Close to the ice edge the *Koonya* unhitched and turned for home, the *Nimrod* sailing on to the edge of the ice shelf in search of the inlet from where the *Discovery*'s balloon launches had been made. The inlet was gone, presumably carved away, and a second inlet – christened Bay of Whales for obvious reasons – could not be reached because of the sea ice.

With the time until the *Nimrod* would have to depart for winter diminishing quickly, Shackleton was forced to break his promise to Scott and cross the 'forbidden' 170°W line for McMurdo Sound, an action that caused him great distress. Unable to reach Discovery Hut because of sea ice, Shackleton built a new hut near Cape Royds, about 35km (22 miles) to the north (and therefore further from the pole: the intended camp on the ice shelf was at least 100km/62 miles – straight-

line distance – closer). With everything unloaded the *Nimrod* left for New Zealand carrying secret orders from Shackleton for the dismissal of her captain, Rupert England. Shackleton had disagreed with England several times over what he saw as the captain's timidity when in the pack ice, and was deeply concerned that any over-caution in 1910 might lead to his team having to be relieved (worse still rescued) by Scott. That he could not allow. Ironically in view of his own departure from the *Discovery*, Shackleton cited England's poor health as the reason for the dismissal. Only when the *Nimrod* arrived back in New Zealand did England discovered he had been sacked. Subsequent details of his conflict led to livid headlines in British newspapers and from those Scott learned that Shackleton had broken his promise not to cross 170°W. The outraged Scott branded Shackleton a liar and swore never to have anything to do with him again, a promise unlikely to have broken Shackleton's heart.

To give his men something to do Shackleton suggested a first ascent of Mount Erebus, though he decided not to go himself when Eric Marshall, the expedition's surgeon refused to allow him to travel unless he was examined. Marshall clearly suspected Shackleton of being ill, and Shackleton refused to be examined, presumably because he was nervous of what Marshall might find, resulting in a conflict between the two. Six men – Marshall, Adams, Brocklehurst, David, Mackay and Mawson – set out in equipment that would have been censurable had not the peak been straightforward. In the absence of climbing equipment they improvised crampons with nails hammered through

Left **Shackleton's hut at Cape Royds.**
Frank Todd, courtesy of Quark Expeditions

Right **The interior of Shackleton's hut at Cape Royds.**
C. Carvalho, courtesy of Quark Expeditions

leather straps which they attached to their boots (though only some of them had time to make these as the decision to climb was taken at short notice). They towed a 270kg (595lb) sledge of equipment. Though gently sloping, Erebus is 3,794m (12,448ft) high, every metre of which had to be climbed from the sea-level hut. After two nights the six left the sledge as a dump. They also left the tent poles as too difficult to carry, so had to sleep under the fabric and cook in the open. One of their sleeping bags was enormous, constructed to accommodate three men, its vastness overburdening whoever carried it. Brocklehurst eventually stopped because of altitude sickness, but the other five reached the top. The five-day struggle was rewarded with a view into the deep, steam-filled crater.

During the winter some of the expedition novices were taught the very basics of snowcraft, involving little more than ski-less manhauling trips. The motor car was driven a few kilometres (a first for Antarctic mechanised transport, but of extremely limited practical use). In New Zealand Shackleton had found nine dogs, the descendants of Borchgrevink's 1900 team, and as an afterthought had taken them; but the winter training did not include any work with these. For the summer Shackleton decided on two objectives. He

Above **Among its many firsts, Shackleton's *Nimrod* expedition was the first to use a motor car on Antarctica. The car – an Arrol-Johnston, the gift of expedition sponsor William Beardmore – was not a great success.**
Richard Sale Collection

Right **Looking into the crater of Mount Erebus after the first ascent.**
Richard Sale Collection

would lead a team of four (himself, Jameson Adams, Eric Marshall and Frank Wild) south, while Edgworth David would lead Douglas Mawson and Alistair Mackay in an attempt to reach the South Magnetic Pole. Of the ten ponies only four remained (in addition to the two which had to be destroyed, four had died). Shackleton would take these. David's team therefore had no ponies and it was decided that they would not use dogs either.

Shackleton's party set out on 29 October 1908. At first they made reasonable time despite the ponies often sinking belly-deep into soft snow, but it soon became clear that ponies were not suited to polar work. They became chilled and had to have blankets draped over them when they stopped, snow walls built to protect them from the wind and their food required thawing. They also did not have the 'advantage' that dogs have of being willing to cannibalise their trace-mates. But ponies do provide a large quantity of 'food on the hoof', early supply dumps being organised around a pony carcass, animals being shot in turn as

they weakened. The men fared better, with no real illnesses (other than Adams having a tooth pulled without anaesthetic, a miserable procedure not helped when Marshall's first attempt merely broke the tooth), though there were inevitable tensions. Marshall's view of Shackleton deteriorated and his concerns over Shackleton's health increased. By contrast, Wild's view of the leader steadily improved: it was on this trip that he first referred to Shackleton as 'the Boss', a nickname which stuck. Despite Wild's fear that they would be lucky to get to the pole and 'luckier still to get back' he was willing to follow wherever the Boss led.

The team passed Scott's furthest south mark and, hauling parallel to the coast, aimed for the 'Golden Gateway', an apparent pass in the mountains (now called the Transantarctic Mountains) ahead. It turned out to be only the entrance to a glacier (named Beardmore by Shackleton after the expedition's sponsor). The glacier was a nightmare; the men had no crampons and Socks, the only remaining pony, disappeared into a crevasse. As they climbed higher the thinning air also became a problem (the pole lies at the centre of a plateau lying at about 3,000m/10,000ft). As time was lost rations were reduced to maintain the possibility of reaching the pole, so the four were constantly hungry. Eventually Shackleton realised that reaching the pole would require an all-or-nothing dash. The four dumped what they could, but it was soon apparent that they were still going too slowly. By 3 January 1909 they were at 87°22'S, still 250km (about 160 miles) short of their goal. They were exhausted, cold (their body temperatures had fallen, a dangerous sign of hypothermia) hungry and dehydrated (fuel, too, being rationed). It was clear they had come to the end, more so when it was realised that even now it was possible that they might miss the *Nimrod* on their return. The weather, which had been excellent early in the trip, was now foul. But Shackleton would not give in. He asked who would continue with him and, with varying degrees of reluctance, all agreed. Shackleton was determined to get within 160km (100 miles) of the pole, so the men dumped half of what little they had and, on 4 January, continued in temperatures sometimes below −30°C, wearing just one layer of underwear, two sweaters and a thin windsuit (but no trousers beneath the leggings) and still hauling over 30kg (66lb) each. But now the weather worsened, a blizzard trapping them in their tents for 60 hours. When it blew over (9 January) the frost-bitten men pushed on one last time, finally reaching 88°23'S. They were 155km (97 miles) from the pole. His target reached, Shackleton bowed to the inevitable defeat and turned around.

The return journey was a nightmare, the four on the edge of starvation for almost the whole 1,170km (730 miles). Several times they ran out of food altogether and only luck allowed them to reach the next of their supply dumps: bad weather would inevitably have meant death. All collapsed at some point, Marshall taking the lead at one stage, Shackleton, who had been very ill, recovering at the end. Yet despite their poor health and limited food their willpower and stamina were phenomenal: one day they marched over 46km (29 miles). Eventually, after 123 days on the trek, and having left the sick Marshall, and Adams as nurse, at a last camp, Shackleton and Wild reached the base hut. The *Nimrod* and everyone had gone, but unbelievably the ship returned at just the right moment, intent on dropping off a wintering crew to search for the quartet's bodies. They had, after all,

Above **Adams, Wild and Shackleton at their furthest south.**
Richard Sale Collection

only 91 days supply of food and so must have perished.

With the return of the ship Shackleton found that the magnetic pole team had triumphed. David, Mackay and Mawson had started three weeks before Shackleton, travelling the first few kilometres of their journey by car before the vehicle became embedded in a snow drift. They then manhauled, starting with loads of 320kg (790lb) including the sledges. The team stayed on the sea-ice edge parallel to the coast, following a route chosen by Mawson who, of the three, had the best nose for a line, but always searching for a way to reach South Victoria Land. It was a precarious route as the sea ice was often fragile, threatening to tip the trio into the sea. Often, too, the ice was wet, making their boots wet and clinging to the sledges so that their daily rate of travel averaged only about 8km (around 5 miles). Mawson was concerned by this slow rate, claiming it was due, in part, to David's age – he was 51, the other two being under 30 – and that as the sea ice might have melted by the time of their return they might run out of food and fuel. He therefore suggested eating seal meat cooked on blubber oil in a biscuit-tin stove, lit with a calico food-bag wick. This saved their supplies, but the sledges remained heavy for a longer period and the change of diet caused acute diarrhoea.

The team's weather was reasonable: on one day it was so warm David gave his feet a snow bath. By 1 December they had reached the Drygalski Ice Tongue,

Above **Mackay, David and Mawson at the South Magnetic Pole.**
Richard Sale Collection

under three weeks, maintaining their target average of 16km (10 miles) each day despite the constant climbing. They estimated their height gain using a hypometer which calculates the boiling point of water and, therefore, the air pressure. The lower boiling point was a matter of contention in the party: how long should tea be allowed to boil before serving? The trip was not straightforward, however. The men had reduced their rations and were all hungry, and the occasional days of intense cold and biting wind had caused the skin of their faces to peel: Mawson's lips were sealed so tight each morning with congealed blood that he had difficulty opening his mouth.

On 16 January they arrived at the mean position of the South Magnetic Pole, as calculated by Mawson, the team's navigator. Because of the relative crudeness of his equipment Mawson was only able to establish the general area of the pole, but by taking several measurements the team were able to move across it. At what they considered the exact spot the three erected a Union Jack for the obligatory photograph and David spoke words given to him by Shackleton, claiming the area around the magnetic pole for the British Empire (an interesting idea given that the pole moves: at present it is offshore of Terre Adélie and regularly sailed over by tourist ships). At the time of the flag raising and photograph, for which the three went bareheaded, the temperature was −18°C.

On the return David hoped they might average 26km (just over 16 miles) daily, so as to meet the *Nimrod* close to the Drygalski Ice Tongue and avoid the potentially dangerous, perhaps impossible, return journey along the coast. At this point his account of the journey became dominated by food: its lack, its relative abundance, its form. He reports an argument when Mawson added sugar to the day's hoosh (what the British called the soup made by mixing pemmican – dried, ground meat and fat – and dry biscuit in boiling water). The variable weather continued, the three men being particularly plagued by strong winds which, with temperatures falling to −30°C, chilled them. But they maintained their target 26km (16 miles) average, in part helped by the fact that they were hauling downhill over reasonable ground and had rigged a mast and sail to the sledge to take advantage of the incessant wind. They reached their dump at the head of the glacier on 30 January, but the descent of the glacier was as arduous as the climb up it. The men fell into crevasses, the sledge overturned often, and Mawson broke through the ice on a glacial pool and went up to his waist in

the ice shelf which defines the southern edge of Terra Nova Bay. Their first attempt to cross this failed, putting the expedition in jeopardy, but a second attempt succeeded, though it took eight days to cross the tongue because of hummocky ice. It took a further two weeks to find a route up the Larsen Glacier on to the plateau, though this included a three-day rest period (on one day of which the sun was so hot their food had to be shielded from it, while two days later there was a blizzard). On a glacier Mawson fell into a crevasse, but was rescued without incident – he even had the presence of mind to excavate some interesting snow crystals while in the crevasse.

Finally the trio emerged on the rising Antarctic plateau, the unbroken view ahead suggesting they were over the worst. They were now at an altitude of about 850m (2,800ft), some 1,350m (4,460ft) below the magnetic pole – though they did not know this – and about 300km (185 miles) from it. After making a dump of some of their supplies they covered this distance in freezing water. On 3 February they arrived at the coast and were able to supplement their diet with seal and penguin meat.

The plan had been for the returning *Nimrod* to sail close to the shore looking for the men, but they had no way of knowing whether she had already passed the spot or was still many days away. Fearful of the possibly horrendous journey along the coast the exhausted David gave the leadership of the team to Mawson who, despite an injured leg, had shown himself the most capable of the three. Barely had this transfer been made when a gunshot announced the arrival of the *Nimrod*. On this expedition remarkable coincidences had become commonplace.

Though Shackleton felt the loss of the pole keenly, the expedition had been a major success. It was only 14 years since men had first (officially) stepped on Antarctica, only nine since the first overwintering, barely six since the first attempt to journey inland. Now *Nimrod*'s men had journeyed within 160km (100 miles) of the pole and stood on the South Magnetic Pole; and they had all returned safely. The achievement of David, Mawson and Mackay was overlooked in the praise of Shackleton's team, but it was every bit as magnificent. In 120 days they had travelled almost 2,000km (about 1,200 miles) without serious mishap. Apart from the first few kilometres in the motor car they had manhauled all the way. Irrespective of remarks that can be made about the lack of skis and dogs it had been a marvellous display of courage and willpower. That was true too of Shackleton. He had increased the record for furthest south by the greatest margin since Captain Cook's voyage, a margin that could never be broken. He had shown the way to the pole from McMurdo. If he had completed the same distance from the Bay of Whales he might well have reached the pole, a fact which Amundsen noted eagerly. Shackleton returned home a hero. The British are deeply suspicious of winners, but love a heroic loser; the only thing that could have improved Shackleton's stock was succeeding, but dying. He was knighted and produced a book, *The Heart of Antarctica* (ghosted by the New Zealand journalist Ernest Saunders) which won excellent reviews. Scott and other members of the British 'Antarctic establishment' were civil in public, bitter in private. They spread rumours about the true latitude reached. They could hardly argue with the last sun-spotted position of 87°22' (on 3 January), but raised doubts about later positions. They had a point. Shackleton's claimed position was based on dead reckoning, no sun having been visible for days. Ironically later that day it was, but the theodolite had been left in the last camp to save weight and it was also only 9am when they stopped: by noon they had not yet reached their last camp and, in any case, no one had the strength left to bother to take a reading. The distances claimed for the last dash – 32 nautical miles (59km/37 miles) in ten hours at 3,000m (10,000ft) – do seem implausible. Perhaps Marshall wanted to give Shackleton his 'within 100 miles' so they could all go home. Who can tell? And, apart from Scott and his supporters, who would be churlish enough to deny the four their small victory?

Amundsen: the pole reached

Shackleton gave many lectures. At one, in Christiania (Oslo), Norway, the audience included Nansen and Amundsen. Nansen was secretly relieved that Shackleton had not made the pole as he wanted to make one last trip of his own – and he had decided to go south. In part the reason was that he had agreed to lend the *Fram* to Amundsen who wanted to try for the North Pole (though 'lend' is not really the correct term: the ship was owned by the Norwegian state and Nansen accepted Amundsen's first use). But news had just arrived that both Cook and Peary were claiming to have reached the North Pole.

As a young boy Roald Amundsen was a member of a gang who played in the nearby forests: another member of the group was Carsten Borchgrevink, the first man to officially set foot on Antarctica (perhaps). Amundsen claimed that reading about Franklin's Canada overland trip of 1819/25 made him want to be a polar explorer, a desire hardened by Nansen's crossing of Greenland which inspired a generation of Norwegian youth. Learning from Nansen's success Amundsen practised his skiing. He also recognised early on the advantages of dog-sledging demonstrated by the Peary/Astrup crossing of northern Greenland in 1892. Amundsen enrolled at Christiania (Oslo) University to study medicine, but failed his exams and left unqualified. In need of a job he joined several sealing expeditions, realising that another essential of polar travel was the ability to sail. His experience as a sailor in Arctic waters and his skill as a skier, coupled with his enthusiasm for the trip and his willingness to go without pay, got him a place on board de Gerlache's *Belgica*. There he learned at first hand about the polar winter and soaked up information from Frederick Cook whose Arctic trips made him one of the most experienced polar travellers of the time. On his return from Antarctica Amundsen decided to organise his own trip, choosing the North-West Passage and North Magnetic Pole (the first still to be sailed, the latter reached just once before by Ross in 1831), an objective which Nansen approved. Such was Nansen's status in Norway that just this nod of approval was sufficient to kick-start the expedition. The start of Amundsen's quest for the North-West Passage coincided with Sverdrup's return from his exploration of northern Canada in *Fram*. Sverdrup's experiences with dog-sledging reinforced Amundsen's opinion. He was determined to learn the technique from the Canadian Inuit, which he accomplished brilliantly while the *Gjøa* was overwintering during the passage transit.

Amundsen returned to a newly independent Norway and was heralded as its first hero (despite the massive shadow cast by Nansen). Encouraged to believe that a grateful nation might underwrite another trip he decided to try for the North Pole. He spoke to Nansen about use of the *Fram*, but found him less than keen as he still harboured ambitions to attempt the South Pole himself. Nansen believed (correctly) that Antarctica had an ice cap and that a trip to the South Pole would be merely a longer version of his Greenland crossing. Amundsen, probably surmising that Nansen's dream was just that – a dream – pressed him on the use of *Fram* and eventually Nansen agreed to give up his own priority in favour of the younger man's.

For his proposed North Pole expedition Amundsen chose his men wisely. One was Olav Bjaaland, a brilliant skier who had allied telemark techniques to standard cross-country skiing. He had Helmer Hanssen, who had been on *Gjøa* and was an excellent dog driver, and Hjalmar Johansen, Nansen's companion on the epic attempt to reach the North Pole from *Fram*. Interestingly, he had no doctor, preferring to send two of his men on short courses (and to use his own medical knowledge). The preparations for the trip were well advanced when word came that there were two claimants to the pole.

Amundsen's view of the Cook and Peary claims is strange. He sent his congratulations to his old friend Cook, but declined to confirm whether he believed him. He was equally evasive when asked about Peary's claim. Nevertheless, he was obviously sufficiently concerned to change his own plans, though he decided not to tell anyone until it was too late for them to stop him. He may have been worried about Nansen's reaction, and he was almost certainly nervous of the Norwegian government's view of upsetting the British. Amundsen claimed that Peary's imputation of Cook was based, in part, on his assumed proprietorial rights over the North Pole, and he probably assumed, rightly, that Scott felt the same way about the South Pole; in a letter Scott wrote that he did not 'hold that anyone but an Englishman' should be first at the South Pole. For the same reason Amundsen decided against using McMurdo as his base, choosing instead to go to the Bay of Whales, which also had the advantage of being at least 100km (60 miles) closer to the pole. At his proposed daily rate of travel of 24km (15 miles) that difference amounted to eight days' travel, even if it meant he would be crossing new ground for his entire journey.

Amundsen had special larger skis made, and clothing similar to that of the Inuit in northern Canada. He was meticulous about all the other equipment too, and especially about food. His preparations also included an avoidance of Scott who several times tried to arrange meetings to discuss the sharing of scientific projects: Amundsen could tolerate being called a 'bad sport', but not a liar. On 6 June 1910 the *Fram* sailed from Bundefjord, Amundsen's home, leaving at midnight just as *Gjøa* had done when she set out for the North-West Passage. This was only a proving run; not until 9 August did the *Fram*, with 97 Greenland dogs on board, finally leave Norway. This time Amundsen slipped away in mid-evening rather than midnight, but to ensure that there would be no final farewells (potentially embarrassing because of his real plan, as well as being against his nature) he did not announce his departure and simply raised the anchor as soon as the last dog was loaded.

As the planned trip, sealing *Fram* in the ice just as Nansen had done, was to begin in the Bering Sea, the crew were not surprised to head south to Madeira even though Nansen had taken the North-East Passage: they assumed they were to round Cape Horn and sail north. They were, though, curious about certain aspects of the trip: why take dogs all the way to Alaska when there were dogs easily available there? What was this huge hut for – surely not for erecting on pack ice? It is possible that some of the more astute of Amundsen's team knew there was something going on; if they did, they were proved right at Madeira. There, after sending letters announcing his change of plan to Nansen, King Haakon and several others, Amundsen told the crew. None objected, though Amundsen did couch the change as an 'extension' to the original plan: getting to the South Pole would help finance the 'real' trip to the North Pole. What he did not tell them was where he was

Above **In the Bay of Whales on 3 February 1911, Lt Victor Campbell and *Terra Nova* found the Norwegians and was treated to a demonstration of dog-sledging that made all the British gasp – never had they seen sledges move so fast. It was a show put on specifically for the British by Amundsen, but for all that it was an indication of just what the dog-sledge was capable of as a means of transport.**
USA Library of Congress

Above **Framheim at the Bay of Whales. The Bay of Whales is a semi-permanent feature of the Ross Ice Shelf. The early expeditions knew this though at the time they did not know the reason for its existence. Amundsen surmised that it was actually land. It is not, being formed by Roosevelt Island which perturbs the flow of the shelf ice and so causes an indentation of varying size in the shelf edge.**
USA Library of Congress

planning to land, as he had no wish for this information to reach the British. The 19 Norwegians were now in a race with the 67 Britons on board *Terra Nova* which had left Cardiff on 15 June.

On the journey south the men honed their equipment towards perfection, a task they would complete during the winter on the Ross Ice Shelf. Amundsen was behind the British and though they were not – to Norwegian incredulity – using dogs and skis, they did have motor-sledges which might be quicker than dogs. All possible sources of delay must therefore be eliminated. Amundsen was 480km (300 miles) behind Scott when he entered the Ross Sea, and ten days behind him after unloading in the Bay of Whales and setting up Framheim (*Fram*'s home), his winter base.

In what remained of the austral autumn Amundsen laid out supply dumps southward, reaching 82°S: he was now, effectively, 240km (150 miles) ahead of Scott, and his dumps were better marked and, therefore, easier to find. The description of the Norwegian base

during the winter makes impressive reading. It was a hive of activity as the sledges, traces, skis, clothing and supplies were modified and perfected. The Norwegians were clearly in tune with their environment and with the job at hand in a way in which the British, who had brought England to Antarctica, were not. This can most readily be seen in one detail: Greenland dogs will, if given the chance, eat human excrement. The Norwegians made use of this as a means of keeping their base cleaner: the British stopped any dog that tried.

On 8 September Amundsen started for the pole against the advice of Johansen whose experience with Nansen had taught him the folly of trekking in extreme cold, and who had realised on the depot-laying tours that the cold of the Antarctic was even more brutal than that of the Arctic pack. But Amundsen feared an early move by Scott and insisted. With temperatures falling to –57°C the team soon began to experience frostbite and the dogs became exhausted and injured, blood from their paws staining the ice. The spirit compasses froze and were useless, the vacuum flasks broke into pieces in the cold, and even a reviving bottle of gin froze solid and cracked on thawing. Amundsen was forced to give up. The retreat, begun at 7am, was a shambles. Amundsen decided to go to Framheim in one go rather than the normal two-day trip, and set off on skis towed by Oscar Wisting's sledge. With them was Helmer Hanssen and his sledge. Behind them came the rest: Jørgen Stubberud and Olav Bjaaland, then Sverre Hassel (slowed by frostbite in a big toe). Behind again were Hjalmar Johansen and bringing up the rear Kristian Prestrud, a polar newcomer whose feet were frozen and whose dogs were now useless. Johansen caught Hassel and explained that someone had to wait for Prestrud. Hassel declined, probably fearing the state of his own feet, but gave Johansen a tent. When Prestrud eventually reached Johansen he was in a poor state. Without food or a stove to make drinks Johansen knew it was imperative that he get Prestrud back to Framheim. At times he had to carry him.

Amundsen's team of three reached Framheim at 4pm, the others trailing in between 6 and 6.30. Johansen brought Prestrud – now unable to walk and barely able to stand – in after midnight. In his book Amundsen notes this with the comment, 'Heaven knows what they had been doing on the way!'. What they had been doing was fighting for Prestrud's life, Johansen saving not only that but Amundsen's expedition as well, as there is little doubt that Prestrud's death would have precipitated its collapse. The following morning Amundsen asked Johansen why they had been so late arriving. Johansen's pent-up frustration erupted and he told Amundsen not only why, but exactly what he felt about a leader who abandoned his men without food or fuel in order to save himself. Johansen's view was that the retreat had not been an expedition but a panic, and that in addition to the charge of poor judgement for going too early Amundsen now stood accused of poor leadership.

Though there is good evidence that most of the rest of the team agreed with Johansen they were all too fearful of their position in the pole party to say so. Johansen was isolated. Amundsen noted in his diary that 'this was a sad end to an excellent unity, but I feel the only course after his [Johansen's] behaviour is to exclude him. We can accept no critical elements on our journey and coming from an experienced man like him it would be doubly dangerous.' Amundsen not only excluded Johansen from the pole party, but put him in a team which was to explore King Edward VII Land, a team to be led by Prestrud. This quite deliberate snub led to further aggravation and, according to some sources, a fight.

Johansen noted in his own diary that Amundsen 'feels it as deadly insult because his qualities of leadership have been exposed as hollow… He is not the man I thought he was…' There is some evidence that Amundsen's spitefulness over the incident – which receives no mention in his book on the pole expedition – was not limited to removing Johansen from the team. Johansen left the team as soon as it reached civilisation and travelled back to Norway independently, and there is evidence that Amundsen forced this decision on him. It has also been said that Amundsen gave Johansen no money so that he had to beg cash for a passage home. However, it can be credibly argued that Johansen was given the money he was due and drank it away so that he was penniless when he arrived in Melbourne (from New Zealand). It is also claimed that Amundsen telegraphed to Norway ahead of Johansen's arrival (he arrived before the rest of the team) to ensure that he was not greeted as a hero. But again there is a credible alternative that it was Alexander Nansen, Fridtjof's brother and the expedition's lawyer, who wrote the telegram after hearing from Amundsen of Johansen's 'mutiny'. Whatever the truth it was an unpleasant end to an otherwise successful trip, and one with terrible consequences. Johansen, despite having been Nansen's companion and having saved Prestrud's life, never regained his reputation. His drinking, which had been a serious problem before the trip, increased heavily and he became depressed, eventually committing suicide in 1913 at the age of 46.

Amundsen, with Bjaaland, Hanssen, Hassel and Wisting, left again on 20 October, with 52 dogs pulling four sledges. Usually Bjaaland, the best skier, moved ahead of the convoy, giving the dogs something to chase. At the 80°S dump four dogs were released to make their way back to Framheim. When the team set out again on 24 October they were 240km (150 miles) ahead of Scott: his attempt set out that same day from his McMurdo base. Despite occasional requests from his men to go faster Amundsen set and maintained a daily distance target of 24km (15 miles) so as not to wear out the dogs. By 4 November they were at 82°S, their last dump. Here it was decided to create dumps every 1° south to progressively reduce the weight carried. To help locate the dumps on their return journey cairns were raised along the route. As the load reduced, so did the number of dogs, the weakest being shot to feed the rest.

Left **Amundsen's team on their way to the pole.**
USA Library of Congress

Above **Camp at 84°S on the pole journey.**
USA Library of Congress

Below **The Devil's Glacier, the most difficult part of the Norwegians' journey to the pole.**
USA Library of Congress

Ahead now lay a range of mountains Amundsen named after the Norwegian queen (the Queen Maud Mountains are part of the Transantarctic Range). Amundsen had hoped that the ice shelf rose gently to the polar plateau, but now he, like Shackleton and Scott, had to find a way through the mountains. His route took him to a glacier named for Axel Heiberg, steeper, but shorter, than the Beardmore: its ascent took four hard days. In a camp on the plateau at the top all but 18 dogs were shot, both men and the remaining dogs eating the carcasses. One sledge was left behind and the party moved on again.

Briefly the terrain became difficult – the Norwegians were crossing the start of the Devil's Glacier – then levelled again. The weather too was poor, but Shackleton's mark was passed on 8 December. The next day the last dump was made and marked. Now the weather was fine, the going easy, the only concern being whether Scott had beaten them: in fact, he was 575km (360 miles) behind them. On 14 December 1911

Amundsen was pushed to the front for the last few kilometres. At 3pm they reached what they thought was the pole: the snow was virginal, the Norwegians had won. The obligatory photographs were taken; ironically Amundsen's camera was damaged and took no shots, the iconic photograph being taken on a cheap camera brought by Bjaaland. Amundsen formally named the area around the pole King Haakon VII's Plateau. The pride the men felt at what they had achieved was mixed with a huge sense of relief that it was all over – now they could go home.

In fact the Norwegians stayed at Polheim, their polar camp, for three days, boxing the area with flags as they took readings from the sun to confirm their position. Amundsen's account remarks on the curious motion of the sun at the pole and he wonders if the Norwegians are the first to see it, which implies he believed neither Cook nor Peary had reached the North Pole. It is estimated that on 17 December Bjaaland and Hanssen passed within a few tens of metres of the actual pole: Polheim was probably 2km (1¼ miles) from it. At Polheim Amundsen left a tent, a pole from which flew the Norwegian flag, and a letter for the Norwegian king with a covering note asking Scott to deliver it. (Scott was confused by the letter, not realising that Amundsen left it in case he failed to reach Framheim: a later author noted that by taking the letter Scott had, in one instance, gone from explorer to postman, which seems a gratuitously unkind thing to say.) The letter stated the Norwegian view that the polar plateau was 6,700m (22,000ft) high, about the only mistake Amundsen made on the entire trip, though as they had a hypsometer and took regular (and correct) readings it is more likely to have been a 'spelling' mistake.

On 17 December the Norwegians left, Amundsen still maintaining the 24km (15-mile) daily regime, the men sometimes spending 16 hours each day resting. Around 31 December the Norwegians and British were at the same latitude and probably less than 100km (60 miles) apart. Though they were well out of sight of each other it is interesting to speculate what would have happened had they spotted the other team. Would Scott have turned around?

The Norwegians had a comfortable journey back to Framheim: the dogs ran well, there was adequate food on the days between the dumps, and good supplies at the dumps. At the base of the Axel Heiberg Glacier another note on the expedition was left beneath a cairn: it was found in 1929 by a team led by Laurence Gould, part of Richard Byrd's expedition. Wisting had to have a tooth pulled – the only drama on the journey – and the weather deteriorated, but the daily target was consistently met. At 4am on 26 January 1912 Amundsen crept into the hut and woke the rest of his men by asking if there was any coffee. On 30 January the men boarded the *Fram* and sailed for Hobart where, on 7 March, the world was told of the success.

Scott: the race lost

On 7 March the four survivors of Scott's five-man team were struggling towards what they hoped would be a supply dump laid down for them by the other members of the expedition at McMurdo. Scott's second expedition had been brought to Antarctica by the *Terra Nova* which had accompanied the *Morning* on the second Discovery relief expedition in early 1904. Scott had asked Mawson and Wild to go with him on his second (the British Antarctic) expedition, but both had

Above **Sverre Hansen at the South Pole.**
USA Library of Congress

declined, though two others from Shackleton's *Nimrod* team had accepted. Wilson was going again: for the rest Scott had the pick of several thousand volunteers. The chosen party included Captain Lawrence Edward Grace Oates, ex-Eton, currently a cavalry officer serving in India. Oates was a sports enthusiast and was bored with the quiet of the sub-continent. He appears to have had little idea about Antarctica – when he heard he was likely to be accepted he wrote to his mother that 'the climate is healthy, but inclined to be cold' – but fancied the adventure. Oates' application was undoubtedly helped by the £1,000 cheque he wrote. Volunteers who paid for the privilege of joining were welcome: in addition to Oates there was one more who paid £1,000, Apsley Cherry-Garrard.

Chosen from the no-fee volunteers was Henry Robertson Bowers, a lieutenant in the Royal Indian Marine. He had sailing experience and an enthusiasm for the polar regions, though the latter was gained from books rather than direct experience. From the *Discovery* team came Crean, Lashly and Edgar Evans. The latter should not be confused with Lt (later Admiral Sir) Edward Evans (Teddy Evans) who was made second-in-command to Scott when news of his (Evans') intention to mount a separate expedition became known.

Shackleton, Scott's *bête noire*, had passed 88°S. Recognising this fact alone Scott decided to take ponies as Shackleton had. He also decided to use motor-sledges. When he met Nansen again, the great man was, yet again, aghast. There was nothing he could do about the sledging (though he did manage to cajole Scott into taking a few, token, dogs) but he did persuade Scott to take skis, even 'lending' him Tryggve Gran, a young Norwegian and an expert skier. This contact worked in changing Scott's mind, though not to the extent of him recognising that learning to ski was more than just a weekend's work.

On 15 June 1910 the *Terra Nova* sailed from Cardiff, but without the expedition leader: Scott left a month later, meeting his ship in Cape Town. *Terra Nova* and Scott reached Melbourne on 12 October. The next day he received a telegram from Christiania: 'Beg leave to inform you *Fram* proceeding Antarctic. Amundsen.' The sender was Leon Amundsen, Roald's brother. The story was front-line news in Norway that day and reached Britain soon after. In Britain some were astonished (Shackleton noted that since Amundsen had taken dogs not ponies he was unlikely to reach the pole as dogs 'are not very reliable'), and enraged others (Sir Clements Markham called Amundsen 'a blackguard'). On the *Terra Nova* Tryggve Gran was embarrassed and perplexed – he knew nothing about Amundsen's plans – while Scott tried to persuade himself that Amundsen was heading for the Weddell Sea and would therefore be little threat.

In New Zealand the ponies were loaded on to the *Terra Nova*. Oates, the cavalry officer and horse expert, was not impressed with them. One team member who was rather more impressed with the stay in New Zealand was Teddy Evans. He had been keen to get rid of Edgar Evans for some time as he had no time for over-drinking unfit men. In this he had been thwarted by Scott who had a soft spot for the big sailor. But when Edgar Evans got drunk and fell in the sea at Lyttleton even Scott had had enough. To Teddy Evans' delight Scott dismissed Edgar Evans and *Terra Nova* sailed without him. But, to Teddy Evans' disgust, when Evans appealed to Scott, who had stayed behind in Lyttleton to tie up final loose ends, for one more chance, he was given it and travelled with Scott to rejoin the ship at Port Chalmers.

The team were subjected to the usual stormy crossing of the Southern Ocean (two ponies, two dogs and some stores were lost), McMurdo being reached on 2 January 1911. The ship was unloaded at Cape Evans (north of the Discovery Hut), one of the motor-sledges dropping through the thin sea ice and disappearing – not an auspicious start. After establishing a base Scott began to organise southern supply dumps, but was

Above **The interior of Scott's hut at Cape Evans.**
P.S. Kristensen, courtesy of Quark Expeditions

Above **The photograph of the *Terra Nova* through the opening of a grotto in an iceberg is one of Herbert Ponting's most enduring images from Scott's last expedition. This rarely seen shot, also by Ponting, shows the outside of the Grotto Berg.**
USA Library of Congress

only able to establish the One Ton Depot at 78°28½'S because the ponies found the going hard. Oates, the horse expert, wanted to kill the weakest (dumping them as food) and continue, but Scott refused: the frustrated Oates suggested presciently that Scott would regret the decision. Retreating from his southernmost dump Scott discovered that Amundsen was in the Bay of Whales. He was distraught: Amundsen's dogs could

start earlier than the ponies because they did not sink into the snow and the Norwegians were already closer to the pole. Had Scott, assisted by the show laid on by Amundsen for the *Terra Nova*'s crew, finally understood the value of dogs? Scott was also appalled by Amundsen invading his (Scott's) own territory, the more so as the British had intended to land an exploratory team at the Bay of Whales. To make matters worse, the team returning from the south – Scott had travelled ahead – lost seven out of eight ponies when attempting to cross unstable sea ice.

During the winter that followed Bowers, Cherry-Garrard and Wilson made a trip to Cape Crozier, on the east side of Ross Sea, to obtain the eggs of Emperor penguins, a round trip of some 240km (150 miles). Cherry-Garrard's description of the journey is the central theme of his book on the entire expedition. The chapter is called 'The Worse Journey', the book *The Worst Journey in the World*, which many have claimed to be the finest ever written on an Antarctic trek. The book also includes Cherry-Garrard's description of the early stages of Scott's polar trek and Lashly's account of the return of the final support team, as well as the harrowing description of finding the bodies of Scott, Wilson and Bowers.

Scott called 'the worst journey' 'one of the most gallant stories in polar history'. Considering that its objective was merely to retrieve penguin eggs it could also be termed one of the most ridiculous. Cherry-Garrard opens by noting that of the three men (Wilson, Bowers and himself) who waited to depart one was 'feeling a little frightened'. It was a sensible emotion as he soon discovered. He wrote 'the horror of the 19 days it took us to travel... to Cape Crozier would have to be re-experienced to be appreciated... it is not possible to describe it'. They averaged 2½km (1½ miles) each day. Their clothes froze so solid that it took two men to bend them to shape. Their balaclavas froze to their heads: once Cherry-Garrard raised his head as he stepped from the tent and his clothes solidified so quickly he could not look down for four hours. The temperature fell to –77.5°F (–61°C). Cherry-Garrard noting that temperatures in the minus fifties (about –48°C) seemed luxurious. They were so cold that the agonies of warming extremities became a daily occurrence. In the perpetual darkness they could not see the crevasses. Walking was like playing blind-man's-bluff as they frequently fell, saved only by their sledge harnesses, an experience that frayed the nerves.

Finally they arrived at Cape Crozier becoming the first men to see incubating Emperor penguins. They collected the eggs, but had a nightmare journey back to camp, Cherry-Garrard noting that by now the three were beginning to think of death as a friend. But worse was to come when they were struck by a storm so ferocious it was 'as though the world was having a bit of hysterics'. They had built an igloo beside their tent: the tent blew away, the roof blew off the igloo. They survived by staying in their sleeping bags for 36 hours and allowing snow to drift over them. Cherry-Garrard comforted himself with thoughts of peaches and syrup, and then, knowing that without the tent they were unlikely to survive the return journey, hoped for death. All three survived and then, miraculously, found the tent. The journey back was equally epic, but with less to haul much quicker. Once, when Bowers' balaclava froze so that he was no longer able to look down, he walked into a crevasse. At night – there was twilight now at midday, so they could differentiate night and day – they were so cold in their sleeping bags they could not sleep and often fell asleep as they walked. Finally they arrived back at base and 'thus ended the worst journey in the world'. It had been an amazing journey; and the penguin eggs were brought safely back.

On 24 October 1911 Scott's remaining motor-sledges started from Cape Evans as an advance party. On the same day the Norwegians were leaving their dump at 80°S. The motor-sledges lasted just five days before failing. Two days later, on 1 November, Scott and the main party set off. Within a few days Scott's concerns over the use of dogs must have been heightened considerably when his own teams (driven by Cecil Meares and Dimitri Gerov, a Russian 'acquired' by Meares when he bought the dogs in Siberia) covered his daily distance in considerably less time. But the die was cast, and with the ponies sinking into the snow Scott followed his own, then Shackleton's, route south. By 9 December at the bottom of the Beardmore Glacier the ponies were finished and were shot. Two days later the dog teams turned north, leaving Scott with 11 men. These, some on skis, manhauled up the glacier, back-breaking work, though at least the weather was fine. At the top four men (including Cherry-Garrard) turned and headed north, their job of hauling supplies for intermediate depots completed. The eight who continued were organised in two teams: Scott with Edgar Evans, Oates and Wilson; Teddy Evans with Bowers, Crean and Lashly.

When on 2 January 1912 the time came to choose the final pole party Scott chose his own four as a group. He then, surprisingly, picked Bowers to accom-

Above **Robert Falcon Scott at his desk in the hut at Cape Evans. The photograph was taken in October 1911 two weeks before Scott set out for the pole.**
USA Library of Congress

pany them. The reason seems to have been that no one in his own team was a competent navigator and Bowers was, though Scott's diary does not confirm this. The decision meant that the pole party had to sleep five in a four-man tent and share rations for four. More seriously it meant that Bowers had to haul on foot, while the other four were on skis because on 31 December Scott had ordered Teddy Evans' team to leave their skis behind. He does not explain why, but it has been speculated that he wished to slow the Evans team so that his decision to take his own would appear clearly justified.

The five men of the pole team continued south at a daily rate of about 14km (9 miles), a distance earned by hours of effort. Oates was hindered by an old Boer War wound to his thigh and Evans had an injured hand (cut while working on the sledges). But the men were driven by the thought that Amundsen was still behind them. Then, on 16 January the men detected something ahead: it was one of Amundsen's black flags, the surrounding snow etched with ski and sledge marks and paw prints. The British had lost the race. Scott's diary is matter-of-fact: 'The Norwegians have forestalled us and are first at the pole. It is a terrible

Above **Scott's team at the pole.**
Left to right: Bowers, Evans, Scott, Oates and Wilson.
The camera was triggered by string pulled by Bowers.
USA Library of Congress

Above **The British find the Norwegian tent.**
Left to right: Scott, Oates, Wilson and Evans.
USA Library of Congress

disappointment, and I am very sorry for my loyal companions', but the next day's entry when the British actually reached the pole is a more telling description. 'The pole, Yes, but under very different circumstances from those expected... none of us having slept much after the shock of our discovery... Great God! this is an awful place and terrible enough for us to have laboured to it without reward of priority.' Scott's words are as chilling a statement of defeat and failure as could be imagined. Lately it has become fashionable to depict Scott as an amateur bungler. There is truth in this (certainly in comparison to Amundsen's marvellously professional journey), but faced with Scott's pain at the enormity of his defeat it is hard not to feel sympathy for the man.

On 18 January, close to what they believed was the actual pole, Scott's team found Polheim and the letter for King Haakon. Other cairns and flags led Scott to note 'There is no doubt that our predecessors have made thoroughly sure of their mark'; there was not even the satisfaction of knowing that the British were the first to mark the exact spot even if they had come second in the main race. After the obligatory

photograph there was nothing left but to turn north for home. Scott noted in his diary (on 17 January) 'Now for the run home and a desperate struggle. I wonder if we can do it', a strangely downbeat comment even allowing for the disappointment.

But the homeward journey was indeed a desperate struggle. Food and fuel were short, as was time; yet despite this a gloriously fine half-day on the Beardmore Glacier was spent collecting 16kg (35lb) of rock samples which were then towed for the rest of the journey. The lost time equates to perhaps 8km (5 miles), the extra load perhaps as much again in terms of energy spent. And the last camp was 17.5km (11 miles) from One Ton Depot. The time loss is all the more surprising because Edgar Evans' condition was worsening. His cut hand was pus-filled, his mental health fragmenting. On 17 February Evans collapsed in the snow and was left behind. Later the four went back for him, and that night he died.

Oates was next. He had frost-bitten feet (the austral summer was fast drawing to a close and temperatures were falling), making walking agony and survival unlikely. His condition made hauling near impossible and probably slowed the rest. By 16 March, two weeks after first showing the others the appalling state of his feet (by now they were probably gangrenous, making death a near certainty) Scott says he asked to be left behind. The request was turned down and next morning Scott records that Oates famously said, 'I am just going outside and may be some time', before struggling into a blizzard. Wilson, writing to Oates' mother, does not mention these iconic words.

The last three struggled on until 21 March when they camped 17.5km (11 miles) from One Ton Depot. Scott was finished, his right foot probably gangrenous as he noted that 'amputation is the least I can hope for'. He says that the other two tried to go to the depot on 22nd and 23rd, but could not because of a blizzard. The next entry is 29 March and the gale has been blowing non-stop. Yet it is surprising that neither Bowers nor Wilson made one last effort to reach the depot. With no hope of rescue why do men sit and wait for death for nine days? During that time Scott wrote his poignant letter to the British public and composed the elegies for his companions. The tent, with the three still inside their sleeping bags, was discovered in November 1912 by a British search party. They were buried where they lay.

In his last letters Scott wrote 'we are setting a good example to our countrymen... by facing (hardship, death) like men' and 'we are showing that Englishmen can still die with a bold spirit, fighting it out to the end'. It is hard not to imagine that Scott, having no choice but to taste defeat rather than victory, chose death rather than dishonour, his words chillingly echoing the 'I wonder if we can do it' written at the pole. But even if it can be persuasively argued that Scott was resigned to death, would Bowers and Wilson have been so keen to follow his lead?

Within months many young men would follow Scott's display of dying with a bold spirit on the battlefields of France and Belgium. By then, and even more so after, his death had become a symbol of British heroism, the dubious details of the journey lost in jingoism. 'Great Scott!' became a British exclamation used to denote something supranormal (though the Scott of the expression is said to have been the novelist Sir Walter, the expression had a renaissance after Scott's journey). Scott, it was claimed, had died last – this was printed so many times it became a 'fact' (though it is likely to have been Bowers) – a model of leadership to the end.

Top **The final camp: the tent in which the bodies of Scott, Wilson and Bowers were discovered.**
Scott Polar Research Institute, University of Cambridge, UK

Above **The tent at the final camp had inner and outer fabrics. The inner was dropped over the bodies and a snow cairn was erected over it. The outer was brought back to Britain and erected in Earls Court. A Royal Navy honour guard stood beside it as thousands silently filed past.**
Scott Polar Research Institute, University of Cambridge, UK

Amundsen: victory denied

Amundsen heard of Scott's death soon after learning of Johansen's suicide. He was horrified, devastated. The idea that defeat had broken Scott's heart and spirit haunted Amundsen, as did the thought that had he left more supplies at the pole Scott might have survived. Logic told Amundsen that Scott's death had been both self-inflicted and avoidable, but logic is not as powerful as emotion. Norway, though enraptured with success, were nervous in victory. The British felt cheated and could hardly applaud Amundsen for giving them a hero, the more so as they saw Amundsen as a professional. Amundsen was in part the unwitting architect of this idea, a ludicrous suggestion and one which implied Scott was an amateur, which might have been closer to the truth than the British actually meant to suggest. Amundsen's story implied a comfortable, occasionally fun journey, whereas Scott's diary spoke only of hardship and woe, even before the race was lost. The British also thought Amundsen had used underhand tactics. Scott had manhauled, whereas the Norwegians had been pulled along. Amundsen claimed that at a dinner in London in his honour the president of the Royal Geographical Society had proposed three cheers for the dogs, but none for him. When he complained the Royal Geographical Society declared he had misheard and demanded an apology for his 'insult'. But the same muted praise was heard everywhere he went and, coupled with Amundsen's own doubts and fears, made him a bitter man. He had accomplished so much and so brilliantly, and it had all been taken from him. His death, when it came, was sad, lonely and unnecessary, with little of the glory Scott had found. Even now, despite the revisionist view of his expedition, everyone remembers Scott's name and even those of Bowers, Evans, Oates and Wilson.

Few outside Norway recall those of Amundsen's team. Sverre Hassel died in 1928 while visiting Amundsen, dropping down dead at his old leader's feet. In 1936 the 65-year-old Oscar Wisting asked to be allowed to spend the night on the *Fram* in his old cabin. The next morning he was found dead. Helmer Hanssen died in 1957 aged 87. Olav Bjaaland lived even longer; he was 89 and still living on his Telemark farm when he died in 1961. Not long before he had met Sir Vivian Fuchs, leader of the British 1957/8 expedition, the first Briton to reach the pole overland and return alive. There had been a great fuss over the expedition, but Bjaaland was unimpressed, reckoning that in all probability nothing much had changed there since his visit 45 years before.

Shirase and Filchner

When Amundsen regained his Bay of Whales base he discovered a Japanese expedition had arrived. Led by Nobu (sometimes given as Choku or Naoshi) Shirase, son of a Buddhist priest and a lieutenant in the Japanese navy, the expedition had arrived in the *Kainan Maru* (Southern Pioneer). Shirase had raised the cash for the trip in the face of public apathy and sailed in December 1910. Unable to locate a landing spot on Victoria Land, Shirase retreated to Australia where the expedition spent an unhappy winter camped in a garden, frequently harassed by the pro-Scott local press. Returning to Antarctica the Japanese landed in the bay in mid-January 1912, too late for their intended trip to the pole. A symbolic 'dash patrol' of Shirase and six others (using dog sledges) passed 80°S on 28 January. There they claimed the Ross Ice Shelf for Japan, calling it the Yamato Yukihara – Yamato Snow Plain. On their return to Japan they found the formerly apathetic public ecstatic at their success, though the Japanese government (not surprisingly) did not pursue the name or claim to the ice shelf.

Having encountered the Japanese on the ice shelf, Amundsen met Wilhelm Filchner, leader of the German Antarctic Expedition, in Buenos Aires, finding that he was primarily interested in discovering whether the Weddell and Ross Seas were connected, and that he intended to cross the continent. Filchner had come to some form of understanding with Scott which probably meant the Germans were not trying for the pole (though doubtless would not have been bothered if it lay in their path), but whatever the terms of the understanding they had become irrelevant. Leaving Buenos Aires the *Deutschland* (the renamed Norwegian ship *Bjørn*) reached the southern coast of the Weddell Sea (the Leopold Coast, named by Filchner for the German Prince Regent) and discovered the ice shelf that now bears Filchner's name. Filchner actually named it for Kaiser Wilhelm, but his majesty declined the offer and insisted on it bearing the expedition leader's name. The original Filchner Ice Shelf is now two separate ones, the Filchner and the Ronne – that latter named for the Norwegian Finn Ronne – separated by Berkner Island.

In the Weddell Sea the *Deutschland* became trapped in the pack ice and the Germans were forced to overwinter, their attempt to set up a base on the ice shelf almost ending disastrously when a vast tabular berg (with the base hut on it) cleaved. From the ship Filchner and two others dog-sledged across the ice in midwinter, a remarkable journey as the ship drifted

over 60km (about 40 miles) while they were away and they had to navigate by dead reckoning when their instruments froze. The *Deutschland* was released from the ice in November 1912 and made an uneventful journey home. There Filchner's attempts to raise money for another trip were thwarted by the looming European war.

Mawson: *The Home of the Blizzard*

A third expedition was also on the continent while Amundsen and Scott were striving for the pole. The Australasian Antarctic Expedition was led by Douglas Mawson who had declined Scott's offer of a place on *Terra Nova* in favour of leading his own trip. Mawson was hoping to fill in the gaps on the map between McMurdo and the German discoveries of 1902, a worthy objective for an expedition that was to turn into one of the great survival stories of polar exploration. The expedition left Hobart in December 1911 in the *Aurora*, an ex-Arctic sealer, captained by John Davis. Amongst other things, the ship was carrying the fuselage of a Vickers REP monoplane. The plane had crashed on its trial flight and, devoid of wings, was to be used as an 'air-tractor': it wasn't much better at that job either, managing little more than 30km (20 miles) before the engine seized.

Above **The cold, dense air of high Antarctica drops off the plateau, accelerating under the influence of gravity to speeds of over 300kmph (about 200mph), but the persistence of these katabatic winds (named from the Greek for 'going downhill') only became apparent to Mawson when it was too late. The expedition recorded an average windspeed of 69.4kmph (43.4mph) over a period of one calendar year. In July 1912 the wind averaged over 100kmph (over 62mph) for the whole 31 days. On 15 May the 24-hour average was over 145kmph (90mph). On one day in the winter of 1913 the wind blew at over 160kmph (100mph) for more than eight hours. The wind could hurl men and equipment about: it could also stop abruptly, leaving men who had been leaning into it to fall flat on their faces. It whipped up surface snow to create vicious white-outs, which led Mawson to call his base (and his book on the expedition) *The Home of the Blizzard.***
University of Adelaide, South Australia

Mawson's plan was to land close to, but to the west of, Cape Adare, but the unforgiving terrain forced the *Aurora* much further west, the expedition's chosen base being at Cape Denison (named for a Sydney patron) in Commonwealth Bay, almost 1,300 sea km (800 sea miles) west of Adare. Though apparently hospitable, Cape Denison was soon found to be a windy spot. In

fact, Mawson had inadvertently chosen one of the windiest places on the continent.

Mawson's landing at Cape Dennison was not without incident. Crucial stove parts, thought to be in a box which had fallen overboard into 1.5m (5ft) of water, had to be retrieved by Mawson stripping off and jumping in. The box contained only jam – the stove parts were found elsewhere – and Mawson 'established a new record for myself in dressing'. Then a huge sea elephant – rare on the continental mainland – threatened the dogs. It was shot, and measured at 5.3m (17½ft) long and 3.7m (12ft) around, a truly monstrous specimen which yielded a vast amount of dog food. After dropping Mawson (at the same time that Scott was heading north from the pole) the *Aurora* then left another team, led by Frank Wild – veteran of Scott's *Discovery* trip and Shackleton's furthest south – over 1,600km (1,000 miles) miles away to the west on an ice shelf Wild named for Shackleton. It was planned that Wild's team would explore towards Drygalski's discovered land.

The main party overwintered at Cape Denison, making forays to dump supplies to the south, many in Aladdin's Cave (an excavated ice cavern) on the rare occasions the weather was suitable. When summer came the party divided; the local coast was explored by three teams, while another went south to investigate the area close to the South Magnetic Pole. This team, which included the photographer Frank Hurley whose

record of Shackelton's *Endurance* expedition has brought him lasting fame, got to within 80km (50 miles) of the pole, manhauling against ferocious winds before retreating. Mawson, together with Lt Belgrave Edward Sutton Ninnis, a British army officer who had shown an aptitude with dogs, and Dr Xavier Guillaume Mertz, a Swiss lawyer, ski champion and mountaineer, headed east. The three left the base on 10 November 1912, a late start due to appalling weather, knowing that they had to be back by 15 January 1913 at the latest or the *Aurora* would leave without them. Their journey soon became difficult. Not only was the weather bad but they ran into the tortuous ice and crevasses of two huge glaciers (now called the Mertz and Ninnis Glaciers). Many times the dogs fell into crevasses, some being injured so badly they had to be destroyed, but the team's luck in surviving the falls was amazing. Eventually the luck ran out: on 14 December Ninnis, complete with his dog team and sledge, disappeared into a vast crevasse which Mertz had skied across and Mawson had sledged over. Peering down, Mawson and Mertz could see only a pair of dogs some 45m (150ft) down. Of Ninnis, his sledge, all the dog food and much of their own food, there was no sign.

The situation was immediately perilous. Mawson and Mertz were over 500km (320 miles) from base with food for about ten days, but no food for the remaining dogs. Mawson noted in his diary that they would have

to eat the dogs to survive, then wrote 'May God help us'. Feeding the weakest dog to the strongest the two men set off for base. Soon they were supplementing their own meagre rations with dog meat. The meat from the starving dogs offered little nourishment, but their livers were big.

Mawson and Mertz did not know that the Inuit and Nansen had warned against eating the livers of Arctic carnivores; as a result of their exclusively meat diet these animals store vast quantities of vitamin A in their livers. Earlier in 1912 the Polish-born biochemist Casimir Funk, working in London, had coined the word 'vitamine' (changed to 'vitamin' in 1920 by the Englishman Sir Jack Drummond), but not until the 1930s would George Wald understand the nature of vitamin A, and it was later still that the effects of excess vitamin A on the human body were recognised. Mawson and Mertz were not to know that their apparently life-saving diet of dog liver was poisoning them, causing dysentery and nausea, loss of hair and skin, chronic stomach pain and, eventually, delirium, convulsions and death. Ironically the younger, fitter Mawson gave his companion extra rations thinking it would help him, and in doing so, ensured his own survival.

As the two men became weaker they abandoned surplus weight. One item left behind was the rifle, forcing Mawson to kill the last dog with a spade. The glacier crossings were a nightmare: again they miracu-lously survived crevasse falls. By Christmas Day their skin was peeling, adding the pain of raw flesh to the other effects of vitamin A poisoning. The pair boiled down the bones and sinews of the last dog to a jelly, but by now Mertz could no longer face, or keep down, dog-based food. After harrowing days in which the delirious, convulsing Mertz could not leave his sleeping bag, he died on 8 January. Mawson buried him, then reduced the sledge, cutting it in half with a penknife. When he was ready to start moving again his condition was pitiful. The skin peeling from his thighs and scro-tum meant he had to walk bow-legged, and the entire soles of his feet had come away forcing him to bandage them in place. His whole body seemed to be rotting away. To make matters worse, he was now travelling only 8–10km (5–6 miles) each day and would not make base before 15 January.

The crossing of the Mertz Glacier was a triumph of courage and will. Mawson fell into a crevasse, only held by the rope attaching him to his sledge. He hauled himself to the lip, but fell again. Luckily the sledge held and he hauled himself out at the second attempt. He then made a rope ladder to aid his climb in case the same thing happened again. By 15 January he was still 130km (80 miles) from base and his progress was down to 4–5km (2½–3 miles) each day. He walked at night because the snow was harder, and struggled on in con-ditions that many would have said were impossible. He

Above **Mawson after his arrival back at camp.**
University of Adelaide, South Australia

his raw flash. The nails forced their way back, piercing his boots and flesh. He was now exhausted, both physically and mentally, the nearness of rescue bringing its own despair. It took him four days to reach Aladdin's Cave, but there were no crampons there and a blizzard imprisoned him for a week. When he could move again he saw the smoke of a disappearing ship and realised he might have to spend the winter alone. But then he saw men near the hut. He waved and they rushed towards him. The first to reach him was so shocked by Mawson's appearance that his first question was 'Which one are you?'.

Mawson's expedition was the first to use radio in Antarctica. The men called the *Aurora*, but the ship was unable to come close to shore because of the weather and finally had to abandon the attempt in order to pick up Wild's team who were not equipped to overwinter. Mawson therefore had to overwinter again, though the long months of inactivity helped him recover. Considering his ordeal, his return to full health was remarkable: he later led another Antarctic expedition, was knighted for his work, and died in 1958 at the age of 76.

Shackleton: *Endurance*

In Britain the national grief and euphoria that greeted the news of Scott's death had given way, at the higher levels of government, to a colder reality. There was the Irish crisis, there were the suffragettes: any anti-Norwegian feelings were a sideshow compared to the real unease felt about the rise of German naval power. The war clouds darkening the horizons of Europe were blocking out the view of Antarctica's snowy wastes. When Winston Churchill, the new First Lord of the Admiralty, heard about another southern expedition, he growled that 'enough life and money has been spent on this sterile quest', noting that polar expeditions 'are becoming an industry'. But Ernest Shackleton, the man behind the requests for government support, would not be denied. He was popular, the live hero the people wanted, the man who could restore some national pride, a fact that Chancellor of the Exchequer Lloyd George was more than willing to exploit. If Juvenal was right, that to keep the masses happy what was needed were bread and circuses, Lloyd George was more than willing to have Shackleton provide the circus at a time when difficult decisions needed to be made.

Shackleton's idea was to cross Antarctica from the Weddell Sea to the Ross Sea, going over the pole. He

was knocked over by the persistent wind, but still he kept going. His hair was falling out and he feared he was dying of scurvy, but his will was undaunted, as was his hope that a rescue party would reach him. On 20 January he gained the plateau beyond the glacier. He could now sail his sledge so progress improved. On 29 January he stumbled on a new cairn; inside was food and a note with the news that Amundsen had reached the pole, and the bearing and distance of Aladdin's Cave. The note also said that a rescue party had left the cairn just six hours before: Mawson's last camp was only 8km (5 miles) from that of his rescuers. But there was no hope of catching them: they were three fit men, he was barely alive. Worse, he had abandoned his crampons when he reached the plateau, but the wind had polished it to hard ice. He improvised, knocking nails into pieces of wood which he strapped to his feet, leaving off the shed-skin soles that he had used to protect

needed two ships, buying the *Polaris*, a would-be cruise ship from a failed Arctic venture of de Gerlache, and renaming it *Endurance*, and borrowing the *Aurora* from Mawson. Shackleton would take the *Endurance* to the Weddell: he wanted the navy to take the *Aurora* to the Ross Sea from where supply dumps would be prepared for the arrival of the Weddell men, but Churchill vetoed that idea.

When the *Endurance* sailed under the command of Frank Worsley, on board were Frank Wild, the most experienced Antarctic polar explorer of the age and Shackleton's second-in-command, and the Australian photographer Frank Hurley, veteran of Mawson's expedition, whose photos were to help create the legend. It was 1 August 1914 when the *Endurance* left London. On 4 August Britain declared war on Germany. On 8 August when the ship finally left Plymouth for Antarctica it was only after Shackleton had offered to abort the trip and some men had left for active service. In the way of British legends Shackleton received a one-word telegram: 'Proceed'. In fact, it was the *Endurance* that proceeded, Shackleton not leaving Britain until 26 September on a ship bound for Buenos Aires. The news-

papers claimed that the expedition had popular support and was perceived as every bit as dangerous as going to war, but there is evidence that the nation was not united in its approval, some believing that a fit, active man's place was on the battlefield.

The *Endurance* arrived in South Georgia on 5 November, choosing that island rather than the Falklands to hopefully avoid meeting the fleet of German Admiral von Spee which had recently destroyed

a British squadron off Chile's Cape Coronel. The whaling community of Grytviken was sceptical of Shackleton's chances of penetrating the Weddell Sea: they would have been even more so had they known he intended to freeze the *Endurance* into the ice there because he did not trust Worsley to get back to his base the following year. Shackleton sailed to the South Sandwich Islands, then turned south. His destination was Vahsel Bay. This had been discovered and named by Filchner in 1912. Richard Vahsel, a veteran of the *Gauss*, was captain of the *Deutschland*: when he died soon after the discovery, Filchner changed the name to that of one of his sponsors, but later explorers changed it back.

The *Endurance* made good progress towards Vahsel at first, but was then stopped by heavy pack ice. On 15 January 1915 they reached open water just 130km (80 miles) from the bay, but next day the ice closed around the ship. Despite desperate attempts to free her

Shackleton had to accept that they would never make landfall, throwing the transantarctic trek into doubt. Soon, as the ship drifted north with the ice it became apparent that the great adventure was over.

The men survived the winter well considering the disappointment of losing the trek and the makeshift nature of their quarters. The ship fared less well. Not built to ride the ice as *Fram* had been the *Endurance* was gripped by it, pushed, pulled and compressed. When spring came it was clear that a really powerful squeeze would destroy her timbers. On 15 October the ship broke free, but hope was short-lived. Two days later she was entombed again, ten days more and it was clear that irreparable damage had been sustained and Shackleton ordered his men on to the ice. To his disconsolate and fearful crew he now said, quite simply, 'So now we'll go home'. For all his faults – though he had taken dogs this time he had not learned to drive them or taken men who had; he had not learned to ski; his preparations were poor and hasty; his attitude towards his men sometimes divisive – when backs were against the wall Shackleton came into his own. Amundsen's careful preparation would probably keep

you out of trouble, but if trouble did come, Shackleton would probably get you out of it.

Shackleton decided to haul two loaded boats across the ice to Paulet Island, one of Nordenskjöld's bases which he knew was well stocked, or to Snow Hill Island which was closer; from either a small party could reach the whalers on Deception Island. Worsley disagreed: he was a sailor, not a manhauler, and wanted to wait for the ice to break up and then to use all three boats to head north, but he was overruled. Paulet was about 650km (400 miles) away, a journey of 65 days or more. The trek began on 30 October but was quickly abandoned. The optimism of hauling 10km (6 miles) daily was crushed by a 1.5km (1 mile) reality. A second attempt many weeks later proved equally futile. A camp was now set up on the ice and more equipment was salvaged from the *Endurance*. To save weight Hurley threw away many (perhaps 70 per cent) of his slides – in view of the quality of what he kept, the destruction is enough to make one weep.

On 21 November the crippled *Endurance* finally sank. The marooned men were now at the mercy of the elements and calculations showed food would likely run short. Tempers frayed and it took all of Shackleton's leadership skills to keep the group coherent. Eventually, as the floe on which they were camped was pushed north, penguins and seals arrived, supplementing the diet and allowing reserves to be built up. Finally, on 9 April 1916, after over five months on the ice, the men could take to the boats, heading north across an uneasy sea. The weather drove them south

and east when they wanted to go north and west: they could not hope to reach Deception Island. If they headed north now they might be pushed past the South Shetlands into the Atlantic and almost certain death. Shackleton therefore decided to head for Elephant Island. It was close, but the weather made it an epic voyage. It was so cold that spray whipped up by the wind fell as ice: as two of the boats also leaked the men's feet were often immersed in freezing water. They landed on 15 April 1916, after seven days at sea (though they had been able to camp on floes early in the voyage) and 497 days since last touching land on 5 December 1914. (Shackleton has the landing on 15 April in his book *South*, but also states 'next morning (15 April)' implying the landing was on the 14th.) By then many of the men were in a state of shock or hypothermia. They had had no hot food or any drink for days, and wandered about as though inebriated.

Elephant Island teemed with seals and penguins (a source of food) but was otherwise inhospitable, so much so that the first landing place had to be abandoned for another along the coast – and that was little better. The weather was atrocious, soaking the men and

their sleeping bags before any shelter could be organised. To make matters worse, when they lay down to rest, the heat from their bodies melted the frozen penguin guano on the beach and it stank appallingly. By 19 April the situation was desperate, many of the men apparently so demoralised by finding themselves as badly off on land as they had been on the ice that they were almost ready to give up. Percy Blackborrow, who had stowed away on the ship in Buenos Aires as an adventure-seeking 19-year-old, had frostbite in his toes which threatened gangrene. Aware of the need for urgent action, Shackleton decided not to overwinter on the island, but to risk one boat and six men on a dash to South Georgia. The island was 1,300km (800 miles) away, the seas (as winter approached) likely to be mountainous, the navigational aids rudimentary. The only plus point was that the wind would be on the sailors' side, but it was a small positive against a mass of negatives. Many thought the trip was doomed.

Having decided to go Shackleton set the *Endurance*'s carpenter, Harry McNeish (sometimes written as McNish), to make the *James Caird* (the biggest and most seaworthy of the three boats: it was named

for a major benefactor of the expedition) as ready as could be. McNeish strengthened the keel with the mast of one of the other boats, and constructed a deck framework: as timber was short the decking was canvas. McNeish was one of the chosen crew, which consisted of Shackleton, Frank Worsley, Tom Crean (a veteran of both of Scott's expeditions), John Vincent, Tim McCarthy and McNeish. The choice of McNeish and Vincent is another indication of Shackleton's leadership skills. McNeish had wanted to build a ship from the wreckage of the *Endurance*, a reasonable suggestion Shackleton had vetoed: later the carpenter had 'mutinied', claiming loss of the ship freed him from any obligation to 'The Boss'. It had been a tricky moment, and there were others behind the physically strong Vincent, who was inclined to bully people. Shackleton's choice placed the two potential troublemakers where they would have other concerns to occupy them and could not disrupt the fragile accord on Elephant Island.

The weather was still atrocious, but improved slightly on 24 April. Shackleton launched immediately. Wild was left in charge on the island with orders to overwinter and then sail for Deception Island if rescue did not come. The *James Caird* had four weeks' supply of food – if they had not reached South Georgia in that time they would have died on the way – and bags of blubber oil to quell spiteful seas, an attempt to stop waves breaking over the boat. The 16-day voyage of the *James Caird* to South Georgia was one of the great boat journeys of all time. The crew were permanently soaked almost from the start. The cold was intense: occasionally ice had to be hacked from the canvas deck and the continuous pumping, which had to be done with bare hands, was a freezing nightmare. Sleeping in the claustrophobic space beneath the canvas, in wet, rotting sleeping bags on the boulders loaded as ballast, was near impossible. The sea was rough almost all the time, adding seasickness to the general misery: once a giant wave almost smashed the boat. On occasions the wind was so strong the boat had to be held into it making progress impossible: a hurricane-force blow endured at one stage sank a 500-ton steamer. To compound the agonies, one of the water

Top **The heroic nature of Shackleton's boat journey to South Georgia and his crossing of the island have inspired many subsequent adventurers to undertake sections of the journey again. This photograph was taken during a repeat of the island crossing by Conrad Anker, Reinhold Messner and Stephen Venables. Anker and Messner are descending the Fortuna Glacier towards Fortuna Bay.**
Stephen Venables

Above **Launching the *James Caird* from Elephant Island.**
USA Library of Congress

kegs was spoiled by sea water so that the men had nothing to drink for the last three days. Navigation was by dead reckoning and from very occasional glimpses of the sun, Worsley's successful guidance of the boat to South Georgia therefore amounting to genius.

When seaweed and then seabirds were spotted, indicating that land was close, the men's elation was short-lived, a gale threatening to smash the boat against the sheer cliffs of South Georgia's south-western shore. Shackleton had deliberately made for this coast: though the whaling stations were on the north-eastern coast any failed attempt to reach that side meant the boat would have been pushed into open ocean. At least the southern side gave the chance of trying again on the north if the island had been missed. Only after hours of tacking, and a good dose of fortune, was the boat beached near Cape Rosa at the entrance to King Haakon Bay. The grateful men found that they had landed near a stream. They slept in a handy cave, then added four albatross fledglings to their pot, the first substantial meal they had eaten in two-and-a-half weeks. Shackleton decided that another boat journey was too hazardous and that he would cross the island on foot. On 15 May after a few days of rest the *James Caird* was sailed to the back of King Haakon Bay where a clear pass split the mountains.

There were several whaling stations on South Georgia, the closest of which – at Prince Olav Harbour – was only 11km (7 miles) away, but unsure if it was manned in winter Shackleton decided to head for Husvik which he knew was. He chose Worsley and Crean to accompany him. Carrying food for three days, but no sleeping bags, and with salvaged screws in their boots as crampons, the three set off early on 19 May, after being stormbound at the bay's head for three days. In better weather than they could have hoped for they picked their way across the glaciated heart of South Georgia, sometimes retracing their steps when the terrain proved unyielding. After 36 hours during which they stopped only for short rests and meals they stumbled into Stromness, frightening the first people they met who mistook them for drunks. When the apprehensive whaling station manager asked, 'Who the hell are you?' the dirty, haggard, bearded man in the centre of the three said simply, 'My name is Shackleton.'

Worsley set off to rescue the three in King Haakon Bay – he also rescued the *James Caird* which can still be seen at Dulwich College, England – noting that the vicious storm which had blown up would have killed them on their walk, while Shackleton organised a ship to fetch the men on Elephant Island. The first two attempts failed because the rescue ships could not get through the winter ice. Then, incensed by the British government's decision to send the *Discovery* to rescue the men, which would entail a wait of many weeks, and not to have him as leader of the mission, Shackleton persuaded the Chilean government to lend him the *Yelcho*, an unsuitable steam tug. With Worsley and Crean, and a crew of Chileans, Shackleton set out on 25 August.

On Elephant Island the remaining two boats had been converted into a hut. In this the frost-bitten toes of Blackborrow's left foot were amputated using the last of the chloroform as anaesthetic. The winter was survived on a diet of seal and penguin. Wild had decided that when spring came he would take three men and one boat to Deception Island, but on 29 August the *Yelcho* anchored just 150m (500ft) offshore. The Endurance expedition was over.

The recent explosion of interest in Shackleton means that many could be forgiven for believing that the *Endurance* adventure was the whole story. Too often the *Aurora*'s men – Shackleton's Forgotten Men – are ignored. The *Aurora* left Hobart under the command of Aeneas Mackintosh, a veteran of the *Nimrod*. The ship was late leaving and also under-supplied because of financial problems. After making a base in Scott's hut at Cape Evans, Mackintosh and a party which included Ernest Wild, Frank Wild's brother, laid supply dumps to 80°S in dreadful weather. They returned to the hut to find that the *Aurora* had broken her moorings and drifted out to sea, leaving them and eight others marooned. They only survived because of stores left two years before when the survivors of Scott's expedition had been evacuated. Among the marooned men morale was low. They mistrusted Mackintosh who, as they (rightly) saw it, had abandoned his ship; they had no idea when they would be rescued; and they still had the responsibility of setting up supply dumps for Shackleton all the way to the Beardmore Glacier.

Freed from the ice in which she had become entombed after drifting out to sea the *Aurora* sailed to New Zealand, then, reprovisioned, returned to the Ross Sea. The captain was now John King Davis who had captained the ship for Mawson and been with Shackleton on the *Nimrod*. Shackleton himself, fit again after his Elephant Island/South Georgia exertions, went as a supernumerary officer. What the *Aurora* found was a group of men whose appearance shocked Shackleton as they looked far worse than the men rescued from Elephant Island.

After overwintering a team of six with those dogs that had survived set out to lay a dump at 83°S. It had been a harrowing trip: the men had no skis and the lack of dogs meant they had to manhaul. By the time they reached 83°S they were all suffering from scurvy and one man, the Rev Arnold Spencer-Smith, the first clergyman on Antarctica, had been left in a tent unable to move. Spencer-Smith was collected a week later, but was too ill to walk, the other five dragging him for over 300km (200 miles) to their 80°S dump. Leaving food for Shackleton the men were now dangerously short of supplies, but managed to reach a point just 16km (10 miles) from their next dump. A blizzard erupted, keeping them in camp for five days. Desperately short of food and fearing they would meet the same fate as Scott's team, three men – Joyce, Hayward and Richards – set off for base leaving Ernest Wild with Spencer-Smith and Mackintosh, both too sick to travel. The three miraculously found the dump in the blizzard and returned with food. Hauling Spencer-Smith and Mackintosh, the party set off again, but soon Hayward collapsed. Leaving Mackintosh in a tent Joyce, Richards and Wild hauled Spencer-Smith and Hayward south, but two days before reaching the Discovery hut Spencer-Smith died. He had been hauled almost 500km (300 miles). Leaving Hayward at the hut the three haulers went back to rescue Mackintosh.

The five survivors now waited for many weeks for the sea to freeze so they could reach Cape Evans. But on 8 May the now-recovered Mackintosh and Hayward, though discouraged by the others who were concerned the ice was too fragile, decided they could wait no longer. The others waited a further two months before daring to trust the ice, finally reaching Cape Evans on 15 July 1916, ten months after leaving it, to discover that Mackintosh and Hayward had not arrived.

The world that Shackleton and his men returned to had changed, almost beyond their imagining. The war which would be 'over by Christmas' was grinding on,

countless bodies lying slaughtered on the Western Front. Shackleton's adventure was a momentary distraction for an exhausted nation. Within months of leaving Elephant Island many of The Boss' men were in action. Within four months of the *James Caird* landing on South Georgia, Tim McCarthy, one of the six crewmen, had been killed in action. Shackleton did not seem to understand the change. He had had a hero's reception in Chile, but a much less rapturous one on the Falklands where one islander commented that he should have 'been at the war long ago instead of messing about on icebergs'. When he joined the *Aurora* he was bluntly told that people were 'a little impatient with polar exploration...' and that 'when every man in uniform was either a real, or at least a potential hero, people were also a little impatient of explorers in general'.

Back in Britain Shackleton, too old for active service, was shuffled around the corridors of power, sent to Buenos Aires and then to north Norway and Murmansk to organise transport during the Arctic winter. Before he had a chance to do anything the war ended. In 1920 after dictating *South*, his book on the *Endurance* trip (written by Edward Saunders from the dictated notes and various diaries), and giving numerous lectures, Shackleton decided to head south again. With no clear idea of where he was going to go or why, but perhaps knowing that age and poor health were catching up with him – he had probably had a first heart attack in Tromsø in 1917 – and that he was ill-suited to a humdrum life, he found a ship, the *Quest*, gathered a few old colleagues, including Frank Wild, and set sail. The *Quest* reached South Georgia where, early on 5 January 1922, Shackleton had a massive heart attack and died. He was 47. At the request of his wife he was buried on the island. He was long outlived by many of the *Endurance*'s crew. Worsley, the last survivor of the *James Caird* crew died in 1943, Lionel Greenstreet, the last survivor of all died in March 1979. He was 89.

Over the years it has become *de rigueur* to denigrate Scott as an incompetent establishment man, to lionise Shackleton as the marvellous antithesis. The reality is too complex for such simple characterisations. Shackleton was a superb leader and a marvellous man in a crisis, but he was little better than Scott as a polar explorer. He took ponies on *Nimrod* and though he had dogs on *Endurance* he had no trained dog drivers.

Above **Percy Blackborrow and Harry McNeish's cat, Mrs Chippy. Blackborrow was refused a job on the *Endurance* when his friend, William Bakewell, was taken on in Buenos Aires. Bakewell helped Blackborrow stow away on the ship. When he was discovered Shackleton allowed him to stay – pointing out that he should remember that men on polar expeditions often went hungry and that stowaways were then the first to be eaten. Blackborrow's feet were frost-bitten and the toes of his left foot were amputated on Elephant Island. He returned to his native Wales after the expedition and worked on the docks in Newport. He died in 1949.**

As a carpenter Harry McNeish was a real craftsman, admired by almost everyone. But he was also an abrasive character which did not endear him to either Shackleton or Worsley. McNeish's cat, Mrs Chippy, was the expedition's mascot and the carpenter's true friend. When the *Endurance* sank Shackleton ordered that puppies and the cat should be put down as they could not earn their keep and food was likely to become scarce. McNeish never forgave him for it. After the expedition McNeish returned to his native Scotland, but then emigrated to New Zealand where, unable to work (because, he claimed, the trip had left his hands aching permanently), he became a fixture on Wellington docks, sleeping rough and maintained in drink by the dockers who considered him a hero for his work and voyage on the *James Caird*. It is said that McNeish could manipulate any conversation around to Shackleton and the death of his cat so that he could extol the virtues of the latter and berate the former. When he died in 1957 his coffin was borne on an army gun carriage before being taken to the grave by navy pallbearers.

Scott Polar Research Institute, University of Cambridge, UK

Neither had he learned to ski, nor taken any expert skiers. He had witnessed Amundsen's success, but not really learned from it. It is frequently stated that he never lost a man, yet the survival of the team on his furthest south expedition owed more to good luck than good management, and the deaths of the *Aurora* team members had their roots as much in Shackleton's poor organisation of the expedition as in the poor quality of Mackintosh's leadership. When Shackleton recommended the *Endurance* men for the Polar Medal he pointedly excluded four, including McNeish and Vincent who had been on the *James Caird*. In view of the enormous contribution McNeish made to the success of the boat journey this was a spiteful act whatever the perceived justification, and it outraged several who received the medal, as did the exclusion of Vincent whose only 'crime' was to have collapsed mentally towards the end of the *James Caird* voyage. That Shackleton was a great man is indisputable, but he was not quite as wonderful as he is now usually portrayed, any more than Scott was quite as bad.

Flying to the pole

In the aftermath of the Great War Britain, beaten in the race for the South Pole, and with the North Pole now won, turned its attention to the Third Pole: Everest. Many of the traits seen in the Antarctic trips can be glimpsed in the Everest expeditions of 1921, 1922 and 1924. After the Australian-born George Finch used a duvet jacket and enthusiastically promoted the use of oxygen in 1922 he was dropped from the 1924 team. In 1924 Mallory and Irvine died and became the new British heroes. Their deaths were heroic, like Scott's, and had the advantage that they might have reached the top and that defeat was not at the hands of a tiny, friendly nation of foreigners, but something huge, hostile and inanimate.

Trips south were now carried out in order to fill the gaps on the Antarctic map; but when the next explorers arrived they used aeroplanes. After the faintly ludicrous attempts with snowmobiles and motor cars the era of the engine had truly arrived. First of the 'new generation' was Sir Hubert Wilkins, an Australian who had been a member of the British Imperial Expedition of 1920/2 (a group of four despite its grandiose title, who had fallen out with each other and failed to cross Graham Land) and of Shackleton's *Quest* expedition. Early in 1928 Wilkins had made important Arctic flights and been knighted. Later the same year, backed by the American newspaper baron William Randolph Hearst, he decided to attempt the first flights in Antarctica. His pilot was Carl Ben Eielson, an Alaskan bush pilot remembered in the name of a visitor centre in the Denali National Park, who had been Wilkins' pilot on his Arctic flights. The pair, with a second pilot and an engineering team, shipped two Lockheed Vega monoplanes to Deception Island intending to take off from the sea. The sheltered Deception Harbour (Port Foster) was iced, the ship carrying the planes (the *Hektoria*) ploughing a seaway for the float-fitted planes. Unfortunately the open water was promptly invaded by feeding albatrosses who declined to leave, forcing the levelling of a runway which ran downhill to the sea, a major incentive to a successful take-off. From the runway, on 16 November 1928, Eielson and Wilkins made the first Antarctic flight. One later flight, lasting 11 hours and covering 2,000km (1,300 miles) was over Graham Land. Remembering his struggle on the land expedition to Graham Land, Wilkins enjoyed the 'tremendous sensation of power and freedom' he felt in the air. It was, he noted, the first time new land had been discovered from the air. Wilkins continued to fly, mapping the continent, until 1930.

The first flight over Antarctica was followed by the first flight from the continent. In 1926 the American Richard Evelyn Byrd claimed to have flown to the North Pole (now discounted by most experts) and in June 1927 crossed the Atlantic Ocean just weeks after Charles Lindbergh. His fame attracted rich sponsors including John D. Rockefeller, Edsel Ford and Harold Vanderbilt (and a $1,000 cheque from Lindbergh himself) and a payment of $60,000 from the *New York Times* for exclusive rights to cover his proposed southern expedition. Byrd took three planes – Fokker, Fairchild and Ford Tri-Motor monoplanes – a huge pack of dogs and 650 tons of equipment. A base, Little America, was established on the ice shelf of the Bay of Whales and from it, on 27 January 1929, Byrd, with pilot Bernt Balchen (a Norwegian, but later a naturalised American) made the first flight from the continent, discovering the Rockefeller Mountains. Several more firsts soon followed. A party (led by Laurence Gould, Byrd's deputy) flown in to make a land survey of the mountains, was hit by a 12-day blizzard during which their Fokker transport broke free of its moorings and 'flew' about 800m (875yd) before crashing – Antarctica's first air crash. The men were rescued by another plane – Antarctica's first air rescue.

After overwintering the remaining planes were made ready for flying again. On 28 November 1929 the Ford Tri-Motor (named *Floyd Bennett* after Byrd's pilot on his

Above **The remnants of Byrd's Fokker single-engine Super Universal after the blizzard.**
Richard Sale Collection

North Pole flight who had died in 1927) took off with Balchen as pilot and Harold June as co-pilot, together with Byrd and Ashley McKinley. They had to jettison 135kg (300lb) of emergency food to reduce weight so as to acquire enough height to cross the Transantarctic Mountains (by way of the Liv Glacier), then continued across the plateau. At 1.14am (GMT) on 29 November, after a flight of 8 hours 31 minutes, Byrd radioed Little America that they were over the pole, noting that 'for a few seconds we stood over the spot where Amundsen had stood... and Scott had also stood'. Now 'there was nothing to mark that scene'. No tents or flags stained the 'white desolation and solitude'. As they circled the pole Byrd dropped a USA flag weighted with a stone he had taken from Floyd Bennett's grave. The plane landed at a prepared fuel depot by the Queen Maud Mountains at 4.47am, took off at 6am and was back at Little America at 10.08am. The journey had taken 18 hours 39 minutes, the flight time being 17 hours 26 minutes. Amundsen had taken 99 days, Scott had never returned.

During the flight the *Floyd Bennett* dropped supplies by parachute to a sledge party led by Laurence Gould which was setting out to survey the Queen Maud Mountains. Byrd had also dropped supplies to the team during the flight to create the fuel dump for the pole flight. He wrote 'the men were in harness, pulling with the dogs: the dogs were up to their bellies in snow... If ever a conclusive contrast was struck between the new and old methods of polar travel it was at this moment.' Gould's survey team followed Amundsen's route to the foot of the Axel Heiberg Glacier where they found a cairn erected by the Norwegians as they returned from

Above **Richard Byrd's Ford Tri-Motor *Floyd Bennett* on the way to the pole.**
From a painting by Robert Carlin.
US Navy Historical Centre

Right **Amundsen's cairn on Mount Betty, visited by Laurence Gould's team during the Byrd expedition.**
Richard Sale Collection

the pole. Inside it was a 17-litre (3³/₄-gallon) can of paraffin (still intact), some matches and a tin box holding two pieces of paper. One had the addresses of Hanssen and Wisting who had built the cairn, the other was a note from Amundsen with brief notes on the journey, including the date the pole was reached. The items were extracted, says Gould, 'with reverent hands… without in any way disturbing the shape or structure' of the cairn. Gould goes on 'I think we shall none of us forget the glamour of the moment.' Each of the Americans took a small rock from the cairn as a keepsake. Later, close by, they built a bigger cairn over some of their own supplies.

In 1933 Richard Byrd returned with an even bigger expedition: 56 men, 153 dogs, 4 tractors, 3 airplanes and an autogyro. The base, Little America II, was on the site of the earlier one on the ice shelf and from it the tractors drove over 20,000km (12,500 miles) finally proving the worth of the internal combustion engine in Antarctic travel. The planes explored over 700,000 sq km (270,000 sq miles) of the continent, massively increasing knowledge of it. The expedition was an almost complete success apart from a bizarre incident which almost cost Byrd his life. Byrd built a hut (named the Bolling Advance Weather Station – Bolling after his mother's maiden name) at 80°8'S, some 190km (120 miles) from Little America II, sinking a prefabricated structure 2.5m (8ft) into the ice. Byrd had planned for three men to overwinter in the hut making meteorological observations, but the breakdown of a tractor bringing supplies meant that there was food for only two. Believing that two men, without recourse to a 'referee', would irritate each other beyond reason, Byrd decided to overwinter alone (though in constant radio contact with base). On 28 March he waved goodbye to the last of his team.

His early problems were associated with his daily walk outside the hut. Once he became lost, once almost fell into a crevasse and then, in a blizzard, found the trapdoor access to the hut iced over and was only just able to open it. Being alone was not only perilous outside: in the hut Byrd found the darkness and cold increasingly trying and became lonely and despondent. In May a fault developed in his heating/cooking stove burner which, combined with the hut ventilators being blocked with snow, made him ill from carbon monoxide poisoning. He spotted the problems in time, but soon after the petrol-driven generator developed a fault. The generator was in a small annex, but before he could return along an access tunnel Byrd had been near-poisoned again by fumes. This time the effect on him was irreversible, his health declining. With the worst of the winter to come – and he was the furthest south anyone had ever overwintered – Byrd attempted to prevent his colleagues from realising his condition in case they risked their lives in a rescue. But by early August his radio messages had become so strange the men at Little America II had guessed, and a rescue mission set out. After a false start due to mechanical problems, a tractor reached the hut where a weak, emaciated Byrd – he had lost 30kg (70lb) in weight – welcomed them with hot soup. It was two months before he was well enough to travel back to base. Of his solitary vigil Byrd claimed, 'I learned much, but I never want to go through that experience again.'

The next flyer on the continent was Lincoln Ellsworth, who in 1926 had flown across the Arctic with Amundsen and Nobile in the airship *Norge*. Ellsworth came south in 1933 determined to add a transantarctic flight to his Arctic record. He had his own ship, the *Wyatt Earp* (a renamed Norwegian herring boat) and aircraft (the *Polar Star*, a Northrup monoplane) and a team which included Hubert Wilkins and pilot Bernt Balchen. During this first trip the *Polar Star* was damaged when the ice sheet at the Bay of Whales split, dropping it into the crack. Ellsworth tried again in 1934 but could not find a suitable place for a runway on the Antarctic Peninsula. During the journey home the *Wyatt Earp* was overrun by rats which not only ate all the expedition's boats and snowshoe webbing but, ironically, also killed and ate the ship's cat.

In 1935, but now with a new pilot – Herbert Hollick-Kenyon, a British-born Canadian – Ellsworth tried for a third time. The *Polar Star* took off from Dundee Island, at the northern end of the peninsula, on 23 November and flew along it, heading directly for the Bay of Whales (and Byrd's Little America base). After 14 hours in the air, during which their radio failed (causing a rescue mission to be organised and frantic newspaper headlines written) Hollick-Kenyon landed the plane on the Antarctic plateau. After resting they took off again on 24 November, but were forced down by bad weather after just 30 minutes. The storm lasted three days, and when they took off again they managed only another 50 minutes' flying before bad weather returned, keeping them tent-bound for seven days as a blizzard raged. The plane took a day to free from the drifting snow (Ellsworth used a mug to clear snow from the inner tail section: his description of this notes that he lost all feeling in his left foot during the work but assumed it was just due to the cold!), but it snowed again before they could take off. Finally, after further digging, they took off on 4 December. They landed after four hours to check their position (by sextant): they were 200km (125 miles) from Little America.

Next day they continued, soon sighting the Ross Sea, but then being forced to land when the *Polar Star* ran out of fuel. They were 26km (16 miles) from Little America, though they did not reach it until 15 December after hauling the emergency sledge for more than five times that distance through bad weather. By then Ellsworth's frozen foot was giving him real trouble. The two men settled into Little America and on 19

January 1936 a plane from an Australian rescue ship dropped them food and mail: three days later the *Wyatt Earp* arrived to pick them up.

After Byrd's pioneering flights, in 1929–31 Douglas Mawson led joint Australian, British, New Zealand expeditions to explore the coast between Wilhelm II coast and Coats Land. The team used the *Discovery*, Scott's old ship, but further flights by Ellsworth in 1938 emphasised Byrd's view that exploration and mapping of the continent was quicker and safer from the air. Mawson's expeditions represent the last of the 'old-fashioned' approach to discovering Antarctica. In 40 years Antarctica had gone from an unknown continent on which man had never set foot, one to which men voyaged in sailing ships, to one which had been mapped from the air. In 25 years man had gone from dreaming about reaching the South Pole to being able to fly to it in a matter of hours.

Crossing Antarctica

The 1939–45 war put an end to the Antarctic dream, though Richard Byrd led one more expedition (1939–41) as the Pacific sank towards despair. When peace returned interest in the continent was also revitalised. The Americans, Argentineans, Chileans and French all arrived to map, do scientific research and stake claims. Weather stations were set up: in 1954 the Australians set up Mawson, the first permanent year-round station on the Mac-Robertson Land coast.

All the expeditions were scientific – though it could not have escaped the notice of military planners that the 4,700 sailors involved in the US Operation Highjump would get cold-weather training that might prove valuable if the Cold War developed into Arctic warfare – and culminated in the work of the International Geographical Year (IGY). The IGY – 'the most significant peaceful activity since the Renaissance' to quote the hype of the time – involved tens of thousands of scientists from 60 or more countries. As part of the IGY the Americans set up a base at the South Pole, tactfully named Amundsen-Scott. On 31 October 1956 a DC3 (called the *Que Sera Sera*) piloted by Gus Shinn landed at the pole and Admiral George Dufek became the 11th man, and the first American, to stand there – and the first to have arrived there without days of cold, relentless effort. The following month Lt Richard Bowers – the second Lt Bowers to stand at the pole, but the first to arrive safely back at McMurdo – arrived to supervise construction of the base.

As part of the IGY the British decided to realise Shackleton's dream of crossing Antarctica from the Weddell to the Ross. Ironically the prime minister who committed the country to financing the plan was Winston Churchill, the man who had led the campaign against Shackleton's proposal. In charge of the project was Vivian Fuchs. His team would start from the Weddell

and, after reaching the pole, use supply depots laid by a New Zealand team working from McMurdo to continue to the Ross Sea. The New Zealanders were to be led by Sir Edmund Hillary who, three years earlier had, with Tenzing Norgay, been first to the summit of Everest. In January 1956 the *Theron*, a Canadian sealer captained by Harald Marø, took Fuchs and his team, together with Hillary, to the Weddell where, having reached Vahsel Bay, they established Shackleton base. The *Theron* had ice-spotter planes and radar, which gave her a superb advantage over the *Endurance*, but returning from the bay (eight men were left to overwinter) the ship almost became ice-bound in an eerie replay of Shackleton's trip.

In January 1957 the *Endeavour* took Hillary and his team to McMurdo where the ice-breaker USS *Glacier* helped her reach the continent. Hillary established Scott base at Pram Point from where, using planes, depots were established on the Skelton Glacier and the plateau beyond. Hillary chose the Skelton rather than the Beardmore because, although a longer journey, it was an easier one for vehicles. To test his vehicles, which he secretly hoped to drive south, Hillary repeated the 'Worst Journey in the World' in March taking two days to reach Cape Crozier – where the ruins of the 1911 team's hut were discovered, a search revealing some of Edward Wilson's drawing pencils, a poignant find – and just 14 hours to return. On the other side of the continent Fuchs' team was establishing 'South Ice', an advanced base at 81°40'S, again using planes to transport all the base's supplies. The austral winter passed with teams at the Shackleton, Scott and South Ice bases.

When summer came Fuchs found the journey to South Ice – he was using a combination of dog teams and vehicles – much more difficult for his tractors than he had imagined, taking 37 days to cover the 644km (400 miles): he then flew back to Shackleton in two-and-a-half hours. He finally set out on the transantarctic journey on 24 November.

Fuchs' original plan had been to reach the pole on 25 December and even now he thought 31 December was possible, though this seems to have been a forlorn hope. In a note to Hillary before starting, Fuchs hints as much: using his calculations 10 January was the earliest he could arrive. Fuchs set out with US SnoCats

Above **A camp on the Skelton Glacier during the Trans-Antarctic expedition.**
Canterbury Museum, New Zealand

Above **Edmund Hillary, Vivian Fuchs and Admiral George Dufek at the South Pole, March 1958. Dufek was the 11th man to reach the pole. Hillary led the third team to reach it overland, while Fuchs was the first to complete the traverse of Antarctica.**
Canterbury Museum, New Zealand

and Weasels, reaching South Ice on 21 December and not leaving until 25 December. He then followed a trail forged by dog teams, catching these on 29 December, but continuing to follow them for several more days. Progress was mixed. On the ice shelf the heavy vehicles fell into crevasses the dogs could cross easily, much time and effort being required to extract them. On the plateau, which, in general, was much less heavily ice-ridged and crevassed, the vehicles were much quicker than the dogs. Fuchs had been unsure of the reliability of the vehicles and had been prepared to manhaul if necessary, but in fact lost only one tractor to mechanical failure.

On the Ross Sea side Hillary was establishing two further depots, at 770km and 1,100km (480 and 700 miles) from Scott base. Determined to try his tractors Hillary had driven south, discovering that they were not only reliable, but fast. By 15 December he had reached Depot 700 with three tractors. The plan had been for Fuchs to reach the pole by the 25th, then to travel to Depot 700 from where Hillary would guide him to Scott base. But now this plan was in tatters. Faced with a wait of at least a month and confident of his tractors Hillary decided to go for the pole. He crossed a crevassed area, then managed 65km (40 miles) daily for six days. Even though progress then slowed to just

1.5kmph (1mph) Hillary's team reached the pole at noon on 4 January 1958, the first men to do so overland since Scott in 1912. The next day Fuchs received a message from Hillary suggesting that because of the delay in his (Fuchs') plan a transantarctic journey was now unjustifiably risky and should be abandoned at the pole, then resumed in 1959. Hillary's message and Fuchs' sharp response were released to the press, doing nothing for relations between the two, which had clearly been strained by Hillary's pole dash.

The joint account of the trip glosses over these problems, but they are exposed by Hillary's account in his biography. He had been told that his job was to wait at Depot 700, then reluctantly allowed to continue, the pole dash causing exchanges at a very high level, the New Zealand prime minster supporting the trip, but the British clearly feeling Hillary was stealing Fuchs' thunder. Fuchs even sent a message telling Hillary not to go for the pole but to conserve fuel as he (Fuchs) was running low: this message annoyed Hillary and precipitated his suggestion that Fuchs abandon his journey at the pole. On his return flight from the pole Hillary flew low over Fuchs' team but only George Lowe (a fellow New Zealander and member of the 1953 Everest team) came out to wave. Hillary saw this as a deliberate slight. He was also very aggrieved when

Above **One of the Ferguson tractors used by Hillary on his Antarctic journey. Lovingly restored it is now a centrepiece of the Massey Ferguson tractor museum in Coventry, England.**

Richard Sale, courtesy of Massey Ferguson (AGCO Ltd) UK

Fuchs persuaded the Americans to fly his dogs from the pole to McMurdo as they were tired and slower than the vehicles: as the dogs could not enter New Zealand Hillary had to shoot them, a responsibility he fiercely resented. Overall, though, it is difficult not to see Hillary's dash as less a thumbed nose to the British, than a deliberate (and very successful) attempt to steal Fuchs' thunder.

From the pole Hillary flew to McMurdo, but returned to welcome Fuchs to the pole when he finally arrived on 19 January (20 January pole time, as Shackleton base and the pole station were on opposite sides of the Date Line and had times 12 hours apart). Fuchs left the pole on 24 January. One of his drivers was poisoned by carbon monoxide fumes from his engine and needed oxygen dropped by plane, but otherwise the trip was uneventful. Hillary joined the team at Depot 700 (on 7 February) and Scott base was reached on 2 March 1958 after a journey of 3,450km (2,158 miles) in 98 days, a daily average of 35km (22 miles). Shackleton's great dream had been realised.

With dogs, on foot – again

Fuchs, who at Scott base received the news that he had been knighted, had taken seismic readings every day on his journey to determine ice thickness – the ice shelf at Shackleton was found to be 400m (1,300ft) thick – though the journey had been as much for adventure as science. Future journeys to the pole and across the continent would be exclusively for adventure, though there are occasional, usually doubtful, scientific reasons given as side issues. In general scientific research is better handled by well-fed men landing in planes than by exhausted, under-fed ones arriving after days in the open. The other difference between the recent expeditions and the earlier ones is that nations no longer underwrite adventures, private finance being required. The need for sponsorship has led to increasingly audacious plans, but has also increased the antagonism between groups as unwritten (and, therefore, highly disputable) laws are transgressed – though to date there has been less aggravation and mutual mud-slinging in Antarctica than in the Arctic.

In 1980 the Trans-Globe Expedition, the three-man British team of Charles Burton, Sir Ranulph Fiennes and Oliver Shepard (none with previous Antarctic experience), landed on the Queen Maud Land coast, close to Sanae, the South African base, and the 0° meridian. The expedition was intending to circumnavigate the earth along (or as close as possible to) the prime meridian and, as part of that trip, was intending to cross Antarctica on open snow scooters, a feat which many claimed was not possible because of the extremes of cold and wind. The team also faced hostility from the British, New Zealand and US governments. The three landed from a chartered ship and overwintered in a double-skinned cardboard hut. They set out for the pole on 26 October 1980, towing sledges behind their scooters (ski-doos with 640cc engines) but being resupplied by air (a private twin-Otter piloted by Giles Kershaw). The three men reached the pole on 15 December and continued to Scott base on Ross Island, which they reached on 11 January. They had achieved the second crossing of the continent, covering 4,200km (2,600 miles) in 66 days, a significantly longer journey than the Fuchs traverse, and at almost double the speed. Trans-Globe was picked up by its chartered ship from Ross Island.

The next land journey to the pole, in 1985/6, recreated the journey of Scott's team. 'In the Footsteps of Scott' was the brainchild of Briton Robert Swan. The team sailed the *Southern Quest* from London to McMurdo following the route of the *Terra Nova*, then three of them – Roger Mear, Gareth Wood and Mike Stroud – overwintered, recreating the 'Worst Journey in the World' by manhauling to Cape Crozier, taking 30

days for the trip. Then, almost exactly duplicating Scott's route three men – Swan, Mear and Wood – set off for the pole. They took no radio so as to recreate the same sense of isolation, but had sledges that weighed only half as much – in part because they were not walking out (they had their own air transport), in part because modern foodstuffs and equipment are lighter. Having set out on the same date as Scott they arrived at the pole on 11 January 1986, a week ahead of Scott's schedule. In an uncanny parallel with the disappointment of the 1911/12 expedition they also received bad news at the pole: the *Southern Quest* had been crushed by ice in McMurdo and sunk. They also met hostility from a proprietorial US government which declined to allow them to contact their base, refused permission for their support plane to fly in to meet them, and whisked them back to McMurdo for an immediate onward journey to New Zealand.

The official US line is that private adventures which go wrong can result in expensive rescues which endanger their personnel, a reasonable argument against the

deliberately foolhardy, but one which fails to stand up for the Swan expedition which was meticulously planned and superbly executed. As the team carried no radios and had no supply depots if they ran out of food they would die, though their air transport could have mounted a search if they were overdue. The loss of the *Southern Quest* was unfortunate, but hardly predictable.

Swan's team had two more links with the past, neither foreseen during the planning stage and one deeply ironical. In 1986 the Norwegian Monica Kristensen led a team attempting to recreate Amundsen's journey by dog-sledge from the Bay of Whales to the pole and back. Apart from Kristensen, the team was male; when asked how it felt to be a woman leading a male team she witheringly replied that she had no experience of being anything other than a woman. The team's start was

Above **The Gateway, looking north from Mount Hope on the 'Footsteps of Scott' expedition.**
Roger Mear

delayed until 17 December, much too late, especially as they had to make the return journey. By the end of January 1987 the team had to turn around, 440km (275 miles) short of the pole. If the British success contrasted with the unfortunate Norwegian effort, relations within the British team bore a marked similarity to those on the *Discovery* expedition trek, antagonism between Mear and Swan mirroring that between Scott and Shackleton. Indeed, Wood was only added to the team to keep the peace (Wilson style) between the two.

The 'Footsteps' expedition was the last which used a ship for transport (though by choice rather than a necessity). The air age had truly arrived with the discovery, at Patriot Hills near the south-western edge of the Ronne Ice Shelf, of a natural blue-ice runway which could be used safely by wheeled (as opposed to ski-mounted) aircraft. In 1988 one of the more amazing trips in Antarctic history saw the first commercial ski journey to the pole, a party of six paying 'tourists' being led by five guides of Mountain Travel from Patriot Hills to the pole. Starting on 3 December 1988 the party covered 1,200km (750 miles) in 49 days, a daily

average of 24km (15 miles), arriving on 17 January 1989. The 'tourists' included the Americans Shirley Metz and Victoria Murdon, the first women to reach the pole overland.

Reinhold Messner, the world's greatest high-altitude climber, had pledged himself to climb the 14 8,000m (26,248ft) peaks without supplementary oxygen. When he achieved this feat in October 1986 he acceded to a promise made to his mother and stopped visiting the high hills. But the restless spirit, the relentless striving towards self-imposed goals or pure ambition – whatever it is that drives him – would not let him be, and he decided to attempt a crossing of Antarctica without mechanised transport. As partner he chose the German Arved Fuchs – no relation to Sir Vivian Fuchs – an expert navigator and Arctic veteran. The two wanted to start from the Filchner Ice Shelf, but an inadequate aircraft fuel supply at Patriot Hills – where Messner/ Fuchs met the Steger/Etienne group (see below) – meant a Ronne Shelf start. On 13 November 1989 they were landed at approximately 82°S, 72°W. From there they followed a route through the Thiel Mountains to the plateau, using specially designed parawings to assist with towing their sledges, the wings attached to them rather than their sledges (as Nansen, Shackleton and Scott had used them). The wings offered faster travel when the wind was in a convenient direction – on one day the pair travelled over 100km (more than 60 miles) – but were of limited value if sastrugi (wind-carved ridges of hard snow) lay across the line of travel. Then the sailor's skis could be caught causing tumbling falls. On one occasion Fuchs was picked up by a strong gust and was lucky to escape without breaking his leg. In addition to the sails the pair had global positioning system (a satellite signal-driven device which fixes the user's position to within a few metres) and radios, and were resupplied by air on the journey to the pole and at the pole itself.

They reached the pole on 30 December (or 31 December depending on which side of the Date Line they stood), Fuchs becoming the first man to have reached both poles on foot in one year. The pair then continued along the Shackleton/Scott Beardmore Glacier route, racing against time and hunger as they were not resupplied on this leg. They reached Scott base on 12 February 1990 after a trek of 92 days (during which they averaged 30km/19 miles daily) and sailed to New Zealand with an Italian expedition.

As with the Swan team, Messner and Fuchs were received with popular interest and admiration, tempered by official hostility at the US pole station. They also fell out, Messner becoming increasingly fed up with Fuchs' lack of fitness and slowness in the early stages of the trek. Though he later expressed admiration for Fuchs' willpower and commitment when hunger and fatigue threatened to end the trek, intemperate remarks by Fuchs after the trip, blown into a full-scale row by the media, discoloured what had been a fine, first, unmechanised traverse.

The Steger/Etienne team Fuchs and Messner met at Patriot Hills was multi-national. Joint leaders Will Steger, an American, and Frenchman Jean-Louis Etienne, had met when their tracks crossed (literally) on the way to the North Pole in 1986. They were joined by Victor Boyarsky, a Russian scientist, Qin Dahe, a Chinese glaciologist, and two dog experts, the Japanese Keizo Funatsu and Briton Geoff Somers. The route the team chose was the longest traverse that could be made, starting near the tip of the Antarctic Peninsula and going through the pole to the Russian Mirny Station on the shore of the Davis Sea, a distance of 6,000km (3,750 miles). Because they intended to complete the traverse in one continuous journey they had to start in midwinter, leaving the peninsula's tip on 27 July 1989 (with the temperature a surprisingly balmy –12°C) with three dog teams/sledges. On the journey to the pole the team moved between a dozen previously laid-down supply depots (though several were not located) and were also resupplied by air from Patriot Hills. Sick or exhausted dogs were also replaced. Nevertheless the trip was a great feat of endurance: September was a month of ferocious blizzards with temperatures down to –40°C and wind-chill temperatures much lower: days were lost as leaving the tents became near impossible and travel out of the question. But conditions improved when the peninsula was left behind: travel rates increased and the pole was reached on 11 December after 138 days. Their reception at the pole station was much the same as that of previous trekkers, with the addition of a 'no fraternising' rule that saw the team camp well away from the dome. They were refused facilities such as meals and showers, a situation which greatly embarrassed Steger, the team's lone American. He was appalled by the lack of warmth shown to his Chinese and Russian teammates, and even more so by the constant stream of 'official' visitors who arrived by air, bought souvenir T-shirts their plane had brought in, never went outside (except to get off and on the plane) and showed precious little interest in the scientific work of the station.

The difficult part of the journey now lay ahead. With limited air resupply possible the team had to make it to Vostok, the remote Russian station on the polar plateau across ground that was rumoured to be impassable because of deep powder snow. In reality the crossing was straightforward, Vostok being reached on 18 January 1990. Now the temperature began to fall, with many days continuously around –45°C, and the added hazard of wind. The weather frayed everyone's nerves and led to the most serious confrontation on the trip when Somers poured out his anger over Steger's handling of a sick dog whose death in October, nearly three months before, had, Somers claimed, been due to Steger's neglect. Then, within sight of success, just 25km (16 miles) from Mirny, Funatsu left his tent in a blizzard to feed his dogs, became disorientated and lost, and was forced to dig a ditch in the snow with a pair of pliers. The others, realising he had not returned,

Above **The Steger/Etienne Transarctic Expedition**
Will Steger

searched and shouted for him, all of them attached to a single rope, but without success. Eventually darkness and cold forced them to abandon the search. At dawn they began again, finding Funatsu soon after. In limited clothing he had survived 12 hours in appalling conditions, a tribute to both his fitness and his refusal to panic. The next day the team completed their journey to Mirny. They had trekked for 220 days at a daily average of 27km (17 miles).

Though the Messner/Fuchs and Steger traverses (and another, unheralded, traverse from the Weddell to the pole, then along Amundsen's route by the Norwegians Høibakk, Mehren and the Mørdre brothers) had been great achievements, the idea of an unsupported traverse – and even of an unsupported journey to the pole – was still a target. In 1992/3 the British pair of Ranulf Fiennes and Mike Stroud almost succeeded. Starting on 9 November 1992 from Berkner Island, between the Filchner and Ronne Ice Shelfs, they made it to the pole on 16 January 1993 hauling sledges that started out weighing 225kg (about 500lb). Reversing the Shackleton/Scott route down the Beardmore Glacier they reached the Ross Ice Shelf (and so were able to claim a sea-to-sea traverse), but had to

call for air evacuation on 12 February after 95 days and 2,000km (1,250 miles) of travel when their physical condition had deteriorated to the point where they could no longer manhaul. They were about 400km (250 miles) from McMurdo.

The following year the Norwegian Erling Kagge made the first unsupported, solo journey to the pole. Starting from Berkner Island on 18 November 1993 he reached the pole in 49 days and 13 hours, arriving on 7 January 1994. He had travelled 1,310km (819 miles), starting with a sledge which weighed 120kg (265lb), which included food for 66 days. Kagge's journey was remarkably uneventful: he had some minor injuries and was occasionally so cold that he had to keep moving so as to warm up rather than stopping to pitch his tent. These episodes depressed him, but overall he was in complete command of himself and the trek, and arrived at the pole fit and well, and almost sorry that the trip was over.

Three years later another Norwegian, Børge Ousland (who had already made solo, unsupported journeys to both the North and South Poles) completed the first unsupported traverse. Ousland started out at the same time as Ranulf Fiennes and the Pole Marek Kaminski who were also trying for the elusive first solo traverse. Interestingly his impression of Fiennes was an echo of the opinion of Nansen and Amundsen for their British competitors. He thought Fiennes' equipment heavy and poorly designed, and considered that all his expeditions had been ill-prepared and, consequently, too strenuous. Like the earlier Norwegian he was surprised how little Fiennes had learnt: on this trip he was following his 1992/3 route from Berkner, despite having found it difficult and dangerous then. Why not, he thought, follow the Norwegian-pioneered route which had been shown to be so much easier? By contrast Ousland's own preparations had an Amundsen-like thoroughness: he had a kevlar sledge, carefully designed equipment, and supplies considered to the gram so that his sledge weighed only about 180kg (400lb).

In the event Fiennes contracted kidney stones and had to be evacuated while Kaminski had a near-fatal fall on the ice shelf and, though he continued, had to stop at the pole. Ousland followed a similar route to Kagge from Berkner Island to the pole, reaching it on 19 December after 35 days, then followed Amundsen's route to and down the Axel Heiberg Glacier before crossing the Ross Ice Shelf to McMurdo. He crossed 2,840km (1,775 miles) of the continent in an astonishing 64 days – a daily average of over 44km (27$\frac{1}{2}$ miles).

This high figure was helped by some astonishing sail-skiing: on one day on the Ross Shelf he covered 226km (more than 140 miles).

Despite being a landmark journey, Ousland's solo trek has not marked the end of Antarctic adventure, despite the official frowns and the obvious hazards. In 1997/8 the Belgians Dixie Dansercoer and Alain Hubert followed the TransGlobe route from Queen Maud Land to the pole and on to McMurdo – 3,500km (2200 miles) in 97 days (they needed one resupply flight to replace a broken sledge) – then in 1998/9 the Japanese Mitsuro Ohba followed the same route to the pole before turning right (as it were) towards the Ellsworth Mountains. Sadly he didn't reach the sea: after a solo journey of 3,825km (2,390 miles), the longest in history, he was evacuated to Patriot Hills. Both the Belgians and Ohba were resupplied during their treks, but in the austral summer of 2000/1 the Norwegians Rolf Bae and Eirik Sønneland completed an unsupported journey of 3,800km (2,375

miles), the longest unsupported journey ever made. The pair started out from Queen Maud coast after overwintering at the Norwegian Troll station hauling sledges of 180kg (397lb). They journeyed to the pole, continuing to the Ross Ice Shelf by way of the Axel Heiberg Glacier (Amundsen's route). After 105 days they reached the McMurdo base, a phenomenal achievement.

Others can enjoy a less exacting journey, Adventure Network International offering 60-day ski trips to the pole from the Ronne Ice Shelf, or ten-day 'last degree' ski trips from 89°S. But whether solo unsupported or with the back-up of a commercial operation, Antarctica will continue to exert the same magnetic pull on the inner steel of adventurers that it has since Shackleton first felt compelled to return.

Below **Børge Ousland heads south on the first solo, unsupported traverse of Antarctica**
Børge Ousland

Selected bibliography

Albanov, Valerian. *In the Land of White Death* (Modern Library, NY, 2000)

Amundsen, Roald. *The North West Passage* (Constable, 1907)

Amundsen, Roald. *The South Pole* (John Murray, 1913)

Amundsen, Roald. *Nordostpassagen* (Gyldendal, Kristiania, 1921) (in Norwegian, has not been translated into English)

Amundsen, Roald and Ellsworth, Lincoln. *The First Flight Across the Polar Sea* (Hutchinson, 1926)

Amundsen, Roald. *My Life as an Explorer* (Heinemann, 1927)

Andrée's Story, the Complete Record of his Polar Flight, 1897 (Viking, NY, 1930)

Arlov, Thor. *A Short History of Svalbard* (Norsk Polarinstitutt, Oslo, 1989)

Astrup, Eivind. *With Peary near the Pole* (Pearson, 1898)

Barr, Susan. *Franz Josef Land* (Norsk Polarinstitutt, Oslo, 1995)

Barr, Susan (Editor), Ivar Fosheim. *Storvilt, Is Og Nytt Land* (Aschehoug, Oslo, 1994) (in Norwegian, not translated into English)

Barrow, John. *A Chronological History of Voyages into the Arctic Regions (1818)* (John Murray, 1818)

Baughman, T. H. *Pilgrims on the Ice* (University of Nebraska, 1999)

Beattie, Owen, and Geiger, John. *Frozen in Time* (Bloomsbury, 1987)

Beechey, Frederick. *Narrative of a Voyage to the Pacific and Beering's Strait* (Colburn and Bentley, 1831)

Beechey, Frederick. *A Voyage towards the North Pole* (Bentley, 1843)

Belcher, Edward. *The Last of the Arctic Voyages* (Lovell Reece, 1855)

Berton, Pierre. *The Arctic Grail* (Viking, 1988)

Bertrand, Kenneth. *Americans in Antarctica* (American Geographical Society, NY, 1971)

Best, George. *A True Discourse: George Best's Account of the Frobisher Voyages* (1578)

Bickel, Lennard. *Shackleton's Forgotten Men* (Thunder's Mouth Press, 2000)

Bickel, Lennard. *Mawson's Will* (Steerforth Press, Vermont, 2000)

Bobrick, Benson. *East of the Sun* (Heinemann, 1992)

Bockstoce, John, R. *Whales, Ice and Men* (University of Washington Press, 1986)

Bomann-Larsen, Tor. *Roald Amundsen, En Biografi* (Cappelen, Oslo, 1995) (in Norwegian, not translated into English)

Borchgrevink, Carsten. *First on the Antarctic Continent* (George Newnes, 1901)

Boyarsky, Victor. *Seven Months of Infinity* (Terra, Moscow, 1998) (in Russian, not translated into English)

Bruce, William. *Polar Exploration* (Williams and Norgate, 1911)

Bryce, Robert. *Cook and Peary* (Stackpole Books, 1997)

Byrd, Richard E. *Alone* (Putnam, 1938)

Capelotti, P.J. *By Airship to the North Pole* (Rutgers University Press, 1999)

Chapman, F. Spencer. *Northern Lights* (Chatto and Windus, 1832)

Charcot, Jean-Baptiste. *Le Français au Pôle Sud* (Ernest Flammarion, Paris, 1906)

Cherry-Garrard, Apsley. *The Worst Journey in the World* (Constable, 1922)

Chevigny, Hector. *Russian America* (Binford and Mort, Oregon, 1985)

Conway, Martin. *No Man's Land. A History of Spitsbergen from its Discovery* (CUP, 1906)

Cook, Frederick. *Through the First Antarctic Night* (Doubleday, Page and Co, 1909)

Cook, Frederick. *My Attainment of the Pole* (Polar Publishing, 1911)

Cook, Frederick. *Return from the Pole* (Burke, 1953)

Cookman, Scott. *Ice Blink* (John Wiley, 2000)

Crawford, Janet. *That First Antarctic Winter* (South Latitude Research Limited, 1998)

Cyriax, Richard. *Sir John Franklin's Last Expedition* (Methuen, 1939)

Delgado, James. *Across the Top of the World* (Checkmark Books, NY, 1999)

De Long, E. *The Voyage of the Jeanette. The Ship and Ice Journals of George W. De Long* (Houghton, Mifflin & Co, Boston, 1884)

Drygalski, Erich von. *The Southern Ice-Continent* (translated by Bluntisham Books, 1989)

Dupre, Lonnie. *Greenland Expedition: Where Ice Is Born* (NorthWord Press, Minnesota, 2000) (One or two further volumes of the Dupre/Hoeschler Greenland Expedition will be published soon)

Erngaard, Erik. *Grønland, I Tusinde År, Sesam* (Viborg, 1982) (in Danish, no English translation)

Evans, Edward. *South with Scott* (Collins, 1919)

Fairley, T.C. *Sverdrup's Arctic Adventures* (Longmans, 1959)

Fiala, Anthony. *Fighting the Polar Ice* (Doubleday, Page & Co 1906)

Fisher, Raymond. *The Voyage of Semen Dezhnev in 1648* (Hakluyt Society, 1981)

Fox, Luke. *North-West Fox* (1635)

Franklin, John. *Narrative of Journey to the Shores of the Polar Sea* (John Murray, 1824)

Franklin, John. *Narrative of Second Expedition to the Shores of the Polar Sea* (John Murray, 1828)

Fuchs, Vivian and Hillary, Edmund. *The Crossing of Antarctica* (Cassell, 1958)

Geiger, John and Beattie, Owen. *Dead Silence: the Greatest Mystery in Arctic Discovery* (Bloomsbury, 1993)

Gjeldnes, Rune and Larsen, Torry. *Dead Men Walking* (Larsen and Gjeldnes, 2000)

Gould, Laurence McKinley. *Cold* (Brewer, Warren and Putnam, NY, 1931)

Greely, Adolphus. *Three Years of Arctic Service* (Charles Scribner's Sons, NY, 1886)

Grierson, John. *Challenge to the Pole* (G.T. Foulis and Co, 1964)

Guttridge, Leonard F. *Ghosts of Cape Sabine* (Putnam, NY, 2000)

Guttridge, Leonard F. *Icebound: the Jeanette Expedition's Quest for the North Pole* (Paragon, NY, 1987)

Hall, Charles Francis. *Arctic Researches and Life among the Eskimo* (Harper, NY, 1865)

Harper, Kenn. *Give Me My Father's Body* (Profile Books, 2000)

Hayes, Isaac. *An Arctic Boat Journey in the Autumn of 1854* (Brown, Taggard and Chase, Boston, 1860)

Hayes, Isaac. *The Open Polar Sea* (Hurd and Houghton, NY, 1867)

Henderson, Bruce. *Fatal North* (New American Library, NY, 2001)

Henson, Matthew. *A Negro Explorer at the North Pole* (Frederick A. Stokes, NY, 1912)

Herbert, Wally. *Across the Top of the World* (Longmans, 1969)

Herbert, Wally. *The Noose of Laurels* (Hodder and Stoughton, 1989)

Horwood, Harold. *Bartlett, the Great Canadian Explorer* (Doubleday, NY, 1977)

Huish, Robert. *The Last Voyage of Capt Sir John Ross* (John Saunders, 1835)

Huish, Robert. *A Narrative of the Voyage and Travels of Capt Beechey* (W. Wright, 1836)

Huntford, Roland. *Scott and Amundsen* (Macmillan, 1979)

Huntford, Roland. *Shackleton* (Hodder & Stoughton, 1985)

Huntford, Roland. *Nansen* (Duckworth, 1997)

Jackson, Frederick. *The Great Frozen Land* (Macmillan, 1895)

Jackson, Frederick. *A Thousand Days in the Arctic* (Harper, 1899)

James, Thomas. *The Strange and Dangerous Voyage of Capt Thomas James* (1633)

Jones, A.G.E. *Antarctica Observed* Caedmon of Whitby (1982)

Kane, Elisha Kent. *The US Grinnell Expedition in Search of Sir John Franklin* (Childs and Peterson, Philadelphia, 1856)

Kane, Elisha Kent. *Arctic Explorations: the Second Grinnell Expedition in Search of Sir John Franklin* (Childs and Peterson, NY, 1853)

Kaye Lamb, W. *The Journals and Letters of Sir Alexander Mackenzie* (Hakluyt Society, 1970)

Kish, George. *North East Passage* (Nico Israel, Amsterdam, 1973)

Kvam, Ragnar. *Den Tredje Mann* (Gyldendal, 1997) (a biography of Hjalmar Johansen: not translated into English)

Kushnarev, Evgenii. *Bering's Search for the Straits* (Oregon Historical Society, 1990)

Liljequist, Gösta. *High Latitudes* (Swedish Polar Research Secretariat, 1993)

Loomis, Chauncey. *Weird and Tragic Shores* (Macmillan, 1972)

Lyon, George. *A Brief Narrative of an Unsuccessful Attempt to Reach Repulse Bay* (John Murray, 1825)

M'Clintock, Francis. *The Voyage of the Fox in the Arctic Seas* (John Murray, 1859)

McClure, Robert. *The Discovery of the North West Passage* (Longman, Brown, Green, Longmans and Roberts, 1856)

McGhee, Robert. *Ancient People of the Arctic* (UBC Press, Vancouver, 1996)

McGoogan, Ken. *Fatal Passage* (Harper Flamingo, 2001)

McKinlay, William Laird. *Karluk* (Weidenfeld and Nicolson, 1976)

Mason, Theodore, K. *Two Against the Ice: Amundsen and Ellsworth* (Dodd, Mead and Co, NY, 1982)

Mawson, Douglas. *The Home of Blizzard* (Hodder and Stoughton, 1930)

Mear, Roger and Swan, Robert. *In the Footsteps of Scott* (Jonathan Cape, 1987)

Messner, Reinhold. Antarctica, *Both Heaven and Hell* (Crowood Press, 1991)

Mikkelsen, Ejnar. *Lost in the Arctic* (Heinemann, 1913)

Mirsky, Jeannette. *To the Arctic* (Wingate, 1934)

Nansen, Fridtjof. *In Northern Mists* (Heinemann, 1911)

Nansen, Fridtjof. *Farthest North* (Archibald Constable, 1897)

Nares, George. *The Official Record of the Recent Arctic Expedition* (John Murray, 1876)

Nares, George. *Narrative of a Voyage to the Polar Sea during 1875–6* (Sampson, Low, Marston, Searle and Rivington, 1878)

Newman, Peter. *Company of Adventurers* (Penguin Books, Canada, 1985)

Newman, Peter. *Caesars of the Wilderness* (Penguin Books, Canada, 1987)

(The Newman books are a history of the Hudson's Bay Company in two volumes)

Niven, Jennifer. *The Ice Master* (Macmillan, 2000)

Nobile, Umberto *With the Italia to the North Pole* (George Allen and Unwin, 1930)

Nobile, Umberto. *My Polar Flights* (Frederick Muller, 1961)

Nordenskiöld, Adolf. *The Voyage of the Vega around Asia and Europe* (Macmillan, 1881)

Oleson, Tryggvi. *Early Voyages and Northern Approaches* (McClelland and Stewart, 1963)

Ousland, Børge. *Alone Across Antarctica* (Ousland, 1997)

Ousland, Børge. *Alone to the North Pole* (Ousland, 1994)

Ousland, Børge. *Arctic Traverse* (Ousland, to be published)

Papanin, Ivan. *Life on an Ice Flow* (Julian Messner, NY, 1939)

Parry, William Edward. *Journal of a Voyage for the Discovery of a North-West Passage* (John Murray, 1821)

Parry, William Edward. *Journal of a Second Voyage for the Discovery of a North-West Passage* (John Murray, 1824)

Parry, William Edward. *Journal of a Third Voyage for the Discovery of a North-West Passage* (John Murray, 1826)

Parry, William Edward. *Narrative of a Journey to reach the North Pole* (John Murray, 1828)

Pasetskiy, B.M. *Russian discoveries in the Arctic, Volume 1* (Admiralteistovo, St. Petersburg 2000) (in Russian, not translated into English)

Payer, Julius. *New Lands within the Arctic Circle* (Macmillan, 1876)

Peary, Robert E. *Northward over the Great Ice* (Methuen, 1898)

Peary, Robert E. *Nearest the Pole* (Hutchinson, 1907)

Peary, Robert E. *The North Pole* (Hodder and Stoughton, 1910)

Ponting, Herbert. *The Great White South* (Duckworth, 1921)

Powys, Llewelyn. *Henry Hudson* (The Bodley Head, 1927)

Rasmussen, Knud. *Across Arctic America. Narrative of the Fifth Thule Expedition* (Putnam, 1933)

Richardson, John. *Arctic Searching Expedition* (Harper, 1851)

Ross, James Clark. *A Voyage of Discovery and Research in the Southern and Antarctic regions* (John Murray, 1847)

Ross, John. *A Voyage of Discovery under the Orders of the Admiralty* (John Murray, 1819)

Ross, John. *Narrative of a Second Voyage in search of a North-West Passage* (Webster, 1835)

Savoia, Luigi Amedeo di, Duke of the Abruzzi. *On the Polar Star in the Arctic Seas* (Hutchinson, London, 1903)

Savours, Ann. *The Search for the North West Passage* (St Martin's Press, NY, 1999)

Schley, W.S. and Soley J.R. *The Rescue of Greely* (Charles Scribner's Sons, 1889)

Scoresby, William. *An Account of the Arctic Regions* (Archibald Constable, 1820)

Scott, Robert F. *The Voyage of the Discovery* (Smith, Elder and Co, 1907)

Scott's Last Expedition (Smith, Elder and Co, 1913)

Shackleton, Ernest. *The Heart of Antarctica* (Heinemann, 1909)

Shackleton, Ernest. *South* (Heinemann, 1919)

Shelvocke, George, A Voyage round the World by way of the Great South Sea, J Senex, 1728

Simpson, A. *The Life and Travels of Thomas Simpson, the Arctic Discoverer* (Richard Bentley, 1845)

Simpson, Thomas. *Narrative of the Discoveries on the North Coast of America effected by the Officers of the Hudson's Bay Company* (Richard Bentley, 1843)

Spufford, Francis. *I May Be Some Time* (Faber and Faber, 1996)

Stefansson, Vilhjalmur. *The Friendly Arctic* (Macmillan, 1922)

Steger, Will, and Schurke, Paul. *North to the Pole* (Macmillan, 1987)

Steger, Will and Bowermaster, Jon. *Crossing Antarctica* (Bantam Press, 1991)

Struzik, Edward. *North West Passage* (Blandford, 1991)

Sverdrup, Otto. *New Land* (Longman Green, 1904)

Tyrell, James. *Across the Sub-Arctics of Canada* (William Briggs, Toronto, 1908)

Uemura. *Hokkyokuten Gurinrando tandokuk (Solo Journeys to the North Pole and across Greenland)* (Bungei Shunju, 1978) (in Japanese, not translated into English)

Urvantsev, Nikolai. *Severnaya Zemlya* (Arctic Institute, Leningrad, 1933) (in Russian, not translated into English)

Ushakov, George. *On Untrodden Land* (Molodaya Gvardiya, Moscow, 1953) (in Russian, not translated into English)

Vaughan, Richard. *North West Greenland: A History* (University of Maine Press, 1991)

Vaughan, Richard. *The Arctic, a History* (Alan Sutton, 1994)

The Voyage of the Chelyuskin (Chatto and Windus, 1935)

Weber, Richard and Malakhov, Mikhail. *Polar Attack* (McClelland and Stewart, 1996)

Weddell, James. *A Voyage towards the South Pole* (Longman, Rees, Orme, Brown and Green, 1825)

Wellman, Walter. *The Aerial Age* (Keller and Co, NY, 1911)

Wilkes, Charles. *Narrative of the US Exploring Expedition* (Lea & Blanchard, Philadelphia, 1845)

Woodman, David. *Unravelling the Franklin Mystery* (McGill-Queen's University Press, 1991)

Worsley, F.A. *Endurance* (Norton and Co, 1999)

Index

Adams, Jameson 180–1
Advance 109
Adventure 148, 150
Alabama 87–9
Albanov, Valerian 10, 74, 104–5, 119, 141
Alert 111, 118, 127
Amedeo, Luigi, Duke of the Abruzzi 125
America 133, 135, 140
Amundsen, Roald Engebreth Gravning 10–11, 40, 44, 53, 58–9, 60–1, 63, 66, 73, 75–6, 82, 84, 130, 135–41, 148, 152, 161, 164, 167, 178, 183–90, 192, 194–5, 198, 200, 207–9, 210–11, 215, 218–19
Andrée, Salomon August 121–4, 133, 135
Antarctic (Kristensen) 159–60, 169
Antarctic (Nordenskjöld) 174–6
Antarctic Circle 148, 150, 152, 159, 161, 174
Archer 118, 164, 169
Arctic Circle 13, 40
Arctic Ocean Hydrographic Expedition 102
Arktika 142
Assistance 53
Astrup, Eivind 84, 85, 86, 132
Aurora 195–6, 198–9, 205–7
Austin, Horatio 53, 167
Australasian Antarctic Expedition 195
Austro-Hungarian Expedition 98

Back, George 40, 42–3, 46–8
Balchen, Bernt 208, 210
Baldwin, Evelyn 126
Balleny, John 157
Bancroft, Anne 143
Banks, Sir Joseph 37, 148
Barents, Willem 23–4
Barrow, John 36–8, 40, 46, 48–9, 51
Bartlett, Bob 76–9, 128
Bartlett, Moses 129
Bear 78, 114
Beattie, Professor Owen 58
Beaumont, Lewis 111–12
Beechey, Frederick 42–3, 58
Belcher, Sir Edward 55, 107, 111
Belgica 60, 160–2, 164, 167, 173, 177, 183
Bellingshauzen, Faddey Faddeyevich *see* von Bellingshausen, Thaddens
Bellot, Joseph Rene 54
Bering, Vitus Jonassen 67, 68–9

Bernier, Joseph Elzear 76
Bessels, Emil 109–10
Biscoe, John 157
Booth, Felix 44
Borchgrevink, Carsten 159–60, 164–70, 172, 179, 183
Bowers, Henry Robertson 189–91, 193–4
Bowers, Lt Richard 211
Bransfield, Captain Edward 151–2, 160
British Arctic Air-Route Expedition 91
British TransArctic Expedition 143
Brönlund, Jorgen 87–9
Bruce, William 169
Brusilov, Georgi 104
Buchan, David 37, 106–7
Budington, Sidney 109–10
Burrough, Stephen 20
Burton, Charles 214
Byrd, Richard 10, 91, 135–6, 188, 208, 210–11

Cabot, John *see* Caboto, Giovanni
Cabot, Sebastian (Grand Pilot of England) 19, 30
Caboto, Giovanni 18–19
Cagni, Umberto 126–7
Calvert, James 142
Camell, William 148
Canadian Arctic Expedition 76
Capella 125–6
Carcass 106
Cartier, Jacques 30–1
Castor 48
Cecilia 160
Challenger 159
Chancellor, Richard 19, 64
Charcot, Dr Jean-Baptiste 176–7
Charles 28–9
Chelyuskin 74
Chelyuskin, Semen 70
Cherry-Garrard, Apsley 189–91
Chichagov, Vasili 71
Chirikov, Aledsandr 68
Cholet, Captain Ernest 177
Citta di Milano 138
Clarke, Charles 148
Collinson, Richard 51, 53, 61
Columbus, Christopher, 18–19
Conway, Sir Martin 94
Cook, Dr Frederick 10, 51, 84–6, 126–7, 129–30, 132–33, 135–6, 140–1, 184
Cook, Frederick Albert MD 160–4, 183
Cook, James 32, 68–9, 148–50, 152, 156
Courtauld, Augustine 91
Crean, Tom 189, 191, 202, 204–5
Crozier, Captain F.R.M. 57, 59
Cunningham, John 28

Dalager, Lars 81
Danenhower, John 116, 118
David, Edgworth 77, 180–3
Davis, John 160

de Champlain, Samuel 31
de Gerlache, Adrian 161–2, 164, 173, 177, 183, 199
De Halve Maan 27
de Larramendi, Ramón Hernando 63
De Long, George Washington 116–18
De Swane 23
Dease, Peter 47–8
del Cano, Sebastian 146
Denmark 87
Deutschland 194–5, 200
Dezhnev, Semen Ivanovich 66–7, 68
Diaz, Bartolomeo 146
Discovery (Hudson) 27–8, 30
Discovery (Nares) 111–12
Discovery (Scott) 168–70, 172, 173–4, 177–8, 189, 196, 205, 211, 216
Dove 152
Dragon 160
Drake, Sir Francis 20, 147
Dufek, Admiral George 211
Dumont d'Urville, Jules-Sébastien-César 157, 159
Dupre, Lonnie 11, 97, 100

Eagle 121–4
Egede, Hans Povelsen 80
Eielson, Carl 139, 208
Eirik the Red 16, 17, 92
Eiriksson, Liefur 16
Ekholm, Nils 122
Ellen 23
Ellsworth, Lincoln 6, 135–8, 210–11, 219
Endurance 76, 178, 196, 198–202, 205–7, 212
Enterprise 51, 53
Erebus 48, 49, 51, 53, 57–9
Ermak 103
Etienne, Jean-Louis 143, 217
Evans, Edgar 172, 189
Evans, Lt Edward (Teddy) 189, 191–2, 194

Fanning, Edmund 147, 153; Fanning–Pendleton expedition 153
Farm 135
Fiala, Anthony 126
Fiennes, Sir Ranulf 214, 218
Filchner, Wilhelm 194–5, 200
Floyd Bennett 208
Foxe, Luke 28–30
Foyn, Svend 155, 159–60
Fram 10, 60, 63, 73, 75, 77, 82, 84, 86, 118–21, 135, 164, 169, 178, 183–5, 188–9, 194, 200
Français 176, 177
Francke, Rudolphe 129
Franklin, Lady Jane 51, 54, 56, 59, 107
Franklin, Sir John 6, 9–10, 16, 37, 40–4, 46–9, 51–6, 58–60, 80, 82, 89, 91, 100, 106–7, 109, 111, 116, 132, 159, 167, 183
Frithjof 125–6

de Champlain, Samuel 31
Frobisher, Martin 9, 20
Frœnkel, Knut 123, 125
Fuchs, Sir Vivian 194, 211–14, 216–18
Furneaux, Tobias 148
Fury 42, 44

Garlington, Ernest 113–16
Gauss 173, 174, 200
Gauss, Karl 173
German Antarctic Expedition 173, 194
German Polar Expedition 80
Germania 81
Gherritz, Dirck 147
Gibson, Langdon 84
Gilles, Cornelis 120
Gjeldnes, Rune 11, 92, 144
Gjøa 60–1, 63, 66, 73, 118, 184
Glacier 212
Golden Hind 147
Gould, Laurence 188, 208–9
Great Northern Expedition 69, 71
Greely, Adolphus Washington 51, 86, 112–16, 118
Greene, Henry 27
Greyhound 23
Grinnell, Henry 51, 53, 107
Griper 42

Hagen, Hoeg 87–8
Hall, Charles Francis 51, 58
Hall, James 28
Hansa 81
Hanson, Nicolai 165, 167, 170
Hanssen, Helmer 10, 60–1, 184, 186, 188, 194, 209
Hansson, Charles 61
Hayes, Isaac Israel 109
Hazen, William 112
Hearne, Samuel 31, 33–4, 37, 40–1
Hecla 42, 106–7
Hendrik, Hans 109–11
Henrietta Maria 29
Henry, Charles 114
Henson, Matthew 129–30
Hepburn, John 40–2
Herald 100
Herbert, Wally 143
Herjolfsson, Bjarni 16
l'Hermite, Jacob 147
Hillary, Sir Edmund 212–14
Hobson, Lt William 58
Hoelscher, John 11, 97, 100
Hollick-Kenyon, Herbert 210
Hood, Robert 40–2, 46
Hopewell 25–6
Hudson, Henry 25–8, 30, 106
Hudson's Bay Company 31–2, 34, 35, 40, 47, 55, 58–9, 73, 76
Hurley, Frank 199, 201

Inglefield, Edward 107, 109
Investigator 51–3
Isabel 107
Isabella 37, 46, 107
Isbjørn 101–2
Italia 138–40

Iversen, Iver 88–9
Jackson, Andrew 49,
Jackson, Frederick 10, 104–5,
120, 125–6, 178
James Caird 202–7
James, Thomas 29–30
Jason 82, 174
Jeanette 77, 104, 112, 116,
117, 118
Jerez, Gregorio 149
Johansen, Hjalmar 118–19,
120–1, 139, 184–6, 194
John A. Macdonald 63
John R. Bradley 129
Josephine Ford 135–6
Juet, Robert 26–7

Kagge, Erling 11, 144, 218
Kamchatka Expedition 68–9
Kaminski, Marek 218
Karluk 76–9, 104, 128
Kellett, Henry 53, 55, 100
Kent Kane, Elisha 6, 107
King and Winge 78
Kite 84
Knight, John 28, 33
Koch, Johan Peter 87, 89, 91
Kolchak, Alexander 103
Konrad, Alexander 105, 141
Kopylov, Dimitri 66
Krasny Oktyobr 100
Krassin 138

Larsen, Torry 11, 63, 79, 92,
144, 174
Lashly, 189–90
Le Maire, Jacob 146
Leigh Smith, Benjamin 105
Lena 71–2
Liddon, Matthew 38
Lockwood, James 112, 119
Lok, Michael 21–2
Lomonosov, Mikhail 71
Longyear, John Munroe 94
Lundborg, Einar 138
Lutwidge, Skeffington 106
Lyon, George 42

Mackay, Alastair 77, 78
Mackay, Alistair 179–81, 183
Mackenzie, Alexander 34–6,
40, 53
Mackintosh, Aeneas 205, 207
Magdalena 94
Magellan, Ferdinand 6, 9,
146–7
Makarov, Vice-Admiral 103
Malakhov, Mikhail 144
Malmgren, Finn 138–9
Manhattan 63, 79
Mariano, Adalberto 138–9
Markham, Albert 111–12,
167–70, 172, 177, 189
Marshall, Eric 180–1, 183
Maud 73, 135, 140
Mawson, Douglas 77, 178,
180–3, 188, 195–9, 205, 211
McClintock, Francis 56–8
McClure, Robert 51–3, 55, 59
McFarlane, John 160
McKinlay, William Laird 79
McNeish, Harry 202, 207

Melville, George 116–18
Mercurius 23
Mertz, Dr Xavier Guillaume
196–7
Messner, Reinhold 216–18
Middleton, Christopher 33, 42
Mikkelsen, Ejnar 87–90
Minin, Fedor 70
Mirnyi 150, 152
Monroe, James 152
Moore, William 33
Morning 172
Morrell, Ben 156
Moys, William 63
Munk, Jans 28–9
Murray, James 77
Mylius-Erichsen, Ludvig 60,
87–8, 90

Nagursky, Jan 141
Nai, Cornelius 23
Nansen, Fridtjof 6, 10–11,
75, 80–6, 91, 104, 118–19,
120–1, 126, 140–1, 152,
163–4, 169–70, 174, 178,
183–6, 189, 197, 217–18
Nares, George 109, 111–14,
118
Nautilus 142
Nelson, Horatio 106
Neptune 113, 151
Newnes, George 164–5, 167–8
Nimrod 77, 177–83, 189, 205–6
Ninnis, Edward Sutton 196
Nobile, Umberto 135–9, 210
Nonsuch 32
Nordenskiöld, Adolf Erik
71–2, 81–2, 94, 103, 174
Nordenskjöld, Otto 174–7, 201
Norge 136–8, 140, 210
North Magnetic Pole 38, 43,
45–6, 60–1, 157, 159, 184
North Pole 87, 92, 100,
103–4, 106–7, 109, 111,
116, 118, 121, 127, 130,
135, 141, 145, 161, 183–4,
188, 207–8, 217
North-East Passage 19, 23,
25–6, 28, 64, 70–2, 74,
101, 103–4, 135, 174, 184
Northern Land Expedition 103
North-West Passage 9–10, 19,
23, 26, 28, 30, 32, 36–7,
40, 44, 48, 52–3, 59–61,
66, 69, 75–6, 80, 91, 97,
106–7, 159, 164, 184

Oates, Captain Lawrence
Edward Grace 189, 190–4
Ousland, Borge 11, 144–5,
218–19

Palmer, National 152–3
Papanin, Ivan 141–2
Parry, William Edward 38,
40, 42, 44–5, 48, 51–2,
106–7, 159
Peary, Robert Edwin 10, 14,
51, 76, 81–2, 84–8, 90, 121,
126–30, 132–3, 135–6,
140–1, 169, 183–4, 188
Pelican see Golden Hind

Pendleton *see* Fanning,
Edmund
Phipps, Constantine 106
Phipps, John 94
Pim, Lt 53
Plaisted, Ralph 143
Polar Star 210
Polaris 109, 199
Pollux 48, 164
Pond, Peter 34
Powell, George 152–3
Prester, John 9
Prince Albert 54
Pronchishchev, Vasily 70
Proteus 113

Quest 206–7

Racehorse 106
Rae, Dr John 48, 53, 55–6, 59
Riip, Jan Cornelius 24
Ristvedt, Peder, Knud 61
Rønnbeck, Nils Fredrik 1019
Roosevelt, 128–9
Ross, James Clark 37–8,
44–5, 51, 53, 57, 61
Ross, John 37
Roys, Thomas 100
Rusanov, V.A. 103
Ruser, Hans 173

Saint Anna 10, 104–5, 141
Saint Foka 105
Schley, Winfield 114
Schouten, Willem 146
Schyberg, Birger 138
Scoresby Jnr, William, 80
Scoresby Snr, William 36–7, 80
Scott, Robert Falcon 9–10,
126, 140, 159, 164,
167–73, 177–80, 183–96,
198, 205–8, 211–18
Searchthrift 20
Sedov, Georgi 104–5, 141
Shackleton, Sir Ernest 10–11,
76–7, 79, 157, 169–72,
177–83, 187, 189, 191,
196, 198–207, 211–12,
214, 216, 218–19
Shelvocke, George °147–8
Shepard, Oliver 214
Shirreff, Captain William 151
Sibiryakov, Aledsandr 74
South Pole 60, 73, 75, 135–6,
140, 148, 161, 164, 184,
207, 211, 218
Southern Cross 164–8, 172
Southern Quest 214–15
Speedwell 147–8
Spidsbergen 101
St Roch 63, 79
Stefansson, Vilhjalmur 76, 100
Stella Polare 126
Steller, Georg W. 68
Suersaq *see* Hendrik, Hans
Superior 100
Svea 121
Sverdrup, Otto 60, 75–6, 79,
120–2, 132
Swan 214–17

Taimyr 103

Tasman, Abel 146
Taylor, Zachary 51
Tegetthoff 101–5, 125
Tegetthoff, Wilhelm 101
Teroahauté, Michel 41–2
Terror 48–9, 51, 53, 57–9, 170
The Flying Dutchman 20
Thorfinnsson, Snorri 17
Timofeyevich, Vasily 64
Torell, Otto 94
TransAntarctic Expedition 143
Trans-Globe Expedition 214

Uemura, Naomi 63, 92, 143
Urvantsev, Nikolai 103
Ushakov, George 103

van Heemskerk, Jacob 24, 25
van Payer, Julius 101
Van Tunzelman, Alexander 160
Vanhöffen, Ernst 174
Vasco de Gama 146
Vaygach 103
Vega 71–2, 139
Verhoeff, John 84, 86, 132
Vespucci, Amerigo 147
Victory 44–6, 49, 57, 58
Viltiski, Boris 103
von Bellingshausen, Thaddens
36, 150, 152, 160
von Drygalski, Erich 173–4
von Wrangel, Baron
Ferdinand 100
Voronin, Vladimir 74
Vostock 150, 152

Wafer, Lionel 147
Wasp 156
Waterman, Jonathan 63
Watkins, Henry George (Gino)
91
Weber, Richard 144
Weddell, James 152, 156, 168
Wegener, Alfred 91
Wellman, Walter 125–6, 133,
135
Weyprecht, Karl 101–2, 112
Whymper, Eric 81
Wiencke, Carl 163
Wild, Frank 180–1, 188, 196,
198–9, 203, 205–6
Wildes, Frank 113, 115–16
Wilkes, Lt Charles 157, 159
Wilkins, Hubert 77, 139,
142–3, 207–8, 210
Williams 150–1, 153
Williwaw 63
Wilson, Edward 6, 28, 167,
168–9, 172, 178, 212
Windward 120
Wisting, Oscar 73, 136–7,
186, 188, 194, 209
Worsley, Frank 199–202, 204–6
Wyatt Earp 210–11

Yantic 113–14

Zappi, Filippo 138–9
Zeigler, William 126
Zhuravlev, Sergei 103
Ziegler-Baldwin expedition
87, 105

WORLD CRICKET RECORDS

The joy of cricket: a bat, a ball and an open space are all that is required to enjoy this most traditional of games.

First published in 2010
Second edition 2011
Third edition 2012

Copyright © Carlton Books Limited 2010, 2011, 2012

Carlton Books Limited
20 Mortimer Street
London W1T 3JW

A CIP catalogue record for this book is available from the British Library

10 9 8 7 6 5 4 3 2 1

ISBN: 978-1-78097-101-8

Editor: Martin Corteel
Project art editor: Luke Griffin
Picture research: Paul Langan
Production: Rachel Burgess

Printed in Dubai

WORLD CRICKET RECORDS

THIRD EDITION

CHRIS HAWKES

CARLTON
BOOKS

CONTENTS

🏏 **INTRODUCTION** 8

🏏 **PART I: TEST CRICKET** 10

Team Records 12   Ground Records 22   Batting Records 24   Bowling Records 34

Wicketkeeping Records 42   Fielding Records 44   All-Round Records 46   Partnership Records 48

Test Records: By Team 50

Australia 52   England 56   India 60   New Zealand 64

Pakistan 68   South Africa 72   Sri Lanka 76   West Indies 80

Bangladesh 84   Zimbabwe 85

Test Records: By Series 86

Australia v England 88   South Africa v England 90   South Africa v Australia 92

England v West Indies 94   New Zealand v England 96   Australia v West Indies 98

New Zealand v South Africa 100   England v India 102   New Zealand v Australia 104

Australia v India 106   India v West Indies 108   New Zealand v West Indies 110

India v Pakistan 112   England v Pakistan 114   Pakistan v New Zealand 116

India v New Zealand 118   Pakistan v Australia 120   West Indies v Pakistan 122

Pakistan v Sri Lanka 124   India v Sri Lanka 126   Sri Lanka v England 127

New Zealand v Sri Lanka 128   Sri Lanka v Australia 129   West Indies v South Africa 130

Zimbabwe v India 131   Zimbabwe v New Zealand 132   South Africa v India 133

Sri Lanka v South Africa 134   Sri Lanka v West Indies 135   Zimbabwe v Sri Lanka 136

South Africa v Pakistan 137   Pakistan v Zimbabwe 138   South Africa v Zimbabwe 139

Zimbabwe v England 140   Zimbabwe v Australia 141   West Indies v Zimbabwe 142

Bangladesh v India 143   Pakistan v Bangladesh 144   New Zealand v Bangladesh 145

Sri Lanka v Bangladesh 146   South Africa v Bangladesh 147   Bangladesh v West Indies 148

Australia v Bangladesh 148   Bangladesh v England 149

🏏 **PART II: ONE-DAY INTERNATIONAL CRICKET** 150

ICC World Cup: Team Records 152   ICC World Cup: Batting Records 154

ICC World Cup: Bowling Records 156   ICC World Cup: Other Records 158

ICC Champions Trophy 160   ODI Cricket: Team Records 162

ODI Cricket: Batting Records 166   ODI Cricket: Bowling Records 170

ODI Cricket: Other Records 174   ICC Trophy 176

ODI Records: By Team 178

Australia: ODI Records 180   **England: ODI Records** 182   **India: ODI Records** 184
New Zealand: ODI Records 186   **Pakistan: ODI Records** 188   **South Africa: ODI Records** 190
Sri Lanka: ODI Records 192   **West Indies: ODI Records** 194   **Bangladesh: ODI Records** 196
Ireland: ODI Records 197   **Kenya: ODI Records** 198   **Netherlands: ODI Records** 199
Scotland: ODI Records 200   **Zimbabwe: ODI Records** 201   **Other Teams: ODI Records** 202

PART III: TWENTY20 CRICKET 204

ICC World Twenty20: Team Records 206   **ICC World Twenty20: Batting Records** 208
ICC World Twenty20: Bowling Records 210   **ICC World Twenty20: Other Records** 212
International Twenty20 214

PART IV: DOMESTIC CRICKET RECORDS 216

First-Class Team Records 218   **First-Class Batting Records** 220
First-Class Bowling Records 224   **First-Class Other Records** 228
List A Team/Batting Records 230   **List A Bowling/Other Records** 232
Twenty20 Records 234   **Indian Premier League Records** 238

PART V: OTHER CRICKET 242

Women's Test Cricket 244   **Women's ODI Cricket** 246
Women's Twenty20 Internationals 248   **Youth Test/ODI Cricket** 250

INDEX 252

CREDITS 256

Opposite, top to bottom: Mahela Jayawardene (Sri Lanka),
Jacques Kallis (South Africa), Charlotte Edwards (England);
this page, top to bottom: Graeme Swann (England),
Michael Clarke (Australia), Younus Khan (Pakistan)

Andrew Strauss (far right) and the England team celebrate at The Oval in 2011 after their 4–0 series whitewash of India took them to No. 1 in the ICC World Test Rankings.

INTRODUCTION

WELCOME to the third edition of a new venture in international cricket publishing – **World Cricket Records**. Ranging across the length and breadth of world cricket and including the men's game, women's cricket and youth cricket, the intention of this book is to explore, explain and intrigue the reader with the people, places and competitions that have made the game of cricket one of the most popular and widespread sports on the planet.

One of the enduring fascinations of the game of cricket, in all its forms (timed matches, limited-overs matches and the new kid on the block, Twenty20 cricket) is that the game can be broken down into the minutest of details. Every ball of every match played in the professional game over the years has been recorded for posterity, meaning that fans from all over the world can dip in and out of the game's records and ascertain any number of facts. Few other sports can be scrutinized to such an extent as cricket.

First and foremost, **World Cricket Records** is not a history book. It is a celebration of both the best and the worst of performances in Test cricket, one-day international cricket, the Twenty20 game, first-class domestic cricket, women's cricket and youth international cricket. It is an exposition of benchmarks – those to which every player in the game would wish to aspire and surpass as well as those that players would want to avoid. For every one of the game's most wanted records, there is a plethora of unwanted ones.

Such a book, of course, would not be possible without the considerable efforts of others. Cricket is blessed with numerous and comprehensive archives, with scorecards and statistics dating back to the game's earliest days in the 19th century. And all are available to the general public at the touch of a button. It has been a privilege to spend months trawling through these archives to find the hidden gems dotted throughout this book, to bring performances that could have been lost in the mists of time back to life and to introduce readers to the feats of players whose achievements could, otherwise, have been consigned to unopened books on dusty shelves. A sport can only be as rich as its history and, in that regard, cricket is blessed with considerable treasures.

Because cricket has become a 12-month sport, clearly there had to be a cut-off point. As such, all statistics in the book are correct as of 26 April 2012.

Particular thanks are also due to Martin Corteel, whose encouragement while putting a book of this type together is both morale-boosting and invaluable, to Jim Lockwood and Luke Griffen for their keen eye for design, to David Ballheimer for his assiduous attention to the minutest of cricketing details, to Paul Langan, for his painstaking search through cricket's photo archives and to Rachel Burgess for her huge efforts with the book's production. This project would not have come together without their considerable input.

Chris Hawkes, London, April 2012

India's Sachin Tendulkar became the first man to score 100 international centuries, reaching the landmark against Bangladesh in March 2012.

PART I: TEST CRICKET

Cricket had been played in various countries around the world for decades, but when, on the morning of Thursday, 15 March 1877, England's Arthur Shaw bowled to Australia's Charles Bannerman in Melbourne, a new phenomenon was born: Test cricket. More than 130 years later, the game has spread around the world and has left an indelible mark wherever it has settled.

Nobody is quite sure how it got its name, but Test cricket is just that: a complete and total test of a player's technique, his mental surety and, particularly in the modern game, his physical prowess. Its enduring fascination to players and spectators, of course, is that it is many other things beyond that: it can be an epic battle between bat and ball; it is a game in which, at any point during the five days, the balance of power can shift in an instant – an awe-inspiring catch, an unplayable delivery, an ill-advised shot or a farcical, out-of-the-blue run-out all have the ability to trigger a magical chain of events that appeared outrageously improbable only moments earlier.

As one might expect, a section on Test cricket's all-time record-breakers contains a legion of the game's most revered names – Donald Bradman, Garfield Sobers, Sachin Tendulkar and Shane Warne to name but four – but there are also some more unusual, less heralded entrants. Who, for example, was the first bowler to take nine wickets in an innings, or which wicketkeeper holds the record for the highest score in Test cricket?

Lord's, the home of cricket: there is no better place to be on a fine summer's day.

TEAM RECORDS

RESULTS SUMMARY

Team	Span	Mat	Won	Lost	Tied	Draw	W/L	%W	%L	%D
Australia	1877–2012	744	350	194	2	197	1.80	47.04	26.07	26.61
Bangladesh	2000–2011	73	3	63	0	7	0.04	4.10	86.30	9.58
England	1877–2012	920	327	265	0	328	1.23	35.54	28.80	35.65
India	1932–2012	462	112	147	1	202	0.76	24.24	31.81	43.72
New Zealand	1930–2012	371	71	149	0	151	0.47	19.13	40.16	40.70
Pakistan	1952–2012	367	115	100	0	152	1.15	31.33	27.24	41.41
South Africa	1889–2012	366	129	126	0	111	1.02	35.24	34.42	30.32
Sri Lanka	1982–2012	212	63	76	0	73	0.82	29.71	35.84	34.43
West Indies	1928–2012	481	154	160	1	166	0.96	32.01	33.26	34.51
Zimbabwe	1992–2012	87	9	52	0	26	0.17	10.34	59.77	29.88
ICC World XI	2005	1	0	1	0	0	0.00	0.00	100.00	0.00*

* An ICC World XI played a one-off "Super" Test against Australia in 2005 – the match was given official Test status by the ICC and so appears in all Test records.

The 40-year wait

No country has been forced to endure a longer wait for a series victory than New Zealand. Between the country's first-ever Test match (against England) in 1929 and 1969, they suffered 21 series defeats (with nine drawn) before a draw in the Third Test against Pakistan in Dacca (now in Bangladesh) in November 1969 secured a 1–0 series victory to end their record-breaking sequence of 30 Test series without a victory.

The West Indies by a whisker

When Australia's off-spinner Tim May took 5 for 9 in 6.5 overs to help dismiss the West Indies for 146 in the Fourth Test at Adelaide in January 1993, it left the home side needing a modest 186 runs for a victory that would hand them an unassailable 2–0 lead in the five-match series. Australia slipped to 144 for 9, before a rearguard action from May and Craig McDermott brought them within agonizing reach of the winning line. Then tragedy struck: a **Courtney Walsh** (right) delivery found the edge of McDermott's bat; Junior Murray claimed the catch; and the West Indies had won one of the greatest Test matches in history by a single run – the smallest margin of victory (by runs) in Test history.

England crush sorry Australia

England, inspired by 22-year-old **Len Hutton** (who made a world record 364), put on a batting masterclass for two-and-a-half days of the final Test of the 1938 Ashes series, played at The Oval. Trailing 1–0 in the series, the home side compiled a massive 903 for 7 in their first innings to leave Australia with a daunting mountain to climb. They failed miserably, falling to 201 all out in their first innings and 123 all out in their second. The margin of defeat – an innings and 579 runs – is the largest (by an innings) in Test history.

England off to a flyer

A fine innings of 169 by **Patsy Hendren** helped England to a commanding first-innings score of 521 all out in the first Test of the 1928–29 Ashes series, played at Brisbane. In reply, Australia – featuring debutant Donald Bradman – limped to 122 all out – 399 runs in arrears. England, declining to enforce the follow-on, piled on the pressure, hitting 342 for 8 in their second innings to set Australia an unlikely victory target of 742. The home side wilted under the pressure, subsiding to 66 all out in 25.3 overs to lose by 675 runs – the largest losing margin (by runs) in Test history.

First whitewash

The 1920–21 Ashes series was nothing short of a nightmare for England. They were trounced by 377 runs in Sydney, by an innings and 91 runs in Melbourne, by 119 runs in Adelaide, by eight wickets back in Melbourne, and by nine wickets back in Sydney to become the first team in history to suffer a "whitewash" in a five-Test series.

The taming of the Tigers

Having attained Test status in June 2000, Bangladesh's cricketers struggled to establish themselves in the highest echelon of the game. After losing their first-ever Test match (and series) to India, the Tigers went a further 36 Tests and a record-breaking 16 series before recording their first series win. When it finally happened – following a 1–0 series victory against Zimbabwe in January 2005 – it sparked mass celebrations on the streets of cricket-mad Bangladesh.

Pick and mix for England

England simply could not find a winning formula in the 1921 home Ashes series. Defeat by ten wickets at Trent Bridge prompted six changes for the Second Test at Lord's; Australia won the match by eight wickets. Seven changes ensued for the Third Test at Headingley, as well as the appointment of **Lionel Tennyson** as captain; Australia won by 219 runs. Six changes were made at Old Trafford (match drawn) and a further two at The Oval (match drawn), and in all England used 30 different players, a record for a five-match series.

The first tied Test match

In December 1960, in the First Test against the West Indies at Brisbane, the Australians, after holding a 52-run first-innings lead, were set 233 runs to win. They slipped to 92 for 6 before a record-breaking 134-run seventh-wicket stand between Alan Davidson (who became the first player to score 100 runs and take 10 wickets in a Test match) and captain Richie Benaud brought them to within six runs of victory. Then disaster struck: Davidson was run out for 80 and Benaud (52) followed two runs later. Panic set in, and Australia lost their last two wickets – both run-outs – for only four runs. The match had ended in a tie: the first of only two instances of a tied match in Test cricket.

Longest unbeaten streak

With a battery of fast bowlers capable of intimidating any opposition line-up and an array of batting talent to rival any in the game, the West Indies side of the 1980s and early 1990s was the most formidable in modern cricket and, for a period, they were virtually unbeatable. Following their 1–0 series win over England in 1980, the Caribbean side did not lose a series over a 15-year period (in which they lost only 15 Test matches) before finally losing to Australia at home (2–1), in May 1995.

Honours even

When England ended Zimbabwe's second innings on 234 at Bulawayo in December 2006, it left them with a target of 205 runs off 37 overs to secure a 1–0 lead in the two-match series. Often up with the rate, but never comfortably ahead of it, England eventually needed three runs off the final delivery (from Heath Streak) for victory. Nick Knight only managed two and the match – with England on 204 for 6 – ended in a draw. On two occasions a Test has been tied (the side batting last having been bowled out), but this was the first Test match ever to end in a draw with the scores level; the second came between India and the West Indies at Mumbai in November 2011.

A come-from-behind victory for England

Being forced to follow on in the opening Test of the 1894–95 Ashes series, at Sydney, could have left England floundering, but instead it inspired them. Trailing by 263 runs, a fine 117 from Albert Ward was the basis of a fighting second-innings total of 437, before **Bobby Peel** took 6 for 67 to help England dismiss Australia for 166, 11 runs short of their victory target. It was the first of only three instances in Test cricket of a side coming back to win the match after being forced to follow on.

HIGH INNINGS TOTALS: TOP 10

	Team	Score	Overs	RR	Inns	Opposition	Venue	Match start
1	Sri Lanka	952/6d	271.0	3.51	2	India	Colombo	2 Aug 1997
2	England	903/7d	335.2	2.69	1	Australia	The Oval	20 Aug 1938
3	England	849	258.2	3.28	1	West Indies	Kingston	3 Apr 1930
4	West Indies	790/3d	208.1	3.79	2	Pakistan	Kingston	26 Feb 1958
5	Pakistan	765/6d	248.5	3.07	2	Sri Lanka	Karachi	21 Feb 2009
6	Sri Lanka	760/7d	202.4	3.75	2	India	Ahmedabad	16 Nov 2009
7	Australia	758/8d	245.4	3.08	2	West Indies	Kingston	11 Jun 1955
8	Sri Lanka	756/5d	185.1	4.08	2	South Africa	Colombo	27 Jul 2006
9	West Indies	751/5d	202.0	3.71	1	England	St John's	10 Apr 2004
10	West Indies	749/9d	194.4	3.84	2	England	Bridgetown	26 Feb 2009

When ten days were not enough

Before the 1938–39 series, England and South Africa had agreed to make the Fifth Test, at Durban, "timeless" – played to a conclusion – if the scores going into the final match were level or if either side was one up in the series. England led 1–0. Play got under way on a bright, sunny morning on 3 March 1939. The batsmen had a field day. Ten days later, with the pitch showing few discernible signs of wear, England, chasing 696 for victory, had battled their way to 654 for 5 before play was abandoned at tea on 13 March to allow the England players time to undertake a two-day journey to Cape Town to catch the mail boat home. It remains the highest fourth-innings score in history.

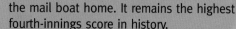

India's batsmen prosper

For six Test matches, between October 1986 and February 1987, all played on Indian soil, India's batsmen were on fire, notching up an all-time record six consecutive scores of 400-plus – with a highest of 676 for 7 declared, including centuries for **Mohammad Azharuddin** (199), Sunil Gavaskar (176) and Kapil Dev (163) against Sri Lanka at Kanpur – before the run finally came to an end after they declared their second innings on 181 for 3 in the drawn Second Test against Pakistan at Kolkata in February 1987.

Digging deep

Faced with a mighty West Indies first-innings total of 575 for 9 declared in the First Test at Bridgetown, Barbados, in January 1958, Pakistan produced a woeful reply, limping to a paltry 106 all out in 42.2 overs. To their great credit, however, they dug deep in spectacular fashion second time round, thanks in no small part to **Hanif Mohammad**'s massive 337, to score 657 for 8 and hold out for a remarkable draw. The difference in runs between the two innings, 551, is the largest in history.

Indian wickets tumble

Already two matches down to England in a four-match series, India travelled to Old Trafford in July 1952 in understandably low spirits. And it showed. After England compiled a steady 347 for 9 declared over two rain-interrupted days, on the third day India slipped to 58 all out and, following on, 82 all out to lose by a mighty innings and 207 runs. They became the first of three Test teams ever to lose all 20 wickets in a single day. **Fred Trueman**, Alec Bedser and Tony Lock took nine, seven and four wickets, respectively.

BELOW: Captains **Andrew Strauss** (right) and **Chris Gayle** (left) discuss the state of play with the umpires. Moments later, the Second Test at Antigua was abandoned.

The shortest match

Much to the West Indies Cricket Board's chagrin, just ten deliveries, 1.4 overs, of the Second Test between the West Indies and England at the Sir Vivian Richards Stadium in Antigua were enough to establish that the sandy outfield was unsafe for bowlers and the match, amid much embarrassment and blame, was abandoned as a draw. The fiasco did produce one record, however: it remains the shortest completed Test match in history.

History-making run-chase

Australia may have slipped from 242 for 0 to 417 all out in their second innings in the Fourth Test against the West Indies at St John's, Antigua, in May 2003, but they would still have fancied their chances of winning the match and securing a 4–0 series victory. The West Indies batsmen had other ideas, however. Chasing 418 – the scores were level after completion of the first innings – and helped by centuries from Ramnaresh Sarwan (105) and **Shivnarine Chanderpaul** (104), the home side cantered to the target with three wickets to spare. It remains the highest successful run-chase in Test history.

Blink and you've missed it

South Africa's 1924 tour to England got off to a dreadful start at Edgbaston. After England had compiled 438 all out, South Africa subsided to a meagre 30 all out in just 12.3 overs – at 75 balls, it remains the shortest completed innings in Test history. They did better second time around (scoring 390), but England still went on to win the game by an innings and 18 runs.

LOWEST TOTALS: TOP 10

	Score	Team	Overs	RR	Inns	Opposition	Venue	Match start
1	26	New Zealand	27.0	0.96	3	England	Auckland	25 Mar 1955
2	30	South Africa	18.4*	1.91	4	England	Port Elizabeth	13 Feb 1896
=	30	South Africa	12.3	2.40	2	England	Birmingham	14 Jun 1924
4	35	South Africa	22.4*	1.84	4	England	Cape Town	1 Apr 1899
5	36	South Africa	23.2	1.54	1	Australia	Melbourne	12 Feb 1932
=	36	Australia	23.0	1.56	2	England	Birmingham	29 May 1902
7	42	New Zealand	39.0	1.07	1	Australia	Wellington	29 Mar 1946
=	42	Australia	37.3#	1.66	2	England	Sydney	10 Feb 1888
=	42	India	17.0	2.47	3	England	Lord's	20 Jun 1974
10	43	South Africa	28.2#	2.26	3	England	Cape Town	25 Mar 1889

* match played with five-ball overs; # match played with four-ball overs

The longest wait for victory

Following an eight-wicket defeat by England in their first-ever Test match, at Christchurch in January 1930, life was tough for New Zealand cricketers. For the next 26 years, over a period of 44 Test matches (a record), New Zealand failed to produce a single Test victory. The magic moment, which saw local offices close and crowds stream into Eden Park, finally arrived in Auckland on 13 March 1956, as New Zealand, already three down in the four-match series, bowled out the West Indies for 77 in the second innings to record their first-ever Test victory, by 190 runs.

Bangladesh just can't shake that losing feeling

The argument that a team can only improve by pitting them-selves against the best in the business was sorely tested when Bangladesh were granted Test status in June 2000. The country may have been a mine of untapped talent, but the Tigers' initial forays into Test cricket were nothing short of disastrous. Between 15 November 2001 and 19 February 2004, Bangladesh crashed to a record 21 consecutive defeats (12 of them by an innings or more) before the run came to an end following a rain-hit draw against Zimbabwe in Bulawayo in March 2004.

*Australia's record-breaking run without a draw included a 4–1 series win over England in the 2001 Ashes series. **Steve Waugh** holds the trophy after Australia's innings-and-25-run victory in the Fifth Test at The Oval.*

Forcing a result

Having a rich, deep seam of talent at their disposal may have been the principal factor, but a large, and much heralded, part of Australia's success in world cricket in recent times was the positive manner in which they approached the game. Their philosophy was one based on attack: to score runs as quickly as possible to give yourself time to bowl out an opponent and force a result. As a consequence, it comes as little surprise that, between October 1999 and August 2001, Australia played out 23 Test matches (20 wins, three defeats) – an all-time record – without recording a single draw.

Most consecutive draws

In recent times, pitches throughout the Caribbean have come under fire for their inability to produce a result, but this is no new phenomenon. It seems that wickets in the islands were equally lifeless back in the 1970s. Between the last three Tests of the West Indies' five-match series against India in 1970–71, a drawn five-match series against New Zealand in 1971–72, and the first two Test matches of the 1972–73 series against Australia, the West Indies played out ten consecutive draws (all of them at home). The record drawing streak finally came to an end in the Third Test against Australia at Port of Spain in March 1973, which the West Indies lost by 44 runs.

Most miss-able day's play

The most turgid five-and-a-half hours' play in Test cricket? Look no further than the first day's play of the first-ever Test match between Pakistan and Australia, played at Karachi between 11 and 17 October 1956. Australia won the toss, elected to bat and, mesmerized by the guile of opening bowlers **Fazal Mahmood** (who took 6 for 34 off 27 overs) and Khan Mohammad (4 for 43 off 26.1 overs), produced a 53.1-over crawl to 80 all out. By the close of play, Pakistan had reached 15 for 2 and the day had produced a meagre 95 runs.

Taking the positive approach

During the 1902–03 Test series in South Africa, Australia's reply to South Africa's first-innings total of 454 in the First Test, played at the Old Wanderers ground in Johannesburg, was all-out attack. And, although they fell for 296 – to trail by 158 runs – and were forced to follow on, they had compiled their total at a record rate of 5.80 runs per over (a record that stands to this day). Australia rallied in their second innings, hitting 372 for 7 – at a more leisurely rate of 4.76 runs per over – to force a draw.

MOST RUNS IN A DAY: TOP 10

	Runs	Team	Opposition	Day	Wkts	Venue	Date
1	588	England	India	2	6	Manchester	25 Jul 1936
2	522	England	South Africa	2	2	Lord's	28 Jun 1924
3	509	Sri Lanka	Bangladesh	2	9	Colombo	21 Jul 2002
4	508	England	South Africa	3	8	The Oval	17 Aug 1935
5	496	England	Pakistan	2	4	Nottingham	1 Jul 1954
6	494	Australia	South Africa	1	6	Sydney	9 Dec 1910
7	492	England	South Africa	2	8	The Oval	17 Aug 1935
8	491	England	New Zealand	3	7	Leeds	11 Jun 1949
9	482	Australia	India	3	10	Sydney	2 Jan 2000
10	475	England	Australia	1	2	The Oval	18 Aug 1934

RIGHT: Walter Hammond scored 167 of England's 588 runs on the second day of the Second Test against India at Old Trafford in July 1936.

Hitting an all-time low

Just when New Zealand cricket fans thought things could not get much worse – their side had remained winless in 32 matches since the country's first-ever Test match, against England in 1930 – their players hit an all-time low. Facing a meagre first-innings deficit of 46 against England at Auckland in March 1955, and very much in with a chance of getting something out of the match, they capitulated to an all-time Test low score of 26 all out – compiled at an all-time low run-rate of 0.96 runs per over – to hand England victory by an innings and 20 runs.

All in a day's play

There has been no harder day to bat in Test history than on 16 July 1888, the second day of the First Test (of three) between England and Australia, at Lord's. Resuming on 18 for 3 on the second morning, after a rain-affected first day had seen Australia amass a less than confident 116 all out, England limped their way to 53 all out. Australia made 60 in their second innings to set England an achievable 124 runs for victory, but the home side did not come close, slipping to 62 all out to lose the match by 61 runs. A total of 27 wickets fell on the second day, which remains an all-time record in Test cricket.

Beat us if you can

For a period in the early 1980s, the West Indies – powered with the bat by **Viv Richards**, Gordon Greenidge, Desmond Haynes and co at their peak and with the ball by the most fearsome attack in the game's history – were literally unbeatable. From January 1982 (a drawn match against Australia at Sydney) to December 1984 (a draw against the same opposition in Melbourne), the men from the Caribbean did not lose a single one of their 27 matches. It remains the longest unbeaten streak in Test history.

Record-breakers

With a heady mix of batting talent, a world-class wicketkeeper-batsman and a bowling attack (including **Glenn McGrath** and legendary leg-spinner Shane Warne) as complete as any the game has ever seen, Australia dominated world cricket in the late 1990s and the first decade of the new millennium. Twice during that period (between October 1999 and February 2001, and again between December 2005 and January 2008) they put together a sequence of 16 consecutive victories. It is an all-time record in Test cricket.

MOST SIXES IN A MATCH: TOP 10

	6s	Team 1	Team 2	Match winner	Venue	Match start
1	27	Pakistan	India	drawn	Faisalabad	21 Jan 2006
2	23	New Zealand	England	England	Christchurch	13 Mar 2002
3	22	Pakistan	New Zealand	drawn	Karachi	30 Oct 1976
=	22	West Indies	South Africa	drawn	Basseterre	18 June 2010
5	20	India	Sri Lanka	India	Mumbai	2 Dec 2009
=	20	Zimbabwe	New Zealand	New Zealand	Bulawayo	1 Nov 2011
7	19	West Indies	England	West Indies	St John's	11 Apr 1986
=	19	India	Pakistan	drawn	Chennai	3 Feb 1987
=	19	India	Australia	India	Chennai	18 Mar 2001
=	19	Australia	Zimbabwe	Australia	Perth	9 Oct 2003
=	19	New Zealand	South Africa	New Zealand	Auckland	18 Mar 2004
=	19	Pakistan	England	drawn	Faisalabad	20 Nov 2005
=	19	New Zealand	Bangladesh	New Zealand	Hamilton	15 Feb 2010

LEFT: Shahid Afridi hit six of Pakistan's world record 27 sixes in the match in his first-innings knock of 156 against India at Faisalabad in January 2006.

Sixes galore

Aided in no small part by **Matthew Hayden**'s then world record contribution of 380, Australia's massive first-innings total of 735 for 6 declared (the 12th highest innings total of all time) against Zimbabwe at Perth in October 2003 contained a single-innings record 17 sixes – Hayden struck 11 of them, Steve Waugh and Darren Lehmann hit one each, and wicketkeeper-batsman Adam Gilchrist plundered the other four.

Most ducks recorded in a single innings

The record for the most ducks in a single innings is six, an event that has occurred on three occasions, all of them in the subcontinent. First in December 1980, when Pakistan slipped to 128 all out against the West Indies in the First Test in Karachi; second when South Africa collapsed to 105 all out and defeat in their fourth innings against India in Ahmedabad in November 1996; and third when Bangladesh slumped to 80 all out in their second innings against the West Indies in Dacca in December 2002 to lose by a mighty innings and 310 runs.

Chipping in for the cause

Facing a first-innings deficit of 48 (which could have been far worse given that they were all out for 75 on the first day), England required a more fruitful second innings in the second Test against Australia at Melbourne in December 1894 if they wanted to maintain or extend their 1–0 series lead. Their 475 all out was significant for two reasons: it helped them seal a 2–0 Ashes series lead and was the first instance in Test history of all 11 batsmen making double figures in a single innings.

Finding the boundary rope

High-scoring draws are not always the most palatable affairs for spectators, but the drawn Fourth Test match between Australia and India at Sydney in January 2004 was notable for more than the consistently high standard of batting on display. Of the 1,747 runs scored in the match, 952 of them came from 238 fours – the most in Test history.

All 11 fail to make a mark

South Africa's sorry 75-ball capitulation to 30 all out against England in the First Test in June 1924, at Edgbaston – the shortest completed innings (by balls) in history – was significant for another reason: it remains the only instance in Test history in which all 11 batsmen failed to make a double-figure score (extras were the top scorer with 11).

Record-shattering performance

Memorable principally for being the highest innings total and containing the highest partnership in Test history (**Mahela Jayawardene**, left, and **Kumar Sangakkara**'s, facing camera, epic second-wicket stand of 624), Sri Lanka's colossal first-innings total of 952 for 6 declared in the First Test against India at Colombo in July 2006 also broke the record for the most fours scored in a single innings (109) as well as the record for the most runs scored in an innings from fours and sixes (448).

Running riot

There have been two instances in Test cricket of five batsmen scoring a century in a single innings. The first came at Kingston, Jamaica, in June 1955, when Australia's Colin McDonald (127), Neil Harvey (204), Keith Miller (109), Ron Archer (128) and Richie Benaud (121) all passed three figures against the West Indies in the Fifth Test. The second came at Multan, Pakistan, in August 2001, when the home side's Saeed Anwar (101), Taufeeq Umar (104), Inzamam-ul-Haq (105), Mohammad Yousuf (102 not out) and Abdul Razzaq (110 not out) ran riot against an inexperienced Bangladesh attack in the First Test.

Combining to great effect

Remembered as the match in which Arthur Morris (182) and Don Bradman (173) combined with devastating effect in the fourth innings to chase down a then world record victory target of 404 to secure an unassailable 3–0 lead in the 1948 Ashes series, the Third Test at Headingley – in which England, despite defeat, scored a commendable 861 runs – also saw the record for the most century partnerships in a single Test match (eight – five by England and three by Australia).

Getting off to a good start

The maxim that the foundations of a good innings are more than often based on a solid opening partnership has been around for many years, but it wasn't until August 1899 – 22 years and 63 matches after the first-ever Test match – that two openers from the same team both scored a century in the same innings in a Test match. Stanley Jackson (118) and **Tom Hayward** (137) got England off to a flying start against Australia in the Fifth Test at The Oval, posting an opening partnership of 185. England could not capitalize on the situation, however, the match ended in a draw and Australia clinched the series 1–0.

A run-fest in Antigua

Already holding an unassailable 2–0 lead in the four-Test series, South Africa would have been more than happy with their first-innings total of 588 for 6 – including centuries for A.B. de Villiers (114), Graeme Smith (126), Jacques Kallis (147) and Ashwell Prince (131) – in the Fourth Test at St John's, Antigua, in April–May 2005. But rather than capitulating, the West Indies batsmen dug deep and carved out a magnificent 747 in reply, with **Chris Gayle** (317), Ramnaresh Sarwan (127), Shivnarine Chanderpaul (127) and Dwayne Bravo (107) all passing three figures. The eight centuries scored in the match (which ended in a draw) is an all-time record.

Giving everyone a go

With the game long since destined for a draw, the Third Test (of five) between South Africa and England, at Cape Town in January 1965, produced a cricket peculiarity. During South Africa's second innings, which put the result beyond doubt, all ten England fielders had bowled. Then, with England needing an impossible 406 runs to win off eight overs, South Africa's captain **Trevor Goddard** elected to bowl the four members of his side who had not bowled in the first innings. For the only time in Test history, all 20 fielders had bowled in the match.

Unwanted record for makeshift keeper

In the final Test at The Oval in 1934, with the Ashes series locked at 1–1, England went in to bat facing a massive Bradman- and Ponsford-inspired Australian first-innings total of 701. Things really started to unravel for the home side after their wicket-keeper Les Ames was forced to retire hurt with a strained back and took no further part in the game. England fell to 321 all out. Australia, electing not to enforce the follow-on, batted again, scoring 327 – an innings that saw 47-year-old Frank Woolley take over the gloves for England (and concede a world record 37 byes) – to set England an improbable 708 runs for victory. They did not come close, capitulating to 145 all out as Australia won by 562 runs to regain the Ashes.

Most wides in a match

The opening second-innings stand of 223 between **Phil Jacques** (left, 108) and **Simon Katich** (right, 157), which effectively batted the West Indies out of the game, took all the plaudits as Australia won the Third and final Test match by 87 runs at Bridgetown, Barbados, in June 2008 to win the series 2–0. Newspaper reports at the time failed to point the finger of blame at the West Indies' bowling attack, but perhaps they should have done, as during the match they bowled an all-time record 34 wides.

Combining to great effect

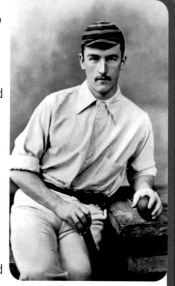

It is a captain's dream: not one but two of his bowlers firing on all cylinders to send an opponent packing. There have been 52 instances in Test cricket of two bowlers taking five wickets in the same innings, the first of which occurred in February 1887, in the 26th Test match in history, when Australia's **J.J. Ferris** (5 for 71) and Charlie Turner (5 for 41) combined to dismiss England for 151 in their first innings at Sydney. Not that the pair's effort changed the course of the match, however. England's George Lohmann took 10 wickets of his own (for 87 runs) as the visitors won the match by 71 runs to take a 2–0 series lead.

Most players out caught

A more common phenomenon than one might think, there have been 58 instances in Test cricket – the first happening in the Second Test between Australia and England at Melbourne in January 1904 – in which all ten batsmen have been out caught in the same innings. The record for the most players caught in a match is 33, in the Fifth Test between Australia and India at Perth in February 1992.

Finding the target

It may be that batsmen's techniques have improved over the years or that modern-day cricketers simply do not bowl straight enough, but both instances in Test history of nine players being bowled out in the same innings occurred in the 19th century. First at Cape Town in March 1889, when England bowled out South Africa for 43 in their second innings; and then in August 1890, when England dismissed Australia for 102 in the second innings of the Second Test, played at The Oval.

MOST EXTRAS IN AN INNINGS: TOP 10

	Extras	(b, lb, w, nb)	Team	Opposition	Venue	Match start
1	76	(35, 26, 0, 15)	Pakistan	India	Bangalore	8 Dec 2007
2	74	(35, 12, 11, 16)	West Indies	England	Port of Spain	6 Mar 2009
3	71	(21, 8, 4, 38)	Pakistan	West Indies	Georgetown	2 Apr 1988
4	68	(29, 11, 0, 28)	Pakistan	West Indies	Bridgetown	18 Feb 1977
5	65	(10, 18, 1, 36)	Zimbabwe	Sri Lanka	Harare	11 Oct 1994
6	64	(4, 18, 6, 36)	South Africa	Pakistan	Johannesburg	19 Jan 1995
=	64	(18, 11, 1, 34)	England	West Indies	Manchester	27 Jul 1995
=	64	(12, 25, 0, 27)	India	West Indies	Kolkata	26 Dec 1987
=	64	(25, 21, 5, 13)	South Africa	England	Lord's	31 Jul 2003
10	63	(11, 34, 3, 15)	England	India	Birmingham	10 Aug 2011

RIGHT: The 35 byes conceded by wicketkeeper **Dinesh Kartik** was a major factor in India conceding a world-record 35 byes against Pakistan in December 2007.

An incidental record

The Third Test between England and South Africa at Edgbaston in July–August 2008 will best be remembered for the ruthless manner in which South Africa, inspired by captain Graeme Smith's unbeaten 154, chased down a victory target of 281. The five-wicket win saw South Africa take an unassailable 2–0 lead in the four-match series, prompting the tearful resignation of long-standing England captain Michael Vaughan. It is South Africa's first-innings total of 314 all out that makes the record books, however, as it contained a world record 35 leg-byes.

Most players out lbw in a single Test match

Umpires Billy Bowden and Tony Hill had never been busier than during the First Test between the West Indies and Pakistan at Guyana in May 2011. During the match, which the West Indies won by 40 runs to take a 1–0 lead in the two-match series, the pair combined to give 20 players out lbw – a record for a Test match. The record for the most batsmen out lbw in a single Test innings is seven, an event that has occurred on two occasions: Zimbabwe against England at Chester-le-Street in June 2003; and New Zealand against Australia at Christchurch in March 2005.

Overstepping the mark

The First Test of the five-match series between the West Indies and Pakistan in 1976–77 got off to an exhilarating start at the Kensington Oval, Bridgetown, Barbados. In a high-scoring match, the home side – set 306 runs for victory – clung on for a hard-fought draw. The game has forced its way into the record books for another reason, however. As bowlers strained every sinew to force a breakthrough, no-balls blighted the game, a staggering 103 of them, an all-time record. The total number of extras conceded in the match – 173 (b37, lb31, w2, nb103) – is also a record.

Run-out madness

The run-out is possibly the most demoralizing dismissal in cricket; a basic misjudgement that leads to the cheap loss of a wicket. Losing one player to a run-out in an innings may be bad enough, but over the years four players have been run out in a single innings on two occasions: India against Pakistan at Peshawar in February 1955; and Australia against the West Indies at Adelaide in January 1969. On both occasions the match ended in a draw.

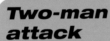

Two-man attack

Monty Noble (left, 7 for 17 and 6 for 60) and **Hugh Trumble** (right, 3 for 38 and 4 for 49) were the scourge of England's batsmen in the Second Test at Melbourne in January 1902, combining to devastating effect as Australia won the match by 229 runs to level the Ashes series at 1–1. It was the first of six instances in Test cricket in which two bowlers have taken all 20 wickets in a match.

GROUND RECORDS

Ground	Span	Mat	Ground	Span	Mat
Lord's, London, England	1884–2011	123	Harare Sports Club, Zimbabwe	1992–2011	27
Melbourne Cricket Ground, Australia (below left)	1877–2011	104	Iqbal Stadium, Faisalabad, Pakistan	1978–2006	24
Sydney Cricket Ground, Australia	1882–2012	100	St George's Park, Port Elizabeth, South Africa	1889–2007	23
Kennington Oval, London, England (below right)	1880–2011	94	Old Wanderers, Johannesburg, South Africa	1896–1939	22
Old Trafford, Manchester, England	1884–2010	74	Antigua Recreation Ground, St John's, Antigua	1981–2009	22
Headingley, Leeds, England	1899–2010	70	Wankhede Stadium, Mumbai, India	1975–2011	22
Adelaide Oval, Australia	1884–2012	70	Green Park, Kanpur, India	1952–2009	21
Queen's Park Oval, Port of Spain, Trinidad	1930–2012	58	Asgiriya Stadium, Kandy, Sri Lanka	1983–2007	21
Trent Bridge, Nottingham, England	1899–2011	57	M. Chinnaswamy Stadium, Bangalore, India	1974–2010	19
Woolloongabba, Brisbane, Australia	1931–2011	54	Seddon Park, Hamilton, New Zealand	1991–2012	19
Basin Reserve, Wellington, New Zealand	1930–2012	53	Queens Sports Club, Bulawayo, Zimbabwe	1994–2011	19
Newlands, Cape Town, South Africa	1889–2012	48	Galle International Stadium, Sri Lanka	1998–2012	19
Kensington Oval, Bridgetown, Barbados	1930–2012	48	Brabourne Stadium, Mumbai, India	1948–2009	18
Eden Park, Auckland, New Zealand	1930–2006	47	Bangabandhu National Stadium, Dhaka, Bangladesh	1955–2005	17
Edgbaston, Birmingham, England	1902–2011	46	P. Sara Oval, Colombo, Sri Lanka	1982–2012	16
Sabina Park, Kingston, Jamaica	1930–2011	45	SuperSport Park, Centurion, South Africa	1995–2010	16
National Stadium, Karachi, Pakistan	1955–2009	41	McLean Park, Napier, New Zealand	1979–2012	11
AMI Stadium, Christchurch, New Zealand	1930–2006	40	Sardar Patel (Gujarat) Stadium, Ahmedabad, India	1983–2010	11
Gaddafi Stadium, Lahore, Pakistan	1959–2009	40	Carisbrook, Dunedin, New Zealand	1955–97	10
Kingsmead, Durban, South Africa	1923–2011	39	Punjab C.A. Stadium, Mohali, India	1994–2010	10
W.A.C.A. Ground, Perth, Australia	1970–2011	39	Bellerive Oval, Hobart, Australia	1989–2011	10
Eden Gardens, Kolkata, India	1934–2011	37	Z.A. Chowdhury Stadium, Chittagong, Bangladesh	2006–11	10
Sinhalese Sports Club Ground, Colombo, Sri Lanka	1984–2011	35	Nehru Stadium, Chennai, India	1956–65	9
The Wanderers Stadium, Johannesburg, South Africa	1956–2011	33	Vidarbha C.A. Ground, Nagpur, India	1969–2006	9
Feroz Shah Kotla, Delhi, India	1948–2011	31	Rawalpindi Cricket Stadium, Pakistan	1993–2004	8
Bourda, Georgetown, Guyana	1930–2005	30	M.A. Aziz Stadium, Chittagong, Bangladesh	2001–2005	8
M.A. Chidambaram Stadium, Chennai, India	1934–2008	30	Shere Bangla National Stadium, Dhaka, Bangladesh	2007–11	8

Ground	Span	Mat
R. Premadasa Stadium, Colombo, Sri Lanka	1992–2010	7
Ellis Park, Johannesburg, South Africa	1948–54	6
Arbab Niaz Stadium, Peshawar, Pakistan	1995–2003	6
Niaz Stadium, Hyderabad, India	1973–84	5
Multan Cricket Stadium, Pakistan	2001–06	5
Sharjah C.A. Stadium, UAE	2002–11	5
Lord's, Durban, South Africa	1910–21	4
Jinnah Stadium, Sialkot, Pakistan	1985–95	4
Tyronne Fernando Stadium, Moratuwa, Sri Lanka	1992–93	4
Chevrolet Park, Bloemfontein, South Africa	1999–2008	4
Riverside Ground, Chester-le-Street, England	2003–09	4
University Oval, Dunedin, New Zealand	2008–12	4
Dubai International Cricket Stadium, UAE	2010–12	4
Bagh-e-Jinnah, Lahore, Pakistan	1955–59	3
Lal Bahadur Shastri Stadium, Hyderabad, India	1955–88	3
Colombo Cricket Club Ground, Sri Lanka	1984–87	3
Beausejour Cricket Ground, Gros Islet, St Lucia	2003–06	3
Vidarbha Cricket Association Stadium, Nagpur, India	2008–10	3
Warner Park, Basseterre, St Kitts	2006–11	3
Sheikh Zayed Stadium, Abu Dhabi, UAE	2010–12	3
Exhibition Ground, Brisbane, Australia	1928–31	2
Barabati Stadium, Cuttack, India	1987–95	2
Sheikhupura Stadium, Pakistan	1996–97	2
Arnos Vale Ground, Kingstown, St Vincent	1997–2009	2
National Cricket Stadium, St George's, Grenada	2002–09	2
Marrara Cricket Ground, Darwin, Australia	2003–04	2
Cazaly's Stadium, Cairns, Australia	2003–04	2

Ground	Span	Mat
Sir Vivian Richards Stadium, North Sound, Antigua	2008–09	2
Providence Stadium, Guyana	2008–11	2
Sophia Gardens, Cardiff, Wales	2009–11	2
Pallekele International Cricket Stadium, Sri Lanka	2010–11	2
Windsor Park, Roseau, Dominica	2011–12	2
Bramall Lane, Sheffield, England	1902	1
Gymkhana Ground, Mumbai, India	1933	1
University Ground, Lucknow, India	1952	1
Bahawal Stadium, Bahawalpur, Pakistan	1955	1
Peshawar Club Ground, Pakistan	1955	1
Pindi Club Ground, Rawalpindi, Pakistan	1965	1
Ibn-e-Qasim Bagh Stadium, Multan, Pakistan	1980–81	1
Gandhi Stadium, Jalandhar, India	1983	1
Sawai Mansingh Stadium, Jaipur, India	1987	1
Sector 16 Stadium, Chandigarh, India	1990	1
Jinnah Stadium, Gujranwala, Pakistan	1991	1
Bulawayo Athletic Club, Zimbabwe	1992	1
Southend Club Cricket Stadium, Karachi, Pakistan	1993	1
K.D. Singh "Babu" Stadium, Lucknow, India	1994	1
Buffalo Park, East London, South Africa	2002	1
Senwes Park, Potchefstroom, South Africa	2002	1
Shaheed Chandu Stadium, Bogra, Bangladesh	2006	1
K. Shaheb Osman Ali Stadium, Fatullah, Bangladesh	2006	1
Rajiv Gandhi International Stadium, Hyderabad, India	2010	1
The Rose Bowl, Southampton, England	2011	1

BATTING RECORDS

MOST CAREER RUNS: TOP 10

Pos	Player	Span	Mat	Inns	NO	Runs	HS	Ave	100	50	0
1	S.R. Tendulkar (Ind)	1989–2012	188	311	32	15,470	248*	55.44	51	65	14
2	R.T. Ponting (Aus)	1995–2012	165	282	29	13,346	257	52.75	41	62	16
3	R. Dravid (ICC/Ind)	1996–2012	164	286	32	13,288	270	52.31	36	63	8
4	J.H. Kallis (ICC/SA)	1995–2012	152	257	39	12,379	224	56.78	42	55	14
5	B.C. Lara (ICC/WI)	1990–2006	131	232	6	11,953	400*	52.88	34	48	17
6	A.R. Border (Aus)	1978–94	156	265	44	11,174	205	50.56	27	63	11
7	S.R. Waugh (Aus)	1985–2004	168	260	46	10,927	200	51.06	32	50	22
8	D.P.M.D. Jayawardene (SL)	1997–2012	130	217	13	10,440	374	51.17	31	41	11
9	S.M. Gavaskar (Ind)	1971–87	125	214	16	10,122	236*	51.12	34	45	12
10	S. Chanderpaul (WI)	1994–2011	140	239	38	10,055	203*	50.02	25	59	13

Lindsay's heroics help South Africa sink Australia

South Africa's epic 3–1 home series victory over Australia in 1966–67 created many legends – Graeme Pollock (with 537 runs) and Trevor Goddard (with 26 wickets) for example – but the real star of the series was South Africa wicketkeeper Denis Lindsay, whose 606 runs at an average of 86.57 (with three centuries, including an innings of 182 in the First Test at Johannesburg) remains the highest series total by a wicketkeeper in Test history.

Prospering on home turf

It would be safe to assume that the Sinhalese Sports Club ground in Colombo is the former Sri Lanka captain **Mahele Jayawardene**'s favourite venue. Since playing there for the first time in 1997, the right-hander has scored ten centuries and eight 50s at the ground (with a highest score of 374 against South Africa in July 2006) and amassed 2,697 runs (at an average of 79.32). It is the highest amount of runs scored by a player at a single ground in Test history.

Gillespie shows the way

Under normal circumstances, the most one could expect from a nightwatchman would be to see out the last few overs of a day and then to add a few quick runs the following morning before leaving the serious business of batting to the batsmen. But after successfully negotiating the final 6.4 overs of the first day (5 not out overnight) of the Second Test against Bangladesh at Chittagong in April 2006, and adding a further 14 runs on a rain-affected second day, Australia's nightwatchman Jason Gillespie had other ideas. On day three, the Australian fast bowler collected a further 83 runs to record his first Test century; on the fourth day, incredibly, he had reached 201 not out before Australia's declaration. It is the highest-ever score by a nightwatchman in Test cricket.

Gooch's Indian summer

Graham Gooch, the 11th-highest run-scorer of all time in Test cricket, reached the peak of his considerable powers in the First Test (of three) against India, at Lord's, in 1990. Leading by example, the England captain smashed 333 in the first innings and plundered a 113-ball 125 in the second as England romped to victory by 247 runs. The Essex man's 456 runs in the match is an all-time Test record.

A year to remember

In 2006, **Mohammad Yousuf** produced the best 12 months of batting form Test cricket has ever seen. He started the year with a century (173 against India in Lahore) and ended it in the same fashion (with a match-winning 124 against the West Indies in Karachi). In between times, the Pakistan right-hander registered nine centuries (a record for a calendar year), with a highest of 202 against England at Lord's, and amassed 1,788 runs – an all-time Test record for runs scored in a calendar year.

Test cricket's most productive over

While six sixes in an over have been achieved in one-day international cricket (Herschelle Gibbs), Twenty20 international cricket (Yuvraj Singh) and first-class cricket (Garfield Sobers and Ravi Shastri), to date no one has completed the feat in Test cricket, where the most runs scored off one over is 28 (4,6,6,4,4,4) by Brian Lara off South Africa's slow left-armer Robin Peterson at Johannesburg in December 2003.

Lone resistance

It is not often that a batsman of a team that has just lost a Test match early on the fifth day takes all the plaudits, but the whole world knew that Sri Lanka's ten-wicket victory over the West Indies in the Third Test at Colombo in November–December 2001 would have been far greater had it not been for the efforts of Brian Lara. The Trinidad left-hander hit 221 (of 390) in the first innings and 130 (of 262) in the second. His 351 runs in the match are the most in Test history by any player to end up on the losing side.

The Don plunders the England attack

That Australia recovered from losing the opening match of the 1930 series against England to regain the Ashes had much to do with the formidable talent of **Donald Bradman**. Not that the New South Wales batsman could have been blamed in any way for the 93-run defeat at Trent Bridge, scoring as he did 195 of Australia's 479 runs. His good form continued at Lord's, where his first-innings 254 did much to secure an Australian seven-wicket victory. At a drawn match at Headingley, the Don plundered a then world record score of 334 (including a record 309 runs on the first day). He failed in the rain-affected Fourth Test at Old Trafford, but resumed normal service with a sublime 232 runs in the deciding Test at The Oval; the innings was a major factor in Australia's innings-and-39-run victory. Bradman's 974 runs in the series (at an average of 139.14) is an all-time record.

Lara's moment of magic

England's bowlers had every reason to be sick of the sight of **Brian Lara** in the 1990s and after the turn of the century. In April 1994, at St John's, Antigua, the left-hander had plundered a world record 375 off their bowlers; a decade later at the same venue – having lost his record to Australia's Matthew Hayden (380 v Zimbabwe at Perth in October 2003) – the West Indies maestro did it again, smashing England's frustrated bowlers for 43 fours and four sixes en route to a world record score of 400 not out.

Flower blooms in Nagpur

If you had to pick one innings to confirm Zimbabwe wicketkeeper-batsman Andy Flower's credentials as a Test player of the highest quality, the obvious choice would be his second-innings performance against India in the Second Test at Nagpur in November 2000. Striding to the crease with his side in dire straits at 61 for 3, still 156 runs behind after following on, Flower dug deep for over nine hours, hitting an unbeaten 232 to take his side to 503 for 6 and safety. It is the highest individual score by a wicketkeeper in Test history.

HIGHEST CAREER BATTING AVERAGE: TOP 10

Pos	Ave	Player	Career span	Mat	Inns	NO	Runs	HS	100	50	0
1	99.94	D.G. Bradman (Aus)	1928–48	52	80	10	6,996	334	29	13	7
2	60.97	R.G. Pollock (SA)	1963–70	23	41	4	2,256	274	7	11	1
3	60.83	G.A. Headley (WI)	1930–54	22	40	4	2,190	270*	10	5	2
4	60.73	H. Sutcliffe (Eng)	1924–35	54	84	9	4,555	194	16	23	2
5	59.23	E. Paynter (Eng)	1931–39	20	31	5	1,540	243	4	7	3
6	58.67	K.F. Barrington (Eng)	1955–68	82	131	15	6,806	256	20	35	5
7	58.61	E.D. Weekes (WI)	1948–58	48	81	5	4,455	207	15	19	6
8	58.45	W.R. Hammond (Eng)	1927–47	85	140	16	7,249	336*	22	24	4
9	57.78	G.S. Sobers (WI)	1954–74	93	160	21	8,032	365*	26	30	12
10	56.94	J.B. Hobbs (Eng)	1908–30	61	102	7	5,410	211	15	28	4

Foster in tip-top form

One of seven brothers to represent Worcestershire before the First World War, **Tip (Reginald Erskine) Foster** was undoubtedly the most talented of them. The highlight of his brief eight-Test career came at Sydney, in the opening Test of the 1903–04 Ashes series, when he became the first player in Test history to pass the 250-run mark, hitting 287 – a figure that would remain as Test cricket's highest individual score for the next 26 years.

Bowing out in style

Often forced to play second fiddle to opening partner Jack Hobbs during his England career, **Andy Sandham** bowed out of Test cricket (after 14 Tests over nine years) with a truly headline-grabbing performance. As England piled on a massive 849 in their first innings against the West Indies at Kingston, Jamaica, in April 1930, Sandham, in his 40th year, batted for 10 hours, faced 640 balls and hit 28 fours en route to becoming the first player in Test history to score a triple-century. His innings of 325 remained a Test best for less than three months.

Top of the class

In the history of Test cricket, two players have scored a hundred in both innings of a Test match on three separate occasions: **Sunil Gavaskar** (124 and 220, India against the West Indies at Port of Spain in April 1971; 111 and 137, India against Pakistan at Karachi in November 1978; 107 and 182 not out, India against the West Indies at Kolkata in December 1978) and Ricky Ponting (149 and 104 not out, Australia against the West Indies at Brisbane in November 2005; 120 and 143 not out, Australia against South Africa at Sydney in January 2006; 103 and 116, Australia against South Africa at Durban in March 2006).

Dramatic debuts

Five players have made a double-century in their first-ever Test match: Tip Foster (287 for England against Australia at Sydney in December 1903); Lawrence Rowe (214 for the West Indies against New Zealand at Kingston, Jamaica, in February 1972); Brendon Kuruppu (201 not out for Sri Lanka against New Zealand at Colombo in April 1987); **Mathew Sinclair** (214 for New Zealand against the West Indies at Wellington in December 1999); and Jacques Rudolph (222 not out for South Africa against Bangladesh at Chittagong in April 2003).

Off to a blistering start

Test cricket did not have to wait long to witness the first-ever century. Indeed, the man who faced the first-ever ball in Test cricket, Australia's **Charles Bannerman** (against England at Melbourne in March 1877), went on to bat for a further four-and-three-quarter hours before retiring hurt on 165 (out of an Australian total of 245 all out). Australia went on to win the low-scoring match by 45 runs.

Starting as you mean to go on

Hometown boy Lawrence Rowe made the most impressive start to an international career in Test history against New Zealand at Sabina Park, Kingston, Jamaica, in February 1972. Unleashing a barrage of trademark cuts and pulls, the elegant right-hander made 214 in the first innings of the match and an unbeaten century in the second; his 314 runs in the match are the most by any player on debut in Test history. Rowe went on to make 30 Test appearances for the West Indies over eight years.

Finishing with a flourish

Having seen his side reach an overwhelmingly dominant position in the Second Test against South Africa at Auckland in March 2004 – requiring just 54 runs for victory in their second innings – Kiwi captain **Stephen Fleming** decided to produce some fireworks. His 31 off 11 balls, which took his side past the winning line for the first time against South Africa on home soil, was hit at a rate of 281.81 runs per 100 balls – the highest strike-rate in an innings in Test history.

Two hundreds in a match

That Australia held out for a draw in serene fashion in the Fifth Test of the 1909 Ashes campaign at The Oval to complete a 2–1 series victory had much to do with the history-making performance of their opener, Warren Bardsley. The New South Wales left-hander hit 136 in the first innings and 130 in the second to become the first player in Test history to score a century in both innings of a match, a feat since repeated on 67 occasions.

Leading by example

His country's finest batsman of the early 1880s and team captain, Billy Murdoch led the way as Australia put England's bowlers to the sword in the first innings of the Third Test at The Oval in August 1884. As the visitors compiled an accomplished 551 all out, Murdoch batted for 490 minutes, faced 525 balls and struck 24 fours en route to becoming the first player in Test history to score a double-century (211). England recovered well, however, to claim a draw and a 1–0 series win.

Ending a 92-year wait

In February 1969, at Sydney, Australia's Doug Walters made history. In the first innings of the Fifth Test against the West Indies he struck a majestic 242; he then crafted a patient 103 in the second innings to become, in the 646th Test match, the first player in 92 years of Test cricket to record a double-century and a century in the same match. Five players (Sunil Gavaskar, Lawrence Rowe, Greg Chappell, Graham Gooch and Brian Lara) have gone on to emulate the feat.

MOST HUNDREDS IN A CAREER: TOP 10

Pos	100s	Player	Career span	Mat	Inns	NO	Runs	HS	Ave	50	0
1	51	**S.R. Tendulkar (Ind)**	1989–2012	188	311	32	15,470	248*	55.44	65	14
2	42	J.H. Kallis (ICC/SA)	1995–2012	152	257	39	12,379	224	56.78	55	14
3	41	R.T. Ponting (Aus)	1995–2012	165	282	29	13,346	257	52.75	62	16
4	36	R. Dravid (ICC/Ind)	1996–2012	164	286	32	13,288	270	52.31	63	8
5	34	S.M. Gavaskar (Ind)	1971–87	125	214	16	10,122	236*	51.12	45	12
=	34	B.C. Lara (ICC/WI)	1990–2006	131	232	6	11,953	400*	52.88	48	17
7	32	S.R. Waugh (Aus)	1985–2004	168	260	46	10,927	200	51.06	50	22
8	31	D.P.M.D. Jayawardene (SL)	1997–2012	130	217	13	10,440	374	51.17	41	11
9	30	M.L. Hayden (Aus)	1994–2009	103	184	14	8,625	380	50.73	29	14
10	29	D.G. Bradman (Aus)	1928–48	52	80	10	6,996	334	99.94	13	7

MOST HUNDREDS AGAINST ONE TEAM: TOP 10

Pos	100	Player	Opponent	Mat	Inns	NO	Runs	HS	Ave
1	19	D.G. Bradman (Aus)	England (1928–48)	37	63	7	5,028	334	89.78
2	13	S.M. Gavaskar (Ind)	West Indies (1971–83)	27	48	6	2,749	236*	65.45
3	12	J.B. Hobbs (Eng)	Australia (1908–30)	41	71	4	3,636	187	54.26
4	11	S.R. Tendulkar (Ind)	Australia (1991–2012)	35	67	7	3,438	241*	57.30
5	10	G.S. Sobers (WI)	England (1954–74)	36	61	8	3,214	226	60.64
=	10	S.R. Waugh (Aus)	England (1986–2003)	46	73	18	3,200	177*	58.18
7	9	S.R. Tendulkar (Ind)	Sri Lanka (1990–2010)	25	36	3	1,995	203	60.45
=	9	R.B. Richardson (WI)	Australia (1984–95)	29	48	4	2,175	182	49.43
=	9	W.R. Hammond (Eng)	Australia (1928–47)	33	58	3	2,852	251	51.85
=	9	B.C. Lara (ICC/WI)	Australia (1992–2005)	31	58	2	2,856	277	51.00
=	9	G.S. Chappell (Aus)	England (1970–83)	35	65	8	2,619	144	45.94
=	9	D.I. Gower (Eng)	Australia (1978–91)	42	77	4	3,269	215	44.78

A good morning's work

There have been four instances in history of a player scoring a century before lunch on the first day of a Test match: Victor Trumper, 103 not out for Australia against England at Lord's in 1902; Charlie Macartney, 112 not out for Australia against England at Leeds in 1926; Donald Bradman, 105 not out for Australia against England at Leeds in 1930; and Majid Khan, 108 not out for Pakistan against New Zealand at Karachi in 1976.

Six in a row

When **Donald Bradman** passed three figures (103) in Australia's first innings against England at Headingley in July 1938, he achieved something that no player before or since has equalled. Starting with the Third Test match of the 1936–37 Ashes series at Melbourne, Bradman had recorded a century in six consecutive matches. Three players (Jacques Kallis, Mohammad Yousuf and Gautham Gambhir) have scored centuries in five consecutive matches.

Test cricket's youngest-ever centurion

In general, Bangladesh's early forays in the Test arena brought them nothing but disappointment, but there were some brighter moments, notably in September 2001 in the Second Test against Sri Lanka at Colombo. The record books may show that the home side cantered to an innings-and-137-run victory, but Bangladesh's second-innings score of 328 (after a pitiful 90 all out in their first innings) provided a moment of history. Playing in his first Test match, Mohammad Ashraful crafted a 212-ball 114 to become, aged 17 years 61 days, the youngest centurion in Test history.

Bradman leads the way for Australia

If the mark of a good batsman is to push on once settled and register a big score, then there has been no finer exponent than **Donald Bradman**. The Australian maestro made an all-time record 12 double-centuries in his 20-year Test career – including a record three in a series against England in 1930 – and is one of only four batsmen in the game's history (along with Brian Lara, Virender Sehwag and Chris Gayle) to have passed 300 runs in a single innings twice in his Test career.

Brutal Richards destroys England

With England already 4–0 down in the five-match series and facing a first-innings deficit of 164, West Indies captain **Viv Richards** strode to the crease with his side on 100 for 1 in the Fifth Test at St John's, Antigua, and decided to put on a batting masterclass for the home fans. By the time he declared his side's innings on 246 for 2, Richards had plundered an unbeaten 110 off 58 balls – he reached three figures off a mere 56 balls, to record the fastest century Test cricket has ever seen.

Sobers strides into the history books

Garfield Sobers's first-innings score of 365 not out in the Third Test against Pakistan at Sabina Park, Kingston, Jamaica, in February–March 1958 was remarkable for a number of reasons. It was the highest-ever maiden century in the history of the game (in 16 previous Tests Sobers's highest score had been 80), it broke the world record for the highest individual score (Len Hutton's 364 against Australia in 1938) and meant that, at 21 years 213 days, Sobers had become the youngest player in Test history to score a triple-century.

Resilient in defeat

The West Indies may have crashed to a 3–0 loss in their home five-match series against Australia in the spring of 1955, but one of their defeated team could hold his head up high. Stylish right-hander Clive Walcott scored 698 runs in the series – including a series record five centuries in the five Tests (108 in the First, 126 and 110 in the Second and 155 and 110 in the Fifth) – at an average of 87.25.

Miandad makes his mark

Javed Miandad's introduction to Test cricket was nothing short of remarkable. In his very first innings for Pakistan at the highest level of the game, he scored 163 against New Zealand at Lahore on 9–13 October 1976; three weeks later, in only his third Test – against the same opponents, in Karachi – he hit a brilliant 206 to become, aged 19 years 140 days, the youngest double-centurion in Test history.

Five in five for Weekes

A fine second-innings knock of 141 by Everton Weekes in the Fourth Test against England at Kingston, Jamaica, in March 1948 did much to guide the West Indies to a ten-wicket victory and a 2–0 series win. Eight months later, the stocky right-hander picked up in the three-match series against India where he had left off against England, rattling off scores of 128 (in the First Test), 194 (in the Second Test) and 162 and 101 (in the Third Test) to become the first, and to date only, player in Test history to score five centuries in five consecutive innings.

The oldest centurion in Test history

The 1928–29 Ashes series was an unqualified success for England, who won the first four Tests, but for **Jack Hobbs** (left) looking to bow out of his final overseas tour in style (21 years after making his Test debut), those matches had been a bitter disappointment – he had scored just 224 runs in seven innings. That all changed in Melbourne: in the first innings Hobbs hit a peerless 142 to become, aged 46 years 82 days, the oldest centurion in Test history.

Making Test cricket look easy

Mohammad Azharuddin's initial forays into Test cricket for India were the most spectacular in the game's history. Handed his debut in the Third Test against England at Kolkata in January 1985, the 21-year-old hit a sublime first-innings 110 before the match ended in a draw. Retaining his place for the Fourth Test at Chennai, he hit a second-innings 105, only to see India lose the match by nine wickets. His first-innings 122 in the drawn fifth and final Test at Kanpur meant he had become the first, and to date only, player in Test history to register three centuries in his first three matches.

The Lahore crawl

Pakistan's crawl to 407 for 9 over the first two-and-a-half days of the First Test against England at Lahore in December 1977 may have been painful to watch, but it did contain a moment of history. When opener **Mudassar Nazar** finally reached three figures – after 9 hours and 57 minutes of batting – he had recorded the slowest Test century in history.

MOST SCORES OF 50-PLUS IN A CAREER: TOP 10

Pos	50+	Player	Span	Mat	Inns	NO	Runs	HS	Ave	100	50
1	116	S.R. Tendulkar (Ind)	1989–2012	188	311	32	15,470	248*	55.44	51	65
2	102	R.T. Ponting (Aus)	1995–2012	162	276	29	13,290	257	53.44	41	61
3	99	R. Dravid (ICC/Ind)	1996–2012	164	286	32	13,288	270	52.31	36	63
4	97	J.H. Kallis (ICC/SA)	1995–2012	152	257	39	12,379	224	56.78	42	55
5	90	A.R. Border (Aus)	1978–94	156	265	44	11,174	205	50.56	27	63
6	84	S. Chanderpaul (WI)	1994–2012	140	239	38	10,055	203*	50.02	25	59
7	82	B.C. Lara (ICC/WI)	1990–2006	131	232	6	11,953	400*	52.88	34	48
=	82	S.R. Waugh (Aus)	1985–2004	168	260	46	10,927	200	51.06	32	50
9	79	S.M. Gavaskar (Ind)	1971–87	125	214	16	10,122	236*	51.12	34	45
10	73	V.V.S. Laxman (Ind)	1996–2012	134	225	34	8,781	281	45.97	17	16

Getting off the mark

It is ironic given he was always seen as a nervous starter, but the record for the most consecutive innings in Test cricket without a duck is 119, set by England's **David Gower** between August 1982 and December 1990.

Duck avoidance

Now one of the first names on the South Africa team-sheet, **A.B. de Villiers**'s first forays in Test cricket were smooth if not spectacular. He scored a maiden century in his fifth Test (against England at Centurion in January 2005) and endured the highs and lows every Test player suffers. Unremarkable in every way but one: between his debut in December 2004 and November 2008, he went a record 78 innings before recording his first duck (against Bangladesh at Centurion).

Left stranded on 99

There are few more frustrating feelings for a batsman than being left stranded on 99 not out. The phenomenon has occurred five times in Test cricket: Geoffrey Boycott (England against Australia at Perth in December 1979); Steve Waugh (Australia against England at Perth in February 1995); Alex Tudor (England against New Zealand at Birmingham in July 1999); Shaun Pollock (South Africa against Sri Lanka at Centurion in November 2002); and Andrew Hall (South Africa against England at Headingley in August 2003). One player has been left stranded on 199 not out (Andy Flower, Zimbabwe against South Africa at Harare in September 2001), and one player on 299 not out (Donald Bradman, Australia against South Africa at Adelaide in January–February 1932).

On a roll

The 12 months in which he truly established himself as an international batsman of genuine class, 1976 was a golden year for Viv Richards. The West Indian master-blaster swatted 1,710 runs (a record at the time for runs in a calendar year), blasted seven centuries (including a majestic 291 against England at The Oval) and laid the foundations for a record that has not been surpassed for more than 35 years: between January 1976 and February 1977, Richards posted 50 or more in 11 consecutive matches. Two Indian batsmen have since equalled his feat: Gautham Gambhir and Virender Sehwag.

Out in the nervous 90s

Three players hold the record for being out in the 90s the most times in a career: India's Rahul Dravid and Sachin Tendulkar and Australia's Steve Waugh have all been out in the 90s on 10 occasions.

Most times dismissed on 99 in Test cricket

Five players have been dismissed on 99 twice in their Test careers: Richie Richardson (West Indies against India at Port of Spain in April 1989; West Indies against Australia at Bridgetown in April 1991); John Wright (New Zealand against Australia at Melbourne in December 1987; New Zealand against England at Christchurch in January 1992); **Michael Atherton** (England against Australia at Lord's in June 1993; England against South Africa at Headingley in August 1994); Greg Blewett (Australia against the West Indies at Adelaide in January 1997; Australia against New Zealand at Hobart in November 1997); and Sourav Ganguly (India against Sri Lanka at Nagpur in November 1997; India against England at Trent Bridge in August 2002).

Fastest 50

A sorry mismatch between South Africa and Zimbabwe at Cape Town in March 2005, which the home side won by an innings and 21 runs inside two days, provided **Jacques Kallis** with a record-breaking opportunity. Coming to the crease with his side on a commanding 234 for 2 (already 184 ahead), Kallis reached his 50 off just 24 balls (ending on 54 not out): it is the fastest half-century (by balls faced) in Test history.

True grit

Trailing by 52 runs in the First Test of the 1958–59 Ashes series at Brisbane, England needed to dig deep in their second innings if they were going to post a remotely challenging victory target. And nobody dug deeper than Trevor Bailey (batting). The Essex all-rounder limped to 50 off a record slow (by balls faced) 350 balls before falling for a commendable 68. Sadly for England, Bailey's efforts made little difference to the outcome of the match: Australia won by eight wickets.

The first to fall short

Lower-order resistance was the key to Australia's 229-run victory over England at Melbourne in the Second Test of the 1901–02 Ashes campaign, which saw the home side level the series at 1–1. Reggie Duff's battling 104 may have grabbed the majority of the headlines, but it was Clem Hill's innings that stole a place in the record books. The left-hander was out for 99; the first of 79 instances of such a feat.

Most ducks in a series

Not only was the 1978–79 Ashes series one to forget for Australia, England having crushed them 5–1, it was also a record-breaking one for Alan Hurst. The renowned Victorian fast bowler batted 12 times during the campaign, scored a meagre 44 runs and recorded six ducks – an all-time record in a series.

MOST DUCKS IN A CAREER: TOP 10

Pos	0	Player	Span	Mat	Inns	NO	Runs	HS	Ave	100	50
1	43	C.A. Walsh (WI)	1984–2001	132	185	61	936	30*	7.54	0	0
2	35	G.D. McGrath (Aus)	1993–2007	124	138	51	641	61	7.36	0	1
3	34	S.K. Warne (Aus)	1992–2007	145	199	17	3,154	99	17.32	0	12
4	33	M. Muralitharan (ICC/SL)	1992–2009	130	159	54	1,203	67	11.45	0	1
=	33	C.S. Martin (NZ)	2000–12	68	98	49	119	12*	2.42	0	0
6	26	M. Dillon (WI)	1997–2004	38	68	3	549	43	8.44	0	0
=	26	C.E.L. Ambrose (WI)	1988–2000	98	145	29	1,439	53	12.40	0	1
8	25	Danish Kaneria (Pak)	2000–10	61	84	33	360	29	7.05	0	0
=	25	Zaheer Khan (Ind)	2000–12	83	113	23	1,114	75	12.37	0	3
10	23	D.K. Morrison (NZ)	1987–97	48	71	26	379	42	8.42	0	0

Mr Maximum

In all probability the finest wicketkeeper-batsman Test cricket has ever seen, **Adam Gilchrist** played for Australia on 96 occasions, scoring 5,570 runs (at an average of 47.60, including a highest score of 204 not out against South Africa in Johannesburg) and struck an all-time career Test record 100 sixes.

Consecutive fours

The record for the most consecutive fours is six. Three players have achieved the feat: Chris Gayle (off Matthew Hoggard, West Indies against England at The Oval in 2004); Ramnaresh Sarwan (off Munaf Patel, West Indies against India at St Kitts in 2006); and Sanath Jayasuriya (off James Anderson, Sri Lanka against England at Kandy in 2007).

Stealing the limelight

Seven players have batted on each day of a five-day match: Motganhalli Jaisimha (India against Australia at Kolkata in January 1960); Geoffrey Boycott (England against Australia at Trent Bridge in July 1977); Kim Hughes (Australia against England at Lord's in August 1980); Allan Lamb (England against the West Indies at Lord's in June 1984); Ravi Shastri (India against England at Kolkata in December 1984); Adrian Griffith (West Indies against New Zealand at Hamilton in December 1999); and Andrew Flintoff (England against England at Mohali in March 2006).

The worst of starts

Two players share the record for being dismissed by/off the first ball of a Test match. India's Sunil Gavaskar (against England by Geoff Arnold at Birmingham in 1974, against Pakistan by Imran Khan in Jaipur in 1986–87, and against the West Indies by Malcolm Marshall in Kolkata in 1983–84) and Bangladesh's Hannan Sarkar (each time against the West Indies by Pedro Collins, at Dhaka in 2002–03, at Gros Islet in 2004 and at Kingston in 2004) have both suffered the ignominious fate on three occasions.

Waqar's unusual record

One of the game's deadliest operators with the ball, where his ability to swing the ball late and at pace created havoc among opposition batsmen, Waqar Younis claimed 373 wickets in 87 Test matches between 1989 and 2003. His batting skills also found a place in the record books: with a highest score of 45, he remains the only player in history to score 1,000 career runs in Test cricket without scoring a single half-century.

Most fours in an innings

A selector's dream – a technically gifted opening batsman who knew both his limitations and which ball to put away – **John Edrich** played 77 Test matches for England between 1963 and 1976, scoring 5,138 runs. The highlight of his career came against New Zealand at Headingley in July 1965, when he batted for eight minutes short of nine hours and faced 450 balls en route to compiling an unbeaten 310: the innings contained a world record 52 fours (and five sixes).

HIGHEST SCORES BY BATTING POSITION

Pos	Player	Runs	Mins	Balls	4s	6s	Team	Opposition	Venue	Match start
1/2	M.L. Hayden	380	622	437	38	11	Australia	Zimbabwe	Perth	9 Oct 2003
1/2	L. Hutton	364	797	847	35	0	England	Australia	The Oval	20 Aug 1938
3	B.C. Lara	400*	778	582	43	4	West Indies	England	St John's	10 Apr 2004
4	D.P.M.D. Jayawardene	374	752	572	43	1	Sri Lanka	South Africa	Colombo	27 Jul 2006
5	M.J. Clarke	329*	609	468	39	1	Australia	India	Sydney	3 Jan 2012
6	K.D. Walters	250	394	342	30	2	Australia	New Zealand	Christchurch	18 Feb 1977
7	D.G. Bradman	270	458	375	22	0	Australia	England	Melbourne	1 Jan 1937
8	Wasim Akram	257*	490	363	22	12	Pakistan	Zimbabwe	Sheikhupura	17 Oct 1996
9	I.D.S. Smith	173	237	136	23	3	New Zealand	India	Auckland	22 Feb 1990
10	W.W. Read	117	120	155	20	0	England	Australia	The Oval	11 Aug 1884
11	Z. Khan	75	123	115	10	2	India	Bangladesh	Dhaka	10 Dec 2004

UNUSUAL DISMISSALS

Player	Dismissal	Runs	Team	Opposition	Venue	Match start
L. Hutton	obstructing the field	27	England	South Africa	The Oval	16 Aug 1951
W.R. Endean	handled the ball	3	South Africa	England	Cape Town	1 Jan 1957
A.M.J. Hilditch	handled the ball	29	Australia	Pakistan	Perth	24 Mar 1979
Mohsin Khan	handled the ball	58	Pakistan	Australia	Karachi	22 Sep 1982
D.L. Haynes	handled the ball	55	West Indies	India	Mumbai	24 Nov 1983
G.A. Gooch	handled the ball	133	England	Australia	Manchester	3 Jun 1993
S.R. Waugh	handled the ball	47	Australia	India	Chennai	18 Mar 2001
M.S. Atapattu	retired out	201	Sri Lanka	Bangladesh	Colombo	6 Sep 2001
D.P.M.D. Jayawardene	retired out	150	Sri Lanka	Bangladesh	Colombo	6 Sep 2001
M.P. Vaughan	handled the ball	64	England	India	Bangalore	19 Dec 2001

Consecutive sixes

The record for the most consecutive sixes in Tests is four. Three players have achieved the feat: Shahid Afridi (off Harbhajan Singh, for Pakistan against India at Lahore in 2006); Kapil Dev (off Eddie Hemmings, for India against England at Lord's in 1990); and A.B. de Villiers (off Andrew McDonald, for South Africa against Australia at Cape Town in 2008–09).

Fastest to 10,000 runs

Nine players in the history of the game have achieved the heady feat of accumulating over 10,000 Test runs. The fastest to do so were Brian Lara and Sachin Tendulkar, both of whom passed the milestone in their 195th Test innings.

Hitting the most boundaries

No batsman in Test history has struck more fours than the sport's all-time leading run-scorer, **Sachin Tendulkar.** The Mumbai-born maestro has found the boundary on 1,995 occasions in 188 Tests since he made his debut against Pakistan in Karachi in November 1989.

Des stands his ground

Desmond Haynes holds the all-time Test record for carrying his bat (batting throughout his side's innings and remaining not out) on the most occasions. The right-handed opener stood firm while all around him capitulated three times during his Test career: 88 not out of the West Indies' 211 all out against Pakistan in Karachi in November 1986; 75 not out of the West Indies' 176 all out against England at The Oval in August 1991; and 143 not out of the West Indies' 382 all out against Pakistan at Port of Spain in April 1993.

The longest individual innings in Test history

Len Hutton's legendary innings of 364 against Australia at The Oval in August 1938 was not only the highest individual score in Test history at the time (Garfield Sobers broke it in 1958 with 365 not out against Pakistan), but it was also, and remains, the longest Test innings of all time. Hutton faced 847 balls.

Most sixes in an innings

Wasim Akram showed his true credentials as a genuine all-rounder in spectacular fashion in the First Test against Zimbabwe at Sheikhupura in October 1996. The Pakistan captain smashed an imperious 257 off 363 balls (the highest innings by a No. 8 in Test history), an innings that included a world record 12 sixes.

BOWLING RECORDS

MOST WICKETS IN A CAREER: TOP 10

Pos	Wkts	Player	Span	Mat	Balls	Runs	BBI	BBM	Ave	5	10
1	800	M. Muralitharan (ICC/SL)	1992–2010	133	44,039	18,180	9/51	16/220	22.72	67	22
2	708	S.K. Warne (Aus)	1992–2007	145	40,705	17,995	8/71	12/128	25.41	37	10
3	619	A. Kumble (Ind)	1990–2008	132	40,850	18,355	10/74	14/149	29.65	35	8
4	563	G.D. McGrath (Aus)	1993–2007	124	29,248	12,186	8/24	10/27	21.64	29	3
5	519	C.A. Walsh (WI)	1984–2001	132	30,019	12,688	7/37	13/55	24.44	22	3
6	434	Kapil Dev (Ind)	1978–94	131	27,740	12,867	9/83	11/146	29.64	23	2
7	431	R.J. Hadlee (NZ)	1973–90	86	21,918	9,611	9/52	15/123	22.29	36	9
8	421	S.M. Pollock (SA)	1995–2008	108	24,353	9,733	7/87	10/147	23.11	16	1
9	414	Wasim Akram (Pak)	1985–2002	104	22,627	9,779	7/119	11/110	23.62	25	5
10	406	Harbhajan Singh (Ind)	1998–2011	98	29,651	13,084	8/34	15/217	32.22	25	5

Walsh flattens Kiwis

New Zealand's batsmen could find no answers to the many questions posed to them by Courtney Walsh in the Second Test at Wellington in February 1995. The West Indies captain took 7 for 37 in the first innings and 6 for 18 in the second to lead his side to a colossal innings-and-322-run victory. Walsh's 13 for 55 are the best match figures by a captain in Test history.

Laker's Test

England's innings-and-71-run victory over Australia in the Fourth Test at Old Trafford in July 1956 to retain the Ashes will always be remembered as **Jim Laker**'s Test. The Surrey off-break bowler took 9 for 37 in Australia's first innings and 10 for 53 in the second to become the first person in Test history to take ten wickets in an innings (a feat repeated only once, by Anil Kumble, who took 10 for 74 against Pakistan in 1999). Laker's match figures of 19 for 90 remain the best in Test history. It was also the first of six instances of a bowler dismissing all 11 batsmen in a match.

There's no place like home

Despite being the leading wicket-taker (with 800 wickets) and the record-holder for the most five-wicket (67) and 10-wicket hauls (22) in Test history, the argument against Muttiah Muralitharan being the greatest bowler of all time is that he has the good fortune to play the majority of his games on the helpful wickets of Sri Lanka. And how he has prospered in his homeland: his 166 wickets at Colombo's Sinhalese Sports Club Ground, his 117 Test wickets at the Asgiriya Stadium in Kandy and his 111 Test wickets at Galle's International Stadium occupy the top three places on the all-time list for the most Test wickets taken by a player at a single ground.

Lone resistance

Javagal Srinath's commendable effort of taking 5 for 46 in the first innings and 8 for 86 in the second were not enough to prevent India from slipping to a 46-run defeat in the First Test against Pakistan in Kolkata in February 1999. The paceman's 13 for 132 are the best match figures by a player who has ended up on the losing side in Test history.

First nine-wicket haul

The chief architect of England's comprehensive innings-and-197-run victory over South Africa at Johannesburg in March 1896 was George Lohmann. The Surrey man ripped the heart out of their batting line-up to take 9 for 28. It was the first instance (of 15) in Test history of a bowler taking nine wickets in an innings.

Fiery Fred the first to 300

No one will ever know how much more **Fred Trueman** could have achieved had not an insubordinate nature and a sharp tongue stood in his way. The Yorkshireman, a bowler with genuine pace, was selected for only 67 of a possible 118 Tests throughout his career, but when he played, he prospered. In his 65th Test, against Australia at The Oval in August 1964, he dismissed Neil Hawke (above) to become the first bowler in history to take 300 Test wickets.

England's Briggs casts a spell on South Africa

Dismissed for 292 in their first innings against South Africa in the Second and final Test at Cape Town in March 1889, England knew that, barring an outstanding performance with the ball, they would have to bat again. Cue Johnny Briggs. The Lancashire slow left-armer bewitched the hosts, taking 7 for 17 in the first innings and 8 for 11 in the second to secure an England victory by an innings and 202 runs and to become the first player (of 12) in Test history to take 15 wickets or more in a match.

Going out on a high

The star of England's 4–0 series win over South Africa in 1913–14 was S.F. Barnes. Despite playing in only four of the five Tests, the Staffordshire-born fast bowler was unplayable, taking an all-time record 49 wickets in the series, including seven five-wicket hauls – with a best of 9 for 103 in the Second Test at Johannesburg – and three ten-wicket match hauls. It turned out to be some swansong: these were the final Test matches of Barnes's career.

All in vain

Nobody could point the finger of blame at Kapil Dev following India's 138-run defeat to the West Indies in the Third Test at Ahmedabad in November 1983. India's captain led from the front in the West Indies' second innings, taking 9 for 83: the best bowling performance in an innings by a captain and the best figures in an innings by a bowler who has ended up on the losing side in Test history.

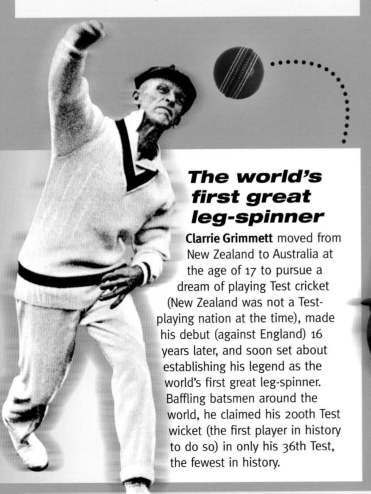

The world's first great leg-spinner

Clarrie Grimmett moved from New Zealand to Australia at the age of 17 to pursue a dream of playing Test cricket (New Zealand was not a Test-playing nation at the time), made his debut (against England) 16 years later, and soon set about establishing his legend as the world's first great leg-spinner. Baffling batsmen around the world, he claimed his 200th Test wicket (the first player in history to do so) in only his 36th Test, the fewest in history.

Golden year

The legendary zip of his leg-spinner's action may have diminished over the years, but, by 2005, **Shane Warne**'s experience, craft and guile were more than a match for his opponents. In the 15 Tests he played during that year, the spin wizard took 96 wickets – including a sensational 40 in a losing Ashes campaign – to set the record for the most Test wickets in a calendar year.

BEST ECONOMY RATE IN AN INNINGS: TOP 10
(minimum of 10 overs)

Pos	Econ	Player	O	M	R	W	Team	Opposition	Venue	Match start
1	0.15	R.G. Nadkarni	32.0	27	5	0	India	England	Chennai	10 Jan 1964
2	0.21	G.S. Sobers	14.0	11	3	1	West Indies	New Zealand	Wellington	3 Mar 1956
=	0.21	R.G. Nadkarni	14.0	11	3	0	India	England	Mumbai (BS)	21 Jan 1964
4	0.30	Majid Khan	10.0	8	3	0	Pakistan	West Indies	Port of Spain	1 Apr 1977
=	0.30	R.E.S. Wyatt	13.0	10	4	3	England	South Africa	Durban	21 Jan 1928
=	0.30	H. Verity	13.0	11	4	0	England	South Africa	Leeds	13 Jul 1935
7	0.37	J.C. Laker	14.1*	9	7	2	England	South Africa	Cape Town	1 Jan 1957
8	0.40	J.W. Burke	15.0*	10	8	0	Australia	South Africa	Johannesburg	7 Feb 1958
9	0.41	H. Verity	12.0	9	5	2	England	South Africa	Leeds	13 Jul 1935
10	0.41	Pervez Sajjad	12.0	8	5	4	Pakistan	New Zealand	Rawalpindi	27 Mar 1965

* The match was played using eight-ball overs.

The best bowler in history?

The first bowler to take nine wickets in an innings and the fastest to the 100-wicket milestone in Test history, on statistics alone **George Lohmann** has a rightful claim to being the greatest bowler in the game's history. In 18 Test matches between 1886 and 1896, the medium-pacer took 112 wickets at 10.75 (the lowest average in history) at a strike-rate of a wicket every 34.1 balls (also the lowest in history).

The mean machine

Few players in the history of the game have frustrated batsmen as much as William Attewell, a bowler of metronomic accuracy who relied on the principle of bowling the ball at off stump and setting an off-side field. In ten Tests between 1884 and 1894, the Nottinghamshire medium-pacer bowled 2,850 balls in Test cricket (taking 28 wickets) at an economy rate of 1.31 runs per over. Of bowlers to have bowled 2,000 balls or more in Test cricket, it is the lowest economy rate in the game's history.

Lean times with the ball

Now considered one of his country's finest umpires, Asoka de Silva did not enjoy the best of careers as a player. Capped ten times for Sri Lanka between 1985 and 1991, the left-arm googly bowler set two dubious records: of bowlers to have bowled 2,000 balls or more, he has the worst career bowling average (129.00 – 8 wickets for 1,032 runs) and the worst career strike-rate (a wicket every 291.0 balls).

On a hot streak

Although Australia lost the 1888 Ashes series 2–1 to England, none of the team's detractors would have apportioned any blame to Charlie Turner. Despite the loss, the fast-medium bowler was in inspired form with the ball, taking 5 for 44, 7 for 43, 5 for 27, 5 for 36, 6 for 112 and 5 for 86 to become the only player in Test history to claim five-wicket hauls in six consecutive innings.

Taking the brunt of it

Len Hutton and the rest of his England team-mates were not the only ones to enter the record books following their historic innings-and-579-run victory over Australia at The Oval in August 1938. The main victim of England's massive first-innings 903 for 7 declared was Australia's **Chuck Fleetwood-Smith**. The left-arm chinaman bowler delivered 87.0 overs and took just one wicket; his strike-rate of 522.0 is the worst in a single innings in Test history.

Best strike-rate in an innings

It took just 19 balls in India's first innings of the First Test at Brisbane in November–December 1947 for Australia's **Ernie Toshack** to claim a place in the record books. The left-arm medium-pace bowler took five wickets for two runs in 2.3 eight-ball overs to help reduce India to 58 all out. At 3.8 balls per wicket, it is the best strike-rate in Test history of any bowler who has taken four or more wickets in an innings.

Into the lion's den

Fast-tracked into the Bangladesh Test side as an 18-year-old in 2005 after being discovered at a talent-spotting camp, fast bowler **Shahadat Hossain** found his early forays in international cricket to be a chastening experience. He claimed 68 wickets in 33 matches, but, of all the bowlers to have bowled 2,000 or more balls in Test cricket, he holds the record for the worst career economy rate (4.20 runs per over) and for the worst economy rate in an innings (8.41 – against England at Lord's in May 2005, when his figures were 12-0-101-0).

Lacking a cutting edge

A standout performer at youth international level, Roger Wijesuriya failed to make his mark in Test cricket. In four Tests for Sri Lanka between 1982 and 1985, the slow left-armer bowled 97.4 overs, conceded 294 runs and claimed just one Test victim (Pakistan's Abdul Qadir). His career bowling average of 294.0 is the worst, without qualification, in Test history.

Making an early mark

With Australia already 2–0 down in the 1894–95 Ashes series, it was time to make changes for the Third Test at Adelaide. In came Albert Trott, and the Victoria slow bowler got off to a blistering start, taking a match-winning 8 for 43 in England's second innings to lead Australia to a 382-run victory. They are the best single-innings figures by a player on debut in the game's history.

Youngest and oldest

The youngest player to take five wickets in an innings is Nasim-ul-Ghani, who took 5 for 116 for Pakistan against the West Indies at Georgetown in March 1958 aged 16 years 303 days. The oldest player to achieve the feat is **Bert Ironmonger**, who took 6 for 18 for Australia against South Africa in Melbourne in February 1932 aged 49 years 311 days. The performance also saw Ironmonger become the oldest player to take ten wickets in a match.

Hirwani's heroics

Drafted into the India team for the first time for the Fourth Test against the West Indies at Chennai in January 1988, **Narendra Hirwani**'s introduction to Test cricket was the most spectacular in the game's history. The slow left-armer took 8 for 61 in the first innings and 8 for 75 in the second as India won by 255 runs to draw the series 1–1. Hirwani's match figures of 16 for 136 are a record for a Test debutant.

MOST RUNS CONCEDED IN A CAREER: TOP 10

Pos	Runs	Player	Span	Mat
1	18,355	A. Kumble (Ind)	1990–2008	132
2	18,110	**M. Muralitharan** (ICC/SL)	1992–2010	133
3	17,995	S.K. Warne (Aus)	1992–2007	145
4	13,084	Harbhajan Singh (Ind)	1998–2011	98
5	12,867	Kapil Dev (Ind)	1978–94	131
6	12,688	C.A. Walsh (WI)	1984–2001	132
7	12,265	D.L. Vettori (ICC/NZ)	1997–2012	111
7	12,186	G.D. McGrath (Aus)	1993–2007	124
9	11,242	M. Ntini (SA)	1998–2009	101
10	10,878	I.T. Botham (Eng)	1977–92	102

Hitting the right spot

Anil Kumble, India's legendary leg-spinner who, with 619 Test wickets, stands third on the all-time list of wicket-takers, may not have been the biggest turner of a cricket ball, but what he may have lacked in zip, he more than made up for with a nagging accuracy. The reward for his unremitting line-and-length policy was 156 lbw victims (25.2 per cent of his wickets) and 35 caught-and-bowled victims (5.65 per cent of his wickets). Both are an all-time Test record (the latter shared with Sri Lanka's Muttiah Muralitharan).

All-time leader

Perhaps not surprising given his status as the leading Test wicket-taker of all time, **Muttiah Muralitharan** holds the record for the most wickets taken bowled (167, 20.87 per cent of his wickets), the most wickets taken caught (435 – 54.37 per cent of his wickets) and for most wickets stumped (47, 5.87 per cent of his wickets). He also shares the record (with Anil Kumble) for the most caught-and-bowled victims (35).

Most deliveries

No bowler has bowled more deliveries in Test cricket than **Muttiah Muralitharan**. Sri Lanka's spinning legend, the all-time leading Test wicket-taker and the holder of numerous other records, has completed 44,039 deliveries in 133 Test matches between 1992 and 2010.

Spofforth's strikes leave England reeling

Australia may already have been in dreamland after reducing England to 26 for 4 on the opening morning of the only Ashes Test of the tour, played at Melbourne in January 1879, but even better things were to follow. Fast bowler **Fred Spofforth** dismissed Vernon Royle, Francis Mackinnon and Tom Emmett in successive deliveries to leave England on a desperate 26 for 7 (a position from which they never recovered; Australia won the game by ten wickets) and record the first of 39 hat-tricks in Test history.

Most wickets taken hit-wicket

Australia's best fast bowler of the 1960s, **Graham McKenzie** had a languid action and surprising pace, which brought him 246 Test wickets in a ten-year career between 1961 and 1971. Uniquely, an all-time Test record four of those scalps were out hit-wicket.

Two hat-tricks in a day

The triangular tournament between England, Australia and South Africa – held in England – in 1912 may have been an unusual occurrence in itself, but the match between Australia and South Africa at Old Trafford provided a unique moment in Test history. In South Africa's first innings, leg-break bowler Jimmy Matthews took the eighth hat-trick in Test history. Later in the day, with South Africa following on, he took another. Bizarrely they were the only wickets he took in the match, but Matthews remains the only man in history to have achieved the feat of taking two hat-tricks in a single Test match.

Earning a crust

Trailing the West Indies by a massive 288 runs after the first innings in the First Test at Edgbaston in May–June 1957, England had to dig deep. And no one dug deeper than captain Peter May (285 not out) and Colin Cowdrey (154 not out) as the home side ground out a patient 583 for 4 declared off a mighty 258 overs; Sonny Ramadhin delivered 98 of those overs (588 deliveries) – a single-innings record – to take 2 for 179. The match ended in a draw.

Four wickets in five balls

There have been three instances in Test cricket of a bowler taking four wickets in five balls: Maurice Allom, W-WWW, on debut for England against New Zealand at Christchurch in 1929–30; **Chris Old**, WW-WW, for England against Pakistan at Birmingham in 1978; and Wasim Akram, WW-WW, for Pakistan against the West Indies at Lahore in 1990–91.

Finding the corridor of uncertainty

The most successful fast bowler in the game's history and fourth on the all-time list of wicket-takers, **Glenn McGrath** used methods not based on express pace but on a metronomic ability to bowl the ball on the line of off stump or just outside. As a result, a record 152 of his 563 Test victims (26.99 per cent of his career haul) were out caught behind.

BOWLER/BATSMAN COMBINATION: TOP 10

Pos	Wkts	Bowler	Batsman	Span	Mat	Ave	Ducks
1	19	**G.D. McGrath** (Aus)	**M.A. Atherton** (Eng)	1994–2001	17	9.89	3
2	18	A.V. Bedser (Eng)	A.R. Morris (Aus)	1946–54	21	32.11	2
3	17	C.E.L. Ambrose (WI)	M.A. Atherton (Eng)	1991–2000	26	25.76	4
=	17	C.A. Walsh (WI)	M.A. Atherton (Eng)	1991–2000	27	22.64	1
5	16	M.D. Marshall (WI)	G.A. Gooch (Eng)	1980–91	21	28.50	2
6	15	H. Trumble (Aus)	T.W. Hayward (Eng)	1896–1904	22	26.26	4
=	15	C.E.L. Ambrose (WI)	M.E. Waugh (Aus)	1991–99	22	35.06	3
=	15	G.D. McGrath (Aus)	B.C. Lara (ICC/WI)	1995–2005	24	41.40	2
=	15	C.A. Walsh (WI)	I.A. Healy (Aus)	1988–99	28	12.53	5
10	14	G.F. Lawson (Aus)	D.I. Gower (Eng)	1981–89	21	40.85	0
=	14	S.K. Warne (Aus)	A.J. Stewart (Eng)	1993–2002	23	26.64	2
=	14	M.A. Noble (Aus)	A.F.A. Lilley (Eng)	1899–1909	29	14.85	2

BOWLERS NO-BALLED FOR THROWING

Bowler	Team	Opposition	Venue	Year
E. Jones	Australia	England	Melbourne	1898
G.A.R. Lock	England	West Indies	Kingston	1954
G.M. Griffin	South Africa	England	Lord's	1960
Haseeb Ahsan	Pakistan	India	Mumbai	1960
I. Meckiff	Australia	South Africa	Brisbane	1963
Abid Ali	India	New Zealand	Christchurch	1968
S.M.H. Kirmani	India	West Indies	Bridgetown	1983
D.I. Gower	England	New Zealand	Nottingham	1986
H. Olonga	Zimbabwe	Pakistan	Harare	1995
M. Muralitharan	Sri Lanka	Australia	Melbourne	1995
G.W. Flower	Zimbabwe	New Zealand	Bulawayo	2000

The most unusual hat-trick

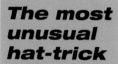

In the Second Test of the 1988–89 series between Australia and the West Indies, at Perth, **Merv Hughes** dismissed Gus Logie with the final ball of his 36th over of the first innings, and then Patrick Patterson with the first ball of his 37th over to end the West Indies' innings. When he trapped Gordon Greenidge lbw first ball in the West Indies' second innings, he had completed Test cricket's most unusual hat-trick.

Players to take a hat-trick on Test debut

Three players in Test history have taken a hat-trick on debut: Maurice Allom, for England against New Zealand at Christchurch in 1929–30; Peter Petherick, for New Zealand against Pakistan at Lahore in 1976–77, and Damien Fleming, for Australia against Pakistan at Rawalpindi in 1994–95.

A spectacular introduction

Picture the scene. A bowler is appearing in his first Test match. The captain has just thrown him the ball; he is standing at the end of his run-up, ball in sweaty hand; the crowd is hushed, and the nerves are jangling. But the debutant gets off to the perfect start: he takes a wicket with his first-ever ball. Thirteen players in Test history have enjoyed such an experience.

Fastest to 250 and 300

After breaking on to the international scene in the early 1970s, with his fearsome pace and legendary stamina it did not take **Dennis Lillee** long to win the hearts of Australian cricket fans or to strike terror into batsmen around the world. As the fans chanted his name, Lillee responded in style: no player has taken 250 (48 matches) or 300 Test wickets (56 matches) in a shorter time.

Fastest to 50

One of the best bowlers Australia has ever produced, Charlie Turner was a skilful right-arm fast-medium bowler with an effortless action. He made a blistering start to his Test career, reaching the 50-wicket milestone in only his sixth Test match and remains the fastest to achieve the feat in Test history.

Fastest to 150

The finest bowler of the early part of the 20th century, England's **S.F. Barnes** was one of the first bowlers to make use of a new ball's seam and, as a result, terrorized batsmen throughout his 13-year, 27-Test career. He claimed his 150th scalp in only his 24th Test – it is a record that stands to this day.

ALL-TIME LEADING TEST WICKET-TAKER: PROGRESSIVE RECORD HOLDERS FROM THE START OF 20TH CENTURY

Record broken	Player	New record
1900	Johnny Briggs (England)	119
January 1904	Hugh Trumble (Australia)	141
December 1913	Sydney (S.F.) Barnes (England)	189
January 1936	Clarrie Grimmett (Australia)	216
July 1953	Alec Bedser (England)	236
January 1963	Brian Statham (England)	242
March 1963	Fred Trueman (England)	307
February 1976	Lance Gibbs (West Indies)	309
December 1981	Dennis Lillee (Australia)	355
August 1986	Ian Botham (England)	383
November 1988	**Richard Hadlee** (New Zealand)	431
January 1994	Kapil Dev (India)	434
March 2000	Courtney Walsh (West Indies)	519
May 2004	Muttiah Muralitharan (Sri Lanka)	520
July 2004	Shane Warne (Australia)	527*
August 2004	Muttiah Muralitharan (Sri Lanka)	532
October 2004	Shane Warne (Australia)	708
December 2007	Muttiah Muralitharan	800

* Warne equalled Muralitharan's total of 527 wickets, before the Sri Lankan moved ahead in the race in August 2004.

More Murali records

Among Sri Lanka spin wizard Muttiah Muralitharan's many records is the speed at which he has reached various wicket milestones. He took his 350th Test wicket in a record low 66 matches; his 400th wicket in a record 72 matches; his 450th Test wicket in a record 80 matches; his 500th Test wicket in a record 87 matches; his 600th wicket in a record 101 matches; his 700th wicket in a record 113 matches; and, of course, he is the only player in history to have reached the 800-wicket milestone (in 133 Tests).

The first hat-trick in Tests to be split over two innings

There have been two instances in Test history of a bowler taking a hat-trick split over two innings. In the First Test of the 1988–89 series between Australia and the West Indies at Brisbane, Courtney Walsh dismissed Tony Dodemaide with his final ball of Australia's first innings and Mike Veletta and Graeme Wood with his first two balls of the second to complete Test cricket's first "split" hat-trick. The second instance involved Merv Hughes (see left).

No need for change

For two bowlers to bowl unchanged throughout an innings is a rare event in Test cricket; there have been only 24 such occurrences in the game's history (and none since 1999). It usually occurs only when opening bowlers get into an unplayable groove and dismiss a side cheaply, but that is not always the case. In the first-ever instance of the feat, in the Second Test of the 1881–82 Ashes series, at Melbourne, Australia's Joey Palmer and Edwin Evans combined for an unchanged 115 (four-ball) overs in England's first innings.

BEST FIGURES IN AN INNINGS: PROGRESSIVE RECORD

Rank	Bowling	Player	Match	Venue	Season
1	7–55	Tom Kendall (Aus)	Australia v England	Melbourne	1876–77*
2	7–44	Fred Spofforth (Aus)	England v Australia	The Oval	1882
3	7–28	Billy Bates (Eng)	Australia v England	Melbourne	1882–83
4	8–35	George Lohmann (Eng)	Australia v England	Sydney	1886–87
5	8–11	Johnny Briggs (Eng)	South Africa v England	Cape Town	1888–89
6	8–7	George Lohmann (Eng)	South Africa v England	Port Elizabeth	1895–96
7	9–28	George Lohmann (Eng)	South Africa v England	Johannesburg	1895–96
8	10–53	Jim Laker (Eng)	England v Australia	Manchester	1956

* Kendall took his 7 for 55 in the inaugural Test Match

WICKETKEEPING RECORDS

MOST DISMISSALS IN A CAREER: TOP 10

Pos	Dismissals	Player	Span	Mat	Inns	Ct	St	Dis/Inn
1	555	**M.V. Boucher** (ICC/SA)	1997–2012	147	281	532	23	1.97
2	416	A.C. Gilchrist (Aus)	1999–2008	96	191	379	37	2.178
3	395	I.A. Healy (Aus)	1988–99	119	224	366	29	1.763
4	355	R.W. Marsh (Aus)	1970–84	96	182	343	12	1.950
5	270	P.J.L. Dujon (WI)	1981–91	81	150	265	5	1.800
6	269	A.P.E. Knott (Eng)	1967–81	95	174	250	19	1.545
7	241	A.J. Stewart (Eng)	1990–2003	133	141	227	14	1.709
8	228	Wasim Bari (Pak)	1967–84	81	146	201	27	1.561
9	220	M.S. Dhoni (Ind)	2005–12	67	123	192	28	1.788
10	219	R.D. Jacobs (WI)	1998–2004	65	122	207	12	1.795
=	219	T.G. Evans (Eng)	1946–59	91	175	173	46	1.251

Bore draw brings a record

At first glance, the Second Test between the West Indies and New Zealand at St John's, Antigua, in April 1996 was an inspiring draw brought to life, only briefly, by the West Indies' mini-collapse in the second innings, only for New Zealand to run out of time in their chase for victory. However, dig deeper and you will find that the match was a record-breaking one: the 1,299 runs scored in the match did not contain a single bye; it is the highest match aggregate with no byes conceded in Test history.

Most dismissals in a single Test match

The Second Test between England and South Africa at Johannesburg in November–December 1995 was a memorable occasion for Jack Russell. The England wicketkeeper took six catches in the first innings and five in the second to set the all-time record for the most dismissals in a match (11). He then hung on grimly with the bat, facing 234 balls for an unbeaten 29 as England held out for an unlikely draw.

Most dismissals in a series

Rod Marsh may not have made much of an impact with the bat during Australia's 2–1 Ashes victory over England in 1982–83 (scoring 124 runs at an average of 17.71), but he certainly shone behind the stumps. The Western Australian gloveman claimed 28 catches in the series – an all-time record.

Most dismissals in an innings

The record for the most dismissals in an innings by a wicketkeeper is seven, a feat that has been achieved on four occasions: Wasim Bari (7ct), Pakistan against New Zealand at Auckland in February 1979; Bob Taylor (7ct), England against India at Mumbai in February 1980; Ian Smith (7ct), New Zealand against Sri Lanka at Hamilton in February 1991; and Ridley Jacobs (7ct), West Indies against Australia at Melbourne in December 2000.

Setting a series benchmark

The West Indies may have crashed to a 2–1 home series defeat against Australia in 1960–61, but it was not for any lack of effort by Gerry Alexander. The wicketkeeper-batsman not only topped the West Indies' batting averages, with 484 runs at an average of 60.50, he also excelled behind the stumps, taking 16 catches: it was the first time of 17 instances in history that a wicketkeeper has scored 300 runs and taken 15 dismissals in a series.

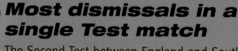

Dujon's standout performances

The only wicketkeeper in Test history to score 300-plus runs and take 15-plus dismissals in a series on three occasions is **Jeff Dujon**. The West Indies keeper achieved the feat against India in 1983–84 (367 runs and 16 dismissals), against Australia in 1984–85 (341 runs and 19 dismissals) and against England in the 1988 series (305 runs and 20 dismissals).

Evans sets a career benchmark

By the time **Godfrey Evans** finished his 91-match, 13-year England career in 1959 he was considered a true technician behind the stumps and one of the greatest wicketkeepers the game has ever seen. His career haul of 219 dismissals (173ct, 46st) and 2,439 runs became a target for other keepers to aim at. In modern times, 200 dismissals and 2,000 career runs is considered a fair benchmark by which to judge a wicketkeeper. Evans was the first of 12 players in Test history to achieve the feat.

Scant consolation for Prasanna Jayawardene

Sri Lanka may ultimately have lost the match (by an innings and 24 runs) and with it the series (2–0) in the third Test against India at the Brabourne Stadium in Mumbai in December 2009, but for their wicketkeeper **Prasanna Jayawardene** the bitterness of defeat was offset by the fact that his performances behind the stumps earned him a place in the history books. During India's massive first-innings total of 726 for 9 declared (in which Virender Sehwag top-scored with 293), Jayawardene did not concede a single bye. It is the largest innings total in Test history in which no byes were conceded.

Most stumpings in a career

With his rapid reflexes and boundless enthusiasm, Australia's Bert Oldfield was the first of the game's great wicket-keepers. A master of the stumping – he is the only man to have taken four stumpings in an innings on four occasions – he made more stumpings in his 17-year, 54-Test career (1920–37) than any other wicketkeeper in history (52).

Most stumpings in a match

The main beneficiary of Narendra Hirwani's record-breaking 16-wicket haul on debut for India in the Fourth Test against the West Indies on an under-prepared, spinner-friendly surface at Chennai in January 1988 was wicketkeeper Kiran More. As the West Indies batsmen floundered against the spinning ball throughout the match, More picked up an all-time record six stumpings – one of them in the first innings and five of them coming in the second.

Most stumpings in a series

The record for the most stumpings in a series is jointly held by two players: Percy Sherwell, with nine stumpings for South Africa against Australia in the 1910–11 series in Australia; and Dick Lillee, with nine stumpings for England against Australia in the 1903–04 Ashes series.

SCORING 100 AND FIVE DISMISSALS IN AN INNINGS

Player	Bat	Field	Team	Opposition	Venue	Match start
D.T. Lindsay	182	6ct/0st	South Africa	Australia	Johannesburg	23 Dec 1966
I.D.S. Smith	113*	4ct/1st	New Zealand	England	Auckland	10 Feb 1984
S.A.R. Silva	111	5ct/0st	Sri Lanka	India	Colombo	6 Sep 1985
A.C. Gilchrist	133	4ct/1st	Australia	England	Sydney	2 Jan 2003
M.J. Prior	118	5ct/0st	England	Australia	Sydney	3 Jan 2011

FIELDING RECORDS

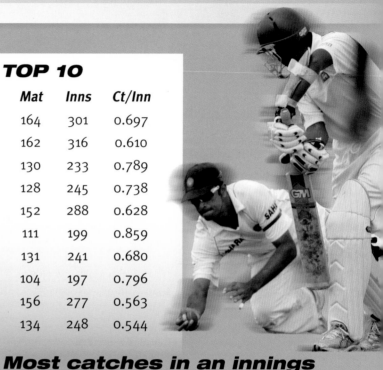

MOST CATCHES IN A CAREER: TOP 10

Pos	Catches	Player	Span	Mat	Inns	Ct/Inn
1	210	**R. Dravid** (ICC/Ind)	1996–2012	164	301	0.697
2	193	R.T. Ponting (Aus)	1995–2012	162	316	0.610
3	184	D.P.M.D. Jayawardene (SL)	1997–2012	130	233	0.789
4	181	M.E. Waugh (Aus)	1991–2002	128	245	0.738
=	181	J.H. Kallis (ICC/SA)	1995–2012	152	288	0.628
6	171	S.P. Fleming (NZ)	1994–2008	111	199	0.859
7	164	B.C. Lara (ICC/WI)	1990–2006	131	241	0.680
8	157	M.A. Taylor (Aus)	1989–99	104	197	0.796
9	156	A.R. Border (Aus)	1978–94	156	277	0.563
10	135	V.V.S. Laxman (Ind)	1996–2012	134	248	0.544

Most catches in an innings by a fielder

The record for the most catches in an innings by a non-wicketkeeper is five, a feat that has occurred on five occasions: by Vic Richardson for Australia against South Africa at Durban in February 1936; by Yajurvindra Singh for India against England at Bangalore in January 1977; by Mohammad Azharuddin for India against Pakistan at Karachi in November 1989; by Kris Srikkanth for India against Australia at Perth in February 1992; and by Stephen Fleming for New Zealand against Zimbabwe at Harare in September 1997.

Most catches in a match

The record for the most catches in a match is seven, a feat that has been achieved on five occasions: by Greg Chappell for Australia against England at Perth in December 1974; by Yajurvindra Singh for India against England at Bangalore in January 1977; by Hashan Tillakaratne for Sri Lanka against New Zealand at Colombo in December 1992; by Stephen Fleming for New Zealand against Zimbabwe at Harare in September 1997, and by Matthew Hayden for Australia against Sri Lanka at Galle in March 2004.

Slip-fielding all-time greats: MARK WAUGH (Australia)

An elegant and gifted strokemaker with the bat (scoring 8,029 runs at an average of 41.81 for Australia in 128 Test matches between 1991 and 2002) and a talented off-spinner (with 59 Test wickets), **Mark Waugh** was equally at home in the hotbed of the slip cordon. By the time he finished his career, the younger of the Waugh twins had taken 128 catches, a mark that stood as a world record until Rahul Dravid broke it in April 2009.

Most catches in a series

There were many heroic Australian performances during their 5–0 whitewash of England in the 1920–21 series. Warwick Armstrong's three centuries and Arthur Mailey's 36 wickets in the series won the highest acclaim, but one perhaps more obscure performance entered the record books and has stood the test of time: Jack Gregory's 15 catches in the series has never been beaten.

Fielding all-time greats:
JONTY RHODES (South Africa)

A man selected as much for his prowess in the field as for his ability with the bat (particularly in the one-day game), South Africa's **Jonty Rhodes** inspired more fear in batsmen than almost any other fielder in the game's history. Razor-sharp reflexes, dives like a leaping salmon at backward point and deadly accurate throws even when off balance became the trademark of his eight-year, 52-Test career between 1992 and 2000.

Fielding all-time greats:
ROGER HARPER
(West Indies)

He was neither a world-beating off-spinner (25 Tests between 1983 and 1993 brought him a mere 46 wickets) nor a great batsman (he averaged 18.44 with the bat), but there have been few finer fielders in the game than Roger Harper. Just ask Graham Gooch. Batting for the MCC against the World XI at Lord's in 1987, the England opener drilled an on-drive off Harper's bowling and stepped out of his crease in anticipation, only to see Harper's telescopic arm reach down, grab the ball and throw down Gooch's stumps to run him out.

Slip-fielding all-time greats:
BOBBY SIMPSON (Australia)

A first-rate opening batsman (he scored 4,869 runs at an average of 46.81 in 62 Tests for Australia between 1957 and 1978) and, with 71 Test wickets to his name, a handy leg-break bowler, Bobby Simpson also had electric reflexes – demonstrated in his youth when he used to catch flies with his bare hands to amuse his school-mates – that turned him into arguably the greatest slip fielder in the history of the game. He ended his career with 110 Test catches.

Fielding all-time greats:
COLIN BLAND
(South Africa)

The hours spent honing his skills by throwing at a single stump certainly paid dividends for **Colin Bland,** who was born in Zimbabwe (then Rhodesia). Although a more than capable batsman (he scored 1,669 runs at an average of 49.08 for South Africa in a 21-Test career between 1961 and 1966), it was his speed, balance and powerful arm in the field that thrilled spectators and opponents around the world in equal measure. He was the world's first truly great fielder.

Proving a point

Left out of the side and watching on from the sidelines as five of his team-mates went on to score centuries in the First Test against newcomers Bangladesh at Multan in August 2001, Pakistan's Younis Khan must have been kicking his heels. And when his chance to impress in the field finally came (on as a substitute for Inzamam-ul-Haq), he grabbed it with both hands, literally, taking an all-time record (for a substitute fielder) four catches in Bangladesh's second innings.

Most catches by a substitute in a match

The record for most catches in a match by a substitute is four, a feat that has been achieved on three occasions: by Gursharan Singh for India against the West Indies at Ahmedabad in November 1983; by Younis Khan for Pakistan against Bangladesh at Multan in August 2001; and by Virender Sehwag for India against Zimbabwe at Nagpur in February 2002.

Perfect partners

The most successful bowler-fielder combination in Test history is that of Sri Lanka's Muttiah Muralitharan and Mahela Jayawardene. The pair have combined for a world-record 77 dismissals between 1997 and 2010.

ALL-ROUND RECORDS

ALL-ROUNDERS TO HAVE SCORED 3,000 RUNS AND TAKEN 200 TEST WICKETS (RANKED BY ORDER OF DEBUT)

Player	Span	Mat	Runs	HS	Ave	100	Wkts	BBI	Ave	5	Ct	St
G.S. Sobers (WI)	1954–74	93	8,032	365*	57.78	26	235	6/73	34.03	6	109	0
Imran Khan (Pak)	1971–92	88	3,807	136	37.69	6	362	8/58	22.81	23	28	0
R.J. Hadlee (NZ)	1973–90	86	3,124	151*	27.16	2	431	9/52	22.29	36	39	0
I.T. Botham (Eng)	1977–92	102	5,200	208	33.54	14	383	8/34	28.40	27	120	0
Kapil Dev (Ind)	1978–94	131	5,248	163	31.05	8	434	9/83	29.64	23	64	0
C.L. Cairns (NZ)	1989–2004	62	3,320	158	33.53	5	218	7/27	29.40	13	14	0
S.K. Warne (Aus)	1992–2007	145	3,154	99	17.32	0	708	8/71	25.41	37	125	0
W.P.U.J.C. Vaas (SL)	1994–2009	111	3,089	100*	24.32	1	355	7/71	29.58	12	31	0
S.M. Pollock (SA)	1995–2008	108	3,781	111	32.31	2	421	7/87	23.11	16	72	0
J.H. Kallis (ICC/SA)	1995–2012	152	12,379	224	56.78	42	276	6/54	32.45	5	181	0
D.L. Vettori (ICC/NZ)	1997–2012	111	4,486	140	30.31	6	3569	7/87	34.16	20	57	0
A. Flintoff (Eng/ICC)	1998–2009	79	3,845	167	31.77	5	226	5/58	32.78	3	52	0

100 runs and ten wickets in a match

Only three players in Test history have achieved the feat of scoring 100 runs and taking ten wickets in a Test match: **Alan Davidson**, 124 runs and 11 wickets for Australia against the West Indies at Brisbane in December 1960; Ian Botham, 114 runs and 13 wickets for England against India at Mumbai in February 1980; and Imran Khan, 117 runs and 11 wickets for Pakistan against India at Faisalabad in January 1983.

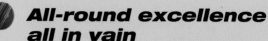

All-round excellence all in vain

Working on the basic principle of hitting the ball as hard and bowling the ball as fast as he could, Jimmy Sinclair did much to put South African cricket on the map. The peak of his 15-year, 25-match career came against England at Cape Town in April 1899 when – despite an eventual 210-run win for England – he took 6 for 26 in England's first innings and then scored 106 to become the first of 28 players in history to score 100 and take five wickets in an innings in a Test match.

A cut above the rest

The only player in history to score 100 runs and take five wickets in an innings on five occasions is Ian Botham. The legendary England all-rounder achieved the feat against New Zealand at Christchurch in February 1978 (103 and 5 for 73); against Pakistan at Lord's in June 1978 (108 and 8 for 34); against India at Mumbai in February 1980 (114 and 6 for 58/7 for 48); against Australia at Headingley in July 1981 (149 not out and 6 for 95); and against New Zealand at Wellington in January 1984 (138 and 5 for 59).

The first great all-rounder

A fine batsman in defence, an excellent driver of the ball and a right-arm medium-pace bowler who relied on spin, guile and variations in flight and pace, Australia's **George Giffen** was Test cricket's first truly great all-rounder. In 31 Tests between 1881 and 1896, he became the first of 54 players in history to score 1,000 runs (1238) and take 100 wickets (103).

Major contributions

A cornerstone of the England team for 58 Tests over 31 years from the turn of the 20th century, Wilfred Rhodes was the greatest slow left-armer of his day and a capable batsman (he once shared an opening stand of 323 with Jack Hobbs), who more than held his own in the field. He was the first of 22 players in history to score 1,000 runs (2,325), take 50 wickets (127) and snare 50 catches (60) in Test cricket.

The first of the fielding all-rounders

A superb batsman (scoring 7,249 runs for England at an average of 58.45, including 22 centuries), Walter Hammond ranks among the finest players ever to have played the game. A naturally gifted athlete, he also proved his worth in the field, taking 110 catches in his 20-year, 85-Test career to become the first of 64 players in history to score 5,000 runs and take 50 catches in Test cricket.

All-time great all-rounders: IAN BOTHAM (England)

Few players in the game's history have been able to galvanize a crowd like **Ian Botham**. A fast-medium swing bowler with an almost unique wicket-taking ability (by the time he ended his 15-year Test career in 1992 he was the world's leading wicket-taker with 383 wickets), Botham was also a hard-hitting batsman capable of turning a match on its head (few who saw it will ever forget his Ashes-turning 149 not out against Australia at Headingley in July 1981) and a world-class slip fielder, who bagged 120 catches in 102 matches.

All-time great all-rounders: KAPIL DEV (India)

Without doubt the finest fast bowler India has ever produced, **Kapil Dev** also made some hefty contributions to the Indian cause with the bat, plundering 5,238 runs – with a highest score of 163 against Sri Lanka at Kanpur in December 1986 – in a 16-year, 131-Test career between 1978 and 1994. However, it was Kapil Dev's relentless march to, and beyond, Richard Hadlee's then world record haul of 431 Test wickets that guaranteed his status among the game's all-time greats.

All-time great all-rounders: GARFIELD SOBERS (West Indies)

Garfield Sobers was the most complete cricketer in the game's history. In a 93-Test career for the West Indies spanning 20 years, he was a world-class performer with both bat (scoring 8,032 runs at an average of 57.78, including a then world record score of 365 not out against Pakistan at Kingston in February 1958), and ball (taking 235 wickets, as either a left-arm fast-medium or slow left-arm bowler), and also excelled in the field, taking 109 catches.

PARTNERSHIP RECORDS

HIGHEST PARTNERSHIPS BY WICKET: TOP 10

Wkt	Runs	Partners	Match	Venue	Match date
1st	415	N.D. McKenzie/G.C. Smith	SA v Bang	Chittagong (CDS)	29 Feb 2008
2nd	576	S.T. Jayasuriya/R.S. Mahanama	SL v Ind	Colombo (RPS)	2 Aug 1997
3rd	624	K.C. Sangakkara/D.P.M.D. Jayawardene	SL v SA	Colombo (SSC)	27 Jul 2006
4th	437	D.P.M.D. Jayawardene/T.T. Samaraweera	SL v Pak	Karachi	21 Feb 2009
5th	405	S.G. Barnes/D.G. Bradman	Aus v Eng	Sydney	13 Dec 1946
6th	351	D.P.M.D. Jayawardene/H.A.P.W. Jayawardene	SL v Ind	Ahmedabad	16 Nov 2009
7th	347	D.S. Atkinson/C.C. Depeiaza	WI v Aus	Bridgetown	14 May 1955
8th	332	**I.J.L. Trott/S.C. Broad**	Eng v Pak	Lord's	26 Aug 2010
9th	195	M.V. Boucher/P.L. Symcox	SA v Pak	Johannesburg	14 Feb 1998
10th	151	B.F. Hastings/R.O. Collinge	NZ v Pak	Auckland	16 Feb 1973
	151	Azhar Mahmood/Mushtaq Ahmed	Pak v SA	Rawalpindi	6 Oct 1997

Golden pair show Australia the way

Australia's Matthew Hayden and Ricky Ponting loved batting together in the 2005–06 season. Between 14 October 2005 and 9 April 2006 the pair batted together on 12 occasions, notching up seven century stands (the highest: 201 v South Africa in Durban) to amass 1,317 runs – a partnership record for a calendar year.

The Karachi kids

The best partnership in Test history (by average) not involving an opening pair is that of Pakistan's Javed Miandad and Shoaib Mohammad (both Karachi-born). The duo batted together 23 times between 1984 and 1993, hitting eight century and seven 50 partnerships and amassing 2,117 runs at a record average of 91.82 runs per partnership.

Mammoth effort is all in vain

A valiant 363-run partnership between Pakistan's **Mohammad Yousuf** (left, 192) and **Younis Khan** (right, 173) on days two and three of the Third Test against England at Headingley in August 2006 ultimately counted for little. The home side went on to win the match by 167 runs to take an unassailable 2–0 lead in the four-Test series, and the pair's 83.5-over effort remains the highest partnership in a losing cause in Test history.

Stuck in the middle with you

It's a fielding side's worst nightmare. Pakistan were floundering on 176 for 9 chasing Sri Lanka's first-innings 273 in the First Test at Colombo in June 2000. Then Wasim Akram (78) and Arshad Khan (9 not out off 95 balls) held on for 257 balls (42.5 overs in three hours four minutes) to add 90 runs – it is the longest tenth-wicket stand (by balls faced) in Test history.

Standing firm

The record for the most successful partnership in a series (868) is jointly held by England's great opening pair **Jack Hobbs** (left) and **Herbert Sutcliffe** (right) (against Australia in 1924–25, with four century stands) and Australia's Donald Bradman and Bill Ponsford (against England in 1934, including a then world record stand of 451 at Headingley).

Leading from the front

Between 2 October 1964 and 14 May 1965, in ten Tests against India, Pakistan and the West Indies, Australia's **Bill Lawry** (right) and **Bobby Simpson** (left) averaged 66.94 runs when they batted together (with a highest of 382 v West Indies in Barbados), to become the first opening partnership to register 1,000 runs (1,205) in a calendar season.

The best opening pair in history

By some distance, the best opening partnership in Test history (in terms of average runs scored) was that of England's Jack Hobbs and Herbert Sutcliffe. The pair batted together on 38 occasions between 1924 and 1930, recording 15 century stands (highest of 283 v Australia at Melbourne in January 1925) at an average of 87.81 runs per innings – only one other pair in Test history (West Indies' Allan Rae and Jeffrey Stollmeyer) has averaged over 70.

Solid as a rock

The legend of the great West Indies sides of the late 1970s and '80s may have been built on a battery of formidable fast bowlers, but a crucial, if unheralded, factor in the success of those teams was the firm foundation provided by a rock-solid opening partnership. Gordon Greenidge and Desmond Haynes batted together on 148 occasions over 14 years and scored 6,482 runs – the most scored by any partnership in Test history.

Perfect partners

Rahul Dravid and Sachin Tendulkar, who formed the backbone of India's batting line-up for approaching 16 years, and in Tendulkar's case considerably more, hold the all-time Test record for the most century partnerships. The pair added 100 runs or more together on 20 occasions between 1996 and 2012, with a highest effort of 249 (for the third wicket) in the Second Test against Zimbabwe at Nagpur in November 2000.

Test cricket's first century partnership

Test cricket had to wait three years and four matches before witnessing the first century partnership. On the opening morning of the 1880 Oval Test against Australia, England's W.G. Grace (152) put on 91 for the first wicket with his brother, E.M. Grace, and then added 120 runs with Bunny Lucas (55) for the second wicket to lead England to a commanding first-innings score of 420 and an eventual five-wicket victory.

Rescue act

Chasing South Africa's first-innings 169 in the First Test at Colombo on 27 July 2006, Sri Lanka had slipped to 14 for 2 when **Mahele Jayawardene** (right) joined **Kumar Sangakkara** (left) at the crease. 157 overs later, the pair – Sangakkara, 285; Jayawardene, 309 – had amassed a mighty 624-run partnership, smashing the partnership record for any wicket (576) set by compatriots Sanath Jayasuriya and Roshan Mohanama in 1997. Sri Lanka went on to win the match by an innings and 153 runs.

TEST RECORDS:
BY TEAM

The spread of the game around the world was not instantaneous. Australia and England first locked horns in March 1877, but it took 123 years before we reached today's complement of ten Test-playing nations as South Africa (1889), West Indies (1928), New Zealand (1930), India (1932), Pakistan (1952), Sri Lanka (1982), Zimbabwe (1992, before losing their Test status in 2005) and Bangladesh (2000) joined the party. This section looks at the leading Test players on a country-by-country basis and tells you, among other things, who is Australia's all-time leading Test batsman and which Pakistan player has taken the most Test catches.

Sachin Tendulkar holds aloft the Border-Gavaskar trophy after India's 2–0 series victory over Australia in 2010–11.

AUSTRALIA

One of international cricket's original two participants, Australia hosted the first-ever Test match, against England at Melbourne in March 1877. England have appeared in more matches than the other Test-playing nations, but no other country in the game's history has enjoyed as many Test wins (348) or as high a winning percentage (46.96) as Australia.

RESULT SUMMARY

Opposition	Span	Mat	Won	Lost	Tied	Draw	W/L	%W	%L	%D
Bangladesh	2003–06	4	4	0	0	0	-	100.00	0.00	0.00
England	1877–2011	326	133	102	0	91	1.30	40.79	31.28	27.91
ICC World XI	2005	1	1	0	0	0	-	100.00	0.00	0.00
India	1947–2012	82	38	20	1	32	1.90	46.34	24.39	28.04
New Zealand	1946–2011	52	27	8	0	17	3.37	51.92	15.38	32.69
Pakistan	1956–2010	57	28	12	0	17	2.33	49.12	21.05	29.82
South Africa	1902–2011	85	48	19	0	18	2.22	56.47	22.35	21.17
Sri Lanka	1983–2011	23	14	1	0	8	14.00	60.86	4.34	34.78
West Indies	1930–2012	111	54	32	1	24	1.68	48.64	28.82	21.62
Zimbabwe	1999–2003	3	3	0	0	0	-	100.00	0.00	0.00

Hitting an all-time low

Australia did not get off to the most convincing of starts in their 1902 Ashes-winning series. In the First Test, at Edgbaston, after England had reached 376 in their first innings, Australia, on a wicket affected by a heavy downpour, crashed to a cataclysmic 36 all out (the lowest total in the country's history), with only Victor Trumper (18) reaching double figures. The rain came back to save Australia, however, and the three-day match ended in a draw.

Largest victories

By an innings: by an innings and 360 runs against South Africa in Johannesburg in February 2002.

By runs: by 562 runs against England at The Oval in 1934.

By wickets: by ten wickets on 28 occasions.

Smallest victories

By runs: by three runs against England at Manchester in July 1902.

By wickets: by one wicket against the West Indies at Melbourne in December 1951.

Heaviest defeats

By an innings: by an innings and 579 runs against England at The Oval in August 1938.

By runs: by 675 runs, against England at Brisbane in November 1928.

By wickets: by ten wickets on ten occasions.

Australia end Caribbean tour on an all-time high

After watching the West Indies compile 357 in their first innings of the Fifth Test at Kingston, Jamaica, in June 1955, Australia – already holding an unassailable 2–0 series lead – were determined to bow out of their first-ever tour to the Caribbean in style and put on a spectacular show. Centuries from Colin McDonald (127), **Neil Harvey** (204), Keith Miller (109), Ron Archer (128) and Richie Benaud (121) saw them reach an Australian record total of 758 for 8. They went on to win the match by an innings and 82 runs.

Hayden hits the heights

By the end of the second day of the First Test between Australia and Zimbabwe at Perth in October 2003, the fact that Australia had amassed a mighty first-innings score of 735 for 6 – the highest total on Australian soil in 126 years of Test cricket – was all but forgotten. Every one of the following day's headlines would be reserved for one man: Matthew Hayden. The Queensland left-handed opener smashed a then world record 380 (off 437 balls); it remains the highest individual score by an Australian in Test history.

BATTING – MOST RUNS: TOP 10

Pos	Runs	Player	Span	Mat	Inns	NO	HS	Ave	100	50	0
1	13,346	R.T. Ponting	1995–2012	165	282	29	257	52.75	41	62	16
2	11,174	A.R. Border	1978–94	156	265	44	205	50.56	27	63	11
3	10,927	S.R. Waugh	1985–2004	168	260	46	200	51.06	32	50	22
4	8,625	M.L. Hayden	1994–2009	103	184	14	380	50.73	30	29	14
5	8,029	M.E. Waugh	1991–2002	128	209	17	153*	41.81	20	47	19
6	7,696	J.L. Langer	1993–2007	105	182	12	250	45.27	23	30	11
7	7,525	M.A. Taylor	1989–99	104	186	13	334*	43.49	19	40	5
8	7,422	D.C. Boon	1984–96	107	190	20	200	43.65	21	32	16
9	7,110	G.S. Chappell	1970–84	87	151	19	247*	53.86	24	31	12
10	6,996	D.G. Bradman	1928–48	52	80	10	334	99.94	29	13	7

All-time great: DONALD BRADMAN

Donald Bradman made his Test debut for Australia aged 20 against England in the 1928–29 Ashes series and registered the first of his 29 Test centuries in his second Test match. From that moment, he became the scourge of bowlers around the world. In the 1930 Ashes series, he plundered a record 974 runs (including a memorable and Test record-breaking knock of 334 at Headingley) at an average of 139.14 – it was the first of five times he would score 500-plus runs in a series. Going into his final Test, against England at The Oval in 1948, with his legend as the greatest batsman of all time confirmed, he needed a mere four runs to end with a career average of 100.00. Sensationally he was out for 0, but his career average of 99.94 still stands as the greatest of all time.

Ponting's record haul

Australia's best batsman of modern times and the heartbeat of one of his country's best-ever teams, **Ricky Ponting** has a talismanic approach to batting, in which every shot is played with a flourish of the bat, and it has brought him rich rewards. In 162 Tests for his country (77 of them as captain) he has plundered 13,346 runs (at an average of 52.75) with 41 centuries. Both the runs and centuries are all-time national records.

Struggling to get off the mark

The leading wicket-taker of all fast bowlers in Test history (with 563 wickets), Glenn McGrath may well have struck fear into opponents when he had the ball in his hand, but it was an altogether different story when he came out to bat. In 124 Test matches between 1993 and 2007, McGrath amassed just 671 runs (at an average of 7.36) and recorded an Australian record 35 ducks.

BOWLING – MOST WICKETS: TOP 10

Pos	Wkts	Player	Span	Mat	Balls	Runs	BBI	BBM	Ave	Econ	SR	5	10
1	708	S.K. Warne	1992–2007	145	40,705	17,995	8/71	12/128	25.41	2.65	57.4	37	10
2	563	G.D. McGrath	1993–2007	124	29,248	12,186	8/24	10/27	21.64	2.49	51.9	29	3
3	355	D.K. Lillee	1971–84	70	18,467	8,493	7/83	11/123	23.92	2.75	52.0	23	7
4	310	B. Lee	1999–2008	76	16,531	9,554	5/30	9/171	30.81	3.46	53.3	10	0
5	291	C.J. McDermott	1984–96	71	16,586	8,332	8/97	11/157	28.63	3.01	56.9	14	2
6	259	J.N. Gillespie	1996–2006	71	14,234	6,770	7/37	9/80	26.13	2.85	54.9	8	0
7	248	R. Benaud	1952–64	63	19,108	6,704	7/72	11/105	27.03	2.10	77.0	16	1
8	246	G.D. McKenzie	1961–71	60	17,681	7,328	8/71	10/91	29.78	2.48	71.8	16	3
9	228	R.R. Lindwall	1946–60	61	13,650	5,251	7/38	9/70	23.03	2.30	59.8	12	0
10	216	C.V. Grimmett	1925–36	37	14,513	5,231	7/40	14/199	24.21	2.16	67.1	21	7

Magical Mailey destroys downbeat England

Already 3–0 up in the 1921 Ashes series, Australia went into the Fourth Test at Melbourne looking to ram home their advantage over England, and nobody did so more effectively than Arthur Mailey. The New South Wales leg-break bowler took 9 for 121 off 47 overs in England's second innings – the best-ever bowling figures in an innings by an Australian – as the home side went on to win the match by eight wickets to take a 4–0 series lead.

Fantastic Ferris

Of all Australian bowlers to have bowled 2,000 or more deliveries in Test cricket, nobody has a better average than J.J. Ferris. In eight matches between 1887 and 1892, the left-arm swing bowler took 61 wickets – with a best return of 7 for 37 against South Africa in Cape Town in March 1892 (in his final appearance for his country) – at an amazing average of 12.70.

Burke produces the most miserly bowling spell

As South Africa battled in vain to avoid defeat against Australia at Johannesburg in the Fourth Test in 1957–58, Australian off-break bowler Jim Burke made history. His 15 (wicketless, eight-ball) overs cost a mere ten runs – the best economy rate in an innings by an Australian bowler in history (0.40).

All-time great: SHANE WARNE

From the moment at Old Trafford in June 1993 when Shane **Warne** ripped a massive leg-break from outside leg stump past a bemused Mike Gatting's defensive push and into off stump with his first delivery in Ashes cricket, the world knew it was witnessing a bowler with supreme ability. His major tools may have changed over the years as a result of injuries – the frequency of the big-spinning deliveries was replaced with more craft and guile – but Warne's ability to hypnotize opponents continued unabated. By the time he finished his 145-match, 15-year Test career in 2007, Warne had taken more five-wicket hauls (37), more ten-wicket hauls (10) and more wickets (708) than any other Australian bowler in history.

Bob Massie's magical debut

With the exception of India's Narendra Hirwani, no bowler has enjoyed a more spectacular start to his Test career than **Bob Massie**. Playing at Lord's in the Second Test of the 1972 Ashes series, the fast-medium swing bowler destroyed England, taking 8 for 84 in the first innings and 8 for 53 in the second to help Australia to an eight-wicket win. His match figures of 16 for 137 are the best by an Australian bowler in Test history.

WICKETKEEPER – MOST DISMISSALS: TOP 5

Pos	Dis	Player	Span	Mat	Inns	Ct	St	Dis/Inn
1	416	**A.C. Gilchrist**	1999–2008	96	191	379	37	2.178
2	395	I.A. Healy	1988–99	119	224	366	29	1.763
3	355	R.W. Marsh	1970–84	96	182	343	12	1.950
4	187	A.T.W. Grout	1957–66	51	98	163	24	1.908
5	164	B.J. Haddin	2008–12	43	82	160	4	2.000

MOST DISMISSALS: INNINGS/MATCHES/SERIES

Three players (Wally Grout, Rod Marsh and Ian Healy) hold the Australian record for the most dismissals in an innings with six. **Adam Gilchrist** holds the record for the most dismissals in a match with ten (all caught), achieved against New Zealand at Hamilton in March 2000, while Marsh holds the record for the most dismissals in a series, with 28 (all catches) in the 1982–83 Ashes series.

FIELDING – MOST CATCHES: TOP 5

Pos	Ct	Player	Span	Mat	Inns	Max	Ct/Inn
1	194	**R.T. Ponting**	1995–2012	165	322	3	0.602
2	181	M.E. Waugh	1991–2002	128	245	4	0.738
3	157	M.A. Taylor	1989–99	104	197	4	0.796
4	156	A.R. Border	1978–94	156	277	4	0.563
5	128	M.L. Hayden	1994–2009	103	205	4	0.624

MOST CATCHES: INNINGS/MATCHES/SERIES

Vic Richardson holds the Australian record for the most catches in an innings with five, against South Africa at Durban in February 1936. Greg Chappell (against England at Perth in December 1974) and Matthew Hayden (against Sri Lanka at Galle in March 2004) hold the record for the most catches in a match, with seven; and Jim Gregory holds the record for the most catches in a series, having taken 15 against England in 1920–21.

LONGEST-SERVING CAPTAINS: TOP 10

Pos	Mat	Player	Span	W-L-T-D	%W
1	93	**A.R. Border**	1984–94	32-22-1-38	34.40
2	77	R.T. Ponting	2004–10	48-16-0-13	62.33
3	57	S.R. Waugh	1999–2004	41-9-0-7	71.92
4	50	M.A. Taylor	1994–99	26-13-0-11	52.00
5	48	G.S. Chappell	1975–83	21-13-0-14	43.75
6	39	R.B. Simpson	1964-78	12-12-0-15	30.76
7	30	I.M. Chappell	1971–75	15-5-0-10	50.00
8	28	R. Benaud	1958–63	12-4-1-11	42.85
=	28	K.J. Hughes	1979–84	4-13-0-11	14.28
10	25	W.M. Woodfull	1930–34	14-7-0-4	56.00

Most successful captain

A natural successor to Steve Waugh when he took over Australia's Test captaincy in 2004, Ricky Ponting went on to become the most successful captain in his country's history. In his 77 Tests in charge, Ponting recorded 48 wins (seven more than Waugh) with a winning percentage of 62.33.

Record partnership

Australia posted an intimidating and series-clinching first-innings total in the final 1934 Ashes Test at The Oval. Bill Ponsford (266) and Donald Bradman (244) put on 451 for the second wicket (the highest Test partnership by an Australian pair) to help their side to 701 all out and an eventual 562-run win.

ENGLAND

The home of cricket and the nation that gave the game to the world, England played in the first-ever Test match, against Australia at Melbourne in 1877, and have since gone on to play in more Test matches than any other country (918). There have been many highs and lows along the way: England's 321 victories (second only to Australia) are balanced out by a record number of defeats (264).

RESULT SUMMARY

Opposition	Span	Mat	Won	Lost	Tied	Draw	W/L	%W	%L	%D
Australia	1877–2011	326	102	133	0	91	0.76	31.28	40.79	27.91
Bangladesh	2003–10	8	8	0	0	0	-	100.00	0.00	0.00
India	1932–2011	103	38	19	0	46	2.20	36.89	18.44	44.66
New Zealand	1930–2008	94	45	8	0	41	5.62	47.87	8.51	43.61
Pakistan	1954–2012	74	22	16	0	36	1.37	29.72	21.62	48.64
South Africa	1889–2010	138	56	29	0	53	1.93	41.57	21.01	38.40
Sri Lanka	1982–2012	26	10	7	0	9	1.42	38.46	26.92	34.61
West Indies	1928–2009	145	43	53	0	49	0.81	29.65	36.55	33.79
Zimbabwe	1996–2003	6	3	0	0	3	-	50.00	0.00	50.00

Low points

There have been a few too many calamitous days for English cricket fans over the years – 46 all out against the West Indies at Port of Spain in March 1994; 51 all out against the same opposition at Bridgetown in January 2009 – but the lowest point in their history came in the first innings of the First Test of the 1886–87 Ashes series, at Melbourne, when they crashed to a miserable 45 all out. Astonishingly, however, England rallied to win the match by 13 runs.

Largest victories

By an innings: by an innings and 579 runs against Australia at The Oval in August 1938.

By runs: by 675 runs against Australia at Brisbane in November 1928.

By wickets: by ten wickets on 19 occasions.

Smallest victories

By runs: by two runs against Australia at Edgbaston in August 2005.

By wickets: by one wicket on three occasions: against Australia at The Oval in August 1902, against Australia at Melbourne in January 1908 and against South Africa in Cape Town in January 1923.

Heaviest defeats

By an innings: by an innings and 332 runs against Australia at Brisbane in November 1946.

By runs: by 562 runs against Australia at The Oval in August 1934.

By wickets: by ten wickets on 20 occasions.

Records tumble in Ashes finale at The Oval

England's spectacular batting performance in the first innings of the Fifth Test against Australia at The Oval in August 1938, which led to them squaring the Ashes series 1–1, set several benchmarks for future generations of England cricketers to aspire to. The team total (903 for 7 declared) is the highest by an England team in history; **Len Hutton**'s majestic innings of 364 has never been bettered by an Englishman; and the victory margin – by an innings and 579 runs – is the largest (by an innings) in England's history.

BATTING – MOST RUNS: TOP 10

Pos	Runs	Player	Span	Mat	Inns	NO	HS	Ave	100	50	0
1	8,900	G.A. Gooch	1975–95	118	215	6	333	42.58	20	46	13
2	8,463	A.J. Stewart	1990–2003	133	235	21	190	39.54	15	45	14
3	8,231	D.I. Gower	1978–92	117	204	18	215	44.25	18	39	7
4	8,114	G. Boycott	1964–82	108	193	23	246*	47.72	22	42	10
5	7,728	M.A. Atherton	1989–2001	115	212	7	185*	37.69	16	46	20
6	7,624	M.C. Cowdrey	1954–75	114	188	15	182	44.06	22	38	9
7	7,249	W.R. Hammond	1927–47	85	140	16	336*	58.45	22	24	4
8	6,971	L. Hutton	1937–55	79	138	15	364	56.67	19	33	5
9	6,806	K.F. Barrington	1955–68	82	131	15	256	58.67	20	35	5
10	6,744	G.P. Thorpe	1993–2005	100	179	28	200*	44.66	16	39	12

Best opening partnership

Between 1924 and 1930 England were blessed with the greatest opening partnership in their history. During that seven-year span, Jack Hobbs and Herbert Sutcliffe batted together on 38 occasions and scored 3,249 runs with 15 century stands (only Gordon Greenidge and Desmond Haynes of the West Indies, with 16, have done better in Test history – taking 148 innings to achieve the feat). Hobbs and Sutcliffe's average partnership of 87.81 is the best in Test history.

One of England's very best

Revered for his astounding powers of concentration and an exemplary technique, the outbreak of the First World War may have delayed **Herbert Sutcliffe's** entry into county cricket (he was 24 when he made his debut for Yorkshire in 1919), but the Harrogate-born batsman more than made up for lost time, breaking into the England team by 1924 and going on to form one half (alongside Jack Hobbs) of his country's most successful opening partnership of all time. His first century (of 16) came in only his second Test (122 against South Africa at Lord's in June 1924) and by the time he bowed out of international cricket 11 years later (after 54 matches) he had amassed 4,555 runs (with a highest score of 194 against Australia at Sydney in December 1932) at an average of 60.73 – the highest by any England batsman in Test history.

All-time great: WALTER HAMMOND

Without doubt one of the finest batsmen to play the game, **Walter Hammond** was also one of the first players to bring a real sense of dash to Test cricket. A naturally gifted athlete, he was quick on his feet, a dashing stroke player and a sweet timer of the ball who was equally dynamic off both the front and back foot, particularly when driving the ball. In 85 Tests for England between 1927 and 1947, Hammond scored 7,249 runs at an impressive average of 58.45. He also set the national record for the most centuries (22, equalled by Colin Cowdrey and Geoffrey Boycott) and for the most runs in a series (905 against Australia in 1928–29).

Most ducks

The English record for the most ducks in Test cricket is 20, an unfortunate feat achieved by two players of contrasting batting ability: Steve Harmison (in 62 Tests between 2002 and 2009) and Michael Atherton (in 115 Tests between 1989 and 2001).

BOWLING – MOST WICKETS: TOP 10

Pos	Wkts	Player	Span	Mat	Balls	Runs	BBI	BBM	Ave	Econ	SR	5	10
1	383	I.T. Botham	1977–92	102	21,815	10,878	8/34	13/106	28.40	2.99	56.9	27	4
2	325	R.G.D. Willis	1971–84	90	17,357	8,190	8/43	9/92	25.20	2.83	53.4	16	0
3	307	F.S. Trueman	1952–65	67	15,178	6,625	8/31	12/119	21.57	2.61	49.4	17	3
4	297	D.L. Underwood	1966–82	86	21,862	7,674	8/51	13/71	25.83	2.10	73.6	17	6
5	258	J.M. Anderson	2003–12	68	14,630	7,7783	7/43	11/71	30.16	3.16	56.7	12	1
6	252	J.B. Statham	1951–65	70	16,056	6,261	7/39	11/97	24.84	2.33	63.7	9	1
7	248	M.J. Hoggard	2000–08	67	13,909	7,564	7/61	12/205	30.50	3.26	56.0	7	1
8	236	A.V. Bedser	1946–55	51	15,918	5,876	7/44	14/99	24.89	2.21	67.4	15	5
9	234	A.R. Caddick	1993–2003	62	13,558	6,999	7/46	10/215	29.91	3.09	57.9	13	1
10	229	D. Gough	1994–2003	58	11,821	6,503	6/42	9/92	28.39	3.30	51.6	9	0

Most five-wicket hauls

A talismanic all-rounder with an uncanny ability to bring a crowd to its feet through his deeds with both bat and ball, Ian Botham ended his 15-year, 102-Test career in 1992 as the world's leading wicket-taker, with 383 wickets, including 27 five-wicket hauls. Both marks still stand as all-time England Test records.

Laker's record return

No player in history, let alone one from England, has been able to match **Jim Laker**'s amazing achievements with the ball during the Fourth Test against Australia at Old Trafford in July 1956. In an Ashes-retaining performance of sublime quality, the Yorkshire off-spinner took 9 for 37 in the first innings and an all-time best 10 for 53 in the second. His match figures of 19 for 90 are also an all-time record in Test cricket.

Toiling in the summer sun

Not every day for **Ian Botham** was one to remember, however. As Pakistan prospered on a batsman-friendly surface in the Fifth Test at The Oval in August 1987, England's bowlers suffered, and none more so than Botham. The Somerset all-rounder's 52 overs eventually brought him three wickets, but they also cost 217 runs – the most ever conceded in a Test innings by an England bowler.

Keeping it tight

Two players share the England record (0.30) for the most economic spell of bowling (minimum of ten overs) in Test history: Bob Wyatt, who took 3 for 4 off 13 overs against South Africa at Durban in January 1928; and Hedley Verity, who took 0 for 4 off 13 overs against South Africa at Leeds in July 1935

All-time great: S.F. BARNES

England have produced some world-class bowlers over the years – Fred Trueman and Ian Botham to name but two – but none of them has struck as much fear into the hearts of opposing batsmen as the legendary **S.F. Barnes**, the greatest fast bowler of the early part of the 20th century. One of the first bowlers to make full use of the ball's seam and capable of swinging the ball both ways, at pace, Barnes took 189 wickets for England (including a national record seven ten-wicket match hauls) in 27 Tests between 1901 and 1914. In his final Test series, against South Africa, he took a world record 49 wickets in the series, in only four Tests.

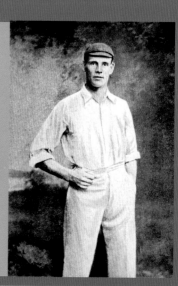

WICKETKEEPER – MOST DISMISSALS: TOP 5

Pos	Dis	Player	Span	Mat	Inns	Ct	St	Dis/Inn
1	269	**A.P.E. Knott**	1967–81	95	174	250	19	1.545
2	241	A.J. Stewart	1990–2003	133	141	227	14	1.709
3	219	T.G. Evans	1946–59	91	175	173	46	1.251
4	174	R.W. Taylor	1971–84	57	106	167	7	1.641
5	165	R.C. Russell	1988–98	54	96	153	12	1.718

MOST DISMISSALS: INNINGS/MATCHES/SERIES

The record for the most dismissals in an innings by an England wicketkeeper is seven by Bob Taylor (7ct) against India in Mumbai in February 1980. Jack Russell holds the record both for the most dismissals in a match – 11 catches in the Second Test of 1995–96 series against South Africa in Johannesburg – and for the most dismissals in a series – 27 (25ct, 2st) against South Africa in the 1995–96 series.

FIELDING - MOST CATCHES: TOP 5

Pos	Ct	Player	Span	Mat	Inns	Max	Ct/Inn
1	120	I.T. Botham	1977–92	102	179	3	0.670
=	120	M.C. Cowdrey	1954–75	114	214	3	0.560
3	115	A.J. Strauss	2004–12	94	179	3	0.642
4	110	W.R. Hammond	1927–47	85	154	3	0.714
5	105	G.P. Thorpe	1993–2005	100	179	4	0.586

MOST CATCHES: INNINGS/ MATCHES/SERIES

The England record for the most catches in an innings is four, a feat achieved on 19 occasions; the record for the most catches in a match is six, a feat achieved on seven occasions; and the record for the most catches in a series is 12, a feat achieved on five occasions.

Most successful captain

His sudden resignation following a five-wicket defeat to South Africa at Edgbaston in August 2008 prevented Michael Vaughan from surpassing **Michael Atherton** as England's longest-serving captain (51 Tests to Atherton's 54), but the history books will record that Vaughan was the most successful England captain in history, recording 26 wins.

The highlight of his captaincy came in 2005, when England won the Ashes for the first time in 18 years.

LONGEST-SERVING CAPTAINS: TOP 10

Pos	Mat	Player	Span	W-L-T-D	%W
1	54	**M.A. Atherton**	1993–2001	13-21-0-20	24.07
2	51	M.P. Vaughan	2003–08	26-11-0-14	50.98
3	45	N. Hussain	1999–2003	17-15-0-13	37.77
4	42	A.J. Strauss	2006–12	21-8-0-13	50.00
5	41	P.B.H. May	1955–61	20-10-0-11	48.78
6	34	G.A. Gooch	1988–93	10-12-0-12	29.41
7	32	D.I. Gower	1982–89	5-18-0-9	15.62
8	31	R. Illingworth	1969–73	12-5-0-14	38.70
=	31	J.M. Brearley	1977–81	18-4-0-9	58.06
10	30	E.R. Dexter	1961–64	9-7-0-14	30.00

INDIA

A Test-playing nation since 1932, India's rise towards the top of world cricket's ranks was gradual. First they became competitive at home, where overseas batsmen struggled against India's legion of spin bowlers on slow, low, turning wickets, and then, with the emergence of an array of batting talent, such as Sunil Gavaskar and Sachin Tendulkar, they started to make waves around the world.

RESULT SUMMARY

Opposition	Span	Mat	Won	Lost	Tied	Draw	W/L	%W	%L	%D
Australia	1947–2012	82	20	38	1	23	0.52	24.39	46.34	28.04
Bangladesh	2000–10	7	6	0	0	1	-	85.71	0.00	14.28
England	1932–2012	103	19	38	0	46	0.50	18.44	36.89	44.60
New Zealand	1955–2010	50	16	9	0	25	1.77	32.00	18.00	50.00
Pakistan	1952–2007	59	9	12	0	38	0.75	15.25	20.33	64.40
South Africa	1992–2011	27	7	12	0	8	0.58	25.92	44.44	29.62
Sri Lanka	1982–2010	35	14	6	0	15	2.33	40.00	17.14	42.85
West Indies	1948–2011	88	14	30	0	44	0.46	15.90	34.09	50.00
Zimbabwe	1992–2005	11	7	2	0	2	3.50	63.63	18.18	18.18

Plummeting to new depths

A trip to Lord's is considered the pinnacle of many players' careers, but that was far from being the case when India played England at the home of cricket in June 1974. Forced to follow on in their second innings, still 327 runs behind, they crashed to a disastrous 42 all out to lose by an innings and 285 runs. It remains India's lowest-ever Test total.

Stellar Sehwag steals the show

After watching South Africa compile a handsome 540 all out in their first innings of the First Test at Chennai in March 2008, India needed a confident performance with the bat if they were to stay in the game. And **Virender Sehwag** duly obliged, batting for 8 hours and 50 minutes, facing 304 balls and hitting 42 fours and five sixes en route to a score of 319. It is the 17th highest score in Test history and the highest by an Indian batsman.

Starting off in style

Sunil Gavaskar, India's first great batsman, burst on to the international scene in spectacular fashion against the West Indies, in the Caribbean, between February and April 1971. Handed his debut in the Second Test of the five-match series, the diminutive opener hit four centuries (with a highest score of 220 in the Fifth Test) and three half-centuries to help India to a sensational 1–0 series win. His haul of 774 runs in the series (at an average of 154.80) is an all-time Indian record.

Largest victories

By an innings: by an innings and 239 runs against Bangladesh in Dhaka in May 2007.

By runs: by 320 runs against Australia at Mohali in October 2008.

By wickets: by ten wickets on seven occasions.

Smallest victories

By runs: by 13 runs against Australia at Mumbai in November 2004.

By wickets: by one wicket against Australia at Mohali in October 2010.

Heaviest defeats

By an innings: by an innings and 336 runs against the West Indies at Kolkata in December 1958.

By runs: by 342 runs against Australia at Nagpur in October 2004.

By wickets: by ten wickets on 15 occasions.

BATTING – MOST RUNS: TOP 10

Pos	Runs	Player	Span	Mat	Inns	NO	HS	Ave	100	50	0
1	15,470	S.R. Tendulkar	1989–2012	188	311	32	248*	55.44	51	65	14
2	13,265	R. Dravid	1996–2012	163	284	32	270	52.63	36	63	7
3	10,122	S.M. Gavaskar	1971–87	125	214	16	236*	51.12	34	45	12
4	8,781	V.V.S. Laxman	1996–2012	134	225	34	281	45.97	17	56	14
5	8,095	V. Sehwag	2001–12	95	165	6	319	50.91	22	31	15
6	7,212	S.C. Ganguly	1996–2008	113	188	17	239	42.17	16	35	13
7	6,868	D.B. Vengsarkar	1976–92	116	185	22	166	42.13	17	35	15
8	6,125	M. Azharuddin	1984–2000	99	147	9	199	45.03	22	21	5
9	6,080	G.R. Viswanath	1969–83	91	155	10	222	41.93	14	35	10
10	5,248	Kapil Dev	1978–94	131	184	15	163	31.05	8	27	16

Sign of things to come

It seemed as it would be a Test debut to forget for **Gundappa Viswanath** when he fell for a duck in India's first innings against Australia at Kanpur in November 1969. But he struck a classy 137 in the second innings – the highest score by an Indian on debut – as the match ended in a draw. It was a record-breaking start to Viswanath's successful 91-Test career that yielded 6,080 runs at an average of 41.93.

All-time great: SACHIN TENDULKAR

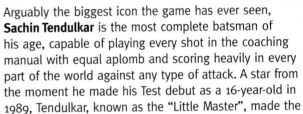

Arguably the biggest icon the game has ever seen, **Sachin Tendulkar** is the most complete batsman of his age, capable of playing every shot in the coaching manual with equal aplomb and scoring heavily in every part of the world against any type of attack. A star from the moment he made his Test debut as a 16-year-old in 1989, Tendulkar, known as the "Little Master", made the first of his all-time record 51 Test centuries aged 17, against England in 1990, and has gone on to enjoy a spectacular career, achieving almost godlike status in cricket-mad India. In 2008 he surpassed Brian Lara as Test cricket's all-time leading run-scorer, with 15,470 runs (at an average of 55.44).

Batting their way to a series win

Already one-nil up in the three-match series and having seen Sri Lanka compile 393 all out in their first innings in the Third Test at Mumbai in December 2009, the equation for India was a simple one: to occupy the crease for as long as possible and bat Sri Lanka out of the game. They did so in record-breaking fashion, as a mighty innings of 293 from Virender Sehwag plus an unbeaten century from Mahendra Singh Dhoni saw them compile a massive 726 for 9 declared – the highest total in India's history – en route to an eventual innings-and-24-run victory and a 2–0 series win.

Hit and miss with the bat

He may have been a huge hit with the ball (taking an impressive 288 wickets in 83 Test matches), but Zaheer Khan has endured more fluctuating fortunes with the bat: he has struck three half-centuries (with a highest score of 75, against Bangladesh at Dhaka in December 2004), but has also failed to trouble the scorers on 25 occasions – a record number of ducks for an India batsman in Tests.

Mankad and Roy power India to series win

One–nil up in the five-match series with one Test to go, at Chennai in January 1956, India won the toss, elected to bat and would have pinned their hopes of series success on their batsmen batting New Zealand out of the game. Their openers, **Vinoo Mankad** (231) and Pankaj Roy (173), responded in spectacular fashion, putting on 413 for the opening wicket – the highest partnership in India's Test history. It provided the perfect foundation for India, who went on to win the match by an innings and 109 runs to take the series 2–0.

BOWLING – MOST WICKETS: TOP 10

Pos	Wkts	Player	Span	Mat	Balls	Runs	BBI	BBM	Ave	Econ	SR	5	10
1	619	A. Kumble	1990–2008	132	40,850	18,355	10/74	14/149	29.65	2.69	65.9	35	8
2	434	Kapil Dev	1978–94	131	27,740	12,867	9/83	11/146	29.64	2.78	63.9	23	2
3	406	Harbhajan Singh	1998–2011	98	27,651	13,084	8/84	15/217	32.22	2.83	68.1	25	5
4	288	Z. Khan	2000–12	83	16,719	9,153	7/87	10/149	31.78	3.28	58.0	10	1
5	266	B.S. Bedi	1966–79	67	21,364	7,637	7/98	10/194	28.71	2.14	80.3	14	1
6	242	B.S. Chandrasekhar	1964–79	58	15,963	7,199	8/79	12/104	29.74	2.70	65.9	16	2
7	236	J. Srinath	1991–2002	67	15,104	7,196	8/86	13/132	30.49	2.85	64.0	10	1
8	189	E.A.S. Prasanna	1962–78	49	14,353	5,742	8/76	11/140	30.38	2.40	75.9	10	2
9	162	M.H. Mankad	1946–59	44	14,686	5,236	8/52	13/131	32.32	2.13	90.6	8	2
10	156	S. Venkataraghavan	1965–83	57	14,877	5,634	8/72	12/152	36.11	2.27	95.3	3	1

Record-breaking achievements with the ball

The fourth and final day of the Second Test match between India and Pakistan at Delhi in February 1999 was a day to remember for Anil Kumble. With Pakistan set an unlikely 420 runs for victory, the leg-spinner became the first Indian, and only the second bowler in Test history, to take all ten wickets in an innings, finishing with 10 for 74 off 26.3 overs. The best match figures by an Indian bowler are 16 for 136, achieved by Narendra Hirwani against the West Indies at Chennai in January 1988.

A miser with the ball

Renowned for his tireless efforts in practice, where he would spend hours bowling at a coin placed on a good length, Bapu Nadkarni was the most miserly bowler in Test history. The left-arm spinner holds the Indian record for both the best economy rate in an innings (0.15 against England at Chennai in January 1964, when his spell of 32-27-5-0 included 22 consecutive maidens) and the best economy rate in a career (his 1,527.3 overs cost him just 1.67 runs per over).

Chandrasekhar too much for England

The star of India's 2–1 home series win over England in 1972–73 was, without doubt, Bhagwath Chandrasekhar. The leg-spinner bewitched England's batsmen throughout, taking four five-wicket hauls (with a best of 8 for 79 in the First Test at Delhi) and ended the series with 35 wickets to his name – an all-time record series haul by an Indian bowler.

All-time great: ANIL KUMBLE

A determined performer who has probably won more matches for India than other bowler in history, **Anil Kumble** owed his success more to a high action that was capable of achieving both metronomic accuracy and an awkward bounce than an inherent ability to turn the ball. After making his debut against England at Old Trafford in 1990, the leg-spinner went on to break virtually every single Indian bowling record. In a 132-Test, 18-year international career he set records for the most wickets (619), the most five-wicket hauls in an innings (35) and the most ten-wicket hauls in a match (8).

A master of his art

A left-arm spin bowler with a masterful control over flight, loop, spin and pace variation, **Bishan Bedi** was an outstanding performer for India from the moment he made his debut against the West Indies at Kolkata in December 1966. In a 67-Test career he took 266 wickets at 28.71 runs per wicket – the lowest average (with a minimum of 2,000 balls bowled) by an Indian in Test history.

WICKETKEEPER – MOST DISMISSALS: TOP 5

Pos	Dis	Player	Span	Mat	Inns	Ct	St	Dis/Inn
1	220	**M.S. Dhoni**	2005–12	67	123	192	28	1.788
2	198	S.M.H. Kirmani	1976–86	88	151	160	38	1.311
3	130	K.S. More	1986–93	49	90	110	20	1.444
4	107	N.R. Mongia	1994–2001	44	77	99	8	1.389
5	82	F.M. Engineer	1961–75	46	83	66	16	0.987

MOST DISMISSALS: INNINGS/MATCHES/SERIES

The Indian record for the most dismissals in an innings is six, a feat achieved on two occasions: by Syed Kirmani (5ct, 1st) against New Zealand at Christchurch in February 1976; and by M.S. Dhoni (6ct) against New Zealand at Wellington in April 2009. The Indian record for the most dismissals in a match is eight, a feat achieved on five occasions – twice by Nayan Mongia and three times by Dhoni.

FIELDING – MOST CATCHES: TOP 5

Pos	Ct	Player	Span	Mat	Inns	Max	Ct/Inn
1	209	**R. Dravid**	1996–2012	163	299	3	0.698
2	122	V.V.S. Laxman	1996–2011	134	248	4	0.544
3	113	S.R. Tendulkar	1989–2012	188	342	3	0.330
4	108	S.M. Gavaskar	1971–87	125	216	3	0.500
5	105	M. Azharuddin	1984–2000	99	177	5	0.593

MOST CATCHES: INNINGS/MATCHES/SERIES

The Indian record for the most catches in an innings is five, achieved on three occasions; the record for the most catches in a match is seven, by Yajurvindra Singh against England at Bangalore in January 1977; the record for the most catches in a series is 13, by **Rahul Dravid** against Australia in 2004–05.

LONGEST-SERVING CAPTAINS: TOP 10

Pos	Mat	Player	Span	W-L-T-D	%W
1	49	S.C. Ganguly	2000–05	21-13-0-15	42.85
2	47	M. Azharuddin	1990–99	14-14-0-19	29.78
=	47	S.M. Gavaskar	1976–85	9-8-0-30	19.14
4	40	Nawab of Pataudi	1962–75	9-19-0-12	22.50
5	37	M.S. Dhoni	2008–12	17-10-0-10	45.94
6	34	Kapil Dev	1983–87	4-7-1-22	11.76
7	25	R. Dravid	2003–07	8-6-0-11	32.00
=	25	S.R. Tendulkar	1996–2000	4-9-0-12	16.00
9	22	B.S. Bedi	1976–78	6-11-0-5	27.27
10	16	A.L. Wadekar	1971–74	4-4-0-8	25.00

Most dismissals in a series

The Indian record for the most dismissals by a wicketkeeper in a series is 19, held jointly by Naren Tamhane (12ct, 7st), against Pakistan in the 1954–55 series in Pakistan, and by Syed Kirmani (17ct, 2st) against Pakistan in 1979–80 in India.

India's most successful captain

Few players in modern times have split opinion as much as the forthright **Sourav Ganguly**, but statistics will tell you he was the best captain India have ever had. When he assumed the captaincy from Sachin Tendulkar in 2000, the Kolkata batsman proved a shrewd and tough leader, and his team thrived under his stewardship. In 49 Tests with Ganguly in charge, India won 21 of them with a winning percentage of 42.85 per cent, an all-time Indian record.

NEW ZEALAND

New Zealand were granted Test status in 1929–30, but it took them 26 years and 44 Tests to record their first victory and 40 years before they could celebrate a first series win. However, the emergence of world-class all-rounder Richard Hadlee in the 1970s inspired a new generation of players to the extent that, today, New Zealand are one of the most competitive sides on the international circuit.

RESULT SUMMARY

Opposition	Span	Mat	Won	Lost	Tied	Draw	W/L	%W	%L	%D
Australia	1946–2011	52	8	27	0	17	0.29	15.38	51.92	32.69
Bangladesh	2001–10	9	8	0	0	1	-	88.88	0.00	11.11
England	1930–2008	94	8	45	0	41	0.17	8.51	47.87	43.61
India	1955–2010	50	9	16	0	25	0.56	18.00	32.00	50.00
Pakistan	1955–2011	50	7	23	0	20	0.30	14.00	46.00	40.00
South Africa	1932–2007	38	4	21	0	13	0.19	10.52	55.26	34.21
Sri Lanka	1983–2009	26	9	7	0	10	1.28	34.61	26.92	38.46
West Indies	1952–2008	37	9	10	0	18	0.90	24.32	27.02	48.64
Zimbabwe	1992–2012	15	9	0	0	6	-	60.00	0.00	40.00

BATTING – MOST RUNS: TOP 10

Pos	Runs	Player	Span	Mat	Inns	NO	HS	Ave	100	50	0
1	7,172	S.P. Fleming	1994–2008	111	189	10	274*	40.06	9	46	16
2	5,444	M.D. Crowe	1982–95	77	131	11	299	45.36	17	18	9
3	5,334	J.G. Wright	1978–93	82	148	7	185	37.82	12	23	7
4	4,702	N.J. Astle	1996–2006	81	137	10	222	37.02	11	24	11
5	4,478	D.L. Vettori	1997–2012	110	169	22	140	30.46	6	23	19
6	3,763	B.B. McCullum	2004–12	64	110	7	225	36.53	6	22	9
7	3,448	B.E. Congdon	1965–78	61	114	7	176	32.22	7	19	9
8	3,428	J.R. Reid	1949–65	58	108	5	142	33.28	6	22	5
9	3,320	C.L. Cairns	1989–2004	62	104	5	158	33.53	5	22	7
10	3,124	R.J. Hadlee	1973–90	86	134	19	151*	27.16	2	15	12

Turner triumphs in the Caribbean

Five consecutive draws between the West Indies and New Zealand in the 1971–72 series played in the Caribbean may not have made for the most entertaining of cricket viewing, but for New Zealand's Glenn Turner the tour was a triumphant one. The right-handed opener's haul of 672 runs in the series, including a highest score of 259 in the Fourth Test at Georgetown, is a New Zealand record.

Largest victories

By an innings: by an innings and 301 runs against Zimbabwe in Napier in January 2012.

By runs: by 204 runs against the West Indies at Bridgetown in June 2002.

By wickets: by ten wickets on four occasions.

Smallest victories

By runs: by 7 runs against Australia at Hobart in December 2011.

By wickets: by one wicket against the West Indies at Dunedin in February 1980.

Heaviest defeats

By an innings: by an innings and 324 runs against Pakistan at Lahore in May 2002.

By runs: by 358 runs against South Africa in Johannesburg in November 2007.

By wickets: by ten wickets on 11 occasions.

Plumbing the depths

New Zealand, still chasing the first Test victory in their history, were still very much in the match after both sides had completed their first innings in the Second Test at Auckland in March 1955, trailing England by just 46 runs. But what followed was the most dramatic collapse in Test history. New Zealand folded to a pitiful 26 all out – the lowest total in Test history – to lose by an innings and 20 runs.

Rearguard action

Facing a 323-run first-innings deficit against Sri Lanka in the First Test at Wellington in January–February 1991, New Zealand needed a performance of epic proportions with the bat in their second innings merely to stay in the game. And they responded in style: led by Martin Crowe (299) and **Andrew Jones** (186), they compiled a mighty 671 for 4 declared – the highest total in New Zealand's history – to force a draw.

All-time great: MARTIN CROWE

Born into a cricketing family (his father Dave played first-class cricket and his elder brother Jeff played 39 Tests for New Zealand), **Martin Crowe** was the most complete batsman his country has ever produced. A right-hander who possessed every shot in the book, and a seemingly limitless amount of time in which to play them, he scored 5,444 runs (at an average of 45.36) in 77 Tests for his country – including 17 centuries and a highest score of 299 (both national records) – before injury brought a premature end to his career in 1995.

Reid tops New Zealand averages list

John F. Reid may not have been as famous as his namesake John R. Reid (who scored 3,428 runs in 58 Tests for New Zealand between 1949 and 1965 and stands seventh on his country's all-time run-scoring list), but the left-hander still put together an impressive Test career. In 19 matches for his country between 1979 and 1986, he scored 1,296 runs (with a highest score of 180, against Sri Lanka in Colombo in March 1984) at an average of 46.28 – the highest by any New Zealand player in Test history.

Most fifties

A sweet timer of the ball and equally strong through the offside or off his pads, **Stephen Fleming** will enter the history books as one of New Zealand's best-ever batsmen. His sole weakness was an inability to convert good starts into big scores. In a 111-Test career for his country between 1994 and 2008, Fleming, New Zealand's most-capped player and all-time leading run-scorer, passed 50 on 55 occasions (a national record), but only managed to convert nine of them into three-figure scores – a conversion rate of just 16.36 per cent.

A rabbit with the bat

In a 68-Test career since making his debut for New Zealand against South Africa in November 2000, **Chris Martin** has taken a commendable 226 wickets, but his hapless performances with the bat are almost as remarkable as his feats with the ball. In 98 innings for his country, Martin has scored just 119 runs (at an average of 2.3842, including a national record 33 ducks.

BOWLING – MOST WICKETS: TOP 10

Pos	Wkts	Player	Span	Mat	Balls	Runs	BBI	BBM	Ave	Econ	SR	5	10
1	431	R.J. Hadlee	1973–90	86	21,918	9,611	9/52	15/123	22.29	2.63	50.8	36	9
2	358	D.L. Vettori	1997–2012	110	28,193	12,154	7/87	12/149	33.94	2.58	78.7	20	3
3	226	C.S. Martin	2000–12	68	13,544	7,593	6/26	11/180	33.59	3.36	59.9	10	1
4	218	C.L. Cairns	1989–2004	62	11,698	6,410	7/27	10/100	29.40	3.28	53.6	13	1
5	160	D.K. Morrison	1987–97	48	10,064	5,549	7/89	8/83	34.68	3.30	62.9	10	0
6	130	B.L. Cairns	1974–85	43	10,628	4,280	7/74	10/144	32.92	2.41	81.7	6	1
7	123	E.J. Chatfield	1975–89	43	10,360	3,958	6/73	10/124	32.17	2.29	84.2	3	1
8	116	R.O. Collinge	1965–78	35	7,689	3,393	6/63	9/166	29.25	2.64	66.2	3	0
9	111	B.R. Taylor	1965–73	30	6,334	2,953	7/74	9/182	26.60	2.79	57.0	4	0
10	102	J.G. Bracewell	1980–90	41	8,403	3,653	6/32	10/106	35.81	2.60	82.3	4	1

A taste for wickets

Among the fastest bowlers on the circuit before his retirement in 2010, **Shane Bond**'s career has been blighted by a succession of injuries since he made his debut against Australia at Hobart in November 2001. When he was able to make it on to the pitch, however, he excelled. In 18 matches for the Blackcaps, Bond took 87 wickets at an average of 22.09 with a wicket every 38.7 balls – the best strike-rate by any New Zealand bowler in history.

Best economy rate: career/innings

Although Jeremy Coney's 52 Test matches brought him only a modest 27 wickets, no bowler (to have bowled more than 2,000 balls) in New Zealand's history can match his economy rate – a mere 2.04 runs per over. The best economy rate in an innings by a New Zealand bowler was achieved by Bev Congdon, whose 18 eight-ball overs against England at Christchurch in February 1978 went for just 14 runs (0.58 runs per over).

The first great Kiwi bowler

After Hadlee, the second best fast bowler New Zealand has ever produced, Jack Cowie played in all nine of New Zealand's Test matches between 1937 and 1949 (by which time he was 37 years old) and prospered, taking 45 wickets (with best figures of 6 for 40 against Australia at Wellington in March 1946) at an average of 21.53 – the best by a New Zealand bowler in history.

Pakistan's batsmen take a liking to Boock

As Pakistan, driven on by Javed Miandad's imperious 271, piled on the runs to reach 616 for 5 in the first innings against New Zealand in the Third Test at Auckland in February 1989, the Blackcaps' slow left-armer Stephen Boock found himself in the record books. His 70 overs in the innings, which brought him one wicket, cost an all-time New Zealand record 229 runs.

All-time great: RICHARD HADLEE

Certainly the finest fast bowler his country has ever produced and one of the greatest all-rounders of all time, **Richard Hadlee** almost single-handedly changed New Zealand's cricket fortunes. In short, when Hadlee was firing on all cylinders with the ball, New Zealand had every chance of winning the game. By the time he ended his 86-match, 17-year Test career, he had taken 431 wickets (at the time an all-time record) and he still holds the New Zealand records for the best bowling in an innings (9 for 52 against Australia at Brisbane in November 1985), the best bowling in a match (15 for 123 in the same match), the most wickets in a series (33 against Australia in the 1985–86 series), the most five-wicket hauls in an innings (36) and the most ten-wicket hauls in a match (9).

WICKETKEEPER – MOST DISMISSALS: TOP 5

Pos	Dis	Player	Span	Mat	Inns	Ct	St	Dis/Inn
1	201	**A.C. Parore**	1990–2002	78	121	194	7	1.661
2	176	I.D.S. Smith	1980–92	63	109	168	8	1.614
3	172	B.B. McCullum	2004–12	64	93	161	11	1.849
4	96	K.J. Wadsworth	1969–76	33	59	92	4	1.627
5	59	W.K. Lees	1976–83	21	42	52	7	1.404

MOST DISMISSALS: INNINGS/MATCHES/SERIES

The New Zealand record for the most dismissals in an innings is seven, achieved by Ian Smith (7ct) against Sri Lanka at Hamilton in February 1991. The New Zealand record for the most dismissals in a match is nine, set by Brendon McCullum (8ct, 1st) against Pakistan at Napier in December 2009. The record for the most dismissals in a series is 23, by Artie Dick (21ct, 2st) against South Africa in South Africa in 1961–62.

FIELDING – MOST CATCHES: TOP 5

Pos	Ct	Player	Span	Mat	Inns	Max	Ct/Inn
1	171	S.P. Fleming	1994–2008	111	199	5	0.859
2	71	M.D. Crowe	1982–95	77	130	4	0.546
3	70	N.J. Astle	1996–2006	81	147	2	0.476
4	64	J.V. Coney	1974–87	52	97	3	0.659
=	64	L.R.P.L. Taylor	2007–12	37	67	3	0.955

LONGEST-SERVING CAPTAINS: TOP 10

Pos	Mat	Player	Span	W-L-T-D	%W
1	80	S.P. Fleming	1997–2006	28-27-0-25	35.00
2	34	J.R. Reid	1956–65	3-18-0-13	8.82
3	32	**D.L. Vettori**	2007–11	6-16-0-10	18.75
4	30	G.P. Howarth	1980–85	11-7-0-12	36.66
5	19	G.T. Dowling	1968–72	4-7-0-8	21.05
6	18	K.R. Rutherford	1993–95	2-11-0-5	11.11
7	17	B.E. Congdon	1972–75	1-7-0-9	5.88
8	16	M.D. Crowe	1990–93	2-7-0-7	12.50
9	15	J.V. Coney	1984–87	5-4-0-6	33.33
10	14	J.G. Wright	1988–90	3-3-0-8	21.42

MOST CATCHES: INNINGS/ MATCHES/ SERIES

The New Zealand record for the most catches in an innings is five, achieved by **Stephen Fleming** against Zimbabwe at Harare in September 1999; he went on to take seven catches in the match (also a national record). Fleming also holds the record for the most catches in a series (10), a feat he achieved twice: against Zimbabwe in 1997–98 and against England in 1999.

Most successful captain

Stephen Fleming proved an inspirational choice as New Zealand captain when, aged just 23 years 321 days, he took over from Lee Germon in 1997. He went on to captain the Blackcaps on 80 occasions and recorded 28 wins – the most, by some distance, of any New Zealand captain in history.

PAKISTAN

Granted Test status in July 1952, following a recommendation from arch-rivals India, Pakistan are one of the most unpredictable Test teams: they can be world-beaters on one day and spectacularly ordinary on another. The country has produced some of Test cricket's all-time great players, such as Javed Miandad and Hanif Mohammad with the bat and Imran Khan and Wasim Akram with the ball.

RESULT SUMMARY

Opposition	Span	Mat	Won	Lost	Tied	Draw	W/L	%W	%L	%D
Australia	1956–2010	57	12	28	0	17	0.42	21.05	49.12	29.82
Bangladesh	2001–11	8	8	0	0	0	-	100.00	0.00	0.00
England	1954–2012	74	17	22	0	36	0.72	21.62	29.72	48.64
India	1952–2007	59	12	9	0	38	1.33	20.33	15.25	64.40
New Zealand	1955–2011	50	23	7	0	20	3.28	46.00	14.00	40.00
South Africa	1995–2010	18	3	8	0	7	0.37	16.66	44.44	38.88
Sri Lanka	1982–2011	40	16	9	0	15	1.77	40.00	22.50	35.13
West Indies	1958–2011	46	16	15	0	15	1.06	34.78	32.60	32.60
Zimbabwe	1993–2011	15	9	2	0	4	4.50	60.00	13.33	26.66

Surrender in Sharjah

Forced to play their home series against Australia in October 2002 at neutral venues as a result of security fears in their own country, Pakistan looked like a fish out of water. In the Second Test at Sharjah (following a 41-run defeat in the First Test at Colombo) they capitulated in spectacular fashion, crashing to 59 all out in their first innings and 53 all out in their second – the two lowest scores in the country's history.

Making hay against the old enemy

There was little doubt as to who was the star of the show during Pakistan's triumphant and comprehensive 3–0 home series victory over arch-rivals India in 1982–83. Mudassar Nazar hit four centuries and one 50 (with a highest score of 231 in the Fourth Test at Faisalabad) to end the six-match series with an all-time Pakistan record haul of 761 runs at an impressive average of 126.83.

A record-breaking response

Any hopes of victory Sri Lanka had after compiling 644 for 7 declared in their first innings of the First Test against Pakistan at Karachi in February 2009 soon turned to frustration. The home side, led by **Younis Khan** (313) and Kamran Akmal (158 not out), responded by posting 765 for 6 declared – the highest score in their history – as the match petered out into a draw.

Largest victories

By an innings: by an innings and 324 runs against New Zealand at Lahore in May 2002.

By runs: by 341 runs against India at Karachi in January 2006.

By wickets: by ten wickets on 11 occasions.

Smallest victories

By runs: by 12 runs against India at Chennai in January 1999.

By wickets: by one wicket on two occasions: against Australia at Karachi in September 1994; and against Bangladesh at Multan in September 2003.

Heaviest defeats

By an innings: by an innings and 225 runs against England at Lord's in August 2010.

By runs: by 491 runs against Australia at Perth in December 2004.

By wickets: by ten wickets on nine occasions.

BATTING – MOST RUNS: TOP 10

Pos	Runs	Player	Span	Mat	Inns	NO	HS	Ave	100	50	0
1	8,832	Javed Miandad	1976–93	124	189	21	280*	52.57	23	43	6
2	8,829	Inzamam-ul-Haq	1992–2007	119	198	22	329	50.16	25	46	14
3	7,530	Mohammad Yousuf	1998–2010	90	156	12	223	52.29	24	33	11
4	6,398	Younis Khan	2000–12	76	133	11	313	52.44	20	25	13
5	5,768	Saleem Malik	1982–99	103	154	22	237	43.69	15	29	12
6	5,062	Zaheer Abbas	1969–85	78	124	11	274	44.79	12	20	10
7	4,114	Mudassar Nazar	1976–89	76	116	8	231	38.09	10	17	7
8	4,052	Saeed Anwar	1990–2001	55	91	2	188*	45.52	11	25	8
9	3,931	Majid Khan	1964–83	63	106	5	167	38.92	8	19	9
10	3,915	Hanif Mohammad	1952–69	55	97	8	337	43.98	12	15	5

Kaneria's unfortunate record

In his ten-year Test career Danish Kaneria has had considerable success with the ball – he has taken 261 wickets in 61 Tests for his country since making his debut in 2000 – but he has enjoyed few high points with the bat: he has been dismissed without scoring on 25 occasions, an all-time record for a Pakistan player.

All-time great: JAVED MIANDAD

Far from conventional (he was one of the first to perfect the reverse sweep) and often at the centre of controversy, **Javed Miandad**'s greatest ability with the bat was his uncanny tendency to score runs at will under any conditions. He burst on to the international scene as a fresh-faced 19-year-old against New Zealand in 1976, scoring 504 runs in three Tests (including 203 in the Third Test to become the game's youngest-ever double centurion) and became a mainstay of Pakistan's batting line-up for the next 17 years. In 124 Tests he scored a Pakistan record 8,832 runs (including 23 centuries) at an average of 52.57 (also a national record).

Yasir hits the ground running

An exquisite timer of the ball whose game is built around a solid technique, Yasir Hameed's Test career got off to a blistering start when he scored 170 in his first-ever Test innings for Pakistan against Bangladesh at Karachi in August 2003 to break Khalid Ibadulla's 39-year national record for the highest score on debut. Not that the right-hander was finished there: he went on to score 105 in the second innings to become only the second player in history (joining the West Indies' Lawrence Rowe) to score two centuries in his debut Test.

Hanif digs Pakistan out of a hole

The first real star of Pakistan cricket, and the first player in Test history to be labelled "The Little Master", Hanif Mohammad showed star quality when his side really needed it in the First Test against the West Indies at Bridgetown in January 1958. With Pakistan forced to follow on in their second innings, still 473 runs in arrears, Hanif played the longest innings in Test history, taking 970 minutes to compile 337 – still the highest individual score by a Pakistan batsman – to help his side save the game.

Inzamam's record haul

Javed Miandad may have edged him out as his country's leading all-time run-scorer, but no Pakistan batsman in history has scored more hundreds or more 50s than **Inzamam-ul-Haq**. In 119 Tests for Pakistan between 1992 and 2007 the right-hander passed the half-century mark on 71 occasions and went on to reach three figures 25 times.

BOWLING – MOST WICKETS: TOP 10

Pos	Wkts	Player	Span	Mat	Balls	Runs	BBI	BBM	Ave	Econ	SR	5	10
1	414	Wasim Akram	1985–2002	104	22,627	9,779	7/119	11/110	23.62	2.59	54.6	25	5
2	373	Waqar Younis	1989–2003	87	16,224	8,788	7/76	13/135	23.56	3.25	43.4	22	5
3	362	Imran Khan	1971–92	88	19,458	8,258	8/58	14/116	22.81	2.54	53.7	23	6
4	261	Danish Kaneria	2000–10	61	17,697	9,082	7/77	12/94	34.79	3.07	67.8	15	2
5	236	Abdul Qadir	1977–90	67	17,126	7,742	9/56	13/101	32.80	2.71	72.5	15	5
6	208	Saqlain Mushtaq	1995–2004	49	14,070	6,206	8/164	10/155	29.83	2.64	67.6	13	3
7	185	Mushtaq Ahmed	1990–2003	52	12,532	6,100	7/56	10/106	32.97	2.92	67.7	10	3
8	178	Shoaib Akhtar	1997–2007	46	8,143	4,574	6/11	11/78	25.69	3.37	45.7	12	2
9	177	Sarfraz Nawaz	1969–84	55	13,951	5,798	9/86	11/125	32.75	2.49	78.8	4	1
10	171	Iqbal Qasim	1976–88	50	13,019	4,807	7/49	11/118	28.11	2.21	76.1	8	2

The prince of Pakistan

Wasim Akram may have been a fine all-rounder, but it was his performances with the ball that will leave an indelible mark in the history books. The most effective left-arm fast bowler Test cricket has ever produced, Wasim ended his 104-Test match career in 2003 as Pakistan's all-time leading wicket-taker (with 414 wickets), including a national record 25 five-wicket hauls (with a best of 7 for 119 against New Zealand at Wellington in March 1994).

The wicket machine

Waqar Younis was the finest exponent of reverse-swing bowling Test cricket has ever seen. In 87 matches for his country between 1989 and 2003, the fast bowler took 373 wickets at 23.56 with a strike-rate of a wicket every 43.4 balls – the best by a Pakistan bowler, the eighth best of all time and the best by any bowler to have bowled more than 10,000 deliveries in Test history.

On the wrong end of a Sobers pummelling

While the Third Test of the 1957–58 series between the West Indies and Pakistan, at Kingston, Jamaica, was one to remember for Garfield Sobers (the 21-year-old hit a then world record score of 365 not out), it was certainly one to forget for two of Pakistan's bowlers. Khan Mohammad's 54 wicketless overs went for 259 runs (an all-time national record) while his team-mate Fazal Mahmood went for 247 runs off 85.2 overs – the second highest number of runs conceded in an innings by a Pakistan bowler.

Keeping things tight

Pervez Sajjad holds the Pakistan record for the best economy rate in a career. In 19 matches for his country between 1964 and 1973, the slow left-armer took 59 wickets at an average of 23.89 and conceded just 2.04 runs per over. Majid Khan holds the record for the best economy rate in an innings. In the West Indies' second innings of the Fourth Test at Port of Spain in April 1977, the off-spinner bowled ten overs for just three runs (0.30 runs per over) with eight maidens.

All-time great: IMRAN KHAN

With his good looks and limitless ability, **Imran Khan** did much to confirm cricket's status as the number-one sport in Pakistan from the moment he made his debut against England in 1971. He was worth a place in the Pakistan side for his ability with the bat alone (he scored 3,807 runs at an average of 37.69), but it was his bowling that made him a truly world-class performer, his bounding, athletic run, high-leaping delivery stride and a huge variety of deliveries – all produced at express pace – striking fear into the hearts of batsmen around the world. In 88 Tests for his country, 48 of them as captain, he set numerous national records: the best bowling figures in a match (14 for 116 against Sri Lanka at Lahore in March 1982), the most ten-wicket match hauls (6), the most wickets in a series (40 against India in Pakistan in 1982–83) and the best career average (22.81).

WICKETKEEPER – MOST DISMISSALS: TOP 5

Pos	Dis	Player	Span	Mat	Inns	Ct	St	Dis/Inn
1	228	**Wasim Bari**	1967–84	81	146	201	27	1.561
2	206	Kamran Akmal	2002–10	53	99	184	22	2.080
3	147	Moin Khan	1990–2004	69	118	127	20	1.245
4	130	Rashid Latif	1992–2003	37	69	119	11	1.884
5	104	Saleem Yousuf	1982–90	32	58	91	13	1.793

MOST DISMISSALS: INNINGS/MATCHES/SERIES

The Pakistan record for the most dismissals in an innings is seven, by **Wasim Bari** (7ct) against New Zealand at Auckland in February 1979. The record for the most dismissals in a match is nine, by Rashid Latif (9ct) against New Zealand at Auckland in February 1994 and by Kamran Akmal (9ct) against the West Indies at Kingston in June 2005. The record for the most dismissals in a series is 18 (17ct, 1st), by Rashid Latif against Bangladesh in 2003.

FIELDING – MOST CATCHES: TOP 5

Pos	Ct	Player	Span	Mat	Inns	Max	Ct/Inn
1	93	**Javed Miandad**	1976–93	124	218	3	0.426
2	86	Younis Khan	2000–12	76	141	3	0.609
3	81	Inzamam-ul-Haq	1992–2007	119	217	4	0.373
4	66	Majid Khan	1964–83	63	116	3	0.568
5	65	Saleem Malik	1982–99	103	184	3	0.353
=	65	Mohammad Yousuf	1998–2010	90	168	3	0.386

MOST CATCHES: INNINGS/MATCHES/SERIES

The Pakistan record for the most catches in an innings is four, a feat achieved on seven occasions. The national record for the most catches in a match is six, set by Taufeeq Umar against South Africa in Faisalabad in October 2003. Umar went on to take nine catches in the series, a record matched by Younis Khan (against South Africa in 2006–07) and Wallis Mathias (against the West Indies in 1957–58).

LONGEST-SERVING CAPTAINS: TOP 10

Pos	Mat	Player	Span	W-L-T-D	%W
1	48	**Imran Khan**	1982–92	14-8-0-26	29.16
2	34	Javed Miandad	1980–93	14-6-0-14	41.17
3	31	Inzamam-ul-Haq	2001–07	11-11-0-9	35.48
4	25	Wasim Akram	1993–99	12-8-0-5	48.00
5	23	A.H. Kardar	1952–58	6-6-0-11	26.08
6	19	Mushtaq Mohammad	1976–79	8-4-0-7	42.10
7	17	Intikhab Alam	1969–75	1-5-0-11	5.88
=	17	Waqar Younis	1993–2003	10-7-0-0	58.82
9	15	Misbah-ul-Haq	2010–12	9-1-0-5	60.00
10	14	Zaheer Abbas	1983–84	3-1-0-10	21.42

Most successful captains

Two Pakistan captains have achieved 14 career wins: **Javed Miandad** (14 wins in 34 Tests as captain with a win percentage of 41.17) and **Imran Khan** (14 wins in 48 matches with a win percentage of 29.16).

SOUTH AFRICA

A 21-year ban from Test cricket between 1970 and 1991 as a result of the South African government's oppressive apartheid policy may have stopped several potentially glittering international careers in their tracks, but since the country's return to the international fold, they have quickly resumed their position as one of the game's most competitive nations.

RESULT SUMMARY

Opposition	Span	Mat	Won	Lost	Tied	Draw	W/L	%W	%L	%D
Australia	1902–2011	85	19	48	0	18	0.39	22.35	56.47	21.17
Bangladesh	2002–08	8	8	0	0	0	-	100.00	0.00	0.00
England	1889–2010	138	29	56	0	53	0.51	21.01	40.47	38.40
India	1992–2011	27	12	7	0	8	1.71	44.44	25.92	29.62
New Zealand	1932–2007	38	21	4	0	13	5.25	55.26	10.52	34.21
Pakistan	1995–2010	18	8	3	0	7	2.66	44.44	16.66	38.88
Sri Lanka	1993–2012	20	10	5	0	5	2.00	50.00	25.00	25.00
West Indies	1992–2010	25	16	3	0	6	5.33	64.00	12.00	24.00
Zimbabwe	1995–2005	7	6	0	0	1	-	85.71	0.00	14.28

Largest victories

By an innings: by an innings and 229 runs against Sri Lanka at Cape Town in January 2001.

By runs: by 358 runs against New Zealand at Johannesburg in November 2007.

By wickets: by ten wickets on seven occasions.

Smallest victories

By runs: by five runs against Australia at Sydney in January 1994.

By wickets: by one wicket against England at Johannesburg in January 1906.

Heaviest defeats

By an innings: by an innings and 360 runs against Australia at Johannesburg in February 2002.

By runs: by 530 runs against Australia at Melbourne in February 1911.

By wickets: by ten wickets on 12 occasions.

Hitting an all-time low

South Africa have crashed to a sorry 30 all out on two occasions: in the First Test against England at Port Elizabeth in February 1896; and against the same opposition in the First Test at Birmingham in June 1924 (an innings in which extras was the highest scorer with 11).

Lording it at the home of cricket

South Africa dominated England in crushing fashion in the Second Test at Lord's in July–August 2003. After dismissing the hosts for 173 in their first innings, the Proteas, led by captain **Graeme Smith** (259) and Gary Kirsten (108), amassed a mighty 682 for 6 declared – the highest score by a South Africa side in history – en route to an innings-and-92-run victory.

BATTING – MOST RUNS: TOP 10

Pos	Runs	Player	Span	Mat	Inns	NO	HS	Ave	100	50	0
1	12,296	J.H. Kallis	1995–2012	151	255	38	224	56.66	42	55	14
2	8,030	G.C. Smith	2002–12	98	172	12	277	50.18	24	32	9
3	7,289	G. Kirsten	1993–2004	101	176	15	275	45.27	21	34	13
4	6,167	H.H. Gibbs	1996–2008	90	154	7	228	41.95	14	26	11
5	5,498	M.V. Boucher	1997–2012	146	204	24	125	30.54	5	35	16
6	5,457	A.B. de Villiers	2004–12	74	125	14	278*	49.16	13	29	3
7	4,554	D.J. Cullinan	1993–2001	70	115	12	275*	44.21	14	20	10
8	4,464	H.M. Amla	2004–12	59	103	8	253*	46.98	14	23	6
9	3,781	S.M. Pollock	1995–2008	108	156	39	111	32.31	2	16	9
10	3,714	W.J. Cronje	1992–2000	68	111	9	135	36.41	6	23	11

All-time great: JACQUES KALLIS

The history books will record that **Jacques Kallis** is one of the greatest batting all-rounders of all time. While his right-arm fast-medium bowling has brought him 276 wickets in a 152-match career, it is his performances with the bat that make him a truly outstanding performer. Not necessarily the most flamboyant of players, he shows a determined, limpet-like resolve at the batting crease that has brought him a national record 12,296 runs (only three players in history have scored more), 42 centuries and 55 half-centuries.

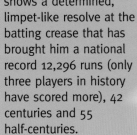

Pollock cut short in his prime

One of a number of exceptional players whose international career was cut short by South Africa's expulsion from international cricket, **Graeme Pollock** was, with the exception of Garfield Sobers, arguably the best left-handed batsman Test cricket has ever seen. In 23 matches for his country between 1963 and 1970, he scored 2,256 runs (with a highest score of 274 against Australia at Durban in February 1970) at an average of 60.97, the highest by any South African player in history to have completed 20 innings.

De Villiers hits new heights

With the two-match series locked at 0–0 after the drawn First Test, South Africa won the toss and elected to bat in the Second Test against Pakistan in Abu Dhabi in November 2010 and immediately ran into trouble, slipping to a worrying 33 for 3. And then A.B. de Villiers strode to the crease: he added 179 for the fourth wicket with Jacques Kallis (105) and by the time South Africa had reached an imposing 584 for 9 declared remained unbeaten on 278 – the highest individual score by a South Africa player in Test cricket. His efforts did not lead his side to victory, however. Pakistan replied with 434 and the match petered out into a draw.

Faulkner flourishes as South Africa fold

Few players in Test cricket have emerged with as much credit following a crushing series defeat as Aubrey Faulkner. As South Africa, struggling on fast, bouncy wickets, crashed to a 4–1 series defeat against Australia in 1910–11, only Faulkner stood tall, hitting 732 runs in the five Tests (a staggering 26.3 per cent of his team's total runs), with a highest score of 204 in the Second Test at Melbourne. His series haul remains a South African record to this day.

Makhaya's misfortune with the bat

The first black African cricketer to play for South Africa when he made his Test debut against Sri Lanka at Cape Town in March 1998, Makhaya Ntini has enjoyed considerable success with the ball in his 101-match career, taking 390 wickets. His performances with the bat have been less impressive, however. His tally of 21 ducks is an all-time South African record.

BOWLING – MOST WICKETS: TOP 10

Pos	Wkts	Player	Span	Mat	Balls	Runs	BBI	BBM	Ave	Econ	SR	5	10
1	421	S.M. Pollock	1995–2008	108	24,353	9,733	7/87	10/147	23.11	2.39	57.8	16	1
2	390	M. Ntini	1998–2010	101	20,834	11,242	7/37	13/132	28.82	3.23	53.4	18	4
3	330	A.A. Donald	1992–2002	72	15,519	7,344	8/71	12/139	22.25	2.83	47.0	20	3
4	276	J.H. Kallis	1995–2012	152	18,894	8,919	6/54	9/92	32.43	2.83	68.7	5	0
5	272	D.W. Steyn	2004–12	54	11,135	6,307	7/51	10/91	23.18	3.39	40.9	17	4
6	170	H.J. Tayfield	1949–60	37	13,568	4,405	9/113	13/165	25.91	1.94	79.8	14	2
7	139	M. Morkel	2006–12	39	7,560	4,174	6/23	7/98	30.02	3.31	54.3	5	0
8	134	P.R. Adams	1995–2004	45	8,850	4,405	7/128	10/106	32.87	2.98	66.0	4	1
9	123	T.L. Goddard	1955–70	41	11,736	3,226	6/53	8/92	26.22	1.64	95.4	5	0
=	123	A. Nel	2001–08	36	7,630	3,919	6/32	10/88	31.86	3.08	62.0	3	1

Super Steyn's greed for wickets

Fast-tracked into the South African side to face England in 2004 little more than a year after making his first-class debut, **Dale Steyn**'s lack of experience was exposed in his early forays in Test cricket, but, once he had found his feet, he demonstrated just how effective he could be. He is genuinely fast, with aggression to match; his 54 matches to date have brought him 272 wickets, and his strike-rate of a wicket every 40.9 deliveries is the best by any South Africa bowler in history.

All-time great: SHAUN POLLOCK

Born into a South African cricketing dynasty – his father Peter and uncle Graeme both starred for the country in the 1960s – **Shaun Pollock** made his Test debut against England in 1996, went on to form an effective new-ball partnership with Allan Donald and soon established himself as an international cricketer of the highest class. His meticulous line-and-length bowling saw him become the first, and to date only, South African bowler to pass the 400-wicket milestone, and he ended his 108-Test match career (26 of them as captain) with 421 scalps to his name.

Makhaya marches into the record books

With an action based on that of Malcolm Marshall, Makhaya Ntini has enjoyed considerable success for South Africa. One of only three of his countrymen to have taken more than 300 Test scalps, the right-arm fast bowler holds the national record for the best figures in a match (13 for 132 against the West Indies at Port of Spain in April 2005) and shares the record for the most ten-wicket match hauls (four) with Dale Steyn.

Adcock's record average

Picked for South Africa to play against New Zealand in December 1953 with only eight first-class matches under his belt, Neil Adcock rewarded the selectors' faith in him in spectacular style. Exploiting his height to create an awkward, sharp-lifting bounce, the fast bowler went on to become the first South Africa bowler in history to take 100 Test wickets, ending his nine-year, 26-match career with 104 wickets at an average of 21.10 – the lowest by any South African bowler to have bowled 2,000 balls or more in Test cricket.

White Lightning strikes

The first genuinely world-class South Africa player since the country's readmission to the international fold in 1992, Allan Donald's searing pace was enough to send shivers down the spines of opposing batsmen. In 72 Tests for his country before his retirement in 2002, the man known as "White Lightning" became the first South Africa bowler in history to claim 300 Test wickets (he finished with 330), and he still holds the national record for the most five-wicket hauls (with 20).

Goddard turns the screw

Renowned more in a 41-Test career between 1955 and 1970 as a solid left-handed opening batsman, Trevor Goddard was as miserly as he was effective with the ball. His left-arm medium pace brought him 123 wickets at an average of 26.22, with his overs costing just 1.64 runs – the best economy rate by any South African to have bowled 2,000 balls or more in Test cricket.

WICKETKEEPER – MOST DISMISSALS: TOP 5

Pos	Dis	Player	Span	Mat	Inns	Ct	St	Dis/Inn
1	553	**M.V. Boucher**	1997–2012	146	279	530	23	1.982
2	152	D.J. Richardson	1992–98	42	77	150	2	1.974
3	141	J.H.B. Waite	1951–65	50	92	124	17	1.532
4	56	D.T. Lindsay	1963–70	19	28	54	2	2.000
5	51	H.B. Cameron	1927–35	26	45	39	12	1.133

MOST DISMISSALS: INNINGS/MATCHES/SERIES

The South Africa record for the most dismissals in an innings is six, a feat achieved by Denis Lindsay (6ct) against Australia at Johannesburg in December 1966 and by **Mark Boucher** on three occasions. The record for the most dismissals in a match is nine, by Dave Richardson (9ct) against India at Port Elizabeth in December 1992 and by Mark Boucher on three occasions. The most dismissals in a series is 26, set by John Waite (23ct, 3st) against New Zealand in 1960–61 and by Mark Boucher (25ct, 1st) against England in 1998.

FIELDING – MOST CATCHES: TOP 5

Pos	Ct	Player	Span	Mat	Inns	Max	Ct/Inn
1	177	**J.H. Kallis**	1995–2012	152	286	4	0.618
2	128	G.C. Smith	2002–12	98	188	3	0.680
3	94	H.H. Gibbs	1996–2008	90	173	4	0.543
4	89	AB de Villiers	2004–12	74	135	3	0.659
5	83	G. Kirsten	1993–2004	101	191	4	0.434

MOST CATCHES: INNINGS/MATCHES/SERIES

The South African record for the most catches in an innings is four, a feat achieved on nine occasions. The record for the most catches in a match is six, by Bert Vogler against England at Durban in January 1910, Bruce Mitchell against Australia at Melbourne in December 1931 and by Jacques Kallis against Sri Lanka at Cape Town in January 2012. Vogler and Mitchell went on to take 12 catches in the series, a national record equalled by Trevor Goddard against England in 1956–57.

LONGEST-SERVING CAPTAINS: TOP 10

Pos	Mat	Player	Span	W-L-T-D	%W
1	90	**G.C. Smith**	2003–12	42-25-0-23	46.66
2	53	W.J. Cronje	1994–2000	27-11-0-15	50.94
3	26	S.M. Pollock	2000–03	14-5-0-7	53.84
4	18	H.W. Taylor	1913–24	1-10-0-7	5.55
5	16	K.C. Wessels	1992–94	5-3-0-8	31.25
6	15	J.E. Cheetham	1952–55	7-5-0-3	46.66
=	15	A.D. Nourse	1948–51	1-9-0-5	6.66
8	14	D.J. McGlew	1955–62	4-6-0-4	28.57
9	13	T.L. Goddard	1963–65	1-2-0-10	7.69
=	13	P.W. Sherwell	1906–11	5-6-0-2	38.46

Smith silences the critics

He may have been a surprise choice as South African captain following the Proteas' dismal showing at the 2003 ICC World Cup, but **Graeme Smith**, just 23 years old at the time of his appointment, has gone on to become the most successful captain in South Africa's history, winning 42 of his 90 Tests in charge between 2003 and 2012.

SRI LANKA

Sri Lanka were granted Test status in 1981 to become the eighth Test-playing nation and, such were the strides they made, by the mid-1990s, they were considered a major force in international cricket. Their success has been founded on the emergence of a host of world-class batsmen and, in Muttiah Muralitharan, the most prolific bowler Test cricket has ever seen.

RESULT SUMMARY

Opposition	Span	Mat	Won	Lost	Tied	Draw	W/L	%W	%L	%D
Australia	1983–2011	23	1	14	0	8	0.07	4.34	60.86	34.78
Bangladesh	2001–09	12	12	0	0	0	-	100.00	0.00	0.00
England	1982–2012	26	7	10	0	9	0.70	26.92	38.46	34.61
India	1982–2010	35	6	14	0	15	0.42	17.14	40.00	42.85
New Zealand	1983–2009	26	7	9	0	10	0.77	26.92	34.61	38.46
Pakistan	1982–2009	40	9	16	0	15	0.56	22.50	40.00	37.50
South Africa	1993–2012	20	5	10	0	5	0.50	25.00	50.00	25.00
West Indies	1993–2010	15	6	3	0	6	2.00	40.00	20.00	40.00
Zimbabwe	1994–2004	15	10	0	0	5	-	66.66	0.00	33.33

Capitulation in Kandy

Trailing 1–0 in the series going into the Third and final Test against Pakistan at Kandy in August 1994, Sri Lanka got off to the worst possible start. After losing the toss and being put in to bat, they wilted in the face of some excellent fast bowling from Wasim Akram (4 for 32) and Waqar Younis (6 for 34) and crashed to 71 all out in just 28.2 overs – the lowest total in their history. Pakistan went on to win the match by an innings and 52 runs.

Batting for fun

With India having amassed an impressive 537 for 8 declared in the first innings of the First Test in Colombo in August 1997, it was time for Sri Lanka to produce a batting masterclass of their own if they wanted to stay in the match. They did just that. Bolstered by centuries from **Sanath Jayasuriya** (340), Roshan Mahanama (225) and Aravinda de Silva (126), they reached 952 for 6 declared – the highest total in Test history.

Jayasuriya prospers against India

An explosive performer in all formats of the game, **Sanath Jayasuriya** reserved his best performances in the Test arena for the two-match series against India in August 1997. In three innings he scored 340 (at the time a new national record), 32 and 199. His series haul of 571 runs (at an unbelievable average of 190.33) is an all-time Sri Lankan record.

Murali's struggles with the bat

While Muttiah Muralitharan holds virtually every Sri Lankan bowling record in the book, his performances with the bat have been less eyebrow-raising: in 132 Tests for his country between 1992 and 2010 he has scored 1,259 runs at an average of 11.87 including a national record 32 ducks.

BATTING – MOST RUNS: TOP 10

Pos	Runs	Player	Span	Mat	Inns	NO	HS	Ave	100	50	0
1	10,440	D.P.M.D. Jayawardene	1997–2012	130	217	13	374	51.17	31	41	11
2	9,382	K.C. Sangakkara	2000–12	108	183	12	287	54.86	28	38	7
3	6,973	S.T. Jayasuriya	1991–2007	110	188	14	340	40.07	14	31	15
4	6,361	P.A. de Silva	1984–2002	93	159	11	267	42.97	20	22	7
5	5,502	M.S. Atapattu	1990–2007	90	156	15	249	39.02	16	17	22
6	5,179	T.T. Samaraweera	2001–12	73	118	20	231	52.84	14	28	9
7	5,105	A. Ranatunga	1982–2000	93	155	12	135*	35.69	4	38	12
8	4,722	T.M. Dilshan	1999–2012	79	129	11	193	40.01	12	20	12
9	4,545	H.P. Tillakaratne	1989–2004	83	131	25	204*	42.87	11	20	9
10	3,089	W.P.U.J.C. Vaas	1994–2009	111	162	35	100*	24.32	1	13	12

Largest victories

By an innings: by an innings and 254 runs against Zimbabwe at Bulawayo in May 2004.

By runs: by 465 runs against Bangladesh at Chittagong in January 2009.

By wickets: by ten wickets on seven occasions.

Smallest victories

By runs: by 42 runs against Pakistan at Faisalabad in September 1995.

By wickets: by one wicket against South Africa at Colombo in August 2006.

Heaviest defeats

By an innings: by an innings and 229 runs against South Africa at Cape Town in January 2001.

By runs: by 301 runs against Pakistan at Colombo in August 1994.

By wickets: by ten wickets on four occasions.

Super Sangakkara

Hauled into the Test side in 2000 at the age of 22 despite modest performances in first-class cricket, **Kumar Sangakkara** has more than repaid the faith the Sri Lankan selectors showed in him. In 108 Tests for his country, the classy left-hander has scored 9,382 runs (with a highest score of 287 against South Africa at Colombo in July 2006) at an average of 54.86 – the highest by any Sri Lankan batsman in history.

All-time great: MAHELA JAYAWARDENE

From the moment **Mahela Jayawardene** stepped into the Test arena, with his side on 790 for 4 against India at Colombo in August 1997, he knew the benchmark to which he must aspire. And he has not disappointed. A well-organized right-hand batsman with limitless concentration and application, Jayawardene has consistently delivered the goods and holds the Sri Lankan record for the most runs scored (10,440), the highest individual score (a stunning knock of 374 against South Africa at Colombo in July 2006, as part of an all-time record partnership of 624 with Kumar Sangakkara), the most centuries (31) and the most scores of 50 or over (72).

BOWLING – MOST WICKETS: TOP 10

Pos	Wkts	Player	Span	Mat	Balls	Runs	BBI	BBM	Ave	Econ	SR	5	10
1	795	M. Muralitharan	1992–2010	132	43,715	18,023	9/51	16/220	22.67	2.47	54.9	67	22
2	355	W.P.U.J.C. Vaas	1994–2009	111	22,438	10,501	7/71	14/191	29.58	2.68	66.0	12	2
3	139	H.M.R.K.B. Herath	1999–2012	37	9,452	4,461	7/157	12/171	32.09	2.83	68.0	10	1
4	101	S.L. Malinga	2004–10	30	5,209	3,349	5/50	9/210	33.15	3.85	51.5	3	0
5	98	S.T. Jayasuriya	1991–2007	110	8,188	3,366	5/34	9/74	34.34	2.46	83.5	2	0
6	97	C.R.D. Fernando	2000–11	39	5,971	3,662	5/42	7/95	33.35	3.67	61.5	3	0
7	85	G.P. Wickramasinghe	1991–2001	40	7,260	3,559	6/60	6/80	41.87	2.94	85.4	3	0
8	73	R.J. Ratnayake	1983–92	23	4,961	2,563	6/66	9/125	35.10	3.09	67.9	5	0
9	69	H.D.P.K. Dharmasena	1993–2004	31	6,939	2,920	6/72	8/183	42.31	2.52	100.5	3	0
10	64	D.N.T. Zoysa	1997–2004	30	4,422	2,157	5/20	8/73	33.70	2.92	69.0	1	0

Mr Economy

Don Anurasiri found it difficult to cement a permanent place in the Sri Lanka side after making his Test debut at the age of 20 against Pakistan in Colombo in March 1986 (he played just 18 times for his country over a 12-year period), but when the slow left-armer did play, he was the epitome of both accuracy and economy. He holds the Sri Lanka record for both best career economy rate (2.33) and for the best economy rate in an innings – 0.60 (15-11-9-0) in the Third Test against Pakistan at Colombo in March 1986.

Part-time success

Tillakaratne Dilshan is renowned chiefly for his prowess with the bat (he has scored 4,722 runs in 79 Tests at an average of 40.01), but his part-time off-spin has earned him a place in the record books. The figures for his spell of bowling in the Second Test against Bangladesh at Chittagong in January 2009 – 4.2-1-10-4 – represent the best strike-rate by a Sri Lanka bowler in Test history (a wicket every 6.5 deliveries).

Slinga Malinga

The fastest bowler Sri Lanka has ever produced, **Lasith Malinga** was a batsman's worst nightmare. Generating genuine pace with an old or new ball, his low-slung, round-arm action made him almost impossible to pick up, and when he was fit – injuries kept him out of Test cricket between December 2007 and July 2010 before he retired from Test cricket in April 2011 – he was deadly: he took 101 wickets in 30 Tests at a strike-rate of a wicket every 51.5 deliveries, an all-time Sri Lankan record.

All-time great: MUTTIAH MURALITHARAN

Predictably enough, **Muttiah Muralitharan**, Test cricket's all-time leading wicket-taker with 800 wickets (which includes the five wickets he took for the ICC), holds virtually every single Sri Lankan bowling record. He leads the way for the best bowling figures in an innings (9 for 51 against Zimbabwe at Kandy in January 2002), the best bowling figures in a match (16 for 220 against England at The Oval in August 1998), the best average of any Sri Lanka bowler to have bowled 2,000 or more balls in Test cricket (22.67), the most five-wicket hauls in an innings (67), the most ten-wicket hauls in a match (22) and the most runs conceded in an innings (224 against Australia in Perth in December 1995).

The other hat-trick man

The only Sri Lanka bowler in Test history to take a hat-trick is Nuwan Zoysa. The left-arm fast-medium bowler dismissed Trevor Gripper (lbw), Murray Goodwin (caught behind) and Neil Johnson (lbw) in the first innings of the Second Test against Zimbabwe in Harare in November 1999 to create his own slice of Sri Lankan cricket history.

WICKETKEEPER – MOST DISMISSALS: TOP 5

Pos	Dis	Player	Span	Mat	Inns	Ct	St	Dis/Inn
1	151	**K.C. Sangakkara**	2000–12	108	90	131	20	1.677
2	119	R.S. Kaluwitharana	1992–2004	49	85	93	26	1.400
3	111	H.A.P.W. Jayawardene	2000–12	45	77	84	27	1.441
4	35	H.P. Tillakaratne	1989–2004	83	18	33	2	1.944
5	34	S.A.R. Silva	1983–88	9	15	33	1	2.266

MOST DISMISSALS: INNINGS/MATCHES/SERIES

The Sri Lanka record for the most dismissals in an innings is six, by Amal Silva (6ct) against India at the Sinhalese Sports Club Ground in Colombo in August 1985; he went on to achieve nine dismissals in the match and repeated the feat in the following Test (8ct, 1s) at the P. Sara Oval ground in Colombo to end the series with a record 22 dismissals to his name.

FIELDING – MOST CATCHES: TOP 5

Pos	Ct	Player	Span	Mat	Inns	Max	Ct/Inn
1	184	D.P.M.D. Jayawardene	1997–2012	130	233	4	0.789
2	89	H.P. Tillakaratne	1989–2004	83	123	4	0.723
3	78	S.T. Jayasuriya	1991–2007	110	196	3	0.397
4	73	T.M. Dilshan	1999–2012	79	18	4	0.528
5	70	M. Muralitharan	1992–2009	131	229	2	0.305

MOST CATCHES: INNINGS/MATCHES/SERIES

The Sri Lanka record for the most catches in an innings is four, a feat achieved on ten occasions. The record for the most catches in a match is seven, by Hashan Tillakaratne against New Zealand in Colombo in December 1992. Mahela Jayawardene holds the Sri Lanka record for the most catches in a series, with ten against Bangladesh in 2007.

LONGEST-SERVING CAPTAINS: TOP 10

Pos	Mat	Player	Span	W-L-T-D	%W
1	56	**A. Ranatunga**	1989–99	12-19-0-25	21.42
2	38	S.T. Jayasuriya	1999–2002	18-12-0-8	47.36
3	30	D.P.M.D. Jayawardene	2006–12	16-8-0-6	53.33
4	19	L.R.D. Mendis	1982–87	2-8-0-9	10.52
5	18	M.S. Atapattu	2002–05	8-6-0-4	44.44
6	15	K.C. Sangakkara	2009–11	5-3-0-7	33.33
7	11	H.P. Tillakaratne	1999–2004	1-4-0-6	9.09
=	11	T.M. Dilshan	2011–12	1-5-0-5	9.09
9	6	P.A. de Silva	1991–99	0-4-0-2	0.00
10	4	B. Warnapura	1982	0-3-0-1	0.00

Most successful captain

Certainly the most barnstorming batsman Sri Lanka has ever produced, **Sanath Jayasuriya** is also the most successful Sri Lankan captain in history. In 38 Tests in charge of his country between 1999 and 2002 he led his side to 18 wins with a win percentage of 47.36 per cent.

WEST INDIES

Granted Test status in 1928 to become the fourth Test-playing nation, the West Indies enjoyed only sporadic success until the late 1970s and early '80s, when a mix of dashing stroke players and fearsome fast bowlers took them to the top of the world game. In recent years, however, the men from the Caribbean have struggled to recapture the glorious successes of those golden years.

RESULT SUMMARY

Opposition	Span	Mat	Won	Lost	Tied	Draw	W/L	%W	%L	%D
Australia	1930–2009	111	32	54	1	24	0.60	28.82	47.74	21.62
Bangladesh	2002–11	8	4	2	0	2	2.00	50.00	25.00	25.00
England	1928–2009	145	53	43	0	49	1.23	36.55	29.65	33.79
India	1948–2011	88	30	14	0	44	2.14	34.09	15.90	50.00
New Zealand	1952–2008	37	10	9	0	18	1.11	27.02	24.32	48.64
Pakistan	1958–2011	46	15	16	0	15	0.93	32.60	34.78	32.60
South Africa	1992–2010	25	3	16	0	6	0.18	12.00	64.00	24.00
Sri Lanka	1993–2010	15	3	6	0	6	0.50	20.00	40.00	40.00
Zimbabwe	2000–03	6	4	0	0	2	-	66.66	0.00	33.3

Harmison blows the Windies away

It was a collapse of spectacular proportions. Trailing England by just 28 runs after the first innings in the First Test at Kingston, Jamaica, in March 2004, the West Indies capitulated to 47 all out in 25.3 overs, with Steve Harmison doing most of the damage for England, taking 7 for 12. It remains the lowest total in the islanders' history.

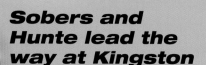

Sobers and Hunte lead the way at Kingston

Garfield Sobers's then world record score of 365 not out in the Third Test against Pakistan at Kingston, Jamaica, in February–March 1958, coupled with Conrad Hunte's innings of 260 (the pair added 446 for the second wicket), provided the platform for the West Indies' highest-ever total – 790 for 3 declared. It is one of four 700-plus scores by the islanders.

Largest victories

By an innings: by an innings and 336 runs against India at Kolkata in December 1958.

By runs: by 425 runs against England at Manchester in July 1976.

By wickets: by ten wickets on 22 occasions.

Smallest victories

By runs: by one run against Australia at Adelaide in January 1993.

By wickets: by one wicket on two occasions – against Australia at Bridgetown in March 1999 and against Pakistan at St John's in May 2000.

Heaviest defeats

By an innings: by an innings and 283 runs against England at Leeds in May 2007.

By runs: by 382 runs against Australia at Sydney in February 1969.

By wickets: by ten wickets on 15 occasions.

Walsh's woes with the bat

You never knew quite what to expect when Courtney Walsh marched to the wicket with a bat in his hands, but the odds were that it would be as brief as it would be entertaining. In 132 Test matches between 1984 and 2001, Test cricket's one-time leading wicket-taker racked up an all-time record 43 ducks.

BATTING – MOST RUNS: TOP 10

Pos	Runs	Player	Span	Mat	Inns	NO	HS	Ave	100	50	0
1	11,912	B.C. Lara	1990–2006	130	230	6	400*	53.17	34	48	17
2	10,055	S. Chanderpaul	1994–2012	140	239	38	203*	50.02	25	59	13
3	8,540	I.V.A. Richards	1974–91	121	182	12	291	50.23	24	45	10
4	8,032	G.S. Sobers	1954–74	93	160	21	365*	57.78	26	30	12
5	7,558	C.G. Greenidge	1974–91	108	185	16	226	44.72	19	34	11
6	7,515	C.H. Lloyd	1966–85	110	175	14	242*	46.67	19	39	4
7	7,487	D.L. Haynes	1978–94	116	202	25	184	42.29	18	39	10
8	6,373	C.H. Gayle	2000–10	91	159	6	333	41.65	13	33	15
9	6,227	R.B. Kanhai	1957–74	79	137	6	256	47.53	15	28	7
10	5,949	R.B. Richardson	1983–95	86	146	12	194	44.39	16	27	8

All-time great: BRIAN LARA

No player since Don Bradman has had such an appetite for building big scores and few players have broken as many records during their career as **Brian Lara**. Twice the left-hander broke the record for the all-time highest score in Test cricket, first with a brilliant knock of 375 against England at St John's, Antigua, in April 1994 and then with a blistering 400 not out against the same opponents at the same venue almost exactly a decade later. He finished his 131-Test, 16-year career in 2006 as the leading run-scorer of all time (his tally of 11,912 runs has since been broken by Sachin Tendulkar) and as the holder of several West Indian records: the most hundreds (34) and the most scores of 50 plus (82).

The "Black Bradman"

The first of the great black batsmen to emerge from the islands at a time when the West Indies team comprised mostly white players, **George Headley** performed such feats with the bat that he was dubbed the "Black Bradman". In 22 Tests for the islanders between 1930 and 1954 he scored 2,190 runs, including 10 centuries (with a highest score of 270 not out against England at Kingston, Jamaica, in March 1935), at an average of 60.83 – the highest by any West Indian batsman in history.

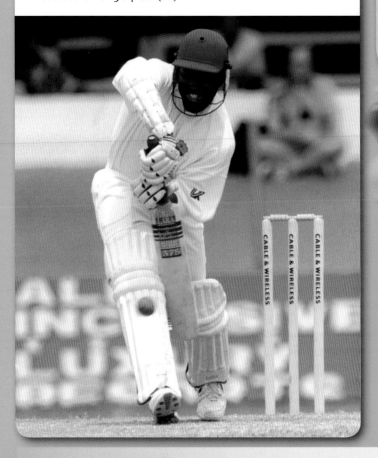

The master blaster runs riot

Viv Richards was at his swaggering best during the West Indies' 3–0 series win over England in 1976. In seven innings during the five-match series – he missed the Second Test at Lord's through injury – the master blaster smashed three centuries and two half-centuries (with a highest score of 291 at The Oval in the Fifth Test) en route to amassing 829 runs at an average of 118.42. It remains the highest series haul by any West Indian batsman.

BOWLING – MOST WICKETS: TOP 10

Pos	Wkts	Player	Span	Mat	Balls	Runs	BBI	BBM	Ave	Econ	SR	5	10
1	519	C.A. Walsh	1984–2001	132	30,019	12,688	7/37	13/55	24.44	2.53	57.8	22	3
2	405	C.E.L. Ambrose	1988–2000	98	22,103	8,501	8/45	11/84	20.99	2.30	54.5	22	3
3	376	M.D. Marshall	1978–91	81	17,584	7,876	7/22	11/89	20.94	2.68	46.7	22	4
4	309	L.R. Gibbs	1958–76	79	27,115	8,989	8/38	11/157	29.09	1.98	87.7	18	2
5	259	J. Garner	1977–87	58	13,169	5,433	6/56	9/108	20.97	2.47	50.8	7	0
6	249	M.A. Holding	1975–87	60	12,680	5,898	8/92	14/149	23.68	2.79	50.9	13	2
7	235	G.S. Sobers	1954–74	93	21,599	7,999	6/73	8/80	34.03	2.22	91.9	6	0
8	202	A.M.E. Roberts	1974–83	47	11,135	5,174	7/54	12/121	25.61	2.78	55.1	11	2
9	192	W.W. Hall	1958–69	48	10,421	5,066	7/69	11/126	26.38	2.91	54.2	9	1
10	161	I.R. Bishop	1989–98	43	8,407	3,909	6/40	8/57	24.27	2.78	52.2	6	0

Whispering Death destroys England

Nicknamed "Whispering Death" for his graceful, stealth-like approach to the bowling crease and an effortless action that produced deliveries at a blistering pace, **Michael Holding** was one of the most feared bowlers of his day. In 60 Tests for the West Indies between 1975 and 1987 he took 249 wickets, with his best performance coming against England at The Oval in August 1976. He took 8 for 92 in the first innings and 6 for 57 in the second: his match haul of 14 for 149 is an all-time West Indies record.

Brief but mightily effective for Lawson

After bursting on to the international scene in December 2002, with 6 for 3 in only his third Test match, against Bangladesh at Chittagong, followed by a career-best 7 for 78 against the all-conquering Australians the following May, Jermaine Lawson's career started to unravel. As the ICC started to question the legitimacy of his action, he struggled to hold a place in the West Indies line-up and by 2005 his international career was over. However, his 51 wickets in 13 Tests came at a strike-rate of a wicket every 46.3 deliveries – an all-time record for a West Indies bowler.

Keeping it tight

Gerry Gomez was the most economical bowler in West Indies cricket history. In 29 Tests for the islanders between 1939 and 1954, his 5,236 deliveries of medium-pace bowling went for just 1.82 runs per over. Garfield Sobers holds the national record for the best economy rate in an innings: he produced a spell of 14-11-3-1 against New Zealand at Wellington in March 1956 – an economy rate of just 0.21 runs per over.

All-time great: MALCOLM MARSHALL

Of the battery of world-class fast bowlers to have emerged from the Caribbean islands over the years, **Malcolm Marshall** was the best of them. Relatively short for a fast bowler, standing at just 5ft 9in, he made up for any lack of height with express pace and an ability to swing the ball both ways. In 81 Tests for the West Indies between 1978 and 1991 he took 376 wickets and set national records for: the best average (20.94), the best strike-rate in an innings (6.5 – against Pakistan at Faisalabad in November 1990, where his figures were 4.2-0-24-4), the most five-wicket hauls (22, shared with Curtly Ambrose and Courtney Walsh), the most ten-wicket match hauls (4) and the most wickets in a series (35, against England in 1988).

Bucking the trend

Given that the golden years of cricket in the Caribbean were based on a fearsome, four-pronged pace attack, it may seem strange that the best bowling figures ever recorded by a West Indian bowler were produced by an off-spinner. In only his second Test match, against India at Port of Spain, Trinidad, in March 1971, 35-year-old Jack Noreiga took 9 for 95. It remains the only nine-wicket innings haul in West Indies cricket history.

WICKETKEEPER – MOST DISMISSALS: TOP 5

Pos	Dis	Player	Span	Mat	Inns	Ct	St	Dis/Inn
1	270	**P.J.L. Dujon**	1981–91	81	150	265	5	1.800
2	219	R.D. Jacobs	1998–2004	65	122	207	12	1.795
3	189	D.L. Murray	1963–80	62	119	181	8	1.588
4	122	D. Ramdin	2005–10	42	76	119	3	1.605
5	101	J.R. Murray	1993–2002	33	57	98	3	1.771

MOST DISMISSALS: INNINGS/MATCHES/SERIES

The West Indies record for the most dismissals in an innings is seven, achieved by Ridley Jacobs (7ct) against Australia at Melbourne in December 2000. Jacobs went on to take a national record nine dismissals in the match (8ct, 1st), equalling previous performances by David Murray (9ct) against Australia at Melbourne in December 1981 and by Courtney Browne against England at Nottingham in August 1995. Murray also holds the record for the most dismissals in a series, 24 (22ct, 2st) against England in 1963.

FIELDING – MOST CATCHES: TOP 5

Pos	Ct	Player	Span	Mat	Inns	Max	Ct/Inn
1	164	**B.C. Lara**	1990–2006	130	239	4	0.686
2	122	I.V.A. Richards	1974–91	121	232	4	0.525
3	115	C.L. Hooper	1987–2002	102	189	4	0.608
4	109	G.S. Sobers	1954–74	93	172	4	0.633
5	96	C.G. Greenidge	1974–91	108	208	3	0.461

MOST CATCHES: INNINGS/MATCHES/SERIES

The West Indies record for the most catches in an innings is four, a feat achieved on 12 occasions. The record for most catches in a match is six, by Garfield Sobers against England at Lord's in August 1973 and by Jimmy Adams against England at Kingston in February 1994. **Brian Lara** holds the national record for the most catches in a series with 13, a feat he achieved on two occasions (against England in 1997–98 and against India in 2006).

LONGEST-SERVING CAPTAINS: TOP 10

Pos	Mat	Player	Span	W-L-T-D	%W
1	74	C.H. Lloyd	1974–85	36-12-0-26	48.64
2	50	I.V.A. Richards	1980–91	27-8-0-15	54.00
3	47	B.C. Lara	1997–2006	10-26-0-11	21.27
4	39	G.S. Sobers	1965–72	9-10-0-20	23.07
5	24	R.B. Richardson	1992–95	11-6-0-7	45.83
6	22	J.D.C. Goddard	1948–57	8-7-0-7	36.36
=	22	C.L. Hooper	2001–02	4-11-0-7	18.18
=	22	C.A. Walsh	1994–97	6-7-0-9	27.27
9	20	C.H. Gayle	2007–10	3-9-0-8	15.00
10	18	F.C.M. Alexander	1958–60	7-4-0-7	38.88

Golden times under Lloyd

Blessed no doubt by having a myriad of world-class talent at his disposal, **Clive Lloyd** is the most successful captain in the West Indies' long cricket history. Between 1974 and 1985 he captained the islanders on 74 occasions, notching up 36 wins with a winning percentage of 48.64.

BANGLADESH

Test cricket's newest incumbents – they were granted Test status in 2000, to become the game's tenth Test-playing nation – Bangladesh have struggled to find their feet in the hotbed of the Test arena. In 73 matches to date, the Tigers have won just three times: once against struggling Zimbabwe and twice against a severely weakened West Indies outfit.

RESULT SUMMARY

Opposition	Span	Mat	Won	Lost	Tied	Draw	W/L	%W	%L	%D
Australia	2003–06	4	0	4	0	0	0.00	0.00	100.00	0.00
England	2003–10	8	0	8	0	0	0.00	0.00	100.00	0.00
India	2000–10	7	0	6	0	1	0.00	0.00	85.71	14.28
New Zealand	2001–10	9	0	8	0	1	0.00	0.00	88.88	11.12
Pakistan	2001–03	8	0	8	0	0	0.00	0.00	100.00	0.00
South Africa	2002–08	8	0	8	0	0	0.00	0.00	100.00	0.00
Sri Lanka	2001–09	12	0	12	0	0	0.00	0.00	100.00	0.00
West Indies	2002–11	8	2	4	0	2	0.50	25.00	50.00	25.00
Zimbabwe	2001–11	9	1	5	0	3	0.20	11.11	55.55	33.33

Ashraful shows Tigers the way forward

The youngest centurion in Test history (he was aged just 17 years 61 days when he struck 114 on debut against Sri Lanka at Colombo in September 2001), Mohammad Ashraful is one of the few good-news stories to have emerged from Bangladesh's well-documented struggles in the Test arena. The flamboyant right-hander has posted five centuries for his country – a national record – including 158 not out against India at Chittagong, the highest score by any Bangladesh batsman in the country's short Test history.

Bangladeshi bowling bests

Renowned more as a talented, hard-hitting batsman, **Shakib Al Hasan** showed his true all-round potential when he took 7 for 36 against New Zealand at Chittagong in December 2008 with his slow left-arm spin bowling. They are the best figures in an innings ever recorded by a Bangladesh bowler. Another slow left-arm bowler, Enamul Haque Jr, holds the record for the best figures in a match: his 12 for 200 against Zimbabwe at Dhaka in January 2005 did much to ensure his country's first-ever series win.

All-time great: HABIBUL BASHAR

One of the few Bangladesh players of genuine Test quality, **Habibul Bashar** carried his side's batting in their early days as a Test-playing nation. The Tigers' longest-serving captain (he led them on 18 occasions between 2004 and 2007) and one of only two Bangladesh players to have played in 50 Tests (Mohammad Ashraful is the other), the right-hander (and former captain) holds the national record for the most runs (3,026) and the most scores of 50 or over (27).

Leading gloveman

A regular behind the stumps for Bangladesh following their introduction to Test cricket, Khaled Mashud holds the national record for the most dismissals with 87 (78ct, 9st) in 44 Tests between 2000 and 2007.

Left-armer Rafique leads the way with the ball

A slow left-arm bowler who relied on nagging accuracy rather than an ability to spin the ball sharply, Mohammad Rafique was a mainstay of Bangladesh's bowling attack between 2000 and 2008. In 33 Tests for his country, he became the only Tigers bowler in history to claim 100 Test wickets, taking his 100th and final wicket (that of South Africa's Robin Peterson) in his last Test against South Africa at Chittagong in February 2008.

ZIMBABWE

Zimbabwe became the ninth Test-playing nation in 1992 and were perennial strugglers in the longest format of the game until the turn of the century when, although never strong, they were at least competitive. Zimbabwe's political problems, however, led to their expulsion from the Test arena in January 2006, and they have played only four Test matches since then (three in 2011 and one in 2012).

RESULT SUMMARY

Opposition	Span	Mat	Won	Lost	Tied	Draw	W/L	%W	%L	%D
Australia	1999–2003	3	0	3	0	0	0.00	0.00	100.00	0.00
Bangladesh	2001–11	9	5	1	0	3	5.00	55.55	11.11	33.33
England	1996–2003	6	0	3	0	3	0.00	0.00	50.00	50.00
India	1992–2005	11	2	7	0	2	0.28	18.18	63.63	18.18
New Zealand	1992–2012	13	0	9	0	6	0.00	0.00	60.00	40.00
Pakistan	1993–2011	15	2	9	0	4	0.22	13.33	60.00	26.66
South Africa	1995–2005	7	0	6	0	1	0.00	0.00	85.71	14.28
Sri Lanka	1994–2004	15	0	10	0	5	0.00	0.00	66.66	33.33
West Indies	2000–03	6	0	4	0	2	0.00	0.00	66.66	33.33

Leading from the front

Dave Houghton, Zimbabwe's first Test captain, led by example in the Second Test against Sri Lanka at Bulawayo in October 1994. Coming to the crease with his side precariously placed on 5 for 2, the right-hander batted for over 11 hours and faced 541 balls en route to amassing 266 runs – the highest score ever made by a Zimbabwe batsman.

A cut above the rest

The second most capped player in Zimbabwe's history (behind Grant Flower) with 65 appearances for his country between 1993 and 2005 (21 of them as captain), Heath Streak was a fast-medium bowler of genuine quality with a heart and stamina to match. The only Zimbabwe bowler in history to reach the 100-wicket milestone, he ended his career with 216 Test scalps to his name. He is also his country's longest-serving captain, leading his side on 21 occasions (a record shared with Alistair Campbell), and its most successful one, recording four victories with a winning percentage of 19.04 per cent.

All-time great: ANDY FLOWER

The finest batsman Zimbabwe has produced and ranked for a short time in 2000 as the number-one batsman in the world, **Andy Flower** set numerous national records in a 63-Test career spanning a decade between 1992 and 2002. Of all Zimbabwe batsmen he has scored the most runs (4,794), has the highest average (an exceptional 51.54), has scored the most hundreds (12), has the most scores of 50 plus (39) and also holds the national record for the most runs in a series (540 in the two-match series against India in 2000–01). He is also the leading wicketkeeper in Zimbabwe's history with 151 (142ct, 9st) Test victims.

Best bowling in an innings/match

A leg-spinner with the full repertoire, Paul Strang is Zimbabwe's second most prolific wicket-taker of all time with 70 Test wickets to his name in 24 Tests between 1994 and 2001. He holds the record for the best bowling figures in an innings: 8 for 109 against New Zealand at Bulawayo in September 2000. Adam Huckle holds the record for the best match figures: the leg-spinner took 11 for 255 against New Zealand at Bulawayo in September 1997.

TEST RECORDS:
BY SERIES

As some rivalries in cricket stretch back a century or more, it stands to reason that some series carry more weight than others. Take the English summer of 2005. In May, England trudged off the field after beating Bangladesh by an innings and 261 runs at a sparsely populated Lord's; two months later, at the same venue, England's players buzzed with tension in the dressing-room as outside vast crowds desperate to watch the first day of the 2005 Ashes series snaked along the pavement. Some matches mean more than others. The following section looks at records on a series-by-series basis.

England captain **Andrew Strauss** holds aloft the Ashes trophy after completing the 3–1 victory at Sydney in 2010–11. Australia v England is probably Test cricket's most eagerly anticipated series.

AUSTRALIA v ENGLAND

It is the oldest and the most eagerly anticipated rivalry in world cricket. England and Australia have been locking horns on a cricket pitch since 1877, and matches between the two countries have become the stuff of legend. Australia lead the way with 133 wins, to England's 102 (with 91 draws), and matches between the game's oldest rivals remain the highlight of the cricket calendar.

Proving their point

In 1938, with any hopes of regaining the Ashes already dashed, England went into the final Test at The Oval 1–0 down in the series and determined to prove a point. They had a plan: to bat the Australians into submission. England won the toss, batted and, over the next two-and-a-half days, ground out a mammoth 903 for 7, a then world record score and still the highest team total in Ashes history. England went on to win the match by an innings and 579 runs (the largest victory margin in Ashes history).

OVERALL SERIES RECORDS

(326 Tests between 1877 and 2011)

	W	L	T	D	W/L	%W	%L	%D
Australia	133	102	0	91	1.30	40.80	31.29	27.91
England	102	133	0	91	0.76	31.29	40.80	27.91

First match: 15–19 March 1877, Melbourne Cricket Ground

Marsh tops dismissals list

An ever-present behind the stumps for Australia for over a decade, Rod Marsh is the most successful wicketkeeper in Ashes history. The combative Western Australian took 141 catches – c. Marsh b. Lillee became a part of cricket folklore Down Under – and seven stumpings in 42 Ashes Tests between 1970 and 1983.

A Herculean effort from 22-year-old Hutton

The main architect of England's Ashes record 903 for 7 and subsequent innings-and-579-run victory over Australia at The Oval in 1938 was **Len Hutton**. The Yorkshire opener faced 847 balls and batted for 13 hours and 17 minutes to compile an innings of 364 – breaking Walter Hammond's world record score of 336 not out (broken by Garfield Sobers in 1958) and setting an all-time Ashes record.

Captain fantastic

The most successful captain in Ashes history? **Allan Border**. The Queensland batsman reluctantly took over the Australian captaincy in 1984–85, but led the side with great distinction to the top of the world game. He captained Australia in 29 Tests against England over five series between 1985 and 1993, winning three of them and an Ashes record 13 matches.

ABOVE: Len Hutton *receives the congratulations of the Australia players after breaking Walter Hammond's world-record score of 336 at The Oval in 1938.*

Best in the business

In 37 Tests between 1928 and 1948, **Donald Bradman** terrorized English bowling attacks and set numerous Ashes records along the way. No other batsman in history has scored more runs in Ashes encounters (5,028), no batsman has recorded a higher career average (89.78) and no one has scored more Ashes centuries (19) – his nearest rival on the all-time Ashes centuries list is Steve Waugh, with ten.

Making hay at the top of the order

The most productive partnership in all Tests between Australia and England is that of England's Jack Hobbs and Herbert Sutcliffe. The legendary opening pair combined to score 2,452 runs in 30 innings between 1924 and 1930 at an average of 84.55, with 11 century partnerships and nine half-century partnerships.

MOST RUNS: TOP 10

Pos	Player	Runs
1	D.G. Bradman (Australia, 1928–48)	5,028
2	J.B. Hobbs (England, 1908–30)	3,636
3	A.R. Border (Australia, 1978–93)	3,548
4	D.I. Gower (England, 1978–91)	3,269
5	S.R. Waugh (Australia, 1986–2003)	3,200
6	G. Boycott (England, 1964–81)	2,945
7	W.R. Hammond (England, 1928–47)	2,852
8	H. Sutcliffe (England, 1924–34)	2,741
9	C. Hill (Australia, 1896–1912)	2,660
10	J.H. Edrich (England, 1964–75)	2,644

MOST WICKETS: TOP 10

Pos	Player	Wickets
1	S.K. Warne (Australia, 1993–2007)	195
2	D.K. Lillee (Australia, 1971–82)	167
3	G.D. McGrath (Australia, 1994–2007)	157
4	I.T. Botham (England, 1977–89)	148
5	H. Trumble (Australia, 1890–1904)	141
6	R.G.D. Willis (England, 1971–83)	128
7	M.A. Noble (Australia, 1898–1909)	115
8	R.R. Lindwall (Australia, 1946–59)	114
9	W. Rhodes (England, 1899–1926)	109
10	S.F. Barnes (England, 1901–12)	106
=	C.V. Grimmett (Australia, 1925–34)	106

Australia get off to the worst of starts

It was the first match of five in the 1902 Ashes series, at Edgbaston, and a chance for England to avenge the crushing 4–1 series defeat they had suffered in Australia just two months earlier. England batted first and scored 376. Australia, embarrassingly, subsided to a sorry 36 all out – the lowest score in Ashes history. Amazingly, however, because it was only a three-day game, they managed to hold out for the draw, and went on to win the series 2–1.

Ponsford and Bradman dash England's hopes

The outcome of the 1934 Ashes series was still hanging in the balance when the two teams arrived for the Fifth and final Test at The Oval locked at 1–1, but by the end of the first day's play, thanks to stunning performances from Bill Ponsford (266) and Donald Bradman (244), there was only going to be one winner. The pair combined to add an Ashes record 451 runs for the second wicket to propel Australia to a mighty first-innings total of 701 all out and an eventual series-clinching 562-run victory.

Chappell claims the most catches

The outstanding Australian batsman of his generation and a fine captain (he led his country to Ashes success in 1982–83), Greg Chappell is also the most successful fielder in all matches between England and Australia, taking 61 catches in 35 Ashes Tests between 1970 and 1983.

Laker puts Australia in a spin

It was the finest performance by a bowler in Test history. With the 1956 Ashes series locked at 1–1 going into the Fourth Test, off-spinner Jim Laker took 9 for 37 in the first innings and 10 for 53 in the second (the best single-innings haul in Test history) as England romped to victory by an innings and 170 runs. Laker's match haul of 19 for 90 is the best in Test history and his series haul of 49 wickets remains an all-time Ashes record.

S. AFRICA v ENGLAND

The first fixture between the two sides took place in March 1889, making this the second-oldest fixture in Test cricket. England enjoyed an early supremacy over South Africa, but matches in recent times, particularly since the Proteas' readmission to international cricket in 1992, have been much closer affairs with South Africa claiming 11 wins to England's ten.

Best partnership

Having battled to escape with a draw in the First Test against South Africa in the 1947 series, Bill Edrich (189) and Denis Compton (208) ensured that any momentum gained continued to swing in England's favour in the Second Test at Lord's. The pair added 370 for the third wicket – the highest partnership in all Tests between the two countries – as England compiled a first-innings total of 554 en route to a ten-wicket victory and a 1–0 series lead.

OVERALL SERIES RECORDS

(138 Tests between 1889 and 2010)

	W	L	T	D	W/L	%W	%L	%D
South Africa	29	56	0	53	0.51	21.01	40.57	38.40
England	56	29	0	53	1.99	40.57	21.01	38.40

First match: 12–13 March 1889, Port Elizabeth

Brilliant Barnes too good for South Africa

If statistics alone can be proof of greatness, then S.F. Barnes was the best fast bowler England has ever produced and he was at his electrifying best against South Africa during England's 1913–14 tour when, playing on matting wickets, he was virtually unplayable. In the Second Test at Johannesburg, which England won by an innings and 12 runs, he produced match figures of 17 for 159 (a record in Tests between the two countries) and ended the series (despite missing the fifth and final Test match) with 49 wickets to his name (an all-time Test record for a five-match series).

Compton's magical series

Denis Compton's battling 163 in the second innings of the First Test against South Africa at Trent Bridge in 1947 not only helped England save the match (the home side had been forced to follow on still 325 runs in arrears), but also changed the course of the series. England went on to win the five-match series 3–0 with Compton's fine form continuing: he hit 208 at Lord's in the Second Test, 115 at Old Trafford in the Third Test and 113 in the Fifth and final Test at The Oval. The Middlesex star's series haul of 753 runs (at an average of 94.12) is an all-time record in matches between the two countries.

Smith is most successful captain

Graeme Smith has come a long way since he first assumed the South African captaincy in the wake of his country's disastrous showing at the 2003 ICC World Cup and has led his country with distinction to this day. He is the most successful captain in South Africa-England Tests, leading his side to six wins in 18 matches between 2003 and 2010.

Lohmann rips through South Africa

The South African batsmen had no answer to George Lohmann on the matting wicket at the Old Wanderers ground in Johannesburg in March 1896. The right-arm fast-medium bowler, who was renowned for his accuracy, took 9 for 28 in South Africa's first innings as England went on to win the match by an innings and 197 runs. Lohmann's effort remains the best bowling performance in an innings in matches between the two sides.

Kicking England when they were down

Following the sudden resignation of Nasser Hussain as England captain after a drawn First Test at Edgbaston in 2003, South Africa piled more misery on to England when the two sides reconvened at Lord's for the Second Test. First they skittled the home side for 173, then, led by captain **Graeme Smith** (259) and Gary Kirsten (108), they compiled 682 for 6 declared – the highest total in all matches between the two sides – en route to completing a convincing innings-and-92-run victory.

New captain Smith answers his critics in style

In the first innings of the First Test against England at Edgbaston in July 2003, South Africa's Graeme Smith, in only his third Test as captain, did much to silence the doubters who thought that, at 22 years of age, he was both too young and too inexperienced to lead his country into a new golden age. The left-handed opener smashed 277 off 373 balls (including 35 fours) – the highest individual score in all matches between the two countries.

Edrich finally masters the South Africans

Having scored a meagre 21 runs in his first five innings against South Africa on the 1938–39 tour, it could be argued that a battling 219 in the Fifth "timeless" Test at Durban saved Bill Edrich's career. He was full of confidence when South Africa toured England in 1947, hitting two half-centuries in the First Test, 189 in the Second Test at Lord's and a brilliant 191 in the Third Test at Old Trafford. In 12 innings against South Africa, Edrich scored 792 runs at an average of 72.00, the highest average of any player to have batted ten times or more in Tests between the two countries.

Most catches

A stalwart of the South Africa side who appeared in 42 consecutive Tests for his country between 1929 and 1949, **Bruce Mitchell** was a fine batsman (scoring 1,380 Test runs at an average of 51.11) and an excellent fielder. He holds the record for the most catches by a player in Tests between England and South Africa, with 43 in 30 Tests between 1929 and 1949.

Most dismissals

A standout performer for South Africa for over a decade, and one of the finest wicketkeeper-batsmen in history, Mark Boucher holds the all-time record for the most dismissals in Test matches between England and South Africa. The East London-born keeper has claimed 105 dismissals (103 catches and two stumpings) in 25 Tests against England between 1998 and 2010.

Most productive partnership

The most productive partnership in all Tests between England and South Africa is that between Len Hutton and Cyril Washbrook. In 19 innings between 1947 and 1949, the pair combined to score 1,371 runs at an average of 80.64.

MOST WICKETS: TOP 10

Pos	Player	Wickets
1	**S.M. Pollock** (South Africa, 1995–2005)	91
2	A.A. Donald (South Africa, 1994–2000)	86
3	S.F. Barnes (England, 1912–14)	83
4	H.J. Tayfield (South Africa, 1955–60)	75
5	C.L. Vincent (South Africa, 1927–35)	72
6	M. Ntini (South Africa, 1998–2009)	70
7	J.B. Statham (England, 1951–65)	69
8	G.A. Faulkner (South Africa, 1906–24)	68
9	T.L. Goddard (South Africa, 1955–65)	63
10	A.E.E. Vogler (South Africa, 1906–10)	60

MOST RUNS: TOP 10

Pos	Player	Runs
1	B. Mitchell (South Africa, 1929–49)	2,732
2	H.W. Taylor (South Africa, 1912–31)	2,287
3	D.C.S. Compton (England, 1947–57)	2,205
4	W.R. Hammond (England, 1927–39)	2,188
5	A.D. Nourse (South Africa, 1935–51)	2,037
6	J.H. Kallis (South Africa, 1995–2010)	1,879
7	G.C. Smith (South Africa, 2003–10)	1,779
8	G. Kirsten (South Africa, 1994–2003)	1,608
9	L. Hutton (England, 1938–51)	1,564
10	J.B. Hobbs (England, 1910–29)	1,562

S. AFRICA v AUSTRALIA

Australia hold a dominating lead in all Tests between the two countries, with 48 wins to South Africa's 19, but in recent times clashes between the two sides have been close affairs, with the series-winning side often considered the best team on the planet.

Classy Grimmett leaves South Africa in a spin

South Africa's batsmen continually failed to come to terms with Clarrie Grimmett's mastery of leg-spin bowling. In ten Tests against the South Africans, the spin wizard claimed 77 scalps (35.65 per cent of his Test victims), including 14 for 199 in the Fourth Test at Adelaide in January–February 1932 (a record match haul in Tests between the two countries) and a series record 44 wickets in the home series in 1935–36.

OVERALL SERIES RECORDS

(85 Tests between 1902 and 2011)

	W	L	T	D	W/L	%W	%L	%D
South Africa	19	48	0	18	0.39	22.35	56.47	21.17
Australia	48	19	0	18	2.52	56.47	22.35	21.17

First match: 11–14 October 1902, Johannesburg

Prolific Ponting an all-round record-breaker

Ricky Ponting has enjoyed some great moments against South Africa. He is the leading run-scorer in all Tests between the two countries (2,100 runs), the most successful captain (eight wins) and a member (along with Matthew Hayden) of the most productive partnership. He also holds the record for the most catches, with 33 in 23 Tests between 1997 and 2011.

Australian batsmen find their form

The Australians made a huge statement of intent in the opening Test of their 2001–02 tour to South Africa at Johannesburg. Having won the toss and elected to bat they put South Africa's bowlers to the sword, with Adam Gilchrist (204), Damien Martyn (133) and Matthew Hayden (122) all making hefty contributions as Australia amassed the highest-ever total in all Tests between the two countries – 652 for 7 declared. Australia went on to win the match by an innings and 360 runs.

Brilliant Boucher leads the way

The most prolific wicketkeeper in history, **Mark Boucher** leads the dismissals list in Tests between Australia and South Africa. In 20 Tests against the Aussies between 2001 and 2011, the South Africa gloveman has claimed 66 dismissals, with 64 catches and two stumpings.

South Africa down and out

Already 4–0 down in the series, the South African tourists had any urge to continue the fight knocked out of them as they returned to Melbourne for the Fifth and final Test against Australia in February 1932. And how it showed. After winning the toss and choosing to bat, they collapsed to a miserable 36 all out in a little under 90 minutes – the lowest-ever total in matches between the two sides. Australia went on to win the Test by an innings and 72 runs to complete a series whitewash.

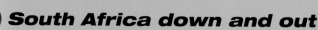

Best partnership

When **Greg Blewett** (left) joined **Steve Waugh** (right) with Australia on 174 for 4, still 128 runs behind South Africa in the First Test at Johannesburg in February–March 1997, the home side would have felt very much as though they were still in the game. Not for long, however. Over the next day and a half the pair – Waugh (160), Blewett (214) – combined to add an Australia-South Africa Test-best partnership of 385 runs to help Australia to 628 for 8 declared and an eventual innings-and-196-run victory.

Most productive partnership

The most productive partnership in all Tests between South Africa and Australia is that of Matthew Hayden and Ricky Ponting. The pair combined to score 1,136 runs in 14 innings between 2001 and 2009 at an average of 87.38.

Most successful captain

The most successful Test captain of all time (with 46 wins), Ricky Ponting enjoyed considerable success as Australia's skipper against South Africa. In 12 Tests against them between 2005 and 2009, the Tasmanian has led his side to a record eight wins.

The Don's batting masterclass

Having already posted scores of 226 and 112 in his first two Tests against South Africa, Donald Bradman reserved his best performance of the 1931–32 series for the Fourth Test at Adelaide, hitting a magnificent unbeaten 299 – the highest individual score in all matches between the two countries. Ironically, he was left stranded after running out No. 11 Pud Thurlow in a scrambled, and ultimately misguided, attempt to reach 300.

Harvey's heroics in vain in drawn series

An electrifying batsman who thrilled crowds with his stunning strokeplay and frustrated opponents with his seemingly limitless powers of concentration, Neil Harvey was at his best during the scintillating 2–2 series draw against South Africa in 1952–53. The left-hander hit four centuries and three half-centuries (with a highest score of 205 in the Fifth Test at Melbourne) to end the series with 834 runs at an average of 92.66. His tally remains the highest series haul by any batsman in all Tests between the two countries. He also holds the record for the highest batting average of all batsmen to have batted in at least ten innings in matches between Australia and South Africa, scoring 1,625 runs at an average of 81.25 in 23 innings against South Africa between 1949 and 1958.

MOST RUNS: TOP 10

Pos	Player	Runs
1	**R.T. Ponting** (Australia, 1997–2011)	2,100
2	J.H. Kallis (South Africa, 1997–2011)	1,639
3	R.N. Harvey (Australia, 1949–58)	1,625
4	M.L. Hayden (Australia, 1994–2009)	1,486
5	R.G. Pollock (South Africa, 1963–70)	1,453
6	E.J. Barlow (South Africa, 1963–70)	1,149
7	S.R. Waugh (Australia, 1994–2002)	1,147
8	M.E. Waugh (Australia, 1993–2002)	1,135
9	G. Kirsten (South Africa, 1993–2002)	1,134
10	T.L. Goddard (South Africa, 1957–70)	1,090

MOST WICKETS: TOP 10

Pos	Player	Wickets
1	S.K. Warne (Australia, 1993–2006)	130
2	C.V. Grimmett (Australia, 1931–36)	77
3	H.J. Tayfield (South Africa, 1949–58)	64
4	M. Ntini (South Africa, 2001–09)	58
5	G.D. McGrath (Australia, 1994–2006)	57
6	T.L. Goddard (South Africa, 1957–70)	53
=	A.A. Donald (South Africa, 1993–2002)	53
8	R. Benaud (Australia, 1952–64)	52
=	P.M. Pollock (South Africa, 1963–70)	52
10	W.J. Whitty (Australia, 1910–12)	50
=	B. Lee (Australia, 2001–08)	50

Johnson's record-breaking performance

Mitchell Johnson produced one of the most devastating spells of fast bowling in recent times in the First Test against South Africa at Perth in December 2008, taking five wickets for two runs in 21 balls to end with figures of 8 for 61 – the best in all matches between the two countries. His record-breaking efforts were all in vain, however, as the Proteas rallied to win the match by six wickets.

ENGLAND v W. INDIES

Behind the Ashes this is the second most contested fixture in international cricket. Fortunes have wavered for both England and the West Indies since the two countries played a Test match for the first time in 1928, with both sides enjoying periods of dominance, none more extreme than when the West Indies went unbeaten in 29 straight Tests against England between June 1976 and February 1990.

OVERALL SERIES RECORDS

(145 Tests between 1928 and 2009)

	W	L	T	D	W/L	%W	%L	%D
England	43	53	0	49	0.81	29.66	36.55	33.79
West Indies	53	43	0	49	1.23	36.55	29.66	33.79

First match: 23–6 June 1928, Lord's

Most catches

Brian Lara not only terrorized England with the bat between 1994 and 2004, he also caused havoc in the field. In 30 Tests against the English, the Trinidad star snared 45 catches, an all-time record for any player in Tests between the two countries.

Most productive partnership

The most productive partnership in all Tests between England and the West Indies is that between Gordon Greenidge and Desmond Haynes, who combined to score 1,862 runs in 37 innings at an average of 51.72.

The master blaster's golden summer

Viv Richards established himself as a player of true international class during the West Indies' 1976 tour to England. He hit 232 in the First Test at Trent Bridge, 135 in the Third Test at Old Trafford (after missing the Second Test through injury) and a magnificent 291 in the Fifth and final Test at The Oval. His series haul of 829 runs (at an average of 118.42) remains an all-time high in all matches between the two countries.

Lara's love-in at Antigua

Brian Lara seemed to reserve his greatest performances for matches against England at St John's, Antigua. In April 1994 he plundered the England attack for a then world record 375. A decade later he was at it again, this time amassing a new all-time Test record score of 400 not out (off 582 balls) with 43 fours and four sixes.

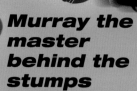

Murray the master behind the stumps

A regular behind the stumps for the West Indies for 17 years between 1963 and 1980, Deryck Murray holds the record for the most dismissals in Tests between England and the West Indies. In 28 matches against England, the Trinidad keeper claimed 94 scalps (90 catches and four stumpings).

Most successful captain

Viv Richards had the good fortune to captain the West Indies during the islanders' golden era, and remains the most successful captain in Test matches between the two countries, leading his side to 13 wins in 19 Tests between 1980 and 1991.

MOST RUNS: TOP 10

Pos	Player	Runs
1	G.S. Sobers (West Indies, 1954–74)	3,214
2	B.C. Lara (West Indies, 1994–2004)	2,983
3	I.V.A. Richards (West Indies, 1976–91)	2,869
4	D.L. Haynes (West Indies, 1980–94)	2,392
5	C.G. Greenidge (West Indies, 1976–90)	2,318
6	R.B. Kanhai (West Indies, 1957–74)	2,267
7	G. Boycott (England, 1966–81)	2,205
8	G.A. Gooch (England, 1980–91)	2,197
9	S. Chanderpaul (W. Indies, 1994–2009)	2,124
10	C.H. Lloyd (West Indies, 1968–84)	2,120

MOST WICKETS: TOP 10

Pos	Player	Wickets
1	C.E.L. Ambrose (W. Indies, 1988–2000)	164
2	C.A. Walsh (West Indies, 1986–2000)	145
3	M.D. Marshall (West Indies, 1980–91)	127
4	G.S. Sobers (West Indies, 1954–74)	102
5	L.R. Gibbs (West Indies, 1963–74)	100
6	M.A. Holding (West Indies, 1976–86)	96
7	J. Garner (West Indies, 1980–86)	92
8	F.S. Trueman (England, 1954–63)	86
9	S. Ramadhin (W. Indies, 1950–60)	80
10	J.A. Snow (England, 1966–76)	72

England prosper in Kingston

With the 1929–30 series locked at 1–1, it was decided that the Fourth and final Test match, at Kingston, Jamaica, should be a timeless one. England won the toss, elected to bat and, led by Andy Sandham's 325, batted themselves into an impregnable position, amassing 849 all out. The score remains the highest total in all matches between the two countries, but it wasn't enough to win the match. After rain on days eight and nine prevented any further play, the two teams agreed on a draw.

Marshall produces his menacing best

The sheer pace and consistent excellence that became the trademark of **Malcolm Marshall**'s career proved too much for England's batsmen during the West Indies' comprehensive 4–0 series win in 1988. Using his unorthodox, open-chested action to swing the ball both ways at frightening pace, Marshall took 35 wickets in the series (an all-time record in Tests between the two countries) with a best of 7 for 22 in the Third Test at Old Trafford.

Cowdrey and May rescue England with record-breaking partnership

With England trailing the West Indies by a mighty 288 runs after the completion of the first innings of the First Test at Edgbaston in May–June 1957, Colin Cowdrey and Peter May came to the rescue when their country truly needed them. The pair added a record 411 runs for the fourth wicket to lead England to 583 for 4 declared and the eventual safety of a draw.

Hutton tops the averages

One of the finest batsmen Test cricket has produced, Len Hutton enjoyed some particularly good times against the West Indies. In 13 matches against the islanders he hit five centuries – with a highest score of 202 not out at The Oval in August 1950 – and amassed 1,661 runs at an average of 79.09 – the highest of any player to have batted in ten innings in matches between England and the West Indies.

Whispering Death makes his deadly mark

Nicknamed "Whispering Death" because of his stealth-like approach to the bowling crease, Michael Holding truly found his stride in the Fifth Test against England at The Oval in August 1976. The Jamaican paceman took 8 for 92 in the first innings and 6 for 57 in the second to end up with match figures of 14 for 149: an all-time West Indian record and a record in all Tests between England and the West Indies.

Sorry England capitulate in Trinidad

Set just 194 runs to win the Third Test of the 1993–94 series at Port of Spain, Trinidad, England collapsed in spectacular and record-breaking style. The tone was set when they lost captain Michael Atherton to the first ball of the innings. Just 19.1 overs later, they had been dismissed for a paltry 46 all out – the lowest score in England–West Indies matches – with Curtly Ambrose (6 for 24) the chief destroyer.

Ambrose the destroyer

English batsmen could find few answers to the hostile pace and bounce of **Curtly Ambrose** over a 12-year period between 1988 and 2000. In 34 Tests against England, the 6ft 7in Antiguan took 164 wickets (40.49 per cent of his career Test wicket haul) with a best of 8 for 45 (at Bridgetown, Barbados, in April 1990). Both are all-time records in Test matches between the two countries.

NZ v ENGLAND

It took New Zealand 47 Test matches over 48 years before they finally managed to record their first-ever victory over England – at Wellington in February 1978 – but, helped by the emergence of several players of true international class, matches between the two countries have been more closely fought encounters in recent years.

OVERALL SERIES RECORDS

(94 Tests between 1930 and 2008)

	W	L	T	D	W/L	%W	%L	%D
New Zealand	8	45	0	41	0.17	8.51	47.87	43.62
England	45	8	0	41	5.62	47.87	8.51	43.62

First match: 10–13 January 1930, Christchurch

Lock's spell in the limelight

An aggressive left-arm spinner who for the most part had to play second fiddle to Jim Laker throughout his 49-Test match career, Tony Lock enjoyed a spell in the limelight against New Zealand in 1958. The Surrey left-arm spinner took 34 wickets in the series (with three five-wicket hauls and a best return of 7 for 35 in the Fourth Test at Old Trafford). No bowler has taken more wickets in an England-New Zealand series.

Most catches

One of the most prolific slip catchers Test cricket has ever seen, **Stephen Fleming** has bagged more catches in England–New Zealand Test matches than any other player. The former Kiwi captain took 33 catches in 19 Tests against England between 1994 and 2008.

The Edrich and Barrington show

Already 2–0 up in the 1965 series going into the Third Test at Headingley in July 1965, England were able to build on their advantage over New Zealand thanks to the batting of John Edrich (310 not out) and Ken Barrington (163). Coming together in the first innings with the score on 13 for 1, the pair added 369 for the second wicket – an all-time record partnership in matches between the two countries – to propel England to a first-innings total of 546 for 4 declared and an eventual innings-and-187-run victory.

Happy days for Vaughan

Michael Vaughan is the most successful captain in the history of Test cricket between England and New Zealand. The Yorkshire star led England to six wins over the Kiwis in eight Tests between 2004 and 2008.

Most productive partnership

The most productive partnership in all Tests between England and New Zealand is that between Michael Atherton and Alec Stewart. The England opening pair combined to score 809 runs in 14 innings at an average of 57.78 (with a highest partnership of 182 runs in the First Test at Auckland in January 1997).

Starting as you mean to go on

There is no better time to make a statement of intent than in the first innings of the opening Test of a series and, in February 1975 at Auckland, England, recently arrived in New Zealand licking their wounds following a 4–1 thumping in the Ashes series, did just that. Helped by superb innings from Keith Fletcher (216) and captain Mike Denness (181), they compiled 593 for 6 declared – the highest innings total in all matches between the two countries – en route to winning the match by an innings and 83 runs.

MOST RUNS: TOP 10

Pos	Player	Runs
1	**J.G. Wright** (New Zealand, 1978–92)	1,518
2	M.D. Crowe (New Zealand, 1983–94)	1,421
3	S.P. Fleming (New Zealand, 1994–2008)	1,229
4	G.A. Gooch (England, 1978–94)	1,148
5	A.J. Stewart (England, 1990–99)	1,145
6	B.E. Congdon (New Zealand, 1965–78)	1,143
7	M.C. Cowdrey (England, 1955–71)	1,133
8	M.A. Atherton (England, 1990–99)	1,088
9	D.I. Gower (England, 1978–86)	1,051
10	B. Sutcliffe (New Zealand, 1947–65)	1,049

MOST WICKETS: TOP 10

Pos	Player	Wickets
1	R.J. Hadlee (New Zealand, 1973–90)	97
2	I.T. Botham (England, 1978–92)	64
3	R.G.D. Willis (England, 1971–84)	60
4	R.O. Collinge (New Zealand, 1965–78)	48
=	**D.L. Underwood** (England, 1969–75)	48
6	G.A.R. Lock (England, 1958–59)	47
=	C.L. Cairns (New Zealand, 1992–2004)	47
=	A.R. Caddick (England, 1997–2002)	47
9	D.L. Vettori (New Zealand, 1997–2008)	45
10	R.J. Sidebottom (England, 2008)	41

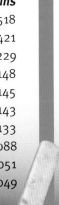

Underwood spins England to a comprehensive victory

England's most successful spin bowler of all time, **Derek Underwood** produced a match-winning performance of star quality in the First Test against New Zealand at Lord's in July 1969. With New Zealand set an improbable 362 runs to win, the Kent left-arm spinner took 7 for 32 off 31 overs to propel England to a 230-run victory. They are the best single-innings figures in England–New Zealand Tests.

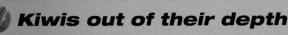

Kiwis out of their depth

Early matches between England and New Zealand were a sorry mismatch and the Kiwis hit an all-time low in the Second Test of the 1954–55 series at Auckland. Trailing England by 46 runs after the completion of the first innings, they crashed to the lowest score in Test history: a miserable 26 all out in 27 overs.

Classy Hammond the pick of the crop

One of Test cricket's all-time great batsmen, **Walter Hammond** flourished against all opponents in the Test arena, but particularly against New Zealand. In the Second Test against the Kiwis in Auckland in March–April 1933, he struck a then world record score of 336 not out (still the highest individual score in all matches between the two countries), an innings that included ten sixes (a world record that stood for 63 years). He ended the series with 563 runs (another all-time high in England-New Zealand Tests) and finished his Test career averaging 112.77 against New Zealand (the highest average of any player to have completed ten or more innings in matches between the two countries).

Deadly Derek strikes again

Nicknamed "Deadly" by his team-mates because of his effectiveness on rain-affected pitches, **Derek Underwood** lived up to his reputation in the First Test match against New Zealand at Christchurch in February 1971. On a damp wicket, he took 6 for 12 in the first innings and 6 for 85 in the second to lead England to an eight-wicket victory. His match haul of 12 for 97 is an all-time record in matches between the two countries.

The most successful keeper? That's Parore

An able performer with the bat and, arguably, the most consistent wicketkeeper in world cricket in the 1990s, Adam Parore claimed more dismissals in England-New Zealand Test matches than any other keeper in history. In 15 matches against England between 1990 and 2002, the Auckland gloveman bagged 46 scalps (45 catches and one stumping).

AUSTRALIA v W. INDIES

This is the sixth-oldest fixture in international cricket and, over the years, one of the most closely contested. Australia lead the way with 54 wins to the West Indies' 32 and in recent times have enjoyed a period of dominance over the islanders, but that has not always been the case.

Walters's West Indian love affair

Renowned as much for his off-the-field antics as for his skills on a cricket pitch, Doug Walters liked nothing more than a battle and reserved some of his best performances for matches against the West Indies fast bowlers. In nine matches against the islanders between 1968 and 1973, the New South Wales stroke player hit six centuries (with a highest score of 242 in the Fifth Test at Sydney in February 1969) and scored 1,196 runs at an average of 92.00 – the highest of any player to have completed ten innings or more in matches between the two countries.

OVERALL SERIES RECORDS

(111 Tests between 1930 and 2012)

	W	L	T	D	W/L	%W	%L	%D
Australia	54	32	1	24	1.68	48.64	28.82	22.52*
West Indies	32	54	1	24	0.59	28.82	48.64	22.52*

First match: 12–16 December 1930, Adelaide
* One match tied

West Indies crash to a record-breaking low in crushing defeat

The golden years of West Indian dominance seemed like a distant memory in the First Test of the 1999 series against Australia at Port of Spain, Trinidad. Set 364 runs to win the opening rubber, the West Indies crashed in spectacular style to 51 all out in a paltry 19.1 overs and a crushing 312-run defeat. It is the lowest team total in all Tests between the two countries.

Most productive partnership

The most productive partnership in all Tests between Australia and the West Indies is that of Gordon Greenidge and Desmond Haynes. The legendary opening batsmen combined to score 2,252 runs in 48 innings between 1978 and 1991 at an average of 53.61.

Captain Lloyd leads the way

Clive Lloyd is the most successful of all captains in the history of Test matches between Australia and the West Indies. In 22 Tests against Australia between 1975 and 1985, Lloyd led the islanders to 12 victories.

Lawry and Simpson dig deep

Having lost two of the first three matches of the 1964–65 series against the West Indies, Australia needed to show considerably more fight when the two teams arrived at Bridgetown, Barbados, for the Fourth Test in May 1965. And Bill Lawry (210) and captain Bobby Simpson (201) did just that, putting on 382 runs for the opening wicket – the best partnership in the history of Australia–West Indies Tests. Unfortunately for the tourists, the West Indies held out for a draw to secure a series victory.

Lone defiance from Walcott

Rarely has a player prospered so much in a losing cause. Australia may have eased to a 3–0 victory over the West Indies in the 1954–55 series in the Caribbean, but they did so despite the best efforts of **Clyde Walcott**. The Bajan right-hander hit five centuries and two half-centuries (with a highest score of 155 in the Fifth Test at Kingston, Jamaica) to end the series with 827 runs at an average of 82.70. It remains the highest series run haul by any batsman in the history of Australia-West Indies matches.

Australia bow out of tour in record-breaking style

In June 1955 Australia held an unassailable 2–0 lead going into the Fifth and final Test at Kingston, Jamaica, and with the series already in the bag, and the pressure off, the tourists put on a show. After watching the home side compile a steady 357 all out, five Australian batsmen passed three figures as they amassed a mighty 758 for 8 declared (the highest total in all Tests between the two sides) on the way to an innings-and-82-run victory.

McKenzie makes the most of helpful conditions

Garth McKenzie took full advantage of both the bitterly cold Boxing Day conditions and the green tinge of the Melbourne wicket in the Second Test against the West Indies in December 1968. The Western Australian fast bowler took 8 for 71 – the best single-innings figures by any bowler in Australia–West Indies Tests – to help his side to an innings-and-30-run victory.

Trio share record for most wickets in a series

Three bowlers hold the record for the most wickets in a series between Australia and the West Indies with 33: Clarrie Grimmett in Australia's 4–1 series victory in the Caribbean in 1930–31; Alan Davidson, in Australia's 2–1 home series win in 1960–61; and Curtly Ambrose, in the West Indies 2–1 series win in Australia in 1992–93.

Most catches

The possessor of one of the safest pairs of hands in Test history, Mark Waugh holds the record for the most catches in Test matches between Australia and the West Indies: the younger of the Waugh twins took 45 catches in 28 Test matches against the islanders between 1991 and 2001.

Most dismissals

Jeff Dujon heads the list of most successful wicketkeepers in matches between Australia and the West Indies. The Jamaican keeper claimed 86 scalps (85 catches and one stumping) in 23 matches against Australia between 1981 and 1991.

Lara makes a name for himself

It was in the Third Test at Sydney, in January 1993, that **Brian Lara** announced himself to the world as a player of exceptional talent. With the West Indies under intense pressure following Australia's first-innings total of 503 for 9 declared, the Trinidad star produced a batting display of breathtaking quality, facing 372 balls and hitting 38 fours en route to compiling a magnificent 277 – the highest individual score in all matches between the two countries.

MOST RUNS: TOP 10

Pos	Player	Runs
1	**B.C. Lara** (West Indies, 1992–2005)	2,815
2	I.V.A. Richards (West Indies, 1975–91)	2,266
3	D.L. Haynes (West Indies, 1978–93)	2,233
4	C.H. Lloyd (West Indies, 1968–85)	2,211
5	S.R. Waugh (Australia, 1988–2003)	2,192
6	R.B. Richardson (West Indies, 1984–95)	2,175
7	A.R. Border (Australia, 1979–93)	2,052
8	R.T. Ponting (Australia, 1996–2012)	1,977
9	M.E. Waugh (Australia, 1991–2001)	1,858
10	C.G. Greenidge (West Indies, 1975–91)	1,819

Big Merv batters the Windies at Perth

A lion-hearted fast bowler who played a major role in helping Australia to climb to the top of world cricket, **Merv Hughes** was at his menacing best in the Second Test against the West Indies at Perth in December 1988. He took 5 for 130 in the first innings and a magnificent 8 for 87 in the second to propel his side to a 169-run victory. His match figures of 13 for 217 are the best by any bowler in all Test matches between the two countries.

MOST WICKETS: TOP 10

Pos	Player	Wickets
1	**C.A. Walsh** (West Indies, 1984–2001)	135
2	C.E.L. Ambrose (West Indies, 1988–99)	128
3	G.D. McGrath (Australia, 1995–2005)	110
4	L.R. Gibbs (West Indies, 1961–76)	103
5	J. Garner (West Indies, 1978–85)	89
6	M.D. Marshall (West Indies, 1984–91)	87
7	M.A. Holding (West Indies, 1975–85)	76
8	S.K. Warne (Australia, 1992–2005)	65
9	B. Lee (Australia, 2000–08)	64
10	J.R. Thomson (Australia, 1975–82)	62

NZ v S. AFRICA

A combination of New Zealand's geographical isolation and South Africa's ostracism from world cricket meant that Test matches between the two countries were few and far between for decades following the sides' first meeting in 1932. In recent times, however, they have met on a more regular basis and South Africa have dominated the encounters, winning 12 out of 21 Tests since 1995.

OVERALL SERIES RECORDS

(38 Tests between 1932 and 2012)

	W	L	T	D	W/L	%W	%L	%D
New Zealand	4	21	0	13	0.19	10.52	55.26	34.21
South Africa	21	4	0	13	5.25	55.26	10.52	34.21

First match: 27 February–1 March 1932, Christchurch, New Zealand

Amla and Kallis conquer batting demons in Johannesburg

After 22 wickets had fallen over the first day-and-a-half of the First Test between South Africa and New Zealand at Johannesburg in November 2007, Hashim Amla (176 not out) and Jacques Kallis (186) finally made batting look easy. The pair added 330 for the third wicket – an all-time high in Tests between the two countries – to help South Africa to a second-innings total of 422 for 3 declared and an eventual 358-run victory. Amla and Kallis have also enjoyed the most productive partnership in South Africa-New Zealand Tests, combining to score 756 runs in six innings at an average of 126.00.

Goofy by name but not by nature

A 6ft 5in fast bowler who relied more on hard work than on natural ability, Godfrey "Goofy" Lawrence appeared in only five Test matches for South Africa, but he more than made his mark in the second innings of the Second Test against New Zealand at Johannesburg in December 1961, taking 8 for 53 – the best single-innings figures in all Tests between South Africa and New Zealand. Unfortunately for Lawrence and South Africa, his performance did not turn out to be a match-winning one: the game petered out into a bore draw. Lawrence ended the series with 28 wickets to his name – another record in Tests between the two countries – but, owing to South Africa's limited Test schedule, never played for his country again.

Wicketkeeper Waite leads the way

The best wicketkeeper in South Africa's history until the arrival of Mark Boucher in the 1990s, and the first South African player to win 50 caps, Johnny Waite is the most successful keeper in the history of Test matches between South Africa and New Zealand. In 15 Tests against the Kiwis between 1953 and 1964, he claimed 56 dismissals, with 47 catches and ten stumpings.

Martin leads Kiwis to memorable victory

Chris Martin was a key figure for his country as New Zealand secured only their fourth-ever victory over South Africa, in the Second Test at Auckland in March 2004. The Kiwi paceman took 6 for 76 in the first innings and 5 for 104 in the second to help his side to a nine-wicket victory. His match haul of 11 for 180 is the best in all Tests between the two sides.

Most successful captain

Graeme Smith is the most successful captain in South Africa-New Zealand Tests. He has led South Africa to six victories in 11 Tests – a winning percentage of 54.54. **Jack Cheetham** won five in seven for the Springboks 1953-54.

Reid leads by example

John Reid was the star of the show as New Zealand fought back to claim a 2–2 draw in the five-match series in South Africa in 1961–62. The New Zealand captain led from the front, hitting four half-centuries and a century (142 in the Fourth Test at Johannesburg) to end the series with 546 runs – an all-time high in series between the two countries – at an average of 60.66.

Most catches

Jacques Kallis, perhaps the most underrated all-rounder in Test history, is the leading fielder in Tests between South Africa and New Zealand. In 16 Tests against the Blackcaps between 1999 and 2007, the all-rounder has taken 15 catches.

South Africa benefit from poor captain's choice

South Africa's batsmen made New Zealand captain Dion Nash's decision to bowl first in the First Test at Auckland in February–March 1999 look like one of Test cricket's more regrettable choices when they put on 621 for 5 over the first two-and-a-half days – the highest score in all Tests between the two countries. Fortunately for Nash, South Africa's bowlers also struggled on the lifeless pitch and the match ended in a draw.

New Zealand batsmen throw away solid position

Having seen South Africa struggle to 243 all out on a damp wicket at Johannesburg in the Fourth Test of the 1953–54 series, New Zealand, 2–0 down in the series, would have felt confident of getting something out of the game. Instead, the wheels fell off in spectacular style: the Kiwis slipped to 79 all out – the lowest score in Tests between the two countries – and went on to lose the match by nine wickets.

Cullinan prospers against New Zealand

Daryll Cullinan was the main beneficiary of Dion Nash's dubious decision to put South Africa in to bat in the First Test at Auckland in February–March 1999. The elegant No. 4 batsman put New Zealand's bowlers to the sword, hitting an unbeaten 275 (off 490 balls with 27 fours and two sixes), which is not only the highest individual score in matches between the two countries but also the third highest score by a South African in Test cricket. Cullinan also holds the record for the highest average by any batsman to have completed ten or more innings in New Zealand-South Africa Tests: he scored 823 runs in 16 innings against New Zealand between 1994 and 2000 at an average of 68.58.

MOST RUNS: TOP 10

	Player	Runs
1	J.H. Kallis (South Africa, 1999–2012)	1,475
2	D.J. McGlew (South Africa, 1953–62)	1,100
3	S.P. Fleming (New Zealand, 1994–2007)	1,072
4	G. Kirsten (South Africa, 1994–2004)	951
5	J.R. Reid (New Zealand, 1953–64)	914
6	D.J. Cullinan (South Africa, 1994–2000)	823
7	G.C. Smith (South Africa, 2004–12)	792
8	H.H. Gibbs (South Africa, 1999–2007)	790
9	H.M. Amla (South Africa, 2006–12)	643
10	J.H.B. Waite (South Africa, 1953–64)	643

MOST WICKETS: TOP 10

	Player	Wickets
1	C.S. Martin (New Zealand, 2000–12)	52
2	M. Ntini (South Africa, 2000–07)	46
3	D.W. Steyn (South Africa, 2006–12)	45
4	S.M. Pollock (South Africa, 1999–2006)	43
5	J.R. Reid (New Zealand, 1953–64)	37
6	N.A.T. Adcock (South Africa, 1953–62)	33
7	P.M. Pollock (South Africa, 1961–64)	32
8	H.J. Tayfield (South Africa, 1953–54)	31
9	F.J. Cameron (New Zealand, 1961–64)	29
10	G.B. Lawrence (South Africa, 1961–62)	28

ENGLAND v INDIA

Since the fixture was first contested in 1932, England have enjoyed the upper hand against India in home Test matches (winning 27 of the 52 matches played and losing just five), but contests on the slow, low, spin-friendly surfaces of the subcontinent have proved to be altogether closer affairs, with India leading the way with 14 wins to England's 11.

OVERALL SERIES RECORDS

(103 Tests between 1932 and 2011)

	W	L	T	D	W/L	%W	%L	%D
England	38	19	0	46	2.00	36.89	18.44	44.66
India	19	38	0	46	0.50	18.44	34.34	44.66

First match: 25–28 June 1932, Lord's

The leading wicketkeeper

Arguably the most complete wicketkeeper England has ever produced and without doubt the best when standing up to spin bowlers (his partnership with Derek Underwood for both Kent and England is legendary), Alan Knott is the most successful wicketkeeper in the history of England-India Test matches. In 16 Tests against India between 1971 and 1977 he claimed 54 dismissals, with 49 catches and five stumpings.

Beefy Botham on fire in Mumbai

The Golden Jubilee Test, played at Mumbai in February 1980, was the Test match which showed the world that, in Ian Botham, England possessed an all-rounder of the highest quality. The Somerset man took 6 for 58 in India's first innings, helped himself to 114 runs when England batted, and then took 7 for 48 in India's second to become only the second player in history (Australia's Alan Davidson being the other) to score a century and take 10 wickets in a Test match. Botham's match haul of 13 for 106 remains an all-time record in England–India Tests.

Most productive partnership

The most productive partnership in all Tests between England and India is that between **Rahul Dravid** and Sachin Tendulkar, who combined to score 1,001 runs in 23 innings between 1996 and 2011 at an average of 43.52.

Bell and Pietersen confirm England dominance

England held an unassailable 3–0 lead over India going into the fourth and final Test at The Oval in August 2011, but there was still plenty for both sides to play for: an England victory would see them overtake India as the no.1 ranked side in Test cricket. England batted after winning the toss, but slipped to 97 for 2. Then **Ian Bell** (left, 235) and **Kevin Pietersen** (175) added an all-time series record 350 runs for the third wicket. After posting 591 for 6 declared, England won the match by an innings and 8 runs to complete a 4–0 series whitewash and claim the no.1 ranking.

England post record total in massive win

Having dismissed India for a below-par 224 in their first innings in the third Test at Edgbaston in August 2011, England were keen to maintain their advantage over the visitors ... and how they did so. Led by Alastair Cook (294 – the second highest individual score in matches between the two sides) and Eoin Morgan (104), the home side posted 710 for 7 – the highest total in England–India Tests – and went on to win the match by an innings and 242 runs to take an unassailable 3–0 lead in the four-match series.

Gavaskar proves his worth in the field

Not only is Sunil Gavaskar the leading run-scorer in Test matches between England and India (with 2,483 runs), he is also the most successful fielder. In 38 Tests against England between 1971 and 1986, the diminutive opening batsman took a record 35 catches.

MOST RUNS: TOP 10

Pos	Player	Runs
1	S.M. Gavaskar (India, 1971–86)	2,483
2	S.R. Tendulkar (India, 1990–2011)	2.423
3	R. Dravid (India, 1996–2011)	1,950
4	G.R. Viswanath (India, 1971–82)	1,880
5	G.A. Gooch (England, 1979–93)	1,725
6	D.B. Vengsarkar (India, 1977–90)	1,589
7	D.I. Gower (England, 1979–90)	1,391
8	K.F. Barrington (England, 1959–67)	1,355
=	Kapil Dev (India, 1979–93)	1,355
10	M. Azharuddin (India, 1984–96)	1,278

MOST WICKETS: TOP 10

Pos	Player	Wickets
1	B.S. Chandrasekhar (India, 1964–79)	95
2	A. Kumble (India, 1990–2007)	92
3	B.S. Bedi (India, 1967–79)	85
=	Kapil Dev (India, 1979–93)	85
5	D.L. Underwood (England, 1971–82)	62
=	R.G.D. Willis (England, 1974–82)	62
7	I.T. Botham (England, 1979–82)	59
8	M.H. Mankad (India, 1946–52)	54
9	F.S. Trueman (England, 1952–59)	53
10	J.K. Lever (England, 1976–86)	45
=	J.M Anderson (England, 2006–11)	45

Most successful captain

One of the quirks of England's destruction of India in the much-hyped but ultimately anti-climatic 2011 series was that Andrew Strauss became the most successful captain in England–India Test matches, having recorded four wins at the helm.

Fiery Fred routs India

Batting on an already green wicket that had been further softened by rain, India's batsmen could find no answer to the pace and hostility of **Fred Trueman** in the Third Test of the 1952 series at Old Trafford. In 8.4 electrifying overs, the legendary Yorkshire fast bowler took 8 for 31 – the best single-innings figures in all Tests between England and India – to propel England to an eventual innings-and-207-run victory.

Gooch's Indian summer

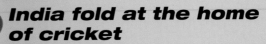

Graham Gooch, England's all-time leading run-scorer, was in the form of his life in the 1990 series against India. In the First Test at Lord's he hit 333 in the first innings (the highest individual score in all Tests between the two countries) and 123 in the second – his match aggregate of 456 runs is the highest in Test history. The Essex man's rich vein of form continued in the Second Test at Old Trafford, where he made 116 and 7, and knocks of 85 and 88 in the third and final Test at The Oval meant that he finished the three-match series with an England-India series record 752 runs to his name at the impressive average of 125.33.

India fold at the home of cricket

Trailing England by 327 runs after the completion of the first innings in the Second Test at Lord's in June 1974, India were asked to follow on and then gave up the fight in sorry fashion, subsiding to an embarrassing 42 all out in just 17 overs – the lowest total in all Test matches between England and India – and losing the match by the massive margin of an innings and 285 runs.

Barrington reserves his best for India

A player who learnt to curb his natural attacking instincts to become one of the most obdurate batsmen England has ever produced, Ken Barrington enjoyed some particularly good times against India. In 14 matches against them between 1959 and 1967 he scored 1,355 runs (with three centuries and a highest score of 172 at Kanpur in December 1961) at an average of 75.27 – the highest of any batsman to have completed ten or more innings in Test matches between the two countries.

Chandra's box of tricks confounds England

One of the major factors behind India's 2–1 series victory over England in 1972–73 was the England batsmen's continued inability to unravel the secrets of leg-spinner Bhagwath Chandrasekhar's box of tricks. The Karnataka spin wizard used his dazzling array of leg-spinners, top-spinners, googlies and sliders to great effect, taking four five-wicket hauls in five Tests (with a best of 8 for 79 in the First Test at Delhi), and ended the series with 35 wickets to his name – a record for an England-India series.

NZ v AUSTRALIA

Given that New Zealand have been playing Test cricket since 1930, it seems strange that they had to wait 16 years before playing near-neighbours Australia for the first time – at Wellington, a match they ended up losing by an innings and 103 runs. And Australia have generally dominated the Kiwis from that moment on, winning 27 of the 52 Test matches played and losing only eight.

Most productive partnership

The most productive partnership in all Tests between New Zealand and Australia is that between Matthew Hayden and Justin Langer. The Aussie pair combined to score 961 runs in 13 innings between 2000 and 2005 at an average of 73.92.

OVERALL SERIES RECORDS

(52 Tests between 1946 and 2011)

	W	L	T	D	W/L	%W	%L	%D
New Zealand	8	27	0	17	0.29	15.36	51.42	32.69
Australia	27	8	0	17	3.37	51.42	15.36	32.69

First match: 29–30 March 1946, Wellington, New Zealand

Most catches

The seventh most prolific fielder in Test history (with 156 catches), Allan Border leads the fielding list in Australia-New Zealand clashes. The former Australian captain bagged 31 catches in 23 Tests against New Zealand between 1980 and 1993.

Australia secure series win in style

Holding a 1–0 lead in the 1993–94 series going into the Third and final Test at Brisbane, Australia soon extinguished any hopes New Zealand might have had of squaring the series. First they dismissed New Zealand for 233; then, with Steve Waugh (147 not out) and Allan Border (105) starring, they batted their opponents out of the game, compiling a massive 607 for 6 declared – the highest team total in all matches between the two countries – en route to completing an innings-and-96-run victory.

Most dismissals

Rod Marsh heads the wicketkeeping list in all Tests between Australia and New Zealand. The Western Australian gloveman claimed 58 scalps in 14 Tests against New Zealand between 1973 and 1982 with 57 catches and one stumping.

Brothers in arms

Coming to the wicket with Australia in trouble at 55 for 2 in the First Test against New Zealand at Wellington in March 1974, brothers **Ian** (right, 145) and **Greg Chappell** (left, 247 not out) combined to record-breaking effect, putting on 264 runs for the third wicket (an all-time record in Australia-New Zealand Tests) to help their side to 511 for 6 declared. The match eventually fizzled out into a draw.

Ponting prospers against New Zealand

Ricky Ponting is the most successful captain in the history of Tests between Australia and New Zealand. The Australian captain, the most successful skipper in Test history, led his side to eight wins over New Zealand in nine Tests between 2004 and 2010.

Katich prospers against Black Caps

An obdurate middle-order batsman in the early part of his career who became an effective opener for Australia, Simon Katich enjoyed many highlights in matches against New Zealand. In seven Tests against the Black Caps between 2005 and 2010, the Western Australian plundered 643 runs (with three centuries and a highest score of 131 not out in the first Test at Brisbane in November 2008) at an average of 80.37 – the highest of any batsman to have completed ten or more innings in Australia-New Zealand Tests.

Inauspicious beginnings

New Zealand got off to the worst possible start in their first-ever Test match against Australia at Wellington in March 1946. Having won the toss and elected to bat, they capitulated to a sorry 42 all out in 39 overs – the lowest total in Australia-New Zealand Test matches. The Kiwis fared little better in the second innings, limping to 54 all out – the second-lowest total in the series – to lose the match by an innings and 103 runs.

Walters digs Australia out of a considerable hole

With Australia struggling on 112 for 4 in the First Test against New Zealand at Christchurch in February 1977, they were in desperate need of a rescue act from one of their batsmen. And Doug Walters came to the party in style, hitting a magnificent 342-ball 250, the highest individual score in all Australia-New Zealand Tests, to help his side to 552 all out. It wasn't enough to win the match, however, as New Zealand eventually held on to force a draw.

Chappell cashes in against the Kiwis

Greg Chappell was the star of the show as Australia came back from 1–0 down to square the series against New Zealand in 1973–74. The middle-order batsman hit two centuries in three Tests, with a highest score of 247 not out in the First Test at Wellington, and ended the series with 449 runs – a record for Test matches between the two countries – at an average of 89.80.

MOST RUNS: TOP 10

Pos	Player	Runs
1	**A.R. Border** (Australia, 1980–93)	1,500
2	J.G. Wright (New Zealand, 1980–93)	1,277
3	M.D. Crowe (New Zealand, 1982–93)	1,255
4	J.L. Langer (Australia, 1993–2005)	1,196
5	D.C. Boon (Australia, 1985–93)	1,187
6	S.R. Waugh (Australia, 1986–2001)	1,117
7	G.S. Chappell (Australia, 1973–82)	1,076
=	R.T. Ponting (Australia, 1997–2011)	1,076
9	N.J. Astle (New Zealand, 1997–2005)	930
10	A.C. Gilchrist (Australia, 2000–05)	923

MOST WICKETS: TOP 10

Pos	Player	Wickets
1	R.J. Hadlee (New Zealand, 1973–90)	130
2	S.K. Warne (Australia, 1993–2005)	103
3	D.L. Vettori (New Zealand, 1997–2011)	65
4	G.D. McGrath (Australia, 1993–2005)	57
5	C.J. McDermott (Australia, 1985–93)	48
6	B. Lee (Australia, 2000–08)	44
7	C.L. Cairns (New Zealand, 1989–2001)	39
8	D.K. Lillee (Australia, 1977–82)	38
=	J.G. Bracewell (New Zealand, 1980–90)	38
10	D.K. Morrison (New Zealand, 1987–93)	37

Sir Richard stuns Australia

One of the outstanding bowlers in Test cricket's long history, **Richard Hadlee** finished his Test career in 1990 with 431 wickets, and between 1988 and 1994 he was the game's all-time leading wicket-taker in Tests. Hadlee, perhaps more than any other bowler for any country, often carried New Zealand's fortunes on a cricket pitch and the fast bowler was often at his brilliant best against Australia. In November 1985 at Brisbane, he decimated Australia with 9 for 52 in the first innings (the best single-innings figures in all Tests between the two countries) and ended with match figures of 15 for 123 (another record). He completed the three-match series – which New Zealand won 2–1 (their only series win on Australian soil) – with 33 wickets (another record in Australia-New Zealand clashes).

AUSTRALIA v INDIA

Although Australia enjoyed a sustained period of dominance over India – they won six and drew one of the first seven series – since 1979 series wins on the subcontinent have almost proved as elusive as the Holy Grail for the men from Down Under. They have recorded only one victory (as opposed to India's six) in their last eight attempts on Indian soil.

Most dismissals

The history books will record that Adam Gilchrist was a hard-hitting batsman who had the ability to take a match away from the opposition in one innings, but he was also a more than capable wicketkeeper who enjoyed considerable success against India. In 18 Tests against them between 1999 and 2008 he claimed 75 scalps, with 73 catches and two stumpings – an all-time record in Tests between the two countries.

OVERALL SERIES RECORDS

(82 Tests between 1947 and 2012)

	W	L	T	D	W/L	%W	%L	%D
Australia	38	20	1	23	1.90	46.34	24.39	28.04
India	20	38	1	23	0.52	24.39	46.34	28.04

First match: 28 November–4 December 1947, Brisbane, Australia

India challenge Australia's dominance

It was decisive proof of just how much India's fortunes had improved on Australian soil. With the series tied at 1–1 going into the Fourth and final Test at Sydney in January 2004, India won the toss, elected to bat, and batted Australia out of the game. Stunning batting from **Sachin Tendulkar** (241 not out) and V.V.S. Laxman (178), helped them to compile a massive 705 for 7 over seven sessions of the match – the highest total in all Tests between the two countries. The match ended in a draw, ensuring that India retained the Border-Gavaskar trophy.

Brilliant Bradman puts India to the sword

Just as England, South Africa and the West Indies had discovered before them, India found out how good a player **Donald Bradman** was when Test cricket's greatest-ever batsman played his one and only series against them in 1947–48. Bradman struck four centuries in six innings, with a highest score of 201 in the Fourth Test at Adelaide, and ended the series with a haul of 715 runs (a record for an Australia-India series) at the astonishing average of 178.75.

Patel powers India to historic victory

Jasubhai Patel's sensational bowling performance in the Second Test at Kanpur in December 1959 was a major factor in India's first-ever Test victory over Australia. The off-spinner took 9 for 69, the best single-innings figures in Australia-India Test matches, in the first innings and 5 for 55 in the second as India won the match by 119 runs.

Shastri shines against Australia

An obdurate batsman who enjoyed considerable success both as an opener and in the middle order, and a player of huge importance to India for over a decade, Ravi Shastri enjoyed particular success against Australia. In nine Tests against them between 1985 and 1992 he scored 622 runs, including two centuries (with a highest score of 206 at Sydney in January 1992) at an average of 77.75 – the highest of any player in history to have completed ten or more innings in all Tests between the two countries.

Most successful captain

Bobby Simpson of Australia is the most successful captain in all Australia–India Tests. In ten Tests against the Indians between 1964 and 1978 (when he emerged from retirement, aged 41, to lead a side decimated by the departure of several players to World Series cricket), he led Australia to six wins.

Clarke leads from the front

With Australia holding a 1–0 series lead after a 122-run victory in the first Test and dismissing India for a sub-standard 191 in the first innings of the second Test at Sydney in January 2012, the Aussies were ready to put the visitors to the sword. Instead, they slipped to 37 for 3. Then Michael Clarke, the Australian captain, produced an innings of the highest quality: batting for 609 minutes, he faced 468 balls and struck 329 not out – the highest innings in Australia-India Tests. Australia declared on 659 for 4 and won by an innings and 68 runs.

Most catches

The safest pair of hands in Test history – with 210 catches he has taken more catches than any other player – Rahul Dravid also heads the Australia-India fielding list, taking 46 catches in 32 Tests against Australia between 1996 and 2012.

India bewildered in Brisbane

Unfortunate in many ways to be caught on a treacherous pitch in their first-ever Test match against Australia at Brisbane in November–December 1947, India's batsmen were horribly out of their depth. Having seen Australia compile 382 for 8 declared in the first innings, India collapsed to 58 all out in 21.3 (eight-ball) overs – the lowest-ever total in Australia-India Tests. Following on, they fared little better in the second innings, dismissed for 98 to lose the match by an innings and 226 runs.

MOST WICKETS: TOP 10

Pos	Player	Wickets
1	**A. Kumble** (India, 1996–2008)	111
2	Harbhajan Singh (India, 1998–2010)	90
3	Kapil Dev (India, 1979–92)	79
4	Z. Khan (India, 2001–12)	61
5	E.A.S. Prasanna (India, 1967–78)	57
6	B.S. Bedi (India, 1968–78)	56
7	N.S. Yadav (India, 1979–86)	55
8	B. Lee (Australia, 1999–2008)	53
9	R. Benaud (Australia, 1956–60)	52
10	G.D. McGrath (Australia, 1996–2004)	51

MOST RUNS: TOP 10

Pos	Player	Runs
1	S.R. Tendulkar (India, 1991–2012)	3,438
2	R.T. Ponting (Australia, 1996–2012)	2,555
3	V.V.S. Laxman (India, 1998–2012)	2,434
4	R. Dravid (India, 1996–2012)	2,143
5	M.L. Hayden (Australia, 2001–08)	1,888
6	V. Sehwag (India, 2003–12)	1,711
7	M.J. Clarke (Australia, 2004–12)	1,628
8	A.R. Border (Australia, 1979–92)	1,567
9	S.M. Gavaskar (India, 1977–86)	1,550
10	G.R. Viswanath (India, 1969–81)	1,538

The Turbanator torments Australia

In March 2001, having sneaked a sensational come-from-behind victory to level the series in the Second Test at Kolkata, India carried their momentum into the Third and final Test of the series at Chennai, largely thanks to **Harbhajan Singh**. "The Turbanator" took 7 for 133 in Australia's first innings and 8 for 84 in the second – his match figures of 15 for 217 are the best in all matches between the two countries – to help India to a two-wicket win and a memorable series victory. Harbhajan's 32 wickets in the series is also a record in Australia-India Tests.

Partners in crime

The most productive partnership in all Tests between Australia and India has been that of Sachin Tendulkar and Rahul Dravid, The pair has batted together on 28 occasions and have produced 1,564 runs (with an average partnership of 60.15 runs and a highest of 169, in the third Test at Chennai in March 2001). The highest partnership in Tests between the two countries is 386, between Michael Clarke (210) and Ricky Ponting (221) in the fourth Test at Adelaide in January 2012; a match Australia went on to win by 298 runs.

INDIA v WEST INDIES

In the early days of this fixture, India's misfortunes were blamed on a lack of experience of playing on hard, bouncy surfaces against a battery of fast bowlers, but in recent times the balance of power has started to shift in India's favour. Of their total of 14 victories against the islanders (in contrast the West Indies have won 30 times), nine of those have come in the 18 Tests played since 2002.

Most catches

No player in the history of India-West Indies Test matches has taken more catches than Viv Richards. The legendary Antiguan claimed 39 victims in 28 Tests against India between 1974 and 1989.

OVERALL SERIES RECORDS

(88 Tests between 1948 and 2011)

	W	L	T	D	W/L	%W	%L	%D
India	14	30	0	44	0.46	15.90	34,09	50.00
West Indies	30	14	0	44	2.14	34,09	15.90	50.00

First match: 10–14 November 1948, Delhi, India

Most productive partnership

The most productive partnership in all Tests between India and the West Indies is that of Gordon Greenidge and Desmond Haynes. The formidable opening pair combined to score 1,325 runs in 30 innings between 1983 and 1989 at an average of 45.68.

Magical debut for Hirwani

It was the most remarkable bowling performance by a debutant in Test history. In the Fourth Test against the West Indies at Chennai in January 1988, India's leg-spinner Narendra Hirwani took 8 for 61 in the first innings and 8 for 75 in the second to bowl his side to a 255-run victory. His match figures of 16 for 136 – the best by a Test debutant in history – are the best in all matches between the two countries.

Dujon heads the dismissals list

The most successful West Indian wicketkeeper in Test history (with 270 dismissals to his name), Jeff Dujon also heads the list in matches between the West Indies and India. In 19 Tests against the Indians between 1983 and 1989, he claimed 60 scalps (with 58 catches and two stumpings).

Magnificent Marshall leads the way

• **Malcolm Marshall** played a significant role in the West Indies' 3–0 series victory in India in 1983–84. The Barbados paceman took two five-wicket hauls, the best being 6 for 37 in the Fifth Test at Kolkata, to end the series with 33 wickets – an all-time series record between the two countries.

India lose the initiative in record-breaking style

India made the worst possible start to the 1987–88 home series against the West Indies in November 1987. Having won the toss and elected to bat, they would have been planning to compile a first-innings total in the region of 400 and put the islanders under pressure; instead they folded to 75 all out – the lowest total in all matches between the two sides – and went on to lose the match by five wickets.

A maiden century to remember

A regular in a strong West Indies batting line-up for 16 years, Rohan Kanhai had to wait until his 13th Test, 19 months after making his debut, to record his first three-figure score in international cricket, but rarely has a wait been so worthwhile. In the Third Test of the 1958–59 series at Kolkata, the diminutive right-hander plundered a magnificent 256 – the highest individual score in all matches between the two countries – and the West Indies went on to win the match by an innings and 336 runs.

644 is the limit

Both sides have recorded totals of 644 in Tests between the two countries: India achieved the total (for the loss of seven wickets) in the Sixth and final Test of the 1978–79 series at Kanpur – a match which they drew to secure a 1–0 series victory; the West Indies achieved the same total (for the loss of eight wickets) in the Fifth and final Test of the 1958–59 series in Delhi – that match also ended in a draw, which was enough to see the islanders claim the series 3–0.

A record-breaker in a losing cause

The West Indies eventually emerged victorious in the Third Test against India at Ahmedabad in November 1983 (winning the match by 138 runs), but only after being on the receiving end of a record-breaking effort by Kapil Dev. The greatest fast bowler India has ever produced took 9 for 83 in the West Indies' second innings – the best single-innings figures in all Tests between the two countries – to haul his side back into the match, only to see India's batsmen (chasing 242 for victory) slip to a sorry 103 all out in 47.1 overs.

Most successful captain

Clive Lloyd is the most successful captain in the history of Test matches between India and the West Indies. The legendary leader recorded ten wins in 20 Tests against India between 1974 and 1983.

Gavaskar and Vengsarkar make hay in the Kolkata sun

Taking advantage of a lifeless pitch, **Sunil Gavaskar** (with his 182 not out, following on from 107 in the first innings, he became the first batsman in history to score two hundreds in a Test on three occasions) and Dilip Vengsarkar (157 not out) prospered in record-breaking style in the second innings of the Third Test against the West Indies at Kolkata in 1978–79. The pair added 344 for the second wicket – an all-time record in matches between the two countries – to set the West Indies 335 runs for victory. The men from the Caribbean hung on in nervous style, however, finishing on 197 for 9 to secure a draw.

Wonderful Weekes prospers against India

Rarely has a batsman enjoyed such a continued streak of fine form in Test cricket's long history. In the West Indies' 1–0 series win in India, in 1948–49, **Everton Weekes** produced successive scores of 152, 194, 162, 101, 90, 56 and 48 to end the series with 779 runs to his name – an all-time record for a series between India and the West Indies – at an average of 111.28. Weekes's career average against the Indians (106.78 in ten Tests between 1948 and 1953) is also a record.

MOST RUNS: TOP 10

Pos	Player	Runs
1	**S.M. Gavaskar** (India, 1971–83)	2,749
2	C.H. Lloyd (West Indies, 1966–83)	2,344
3	S. Chanderpaul (W. Indies, 1994–2011)	2,038
4	R. Dravid (India, 1997–2011)	1,978
5	I.V.A. Richards (West Indies, 1974–89)	1,927
6	G.S. Sobers (West Indies, 1958–71)	1,920
7	V.V.S. Laxman (India, 1997–2011)	1,715
8	R.B. Kanhai (West Indies, 1958–71)	1,693
9	C.G. Greenidge (West Indies, 1974–89)	1,678
10	D.B. Vengsarkar (India, 1976–89)	1,596

MOST WICKETS: TOP 10

Pos	Player	Wickets
1	Kapil Dev (India, 1978–89)	89
2	M.D. Marshall (West Indies, 1978–89)	76
3	A. Kumble (India, 1994–2006)	74
4	S. Venkataraghavan (India, 1966–83)	68
5	A.M.E. Roberts (West Indies, 1974–83)	67
6	W.W. Hall (West Indies, 1958–67)	65
=	B.S. Chandrasekhar (India, 1966–79)	65
=	C.A. Walsh (West Indies, 1987–97)	65
9	L.R. Gibbs (West Indies, 1958–75)	63
10	B.S. Bedi (India, 1966–79)	62

NZ v WEST INDIES

Few contests in Test cricket demonstrate more clearly how much fortunes can change than those between New Zealand and the West Indies. Having previously won just two of 23 Tests against the islanders over a period of 35 years, New Zealand have now not lost a Test match against the West Indies since April 1996.

OVERALL SERIES RECORDS

(37 Tests between 1952 and 2008)

	W	L	T	D	W/L	%W	%L	%D
New Zealand	9	10	0	18	0.90	24.32	27.03	49.65
West Indies	10	9	0	18	1.11	27.03	24.32	49.65

First match: 8–12 February 1952, Christchurch, New Zealand

Down and out in Dunedin

New Zealand's early struggles against the West Indies were epitomized in the First Test at Dunedin in February 1956. Having won the toss and elected to bat, the home side's batsmen could find no answer to the spin bowling of Sonny Ramadhin (who took 6 for 23) and were dismissed for a paltry 74 all out – the lowest total in all Test matches between the two countries.

The Turner and Jarvis Show

Having seen the West Indies reach 365 for 7 declared in their first innings in the Fourth Test against New Zealand at Georgetown, Guyana, in April 1972, Glenn Turner (259) and Terry Jarvis (182) ensured New Zealand's reply got off to the perfect start. The opening pair added 387 runs for the first wicket – an all-time record in New Zealand-West Indies matches – to help their side to 543 for 3 declared. The game, however, petered out into a bore draw.

Most successful captain

The most successful captain in the history of Test matches between New Zealand and the West Indies is **Stephen Fleming**. The former New Zealand captain led his side to five wins in seven Tests between 1999 and 2006.

West Indies batsmen find their form when it matters

There is no better way of putting an opponent under pressure than compiling a huge first-innings total, and certainly no better time to do so than in a series-deciding Test match. That is exactly what the West Indies did in the Second Test against New Zealand at Wellington in February 1995, as centuries from Jimmy Adams (151), Brian Lara (147) and Junior Murray (101 not out) propelled them to 660 for 5 declared – the highest score in all Tests between the two countries – en route to an innings-and-322-run victory and a 1–0 series success.

Cairns turns match on its head

With the West Indies cruising on 276 for 0 towards the end of the first day's play in the First Test against New Zealand at Hamilton in December 1999, the chances of a home victory seemed remote. However, they ended up winning the match by nine wickets, and it had much to do with the second-innings bowling display of **Chris Cairns**. The all-rounder bagged 7 for 27 off 22.5 overs – the best figures in New Zealand-West Indies Tests and the best figures by any New Zealand bowler other than Richard Hadlee in history – to help dismiss the West Indies for 97 and pave the way for an unlikely victory.

Turner's Caribbean triumph

Glenn Turner was outstanding for New Zealand in the country's first-ever tour to the Caribbean in 1971–72. In a drawn five-match series – a result considered a huge triumph for New Zealand at the time – the straight-batted, dogged opener hit two memorable double-centuries, with a best of 259 in the Fourth Test at Georgetown, Guyana (the highest individual score in all matches between the two countries), and ended the series with 672 runs (at an average of 96.00). It is the highest series haul in the history of New Zealand-West Indies Test matches.

Courtney ensures New Zealand crumble

With his batsmen having put his side in a commanding position in the Second Test against New Zealand at Wellington in February 1995, amassing a mighty first-innings total of 660 for 5 declared, it was time for West Indies captain Courtney Walsh to turn the screw. He took 7 for 37 in New Zealand's first innings and 6 for 18 in their second to lead his side to a series-clinching innings-and-332-run victory. His match figures of 13 for 55 are the best in all Tests between the two countries.

A record shared

The record for the most wickets in a series between the two countries is 27, a feat achieved by two bowlers: New Zealand's Bruce Taylor in the 1971–72 series in the Caribbean; and Malcolm Marshall of the West Indies in the 1984–85 series in New Zealand.

Most dismissals

West Indies wicketkeeper Jeff Dujon leads the dismissals list in all Tests between the two countries. The Jamaican gloveman claimed 20 scalps (all catches) in seven Tests against New Zealand between 1985 and 1987.

MOST RUNS: TOP 10

Pos	Player	Runs
1	C.G. Greenidge (West Indies, 1980–87)	882
2	G.M. Turner (New Zealand, 1969–72)	855
3	D.L. Haynes (West Indies, 1980–87)	843
4	C.H. Gayle (West Indies, 2002–08)	820
5	B.E. Congdon (New Zealand, 1969–72)	764
6	S. Chanderpaul (W. Indies, 1995–2008)	729
7	N.J. Astle (New Zealand, 1996–2006)	715
8	B.C. Lara (West Indies, 1995–2006)	704
9	**S.P. Fleming** (New Zealand, 1995–2006)	703
10	S.L. Campbell (West Indies, 1995–99)	598
=	L.G. Rowe (West Indies, 1972–80)	598

MOST WICKETS: TOP 10

Pos	Player	Wickets
1	R.J. Hadlee (New Zealand, 1980–87)	51
2	C.A. Walsh (West Indies, 1985–99)	43
3	J. Garner (West Indies, 1980–87)	36
4	M.D. Marshall (West Indies, 1985–87)	36
5	D.L. Vettori (New Zealand, 1999–2008)	33
6	B.R. Taylor (New Zealand, 1969–72)	32
=	S. Ramadhin (West Indies, 1952–56)	32
8	A.L. Valentine (West Indies, 1952–56)	23
=	E.J. Chatfield (New Zealand, 1985–87)	23
10	S.E. Bond (New Zealand, 2002–06)	20
=	G.B. Troup (New Zealand, 1980–85)	20

Gayle saves his best for New Zealand

A hard-hitting left-hand opening batsman who has gained a reputation for treating all types of bowling with contempt, **Chris Gayle** has, unlike the rest of his team-mates in recent times, prospered against New Zealand. In seven Tests against the Kiwis he has hit 820 runs, including two centuries (with a highest score of 204 at St George's, Grenada, in June 2002) at an average of 75.54 – the highest of any batsman to have completed ten or more innings in all matches between the two teams.

INDIA v PAKISTAN

Given the historic and uneasy relationship between the two countries – they were born out of the bitterness of India's partition in 1947 – this is the most tension-fuelled and politically driven fixture in international cricket. Since the contest was first played back in 1952, Pakistan lead the way with 12 wins to India's nine.

Wasim Bari heads the keepers list

A veteran of 81 Test matches for Pakistan, Wasim Bari has claimed more dismissals than any other wicketkeeper in Tests between India and Pakistan. In 18 matches against India between 1978 and 1983, the greatest keeper his country has ever produced bagged 55 victims (with 50 catches and five stumpings).

India all at sea as they take their bow in Pakistan

India's batsmen played like fish out of water on the jute-matting pitch used for the first-ever Test match between the two countries to be played in Pakistan. Having won the toss and elected to bat, India slipped to 106 all out in 55.1 overs in three hours 20 minutes – still the lowest-ever team total in matches between India and Pakistan – and went on to lose by an innings and 43 runs.

Super Sehwag at his brilliant best

A stunning innings by **Virender Sehwag** was at the heart of India's innings-and-52-run victory over Pakistan in the First Test at Multan in March–April 2004. The free-scoring opener smashed a sensational 309 runs off 375 balls (with 39 fours and six sixes) – the highest individual score in all matches between the two countries – to help his side to a mighty first-innings total of 675 for 5 declared. And this was far from an isolated case of success against Pakistan: Sehwag's career average against them of 91.14 – in nine Tests between 2004 and 2006 (which includes three double-centuries) – is the highest of any player to have completed ten or more innings in India-Pakistan matches.

OVERALL SERIES RECORDS

(59 Tests between 1952 and 2007)

	W	L	T	D	W/L	%W	%L	%D
India	9	12	0	38	0.75	15.25	20.34	64.41
Pakistan	12	9	0	38	1.33	20.34	15.25	64.41

First match: 16–18 October 1952, Delhi, India

Priority lies in building a big score

The fear of defeat lies at the very heart of this fixture: as a result, 38 of the 59 Tests contested between the two countries have been drawn, and the overriding mentality appears to be to bat yourself into a position of absolute safety before even thinking about trying to win the game. As a result, there have been nine scores of 600 plus in matches between the two countries, the highest of which was 699 for 5 declared, achieved by Pakistan in the Third Test at Lahore in December 1989 – a match that, not surprisingly, ended in a draw.

Kumble puts Pakistan in a spin

It will go down in history as one of the best single-innings bowling performances in Test history, bettered, indeed, only by Jim Laker's remarkable effort against Australia at Old Trafford in 1956. Having taken 4 for 75 in Pakistan's first innings in the Second Test at Delhi in February 1999, **Anil Kumble** became only the second bowler in Test history to take ten wickets in an innings (10 for 74) to bowl India to a 212-run victory. Kumble's match figures of 14 for 149 are the best in all Tests between the two countries.

MOST RUNS: TOP 10

Pos	Player	Runs
1	Javed Miandad (Pakistan, 1978–89)	2,228
2	S.M. Gavaskar (India, 1978–87)	2,089
3	Zaheer Abbas (Pakistan, 1978–84)	1,740
4	**Mudassar Nazar** (Pakistan, 1978–84)	1,431
5	Younis Khan (Pakistan, 2005–07)	1,321
6	D.B. Vengsarkar (India, 1978–87)	1,284
7	V. Sehwag (India, 2004–06)	1,276
8	Mohammad Yousuf (Pakistan, 1999–2007)	1,247
9	R. Dravid (India, 1999–2007)	1,236
10	**Imran Khan** (Pakistan, 1978–89)	1,091

MOST WICKETS: TOP 10

Pos	Player	Wickets
1	Kapil Dev (India, 1978–89)	99
2	Imran Khan (Pakistan, 1978–89)	94
3	A Kumble (India, 1999–2007)	81
4	Wasim Akram (Pakistan, 1987–99)	45
5	Fazal Mahmood (Pakistan, 1952–61)	44
6	Danish Kaneria (Pakistan, 2004–07)	43
7	Mahmood Hussain (Pakistan, 1952–61)	39
8	M.H. Mankad (India, 1952–55)	37
9	Sarfraz Nawaz (Pakistan, 1978–83)	36
10	S.P. Gupte (India, 1952–61)	34
=	Iqbal Qasim (Pakistan, 1978–87)	34

Imran's record-breaking haul sparks Pakistan

Where Mudassar Nazar excelled with the bat in Pakistan's stunning 3–0 series victory over arch-rivals India in 1982–83, Imran Khan was the star of the show with the ball. The Pakistan captain took four five-wicket hauls (with a best of 8 for 60 in the Second Test at Karachi) and two ten-wicket match hauls to end the victorious series with 40 wickets – an all-time record series haul in all matches between India and Pakistan.

Imran is the most successful leader

In a fixture not renowned for producing a result – only 35.59 per cent of matches between India and Pakistan have produced a victory for either side – Pakistan's **Imran Khan** is the most successful captain in contests between the two countries, recording four wins in 15 Tests between 1982 and 1989.

Most productive partnership

The most productive partnership in all Tests between India and Pakistan is that of Younis Khan and Mohammad Yousuf. The pair have combined to score 1,372 runs in nine innings between 2005 and 2007 at an average of 171.50.

Leading Pakistan to safety in record-breaking style

With Pakistan losing two wickets in successive deliveries to fall to 60 for 2 and into potential danger against India in the Fourth Test at Hyderabad in January 1983, Mudassar Nazar (231, and in the form of his life) and Javed Miandad (280 not out) steadied the ship in spectacular style. The pair added 451 for the third wicket – the highest partnership in all matches between the two countries – paving the way to Pakistan's 581 for 3 declared and an eventual innings-and-119-run victory.

A safe pair of hands

The record for the most catches in matches between India and Pakistan is 19, a feat achieved by two players: Sunil Gavaskar (India) in 24 Tests between 1978 and 1987; and Rahul Dravid (India) in 15 Tests between 1999 and 2007.

Magical Mudassar piles on the runs

Mudassar Nazar laid the foundations for Pakistan's 3–0 series victory over India in 1982–83. The opener was in sensational form with the bat, hitting four centuries – with a highest score of 231 in the Fourth Test at Hyderabad – and ending the series with 761 runs to his name (at an average of 126.83), an all-time record haul in Test matches between the two countries.

ENGLAND v PAKISTAN

Test matches between England and Pakistan have never been short of drama – who could forget Mike Gatting's finger-pointing rant at umpire Shakoor Rana at Faisalabad in December 1987 or Pakistan's refusal to play after the tea interval following ball-tampering allegations at The Oval in August 2006? But they are also closely contested affairs, with England recording 22 wins to Pakistan's 16.

Strauss is most successful captain

England's Andrew Strauss is the most successful captain in the history of matches between England and Pakistan. He has recorded six wins in eight Tests against Pakistan between 2006 and 2010.

OVERALL SERIES RECORDS

(74 Tests between 1954 and 2012)

	W	L	T	D	W/L	%W	%L	%D
England	22	16	0	36	1.37	29.72	21.62	48.64
Pakistan	16	22	0	36	0.72	21.62	29.72	48.64

First match: 10–15 June 1954, Lord's

Most dismissals

Wasim Bari, Pakistan's most successful wicket-keeper of all time, is the most prolific keeper in all Tests between England and Pakistan. In 24 matches against England between 1967 and 1982 he claimed 54 dismissals, with 50 catches and four stumpings.

Record-breaking effort in a losing cause for Pakistan

For the time being, at least, it was a partnership that kept Pakistan in the Second Test at Headingley in August 2006. Pakistan were trailing 1–0 in the series, and having seen England compile a healthy first-innings total of 515 all out, and then both openers fall in quick succession, the visitors needed senior players Mohammad Yousuf and Younis Khan to stand up and deliver. They did so in magnificent style, putting on 363 for the third wicket (Yousuf with 192 and Khan with 173) – the highest partnership in all matches between the two countries – to help Pakistan to 538 all out. But their effort was all in vain: Pakistan's second-innings collapse (155 all out) saw England win the game by 167 runs.

Most productive partnership

The most productive partnership in all Tests between England and Pakistan is that of Mohammad Yousuf and Inzamam-ul-Haq. The pair combined to score 901 runs in nine innings between 2000 and 2006 at an impressive average of 112.62.

Compton cashes in against uncertain Pakistan

Denis Compton made the most of Pakistan's problems in adjusting to both the cold weather and a damp wicket in the Second Test at Trent Bridge in July 1954. The Middlesex star crashed his highest Test score of 278 (with 34 fours and one six) – also the highest score in matches between the two countries – to help England to a massive first-innings total of 558 for 6 declared and an eventual innings-and-129-run victory.

Dexter saves his best for Pakistan

Ted Dexter enjoyed plenty of good times with the bat against Pakistan. In ten innings he recorded his highest Test score, 205 in the Third Test at Faisalabad in February 1962, and compiled 749 runs at an average of 93.62 – the highest of any batsman to have completed ten or more innings in Tests between the two countries.

Pakistan flattened at Edgbaston

One-nil down in the four-match series going into the Second Test against England at Edgbaston in August 2010, Pakistan won the toss, elected to bat and, in the face of fine seam bowling from James Anderson (4 for 20) and Stuart Broad (4 for 38), collapsed in spectacular fashion to 72 all out – the lowest score in all Tests between the two countries. But England, set only 145 in the second innings to win the second Test of a three-match series in the UAE, equalled Pakistan's sorry feat, and lost by 72 runs.

Batsmen power Pakistan to historic series win

It was some way to secure a first-ever series victory on English soil. Holding a 1–0 lead going into the fifth and final Test at The Oval in August 1987, Pakistan won a crucial toss, elected to bat, and soon extinguished any hopes England might have had of winning the match when they compiled a massive 708 all out, with centuries from Javed Miandad (260), Saleem Malik (102) and Imran Khan (118 not out). It is the highest total in all matches between the two countries.

Underwood thrives at a rain-sodden Lord's

There has been no more destructive bowler on a rain-affected wicket in Test history than "Deadly" Derek Underwood, and the Kent left-arm spinner took full advantage of the damp conditions in the Second Test against Pakistan at Lord's in August 1974. He took 5 for 20 in the first innings and 8 for 51 in the second to end with match figures of 13 for 71 – the best in all Tests between England and Pakistan. The weather had the final say in the match, however, and it ended in a draw.

Qadir's box of tricks too much for England

England's 1987 tour to Pakistan is best remembered, sadly, for the on-the-field tensions and arguments between the English players and the match officials – all of which completely overshadowed **Abdul Qadir**'s stunning performances with the ball throughout the series. In the First Test at Lahore, the leg-spinner got Pakistan off to the perfect start, taking 9 for 56 to help dismiss England for 175 – the best single-innings figures in all matches between the two countries and a vital factor in Pakistan's eventual innings-and-87-run victory. Two further five-wicket hauls followed and Qadir ended the three-match series, which Pakistan won 1–0, with 30 wickets to his name – an all-time record in England-Pakistan matches.

Yousuf's lone resistance

Although England, the hosts, won the four-match series 3–0, many of the headlines during the 2006 series against Pakistan were reserved for the sensational batting performances of Mohammad Yousuf. The Pakistan middle-order batsman hit three centuries, with a highest score of 202 in the First Test at Lord's, and ended the series with 631 runs at an average of 90.14 – no batsman in the history of England-Pakistan Tests has scored more runs in a series.

Most catches

Javed Miandad holds the record for the most catches taken by a fielder in England-Pakistan Tests. The former Pakistan captain took 20 catches in 22 Tests against England between 1977 and 1992.

MOST RUNS: TOP 10

Pos	Player	Runs
1	**Inzamam-ul-Haq** (Pakistan, 1992–2006)	1,584
2	Mushtaq Mohammad (Pakistan, 1961–74)	1,554
3	Mohammad Yousuf (Pakistan, 2000–10)	1,499
4	Saleem Malik (Pakistan, 1984–96)	1,396
5	Javed Miandad (Pakistan, 1977–92)	1,329
6	D.I. Gower (England, 1978–92)	1,185
7	Zaheer Abbas (Pakistan, 1971–84)	1,086
8	Hanif Mohammad (Pakistan, 1954–69)	1,039
9	A.J. Stewart (England, 1992–2001)	994
10	T.W. Graveney (England, 1954–69)	943

MOST WICKETS: TOP 10

Pos	Player	Wickets
1	Abdul Qadir (Pakistan, 1977–87)	82
2	Wasim Akram (Pakistan, 1987–2001)	57
3	Waqar Younis (Pakistan, 1992–2001)	50
4	Intikhab Alam (Pakistan, 1961–74)	49
5	Imran Khan (Pakistan, 1971–87)	47
6	I.T. Botham (England, 1978–92)	40
7	Sarfraz Nawaz (Pakistan, 1969–84)	37
8	D.L. Underwood (England, 1967–74)	36
=	Saeed Ajmal (Pakistan, 2010–12)	36
10	G.P. Swann (England, 2010–12)	35

PAKISTAN v NZ

Pakistan's innings-and-one-run victory in their first-ever Test match against New Zealand at Karachi in October 1955 seemed to set the tone for contests between these two countries, which Pakistan have dominated: winning 23 of the 50 matches played as opposed to New Zealand's seven.

Record-breaking partnership at Dunedin

Mushtaq Mohammad (201) and Asif Iqbal (175) made the most of a placid wicket in the Second Test match of the 1972–73 series at Dunedin to take Pakistan into a dominant position. The pair added 350 runs for the fourth wicket (the highest partnership in the history of Tests between Pakistan and New Zealand) to lead their side to a commanding 507 for 6 declared and an eventual innings-and-166-run victory.

OVERALL SERIES RECORDS

(50 Tests between 1955 and 2011)

	W	L	T	D	W/L	%W	%L	%D
Pakistan	23	7	0	20	3.28	46.00	14.00	40.00
New Zealand	7	23	0	20	0.30	14.00	46.00	40.00

First match: 13–17 October 1955, Karachi, Pakistan

Pakistan power to huge victory

A massive first-innings score by Pakistan in the First Test against New Zealand at Lahore in May 2002 laid the foundations for the fifth-largest margin of victory in Test history. A century from Imran Nazir (127), playing in his first Test match in 17 months, and a magnificent triple-century from captain Inzamam-ul-Haq (329), propelled the home side to 643 all out – the largest total in all matches between the two countries – and an eventual innings-and-324-run victory.

Javed the king of the fielders

No player has taken more catches in Test matches between Pakistan and New Zealand than Javed Miandad. The former Pakistan captain bagged 20 catches in 18 Tests against the Kiwis between 1976 and 1993.

Inzamam defies injury to produce record-breaking knock

Inzamam-ul-Haq scored more than half of his team's runs (51.17 per cent) as Pakistan compiled the highest score in all matches between the two countries (643 all out) in the First Test at Lahore in May 2002. Crippled by cramp that prevented him from running between the wickets in the latter stages of his innings (and, controversially, denied a runner by New Zealand captain Stephen Fleming, given that he had sustained the injury while batting), he resorted to a boundary-only policy on the way to a magnificent 329 off 436 balls (with 38 fours and nine sixes) – it is the 13th highest score in Test history and the highest individual score in all Pakistan-New Zealand matches.

Most successful captain

Javed Miandad is the most successful captain in the history of Test matches between Pakistan and New Zealand, leading Pakistan to four wins in seven Tests against the Kiwis between 1985 and 1993.

Wily Waqar too good for New Zealand

While Shoaib Mohammad laid the foundations with his bat for Pakistan's 3–0 home series victory over New Zealand in 1990–91, hitting a series record 507 runs, **Waqar Younis** was the chief destroyer with the ball. The paceman took three five-wicket innings hauls and two ten-wicket match hauls (with a best of 12 for 130 in the third and final Test at Faisalabad – the best match haul in all Tests between the two countries) and ended the series with 29 wickets (another record in Pakistan-New Zealand Test matches).

Best bowling in an innings

The best single-innings bowling figures in matches between the two countries is 7 for 52, a feat achieved by two bowlers: Intikhab Alam (Pakistan), in the Second Test at Dunedin in February 1973; and Chris Pringle (New Zealand) in the Third Test at Faisalabad in October 1990.

All-time low for New Zealand in drawn Test

The first-ever series between Pakistan and New Zealand, in 1955, was a one-sided affair, but not a whitewash. However, it was only the heavy rain that fell over the first three days of the Third Test in Dhaka (now in Bangladesh), and not the tourists' batting, that prevented Pakistan from securing a 3–0 series victory, and even then the home side came very close. On a soaked matting wicket, they dismissed New Zealand for 70 all out in their first innings – the lowest team total in all Tests between the two countries – and had the Kiwis reeling on 69 for 6 in the second innings (still 56 runs adrift) before play was finally brought to a halt.

Prolific keeper heads dismissals list

Wasim Bari, Pakistan's most prolific and most capped wicketkeeper of all time, leads the all-time dismissals list in Pakistan-New Zealand Test matches. He claimed 32 scalps (27 catches and five stumpings) in 11 Tests against New Zealand between 1969 and 1979.

Most productive partnership

The most productive partnership in all Tests between Pakistan and New Zealand is that of Majid Khan and Sadiq Mohammad. The pair combined to score 811 runs in ten innings between 1973 and 1976 at an average of 90.11.

MOST RUNS: TOP 10

Pos	Player	Runs
1	Javed Miandad (Pakistan, 1976–93)	1,919
2	Asif Iqbal (Pakistan, 1965–79)	1,113
3	Inzamam-ul-Haq (Pakistan, 1993–2003)	1,059
4	M.D. Crowe (New Zealand, 1984–90)	973
5	Saleem Malik (Pakistan, 1984–96)	946
6	Majid Khan (Pakistan, 1965–79)	936
7	Shoaib Mohammad (Pakistan, 1984–90)	854
8	Mushtaq Mohammad (Pakistan, 1969–79)	779
9	M.G. Burgess (New Zealand, 1969–79)	753
10	Mohammad Yousuf (Pakistan, 2001–09)	747

MOST WICKETS: TOP 10

Pos	Player	Wickets
1	Waqar Younis (Pakistan, 1990–2002)	70
2	Wasim Akram (Pakistan, 1985–95)	60
3	Intikhab Alam (Pakistan, 1965–76)	54
4	R.J. Hadlee (New Zealand, 1973–89)	51
5	Pervez Sajjad (Pakistan, 1965–73)	45
6	Mushtaq Ahmed (Pakistan, 1993–2001)	35
7	C.S. Martin (New Zealand, 2001–11)	33
8	D.R. Tuffey (New Zealand, 2001–09)	32
9	Imran Khan (Pakistan, 1976–89)	31
=	D.K. Morrison (New Zealand, 1989–95)	31

Shoaib shines

Shoaib Mohammad was Pakistan's star with the bat as they trounced New Zealand 3–0 in the home series in 1990–91. The opening batsman scored three centuries in the three matches – with a highest score of 203 not out in the First Test at Karachi – and ended the series with 507 runs to his name (the highest haul by any batsman in a Pakistan-New Zealand series), some 357 runs more than Pakistan's next highest scorer (Javed Miandad, with 150 runs). His career average against New Zealand of 106.75 is the highest of any batsman to have completed 10 or more innings in Test matches between the two countries.

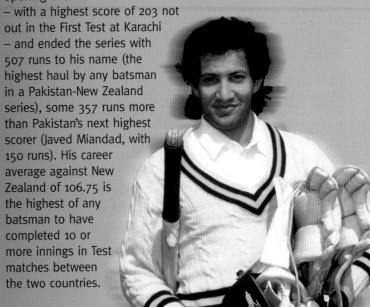

INDIA v NEW ZEALAND

New Zealand did not get off to the best of starts in Tests against India – it took them ten Test matches to record their first-ever victory (at Christchurch in February 1968) – but since that time Tests between the two countries have been reasonably even, with India recording 16 victories to New Zealand's nine.

Captain Dowling steers New Zealand to historic win

Captain Graham Dowling produced a record-breaking performance as New Zealand won the Second Test at Christchurch by six wickets in February 1968 to record their first-ever victory over India. Leading from the front in the first innings, the opener faced 519 balls to score 239 runs. It remains the highest individual score in all matches between the two countries.

OVERALL SERIES RECORDS

(50 Tests between 1955 and 2010)

	W	L	T	D	W/L	%W	%L	%D
India	16	9	0	25	1.77	32.00	18.00	50.00
New Zealand	9	16	0	25	0.56	18.00	32.00	50.00

First match: 19–24 November 1955, Hyderabad, India

Most successful captain

The prime beneficiary of India's early dominance over New Zealand, the Nawab of Pataudi (India) is the most successful captain in all Tests between India and New Zealand. He led his side to five victories in 11 Tests against the Kiwis between 1965 and 1969.

Smith the leading gloveman

A regular behind the stumps for New Zealand for nearly a decade, Ian Smith holds the record for the most dismissals in India-New Zealand Test matches. He pouched 29 victims (all catches) in nine Tests against India between 1981 and 1990.

Mankad and Roy lead India to comprehensive victory

India's Vinoo Mankad (231) and Pankaj Roy (173) dashed any hopes New Zealand might have had of squaring the 1955–56 series (India held a 1–0 lead) in the Fourth and final Test at Chennai. After India had won the toss and elected to bat, the pair put on an opening stand of 413 to help their side to a daunting first-innings total of 537 for 3 declared and an eventual innings-and-109-run victory. It remains the highest partnership in all Tests between the two countries.

Venkat spins India to series success

It took a record-breaking performance from **Srinivas Venkataraghavan** for India to edge to a seven-wicket victory in the Fourth and final Test against New Zealand in 1964–65 at Delhi. Bowling with accuracy and penetration, the off-spinner took 8 for 72 in the first innings (the best single-innings figures in all Tests between the two countries) and 4 for 80 in the second to finish with match figures of 12 for 152 (another India-New Zealand Test record).

Most productive partnership

The most productive partnership in all India-New Zealand Tests is that of India's **Sachin Tendulkar** (right) and **Rahul Dravid** (left). The pair have combined to score 860 runs in 16 innings against New Zealand between 1999 and 2010 at an average of 53.75.

MOST RUNS: TOP 10

Pos	Player	Runs
1	R. Dravid (India, 1998–2010)	1,659
2	S.R. Tendulkar (India, 1990–2010)	1,532
3	G.T. Dowling (New Zealand, 1965–69)	964
4	B. Sutcliffe (New Zealand, 1955–65)	885
5	V.V.S. Laxman (India, 2002–10)	818
6	J.G. Wright (New Zealand, 1981–90)	804
7	M. Azharuddin (India, 1988–99)	796
8	V. Sehwag (India, 2002–10)	755
9	M.G. Burgess (New Zealand, 1968–76)	725
10	B.E. Congdon (New Zealand, 1965–76)	713

MOST WICKETS: TOP 10

Pos	Player	Wickets
1	R.J. Hadlee (New Zealand, 1976–90)	65
2	B.S. Bedi (India, 1968–76)	57
3	E.A.S. Prasanna (India, 1968–76)	55
4	A. Kumble (India, 1994–2003)	50
5	S. Venkataraghavan (India, 1965–76)	44
6	Harbhajan Singh (India, 1998–2010)	43
7	D.L. Vettori (New Zealand, 1998–2010)	40
8	B.S. Chandrasekhar (India, 1965–76)	36
9	Z. Khan (India, 2002–10)	35
10	S.P. Gupte (India, 1955–56)	34

New Zealand compile record-breaking total at Mohali

Following New Zealand's match-saving heroics to deny India victory in the First Test at Ahmedabad, there was still everything to play for when the two sides met at Mohali for the second and final Test of the 2002–03 series. New Zealand won the toss and put themselves in a position of impregnability when – thanks to centuries from Mark Richardson (145), Lou Vincent (106), Scott Styris (119) and Craig McMillan (100 not out) – they amassed a mighty 630 for 6 declared, the highest team total in all matches between the two countries. On a placid wicket, however, New Zealand's bowlers failed to push home the advantage and the match ended in a draw.

Fleming is the catching king

Stephen Fleming, by some distance, is the most prolific fielder in New Zealand's history – he claimed 171 catches in 111 Tests; in second place on the all-time list is Martin Crowe with 71. Fleming also holds the record for the most catches in India-New Zealand Tests: he bagged 20 catches in 13 matches against India between 1994 and 2003.

Sutcliffe shines

The outstanding New Zealand batsman of the post-war period, **Bert Sutcliffe** stood tall while others around him wilted during the 1955–56 series in India. Although the Kiwis lost the series 2–0, the opener scored two centuries, with a highest score of 203 in the Third Test at Delhi, to end the series with 611 runs – a record in any India-New Zealand series. He seemed to prosper against the Indians: in 16 innings against them, he scored 885 runs at an average of 68.07 – the highest by any batsman to have completed ten innings or more in all Tests between the two countries.

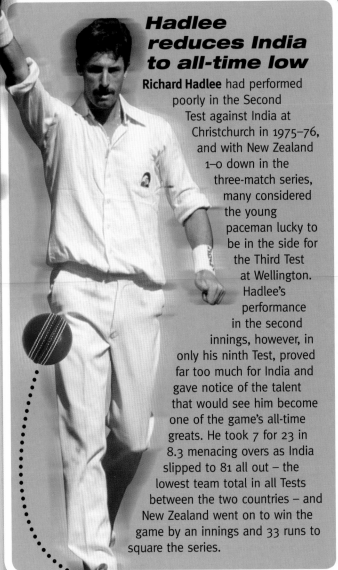

Hadlee reduces India to all-time low

Richard Hadlee had performed poorly in the Second Test against India at Christchurch in 1975–76, and with New Zealand 1–0 down in the three-match series, many considered the young paceman lucky to be in the side for the Third Test at Wellington. Hadlee's performance in the second innings, however, in only his ninth Test, proved far too much for India and gave notice of the talent that would see him become one of the game's all-time greats. He took 7 for 23 in 8.3 menacing overs as India slipped to 81 all out – the lowest team total in all Tests between the two countries – and New Zealand went on to win the game by an innings and 33 runs to square the series.

PAKISTAN v AUSTRALIA

Australia got off to a bad start against Pakistan, losing the first-ever match played between the two countries by nine wickets at Karachi in October 1956, but their overall record against them in subsequent years has been impressive: of the 57 Test matches played, Australia have recorded 28 wins to Pakistan's 12.

Most catches

Mark Waugh is the most successful fielder in all Tests between Australia and Pakistan: he took 23 catches in 15 matches against Pakistan between 1994 and 2002.

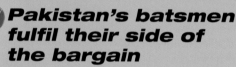

OVERALL SERIES RECORDS

(57 Tests between 1956 and 2010)

	W	L	T	D	W/L	%W	%L	%D
Pakistan	12	28	0	17	0.42	21.05	49.12	29.83
Australia	28	12	0	17	2.45	49.12	21.05	29.83

First match: 11–17 October 1956, Karachi, Pakistan

Pakistan's batsmen fulfil their side of the bargain

Trailing 1–0 in the five-match series, and having seen Australia compile a competitive first-innings score of 465 all out at Adelaide in December 1983, Pakistan knew their only hope of winning the game was to compile a monumental first-innings score and then to bowl out Australia cheaply in their second innings. They fulfilled the first requirement, as centuries from Mohsin Khan (149), Qasim Umar (113) and Javed Miandad (131) propelled them to a mighty 624 all out (the highest team total in all matches between the two countries) and a lead of 159. Their bowlers failed to deliver, however, and the match ended in a draw.

Unplayable Mahmood prospers in Karachi as Australia crumble

Australia could find no answer to the medium-pace bowling of Fazal Mahmood in the first-ever Test match between the two countries, played on a matting wicket at Karachi in October 1956. Pakistan's first great bowler took 6 for 34 in the first innings and 7 for 80 in the second to propel his side to a memorable nine-wicket victory. His match figures of 13 for 114 remain an all-time record in Tests between the two countries.

Pakistan's shocker in Sharjah

Forced to play their three-match series against Australia in October 2002 at neutral venues as a result of safety concerns in their home country, Pakistan played like fish out of water in the Second Test at Sharjah. After winning the toss and electing to bat, they crashed to a dismal 59 all out in their first innings (in 31.5 overs), the lowest score ever made in matches between the two countries. The record did not last for long, however: in the second innings Pakistan fared even worse, subsiding to a sorry 53 all out (in a mere 24.5 overs) to lose the match by an innings and 198 runs.

Super Shane's magic too much for Pakistan

Shane Warne was Pakistan's chief destroyer as Australia romped to a 3–0 series victory in 2002–03. With all the Tests played at neutral venues for safety reasons, the legendary leg-spinner took two five-wicket hauls in three Tests – with a best return of 7 for 94 in the First Test at Colombo, Sri Lanka – to end the series with 27 wickets, an all-time record in Australia-Pakistan matches.

Sensational Sarfraz stuns Australia

With Australia, seven wickets in hand, needing only 77 runs for victory on the fifth day of the First Test at Melbourne in March 1979, **Sarfraz Nawaz** produced one of the greatest bowling performances in Test history. The experienced fast bowler took seven wickets for one run in 33 deliveries to help Pakistan to a stunning 71-run victory and ended with figures of 9 for 86 – the best by any bowler in Australia-Pakistan Test matches.

Taylor leads the way

Mark Taylor holds the highest average of all batsmen to have completed ten or more innings in Pakistan-Australia Test matches. The former captain averaged 79.23 (with 1,347 runs) against Pakistan in 20 innings between 1990 and 1998.

Most dismissals

Rod Marsh leads the all-time dismissals list in Australia-Pakistan Test matches. The legendary gloveman pouched 68 victims (66 catches and two stumpings) in 20 Tests against Pakistan between 1972 and 1984.

Captain Taylor hits an all-time high in Peshawar

With Australia 1–0 up in the three-match series going into the Second Test at Peshawar in October 1998, Australian captain **Mark Taylor** led from the front in record-breaking style. By the end of the second day, after occupying the crease for 12 hours and facing 564 balls, Taylor stood unbeaten on 334 not out – to equal Donald Bradman's all-time highest Test score for an Australian batsman and to leave himself within sight of Brian Lara's world record 375. To the surprise of everyone, however, he made one of Test cricket's most magnanimous gestures: placing his team's need to win the game above any personal glory, he declared. The match ended in a draw, but Taylor's effort is still the highest score by any batsman in Tests between the two countries.

Magical Malik steers Pakistan to victory

Captain Saleem Malik was the star performer as Pakistan edged to a 1–0 home series victory over Australia in 1994–95. Following a modest performance in the victorious First Test at Lahore (he scored 26 and 43 in the course of Pakistan's one-wicket victory), he proceeded to prosper, saving Pakistan in both the drawn Second Test at Rawalpindi (hitting 237 in the second innings as his side was forced to follow on 261 runs in arrears) and again in the Third and final Test at Karachi (where knocks of 75 and 143 did much to secure a draw and, with it, a series victory). His series haul of 557 runs (at the impressive average of 92.83) is an all-time record in Tests between the two countries.

Perfect partners

With Australia already holding an unassailable 2–0 lead in the three-match series going into the Third and final Test against Pakistan at Hobart in January 2010, Michael Clarke joined Ricky Ponting at the crease with their side placed on a precarious 71 for 3 and proceeded to put Pakistan's bowlers to the sword. By the time Clarke (166) departed 102.4 overs later, the pair had added 352 runs for the fourth wicket – an all-time record partnership in Australia-Pakistan Test matches. Australia ended up on 519 for 8 (with Ponting reaching 209) and went on to win the match by 231 runs to secure a 3–0 series whitewash.

On-song Ponting

Ricky Ponting is the most successful captain in the history of Test matches between Australia and Pakistan, leading his side to seven victories in eight Tests against them.

MOST RUNS: TOP 10

Pos	Player	Runs
1	Javed Miandad (Pakistan, 1976–90)	1,797
2	A.R. Border (Australia, 1979–90)	1,666
3	G.S. Chappell (Australia, 1972–84)	1,581
4	R.T. Ponting (Australia, 1998–2010)	1,537
5	Zaheer Abbas (Pakistan, 1972–84)	1,411
6	M.A. Taylor (Australia, 1990–98)	1,347
7	J.L. Langer (Australia, 1994–2005)	1,139
8	Saleem Malik (Pakistan, 1983–98)	1,106
9	Ijaz Ahmed (Pakistan, 1988–99)	1,085
10	K.J. Hughes (Australia, 1979–84)	1,016

MOST WICKETS: TOP 10

Pos	Player	Wickets
1	S.K. Warne (Australia, 1994–2005)	90
2	G.D. McGrath (Australia, 1994–2005)	80
3	D.K. Lillee (Australia, 1972–84)	71
4	Imran Khan (Pakistan, 1976–90)	64
5	Iqbal Qasim (Pakistan, 1976–88)	57
6	Sarfraz Nawaz (Pakistan, 1972–84)	52
7	Wasim Akram (Pakistan, 1990–99)	50
8	Abdul Qadir (Pakistan, 1982–88)	45
9	Mushtaq Ahmed (Pakistan, 1990–99)	35
10	Danish Kaneria (Pakistan, 2002–10)	34

WEST INDIES v PAKISTAN

Having won eight of the last 13 matches played between the two countries, one could easily assume that Pakistan have enjoyed an unrelenting supremacy over the West Indies, but this is only a recent phenomenon: despite the historic ebb and flow of a team's fortunes, matches between Pakistan and the West Indies have, for the most part, been closely fought affairs.

Most dismissals

A solid if not spectacular performer behind the stumps for the West Indies in a 25-Test career, Gerry Alexander holds the record for the most dismissals in Pakistan-West Indies Test matches. In eight games against Pakistan between 1958 and 1959, the former West Indies captain captured 29 victims, with 25 catches and four stumpings.

OVERALL SERIES RECORDS

(44 Tests between 1958 and 2006)

	W	L	T	D	W/L	%W	%L	%D
West Indies	15	16	0	15	0.93	32.60	34.78	32.60
Pakistan	16	15	0	15	10.6	34.78	32.60	32.60

First match: 17–23 January 1958, Bridgetown, Barbados

Windies put on batting masterclass under the Jamaican sun

There were four main factors in the West Indies' crushing victory over Pakistan at Kingston, Jamaica, in February–March 1958: Pakistan's depleted and toothless bowling attack; Garfield Sobers's monumental innings of 365 not out (a new world record); the support Sobers received from Conrad Hunte, who scored 260 (the pair's partnership of 446 for the second wicket is an all-time record in matches between the two countries); and the home side's colossal first-innings total of 790 for 3 declared (the highest team total in Tests between the two countries). Trailing by 462 runs on first innings, Pakistan wilted to 288 all out.

Most catches

Viv Richards holds the record for the most catches in Test matches between Pakistan and the West Indies. The "Master Blaster" from Antigua bagged 23 catches in 16 Tests against Pakistan between 1975 and 1988.

Sobers achieves superstar status

The outstanding performance of a 21-year-old left-handed batsman overshadowed all other events in the Third Test between the West Indies and Pakistan at Kingston, Jamaica, in February–March 1958. **Garfield Sobers** (still waiting to score his first century and playing in his 17th Test match) compiled a peerless innings of 365 not out to break Len Hutton's world record score of 364 against Australia at The Oval in 1938 to prompt 20,000 ecstatic supporters to invade the pitch in wild celebration. He wasn't finished there: in the Fourth Test at Georgetown, Guyana, he scored 125 and 109 not out and ended the series with 824 runs to his name at an imposing average of 137.33 – the highest in any series between Pakistan and the West Indies in history.

Rich pickings against the West Indies

Mohammad Yousuf has enjoyed some good times against the West Indies. In eight Tests against the islanders since 2000 he has scored 1,214 runs, with seven centuries (a highest of 192 in the First Test of the 2006–07 series at Lahore) at an average of 101.16 – the highest of any batsman to complete ten or more innings in matches between the two sides.

West Indies felled to record low in Faisalabad

The West Indies may not have enjoyed the best of times on Pakistani soil – winning only four times in 21 attempts – but they slipped to a record-breaking low in the First Test of the 1986–87 series between the two countries at Faisalabad. Set an achievable 240 for victory, they capitulated in the face of fine bowling from Imran Khan (4 for 30) and Abdul Qadir (6 for 16), subsiding to a miserable 53 all out and a 186-run defeat. It is the lowest team total in all matches between the two countries.

Mahmood's 12-for leads Pakistan to success

Fazal Mahmood was the chief architect of Pakistan's 41-run win in the low-scoring Second Test of the 1958–59 series at Dhaka. He took 6 for 34 in the first innings and 6 for 66 in the second to end with match figures of 12 for 100, the best in all Test matches between Pakistan and the West Indies.

Croft crushes Pakistan

Perhaps the most feared of all the legendary West Indian fast bowlers over the years, owing to his penchant for, and skill at, unleashing a barrage of high-speed, short-pitched deliveries, Colin Croft flattened Pakistan's batsmen into submission in the 1976–77 series in the Caribbean. In the Second Test at Port of Spain, Trinidad, the paceman took 8 for 29 in the second innings (still the best bowling figures by a West Indian in matches between the countries) to lead his side to a six-wicket victory. He ended the series, which the West Indies won 2–1, with 33 wickets to his name, another record in Tests between the two sides.

Most productive partnership

The most productive partnership in all Tests between the West Indies and Pakistan is that between Conrad Hunte and Garfield Sobers. The pair combined to score 723 runs in five innings in the 1957–58 series (with a highest of 446 at Kingston, Jamaica) at an average of 144.60.

Most successful captain

His appointment as captain for the 1957 tour of England was not widely celebrated in the Caribbean, but white, Cambridge-educated, Barbados-born Gerry Alexander proved a popular captain for the West Indies and also a successful one: he led the islanders to four wins over Pakistan in eight Tests between 1958 and 1959 – a record in Pakistan-West Indies Tests.

MOST RUNS: TOP 10

Pos	Player	Runs
1	**Mohammad Yousuf** (Pakistan, 2000–06)	1,214
2	B.C. Lara (West Indies, 1990–2006)	1,173
3	Inzamam-ul-Haq (Pakistan, 1993–2006)	1,124
4	I.V.A. Richards (West Indies, 1975–88)	1,091
5	C.L. Hooper (West Indies, 1988–2002)	998
6	S. Chanderpaul (West Indies, 1997–2011)	986
7	G.S. Sobers (West Indies, 1958–59)	984
8	D.L. Haynes (West Indies, 1980–93)	928
9	Wasim Raja (Pakistan, 1975–81)	919
10	C.G. Greenidge (West Indies, 1977–90)	861

MOST WICKETS: TOP 10

Pos	Player	Wickets
1	**Imran Khan** (Pakistan, 1977–90)	80
2	Wasim Akram (Pakistan, 1986–2000)	79
3	C.A. Walsh (West Indies, 1986–2000)	63
4	Waqar Younis (Pakistan, 1990–2002)	55
5	C.E.H. Croft (West Indies, 1977–81)	50
=	M.D. Marshall (West Indies, 1980–90)	50
7	Abdul Qadir (Pakistan, 1980–90)	42
=	C.E.L. Ambrose (W. Indies, 1988–2000)	42
9	Fazal Mahmood (Pakistan, 1958–59)	41
10	J. Garner (West Indies, 1977–81)	35

PAKISTAN v SRI LANKA

Sri Lanka have played Pakistan on more occasions than they have played against any other Test nation and, despite losing five of their first seven Tests against them, have enjoyed considerable success against their subcontinental near-neighbours. Pakistan still lead the overall series (with 16 wins to Sri Lanka's nine) but, in recent times, matches between the two are regularly competitive.

Most catches

Mahela Jayawardene holds the record for the most catches by a fielder in matches between Pakistan and Sri Lanka: the Sri Lankan has bagged 26 catches in 21 Tests against Pakistan between 1999 and 2009.

OVERALL SERIES RECORDS

(40 Tests between 1982 and 2011)

	W	L	T	D	W/L	%W	%L	%D
Pakistan	16	9	0	15	1.77	40.00	22.50	37.50
Sri Lanka	9	16	0	15	0.56	22.50	40.00	37.50

First match: 5–10 March 1982, Karachi, Pakistan

All-round excellence

Wasim Akram made an impact with both bat and ball for Pakistan in Tests against Sri Lanka. He took 63 wickets in 19 Tests against them (including three five-wicket hauls and a best of 5 for 43 in the first Test at Colombo in August 1994) and also plundered 545 runs at an average of 28.68 (with a highest score of 100 in the first Test at Galle in June 2000). He is the only player in history to have scored more than 500 runs and taken 50-plus wickets in Pakistan-Sri Lanka Tests.

Silky Sangakkara heads averages list

A talented left-handed batsman, Kumar Sangakkara has been an integral member of Sri Lanka's batting for more than a decade. He has enjoyed considerable success against Pakistan over the years, hitting seven of his 28 Test centuries in 13 matches against them – with a highest score of 230 at Lahore in March 2002 – and scoring 1,830 runs at an average of 79.56, the most runs and the highest average of any player to have completed ten or more innings in Pakistan-Sri Lanka Tests. He also holds ther ecord for themost runs in a Test series between the countries (516 in 2010/11)

Muralitharan is the star of the show

Not for the first time in his record-breaking career, **Muttiah Muralitharan** was at the heart of Sri Lanka's 2–1 away series victory over Pakistan in 1999–2000. The wily off-spinner took a series record 26 wickets in the three Tests, with a best of 6 for 71 during Sri Lanka's 57-run, series-clinching victory in the Second Test at Peshawar.

Most dismissals

A veteran of 69 Test matches for Pakistan, Moin Khan is the leading wicketkeeper in Pakistan-Sri Lanka Test matches. The former captain claimed 40 victims (35 catches and five stumpings) in 16 matches against Sri Lanka between 1991 and 2004.

MOST RUNS: TOP 10

Pos	Player	Runs
1	K.C. Sangakkara (Sri Lanka, 2002–1)	1,820
2	Inzamam-ul-Haq (Pakistan, 1994–2006)	1,559
3	S.T. Jayasuriya (Sri Lanka, 1991–2006)	1,490
4	P.A. de Silva (Sri Lanka, 1985–2000)	1,475
5	Younis Khan (Pakistan, 2000–09)	1,356
6	D.P.M.D. Jayawardene (S. Lanka, 1999–2009)	1,217
7	A. Ranatunga (Sri Lanka, 1982–2000)	1,210
8	T.T. Samaraweera (Sri Lanka, 2002–09)	941
9	Saeed Anwar (Pakistan, 1994–2000)	919
10	H.P. Tillakaratne (Sri Lanka, 1991–2002)	820

Pakistan grind out the runs in Karachi

There have been few more turgid stalemates in Test history. On a desperately flat track – the scourge of the modern game – at Karachi in the First Test of the 2008–09 series, Sri Lanka won the toss, elected to bat, and cruised to 644 for 7 declared. Confident Sri Lanka may have been – defeat was now out of the equation – but the Pakistan batsmen, also thriving on the lifeless surface, responded in style. Aided by a magnificent 313 from captain Younis Khan (the highest individual score in Pakistan-Sri Lanka matches) and an unbeaten 158 from Kamran Akmal, Pakistan powered to 765 for 6 declared – the highest total in all matches between the two countries. To the surprise of no one, the match ended in a draw.

MOST WICKETS: TOP 10

Pos	Player	Wickets
1	M. Muralitharan (Sri Lanka, 1994–2009)	80
2	Wasim Akram (Pakistan, 1985–2000)	63
3	Waqar Younis (Pakistan, 1991–2002)	56
4	W.P.U.J.C. Vaas (Sri Lanka, 1994–2009)	47
5	**Imran Khan** (Pakistan, 1982–92)	46
6	H.M.R.K.B. Herath (Sri Lanka, 2000–11)	36
7	Danish Kaneria (Pakistan, 2004–09)	35
8	Saqlain Mushtaq (Pakistan, 1995–2000)	34
9	Saeed Ajmal (Pakistan, 2009–11)	32
=	Umar Gul (Pakistan, 2006–11	32

Perfect partners

Mahela Jayawardene (240) and Thilan Samaraweera (231) were Sri Lanka's driving force in the First Test against Pakistan at Karachi in February 2009. The pair added 437 runs for the fourth wicket to power Sri Lanka to 644 for 7 declared in their first innings and a position of impregnability. It is the highest partnership in all Tests between the two countries. The most productive partnership in Pakistan-Sri Lanka Tests is that between Mahela Jayawardena and Kumar Sangakkara. The have have combined to score 980 runs in 19 innings against Pakistan between 2002 and 2011.

Wasim and Waqar's devastating Kandy blitz

As they had done on many occasions, Pakistan's Wasim Akram and Waqar Younis combined to devastating effect in the Third Test against Sri Lanka at Kandy in August 1994. Wasim took 4 for 32 and Waqar 6 for 34 in 28.2 overs to dismiss Sri Lanka for 71 – the lowest team total in Pakistan-Sri Lanka Tests. Pakistan went on to win the match by an innings and 52 runs to take the series 2–0.

Imran magic inspires Pakistan to crushing victory

Trailing 1–0 in their first-ever series against Pakistan going into the Third and final Test at Lahore in March 1982, but buoyed by a spirited performance in the previous drawn Test at Faisalabad, Sri Lanka then had the misfortune of running into **Imran Khan** at his sublime, but devastating, best. The Pakistan paceman took 8 for 58 in the first innings – the best single-innings figures in all matches between the two countries – and 6 for 58 in the second to lead his side to an innings-and-102-run victory. His match haul of 14 for 116 is another Pakistan-Sri Lanka record.

INDIA v SRI LANKA

While India have enjoyed a prolonged period of success in Test matches against Sri Lanka on home soil – winning ten of 17 Tests and not registering a single defeat – matches in Sri Lanka have always been closer affairs, with India recording only four victories to Sri Lanka's six.

New kid on the block

Ajantha Mendis burst on to the Test cricket scene in spectacular style against India in 2008. Bowling a mixture of leg-spinners, googlies, top-spinners, flippers and speciality "caroms" (released from an unusual snap of the fingers), the Sri Lankan sensation bamboozled India's batsmen. In the First Test at Colombo he became the first Sri Lankan in history to take eight wickets on debut, and he ended the series with 26 wickets – a series record in matches between India and Sri Lanka (and also the best return for a bowler in a three-match debut series, beating Alec Bedser's record haul against India in 1946 by two).

OVERALL SERIES RECORDS

(35 Tests between 1982 and 2010)

	W	L	T	D	W/L	%W	%L	%D
India	14	6	0	15	2.33	40.00	17.14	52.86
Sri Lanka	6	14	0	15	0.42	17.14	40.00	52.86

First match: 17–22 September 1982, Chennai, India

Sri Lanka's batting fun in the Colombo sun

The First Test between Sri Lanka and India at Colombo in August 1997 turned into yet another Test match in the subcontinent in which the bat completely dominated, but at least it was a record-breaking one. Having seen India compile 537 for 8 in their first innings, Sri Lanka, helped by sublime innings from both Sanath Jayasuriya (340) and Roshan Mahanama (225), produced a mammoth response, compiling a mighty 952 for 6 declared – the highest team total in Test history – as the match petered out into an inevitable draw.

Sehwag sparkles against Sri Lanka

A scintillating opening batsman for India with a penchant for compiling huge scores, **Virender Sehwag** has often been in prime form against Sri Lanka: in 18 innings against them he has scored 1,239 runs – including two double-centuries (201 not out at Galle in July 2008, and 293 at Mumbai in December 2009) – at an average of 72.88. It is the highest by any player to have completed ten or more innings in India-Sri Lanka Test matches.

MOST RUNS: TOP 5

Pos	Player	Runs
1	S.R. Tendulkar (India, 1990–2010)	1,995
2	D.P.M.D. Jayawardene (Sri Lanka, 1997–2010)	1,822
3	R. Dravid (India, 1997–2010)	1,508
4	K.C. Sangakkara (Sri Lanka, 2001–10)	1,257
5	P.A. de Silva (Sri Lanka, 1985–99)	1,252

MOST WICKETS: TOP 5

Pos	Player	Wickets
1	M. Muralitharan (Sri Lanka, 1993–2010)	105
2	A. Kumble (India, 1993–2008)	74
3	Harbhajan Singh (India, 1999–2010)	52
4	Kapil Dev (India, 1982–94)	45
5	B.A.W. Mendis (Sri Lanka, 2008–10)	34

SRI LANKA v ENGLAND

Even from the first Test matches between the two countries, England have failed to dominate Sri Lanka – perhaps it was this that prompted a seeming reluctance from the ECB to schedule fixtures against the islanders (the two countries played just five Tests between 1982 and 1993) – and in the 24 Tests played have won only nine to Sri Lanka's six.

OVERALL SERIES RECORDS

(26 Tests between 1982 and 2012)

	W	L	T	D	W/L	%W	%L	%D
Sri Lanka	7	10	0	9	0.70	26.92	38.46	34.61
England	10	7	0	9	1.42	38.46	26.92	34.61

First match: 17–21 February 1982, Colombo, Sri Lanka

Sri Lanka show England how it's done in Colombo

Having seen England compile an under-par first-innings 265 all out in the decisive Third and final Test at Colombo in December 2003 (the series was locked at 0–0 as it reached its finale), Sri Lanka's batsmen put a toothless England attack to the sword, compiling a massive 628 for 8 declared – the highest team total in all matches between the two countries – en route to a comprehensive and series-clinching innings-and-215-run victory.

Lowest score

The lowest team score in the history of England-Sri Lanka matches is 81 all out, a fate that has been suffered on two occasions: by Sri Lanka at Colombo in March 2001; and by England at Galle in December 2007.

Highest individual score

The record for the highest individual score in England-Sri Lanka Test matches is 213, a feat achieved by two Sri Lankan batsmen: **Sanath Jayasuriya** (213 at The Oval in August 1998) and Mahela Jayawardene (213 not out at Galle in December 2007). Jayawardene has prospered against England: in 33 innings against them between 1998 and 2011 he has scored 1,684 runs at an average of 56.13. the record for the highest average of any batsman to have completed ten or more innings in England-Sri Lanka Test matches is held by England's Ian Bell (592 runs at an average 84.57).

MOST RUNS: TOP 5

Pos	Player	Runs
1	D.P.M.D. Jayawardene (Sri Lanka, 1998–2012)	2,038
2	K.C. Sangakkara (Sri Lanka, 2001–12)	1,226
3	A.N. Cook (England, 2006–12)	1,000
4	M.E. Trescothick (England, 2001–06)	957
5	T.M. Dilshan (Sir Lanka, 2001–12)	889

MOST WICKETS: TOP 5

Pos	Player	Wickets
1	M. Muralitharan (Sri Lanka, 1993–2007)	112
2	W.P.U.J.C. Vaas (Sri Lanka, 2001–07)	49
3	M.J. Hoggard (England, 2002–07)	37
4	A.F. Giles (England, 2001–03)	31
5	G.P. Swann (England (2011–12)	28

Best bowling in an innings/match/series

The magical **Muttiah Muralitharan**, Test cricket's all-time leading wicket-taker, holds every major bowling record in the book in England-Sri Lanka matches: he is the only bowler to take more than 100 wickets (112); he recorded the best single-innings bowling figures (9 for 65 at The Oval in August 1998); the best match figures (16 for 220, in the same Test at The Oval); and the most wickets in a series (26 in Sri Lanka's victorious 2003–04 series against England).

NZ v SRI LANKA

That it took nine years and 11 Tests for Sri Lanka to record their first win in matches between the two countries suggests that New Zealand have a firm hold over the Sri Lankans, but while that may have been the case in early clashes, the pendulum has certainly swung back in recent times. Sri Lanka have won five of their last ten Test matches against New Zealand (losing twice) since July 1998.

Vettori's record-breaking efforts all in vain

If only New Zealand's batsmen could have displayed with the bat the skill levels **Daniel Vettori** showed with the ball, the outcome might well have been different. With New Zealand already in trouble in the Second Test against Sri Lanka at Wellington in December 2006 (they were 138 runs behind as Sri Lanka started their second innings), the Kiwi slow left-armer did all he could to bring his side back into the match, taking 7 for 130 – the best single-innings bowling figures in New Zealand-Sri Lanka Tests – to help dismiss the visitors for 365. Set an improbable 504 runs for victory, however, New Zealand slipped to 286 all out and a heavy 217-run defeat.

OVERALL SERIES RECORDS

(26 Tests between 1983 and 2009)

	W	L	T	D	W/L	%W	%L	%D
New Zealand	9	7	0	10	1.28	34.62	26.92	38.46
Sri Lanka	7	9	0	10	0.77	26.92	34.62	38.46

First match: 4–6 March 1983, Christchurch, New Zealand

Sri Lanka stifled in alien conditions

Sri Lanka's batsmen struggled to come to terms with a rain-affected wicket in their second-ever Test against New Zealand, at Wellington in March 1983. Leading by 39 runs after the completion of the first innings, they crashed to 93 all out – the lowest-ever team total in matches between the two countries – and an eventual six-wicket defeat.

Vaas a cut above the rest

It was a performance that propelled Sri Lanka to an unexpected victory on a wicket tailored for New Zealand's fast bowlers and which confirmed Chaminda Vaas's status as the finest fast bowler Sri Lanka has ever produced. In the First Test at Napier in March 1995, the left-arm paceman took 5 for 47 in the first innings and 5 for 43 in the second to lead Sri Lanka to a hefty 241-run victory. His match figures of 10 for 90 are the best in all New Zealand-Sri Lanka Tests.

Nobody can keep up with Jones

One of the pillars upon which New Zealand built their record-breaking recovery against Sri Lanka at Wellington in January–February 1991, hitting 186 (his highest Test score), **Andrew Jones** continued to enjoy good times against Sri Lanka: in six Tests against them he scored 625 runs (with two further centuries) at an average of 62.50 – the highest by any batsman to complete ten or more innings in New Zealand-Sri Lanka Test matches.

MOST RUNS: TOP 5

Pos	Player	Runs
1	S.P. Fleming (New Zealand, 1995–2006)	1,166
2	D.P.M.D. Jayawardene (Sri Lanka, 1998–2009)	928
3	A. Ranatunga (Sri Lanka, 1984–98)	824
4	H.P. Tillakaratne (Sri Lanka, 1991–2003)	819
5	P.A. de Silva (Sri Lanka, 1991–98)	785

MOST WICKETS: TOP 5

Pos	Player	Wickets
1	M. Muralitharan (Sri Lanka, 1992–2009)	82
2	D.L. Vettori (New Zealand, 1997–2009)	51
3	W.P.U.J.C. Vaas (Sri Lanka, 1995–2006)	42
4	R.J. Hadlee (New Zealand, 1983–87)	37
5	V.B. John (Sri Lanka, 1983–84)	24

SRI LANKA v AUSTRALIA

Sri Lanka have not enjoyed the best of times in Tests against Australia since the two sides met for the first time in Kandy in 1983. They have won only once in 23 attempts and, sensationally at Melbourne in 1995, saw their leading bowler, Muttiah Muralitharan, become one of only 11 players in Test history (and the only Sri Lankan) to be no-balled for throwing.

OVERALL SERIES RECORDS

(23 Tests between 1983 and 2011)

	W	L	T	D	W/L	%W	%L	%D
Sri Lanka	1	14	0	8	0.07	4.34	60.86	34.78
Australia	14	1	0	8	14.00	60.86	5.00	34.78

First match: 22–26 April 1983, Kandy, Sri Lanka

MOST RUNS: TOP 5

Pos	Player	Runs
1	**R.T. Ponting** (Australia, 1995–2011)	975
2	P.A. de Silva (Sri Lanka, 1988–99)	803
3	D.P.M.D. Jayawardene (Sri Lanka, 1999–2011)	803
4	M.E.K. Hussey (Australia, 2007–11)	762
5	K.C. Sangakkara (Sri Lanka, 2004–11)	726

MOST WICKETS: TOP 5

Pos	Player	Wickets
1	**S.K. Warne** (Australia, 1992–2004)	59
2	M. Muralitharan (Sri Lanka, 1992–2007)	54
3	W.P.U.J.C. Vaas (Sri Lanka, 1995–2007)	38
4	G.D. McGrath (Australia, 1995–2004)	37
5	C.J. McDermott (Australia, 1988–96)	27

Australia prosper against faltering Sri Lanka

Australia's batsmen took full advantage of an under-performing Sri Lankan bowling attack dogged by accusations of ball-tampering (Sri Lanka became the first team in Test history to be charged with the offence, although the ICC reversed the decision two weeks later) in the First Test of the 1995–96 series at Perth. Led by centuries from Michael Slater, whose 219 is the highest individual score in Australia-Sri Lanka Tests, and Mark Waugh (111), they amassed a colossal 617 for 5 declared – the highest team total in all matches between the two countries – en route to an innings-and-36-run victory.

Sri Lanka down and out in Darwin

Before the Test it was thought that the soft, seaming wicket prepared at Darwin for the First Test of the two-match 2004 series in Australia was unlikely to bring the best out of the Sri Lankan batsmen, and so it proved. Having dismissed Australia comparatively cheaply for 207 in the first innings, Sri Lanka wilted on the unfamiliar surface to 97 all out – the lowest team total in Australia-Sri Lanka Tests. The tourists fared little better second time round: set 312 for victory, they limped to 162 all out – with Michael Kasprowicz taking 7 for 39 (the best single-innings figures in all Tests between the two countries) – and a 149-run defeat.

Happy times for Waugh

The most capped player in Test history (he appeared in 168 Test matches), Steve Waugh enjoyed some fine moments against Sri Lanka. In eight Tests against them between 1988 and 1999, he scored 701 runs (with three centuries – and a highest score of 170 at Adelaide in January 1996) at an average of 87.62 – the highest of any batsman to complete ten or more innings in matches between the two countries.

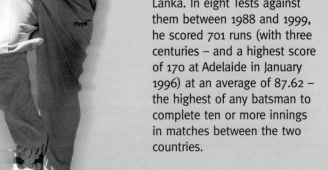

W. INDIES v S. AFRICA

As the two countries first met only in 1992, by which time the shameful policy of apartheid had started to unravel, South Africa, for the most part, have played only against a troubled West Indian side whose glory days seemed far behind them. As a result, South Africa have dominated proceedings, winning 16 of the 25 Tests played to the West Indies' three.

Deadly de Villiers finds his form

A.B. de Villiers has enjoyed some of the finest moments of his already impressive Test career against the West Indies. The right-handed middle-order batsman has hit four of his ten Test centuries against the men from the Caribbean (with a best of 178 at Bridgetown, Barbados, in April 2005) and has hit 1,037 runs in 18 innings at an average of 79.76 – the highest by any batsman to have completed ten innings or more in matches between the two countries.

A run-fest in Antigua

The Antigua Recreation Ground confirmed its reputation as possessing the most benign strip in world cricket when the West Indies met South Africa in the Fourth and final Test of the 2004–05 series. South Africa, holding an impregnable 2–0 series lead, won the toss and batted the West Indies out of the game with 588 for 6 declared. But the West Indies, playing for nothing more than pride, responded bravely. Led by an imperious 317 from Chris Gayle (the highest individual score in all matches between the two countries) and centuries from Ramnaresh Sarwan (127), Shivnarine Chanderpaul (127) and Dwayne Bravo (107), they amassed a colossal 747 all out – the 11th highest team total in Test history and the highest in West Indies-South Africa clashes – as the match meandered towards an inevitable draw.

OVERALL SERIES RECORDS

(25 Tests between 1992 and 2010)

	W	L	T	D	W/L	%W	%L	%D
West Indies	3	16	0	6	0.18	12.00	64.00	24.00
South Africa	16	3	0	6	5.33	64.00	12.00	24.00

First match: 18–23 April 1992, Bridgetown, Barbados

Getting off to the worst of starts

The West Indies have endured a miserable sequence of results against South Africa in recent times (losing 5–0 in 1998–99, 2–1 in 2001 and winning only one of 11 Tests against them between 2003 and 2008), so a good start was essential for both their confidence and morale when the two sides met for the First Test (of three) at Port of Spain in June 2010. South Africa won the toss, elected to bat and reached 352 all out. In reply, the West Indies slumped to 102 all out – the lowest total in all Tests between the two countries – and went on to lose the match by 163 runs.

Most wickets in a series

The record for the most wickets in a West Indies-South Africa series is 29, a feat achieved by two South African players: Shaun Pollock, in South Africa in 1998–99; and Makhaya Ntini, in South Africa in 2003–04.

MOST RUNS: TOP 5

Pos	Player	Runs
1	J.H. Kallis (South Africa, 1998–2010)	2,356
2	B.C. Lara (West Indies, 1992–2005)	1,715
3	S. Chanderpaul (West Indies, 1998–2010)	1,619
4	G.C. Smith (South Africa, 2003–10)	1,593
5	H.H. Gibbs (South Africa, 1998–2008)	1,403

MOST WICKETS: TOP 5

Pos	Player	Wickets
1	**S.M. Pollock** (South Africa, 1998–2008)	70
2	M. Ntini (South Africa, 2001–08)	63
3	A. Nel (South Africa, 2003–08)	52
=	J.H. Kallis (South Africa, 1998–2010)	52
4	C.A. Walsh (West Indies, 1992–2001)	51

ZIMBABWE v INDIA

Apart from a pair of unexpected defeats in Harare (in October 1998 and June 2001, when Zimbabwe cricket was at its strongest), India dominated the few Tests they played against Zimbabwe between 1992 and 2005, winning seven out of 11 and drawing two.

OVERALL SERIES RECORDS

(11 Tests between 1992 and 2005)

	W	L	T	D	W/L	%W	%L	%D
Zimbabwe	2	7	0	2	0.28	18.18	63.64	18.18
India	7	2	0	2	3.50	63.64	18.18	18.18

First match: 18–22 October 1992, Harare, Zimbabwe

MOST RUNS: TOP 5

Pos	Player	Runs
1	A. Flower (Zimbabwe, 1992–2002)	1,138
2	R. Dravid (India, 1998–2005)	979
3	S.R. Tendulkar (India, 1992–2002)	918
4	G.W. Flower (Zimbabwe, 1992–2002)	565
5	S.S. Das (India, 2000–02)	560

MOST WICKETS: TOP 5

Pos	Player	Wickets
1	A. Kumble (India, 1992–2005)	38
2	Harbhajan Singh (India, 1998–2005)	31
3	J. Srinath (India, 1992–2002)	30
=	H.H. Streak (Zimbabwe, 1998–2005)	30
5	Z. Khan (India, 2000–05)	21
=	I.K. Pathan (India, 2005)	21

Records tumble in Nagpur

One-nil up in the series going into the Second and final Test at Nagpur in November 2000, India won the toss and batted Zimbabwe out of the game as centuries from Shiv Sunder Das (110), Rahul Dravid (162) and Sachin Tendulkar (201) propelled them to a mighty 609 for 6 declared – the highest team score in matches between the two sides. When, having dismissed Zimbabwe for 382, they enforced the follow-on, an Indian victory seemed the most probable outcome. In stepped **Andy Flower**, however, hitting an unbeaten 232 – the highest individual score in Zimbabwe-India Tests – to rescue the draw.

Dravid, a.k.a. "The Wall", stands firm

Although Andy Flower may have outgunned him as the all-time leading run-scorer in Zimbabwe-India Tests, no batsman played with more consistency than Rahul Dravid. In 13 innings against Zimbabwe between 1998 and 2005, the man nicknamed "The Wall" hit 979 runs, including five half-centuries and three centuries (with a highest score of 200 not out at Delhi in November 2000), at an average of 97.90 – the highest by any batsman to complete ten or more innings in matches between the two countries.

Disappointment in Delhi for Zim

Trailing India by a mere 25 runs after the completion of the first innings in the Second Test of the two-match 2001–02 series at Delhi, and still very much in the game, Zimbabwe failed to cope with the dual spin threat of Harbhajan Singh and **Anil Kumble**. The former took 6 for 62 and the latter 4 for 58 as Zimbabwe slipped to 146 all out – the lowest team total in Tests between the two countries – and an eventual four-wicket defeat.

Pathan prospers under the African sun

India's comprehensive 2–0 series win over a weak Zimbabwe side in 2005–06 was a personal triumph for Irfan Pathan. Swinging the ball prodigiously, the medium-fast bowler took 5 for 58 and 4 for 53 in India's innings-and-90-run victory in the First Test at Bulawayo, and 7 for 59 (the best single-innings bowling figures in Zimbabwe-India Tests) and 5 for 67 in India's ten-wicket win in the Second Test at Harare. His match figures of 12 for 156 at Harare and his series haul of 21 wickets are both records in matches between the two countries.

ZIMBABWE v NZ

Matches between Zimbabwe and New Zealand have been one-way affairs ever since the two sides met for the first time in Bulawayo in 1992, with New Zealand winning seven of the 13 Test matches played and Zimbabwe failing to record a single victory.

Astle tops the batting charts

A free-scoring middle-order batsman and a veteran of 81 Test matches for his country, **Nathan Astle** has been the outstanding batsman in matches betwee Zimbabwe and New Zealand. The Canterbury star is the leading run-scorer – with 813 runs in 11 Tests between 1996 and 2003 (including three centuries and a highest score of 141 at Wellington in December 2000) – and has the highest average of any batsman to have completed ten or more innings in matches between the two countries (50.81).

OVERALL SERIES RECORDS

(15 Tests between 1992 and 2005)

	W	L	T	D	W/L	%W	%L	%D
Zimbabwe	0	9	0	6	0.0 0	0.0 0	60.00	40.00
New Zealand	9	0	0	6	-	60.00	0.00	40.00

First match: 1–5 November 1992, Bulawayo, Zimbabwe

Zimbabwe back with record defeat

Zimbabwe's one-off Test match against New Zealand at Napier in January 2012 was the first overseas Test they had played in since visiting South Africa in March 2005. Although it was a welcome return to the international fold, it quickly developed into a forgettable match. Having elected to field, Zimbabwe watched Ross Taylor (122) and Bradley-John Watling (102 not out) put their bowlers to the sword, posting 495 for 7 declared (the highest total in all New Zealand-Zimbabwe Tests). the Black Caps then dismissed the visitors for 51 in the first innings and 143 in the second to win by an innings and 301 runs – the largest winning margin in all Tests between the countries.

Strang shines as Zimbabwe stumble

Although Zimbabwe lost the first Test against New Zealand in Bulawayo in September 2000 by seven wickets (despite taking a 12-run first innings lead), no blame for the defeat could be apportioned to Paul Strang. The leg-spinner took 8 for 109 in New Zealand's first innings – the best single-innings figures ever recorded in Test matches between the two countries.

Huckle's spell in the limelight

The brightest moments in Adam Huckle's brief eight-Test career came in the drawn two-match series against New Zealand in 1997–98. In the Second Test at Bulawayo, the leg-spinner took 6 for 109 in the first innings and 5 for 146 in the second as New Zealand, chasing 286 for victory, hung on at 275 for 8 to force a hard-fought, if nervous, draw. Huckle's match haul of 11 for 255 is the best in Zimbabwe-New Zealand Tests, and his series haul of 16 wickets is another record in matches between the two countries.

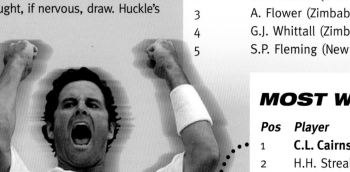

MOST RUNS: TOP 5

Pos	Player	Runs
1	N.J. Astle (New Zealand, 1996–2005)	813
2	G.W. Flower (Zimbabwe, 1992–2000)	780
3	A. Flower (Zimbabwe, 1992–2000)	721
4	G.J. Whittall (Zimbabwe, 1996–2000)	647
5	S.P. Fleming (New Zealand, 1996–2005)	640

MOST WICKETS: TOP 5

Pos	Player	Wickets
1	**C.L. Cairns** (New Zealand, 1996–2000)	39
2	H.H. Streak (Zimbabwe, 1996–2005)	32
=	D.L. Vettori (New Zealand, 1997–2012)	32
4	P.A. Strang (Zimbabwe, 1996–2000)	29
5	D.N. Patel (New Zealand, 1992–96)	23

S. AFRICA v INDIA

Ever since South Africa edged the historic 1992 home series against India (the first team they played against in the post-apartheid era), they have enjoyed a measure of supremacy over them, both at home and away, recording 12 victories in the 27 Tests played to India's six.

India seize their chance

Having lost the First Test of the two-match series against South Africa in February 2010 (by an innings and 6 runs in Nagpur), it was win or bust for the home side when the two teams faced off in Kolkata a week later. And when South Africa slipped to an under-par 296 all out in their first innings, India were handed their chance. They grabbed it with both hands as centuries from **Virender Sehwag** (165), Sachin Tendulkar (106), V.V.S. Laxman (143 not out) and captain Mahendra Singh Dhoni (132 not out) propelled them to a mighty 643 for 6 declared – the highest total in all Tests between the two countries – and an eventual innings-and-57-run victory.

OVERALL SERIES RECORDS

(27 Tests between 1992 and 2011)

	W	L	T	D	W/L	%W	%L	%D
South Africa	12	7	0	8	1.71	44.44	25.93	26.93
India	7	12	0	8	0.58	25.93	44.44	26.93

First match: 13–17 November 1992, Durban, South Africa

Down and out in Durban

India's batsmen failed to cope either with an electric performance from South Africa fast bowler Allan Donald (who took 9 for 54 in the match) or with a lively Durban wicket in the First Test of the 1996–97 series. Set an unlikely 395 runs to win the low-scoring match, they crashed to 66 all out – the lowest team total in Tests between the countries – and a 328-run defeat.

Klusener's cracking debut

Lance Klusener produced one of the most scintillating debut performances in Test history to lead South Africa to a comprehensive victory over India in the Second Test of the 1996–97 series at Kolkata. With the home side set an unlikely 467 runs to win both the match and the series, the all-rounder took 8 for 64. They are the best figures by a debutant in South Africa's history and the best single-innings figures in the history of Tests between South Africa and India. Remarkably, this remained the only five-wicket haul of Klusener's 49-Test career.

Kallis is Mr Consistency

India's batting legend Sachin Tendulkar has scored the most runs (1,741), but no batsman has performed with more consistency in South Africa-India Tests than **Jacques Kallis**. South Africa's legendary all-rounder has scored 1,585 runs in 16 Tests against India since 2000 – with a highest score of 201 not out at Pretoria in December 2010 – at an average of 72.04, the highest by any batsman to complete ten or more innings in matches between the two countries.

MOST RUNS: TOP 5

Pos	Player	Runs
1	S.R. Tendulkar (India, 1992–2011)	1,741
2	J.H. Kallis (South Africa, 2000–11)	1,585
3	V. Sehwag (India, 2001–11)	1,306
4	R. Dravid (India, 1996–2011)	1,252
5	H.M. Amla (South Africa, 2004–11)	1,164

MOST WICKETS: TOP 5

Pos	Player	Wickets
1	A. Kumble (India, 1992–2008)	84
2	J. Srinath (India, 1992–2001)	64
3	Harbhajan Singh (India, 2001–11)	60
4	A.A. Donald (South Africa, 1992–2000)	57
5	D.W. Steyn (South Africa, 2006–11)	53

SRI LANKA v S. AFRICA

The difficulties faced by both sides to adapt to alien conditions have had a major bearing on matches between South Africa and Sri Lanka: South Africa, with a tendency to struggle on spin-friendly, slow, low surfaces, have won only twice in ten attempts in Sri Lanka; the islanders, exposed to fast bowling on livelier South African wickets, have won one, drawn one and lost eight of the ten Test matches.

Standout performer

Quite apart from his headline-grabbing innings of 374 in Colombo in 2006, **Mahela Jayawardene** has excelled against South Africa. In 15 Tests against them since 2000 he has scored 1,604 runs (the most by any batsman in Tests between the two countries), with five centuries (all of them in home matches), at an average of 59.40 – the highest by any batsman to have played in ten or more Test matches in the Sri Lanka–South Africa series.

Murali puts South Africa in a spin

A legion of South African batsmen have failed to fathom the wristy guile of **Muttiah Muralitharan** over the years: of his world record 792 Test wickets, 104 have come against South Africa (only against England has he taken more, 112). And Murali was at his spellbinding best in the First Test of the 2000 series against South Africa at Galle, taking 7 for 84 in the second innings to end the match with 13 for 171 (the latter is a record in Sri Lanka–South Africa Tests) as Sri Lanka won the match by an innings and 15 runs. He ended the series with 26 wickets, another record in a series between Sri Lanka and South Africa.

OVERALL SERIES RECORDS

(20 Tests between 1993 and 2011)

	W	L	T	D	W/L	%W	%L	%D
Sri Lanka	5	10	0	5	0.50	25.00	50.00	25.00
South Africa	10	5	0	5	2.00	50.00	25.00	25.00

First match: 25–30 August 1993, Moratuwa, Sri Lanka

Sri Lanka cruise to record-breaking total in Colombo

Sri Lanka crushed South Africa in comprehensive and record-breaking style in the First Test of the 2006 series in Colombo. In the first innings, having dismissed South Africa for an under-par 169 and then slipped to a worrying 14 for 2 in reply, Sri Lanka needed something magical – and their two most gifted batsmen duly obliged. Mahela Jayawardene (374 – the fourth highest score in Test history, and the highest in Sri Lanka-South Africa Tests) and Kumar Sangakkara (287) added 624 runs for the third wicket (the highest partnership for any wicket in Test history) to propel Sri Lanka to a mighty 756 for 5 declared – the highest team total in all matches between the two countries – and an eventual innings-and-153-run victory.

MOST RUNS: TOP 5

Pos	Player	Runs
1	D.P.M.D. Jayawardene (Sri Lanka, 2000–11)	1,604
2	K.C. Sangakkara (Sri Lanka, 2000–11)	1,362
3	D.J. Cullinan (South Africa, 1993–2001)	917
4	J.H. Kallis (South Africa, 1998–11)	894
5	S.T. Jayasuriya (Sri Lanka, 1993–2006)	857

MOST WICKETS: TOP 5

Pos	Player	Wickets
1	M. Muralitharan (Sri Lanka, 1993–2006)	104
2	S.M. Pollock (South Africa, 1998–2006)	48
3	M. Ntini (South Africa, 1998–2006)	35
4	N. Boje (South Africa, 2000–06)	34
5	A.A. Donald (South Africa, 1993–2001)	29

SRI LANKA v W. INDIES

Aided by a near-impeccable home record against the West Indies (that has seen them win five and draw one of the six Tests played), Sri Lanka have been the dominant force in matches played between the two countries since they met for the first time in 1993, registering six wins to the West Indies' three.

OVERALL SERIES RECORDS

(15 Tests between 1993 and 2010)

	W	L	T	D	W/L	%W	%L	%D
Sri Lanka	6	3	0	6	2.00	40.00	20.00	40.00
West Indies	3	6	0	6	0.50	20.00	40.00	20.00

First match: 8–13 December 1993, Moratuwa, Sri Lanka

Best career average

Of all the batsmen to complete ten or more innings in matches between Sri Lanka and the West Indies, Hashan Tillakaratne has the best average – 89.20 in ten innings between 1993 and 2003, including a career-best 204 not out at Colombo in November-December 2001.

MOST RUNS: TOP 5

Pos	Player	Runs
1	**B.C. Lara** (West Indies, 1993–2003)	1,125
2	K.C. Sangakkara (Sri Lanka, 2001–10)	918
2	R.R. Sarwan (West Indies, 2001–08)	749
4	D.P.M.D. Jayawardene (Sri Lanka, 2001–10)	748
5	T.T. Samaraweera (Sri Lanka, 2001–10)	644

MOST WICKETS: TOP 5

Pos	Player	Wickets
1	M. Muralitharan (Sri Lanka, 1993–2008)	82
2	W.P.U.J.C. Vaas (Sri Lanka, 2001–08)	55
3	C.E.L. Ambrose (West Indies, 1993–97)	14
=	C.D. Collymore (West Indies, 2003)	14
5	D.B.L. Powell (West Indies, 2005–08)	13
=	J.E. Taylor (West Indies, 2003–08)	13

The Colombo run-fest

Already holding an unassailable 2–0 lead in the three-match 2001–02 series going into the final Test at Colombo, Sri Lanka responded in style to the West Indies' first-innings score of 390 (of which **Brian Lara** contributed 221 – the highest individual score in all Tests between the two countries). Led by an unbeaten 204 from Hashan Tillakaratne, they compiled 627 for 9 declared – the highest team total in Sri Lanka-West Indies clashes – en route to a ten-wicket win and a 3–0 series whitewash.

Murali dashes West Indian hopes

Given that Sri Lanka had amassed 375 in their second innings, it was not inconceivable that the West Indies could chase down a victory target of 378 to win the Second Test at Kandy in July 2005 and square the series. But Muttiah Muralitharan had other ideas, hitting top form to take 8 for 46 – the best single-innings figures in Sri Lanka–West Indies Tests – to help dismiss the West Indies for 137 and lead his side to a 240-run win and a 2–0 series victory.

West Indies crawl to record-breaking low

Holding a 58-run first-innings lead and very much in the driving seat in the First Test of the 2005 series at Colombo, the West Indies then capitulated to Sri Lanka in disappointing style. Unable to withstand fine bowling from **Chaminda Vaas** (4 for 15) and Muttiah Muralitharan (6 for 36) they limped to 113 all out in 60 overs – the lowest team total in matches between the two countries – and an eventual six-wicket defeat.

ZIMBABWE v SRI LANKA

Sri Lanka may have been forced to work harder to achieve a victory on Zimbabwean soil – they won three of the eight Tests played there and drew five – but at home against the southern Africans they were invincible, recording seven wins out of seven, and most of them in dominant style.

Sri Lanka cash in against weak Zimbabwe

By 2004, what was effectively the reserve Zimbabwe team had been exposed as being completely out of its depth in international cricket, and when Sri Lanka played against them at Bulawayo in May 2004 they took full advantage. Having seen Zimbabwe struggle to 228 all out, they made the most of the batting-friendly surface. Bolstered by centuries from captain Marvan Atapattu (249), **Kumar Sangakkara** (270 – the highest individual score in Zimbabwe-Sri Lanka Tests) and Mahela Jayawardene (100 not out), they reached 713 for 3 declared (the highest team total in all Tests between the two countries) before bowling out Zimbabwe for 231 second time round to win the match by an innings and 254 runs.

Marvellous Marvan heads averages list

A veteran of 90 Test matches for Sri Lanka over a period of 17 years, **Marvan Atapattu** was a useful opening batsman who seemed to reserve his best performances for matches against Zimbabwe. In ten Test matches against them between 1998 and 2004, he scored 1,145 runs, with five centuries, at an average of 95.41 – the highest by any batsman to complete ten or more innings in matches between the two countries.

Zimbabwe gunned out at Galle

In truth, few thought Zimbabwe capable of chasing down a target of 395 runs from 125 overs to win the Third and final Test of the 2001–02 series – in which Sri Lanka already held a 2–0 lead – but their spectacular collapse still came as a surprise. Failing to come to terms with the dual spin threat of Sanath Jayasuriya (4 for 31) and Muttiah Muralitharan (4 for 24), they folded to 79 all out – the lowest team total in Tests between the countries – and defeat by 315 runs.

OVERALL SERIES RECORDS

(15 Tests between 1994 and 2004)

	W	L	T	D	W/L	%W	%L	%D
Zimbabwe	0	10	0	5	0.00	0.00	66.67	33.33
Sri Lanka	10	0	0	5	0.50	66.67	0.00	33.33

First match: 11–16 October 1994, Harare, Zimbabwe

MOST RUNS: TOP 5

Pos	Player	Runs
1	M.S. Atapattu (Sri Lanka, 1998–2004)	1,145
2	A. Flower (Zimbabwe, 1994–2002)	778
3	S.T. Jayasuriya (Sri Lanka, 1994–2004)	730
4	K.C. Sangakkara (Sri Lanka, 2001–04)	536
5	G.W. Flower (Zimbabwe, 1994–2002)	527

MOST WICKETS: TOP 5

Pos	Player	Wickets
1	M. Muralitharan (Sri Lanka, 1994–2004)	87
2	W.P.U.J.C. Vaas (Sri Lanka, 1994–2004)	48
3	H.H. Streak (Zimbabwe, 1994–2002)	33
4	S.T. Jayasuriya (Sri Lanka, 1994–2004)	20
=	K.R. Pushpakumara (Sri Lanka, 1994–99)	20

S. AFRICA v PAKISTAN

South Africa have played only 18 Test matches against Pakistan since the two sides met for the first time in 1995, but they have already gained a degree of mastery over the men from the subcontinent, recording eight wins to Pakistan's three, with seven of the Tests drawn.

South Africa on cruise control in Cape Town

One–nil up in the two-match series against Pakistan, South Africa got off to a flying start in the Second Test at Cape Town in January 2003. Graeme Smith (151) and **Herschelle Gibbs** (228 – the highest individual score in South Africa-Pakistan clashes) put on 368 runs for the first wicket to propel the home side to 620 for 7 declared (the highest team total in matches between the two countries). Pakistan wilted under the pressure and lost the match by an innings and 142 runs.

Pakistan in freefall in Faisalabad

Pakistan capitulated in spectacular style in the Third and final Test of the 1997–98 series to hand South Africa their first taste of victory on Pakistani soil and an unexpected series win. Set a mere 146 runs for victory, the home side slipped to 92 all out in 37.3 overs – the lowest team total in all matches between the two countries.

Kallis prospers against Pakistan

One of the most effective batsmen of modern times – some claim he is the best – Jacques Kallis has forged a glittering career out of grinding opponents into submission and scoring "dirty" runs. Against no other team has he grafted more successfully than against Pakistan: in 15 Tests against them since 1997 he has scored 1,472 runs (including six centuries, with a highest score of 155 at Karachi in October 2007) at an average of 66.90 – the best by any batsman to complete ten or more innings in South Africa-Pakistan matches.

OVERALL SERIES RECORDS

(18 Tests between 1995 and 2010)

	W	L	T	D	W/L	%W	%L	%D
South Africa	8	3	0	7	2.66	44.44	16.67	38.89
Pakistan	3	8	0	7	0.37	16.67	44.44	38.89

First match: 19–23 January 1995, Johannesburg, South Africa

MOST RUNS: TOP 5

Pos	Player	Runs
1	J.H. Kallis (South Africa, 1997–2010)	1,472
2	G.C. Smith (South Africa, 2002–10)	849
3	G. Kirsten (South Africa, 1995–2003)	838
4	Younis Khan (Pakistan, 2002–10)	750
5	Taufeeq Umar (Pakistan, 2002–10)	730

Most wickets in a series

The record for the most wickets in a South Africa-Pakistan series is 19, a feat achieved by two bowlers: South Africa's Makhaya Ntini, in South Africa in 2006–07; and Pakistan's Mohammad Asif, also in South Africa in 2006–07.

MOST WICKETS: TOP 5

Pos	Player	Wickets
1	**S.M. Pollock** (South Africa, 1997–2007)	45
2	M. Ntini (South Africa, 2002–07)	41
3	Danish Kaneria (Pakistan, 2003–07)	36
4	Mushtaq Ahmed (Pakistan, 1997–2003)	29
5	A.A. Donald (South Africa, 1995–98)	27

PAKISTAN v ZIMBABWE

It may not have been an iron grip, but Pakistan certainly held the upper hand in the 14 Test matches they played against Zimbabwe between 1993 and 2011, winning nine, drawing four and losing only two of them.

Spin-friendly surface suits Saqlain

Saqlain Mushtaq took full advantage of a wicket that offered spin from the first afternoon of the Second Test at Bulawayo in November 2002 to lay the foundations for Pakistan's ten-wicket victory over Zimbabwe to claim a 2–0 series win. The off-spinner took 7 for 66 in the first innings (the best single-innings figures in matches between the two countries) to help dismiss Zimbabwe for 178, a position from which the home side failed to recover.

Wasim's record-breaking rescue act at Sheikhupura

For a short while, with Pakistan struggling on 237 for 7, still 138 runs behind their first-innings score in the First Test of the 1996–97 series at Sheikhupura, Zimbabwe must have felt they stood a reasonable chance of winning the game. But a sensational batting performance from **Wasim Akram**, who hit an unbeaten 257 (the highest score by a No. 8 in Test history and the highest in Pakistan-Zimbabwe clashes), propelled the home side to 553 all out – still the highest team total in all matches between the two countries. Wasim's efforts were not enough to win the match, however, which ended in a draw.

Waqar extinguishes Zimbabwe challenge

Zimbabwe were unfortunate to run into **Waqar Younis** bowling at the peak of his prodigious powers when they faced Pakistan for the first time in a three-match series in 1993–94. The paceman took 7 for 91 and 6 for 44 in the First Test at Karachi (his match haul of 13 for 135 is an all-time Pakistan-Zimbabwe record), 5 for 88 and 4 for 50 in the Second Test at Rawalpindi, and 5 for 100 in the fog- and bad light-affected Third Test at Lahore. Waqar ended the series, which Pakistan won 2–0, with 27 wickets – another all-time record in matches between the two countries.

OVERALL SERIES RECORDS

(15 Tests between 1993 and 2011)

	W	L	T	D	W/L	%W	%L	%D
Pakistan	9	2	0	4	4.50	60.00	13.33	26.66
Zimbabwe	2	9	0	4	0.22	13.33	60.00	26.66

First match: 1–6 December 1993, Karachi, Pakistan

MOST RUNS: TOP 5

Pos	Player	Runs
1	G.W. Flower (Zimbabwe, 1993–2002)	961
2	A. Flower (Zimbabwe, 1993–2002)	931
3	Inzamam-ul-Haq (Pakistan, 1993–2002)	772
4	Mohammad Yousuf (Pakistan, 1998–2002)	616
5	A.D.R. Campbell (Zimbabwe, 1993–2002)	612

MOST WICKETS: TOP 5

Pos	Player	Wickets
1	Waqar Younis (Pakistan, 1993–2002)	62
2	Wasim Akram (Pakistan, 1993–98)	47
3	H.H. Streak (Zimbabwe, 1993–98)	44
4	Saqlain Mushtaq (Pakistan, 1996–2002)	28
5	G.J. Whittall (Zimbabwe, 1993–2002)	23

S. AFRICA v ZIMBABWE

Given their geographical situation as southern African neighbours, it seems strange that South Africa and Zimbabwe contested only seven Test matches in ten years between 1995 and 2005. What is less strange, however, is that South Africa dominated the matches that were played: winning all but one of the matches played and drawing the other.

Happy times in Harare

South Africa's batsmen prospered on a friendly, even surface against a weak Zimbabwe attack in the First Test of the two-match 2001–02 series at Harare. After winning the toss and electing to bat, South Africa's top three batsmen all passed three figures – Herschelle Gibbs (147), Gary Kirsten (220, the highest individual score in South Africa-Zimbabwe Tests) and **Jacques Kallis** (157 not out) – to propel their side to a substantial 600 for 3 declared (the highest team total in all Tests between the two countries) and an eventual nine-wicket win.

Flower blossoms against South Africa

A truly outstanding performer for his country in a 63-Test, decade-long international career, Andy Flower seemed, at times, to provide the sole resistance for Zimbabwe in matches against South Africa. In five Tests against them between 1995 and 2001 he scored 566 runs (with two centuries, two half-centuries and a highest score of 199 not out, at Harare in September 2001) at an average of 70.75 – the highest by any batsman to complete ten or more innings in matches between the two countries.

OVERALL SERIES RECORDS

(7 Tests between 1995 and 2005)

	W	L	T	D	W/L	%W	%L	%D
South Africa	6	0	0	1	-	85.71	0.00	14.29
Zimbabwe	0	6	0	1	0.00	0.00	85.71	14.29

First match: 13–16 October 1995, Harare, Zimbabwe

MOST RUNS: TOP 5

Pos	Player	Runs
1	J.H. Kallis (South Africa, 1999–2005)	679
2	A. Flower (Zimbabwe, 1995–2001)	566
3	G. Kirsten (South Africa, 1995–2001)	330
4	H. Masakadza (Zimbabwe, 2001–05)	278
5	H.H. Gibbs (South Africa, 2001–05)	276

MOST WICKETS: TOP 5

Pos	Player	Wickets
1	S.M. Pollock (South Africa, 1999–2005)	23
2	J.H. Kallis (South Africa, 1999–2005)	21
3	A.A. Donald (South Africa, 1995–99)	14
4	C.W. Henderson (South Africa, 2001)	11
5	B.C. Strang (Zimbabwe, 1995–99)	9
=	A. Nel (South Africa, 2001–05)	9
=	M. Zondeki (South Africa, 2005)	9

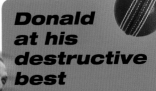

Donald at his destructive best

A blistering performance from **Allan Donald** with the ball in Zimbabwe's second innings paved the way for South Africa's victory in October 1995 at Harare. The legendary fast bowler took 8 for 71 (the best single-innings figures in South Africa-Zimbabwe Tests) to skittle Zimbabwe for 283 and leave South Africa requiring a mere 108 runs for victory; a target they achieved for the loss of three wickets. Donald's match haul (11 for 113) is also a record in South Africa-Zimbabwe matches.

ZIMBABWE v ENGLAND

A record of three victories by an innings and no defeats in the six Test matches they played against Zimbabwe between 1996 and 2000 suggests a complete English dominance over Zimbabwe, but, on occasion, particularly in home Tests, the southern Africans more than held their own.

Johnson's headline-grabbing debut

Richard Johnson made a sensational debut for England against Zimbabwe in the first-ever Test match played at Chester-le-Street in June 2003: he took two wickets in his first over and ended up with figures of 6 for 33 – the best single-innings figures in all England-Zimbabwe matches – as the home side went on to win the match by a innings and 69 runs.

Goodwin shows Zimbabwe the way

Following a comprehensive defeat at Lord's in the first match of the 2000 series, Zimbabwe showed considerable fight in the rain-affected and drawn Second Test at Trent Bridge, and no one more so than Murray Goodwin. The middle-order batsman hit 148 not out in Zimbabwe's first innings, the highest individual score in all Tests between the two countries.

England cash in at Lord's

An undisciplined performance in the field by Zimbabwe allowed England to lay the foundations for an impressive victory inside three days in the First Test of the 2003 series at Lord's. Aided by Mark Butcher's 256-ball 137, and some unforgivably loose bowling from the visitors, the home side reached 472 all out – the highest team total in all matches between the two countries. They then bowled out Zimbabwe twice (for 147 and 233) to win the match by an innings and 92 runs.

All at sea at the home of cricket

Lord's has been a far from happy hunting ground for Zimbabwe – they have played there twice over the years and lost both matches by an innings – but their first visit to the home of cricket, in May 2000, will revive particularly painful memories for the southern Africans. After losing the toss and being put in to bat, they collapsed to 83 all out in 30.3 overs (the lowest-ever total in Zimbabwe-England matches).

OVERALL SERIES RECORDS

(6 Tests between 1996 and 2003)

	W	L	T	D	W/L	%W	%L	%D
Zimbabwe	0	3	0	3	0.00	0.00	50.00	50.00
England	3	0	0	3	-	50.00	0.00	50.00

First match: 18–22 December 1996, Bulawayo, Zimbabwe

MOST RUNS: TOP 5

Pos	Player	Runs
1	**A.J. Stewart** (England, 1996–2003)	483
2	M.A. Atherton (England, 1996–2000)	259
3	N.V. Knight (England, 1996–2000)	248
4	A. Flower (Zimbabwe, 1996–2000)	200
5	N. Hussain (England, 1996–2003)	198

MOST WICKETS: TOP 5

Pos	Player	Wickets
1	**H.H. Streak** (Zimbabwe, 1996–2003)	24
2	D. Gough (England, 1996–2000)	16
3	G.J. Whittall (Zimbabwe, 1996–2000)	13
4	J.M. Anderson (England, 2003)	11
5	P.A. Strang (Zimbabwe, 1996)	10

ZIMBABWE v AUSTRALIA

Australia simply proved too strong for Zimbabwe: the two countries contested only three Test matches between 1999 and 2003 and the Australians won them all, producing some record-breaking performances along the way.

Hayden heroics light up Perth

Matthew Hayden grabbed the headlines in the First Test against Zimbabwe at Perth in October 2003. The Queensland opener, who was nursing a sore back, occupied the crease for ten hours and 22 minutes, faced 437 balls and celebrated wildly as he hit 380 runs to break Brian Lara's record for the highest score in Test cricket (a record Lara would regain seven months later). Hayden's dismissal prompted an Australian declaration: on 735 for 6 – the second-highest team total in Australia's history and the highest in all Australia-Zimbabwe matches.

Part-time bowler Katich steals the show

He went on to become an established presence at the top of the Australian order, but early in his Test career Simon Katich hit the headlines for his part-time left-arm leg-break bowling. In the Second Test against Zimbabwe at Sydney in October 2003, he took 6 for 65 in the second innings (the best bowling figures in Tests between the two countries) to help set up a nine-wicket victory for Australia. Katich also holds the record for the best match figures (6 for 90) – shared with Glenn McGrath, who achieved the feat at Harare in October 1999.

OVERALL SERIES RECORDS

(3 Tests between 1999 and 2003)

	W	L	T	D	W/L	%W	%L	%D
Zimbabwe	0	3	0	0	0.00	0.00	100.00	0.00
Australia	3	0	0	0	-	100.00	0.00	0.00

First match: 14–17 October 1999, Harare, Zimbabwe

MOST RUNS: TOP 5

Pos	Player	Runs
1	M.L. Hayden (Australia, 2003)	501
2	R.T. Ponting (Australia, 1999–2003)	290
=	S.R. Waugh (Australia, 1999–2003)	290
4	T.R. Gripper (Zimbabwe, 1999–2003)	179
5	M.A. Vermeulen (Zimbabwe, 2003)	166

Zimbabwe's highs and lows

The root of Zimbabwe's problems in Test matches against Australia has been their batsmen's inability to amass a total of any real significance: their highest total (321) came after Australia had smashed 735 runs of their own at Perth in October 2003; their lowest effort (194) came in the first-ever match between the two sides at Harare in October 1999.

MOST WICKETS: TOP 5

Pos	Player	Wickets
1	**A.J. Bichel** (Australia, 2003)	10
2	H.H. Streak (Zimbabwe, 1999–2003)	7
3	G.D. McGrath (Australia, 1999)	6
=	S.K. Warne (Australia, 1999)	6
=	S.M. Katich (Australia, 2003)	6
=	B. Lee (Australia, 2003)	6
=	R.W. Price (Zimbabwe, 2003)	6

W. INDIES V ZIMBABWE

Despite their ever-increasing woes against the strongest cricketing nations since the turn of the new millennium, the West Indies enjoyed playing against Zimbabwe. In the six matches between the two countries since they met for the first time in 2000, the men from the Caribbean proved too strong for the southern Africans, winning four of them and drawing the other two.

Batting masterclass from Lara

An imperious innings by Brian Lara ultimately proved the difference between the two sides in the Second Test between Zimbabwe and the West Indies at Bulawayo in November 2003. The masterful left-hander crafted a brilliant 191 off 203 balls – the highest individual score in West Indies-Zimbabwe Tests – in a match the West Indies went on to win by 128 runs.

OVERALL SERIES RECORDS

(6 Tests between 1996 and 2003)

	W	L	T	D	W/L	%W	%L	%D
West Indies	4	0	0	2	-	66.67	0.00	33.33
Zimbabwe	0	4	0	2	0.00	0.00	66.67	33.33

First match: 16–20 March 2000, Port of Spain, Trinidad

MOST RUNS: TOP 5

Pos	Player	Runs
1	**C.H. Gayle** (West Indies, 2000–03)	353
2	C.B. Wishart (Zimbabwe, 2001–03)	331
3	R.R. Sarwan (West Indies, 2001–03)	297
4	H.H. Streak (Zimbabwe, 2000–03)	288
5	W.W. Hinds (West Indies, 2000–03)	281

MOST WICKETS: TOP 5

Pos	Player	Wickets
1	R.W. Price (Zimbabwe, 2001–03)	23
2	H.H. Streak (Zimbabwe, 2000–03)	21
3	R.D. King (West Indies, 2000–01)	16
4	N.C. McGarrell (West Indies, 2001)	12
=	C.E.L. Stuart (West Indies, 2001)	12

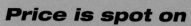

Price is spot on

An impressive left-arm spinner who played 18 Tests for Zimbabwe between 1999 and 2004, **Ray Price** was at his best in the two-match series against the West Indies in November 2003. He took 6 for 73 (the best single-innings figures in West Indies-Zimbabwe matches) and 4 for 88 in the drawn First Test at Harare (his match figures of 10 for 161 are also a record in Tests between the two countries) and 5 for 199 and 4 for 36 in a losing cause in the Second Test at Bulawayo. His series haul of 19 wickets is another West Indies-Zimbabwe record.

Record-breaking rescue act

Trailing by 216 runs at the start of their second innings, Zimbabwe needed to produce an innings of huge proportions to avoid crashing to a second successive heavy defeat in the two-Test 2001 series at Harare. And they did: led by Hamilton Masakadza's 316-ball 119, and bolstered by late-order contributions from Heath Streak (83 not out) and Andy Blignaut (92), Zimbabwe battled to 563 for 9. The highest team total in all matches between the two countries enabled Zimbabwe to evade defeat for the first time against the West Indies.

The worst of starts

Zimbabwe crashed to a morale-crushing defeat in their first-ever Test match against the West Indies, at Port of Spain, Trinidad, in March 2000. Chasing a mere 99 runs for victory, they slumped to 63 all out – the lowest-ever total in West Indies-Zimbabwe Tests.

BANGLADESH v INDIA

India, Bangladesh's first-ever opponents in Test cricket, have dominated the few Test matches played against their subcontinental neighbours, winning six of the seven Tests played (all of them in Bangladesh) and drawing just once.

OVERALL SERIES RECORDS

(7 Tests between 2000 and 2010)

	W	L	T	D	W/L	%W	%L	%D
Bangladesh	0	6	0	1	0.00	0.00	85.71	14.29
India	6	0	0	1	-	85.71	0.00	14.29

First match: 10–13 November 2000, Dhaka, Bangladesh

MOST RUNS: TOP 5

Pos	Player	Runs
1	S.R. Tendulkar (India, 2000–10)	820
2	R. Dravid (India, 2000–10)	560
3	Mohammad Ashraful (Bangladesh, 2004–10)	386
4	G. Gambhir (India, 2004–10)	381
5	S.C. Ganguly (India, 2000–07)	371

MOST WICKETS: TOP 5

Pos	Player	Wickets
1	Z. Khan (India, 2000–10)	31
2	I.K. Pathan (India, 2004)	18
3	Mohammad Rafique (Bangladesh, 2000–07)	15
=	A. Kumble (India, 2004–07)	15
5	Shahadat Hossain (Bangladesh, 2007–10)	12

Pathan plagues Bangladesh

Despite Sachin Tendulkar's star turn with the bat in the First Test against Bangladesh at Dhaka in December 2004, India would not have achieved their massive innings-and-140-run victory without Irfan Pathan's considerable efforts with the ball. The young pace bowler, considered by many to have the potential to become the best Indian fast bowler since Kapil Dev, took 5 for 45 in the first innings and 6 for 51 in the second to end the match with 11 for 96 – the best match figures in all Tests between the two countries. Seven wickets in the Second Test at Chittagong saw Pathan end the series with 18 wickets – another all-time Bangladesh-India record.

India prosper in Dhaka

Having suffered the ignominy of drawing the first of the two Tests in Bangladesh in May 2007, India bounced back in style in the Second Test at Dhaka. Bolstered by centuries from each of their top four batsmen – Dinesh Karthik (129), Wasim Jaffer (138), Rahul Dravid (129) and Sachin Tendulkar (122 not out) – they reached 610 for 3 declared (the highest team total in Bangladesh-India Tests) and went on to win by an innings and 239 runs – their largest-ever Test victory.

Bangladesh let it slip

A sorry second-innings batting display by Bangladesh saw them crash to a six-wicket defeat in the first-ever Test against India at Dhaka in December 2004. The home side crashed to 91 all out – the lowest-ever total in Bangladesh-India clashes.

Tendulkar top of the bill in Dhaka

It may have come against the weakest opponents he has encountered in his illustrious Test career, but **Sachin Tendulkar** cashed in with style in the First Test against Bangladesh at Dhaka in December 2004 to record the highest score of his career (and the best individual score in Bangladesh-India matches). The Little Master faced 379 balls (hitting 35 fours) to compile an unbeaten 248 in a match that India went on to win by an innings and 140 runs.

PAKISTAN v BANGLADESH

Bangladesh's early encounters with Pakistan were humbling – they lost their first three matches against them by an innings – but, although they have lost all eight of the Test matches played, recent encounters have been more competitive as Bangladesh slowly find their feet in the Test arena.

Yousuf shows how it's done

Mohammad Yousuf was in prime batting form for Pakistan in the Second Test of the 2001–02 series against Bangladesh at Chittagong, producing a masterful innings of 204 not out – the highest individual total in matches between the two countries – as Pakistan cruised to 465 for 9. In contrast, Bangladesh's batsmen were woeful, slipping to 148 all out in both innings to lose the match by an innings and 169 runs.

OVERALL SERIES RECORDS

(8 Tests between 2001 and 2011)

	W	L	T	D	W/L	%W	%L	%D
Pakistan	8	0	0	0	-	100.00	0.00	0.00
Bangladesh	0	8	0	0	0.00	0.00	100.00	0.00

First match: 29–31 August 2001, Multan, Pakistan

MOST RUNS: TOP 5

Pos	Player	Runs
1	Taufeeq Umar (Pakistan, 2001–11)	558
2	**Habibul Bashar** (Bangladesh, 2001–03)	554
3	Mohammad Yousuf (Pakistan, 2001–03)	503
4	Mohammad Hafeez (Pakistan, 2003–11)	418
=	Younis Khan (Pakistan, 2002–11)	418

MOST WICKETS: TOP 5

Pos	Player	Wickets
1	**Danish Kaneria** (Pakistan, 2001–03)	34
2	Waqar Younis (Pakistan, 2001–02)	18
3	Umar Gul (Pakistan, 2003–11)	22
4	Shabbir Ahmed (Pakistan, 2003)	17
=	Shoaib Akhtar (Pakistan, 2002–03)	17
=	Mohammad Rafique (Bangladesh, 2003)	17

Most wickets in a series

The record for the most wickets in a Pakistan-Bangladesh series is 17, a feat achieved by two bowlers: Shabbir Ahmed (Pakistan) and Mohammad Rafique (Bangladesh), both in the 2003 series in Pakistan.

Bangladesh lose their nerve

Leading Pakistan by 66 runs after the first innings of the Second Test at Peshawar in August 2003, Bangladesh were in a strong position to win the match. But instead of pushing on to gain a first-ever victory over their subcontinental cousins, Bangladesh's batmen lost their nerve and crashed to 96 all out – the lowest total in all matches between the two sides – and a Test match they should have won was eventually lost by nine wickets.

Kaneria cashes in

One of only four Pakistan bowlers in history to take more than 250 Test wickets (254), **Danish Kaneria** has enjoyed some fine moments against Bangladesh. In the first-ever Test between the two countries at Multan in August 2001 he took 6 for 42 in the first innings and 6 for 52 in the second – his match haul of 12 for 94 is the best in all matches between the two countries – as Pakistan cruised to an innings-and-264-run victory; five months later, in Dhaka, he took 7 for 77 – the best single-innings figures in Pakistan-Bangladesh Tests.

NZ v BANGLADESH

New Zealand have dominated Bangladesh in comprehensive fashion since the two countries met for the first time at Hamilton in December 2001, winning seven of the eight matches played – five of them by an innings – while the other was a rain-affected draw.

Shakib puts New Zealand in a spin

That New Zealand won the First Test of the 2008–09 series at Chittagong by just three wickets shows both how much Bangladesh have improved in Test cricket and how much pressure New Zealand were under following a fine spell of bowling from Shakib Al Hasan. The Bangladesh left-arm spinner took 7 for 36 in New Zealand's first innings – the best single-innings figures in all Tests between the two countries – to guide his side to a 74-run first-innings lead, a position which, ultimately, they ended up squandering.

OVERALL SERIES RECORDS

(9 Tests between 2001 and 2010)

	W	L	T	D	W/L	%W	%L	%D
New Zealand	8	0	0	1	-	88.88	0.00	11.12
Bangladesh	0	8	0	1	0.00	0.00	88.88	11.12

First match: 18–22 December 2001, Hamilton, New Zealand

MOST RUNS: TOP 5

Pos	Player	Runs
1	**B.B. McCullum** (New Zealand, 2004–10)	504
2	S.P. Fleming (New Zealand, 2001–08)	397
3	Shakib Al Hasan (Bangladesh, 2008–10)	358
4	Tamim Iqbal (Bangladesh, 2008–10)	325
=	D.L. Vettori (New Zealand, 2001–10)	325

MOST WICKETS: TOP 5

Pos	Player	Wickets
1	**D.L. Vettori** (New Zealand, 2001–10)	51
2	C.S. Martin (New Zealand, 2001–10)	19
=	I.E. O'Brien (New Zealand, 2008)	15
4	Mashrafe Mortaza (Bangladesh, 2001–08)	14
5	C.L. Cairns (New Zealand, 2001)	13

Fleming leads from the front

Having seen his side brush aside Bangladesh in the First Test of the 2004–05 series (New Zealand won the match at Dhaka by an innings and 90 runs), Stephen Fleming ensured his side carried the momentum into the Second Test at Chittagong. Leading from the front in imperious fashion, the Kiwi captain smashed 202 off 318 balls (the highest individual score in New Zealand-Bangladesh Tests) to help his side reach 545 for 6 declared (the highest team total in matches between the two countries) en route to a comprehensive innings-and-101-run victory.

The worst of starts

Bangladesh's batsmen were all at sea on a bowler-friendly surface at Hamilton against New Zealand in December 2001 – the first-ever Test between the two countries. Having seen the home side scramble to 365 for 9 declared in just 77.1 overs in an attempt to force a result, Bangladesh fell for 205 in the first innings and, following on, 108 in the second (the lowest total in New Zealand-Bangladesh matches) to lose by an innings and 52 runs.

Bangladesh bow to Vettori

Where Stephen Fleming, with his 202, was the star with the bat in the Second Test at Chittagong in October 2004, Daniel Vettori was New Zealand's hero with the ball. The slow left-armer took 6 for 70 in Bangladesh's first innings and 6 for 100 in their second to help bowl his side to an innings-and-101-run victory. His match figures of 12 for 170 are a record in New Zealand-Bangladesh Tests.

SRI LANKA v BANGLADESH

Those who argue that Bangladesh's elevation to Test status was premature could point to their performances against Sri Lanka. They have played 12 Tests against the Sri Lankans (more than against any other country) and have lost every one of them – seven of them by an innings.

Super Sangakkara cashes in

Sri Lanka's complete dominance with the ball in matches against Bangladesh (Test cricket's new boys have posted only one 350-plus score against Sri Lanka in 24 attempts) has given their batsmen both the time and a free rein to craft a big innings. And, in the Third Test of the 2007 series at Kandy, **Kumar Sangakkara** was only too keen to take advantage of the situation. The talented left-hander hit an unbeaten 222 – the highest individual score in Sri Lanka-Bangladesh matches – to help his side reach 500 for 4 declared (in response to Bangladesh's paltry 131 all out) en route to an innings-and-193-run victory.

OVERALL SERIES RECORDS

(12 Tests between 2001 and 2009)

	W	L	T	D	W/L	%W	%L	%D
Sri Lanka	12	0	0	0	–	100.00	0.00	0.00
Bangladesh	0	12	0	0	0.00	0.00	100.00	0.00

First match: 6–8 September 2001, Colombo, Sri Lanka

MOST RUNS: TOP 5

Pos	Player	Runs
1	**K.C. Sangakkara** (Sri Lanka, 2001–09)	876
2	D.P.M.D. Jayawardene (Sri Lanka, 2001–09)	860
3	Mohammad Ashraful (Bangladesh, 2001–09)	858
4	T.M. Dilshan (Sri Lanka, 2005–09)	771
5	T.T. Samaraweera (Sri Lanka, 2001–09)	600

MOST WICKETS: TOP 5

Pos	Player	Wickets
1	**M. Muralitharan** (Sri Lanka, 2001–09)	89
2	C.R.D. Fernando (Sri Lanka, 2002–09)	28
3	S.L. Malinga (Sri Lanka, 2005–07)	27
4	Shahadat Hossain (Bangladesh, 2005–09)	23
5	W.P.U.J.C. Vaas (Sri Lanka, 2001–09)	19

Bangladesh spellbound by Murali magic

One of the arguments against **Muttiah Muralitharan** being the greatest spin bowler ever to play the game – despite his standing as Test cricket's all-time leading wicket-taker (with 792) – will be that he played the majority of his matches in favourable conditions and, in the case of Bangladesh, against favourable opposition. Murali has simply been too good for the Bangladesh batsmen – in 11 Tests he has claimed 89 wickets – and holds all manner of bowling records in matches between the two countries, including: the best bowling in an innings (6 for 18 at Colombo in September 2005); the best bowling in a match (12 for 82 at Kandy in July 2007); and the most wickets in a series (26 in 2007).

Sri Lanka cruise in Colombo

Sri Lanka swept aside Bangladesh with ease in the First Test of a three-match series at Colombo in June 2007. After winning the toss and electing to bowl, they felled Bangladesh for 89 and then – aided by centuries from Michael Vandort (117), Mahela Jayawardene (127), Prasanna Jayawardene (120 not out) and Chaminda Vaas (100 not out) – piled on a massive 577 for 6 declared (the highest team total in Sri Lanka-Bangladesh Tests) and went on to win the match by an innings and 234 runs.

Colombo capitulation

Bangladesh's lowest point against Sri Lanka came in the First Test of the three-match 2007 series at Colombo: they fell to 61 all out in the first innings – the lowest total in all matches between the two countries.

S. AFRICA v BANGLADESH

Bangladesh have enjoyed no success in matches against South Africa: in eight matches played between the two countries since they met for the first time at East London in October 2002 they have lost every time – and on seven of those occasions they have lost by an innings.

OVERALL SERIES RECORDS

(8 Tests between 2002 and 2008)

	W	L	T	D	W/L	%W	%L	%D
South Africa	8	0	0	0	-	100.00	0.00	0.00
Bangladesh	0	8	0	0	0.00	0.00	100.00	0.00

First match: 18–21 October 2002, East London, South Africa

MOST RUNS: TOP 5

Pos	Player	Runs
1	**G.C. Smith** (South Africa, 2002–08)	743
2	J.H. Kallis (South Africa, 2002–08)	317
3	G. Kirsten (South Africa, 2002)	310
4	N.D. McKenzie (South Africa, 2003–08)	306
5	Habibul Bashar (Bangladesh, 2002–08)	301

MOST WICKETS: TOP 5

Pos	Player	Wickets
1	**M. Ntini** (South Africa, 2002–08)	35
2	D.W. Steyn (South Africa, 2008)	22
3	J.H. Kallis (South Africa, 2002–08)	17
4	Shahadat Hossain (Bangladesh, 2008)	15
5	M. Morkel (South Africa, 2008)	14

Hossein gives Bangladesh cause for hope

Although South Africa ultimately won the First Test of the 2007–08 series by five wickets, they did so only after Shahadat Hossain caused them to post their lowest-ever total against Bangladesh. The promising young fast bowler took 6 for 27 in the first innings – the best single-innings figures in matches between the two countries – to help dismiss the visitors for 170.

Dreams dashed in Dhaka

After restricting South Africa to 330 all out in the Second Test of the 2003 series at Dhaka, Bangladesh were very much in the game, but any aspirations they may have had to win the match were soon dashed. In reply, they slipped to 102 all out – the lowest total in South Africa-Bangladesh Tests – and went on to lose by an innings and 18 runs.

Adams spins South Africa to victory

Paul Adams was South Africa's star with the ball as they crushed Bangladesh by an innings and 60 runs in the First Test at Chittagong in April 2003. The unconventional leg-spinner took 5 for 37 in the first innings and 5 for 59 in the second to record match figures of 10 for 106 – a record in South Africa-Bangladesh Test matches.

South Africa crush Bangladesh at Chittagong

Having won the First Test of the 2007–08 series against Bangladesh only by five wickets (thus losing their record of having won every match against them by an innings), South Africa would have been keen to reassert their total supremacy over Test cricket's newest nation in the Second Test at Chittagong. And so they did: **Graeme Smith** hit 232 (the highest individual score in South Africa-Bangladesh Tests) and Neil McKenzie 226 (the pair put on 415 runs for the opening wicket) to send South Africa on their way to a total of 583 for 7 declared (the highest in all matches between the two countries). South Africa went on to win the match by an innings and 205 runs.

BANGLADESH v WEST INDIES

Bangladesh have enjoyed more success against the West Indies than against any other nation since their elevation to Test status in 2001, winning two of the eight Test matches played – both times, admittedly, against a much-weakened West Indies outfit.

OVERALL SERIES RECORDS

(8 Tests between 2002 and 2011)

	W	L	T	D	W/L	%W	%L	%D
Bangladesh	2	4	0	2	0.50	25.00	50.00	25.00
West Indies	4	2	0	2	2.00	50.00	25.00	25.00

First match: 8–10 December 2002, Dhaka, Bangladesh

Sarwan spearheads West Indies victory

The West Indies crushed Bangladesh in the first-ever Test between the two countries at Kingston, Jamaica, in June 2004. A brilliant unbeaten 261 from Ramnaresh Sarwan (the highest individual score in Bangladesh-West Indies Tests) led his side to 559 for 9 declared (another Bangladesh-West Indies record) and an eventual innings-and-99-run victory.

MOST RUNS: TOP 5

Pos	Player	Runs
1	R.R. Sarwan (West Indies, 2002–04)	450
2	Tamim Iqbal (Bangladesh, 2009–11)	383
3	C.H. Gayle (West Indies, 2002–04)	347
4	Shakib Al Hasan (Bangladesh, 2009–11)	327
5	Habibul Bashar (Bangladesh, 2002–04)	284

MOST WICKETS: TOP 5

Pos	Player	Wickets
1	P.T. Collins (West Indies, 2002–04)	26
2	Shakib Al Hasan (Bangladesh, 2009–11)	23
3	D.J.G. Sammy (West Indies, 2009–11)	16
4	K.A.J. Roach (West Indies, 2009–11)	14
5	J.J.C. Lawson (West Indies, 2002–04)	13

AUSTRALIA v BANGLADESH

In Test matches played between the two countries, both at home and away, Bangladesh have proved no match for Australia, losing four Tests out of four, three of them by an innings.

OVERALL SERIES RECORDS

(4 Tests between 2003 and 2006)

	W	L	T	D	W/L	%W	%L	%D
Australia	4	0	0	0	-	100.00	0.00	0.00
Bangladesh	0	4	0	0	0.00	0.00	100.00	0.00

First match: 18–20 July 2003, Darwin, Australia

Gillespie's golden innings

It was the most unexpected performance in Test cricket in recent memory. Coming in as a nightwatchman, Jason Gillespie ended the first day of the Second Test against Bangladesh at Chittagong in April 2006 on 5 not out. Three days later, remarkably, he was still batting, reaching 201 not out (the highest score by a nightwatchman in Test history and the highest individual score in Bangladesh-Australia clashes) before Australia declared on 581 for 4. Gillespie's performance was a match-winning one: the visitors went on to win the match by an innings and 80 runs.

MOST RUNS: TOP 5

Pos	Player	Runs
1	D.S. Lehmann (Australia, 2003)	287
2	Habibul Bashar (Bangladesh, 2003–06)	282
3	R.T. Ponting (Australia, 2003–06)	260
4	S.R. Waugh (Australia, 2003)	256
5	Shahriar Nafees (Bangladesh, 2006)	250

MOST WICKETS: TOP 5

Pos	Player	Wickets
1	S.C.G. MacGill (Australia, 2003–06)	33
2	J.N. Gillespie (Australia, 2003–06)	19
3	S.K. Warne (Australia, 2006)	11
=	Mohammad Rafique (Bangladesh, 2006)	11
5	B. Lee (Australia, 2003–06)	8

BANGLADESH v ENGLAND

Such has been England's dominance over Bangladesh – they have won all six of the Test matches played with ease – that they now see matches against Test cricket's new boys as an opportunity to rest some of their star players in what has become an increasingly congested international schedule.

HIGHS AND LOWS

Highest score (team): 599 for 6 dec – England v Bangladesh at Chittagong in March 2010

Lowest score (team): 104 all out – Bangladesh v England at Chester-le-Street in June 2005

OVERALL SERIES RECORDS

(8 Tests between 2003 and 2010)

	W	L	T	D	W/L	%W	%L	%D
Bangladesh	0	8	0	0	0.00	0.00	100.00	0.00
England	8	0	0	0	-	100.00	0.00	0.00

First match: 21–25 October 2003, Dhaka, Bangladesh

MOST RUNS: TOP 5

Pos	Player	Runs
1	I.R. Bell (England, 2005–10)	633
2	M.E. Trescothick (England, 2003–05)	551
3	Tamim Iqbal (Bangladesh, 2010)	505
4	A.N. Cook (England, 2010)	401
=	I.J.L. Trott (England, 2010)	401

MOST WICKETS: TOP 5

Pos	Player	Wickets
1	M.J. Hoggard (England, 2003–05)	23
2	G.P. Swann (England, 2010)	22
3	S.J. Harmison (England, 2003–05)	19
=	S.T. Finn (England, 2010)	19
5	Shakib Al Hasan (Bangladesh, 2010)	17

Trott tears into Bangladesh

Jonathan Trott produced the standout performance in a commanding display by England against Bangladesh in the First Test of the 2010 series at Lord's. Coming to the crease with England, batting first after being put into bat, the Warwickshire no.3 batted beautifully, hitting 226 – the highest individual score in Bangladesh-England clashes – to lead his side to an imposing 505 all out. England went on to win the match by eight wickets to take a 1–0 series lead.

BOWLING BESTS

Innings: 5 for 35 – S.J. Harmison (England), England v Bangladesh at Dhaka in October 2003

Match: 10 for 217 – G.P. Swann (England), England v Bangladesh at Chittagong in March 2010

Series: 16 – G.P. Swann (England), England in Bangladesh in 2009–10

PART II:
ONE-DAY INTERNATIONAL CRICKET

It was thought merely to have been a one-off arrangement, a means of appeasing a cricket-hungry public following a Boxing Day Test washout, but when Australia played England in a 40-over match at Melbourne on 5 January 1971, one-day international cricket was born, and how the public loved it; 46,000 paying spectators turned up to watch this new phenomenon, and, over the years, the limited-overs game has gone on to form an increasing part of a cricket fan's diet ever since – and is the format used to decide the game's World Cup, the first of which was contested in 1975 (and which was won by the West Indies).

Detractors would suggest a cricket fan is force-fed limited-overs cricket: in the first five years of the 1980s, 402 one-day internationals were played, as opposed to 1,382 between 2000 and 2004 – more than three times as many. But one-day international cricket, particularly in the subcontinent, has become an essential asset for the game's finances – its continued popularity has made it international cricket's cash cow. How long that situation lasts, with the meteoric rise of the Twenty20 game, remains to be seen. The game's detractors will also point out that the abbreviated form of the game brings out the worst in players; that the need for quick runs leads to the breakdown of technique. Its enduring popularity, however, suggests the one-day international game is a platform upon which the best players can dazzle and the enormous success of the 2011 ICC World Cup suggests that the 50-over format of the game will be around for a long time to come.

Crowd-pleasers: **India** beat Sri Lanka by six wickets in the 2011 ICC World Cup final to send the home crowd into raptures.

ICC WORLD CUP

The fourth most watched sporting event on the planet, the ICC World Cup is international cricket's premier 50-over tournament. It has grown in stature over the years: the first edition, held in England in 1975, featured eight pre-invited teams; the 2011 edition, staged on the Subcontinent, featured 14 nations, including four teams that had come through a qualifying tournament.

Largest victories

By runs: by 257 runs – India v Bermuda at Port of Spain, Trinidad, on 19 March 2007 (India 413 for 5 off 50 overs; Bermuda 156 all out in 43.1 overs).

By wickets: by ten wickets on 11 occasions.

Smallest victories

By runs: by one run on two occasions – Australia v India at Chennai, India, on 9 October 1987; and Australia v India at Brisbane on 1 March 1992.

By wickets: by one wicket on four occasions – West Indies v Pakistan at Birmingham on 11 June 1975; Pakistan v West Indies at Lahore on 16 October 1987; South Africa v Sri Lanka at Providence, Guyana, on 28 March 2007; and England v West Indies at Bridgetown, Barbados, on 21 April 2007.

India too hot to handle for Bermuda

One of the consequences of the ICC's commendable drive to expand the World Cup and hand cricket's lesser nations a chance to compete on the international stage has been a growing number of mismatches. When India met Bermuda at Port of Spain, Trinidad, in the 2007 tournament, they eased to 413 for 5 off their 50 overs (with **Virender Sehwag** top scoring with 114) – the highest total in World Cup history – en route to a colossal 257-run victory.

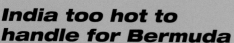

Most matches lost

No side has lost more World Cup matches than Zimbabwe. In 51 matches between 1983 and 2011, the southern Africans have lost 37 matches and won just 10 of them (with one tie and three no-results).

That winning feeling

Three-time winners Australia are the most successful side in World Cup history: in 76 matches between 1975 and 2011, the men from Down Under have won a record 55 matches – 15 more than second-placed New Zealand (with 40).

ICC WORLD CUP WINNERS

Season	Winner	Host
1975	West Indies	(England)
1979	West Indies	(England)
1983	India	(England)
1987	Australia	(India/Pakistan)
1992	Pakistan	(Australia/New Zealand)
1996	Sri Lanka	(India/Pakistan/Sri Lanka)
1999	Australia	(England/Ireland/Netherlands/Scotland)
2003	Australia	(Kenya/South Africa/Zimbabwe)
2007	Australia	(West Indies)
2011	India	(Bangladesh/India/Sri Lanka)

Honours even

There have been four tied matches in World Cup history: Australia v South Africa at Edgbaston on 17 June 1999; South Africa v Sri Lanka at Durban in March 2003; Ireland v Zimbabwe at Kingston, Jamaica, on 15 March 2007; and **India v England** at Bangalore on 27 February 2011.

Runs galore in Bangalore

India were sitting pretty at the halfway mark, as Sachin Tendulkar's 98th international century (120) hoisted them to a healthy total of 338 all out against England in Bangalore at the 2011 World Cup. But comfort soon turned to growing unease as Andrew Strauss (158) led England's noble reply. A late collapse saw the match end in a tie (the fourth in the tournament's history), but it was also a record-breaking encounter: the 676 runs scored is an all-time ICC World Cup high.

Ireland fightback stuns England

When Ireland slumped to 111 for 5 in the 25th over in reply to England's 327 for 8 in the two sides' 2011 World Cup encounter at Bangalore, the match, it seemed, was running to a predictable script. England would gain momentum in the tournament with a comfortable win. Enter **Kevin O'Brien**. The Ireland No.6 bludgeoned a 63-ball 113 – he reached his century off 50 balls (the fastest in ODI history) – to propel Ireland to an unforgettable three-wicket win. England's total (327) is the highest by a team that has gone on to lose the match in the tournament's history.

Canada collapse at Paarl

Canada, making their first World Cup appearance since 1979, proved no match for Sri Lanka when the two sides met at Paarl, South Africa, in February 2003. After losing the toss and being put into bat, they crashed to a dismal 36 all out in 18.4 overs – the lowest total in World Cup history – with **Prabath Nissanka** taking 4 for 12. Sri Lanka eased over the winning line in 4.4 overs for the loss of just one wicket.

Coming back from the dead

When Zimbabwe crashed to 134 all out in 46.1 overs in their group match against England at Albury in 1992, only the most optimistic of their players would have harboured any hopes that they could end their 18-match losing streak in the World Cup stretching back to 1983. But, aided by a bowler-friendly surface, the southern Africans struck back in headline-grabbing fashion, bowling England out for 125 to win the match by nine runs. Their total is the lowest winning total by any side batting first in World Cup history.

ICC WORLD CUP LEAGUE TABLE (RANKED BY WIN-LOSS RATIO)

Pos	Team	W/L	Mat	Won	Lost	Tied	NR
1	**Australia** (1975–2011)	2.89	76	55	19	1	1
2	South Africa (1992–2011)	2.00	47	30	15	2	0
3	England (1975–2011)	1.56	66	39	25	1	1
4	West Indies (1975–2011)	1.52	64	38	25	0	1
5	India (1975–2011)	1.50	67	39	26	1	1
6	Pakistan (1975–2011)	1.38	64	36	26	0	2
7	New Zealand (1975–2011)	1.37	70	40	29	0	1
8	Sri Lanka (1975–2011)	0.96	66	31	32	1	2
9	Bangladesh (1999–2011)	0.47	26	8	17	0	1
10	Ireland (2007–11)	0.40	15	4	10	1	0
11	Kenya (1996–2011)	0.27	29	6	22	0	1
=	Zimbabwe (1983–2011)	0.27	51	10	37	1	3
13	United Arab Emirates (1996)	0.25	5	1	4	0	0
14	Canada (1979–2011)	0.12	18	2	16	0	0
15	Netherlands (1996–2011)	0.11	20	2	18	0	0
16	Bermuda (2007)	0.00	3	0	3	0	0
=	East Africa (1975)	0.00	3	0	3	0	0
=	Namibia (2003)	0.00	6	0	6	0	0
=	Scotland (1999–2007)	0.00	8	0	8	0	0

BATTING RECORDS

MOST RUNS: TOP 10

Pos	Runs	Player	Mat	Inns	NO	HS	Ave	100	50	0
1	2,278	**S.R. Tendulkar** (Ind, 1992–2011)	45	44	4	152	56.96	6	15	2
2	1,743	R.T. Ponting (Aus, 1996–2011)	46	42	4	140*	45.86	5	6	1
3	1,225	B.C. Lara (WI, 1992–2007)	34	33	4	116	42.24	2	7	1
4	1,165	S.T. Jayasuriya (SL, 1992–2007)	38	37	3	120	34.26	3	6	0
5	1,148	J.H. Kallis (SA, 1996–2011)	36	32	7	128*	45.92	1	9	2
6	1,085	A.C. Gilchrist (Aus, 1999–2007)	31	31	1	149	36.16	1	8	1
7	1,083	Javed Miandad (Pak, 1975–96)	33	30	5	103	43.32	1	8	2
8	1,075	S.P. Fleming (NZ, 1996–2007)	33	33	3	134*	35.83	2	5	2
9	1,067	H.H. Gibbs (SA, 1999–2007)	25	23	4	143	56.15	2	8	1
10	1,064	P.A. de Silva (SL, 1987–2003)	35	32	3	145	36.68	2	6	2

King of the big hitters

Renowned for the artful manner in which he constructs an innings and guaranteed to go down in history as one of the greatest batsmen cricket has seen, Ricky Ponting could also mix it with the game's biggest hitters in one-day cricket. In 46 World Cup matches for Australia between 1996 and 2011, the Tasmanian star has struck a tournament record 31 sixes, including a record eight against India in the 2003 World Cup final at Johannesburg.

Most World Cup career ducks

The record for the most World Cup ducks is five, held by two players: Nathan Astle (in 22 matches for New Zealand between 1996 and 2003); and Ijaz Ahmed (in 29 matches for Pakistan between 1987 and 1999).

World Cup final heroics

Six players have scored a century in an ICC World Cup final: Clive Lloyd, 102 for West Indies against Australia at Lord's in 1975); Viv Richards (138 not out for West Indies against England at Lord's in 1979); Aravinda da Silva (107 not out for Sri Lanka against Australia at Lahore in 1996); Ricky Ponting (140 not out for Australia against India at Johannesburg in 2003); Adam Gilchrist (149 for Australia against Sri Lanka at Bridgetown in 2007); and Mahela Jayawardene (103 not out for Sri Lanka against India at Mumbai in 2011). The first five instances saw the star performer end up on the winning side, but there was no such luck for Jayawardene. Despite his heroics, Sri Lanka crashed to a six-wicket defeat.

Klusener crashes his way into the record books

In his early forays in first-class cricket, **Lance Klusener** was considered nothing more than a fast bowler who would bat at No. 11. However, he developed into an all-rounder of true international class and he was at his best in one-day cricket, where his clean ball-striking often gave his side late-order impetus. In 11 World Cup innings for South Africa between 1999 and 2003, Klusener scored 372 runs at an average of 124.00 with a strike-rate of 121.17 runs per 100 balls. Both are World Cup records.

Six sixes in an over

The 29th over of South Africa's 2007 World Cup Group A encounter against Netherlands at St Kitts provided a moment of cricket history. **Heschelle Gibbs** became only the fourth man in the history of the game – and the first in either a World Cup match or a one-day international – to hit six sixes in an over. The unfortunate bowler was Daan van Bunge.

Most sixes in an innings

The most sixes hit in a single innings by a player is eight, a feat achieved by three players: **Ricky Ponting** (Australia) against India at Johannesburg on 23 March 2003; Imran Nazir (Pakistan) against Zimbabwe at Kingston, Jamaica, on 21 March 2007; and by Adam Gilchrist (Australia) against Sri Lanka at Bridgetown, Barbados, on 28 April 2007.

Kirsten cashes in

Gary Kirsten made a mockery of pre-match predictions that the wicket at Rawalpindi for South Africa's 1997 Group B match against United Arab Emirates, having remained under covers for four days because of rain, would be a bowler-friendly surface. The left-handed opener smashed an unbeaten 188 off 159 balls – the highest individual score in World Cup history – as South Africa romped to a 169-run victory.

Gibbs glorious in defeat

It was one of the most scintillating batting performances of the 2003 World Cup. **Herschelle Gibbs** thrilled the partisan Johannesburg crowd with a scintillating innings of 143 to help South Africa to an imposing 306 for 6 in their Pool B encounter with New Zealand. But then the rain came and, with its arrival, South Africa's fortunes changed. New Zealand, chasing a revised target of 226 from 39 overs, and propelled by an unbeaten 134 from captain Stephen Fleming – an innings that contained the most fours in World Cup history (21) – eased to victory with 13 balls to spare. Gibbs's effort is the highest score in a losing cause in World Cup history.

The record breaker

One of the greatest batsmen ever to play the game, India's Sachin Tendulkar has shone in World Cup matches. Having played 45 matches in the tournament between 1992 and 2011, he holds the record for the most runs (2,278), the most balls faced (2,560), the most centuries (6), the most half-centuries (15), and the most runs scored in a single tournament (673 at the 2003 World Cup). The Little Master finally got his hands on a winner's medal in 2011.

Fastest World Cup 50

Although Lou Vincent, with his 101, made the headlines after New Zealand's comfortable 114-run victory over Canada in the two sides' Group C encounter at St Lucia in the 2007 World Cup, it was **Brendon McCullum**, with his late display of power hitting towards the end of New Zealand's innings of 363 for 5, who found a way into the record books. The Kiwi keeper smashed a 20-ball half-century to close out his side's innings – it was the fastest 50 in World Cup history.

BOWLING RECORDS

MOST WICKETS

Pos	Wkts	Player	Mat	O	M	R	BB	Ave	Econ	SR	4w	5w
1	71	G.D. McGrath (Aus, 1996–2007)	39	325.5	42	1292	7/15	18.19	3.96	27.5	0	2
2	68	M. Muralitharan (SL, 1996–2011)	40	343.3	15	335	4/19	19.63	3.88	30.3	4	0
3	55	Wasim Akram (Pak, 1987–2003)	38	324.3	17	1311	5/28	23.83	4.04	35.4	2	1
4	49	W.P.U.J.C. Vaas (SL, 1996–2007)	31	261.4	39	1040	6/25	21.22	3.97	32.0	1	1
5	44	J. Srinath (India, 1992–2003)	34	283.2	21	1224	4/30	27.81	4.32	38.6	2	0
=	44	Z. Khan (India, 2003–11)	23	198.5	12	890	4/42	20.22	4.47	27.1	1	0
7	38	A.A. Donald (SA, 1992–2003)	25	218.5	14	913	4/17	24.02	4.17	34.5	2	0
8	36	J.P.D. Oram (NZ, 2003–11)	23	182.2	21	768	4/39	21.33	4.21	30.3	2	0
9	35	B. Lee (Aus, 2003–11)	17	137.3	15	629	5/42	17.97	4.57	23.5	2	1
10	34	G.B. Hogg (Aus, 2003–07)	21	158.3	10	654	4/27	19.23	4.12	27.9	2	0

Snedden feels the heat

New Zealand's Martin Snedden felt the full force of a blistering England batting display during the two countries' Group A encounter at The Oval in the 1983 World Cup. The medium-pace bowler took two wickets but went for 105 runs off his 12 overs – the most runs conceded in an innings in World Cup history – as England compiled 322 for 6 (off 60 overs) en route to a comprehensive 106-run victory.

Bond's heroics all in vain

At the halfway stage of New Zealand's Super Six match-up against Australia at Port Elizabeth on 11 March 2003, the Kiwis were firmly in the driving seat after **Shane Bond**'s magnificent 6 for 23 – the best one-day international return for New Zealand – had reduced Australia to 208 for 9. But where Bond had prospered with the ball, his team-mates floundered with the bat, crashing to 112 all out in 30.1 overs – the Kiwis' lowest-ever World Cup total – to lose the match by 96 runs. Bond's return is the best spell by any bowler in World Cup history to end up on the losing side.

Super Glenn McGrath

Three-time tournament winner **Glenn McGrath** is the most successful bowler in World Cup history, with 71 wickets. The Australian paceman holds the record for the best figures in an innings (7 for 15 v Namibia at Potchefstroom on 27 February 2003), the best average (18.19), the most wickets in a single tournament (26 in the 2003 World Cup in South Africa) and for the most maidens bowled in a World Cup career (42).

Most five-wicket hauls

The record for the most five-wicket hauls in World Cup history is two, a feat achieved by five players: **Gary Gilmour** (Australia) in two matches in the 1975 World Cup; Vasbert Drakes (West Indies) in six matches in the 2003 World Cup; Ashantha de Mel (Sri Lanka) in nine matches in the 1983 and 1987 World Cups; Glenn McGrath (Australia) in 39 matches between 1996 and 2007; and Shahid Afridi (Pakistan) in 20 matches between 1999 and 2011.

Most four-wicket hauls

The greatest leg-spinner of all time, **Shane Warne** appeared in only two World Cups (he was sensationally dumped from Australia's squad for the 2003 tournament, and subsequently banned from all cricket for a year, after failing a drug test), but when he did play, he more than made his mark: in 17 World Cup matches between 1996 and 1999 he took a record four four-wicket hauls. Muttiah Muralitharan and Shahid Afridi equalled Warne's feat at the 2011 World Cup.

A giant for India

Zaheer Khan's first taste of the World Cup left a sour taste in his mouth: his first over in the 2003 final, the first of the match against Australia, went for 15, the tone was set and Australia romped to an imposing 359 for 2 – en route to a comfortable 125-run victory – with Zaheer conceding 67 off seven (a humiliating 9.57 runs per over). It was an experience that could have knocked lesser men out of their stride, but Zaheer took it in his stride, learned from it and has evolved into one of the deadliest fast bowlers on the ODI circuit; he was a cornerstone of India's bowling attack during the victorious 2011 campaign. In 23 matches in the tournament to date, the left-arm paceman has taken 44 wickets at a strike-rate of one wicket every 27.1 deliveries – the best by any bowler to have bowled 1,000 balls or more in World Cup history.

Lethal weapon

Poker-faced he may have been, but Andy Roberts was arguably the meanest and most deadly of all the great West Indian fast bowlers of the late 1970s and early '80s and played an integral role in his team's World Cup successes in 1975 and 1979. In a World Cup career spanning 16 matches between 1975 and 1983, the Antiguan paceman conceded 552 runs off 170.1 overs (taking 26 wickets) – his economy rate of 3.24 is the best by any bowler in the tournament's history.

Best economy rate in an innings by a bowler

It was the crowning performance of a commanding bowling display by England before rain robbed them of certain victory against Pakistan in the two sides' group match at Adelaide in the 1992 World Cup. As Pakistan floundered to 74 all out, England all-rounder Dermot Reeve bowled five overs for a mere two runs: his economy rate of 0.40 is the best in a single innings by any bowler to bowl five overs or more in World Cup history.

WORLD CUP HAT-TRICKS

Player	For	Against	Venue	Date
Chetan Sharma	India	New Zealand	Nagpur	31 October 1987
Saqlain Mushtaq	Pakistan	Zimbabwe	The Oval	11 June 1999
Chaminda Vaas	Sri Lanka	Bangladesh	Pietermaritzburg	14 February 2003*
Brett Lee	Australia	Kenya	Durban	15 March 2003
Lasith Malinga	Sri Lanka	South Africa	Georgetown	28 March 2007
Kemar Roach	West Indies	Netherlands	New Delhi	28 February 2011
Lasith Malinga	Sri Lanka	Kenya	Colombo	1 March 2011

* Remarkably, Vaas's hat-trick came in the first three deliveries of the match.

OTHER RECORDS

HIGHEST PARTNERSHIP BY WICKET

Wkt	Runs	Partners	Team	Opposition	Venue	Date
1st	282	W.U. Tharanga/T.M. Dilshan	Sri Lanka	Zimbabwe	Pallekele	10 Mar 2011
2nd	318	S.C. Ganguly/R. Dravid	India	Sri Lanka	Taunton	26 May 1999
3rd	237*	R. Dravid/S.R. Tendulkar	India	Kenya	Bristol	23 May 1999
4th	204	M.J. Clarke/B.J. Hodge	Australia	Netherlands	Basseterre	18 March 2007
5th	148	R.G. Twose/C.L. Cairns	New Zealand	Australia	Cardiff	20 May 1999
6th	162	K.J. O'Brien/A.R. Cusack	Ireland	England	Bangalore	2 Mar 2011
7th	98	R.R. Sarwan/R.D. Jacobs	West Indies	New Zealand	Port Elizabeth	13 February 2003
8th	117	D.L. Houghton/I.P. Butchart	Zimbabwe	New Zealand	Hyderabad	10 October 1987
9th	126*	Kapil Dev/S.M.H. Kirmani	India	Zimbabwe	Tunbridge Wells	18 June 1983
10th	71	A.M.E. Roberts/J. Garner	West Indies	India	Manchester	9 June 1983

Most catches in an innings

The record for the most catches in an innings is four, by Mohammad Kaif in India's Super Six match against Sri Lanka at Johannesburg on 10 March 2003. The feat helped India to victory by 183 runs.

Most World Cup catches

No fielder has taken more World Cup catches than Australia's Ricky Ponting. In 46 matches between 1996 and 2011 the Tasmanian has pouched 28 victims. He also holds the record for the most catches in a single tournament (11 at the 2003 World Cup in South Africa).

Most dismissals by a wicketkeeper

Adam Gilchrist was an outstanding performer with the bat for Australia during their period of World Cup dominance between 1999 and 2007 (they claimed three successive tournament wins), and his destructive hitting at the top of the order often propelled his side into an unassailable position. Gilchrist was also a mightily effective, and often underrated, performer behind the stumps. He holds the World Cup record for the most dismissals (52), the most dismissals in an innings (six v Namibia at Potchefstroom on 27 February 2003) and for the most dismissals in a single tournament (21 in the 2003 World Cup in South Africa).

Dravid and Ganguly show eases India to victory

Taking advantage of some undisciplined bowling, a batsman-friendly surface and some favourably short boundaries, **Rahul Dravid** and **Sourav Ganguly** were in record-breaking form in India's Group A encounter with Sri Lanka at Taunton in the 1999 World Cup. The pair added 318 runs in 45 overs for the second wicket – an all-time record for any wicket in one-day international cricket – to help their side to a comfortable 157-run win.

Best attended World Cup

The best attended World Cup in history was the **2003 tournament** held in Kenya, Zimbabwe and South Africa. A total of 626,845 spectators flocked through the turnstiles during the 52 matches played.

First World Cup match played under lights

The first day-night match to be played in World Cup history was the pool match between England and India at Perth during the 1992 World Cup. For the record, England won the closely fought match by nine runs.

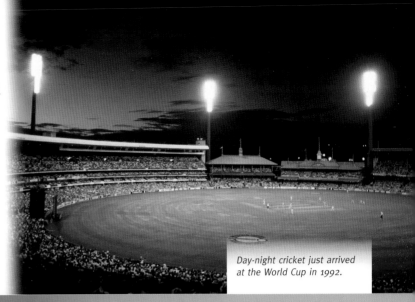
Day-night cricket just arrived at the World Cup in 1992.

Most extras conceded in an innings

As expected, Scotland were comfortably outclassed by Pakistan in the two sides' Group A encounter at Chester-le-Street in the 1999 World Cup, losing the match by 94 runs, but indiscipline with the ball did little to help their cause. During Pakistan's innings, the Scots conceded a World Cup record 59 extras – five byes, six leg-byes, 33 wides and 15 no-balls.

Ponting sets a host of appearance records

Australia's Ricky Ponting holds the distinction of having played in more World Cup matches than any other player. The three-time tournament winner has played 46 games in the competition – 29 of them as captain (another all-time tournament record) – between 1996 and 2011.

Most matches as an umpire

Much-loved English umpire **David Shepherd**, whose death in October 2009 saddened the entire cricket world, holds the record for the most World Cup appearances as an umpire. The former Gloucestershire batsman officiated in 46 matches in the tournament, including the 1996, 1999 and 2003 World Cup finals.

Most World Cup matches staged

Headingley, in Leeds, England, has hosted more World Cup matches than any other ground in history. The home of Yorkshire CCC has staged 12 matches in the tournament between 1975 and 1999.

Most hundreds in a tournament

Big scores were the order of the day at the 2003 World Cup in Kenya, South Africa and Zimbabwe. The tournament saw a tournament record 21 centuries in the 52 matches played – the highest score was Craig Wishart's unbeaten 172 for Zimbabwe against Namibia at Harare on 10 February 2003.

MOST WINS AS CAPTAIN: TOP 5

Pos	Wins	Player
1	26	**R.T. Ponting** (Australia, 2003–11)
2	16	S.P. Fleming (New Zealand, 1999–2007)
3	15	C.H. Lloyd (West Indies, 1975–83)
4	14	Imran Khan (Pakistan, 1983–92)
5	11	A.R. Border (Australia, 1987–92)
=	11	W.J. Cronje (South Africa, 1996–99)
=	11	Kapil Dev (India, 1983–87)
=	11	G.C. Smith (South Africa, 2007–11)

ICC CHAMPIONS TROPHY

Played on a bi-annual basis and considered the second most important one-day competition in world cricket, the ICC Champions Trophy was first contested in Bangladesh in 1998 and has been held on six occasions. Australia are the tournament's only two-time winners.

ICC CHAMPIONS TROPHY WINNERS

Year	Winner	Host
1998	South Africa	(Bangladesh)
2000	New Zealand	(Kenya)
2002	India/Sri Lanka*	(Sri Lanka)
2004	West Indies	(England)
2006	Australia	(India)
2009	Australia	(South Africa**)

* The trophy was shared after the final was washed out by rain.

** The tournament was scheduled to be played in Pakistan but was moved to South Africa because of security fears.

Maharoof mesmerizes West Indians

Bowling full and straight on a low, slow wicket at the Brabourne Stadium in Mumbai, Sri Lanka's Farveez Maharoof proved too much for the West Indies' batsmen in the two sides' qualifying group encounter at the 2002 ICC Champions Trophy. The paceman took 6 for 14 off nine overs – the best bowling figures in the tournament's history – as the West Indies slipped to 80 all out. Sri Lanka eased to victory in 13.2 overs with nine wickets in hand.

Highest individual scores

Two players hold the record for the highest individual score in ICC Champions Trophy history: New Zealand's **Nathan Astle**, 145 not out v USA at The Oval on 10 September 2004; and Zimbabwe's Andy Flower, 145 v India at Colombo on 14 September 2002.

New Zealand take advantage of Uncle Sam

New Zealand cruelly exposed a lack of depth in the USA's bowling attack in the Americans' first-ever match in the ICC Champions Trophy at The Oval on 10 September 2004. Batting first, the Kiwis – propelled by big innings from Nathan Astle (145 not out), Scott Styris (75) and Craig McMillan (64 not out) – amassed a mighty 347 for 4 off their 50 overs (the highest total in the tournament's history) en route to a crushing 210-run win – the largest in ICC Champions Trophy history.

Watson and Ponting crush humbled England

Propelled to a commendable 257 all out (after being on 101 for 6) by a battling 76-ball 80 from Tim Bresnan, England would have had high hopes of containing Australia in the two sides' ICC Champions Trophy tie at Centurion on 2 October 2009. But those hopes were soon dashed: Shane Watson (136 not out) and Ricky Ponting (111 not out) put on 252 runs for the second wicket – the highest partnership in the tournament's history – to ease Australia past the winning post with 8.1 overs to spare.

Most catches

Sri Lanka's Mahela Jayawardene is the leading fielder in all ICC Champions Trophy matches. He has bagged 13 catches in 18 matches between 2000 and 2009.

Most dismissals by a wicketkeeper

Kumar Sangakkara holds the ICC Champions Trophy record for the most dismissals by a wicket-keeper. The Sri Lankan gloveman has pouched 28 victims (24 caught and four stumped) in 18 matches in the tournament between 2000 and 2009.

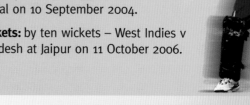

Largest victories

By runs: by 210 runs – New Zealand v USA at The Oval on 10 September 2004.

By wickets: by ten wickets – West Indies v Bangladesh at Jaipur on 11 October 2006.

MOST RUNS: TOP 5

Pos	Runs	Player	M	I	NO	HS	Ave	BF	SR	100	50	0	4s	6s
1	695	C.H. Gayle (WI, 2002–06)	14	14	2	133*	57.91	799	86.98	3	1	1	88	13
2	665	S.C. Ganguly (Ind, 1998–2004)	13	11	2	141*	73.88	800	83.12	3	3	1	66	17
3	653	J.H. Kallis (SA, 1998–2009)	17	17	3	113*	46.64	843	77.46	1	3	0	63	9
4	627	R. Dravid (Ind, 1998–2009)	19	15	2	76	48.23	855	73.33	0	6	0	56	1
5	593	R.T. Ponting (Aus, 1998–2009)	18	18	3	111*	39.53	775	76.51	1	4	1	66	4

MOST WICKETS: TOP 5

Pos	Wkts	Player	Mat	Overs	Mdns	Runs	BBI	Ave	Econ	SR	4	5
1	24	M. Muralitharan (SL, 1998–2009)	17	134.1	11	484	4/15	20.16	3.60	33.5	2	0
2	22	K.D. Mills (NZ, 2002–09)	12	96.0	6	420	4/38	19.09	4.37	26.1	1	0
=	22	B. Lee (Aus, 2000–09)	16	123.1	6	591	3/38	26.86	4.79	33.5	0	0
4	21	G.D. McGrath (Aus, 2000–06)	12	102.0	13	412	5/37	19.61	4.03	29.1	0	1
5	20	J.H. Kallis (SA, 1998–2009)	17	106.3	3	525	5/30	26.25	4.92	31.9	0	1

Sorry USA collapse against Australia

On paper, the match between the USA and Australia at Southampton in the 2004 ICC Champions Trophy was always going to be a mismatch, and so it proved. Put in to bat, the USA were skittled for a paltry 65 all out in 24 overs – the lowest total in the tournament's history. Australia eased to the victory target with nine wickets and a colossal 42.1 overs to spare.

Most extras in an innings

India had an easy win over Kenya at Southampton in the 2004 ICC Champions Trophy, by 98 runs, but many questions would have been posed after their somewhat indifferent performance with the ball. During the course of the Kenyan innings, the Indians conceded a tournament record 42 extras – ten byes, nine leg-byes, a mammoth 19 wides and four no-balls.

Smallest victories

By runs: by ten runs on two occasions – India v South Africa at Colombo on 25 September 2002; and West Indies v Australia at Mumbai on 18 October 2006.

By wickets: by two wickets on three occasions – South Africa v West Indies at Colombo on 13 September 2002; West Indies v England at The Oval on 25 September 2004; and Australia v Pakistan at Centurion on 30 September 2009.

Most successful captain

The only captain in the tournament's history to lift the cup on two occasions, Australia's **Ricky Ponting** is the most successful captain in ICC Champions Trophy history. The Australian skipper has led his side to 12 wins in 16 matches between 2002 and 2009.

ICC CHAMPIONS TROPHY LEAGUE TABLE

Pos	Team (Span)	Mat	Won	Lost	Tied	NR	%
1	Australia (1998–2009)	18	12	5	0	1	70.58
2	India (1998–2009)	19	10	6	0	3	62.50
3	New Zealand (1998–2009)	18	11	7	0	0	61.11
=	Sri Lanka (1998–2009)	20	11	7	0	2	61.11
5	South Africa (1998–2009)	17	10	7	0	0	58.82
6	West Indies (1998–2009)	21	12	9	0	0	57.14
7	England (1998–2009)	16	8	8	0	0	50.00
8	Pakistan (1998–2009)	15	7	8	0	0	46.66
9	Bangladesh (2000–06)	8	1	7	0	0	12.50
10	Kenya (2000–04)	5	0	5	0	0	0.00
=	Netherlands (2002)	2	0	2	0	0	0.00
=	USA (2004)	2	0	2	0	0	0.00
=	Zimbabwe (1998–2006)	9	0	9	0	0	0.00

ODI CRICKET

The first one-day international, a hastily arranged affair after rain washed out the Fifth Test of the 1970–71 Ashes series, was played between Australia and England at Melbourne on 5 January 1971. One-day internationals may not be universally popular, but since then they have become a mainstay of modern cricket: in 2009 alone there were 150 one-day internationals compared to 41 Test matches.

TEAM RECORDS: ONE-DAY INTERNATIONAL RESULT SUMMARY (BY COUNTRY)

Team	Mat	Won	Lost	Tied	NR	%
Afghanistan (2009–12)	21	12	9	0	0	57.14
Africa XI (2005–07)	6	1	4	0	1	20.00
Asia XI (2005–07)	7	4	2	0	1	66.66
Australia (1971–2012)	792	490	268	9	25	64.47
Bangladesh (1986–2011)	262	72	188	0	2	27.69
Bermuda (2006–09)	35	7	28	0	0	20.00
Canada (1979–2011)	70	17	52	0	1	24.63
East Africa (1975)	3	0	3	0	0	0.00
England (1971–2012)	576	278	272	7	19	50.53
Hong Kong (2004–08)	4	0	4	0	0	0.00
ICC World XI (2005)	4	1	3	0	0	25.00
India (1974–2012)	804	397	366	6	35	52.01
Ireland (2006–12)	72	33	35	1	3	48.55
Kenya (1996–2012)	146	39	102	0	5	27.65
Namibia (2003)	6	0	6	0	0	0.00
Netherlands (1996–2011)	69	26	41	0	2	38.80
New Zealand (1973–2012)	620	268	315	5	32	46.80
Pakistan (1973–2012)	769	415	332	6	16	55.51
Scotland (1999–2011)	54	18	33	0	3	35.29
South Africa (1991–2012)	470	294	159	5	12	64.73
Sri Lanka (1975–2012)	662	309	323	4	26	48.89
United Arab Emirates (1994–2008)	11	1	10	0	0	9.09
USA (2004)	2	0	2	0	0	0.00
West Indies (1973–2011)	670	347	293	6	24	54.17
Zimbabwe (1983–2012)	407	107	286	5	9	27.51

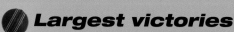

Largest victories

By runs: by 290 runs – New Zealand v Ireland at Aberdeen on 1 July 2008.

By wickets: by ten wickets on 45 occasions.

By balls remaining: 277 – England v Canada at Old Trafford on 13 June 1979.

Narrowest victories

By runs: by one run on 26 occasions.

By wickets: by one wicket on 47 occasions.

By balls remaining: off the last ball of the match on 33 occasions.

Namibia slump to record defeat

It was the biggest mismatch of the 2003 ICC World Cup. Batting first, defending champions Australia cruised to 301 for 6 off the 50-over allocation; in reply, Namibia, in the face of some fine bowling from **Glenn McGrath** (7 for 15), wilted to 45 all out in 14 overs – their innings, which lasted a mere 84 balls, is the shortest completed innings (by balls received) in one-day international cricket history.

HIGHEST TEAM TOTAL: TOP 5

Pos	Score	Team	Inns	Opposition	Venue	Date
1	443–9	Sri Lanka	1	Netherlands	Amstelveen	4 Jul 2006
2	438–9	South Africa	2	Australia	Johannesburg	12 Mar 2006
3	434–4	Australia	1	South Africa	Johannesburg	12 Mar 2006
4	418–5	South Africa	1	Zimbabwe	Potchefstroom	20 Sep 2006
5	418–5	India	1	West Indies	Indore	8 Dec 2011

LOWEST TEAM TOTAL: TOP 5

Pos	Score	Team	Overs	Inns	Opposition	Venue	Date
1	35	Zimbabwe	18.0	1	Sri Lanka	Harare	25 Apr 2004
2	36	Canada	18.4	1	Sri Lanka	Paarl	19 Feb 2003
3	38	Zimbabwe	15.4	1	Sri Lanka	Colombo	8 Dec 2001
4	43	Pakistan	19.5	1	West Indies	Cape Town	25 Feb 1993
=	43	Sri Lanka	20.1	2	South Africa	Paarl	11 Jan 2012

Tied matches

There have been 27 tied matches in one-day international cricket, most famously when **Australia tied with South Africa** in the 1999 World Cup semi-final to progress to the final.

Australia's record-breaking streak

Australia hold the all-time record for the most consecutive one-day international victories. Between 11 January 2003 (a seven-run victory over England at Hobart) and 24 May 2003 (a 67-run win against the West Indies at Port of Spain, Trinidad) they racked up 21 successive victories – a run that included success at the 2003 ICC World Cup. The record-breaking streak came to an end when they slipped to a 39-run defeat by the West Indies at Port of Spain on 25 May 2003.

Runs galore at Johannesburg

With the five-match series evenly poised at 2–2, South Africa and Australia put on a dynamic show of batting brilliance in the fifth and final one-day international at Johannesburg on 12 March 2006. Batting first, Australia romped to a mighty, and apparently match-winning, 434 for 4 off their 50 overs, helped by an innings of 164 from captain Ricky Ponting. Undaunted by the colossal total, however, South Africa, inspired by a sublime, stroke-filled, 111-ball 175 from **Herschelle Gibbs**, sensationally reached the victory target with one ball to spare. The total of 872 runs scored in the match is an all-time record in one-day international cricket.

Most consecutive defeats

Bangladesh's early struggles in the Test arena – they had to wait 35 Tests and four years three months before notching up their first victory – were replicated in one-day internationals. Between 8 October 1999 (a 73-run loss to the West Indies at Dhaka) and 9 October 2002 (a seven-wicket defeat by South Africa at Kimberley), they crashed to a record 23 consecutive defeats. Rain, rather than good play, finally brought the run to an end: their match against the West Indies at Chittagong on 29 November 2002 ended up as a no-result.

Most sixes in an innings

The record for the most sixes in an innings is 18, a feat achieved on four occasions: by South Africa (v Netherlands at Basseterre, St Kitts and Nevis, on 16 March 2007 – a game in which **Herschelle Gibbs** hit six sixes in an over); twice by India (v Bermuda at Port of Spain, Trinidad, on 19 March 2007 and v New Zealand at Christchurch on 8 March 2009); and by New Zealand (v Ireland at Aberdeen on 1 July 2008).

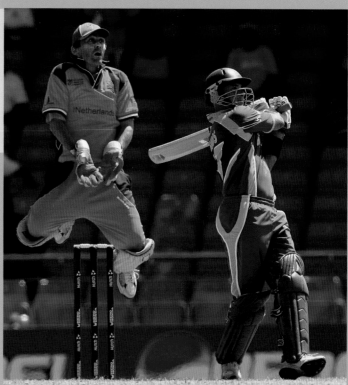

Chappell and Cosier's efforts all in vain

Greg Chappell (5 for 20) and Gary Cosier (5 for 18) created history against England at Edgbaston on 4 June 1977 – it is the only occasion in which two bowlers have taken five wickets in the same innings – but their efforts weren't enough to win Australia the match. England's bowlers rallied in spectacular style to dismiss Australia for 70 and secure a 101-run victory.

Crashing timbers

Having set New Zealand 260 to win the third one-day international at Albion, Guyana, on 14 April 1985, the West Indies' bowlers used the maxim "If you miss, I'll hit" to supreme effect: a record eight Kiwi batsmen were out bowled as the visitors slipped to 129 all out and a 130-run defeat.

Most ducks in a match

The headlines following the West Indies' 92-run victory over England in the **1979 ICC World Cup final** at Lord's were reserved for Viv Richards's stunning innings of 138 not out, but the match was also remarkable because eight batsmen in the match failed to score – an all-time record in one-day international cricket.

Most fours in an innings

Irritated at being asked by the ICC to contest two one-day internationals against the Netherlands hot on the heels of a tough tour of England, Sri Lanka unleashed their frustration in record-breaking fashion in the first of the two matches, played at Amstelveen on 4 July 2006. They smashed a one-day international record 443 for 9 off their 50 overs, an innings that included a remarkable 56 fours (50.56 per cent of their total runs) – another one-day record. Sanath Jayasuriya hit 24 of them in an innings of 157.

Most runs from fours and sixes in an innings

The record for the most runs from boundaries in a one-day international is 256, a feat achieved by two teams: Sri Lanka (43 fours and 14 sixes) v Kenya at Kandy on 6 March 1996; and Australia (43 fours and 14 sixes) v South Africa at Johannesburg on 12 March 2006. **Ricky Ponting** was South Africa's chief destroyer, hitting a majestic 164 with 13 four and nine sixes.

Runs galore in Lahore

When Pakistan, bolstered by centuries from Ijaz Ahmed (111) and Yousuf Youhana (100), posted 315 for 8 off their 50-over allocation against Australia in the third and final one-day international at Lahore on 10 November 1998, they must have felt as though they had done enough to avoid a series whitewash. But Australia had other ideas: propelled by centuries from Adam Gilchrist (103) and Ricky Ponting (124 not out), the tourists reached the victory target with seven balls and four wickets to spare. The four centuries struck in the match set an all-time record in one-day international cricket.

History-making moment in Multan

Mohsin Khan (117 not out) and Zaheer Abbas (118) created a slice of history during Pakistan's 37-run victory over India in the second one-day international at Multan on 17 December 1982: it was the first time in one-day international history that two players from the same side had passed 100 in the same innings. The feat has since been repeated on 98 occasions.

ASSORTED BATTING RECORDS

Most batsmen reaching double figures: 10 – on four occasions
All 11 batsmen failing to reach double figures: two occasions
Most batsmen caught in an innings: 10 – on 14 occasions
Most batsmen lbw in an innings: 6 – on two occasions
Most batsmen run out in an innings: 5 – on nine occasions
Most batsmen stumped in an innings: 3 – on 13 occasions

Openers efforts not enough for Australia

Geoff Marsh (104) and David Boon (111) created history against India at Jaipur on 7 September 1986 – it was the first time in one-day international cricket history that both openers had scored a century in an innings (there have been 22 subsequent instances) – but it wasn't enough to win Australia the match. Chasing 251 for victory, India, thanks in no small part to Kris Srikkanth's 102, won by seven wickets with six overs to spare.

Assorted bowling records

Most bowlers used: 9 – on 13 occasions
Most bowlers taking wickets in a match: 12 – on four occasions
Most ducks in an innings: 6 – on four occasions

Most wides in an innings

The West Indies bowlers' radars were clearly malfunctioning in their Benson and Hedges World Series match against Pakistan at Brisbane on 7 January 1989: during the course of Pakistan's 258 for 7, they delivered a one-day international record 37 wides. Kenya's bowlers equalled the unfortunate feat in their match against Pakistan at Hambantota at the 2011 World Cup.

Most no-balls in an innings

A record number of no-balls (20) ultimately cost Pakistan victory against arch-rivals India in the first one-day international (of seven) at Karachi on 13 March 2004. Chasing 350 for victory, they ultimately fell six runs short.

BATTING RECORDS

MOST CAREER RUNS: TOP 10

Pos	Runs	Player	Mat	Inns	NO	HS	Ave	100	50	0
1	18,426	S.R. Tendulkar (Ind, 1989–2012)	463	452	41	200*	44.83	49	96	20
2	13,704	R.T. Ponting (Aus/ICC, 1995–2012)	375	365	39	164	42.03	30	82	20
3	13,428	S.T. Jayasuriya (Asia/SL, 1989–2009)	444	432	18	189	32.43	28	68	34
4	11,739	Inzamam-ul-Haq (Asia/Pak, 1991–2007)	378	350	53	137*	39.52	10	83	20
5	11,498	J.H. Kallis (Afr/ICC/SA, 1996–2012)	321	307	53	139	45.26	17	85	16
6	11,363	S.C. Ganguly (Asia/Ind, 1992–2007)	311	300	23	183	41.02	22	72	16
7	10,765	R. Dravid (Asia/ICC/Ind, 1996–2009)	339	313	40	153	39.43	12	82	13
8	10,486	D.P.H.D. Jayawardene (Asia/SL, 1998–2012)	373	351	35	144	33.53	15	66	25
9	10,472	K.C. Sangakkara (Asia/SL, 2000–12)	325	306	32	138*	38.21	13	71	10
10	10,405	B.C. Lara (ICC/WI, 1990–2007)	299	289	32	169	40.48	19	63	16

Dhoni puts on batting master-class

It was an innings that confirmed India's **Mahendra Singh Dhoni** as a batsman of the highest class. With his side chasing an imposing 299 for victory against Sri Lanka in the third one-day international at Jaipur on 31 October 2005, Dhoni, batting at No. 3, struck an imperious, chanceless 183 not out in 145 balls to ease his side to a six-wicket victory with 23 balls to spare. It is the highest score by a wicketkeeper in one-day international history.

The one-day international batting king

Sachin Tendulkar, known as the "Little Master", has truly lived up to his reputation in one-day cricket. A veteran of 463 matches (no player in one-day international history has played more), he has scored the most runs (18,426), has recorded the most centuries (49), the most scores of 50-plus (145), the most 90s (18), has been dismissed on 99 more times than any other batsman (3), and holds the record for the most runs in a calendar year (1,894) and the record for the most centuries in a calendar year (9).

Most runs in a career without a hundred

Feared for his bowling, but admired in equal measure for his hard-hitting, late-order exploits with the bat, Pakistan's **Wasim Akram** holds the all-time one-day international cricket record for the most runs scored without ever recording a century. The all-rounder notched up 3,717 runs in 356 matches for Pakistan between 1984 and 2003, with a highest score of 86 coming against Australia at Melbourne on 26 February 1990.

HIGHEST CAREER BATTING AVERAGE (MINIMUM OF 20 INNINGS): TOP 5

Pos	Ave	Player	M	I	NO	Runs	HS	100	50	0
1	67.00	R.N. ten Doeschate (Neth, 2006–11)	33	32	9	1,541	119	5	9	1
2	56.49	H.M. Amla (SA, 2008–12)	57	56	5	2,881	140	9	18	1
3	53.58	M.G. Bevan (Aus, 1994–2004)	232	196	67	6,912	108*	6	46	5
4	51.70	M.S. Dhoni (Ind, 2004–12)	206	184	53	6,773	183*	7	45	6
5	50.06	V. Kohli (Ind, 2008–12)	85	82	11	3,590	18	11	21	5

There's no place like home for Jayasuriya

After Sachin Tendulkar the most experienced one-day international cricketer of all time (444 matches) and the second-leading all-time run-scorer in the 50-over format of the game (with 13,428 runs), Sri Lanka's Sanath Jayasuriya has enjoyed considerable success at the R. Premadasa Stadium in Colombo. In 70 innings there between 1992 and 2009, the left-hander has scored 2,514 runs (with four centuries and a highest score of 130) – the most scored by a player at a single ground in ODI history.

Boom Boom Afridi

A compulsive shot-maker, often to his own detriment, and one of the cleanest strikers of a cricket ball ever to play the game, Pakistan's **Shahid Afridi** is tailor-made for the shorter formats of the game. In 342 one-day internationals for his country between 1996 and 2012 he has scored 7,040 runs (at an average of 23.62 with six centuries) off 6,182 deliveries – the highest career strike-rate of any player to complete 50 innings in one-day international history (113.87).

Hottest batting streaks

The record for the most centuries posted in consecutive innings is three, a feat achieved by four players: Zaheer Abbas (Pakistan) against India between 17 December 1982 and 21 January 1983; Saeed Anwar (Pakistan) against Sri Lanka, West Indies, Sri Lanka between 30 October and 2 November 1993; Herschelle Gibbs (South Africa) against Kenya, India, Bangladesh between 20 September and 3 October 2002; and A.B. de Villiers (South Africa) against India (twice) and the West Indies between 24 February 2010 and 22 May 2010.

Hitting new heights

By 2012, **Sachin Tendulkar** held almost every cricket batting record in the book: he had scored the most runs in Test matches (15,470), the most runs in ODIs (18,426) and had hit more centuries in both forms of the game (100 – 51 in Tests and 49 in ODIs) than any other batsman in history. The Little Master set another record on 24 February 2010, when India played South Africa in the second one-day international at Gwalior.

Opening the batting, Tendulkar smashed an unbeaten 200 off 147 balls (with 25 fours and three sixes) to become the first batsman to score 200 runs a in one-day international innings. Compatriot Virender Sehwag surpassed his total on 8 December 2011 when he scored 219 against the West Indies at Indore.

SCORING 100 ON DEBUT

Player	Runs	Balls	4s	6s	SR	Team	Opposition	Venue	Date
D.L. Amiss	103	134	9	0	76.86	England	Australia	Manchester	24 Aug 1972
D.L. Haynes	148	136	16	2	108.82	West Indies	Australia	St John's	22 Feb 1978
A. Flower	115*	152	8	1	75.65	Zimbabwe	Sri Lanka	New Plymouth	23 Feb 1992
Saleem Elahi	102*	133	7	1	76.69	Pakistan	Sri Lanka	Gujranwala	29 Sep 1995
M.J. Guptill	122*	135	8	2	90.37	New Zealand	West Indies	Auckland	10 Jan 2009
C.A. Ingram	124	126	8	2	98.41	South Africa	Zimbabwe	Bloemfontein	15 Oct 2010
R.J. Nicol	108*	131	11	0	82.44	New Zealand	Zimbabwe	Harare	20 Oct 2011

HIGHEST SCORE: PROGRESSIVE RECORD HOLDERS

Player	Runs	Balls	4s	6s	Team	Opposition	Venue	Date
J.H. Edrich	82	119	4	0	England	Australia	Melbourne	5 Jan 1971
D.L. Amiss	103	134	9	0	England	Australia	Manchester	24 Aug 1972
R.C. Fredericks	105	122	10	1	West Indies	England	The Oval	7 Sep 1973
D. Lloyd	116*	159	8	1	England	Pakistan	Nottingham	31 Aug 1974
G.M. Turner	171*	201	16	2	New Zealand	East Africa	Birmingham	7 Jun 1975
Kapil Dev	175*	138	16	6	India	Zimbabwe	Tunbridge Wells	18 Jun 1983
I.V.A. Richards	189*	170	21	5	West Indies	England	Manchester	31 May 1984
Saeed Anwar	194	146	22	5	Pakistan	India	Chennai	21 May 1997
C.K. Coventry	194*	156	16	7	Zimbabwe	Bangladesh	Bulawayo	16 Aug 2009
S.R. Tendulkar	200*	147	25	3	India	South Africa	Gwalior	24 Feb 2010
V. Sehwag	219	149	25	7	India	West Indies	Indore	8 Dec 2011

Afridi's spectacular entrance on to world stage

Pakistan's Shahid Afridi took the cricket world by storm. Playing in only his second one-day international, but batting for the first time (against Sri Lanka at Nairobi, Kenya, on 4 October 1996) in his fledgling career, the young star (aged just 16 years 217 days at the time) struck 102 off a mere 37 deliveries to record the fastest one-day international century of all time and become the youngest player in history to hit a century in the game's 50-over format.

Richards single-handedly flattens England

Viv Richards (right) produced a virtuoso innings to haul the West Indies into a commanding position in their one-day international against England at Old Trafford on 31 May 1984. While all around him wilted, the master blaster smashed a then one-day international record 189 not out off 170 balls to help his team to 272 for 9. His score remains the highest percentage of a team's total (69.48) in one-day history. And it was enough to secure victory: the West Indies went on to win the match by 104 runs.

Age no deterrent for Jayasuriya

Sri Lanka's **Sanath Jayasuriya**, the second-most capped one-day international cricketer of all time, proved age was no barrier when, on 28 January 2009, aged 39 years 212 days, he struck 107 against India at Dambulla to become the oldest centurion in one-day international cricket history. Sadly for the veteran, it did not turn out to be a match-winning contribution, as India cantered to victory with six wickets and 11 balls to spare.

Troubling the scorers

Kumar Dharmasena became an integral part of Sri Lanka's one-day set-up through his unorthodox, but highly effective, off-spin bowling (playing in 141 one-day internationals between 1994 and 2004), but it was his exploits with the bat that forced him into the record books: the right-hander went 72 innings before recording his first duck – an all-time record in one-day international cricket.

CARRYING BAT THROUGH A COMPLETED INNINGS

Player	Runs	Total	Inns	Team	Opposition	Venue	Date
G.W. Flower	84	205	1	Zimbabwe	England	Sydney	15 Dec 1994
Saeed Anwar	103	219	2	Pakistan	Zimbabwe	Harare	22 Feb 1995
N.V. Knight	125	246	1	England	Pakistan	Nottingham	1 Sep 1996
R.D. Jacobs	49	110	1	West Indies	Australia	Manchester	30 May 1999
D.R. Martyn	116	191	1	Australia	New Zealand	Auckland	3 Mar 2000
H.H. Gibbs	59	101†	2	South Africa	Pakistan	Sharjah	28 Mar 2000
A.J. Stewart	100	192	2	England	West Indies	Nottingham	20 Jul 2000
Javed Omar	33	103	2	Bangladesh	Zimbabwe	Harare	8 Apr 2001

† not all ten wickets fell in the innings

Turner's one-day marathon

It was as much of a marathon innings as you could ever wish to see in a one-day international. Opening the batting for New Zealand against East Africa in the two countries' Group A encounter at Edgbaston in the 1975 World Cup, **Glenn Turner** batted through the entire 60-over innings to reach 171 not out – the 201 balls he faced is a record in one-day international cricket.

Boycott suffers unfortunate landmark

It may not have been the fastest of innings by today's standards (he faced 159 balls), but it was a record-breaking and match-winning one. Playing against Australia at The Oval on 20 August 1980, England opener Geoffrey Boycott became the first player (of 22) in one-day international history to be dismissed (caught Hughes, bowled Lillee) for 99. Buoyed by Boycott's performance, England went on to win the match by 23 runs.

FASTEST TO...

Runs	Player	Innings
1,000	I.V.A. Richards (WI); K.P. Pietersen (Eng/ICC) **I.J.L. Trott** (Eng)	21
2,000	H.M. Amla (SA)	40
3,000	I.V.A. Richards (WI)	69
4,000	I.V.A. Richards (WI)	88
5,000	I.V.A. Richards (WI)	114
6,000	I.V.A. Richards (WI)	141
7,000	S.C. Ganguly (India)	174
8,000	S.C. Ganguly (India)	200
9,000	S.C. Ganguly (India)	228
10,000	S.R. Tendulkar (India)	259
11,000	S.R. Tendulkar (India)	276
12,000	S.R. Tendulkar (India)	300
13,000	S.R. Tendulkar (India)	321
14,000	S.R. Tendulkar (India)	350
15,000	S.R. Tendulkar (India)	377
16,000	S.R. Tendulkar (India)	399
17,000	S.R. Tendulkar (India)	424
18,000	S.R. Tendulkar (India)	440

Watson batters Bangladesh

Although no one genuinely believed Bangladesh's total of 229 for 7 would be enough to challenge Australia in the second one-day international at Dhaka on 11 April 2011, few expected that the Aussies would pass the winning post in as destructive a manner, they had lost one wicket and used only 26 of their 50 overs. And the main reason for this emphatic destruction was hard-hitting opener **Shane Watson**, who plundered an unbeaten 185 off only 96 deliveries, an innings that contained 15 fours and 15 sixes. His 15 sixes in an innings is an all-time record in one-day international cricket.

BOWLING RECORDS

MOST WICKETS: TOP 10

Pos	Wkts	Player	M	B	R	BB	Ave	Econ	SR	4w	5w
1	534	M. Muralitharan (Asia/ICC/SL, 1993–2011)	350	18,881	12,326	7/30	23.08	3.93	35.2	15	10
2	502	Wasim Akram (Pak, 1984–2003)	356	18,186	11,812	5/15	23.52	3.89	36.2	17	6
3	416	Waqar Younis (Pak, 1989–2003)	262	12,698	9,919	7/36	23.84	4.68	30.5	14	13
4	400	W.P.U.J.C. Vaas (Asia/SL, 1994–2008)	322	15,775	11,014	8/19	27.53	4.18	39.4	9	4
5	393	S.M. Pollock (Afr/ICC/SA, 1996–2008)	303	15,712	9,631	6/35	24.50	3.67	39.9	12	5
6	381	G.D. McGrath (Aus/ICC, 1993–2007)	250	12,970	8,391	7/15	22.02	3.88	34.0	9	7
7	377	B. Lee (Aus, 2000–12)	217	11,033	8,740	5/22	23.18	4.75	29.2	14	9
8	341	Shahid Afridi (Asia/ICC/Pak, 1996–2012)	342	14,952	11,482	6/38	33.37	4.60	43.4	4	8
9	337	A. Kumble (Asia/Ind, 1990–2007)	271	14,496	10,412	6/12	30.89	4.30	43.0	8	2
10	322	S.T. Jayasuriya (Asia/SL, 1989–2009)	444	14,838	11,825	6/29	36.72	4.78	46.0	8	4

Imran stands tall as Pakistan falter

A magnificent spell of bowling from Pakistan's Imran Khan (he took 6 for 14 off his ten-over allocation) saw India crash to 125 all out in the opening match of the Four Nations Cup at Sharjah on 22 May 1985. But his magical performance was not enough to win his side the game: in reply, Pakistan slipped to 87 all out to lose the match by 38 runs. Imran's figures are the best by any bowler to end up on the losing side in one-day international cricket history.

Latecomer Harris makes his mark

He may have been a latecomer to the international fold (he was 29 when he finally made his debut for Australia), but, when fit (and numerous injuries have checked his progress), **Ryan Harris** has been the impressive spearhead of Australia's attack in all forms of the game – particularly in one-day international cricket. In 21 matches between 2009 and 2012, the Queensland tearaway fast bowler has taken 44 wickets at an average of 18.90 (with a best bowling performance of 5 for 19 against Pakistan at Perth on 26 January 2010), with a strike-rate of one wicket every 23.4 deliveries – the best by any bowler in one-day international cricket history.

Big Bird puts the breaks on opposition batsmen

There has perhaps been no more fearful sight for batsmen in cricket history: the 6ft 8in **Joel Garner** tearing into the bowling crease ready to unleash an array of searing, fast-paced deliveries from out of the clouds. And the man they called "Big Bird" was at his most potent in one-day cricket: in 98 matches for the West Indies between 1977 and 1987 he took 146 wickets for 2,752 runs at an economy rate of 3.09 runs per over – the best rate by any bowler to have bowled 1,000 deliveries or more in one-day international cricket history.

At the peak of his powers

Pakistan's most effective spin bowler of recent times, Saqlain Mushtaq enjoyed considerable success in the one-day arena. He reached the 100-, 150-, 200- and 250-wicket landmarks faster than any other bowler in history and enjoyed magical years in both 1996 (in which he took 65 one-day international wickets) and 1997 (in which he took 69 wickets – an all-time record number of wickets in a calendar year in one-day international cricket).

Record-breaking success at Sharjah

No fast bowler in history has taken more wickets in one-day international cricket than **Wasim Akram** (502 wickets in 356 matches), and the Pakistan paceman was supremely effective in his country's matches at Sharjah: in 77 matches in the emirate between 1985 and 2002 he took 122 wickets – the most wickets by any bowler at a single ground in ODI history.

A day to forget for Malinga

When he gets it right, Lasith Malinga is one of cricket's most potent bowlers; genuinely quick and with an almost unplayable in-swinging yorker, the Sri Lankan fast bowler has taken 185 wickets in 115 one-day international matches between 2004 and 2012. But even the best in the world can have a day to forget, and Malinga's nadir came against India at Hobart on 28 February 2012: his 7.4 overs went for 96 runs (12.52 runs per over) – the worst-ever economy rate in a one-day international innings.

New boy Edwards hits the headlines

Surprisingly trailing 2–1 in a five-match one-day international series against Zimbabwe in November 2003 the West Indies, desperate to change their fortunes in a match they had to win, handed young paceman Fidel Edwards his debut. It was a masterstroke: the Bajan took 6 for 22 not only to lead his side to a comfortable 72-run victory but also to record the best figures by a debutant in one-day international history.

Lacking the killer punch

A bowler who lacked the pace to make his mark in international cricket, Zimbabwe's Pommie Mbangwa holds the dubious record of having the worst career strike-rate of any bowler to have bowled 1,000 balls or more in one-day international cricket history. The medium-pace swing bowler took 11 wickets for his country in 29 matches between 1996 and 2002 at a strike-rate of a wicket every 124.4 deliveries

Magical McGrath propels Australia to victory

Glenn McGrath was in blistering form with the ball during Australia's successful campaign in the 1998–99 Carlton and United triangular series (which also involved England and Sri Lanka). The fast bowler took 27 wickets in 11 matches – the best by any bowler in history in a one-day tournament – at an average of 15.62 runs per wicket, with a best haul of 5 for 40 against Sri Lanka at Adelaide on 24 January 1999.

Miserly Simmons eases West Indies to victory

Phil Simmons's medium-pace swing bowling proved too much for Pakistan at Sydney on 17 December 1992: the West Indies all-rounder took 4 for 3 off his ten overs – the most economical figures ever recorded in a full spell of bowling in one-day international cricket – in a match the West Indies went on to win by 133 runs.

Vaas rips through Zimbabwe

Sri Lanka's **Chaminda Vaas** was inspirational against Zimbabwe at Colombo on 8 December 2001. The left-arm paceman took a wicket with the first delivery of the match and continued in a similar vein to help rout the visitors for the third lowest score in 50-over cricket (38 all out) and become the first, and to date only, bowler in one-day international cricket history to take eight wickets in an innings. He finished with the astonishing figures of 8 for 19 off eight overs.

BEST CAREER BOWLING AVERAGE: TOP 5 (QUALIFICATION: 50 WICKETS)

Pos	Ave	Player	Mat	Balls	Runs	Wkts	BBI	Econ	SR	4w	5w
1	18.84	J. Garner (WI, 1977–87)	98	5,330	2,752	146	5/31	3.09	36.5	2	3
2	20.05	L.L. Tsotsobe (SA, 2009–12)	31	1,528	1,163	58	4/22	4.56	26.3	4	0
3	20.11	L.S. Pascoe (Aus, 1977–82)	29	1,568	1,066	53	5/30	4.07	29.5	4	1
4	20.35	A.M.E. Roberts (WI, 1975–83)	56	3,123	1,771	87	5/22	3.40	35.8	2	1
5	20.75	B.A.W. Mendis (SL, 2008–12)	59	2,756	1,992	96	6/13	4.33	28.7	4	3

DEADLIEST BOWLER–BATSMAN COMBINATION: TOP 5

Bowler	Batsman	Span	Mat	Wkts	Ave	Ducks
Waqar Younis (Pak)	S.T. Jayasuriya (SL)	1989–2002	45	13	12.76	2
Wasim Akram (Pak)	D.L. Haynes (WI)	1985–93	41	12	16.91	1
S.M. Pollock (ICC/SA)	A.C. Gilchrist (Aus)	1997–2007	43	12	19.41	2
W.P.U.J.C. Vaas (Asia/SL)	S.P. Fleming (ICC/NZ)	1994–2007	29	11	10.09	4
W.P.U.J.C. Vaas (SL)	Saeed Anwar (Pak)	1994–2002	38	11	24.63	0

A poor day at the office

Australia's Mick Lewis had a day to forget as South Africa chased down a victory target of 435 to win by one wicket at Johannesburg on 12 March 2006. The fast-medium bowler went for 113 runs off his 10 overs – the most ever conceded by a bowler to bowl his full allocation of overs in an ODI.

Wasim provides glimpse into a glorious future

Playing in only his fourth one-day international for Pakistan (against Australia at Melbourne on 24 February 1989), **Wasim Akram** gave notice of the talent that would see him become the most successful fast bowler in ODI history. The left-arm paceman took 5 for 21 to become, aged 18 years 66 days, the youngest player to take five wickets in an innings in ODI history. Waqar Younis (18 years 164 days) broke the record (6 for 26 v Sri Lanka) on 29 April 1990.

Magic Malinga carves through South Africa

There have been 31 hat-tricks in the history of one-day international cricket, but there has been only one case of a bowler taking four wickets in four balls: **Lasith Malinga** dismissed Shaun Pollock (bowled), Andrew Hall (caught), Jacques Kallis (caught) and Makhaya Ntini (bowled) in successive deliveries during Sri Lanka's World Cup Super Eight match against South Africa at Providence, Guyana, on 28 March 2007, but still saw his side lose by one run.

Age no barrier for Dhaniram

Sunil Dhaniram created a slice of history during Canada's match against Bermuda at Ontario on 29 June 2008. The Canadian slow left-armer, playing in his 26th one-day international, took 5 for 32 to become, aged 39 years 256 days, the oldest player in history to take five wickets in an innings in a 50-over international. Sadly for Dhaniram, his record-breaking effort did not turn out to be a match-winning one: Bermuda went on to win the rain-affected match by 11 runs.

Breaking the mould

With his late reverse swing that was as likely to crash into the base of the stumps as it was to cannon into a batsman's foot, **Waqar Younis** set a new trend for fast bowlers. He was mightily effective in all formats of the game, but his record in one-day international cricket was truly exceptional: in 262 matches for Pakistan between 1989 and 2003 he took 416 wickets and broke the records for the most five-wicket hauls (13) and the most of four wickets plus (27). He is also the only bowler in one-day international cricket history to take three successive five-wicket hauls.

Most wickets taken...

Bowled: 176 – Wasim Akram (Pakistan, 1984–2003)

Caught: 290 – Muttiah Muralitharan (Sri Lanka, 1993–2011)

Caught and bowled: 35 – Muttiah Muralitharan (Sri Lanka, 1993–2011)

Caught by a fielder: 246 – Muttiah Muralitharan (Sri Lanka, 1993–2011)

Caught by a wicketkeeper: 93 – Wasim Akram (Pakistan, 1984–2003)

LBW: 92 – Wasim Akram (Pakistan, 1984–2003)

Stumped: 56 – Muttiah Muralitharan (Sri Lanka, 1993–2011)

Hit wicket: 3 – Courtney Walsh (West Indies, 1985–2000); and Wasim Akram (Pakistan, 1984–2003)

Most balls bowled in an ODI career

No bowler has bowled more deliveries in one-day international cricket than Muttiah Muralitharan, who bowled 18,811 balls for Sri Lanka in 350 matches between 1993 and 2011. The Sri Lankan spin maestro also holds the record for conceding the most runs in a career (12,326).

Leading from the front

Here's another in the long list of Waqar Younis' ODI records: as Pakistan captain against England at Headingley on 17 June 2001, he took 7 for 36 – the best bowling figures by a captain in ODI history – to lead his side to victory.

Lee makes his mark

One of the quickest bowlers on the international circuit since he made his debut in January 2000, Australia's Brett Lee, mainly as a result of a catalogue of serious injuries, never quite lived up to the hype his searing pace generated. However, he has been a very effective performer in all forms of cricket, particularly One Day Internationals. The New South Wales paceman reached both the 300 and 350-wicket milestones in fewer matches than any other player, in 171 and 202 matches, respectively.

Best bowler-fielder combination

The most successful bowler-fielder combination in one-day international cricket history is that between South Africa's Makhaya Ntini and Mark Boucher. The pair combined for 75 dismissals in 164 matches between 1998 and 2009.

FASTEST TO...

Wkts	Player	Matches
50	**B.A.W. Mendis** (SL)	19
100	Saqlain Mushtaq (Pak)	53
150	Saqlain Mushtaq (Pak)	78
200	Saqlain Mushtaq (Pak)	104
250	Saqlain Mushtaq (Pak)	138
300	B. Lee (Aus)	171
350	B. Lee (Aus)	202
400	Waqar Younis (Pak)	252
450	M. Muralitharan (Asia/ICC/SL)	295
500	M. Muralitharan (Asia/ICC/SL)	324

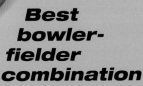

OTHER RECORDS

MOST CATCHES IN A CAREER: TOP 5

Pos	Ct	Player	Mat	Inns
1	190	D.P.M.D. Jayawardene (Asia/SL, 1998–2012)	373	369
2	160	R.T. Ponting (Aus/ICC, 1995–2012)	375	372
3	156	M. Azharuddin (Ind, 1985–2000)	334	332
4	140	S.R. Tendulkar (Ind, 1989–2012)	463	456
5	133	S.P. Fleming (ICC/NZ, 1994–2007)	280	276

A day to forget behind the stumps for Ashraf Ali

Forced to play second fiddle to Wasim Bari for most of his career, Ashraf Ali eventually played 16 one-day internationals for Pakistan between 1980 and 1985 but got his international career off to the worst possible start. In his debut match, against the West Indies at Sialkot on 5 December 1980, he conceded 20 byes – the most by any wicketkeeper in an innings in one-day international cricket – in a game the West Indies went on to win by seven wickets.

Electric Rhodes is the greatest fielder of them all

South Africa's Jonty Rhodes in full flight in the field was as majestic a sight as a bowler or batsman at the very top of his game: in short, he was the greatest fielder to play the game, and a record-breaking one, too. In South Africa's match against the West Indies at Mumbai on 14 November 1993 he took five catches – the most catches in an innings by a fielder in one-day international cricket history.

Most dismissals in a career for Gilchrist

The player who perhaps contributed more than any other to Australia's three successive World Cup triumphs between 1999 and 2007, **Adam Gilchrist** was as colossal behind the stumps as he was destructive at the top of the batting order. In 287 one-day internationals for his country between 1996 and 2008, he claimed a record 472 dismissals, with 417 catches and 55 stumpings.

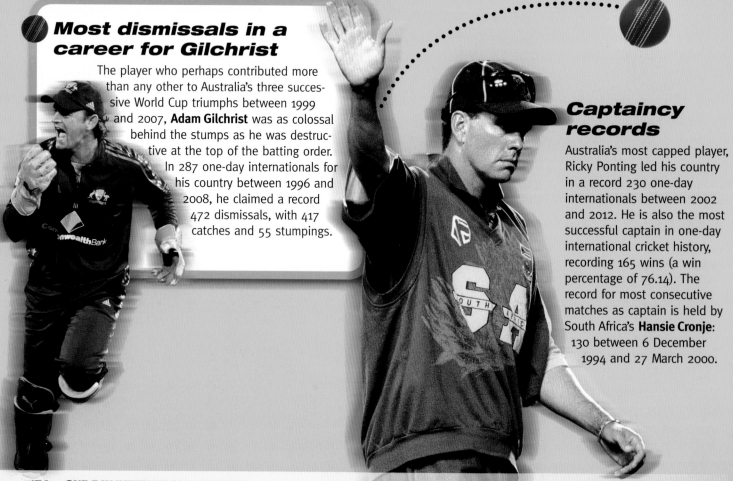

Captaincy records

Australia's most capped player, Ricky Ponting led his country in a record 230 one-day internationals between 2002 and 2012. He is also the most successful captain in one-day international cricket history, recording 165 wins (a win percentage of 76.14). The record for most consecutive matches as captain is held by South Africa's **Hansie Cronje**: 130 between 6 December 1994 and 27 March 2000.

HIGHEST PARTNERSHIP BY WICKET

Wkt	Runs	Partners	Team	Opposition	Venue	Date
1st	286	W.U. Tharanga/S.T. Jayasuriya	Sri Lanka	England	Leeds	1 Jul 2006
2nd	331	S.R. Tendulkar/R. Dravid	India	New Zealand	Hyderabad	8 Nov 1999
3rd	237*	R. Dravid/S.R. Tendulkar	India	Kenya	Bristol	23 May 1999
4th	275*	M. Azharuddin/A. Jadeja	India	Zimbabwe	Cuttack	9 Apr 1998
5th	223	M. Azharuddin/A. Jadeja	India	Sri Lanka	Colombo (RPS)	17 Aug 1997
6th	218	D.P.M.D. Jayawardene/M.S. Dhoni	Asia XI	Africa XI	Chennai	10 Jun 2007
7th	130	A. Flower/H.H. Streak	Zimbabwe	England	Harare	7 Oct 2001
8th	138*	J.M. Kemp/A.J. Hall	South Africa	India	Cape Town	26 Nov 2006
9th	132	A.D. Mathews/S.L. Malinga	Sri Lanka	Australia	Melbourne	3 Nov 2010
10th	106*	I.V.A. Richards/M.A. Holding	West Indies	England	Manchester	31 May 1984

Most matches as an umpire

One of the most respected umpires in the modern game, South Africa's **Rudi Koertzen** has officiated in more one-day internationals than any other umpire. The former bank clerk, famed for his slow finger raise, has stood in the middle on 209 occasions between 1992 and 2012.

The Little Master's other records

The leading run-scorer in one-day international cricket, **Sachin Tendulkar** also holds the record for the most consecutive matches played in the 50-over format of the game. The Little Master appeared in 185 consecutive games for India between 25 April 1990 and 24 April 1998. Tendulkar also holds the record for the most man of the match awards, with 62.

Perfect partners

The most productive partnership in the history of one-day international cricket is that between India's Sachin Tendulkar and Sourav Ganguly. The pair combined to score 8,227 runs in 176 innings for their country between 1992 and 2007, with 26 century stands at an average of 47.55 runs per partnership.

Master blaster Richards shows his all-round skills

Revered throughout world cricket for his power displays with the bat, Viv Richards was also a handy and effective contributor with the ball, particularly in one-day cricket. On 18 March 1987, playing for the West Indies against New Zealand at Dunedin, he hit 119 with the bat and then took 5 for 41 with the ball to become the first player in one-day international cricket history to hit a century and take four or more wickets in a match. The feat has since been repeated on ten occasions.

Tendulkar and Dravid steal the show

Sachin Tendulkar (186 not out) and Rahul Dravid (153) combined to stunning and record-breaking effect as India thrashed New Zealand by 174 runs in the second one-day international of the five-match series between the two countries at Hyderabad on 8 November 1999. The pair added 331 for the second wicket – the highest partnership in one-day international cricket history.

ICC TROPHY

First contested in 1979, the ICC Trophy is a one-day match tournament for non-Test-playing nations. In recent years it has gained extra significance: it serves as a qualifying tournament for the ICC World Cup – the 2009 edition of the tournament saw Ireland, Canada, Netherlands and Kenya qualify for the 2011 World Cup – and the top five finishing teams are awarded ODI status for a four-year period.

ICC TROPHY WINNERS

Year	Winners	Host
1979	Sri Lanka	England
1982	Zimbabwe	England
1986	Zimbabwe	England
1990	Zimbabwe	Netherlands
1994	United Arab Emirates	Kenya
1997	Bangladesh	Malaysia
2001	Netherlands	Canada
2005	Scotland	Ireland
2009	**Ireland**	South Africa

Magic Myles hits tournament best

Simon Myles was the standout performer during Hong Kong's 144-run demolition of Gibraltar in the one-sided Group 2 encounter in the 1986 ICC World Cup, played at Bridgnorth. The Hong Kong batsman smashed a tournament best 172 out of his side's total of 324 for 5. Gibraltar were 180 all out in reply.

Most wickets in a series

The Netherlands' seam bowler Ronnie Elferink was the pick of the bowlers at the 1986 ICC Trophy. In ten matches he took two five-wicket hauls – with a best return of 6 for 14 against Fiji at Gloucester – and ended the tournament with 23 wickets (a record in a single tournament) at an average of 9.82.

Netherlands power past East and Central Africa

It took just 20.5 overs for the Netherlands to dismiss the challenge of East and Central Africa in the two sides' match at the 1997 ICC Trophy in Kuala Lumpur. After winning the toss and electing to bowl, the Netherlands dismissed East and Central Africa for a paltry 26 all out in 15.2 overs – the lowest team total in the tournament's history. The Netherlands reached the minimal victory target in 5.3 overs for the loss of two wickets.

Tau Ao hit to all parts of the ground

Papua New Guinea's Tau Ao bore the brunt of Canada's onslaught during the two sides' Group 2 encounter at Walsall in the 1986 ICC Trophy. As Canada reached an imposing 356 for 5, the Papua New Guinea opening bowler went for 116 off his 12-over allocation – the most runs conceded in an innings by a bowler in the tournament's history.

Largest margin of victory

By runs: by 369 runs – Papua New Guinea v Gibraltar at Cannock on 18 June 1986.

By wickets: by ten wickets on 12 occasions.

By balls remaining: 337 balls remaining – Canada v Gibraltar at Swindon on 20 June 1986.

Smallest margin of victory

By runs: by one run – Bangladesh v Malaysia at Kidderminster on 28 June 1982.

By wickets: by one wicket on seven occasions.

By balls remaining: off the last ball of the match on three occasions.

Longevity the key for Lefebvre

A player who performed with distinction in county cricket for a number of years (he played for Somerset and Glamorgan between 1990 and 1995), **Roland Lefebvre** put his skills to good use in the ICC Trophy for the Netherlands between 1986 and 2001. He holds the record for the most wickets in the tournament's history (71) and also for the most matches played (43).

Kenya pay heavy price for indiscipline in the field

Perhaps the principal reason for Kenya's surprise 37-run loss to Papua New Guinea at The Hague in the two sides' 1990 ICC Trophy encounter was their record-breaking indiscipline in the field. During Papua New Guinea's innings (230 all out), the Kenyans conceded a massive 54 extras (16 leg-byes, 35 wides and three no-balls) – the most in the tournament's history. In reply, the Kenyans slipped to 193 all out.

Prashad prospers as Canada fall short

Although his team failed to progress beyond the group stages of the 1986 ICC Trophy held in England, for Canada's Paul Prashad it was a tournament to remember. In eight innings he hit three centuries (with a highest score of 164 not out against Papua New Guinea at Walsall) and finished with 533 runs to his name – a record for a single ICC Trophy tournament – at an average of 88.83.

Off to a flying start

Rene Schoonheim (117) and R.E. Lifmann (155 not out) provided the perfect platform for the Netherlands during their 125-run victory over Malaysia in the two sides' Group 2 encounter at Redditch in the 1982 ICC Trophy. The pair put on 257 runs for the opening wicket – the highest partnership in the tournament's history.

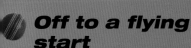

PNG hit the heights

Papua New Guinea were simply too strong for Gibraltar when the two sides met at Cannock in the 1986 ICC Trophy. Batting first, Papua New Guinea amassed a colossal 455 for 9 (off 60 overs), with B. Harry top-scoring with 127. In reply, Gibraltar wilted to a sorry 86 all out to lose the match by 369 runs.

Good things come to those who wait

A star performer for Barbados against the England tourists in 1973–74 (a match in which he hit an imperious 158), **Nolan Clarke** may not have reached the dizzy heights that many at the time predicted he would, but he did go on to enjoy a lengthy and successful career with the Netherlands. In 18 ICC Trophy matches for them between 1990 and 1994 he scored 1,040 runs (with a highest score of 154 against Israel at Amstelveen on 4 June 1990) at an average of 74.28 – the highest by any batsman to have scored 500 runs or more in ICC Trophy history. He also holds the tournament record for the most hundreds scored (five).

Khan records best single-innings bowling figures

Asim Khan was the main destroyer when East and Central Africa slipped to a record-breaking low of 26 all out against the Netherlands at Kuala Lumpur in the 1997 ICC Trophy. The Dutch paceman produced figures of 7 for 9 off 7.2 overs – the best in the tournament's history.

Mortensen makes waves with the ball

A burly seam bowler who performed with great success in county cricket with Derbyshire for over a decade, Ole Mortensen was an outstanding performer in the ICC Trophy for Denmark: in 26 matches in the tournament between 1979 and 1994 he set the all-time records for the best average (10.41), the most four-wicket-plus hauls (seven) and the best strike-rate (taking a wicket every 25.4 deliveries).

MOST RUNS: TOP 5

Pos	Runs	Player	Mat	Inns	NO	HS	Ave	100	50	0
1	1,173	**M.O. Odumbe** (Kenya, 1990–97)	25	24	7	158*	69.00	3	6	1
2	1,040	N.E. Clarke (Neth, 1990–94)	18	18	4	154	74.28	5	3	1
3	772	R. Gomes (Neth, 1986–90)	18	17	4	169*	59.38	3	2	1
4	761	Minhajul Abedin (Bang, 1986–97)	30	28	4	68	31.70	0	4	0
5	747	P. Prashad (Can, 1986–94)	18	18	5	164*	57.46	3	2	0

MOST WICKETS: TOP 5

Pos	Wkts	Player	Mat	Overs	Mdns	Runs	BBI	Ave	Econ	SR	4	5
1	71	R.P. Lefebvre (Neth, 1986–2001)	43	334.4	72	827	5/16	11.64	2.47	28.2	1	1
2	63	O.H. Mortensen (Den, 1979–94)	26	267.4	52	656	7/19	10.41	2.45	25.4	6	1
3	48	A.Y. Karim (Kenya, 1986–97)	30	261.1	41	798	5/20	16.62	3.05	32.6	2	1
4	44	A. Edwards (Berm, 1986–94)	23	218.2	28	764	6/38	17.36	3.49	29.7	0	2
5	42	N.A. Gibbons (Berm, 1979–94)	34	251.3	26	960	4/18	22.85	3.81	35.9	2	0

ODI CRICKET RECORDS:
BY TEAM

One-day international cricket is played more in some parts of the world than in others. For example: Kevin Pietersen (England) and M.S. Dhoni (India) both made their one-day international debuts in 2003 and have been regulars ever since; as of 6 March 2012, however, Pietersen had appeared in 127 ODIs compared to Dhoni's 203. As such, the relative chances of a player featuring among the list of one-day international cricket's all-time cumulative record-holders depend on which country he plays for. To be one's country's all-time ODI leading performer, however, is an altogether different matter and is always a coveted honour.

Record breaker: The highest individual innings in a One Day International, formerly 200 by Sachin Tendulkar, was smashed by **Virender Sehwag** in 2011, when he blasted 219 against the West Indies at Indore.

AUSTRALIA

Australia are the most successful team in the history of one-day international cricket: they have won the most matches (490), have won the ICC World Cup more times than any other country (in 1987, 1999, 2003 and 2007) and are the only team to have won the ICC Champions Trophy on two occasions (emerging victorious in 2006 and 2009).

RESULT SUMMARY

Opposition	Span	Mat	Won	Lost	Tied	NR	%
Bangladesh	1990–2011	19	18	1	0	0	94.73
Canada	1979–2011	2	2	0	0	0	100.00
England	1971–2011	113	67	42	2	2	61.26
ICC World XI	2005	3	3	0	0	0	100.00
India	1980–2012	109	64	37	0	8	63.36
Ireland	2007–10	2	2	0	0	0	100.00
Kenya	1996–2011	5	5	0	0	0	100.00
Namibia	2003	1	1	0	0	0	100.00
Netherlands	2003–07	2	2	0	0	0	100.00
New Zealand	1974–2011	124	85	34	0	5	71.42
Pakistan	1975–2011	86	52	30	1	3	63.25
Scotland	1999–2009	3	3	0	0	0	100.00
South Africa	1992–2011	80	41	36	3	0	53.12
Sri Lanka	1975–2012	84	52	28	0	3	65.00
USA	2004	1	1	0	0	0	100.00
West Indies	1975–2012	130	65	59	3	3	52.36
Zimbabwe	1983–2011	28	26	1	0	1	96.29

Australia's ODI batting master

Despite never really hitting the heights in the Test arena (in which his vulnerability to the short ball meant he only appeared in 18 Tests in the mid-1990s), Michael Bevan suffered no such problems in the 50-over format of the game and went on to form an integral part of Australia's one-day side for a decade, during which he gained a reputation as being one of the best finishers in the business. Relying on exquisite placement and speed between the wickets rather than powerful strokeplay, he amassed an impressive 6,912 runs in 232 one-day internationals between 1994 and 2004 at an average of 53.58 – the best by any Australia batsman in history.

Lillee tops bowling averages

More renowned for his performances in the Test arena, in which he took 355 wickets in 70 Tests, Dennis Lillee was also extremely effective in the one-day game. In 63 matches for Australia between 1972 and 1983 he took 103 wickets at an average of 20.82 – the best by any Australian bowler in history to have bowled 2,000 balls or more in one-day international cricket.

More than six of the best as Watson shines in Dhaka

Australia's victory target of 230 to beat Bangladesh in the second one-day international at Dhaka on 11 April 2011 may not have been too imposing, but **Shane Watson's** performance with the bat made sure they reached it in imperious fashion. The Queensland opener smashed 15 four and an all-time record 15 sixes in his 96-ball unbeaten 185 – the highest score by an Australian batsman in one-day international history – as Australia coasted across the winning line for the loss of just one wicket and with 144 balls to spare.

A true legend of the game

A true rock upon which Australia have built their considerable success in one-day international cricket in recent years, **Ricky Ponting** will go down in history as one of cricket's greatest players, and his record in one-day international cricket is among the best of all time. He holds Australia's all-time records for: most runs (13,589), centuries (29 – with a highest of 164 against South Africa at Johannesburg on 12 March 2006), catches (159) and matches (374). He is also the most successful one-day captain in Australia's history, notching up 164 wins in 229 matches as captain between 2002 and 2012.

Highest and lowest

Highest score: 434 for 4 against South Africa at Johannesburg on 12 March 2006.

Lowest score: 70 all out, against New Zealand at Adelaide on 27 January 1986; and against England at Edgbaston on 4 June 1977.

Biggest victories

By runs: by 256 runs against Namibia at Potchefstroom on 27 February 2003.

By wickets: by ten wickets on four occasions.

By balls remaining (in the second innings): with 253 balls remaining against the United States at Southampton on 13 September 2004.

Smallest victories

By runs: by one run on five occasions.

By wickets: by one wicket on three occasions.

By balls remaining (in the second innings): off the final ball of the match on four occasions.

Watson and Ponting put England to the sword

Shane Watson (136 not out) and Ricky Ponting (111 not out) dashed any hopes England may have had of defending a modest total of 257 in the semi-final of the 2009 ICC Champions Trophy at Centurion on 2 October 2009. Coming together with the score on 6 for 1 in the second over, the pair added an unbeaten 252 runs to see Australia over the winning line with 8.1 overs to spare. It was the highest partnership for Australia in one-day international cricket history.

Magic McGrath leads the way

The most successful one-day bowler in Australia's history (with 380 wickets in 249 matches), **Glenn McGrath** also holds the record for the best figures ever recorded by an Australian bowler in one-day international cricket, with 7 for 15 against Namibia at Potchefstroom in the 2003 World Cup (also a World Cup best).

Most four-wicket-plus innings hauls

One of only three Australian bowlers to have taken a hat-trick in one-day international cricket – the others being Bruce Reid (against New Zealand at Sydney in January 1986) and Anthony Stuart (against Pakistan at Melbourne in January 1997) – Brett Lee has recorded more four-wicket-plus hauls than any other Australian bowler in one-day international cricket history (23 in 217 matches between 2000 and 2012).

Glorious Gilchrist prospers for Australia

Adam Gilchrist will be remembered as the best wicketkeeper-batsman ever to have played the game. In 286 matches for Australia he hit 9,595 runs at a strike-rate of 96.89 runs per 100 balls faced (the best by an Australian in history) and also excelled behind the stumps, claiming 470 dismissals (416 catches and 54 stumpings) – another all-time Australian record.

MOST RUNS: TOP 5

Pos	Runs	Player	Mat	Inns	NO	HS	Ave	100	50	0
1	13,589	R.T. Ponting (1995–2012)	374	364	39	164	41.81	29	82	20
2	9,595	A.C. Gilchrist (1996–2008)	286	278	11	172	35.93	16	55	19
3	8,500	M.E. Waugh (1988–2002)	244	236	20	173	39.35	18	50	16
4	7,569	S.R. Waugh (1986–2002)	325	288	58	120*	32.90	3	45	15
5	6,953	M.J. Clarke (2003–12)	212	194	42	130	45.74	7	51	10

MOST WICKETS: TOP 5

Pos	Wkts	Player	Mat	Balls	Runs	BBI	Ave	Econ	SR	4	5
1	380	G.D. McGrath (1993–2007)	249	12,928	8,354	7/15	21.98	3.87	34.0	9	7
2	377	B. Lee (2000–12)	217	11,033	8,740	5/22	23.18	4.75	29.2	14	9
3	291	S.K. Warne (1993–2003)	193	10,600	7,514	5/33	25.82	4.25	36.4	12	1
4	203	C.J. McDermott (1985–96)	138	7,461	5,018	5/44	24.71	4.03	36.7	4	1
5	195	S.R. Waugh (1986–2002)	325	8,883	6,761	4/33	34.67	4.56	45.5	3	0

ENGLAND

Although they have been runners-up three times in the ICC World Cup (in 1979, 1987 and 1992), England have always struggled to hit the heights in one-day international cricket. In 576 matches played since their opening one-day international against Australia in 1971 they have notched up 278 victories – of all the current Test-playing nations, only Bangladesh, New Zealand and Zimbabwe have recorded fewer.

Bresnan proves his worth on the ODI platform

It took some time, but a string of impressive performances have seen Tim Bresnan finally justify the hype that surrounded him when, in 2001, he became, aged 16, the youngest player to play for Yorkshire for 20 years. Now a regular in England's one-day side, he has the highest strike-rate of any England batsman in history, scoring his 496 runs (in 42 matches) at 94.11 runs per 100 balls faced.

Smith puts on a show at Edgbaston

Australia eventually won the match (and with it the series) against England at Edgbaston on 21 May 1993, but not before they had encountered one of the most destructive one-day innings ever seen on English soil. **Robin Smith** powered his way to a 163-ball unbeaten 167 – the highest score by an England player in one-day international cricket history – as the home side reached 277 for 5. Australia reached the target for the loss of four wickets with nine balls to spare.

RESULT SUMMARY

Opposition	Span	Mat	Won	Lost	Tied	NR	%
Australia	1971–2011	113	42	67	2	2	38.73
Bangladesh	2000–11	15	13	2	0	0	86.66
Canada	1979–2007	2	2	0	0	0	100.00
East Africa	1975	1	1	0	0	0	100.00
India	1974–2011	81	33	42	2	3	43.58
Ireland	2006–11	5	4	1	0	0	80.00
Kenya	1999–2007	2	2	0	0	0	100.00
Namibia	2003	1	1	0	0	0	100.00
Netherlands	1996–2011	3	3	0	0	0	100.00
New Zealand	1973–2009	70	29	35	2	4	45.45
Pakistan	1974–2012	72	42	28	0	2	60.00
Scotland	2008–10	2	1	0	0	1	100.00
South Africa	1992–2011	45	19	23	1	2	45.34
Sri Lanka	1982–2011	50	26	24	0	0	52.00
UAE	1996	1	1	0	0	0	100.00
West Indies	1973–2011	83	38	41	0	4	48.10
Zimbabwe	1992–2004	30	21	8	0	1	72.41

Stewart proves an effective performer behind the stumps

An opening batsman who was forced behind the stumps by the England selectors' desire to find balance in the team, Alec Stewart developed into a top-class wicketkeeper. In 170 one-day internationals between 1989 and 2003 he took an all-time English record 163 dismissals (with 148 catches and 15 stumpings).

England's Mr Dependable

Jonathan Trott's ODI career for England may not have got off to the best of starts – he was dismissed for a five-ball duck on debut against Ireland in Dublin – but, as has become his trademark, the Warwickshire right-hander got his head down, nailed down a place in the England line-up and did what he does best ... score runs, and plenty of them. He posted his first century (of three) against Bangladesh in his sixth innings, became the fastest player (alongside Viv Richards and Kevin Pietersen) to reach 1,000 one-day international runs (in 21 innings), starred for England at the 2011 ICC World Cup and, to date, has scored 1,836 runs in 42 innings at an average of 48.31 – the highest average by any England batsman in history.

MOST RUNS: TOP 5

Pos	Runs	Player	Mat	Inns	NO	HS	Ave	100	50	0
1	5,092	P.D. Collingwood (2001–11)	197	181	37	120*	35.36	5	26	7
2	4,677	A.J. Stewart (1989–2003)	170	162	14	116	31.60	4	28	13
3	4,335	M.E. Trescothick (2000–06)	123	122	6	137	37.37	12	21	13
4	4,290	G.A. Gooch (1976–95)	125	122	6	142	36.98	8	23	4
5	4,205	A.J. Strauss (2003–11)	127	126	8	158	35.63	6	27	9

MOST WICKETS: TOP 5

Pos	Wkts	Player	Mat	Balls	Runs	BBI	Ave	Econ	SR	4	5
1	234	D. Gough (1994–2006)	158	8,422	6,154	5/44	26.29	4.38	35.9	10	2
2	190	J.M. Anderson (2002–12)	154	7,652	6,414	5/23	30.83	5.02	36.7	9	1
3	168	A. Flintoff (1999–2009)	138	5,496	3,968	5/19	23.61	4.33	32.7	6	2
4	145	I.T. Botham (1976–92)	116	6,271	4,139	4/31	28.54	3.96	43.2	3	0
5	142	S.C.J. Broad (2006–12)	87	4,412	3,828	5/23	26.95	5.20	31.0	9	1

The ultimate professional

Paul Collingwood is the perfect example of just how far hard work and professionalism can take you. Widely admired as a gritty, determined performer in the Test arena, he initially cemented his reputation in one-day international cricket, a format in which he has gone on to set numerous all-time records for his country: he is the most capped one-day international cricketer in England's history (winning 197 caps between 2001 and 2011); has taken the most catches (108); and, surprisingly, holds the record for the best bowling figures ever recorded by an England player in a one-day international – 6 for 31 against Bangladesh at Trent Bridge on 21 June 2005 (he also scored a century in the match to become the first player in one-day international cricket history to record a century and take six wickets in a match).

Top performer with the ball

Arguably a finer performer with the ball than with the bat, **Andrew Flintoff** was England's go-to bowler. In 138 one-day internationals between 1999 and 2009 he took 168 wickets for 3,968 runs at an average of 23.61 runs per wicket – the best by any England player to have bowled 2,000 balls or more in one-day international cricket history.

Most successful captain

He may not have performed at his best with the bat in the 50-over format of the game, but Michael Vaughan was the most successful English captain of all time in one-day international cricket, recording 32 wins in 60 matches between 2003 and 2007 – a win percentage of 58.92.

Highest and lowest

Highest score: 391 for 4 against Bangladesh at Trent Bridge on 21 June 2005.

Lowest score: 86 all out against Australia at Old Trafford on 14 June 2001.

Biggest victories

By runs: by 202 runs against India at Lord's on 7 June 1975.

By wickets: by ten wickets on four occasions.

By balls remaining (in the second innings): with 277 balls remaining against Canada at Old Trafford on 13 June 1979.

Smallest victories

By runs: by one run on two occasions: against India at Cuttack on 27 December 1984; and against West Indies at Providence, Guyana, on 20 March 2009.

By wickets: by one wicket on six occasions.

By balls remaining (in the second innings): off the last ball of the match on three occasions.

Gough guns his way into all-time record books

England's best strike bowler since Bob Willis and, with his ability to reverse-swing the ball at pace, an extremely effective "death" bowler, **Darren Gough** is the most successful English bowler in one-day international cricket history (with 235 wickets in 159 matches between 1994 and 2006). He also holds the English record for the most four-wicket-plus hauls, with 12.

INDIA

Cricket-mad India has developed a taste for the one-day game like no other country on earth, playing more matches (801) than any other cricketing nation. And they have enjoyed considerable success, too: sensationally they won the ICC World Cup in 1983, repeated the feat in front of an adoring home crowd in 2011 and have notched up 397 victories – only Australia (490) and Pakistan (415) have more.

RESULT SUMMARY

Opposition	Span	Mat	Won	Lost	Tied	NR	%
Australia	1980–2012	109	37	64	0	8	36.63
Bangladesh	1988–2012	24	21	3	0	0	87.50
Bermuda	2007	1	1	0	0	0	100.00
East Africa	1975	1	1	0	0	0	100.00
England	1974–2011	81	43	33	2	3	56.41
Hong Kong	2008	1	1	0	0	0	100.00
Ireland	2007–11	2	2	0	0	0	100.00
Kenya	1996–2004	13	11	2	0	0	84.61
Namibia	2003	1	1	0	0	0	100.00
Netherlands	2003–11	2	2	0	0	0	100.00
New Zealand	1975–2010	88	46	37	0	5	55.42
Pakistan	1978–2012	121	48	69	0	4	41.02
Scotland	2007	1	1	0	0	0	100.00
South Africa	1991–2011	66	24	40	0	2	37.50
Sri Lanka	1979–2012	134	71	51	1	11	58.13
UAE	1994–2004	2	2	0	0	0	100.00
West Indies	1979–2011	106	46	57	1	2	44.71
Zimbabwe	1983–2010	51	39	10	2	0	78.43

Dashing Dhoni leads averages list

Mahendra Singh Dhoni, who has been a steady performer behind the stumps for India since making his debut against South Africa in December 2004, has more dismissals to his name – 252 (190 catches, 62 stumpings) – than any other wicketkeeper in one-day international history, and has been captain of the side since September 2007. It is Dhoni's swashbuckling performances with the bat, however, that have marked him out as an all-round player of the highest calibre. In 203 one-day internationals he has scored 6,599 runs (with a highest score of 183 not out against Sri Lanka at Jaipur on 31 October 2005) at an average of 51.15 – it is the highest average by any Indian batsman to have completed 25 innings or more in one-day international cricket history.

Superb Sehwag's demolition job

India's **Virender Sehwag** is among the most destructive top-order batsmen in the game's history, going after bowlers from the first ball. And he was at his very best in the fourth one-day international against the West Indies at Indore on 8 December 2011. Leading the side in the absence of Mahendra Singh Dhoni, he reached 50 off 41 balls, 100 off 69, 150 off 112 and 200 off 140 before finally falling for 219 – the highest individual score in one-day international history. India posted 418 for 5 (their highest-ever total) and went on to win the match by 153 runs.

Tendulkar and Dravid combine to devastating effect

Sachin Tendulkar (186 not out) and Rahul Dravid (153) produced a headline-grabbing performance as India beat New Zealand by 174 runs at Hyderabad on 8 November 1999. The pair added 331 runs for the second wicket – an all-time record in one-day international cricket.

Tendulkar's march to cricket greatness

The most complete batsman of his generation, possessing a game without any apparent weaknesses, **Sachin Tendulkar** has become a serial record-breaker in one-day international cricket. In 463 matches for India between 1989 and 2012 (no one in history has played in more) he has set all-time records for the most runs (18,426) and the most centuries (49), and was the fastest to reach every target from 10,000 to 18,000 runs. On 24 February 2010, against South Africa at Gwalior, he smashed 200 not out to become the first player to hit a double-century in ODI cricket.

Haryana Express races into the record books

A legend in Indian cricket both for his all-round brilliance that led India to ICC World Cup success in 1983 and for doggedly chasing down Richard Hadlee's overall aggregate record of Test wickets, **Kapil Dev** – nicknamed the "Haryana Express" by doting cricket fans – was also an exemplary performer in one-day cricket. In 225 matches for his country between 1978 and 1994 he took 253 wickets at an average of 27.45 – the best by any Indian player to have bowled 2,000 balls or more in one-day international cricket history.

Agarkar posts most four-wicket-plus hauls

Tipped as Kapil Dev's natural successor when he first broke into the India set-up in 1998, Ajit Agarkar may not have lived up to the hype in the Test arena (appearing in only 26 Tests between 1998 and 2006), but he more than made his mark in one-day international cricket. In 191 matches between 1998 and 2007, he took 288 wickets – with a best return of 6 for 42 against Australia at Melbourne on 9 January 2004 – including an Indian all-time record 12 four-wicket-plus hauls.

Highest and lowest

Highest score: 418 for 5 against West Indies at Indore on 8 December 2011.

Lowest score: 54 all out against Sri Lanka at Sharjah on 29 October 2000.

Biggest victories

By runs: by 257 runs against Bermuda at Port of Spain, Trinidad, on 19 March 2007.

By wickets: by ten wickets on five occasions.

By balls remaining (in the second innings): with 231 balls remaining against Kenya at Bloemfontein on 12 October 2001.

Smallest victories

By runs: by one run on four occasions: against New Zealand at Wellington on 6 March 1990; against Sri Lanka at Colombo on 25 July 1993; against South Africa at Jaipur on 21 February 2010; and against South Africa at Johannesburg on 15 January 2011.

By wickets: by one wicket, on two occasions, against New Zealand at Auckland on 11 January 2003, and against West Indies at Cuttack on 29 November 2011.

By balls remaining (in the second innings): with one ball remaining on seven occasions.

Most successful captain

Mohammad Azharuddin was the most successful Indian captain in one-day international cricket history, recording 90 wins in 174 matches as captain between 1990 and 1999. He also holds the all-time Indian record for the most catches, taking 156 in 334 matches between 1985 and 2000, when his career was brought to a sudden halt by match-fixing allegations.

MOST RUNS: TOP 5

Pos	Runs	Player	Mat	Inns	NO	HS	Ave	100	50	0
1	18,426	S.R. Tendulkar (1989–2012)	463	452	41	200*	44.83	49	96	20
2	11,221	S.C. Ganguly (1992–2007)	308	297	23	183	40.95	22	71	16
3	10,768	R. Dravid (1996–2011)	340	314	39	153	39.15	12	82	13
4	9,378	M. Azharuddin (1985–2000)	334	308	54	153*	36.92	7	58	9
5	7,959	Yuvraj Singh (2000–11)	271	249	37	139	37.54	13	49	14

MOST WICKETS: TOP 5

Pos	Wkts	Player	Mat	Balls	Runs	BBI	Ave	Econ	SR	4	5
1	334	**A. Kumble** (1990–2007)	269	14,376	10,300	6/12	30.83	4.29	43.0	8	2
2	315	J. Srinath (1991–2003)	229	11,935	8,847	5/23	28.08	4.44	37.8	7	3
3	288	A.B. Agarkar (1998–2007)	191	9,484	8,021	6/42	27.85	5.07	32.9	10	2
4	265	Z. Khan (2000–12)	189	9,569	7,872	5/42	29.70	4.93	36.1	7	1
5	255	Harbhajan Singh (1998–2011)	227	11,939	8,550	5/31	33.52	4.29	46.8	2	3

NEW ZEALAND

From the moment they played their first-ever one-day international in 1973, New Zealand, five-time semi-finalists in the ICC World Cup, have provided dogged opposition in the shortened format of the game and have evolved into one of the most consistent sides on the one-day circuit; the Black Caps are capable of beating anyone on their day.

Most centuries

There is a strong case for regarding the free-scoring **Nathan Astle** as the finest one-day player New Zealand has ever produced. In 223 one-day internationals for his country between 1995 and 2007 he scored 7,090 runs at an average of 34.92 and hit 16 centuries – the most by any New Zealand batsman in one-day international cricket – with a highest score of 145 not out against the United States at The Oval on 10 September 2004.

RESULT SUMMARY

Opposition	Span	Mat	Won	Lost	Tied	NR	%
Australia	1974–2011	124	34	85	0	5	28.57
Bangladesh	1990–2010	21	16	5	0	0	76.19
Canada	2003–11	3	3	0	0	0	100.00
East Africa	1975	1	1	0	0	0	100.00
England	1973–2009	70	35	29	2	4	54.54
India	1975–2010	88	37	46	0	5	44.57
Ireland	2007–08	2	2	0	0	0	100.00
Kenya	2007–11	2	2	0	0	0	100.00
Netherlands	1996	1	1	0	0	0	100.00
Pakistan	1973–2011	89	35	51	1	2	40.80
Scotland	1999–2008	2	2	0	0	0	100.00
South Africa	1992–2012	55	18	33	0	4	35.29
Sri Lanka	1979–2011	74	35	34	1	4	50.71
UAE	1996	1	1	0	0	0	100.00
USA	2004	1	1	0	0	0	100.00
West Indies	1975–2009	51	20	24	0	7	45.45
Zimbabwe	1987–2012	35	25	8	1	1	75.00

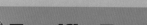

Terrific Turner tops averages list

An uncompromising, straight-playing opening batsman who ensured he wrung every ounce of talent out of his game, Glenn Turner was as successful in one-day cricket for New Zealand as he was in the Test arena. In 41 one-day internationals for his country between 1973 and 1983, he scored 1,598 runs (with a highest score of 171 not out against East Africa in the 1975 ICC World Cup) at an average of 47.00 – the highest by any New Zealand batsman to have completed 20 innings or more in one-day international cricket history.

One of the best in the business

Although his career was blighted by a succession of injuries – many of which kept him out of the game for lengthy periods – **Shane Bond** proved, when fit, that he was one of the finest fast bowlers of his generation. He holds several all-time records for New Zealand in one-day international cricket: for the best bowling in an innings (6 for 19 against India at Bulawayo on 26 August 2005); the best career average (20.88); and the most four-wicket-plus hauls (11 in 82 matches between 2002 and 2010).

Vincent smashes his way into record books

Lou Vincent was at the forefront of New Zealand's 192-run demolition of Zimbabwe – then the largest margin of victory in one-day international cricket history – at Bulawayo on 24 August 2005. The right-handed opener smashed 172 from a mere 120 deliveries – an innings that contained 16 fours and nine sixes – to record the highest-ever individual score by a New Zealand batsman in one-day international cricket.

MOST RUNS: TOP 5

Pos	Runs	Player	Mat	Inns	NO	HS	Ave	100	50	0
1	8,007	S.P. Fleming (1994–2007)	279	268	21	134*	32.41	8	49	17
2	7,090	N.J. Astle (1995–2007)	223	217	14	145*	34.92	16	41	19
3	4,881	C.L. Cairns (1991–2006)	214	192	25	115	29.22	4	25	9
4	4,707	C.D. McMillan (1997–2007)	197	183	16	117	28.18	3	28	9
5	4,704	M.D. Crowe (1982–95)	143	140	18	107*	38.55	4	34	3

MOST WICKETS: TOP 5

Pos	Wkts	Player	Mat	Balls	Runs	BBI	Ave	Econ	SR	4	5
1	274	**D.L. Vettori** (1997–2011)	268	12,663	8,701	5/7	31.75	4.12	46.2	6	2
2	203	C.Z. Harris (1990–2004)	250	10,667	7,613	5/42	37.50	4.28	52.5	2	1
3	200	C.L. Cairns (1991–2006)	214	8,132	6,557	5/42	32.78	4.83	40.6	3	1
=	200	K.D. Mills (2001–12)	135	6,622	5,189	5/25	25.94	4.70	33.1	7	1
5	168	J.P.D. Oram (2001–12)	155	6,677	4,835	5/26	28.77	4.34	39.7	3	2

Cairns Senior powers his way into the record books

Now more famous for being the father of Chris Cairns (who would go on to play in 62 Tests and 215 one-day internationals for New Zealand between 1989 and 2006), **Lance Cairns** was an uncomplicated bully of a cricketer whose performances with the bat in particular often brought crowds to their feet. In 78 one-day internationals for New Zealand between 1974 and 1985 he scored 987 runs from 941 deliveries at a strike-rate of 104.88 runs per 100 balls faced – the best by any New Zealand batsman to have faced 500 balls or more in one-day international cricket history.

The Marshall and McCullum show destroys Ireland

Hamish Marshall (161) and Brendon McCullum (166) produced a rampant performance with the bat at the top of the order to propel New Zealand to a crushing 290-run victory – the highest winning margin in one-day international cricket history – over hapless Ireland at Aberdeen on 1 July 2008. The pair put on 274 runs for the opening wicket – the best partnership of all time for New Zealand in one-day international cricket.

McCullum bags Kiwi record for the most dismissals

First drafted into the New Zealand one-day side as a batsman (against Australia at Sydney in January 2002) following an outstanding career in international youth cricket, **Brendon McCullum** has gone on to become an established and consistent performer behind the stumps. In 21 matches between 2002 and 2012 he has claimed 233 dismissals (with 218 catches and 15 stumpings) – an all-time record for New Zealand in the 50-over format of the game.

Highest and lowest

Highest score: 402 for 2 against Ireland at Aberdeen on 1 July 2008.

Lowest score: 64 all out against Pakistan at Sharjah on 15 April 1986.

Biggest victories

By runs: by 290 runs against Ireland at Aberdeen on 1 July 2008.

By wickets: by ten wickets on six occasions.

By balls remaining (in the second innings): with 264 balls remaining against Bangladesh at Queenstown on 31 December 2007.

Smallest victories

By runs: by one run on four occasions.

By wickets: by one wicket on five occasions.

By balls remaining (in the second innings): off the last ball of the match on four occasions.

Serial record-breaker

Stephen Fleming was a prolific run-scorer for New Zealand in one-day international cricket over a 13-year career stretching from 1994 to 2007 (his 8,007 career runs is the most by any New Zealand batsman in history in one-day international cricket), and the most successful captain his country has ever produced (notching up 98 wins in 218 matches as captain between 1997 and 2007). Fleming also holds the all-time New Zealand records for the most one-day international matches played (279) and for the most catches taken (132).

PAKISTAN

There is no team in world cricket quite like Pakistan, a frustrating blend of sparkling brilliance and overt ordinariness. Their ability to hit heady heights one day and almost laughable lows the next is reflected in their ODI performances. In 1992 their star shone brightly when they won the ICC World Cup; in 2007, however, they failed to progress beyond the group stages.

RESULT SUMMARY

Opposition	Span	Mat	Won	Lost	Tied	NR	%
Afghanistan	2012	1	1	0	0	0	100.00
Australia	1975–2011	86	30	52	1	3	36.74
Bangladesh	1986–2012	31	30	1	0	0	96.77
Canada	1979–2011	2	2	0	0	0	100.00
England	1974–2012	72	28	42	0	2	40.00
Hong Kong	2004–08	2	2	0	0	0	100.00
India	1978–2012	121	69	48	0	4	58.97
Ireland	2007–11	3	2	1	0	0	66.66
Kenya	1996–2011	6	6	0	0	0	100.00
Namibia	2003	1	1	0	0	0	100.00
Netherlands	1996–2003	3	3	0	0	0	100.00
New Zealand	1973–2011	89	51	35	1	2	59.19
Scotland	1999–2006	2	2	0	0	0	100.00
South Africa	1992–2010	57	18	38	0	1	32.14
Sri Lanka	1975–2012	127	76	47	1	0	61.69
UAE	1994–96	2	2	0	0	0	100.00
West Indies	1975–2011	120	52	66	2	0	44.16
Zimbabwe	1992–2011	44	40	2	1	1	94.18

Perfect partners

Aamer Sohail (134) and Inzamam-ul-Haq (137 not out) produced a record-breaking and ultimately match-winning performance against New Zealand at Sharjah on 20 April 1994. The pair put on 263 runs for the second wicket – an all-time record partnership for Pakistan in one-day international cricket – to lead their team to a comfortable 62-run victory.

All-time high strike-rate for "Boom Boom" Afridi

When he is on his game, nobody can demolish an opponent's bowling attack with as much devastating brutality as **Shahid "Boom Boom" Afridi**. In 337 matches for his country between 1996 and 2012 the flamboyant all-rounder has scored 7,003 runs at an average of 23.90 at a strike-rate of 113.79 runs per 100 balls faced – an all-time record in one-day international cricket for any batsman to have faced 500 deliveries or more.

The master opener

A sweet timer of the ball and a graceful stroke-maker, Saeed Anwar stood tall at the top of the Pakistan batting order in all forms of the game for over a decade, but some of his performances in one-day international cricket (he played in 247 matches between 1989 and 2003) were particularly eye-catching. On 21 May 1997, against India at Chennai, he smashed an imperious 194 off 146 balls to break Viv Richards's record for the highest-ever individual score in a one-day international. It was one of 20 one-day centuries compiled in his career – an all-time record for a Pakistan batsman.

The Asian Bradman

Dubbed the "Asian Bradman" in his prime for the single-minded consistency with which he accumulated runs, **Zaheer Abbas** was a refined stroke player who compiled big scores with an array of shots all around the wicket. In 62 one-day internationals for his country between 1974 and 1985 he scored 2,572 runs (with a highest score of 123 against Sri Lanka at Lahore on 29 March 1982) at an average of 47.62 – the highest by any Pakistan player to have completed 20 innings or more in one-day international cricket history.

Highest and lowest

Highest score: 385 for 7 against Bangladesh at Dambulla on 21 June 2010.

Lowest score: 43 all out against the West Indies at Cape Town on 25 February 1993.

Biggest victories

By runs: by 233 runs against Bangladesh at Dhaka on 2 June 2000.

By wickets: by ten wickets on four occasions.

By balls remaining (in the second innings): with 206 balls remaining against New Zealand at Sharjah on 1 May 1990.

Smallest victories

By runs: by one run against the West Indies at Sharjah on 21 October 1991.

By wickets: by one wicket on six occasions.

By balls remaining (in the second innings): off the last ball of the match on five occasions.

Waqar waltzes into record books

Along with Wasim Akram, **Waqar Younis** formed the most destructive new-ball bowling attack in one-day international cricket history. In 262 one-day matches for Pakistan between 1989 and 2003 he took 416 wickets and set his country's all-time records for the best bowling performance in an innings (7 for 36 against England at Headingley on 17 June 2001) and for the most four-wicket-plus innings hauls (27).

Most dismissals

He may have spent most of his career vying with Rashid Latif for the wicketkeeper's berth in the Pakistan line-up but, when he played, Moin Khan proved he was an admirable performer behind the stumps. In 219 one-day international matches for Pakistan between 1990 and 2004, the Rawalpindi keeper claimed 287 dismissals (214 catches and 73 stumpings) – a record for Pakistan in the 50-over format of the game.

Inzamam's inspirational 16-year ODI career

A colossus for his country in 378 one-day internationals between 1991 and 2007 – a record number of matches for a Pakistan player – Inzamam-ul-Haq leads his country's all-time list for the most runs scored (11,701 – putting him fourth on the all-time list – with a top score of 137 not out against New Zealand at Sharjah on 20 April 1994) and, surprisingly given his reputation for slovenliness in the field, is second for the most catches (113, behind Younis Khan with 116).

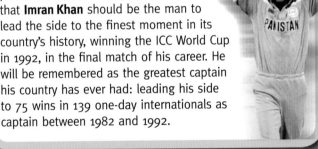

Most successful captain

As the finest cricketer Pakistan has ever produced, it seemed highly appropriate that **Imran Khan** should be the man to lead the side to the finest moment in its country's history, winning the ICC World Cup in 1992, in the final match of his career. He will be remembered as the greatest captain his country has ever had: leading his side to 75 wins in 139 one-day internationals as captain between 1982 and 1992.

MOST RUNS: TOP 5

Pos	Runs	Player	Mat	Inns	NO	HS	Ave	100	50	0
1	11,701	Inzamam-ul-Haq (1991–2007)	375	348	52	137*	39.53	10	83	20
2	9,554	Mohammad Yousuf (1998–2010)	281	267	40	141*	42.08	15	62	15
3	8,824	Saeed Anwar (1989–2003)	247	244	19	194	39.21	20	43	15
4	7,381	Javed Miandad (1975–96)	233	218	41	119*	41.70	8	50	8
5	7,170	Saleem Malik (1982–99)	283	256	38	102	32.88	5	47	19

MOST WICKETS: TOP 5

Pos	Wkts	Player	Mat	Balls	Runs	BBI	Ave	Econ	SR	4	5
1	502	**Wasim Akram** (1984–2003)	356	18,186	11,812	5/15	23.52	3.89	36.2	17	6
2	416	Waqar Younis (1989–2003)	262	12,698	9,919	7/36	23.84	4.68	30.5	14	13
3	342	Shahid Afridi (1996–2012)	342	14,881	11,422	6/38	33.39	4.60	43.5	4	8
4	288	Saqlain Mushtaq (1995–2003)	169	8,770	6,275	5/20	21.78	4.29	30.4	11	6
5	268	Abdul Razzaq (1996–2011)	261	10,851	8,452	6/35	31.53	4.67	40.4	8	3

SOUTH AFRICA

Ever since their return to the international cricket fold after 21 years in the wilderness – their first match back was an ODI against India at Kolkata on 10 November 1991 – South Africa have proved they are a considerable force in the 50-over game. They have the highest winning percentage of any of the current Test-playing nations with 64.73 percent.

Amla's electric arrival on the international scene

His international career is still in its relatively early stages but, after establishing himself in the South Africa team, Hashim Amla – the first player of Indian descent to play for the country – has shown himself to be a player of the highest quality. With his trademark wristy flicks and limitless concentration, he has compiled 2,881 runs in 57 one-day internationals at an average of 56.49 – the highest by any South African batsman to complete 20 innings or more in one-day internationals.

Best career strike-rate

Tipped from an early age to develop into a world-class all-rounder, Albie Morkel may not have lived up to such hype, but he has become a consistent and effective performer in the shorter formats of the game. In 56 one-day internationals for South Africa between 2004 and 2012 he has hit 790 runs from 750 balls faced at a strike-rate of 101.33 runs per 100 balls – the best by any South Africa batsman to have faced 500 balls or more in one-day international cricket.

RESULT SUMMARY

Opposition	Span	Mat	Won	Lost	Tied	NR	%
Australia	1992–2011	80	36	41	3	0	46.87
Bangladesh	2002–11	14	13	1	0	0	92.85
Canada	2003	1	1	0	0	0	100.00
England	1992–2011	45	23	19	1	2	54.65
India	1991–2011	66	40	24	0	2	62.50
Ireland	2007–11	3	3	0	0	0	100.00
Kenya	1996–2008	10	10	0	0	0	100.00
Netherlands	1996–2011	3	3	0	0	0	100.00
New Zealand	1992–2012	55	33	18	0	4	64.70
Pakistan	1992–2010	57	38	18	0	1	67.85
Scotland	2007	1	1	0	0	0	100.00
Sri Lanka	1992–2012	51	25	24	1	1	51.00
UAE	1996	1	1	0	0	0	100.00
West Indies	1992–2011	51	38	12	0	1	76.00
Zimbabwe	1992–2010	32	29	2	0	1	93.54

Highest partnership

Gary Kirsten (115) and Herschelle Gibbs (111) combined to great effect for South Africa against India at Kochi on 9 March 2000, putting on 235 runs for the first wicket – a South African record partnership in one-day international cricket – but their efforts were not enough to win their side the game. India chased down the 302-run victory target with two balls and three wickets to spare.

Kirsten runs riot at Rawalpindi

The opposition may not have been the strongest, but **Gary Kirsten** made a mockery of pre-match predictions that the wicket for South Africa's 1996 ICC World Cup Group B encounter against the United Arab Emirates at Rawalpindi would be a bowler-friendly surface. The left-handed opener batted through the innings to compile a 159-ball unbeaten 188 – the highest score in the tournament's history and the highest-ever score by a South Africa batsman in one-day international cricket.

Glorious Gibbs heads centuries list

One of the most electric stroke players in the modern game – at times it appears no shot is beyond him – **Herschelle Gibbs** has hit more one-day international centuries than any other South African player in history (21). The highlight of his glittering career came when he smashed a 111-ball 175 against Australia at Johannesburg on 12 March 2006 to help his side chase down a seemingly unattainable 435-run victory target.

Deadly Donald delivers the goods

Allan Donald got his international career off to a blistering and eye-catching start – taking 5 for 29 in South Africa's first match back in the international fold, against India at Kolkata on 10 November 1991 – and went on to cement a reputation as the finest bowler his country has ever produced. In 164 one-day internationals between 1991 and 2003 he took 272 wickets – with best figures of 6 for 23 against Kenya at Nairobi on 3 October 1996 – at an average of 21.78, the best by any South African to have bowled 2,000 balls or more in one-day international cricket.

Magic Makhaya sends Australia packing

A devastating spell of bowling from Makhaya Ntini helped South Africa to their biggest-ever victory over Australia at Cape Town on 3 March 2006. Making the most of the seamer-friendly conditions under the Newlands lights, the Mdingi-born paceman took 6 for 22 – the best bowling figures by a South African in one-day international cricket history – to reduce Australia to 93 all out and set up South Africa's crushing 196-run win.

Pollock: South Africa's precision record-breaker

A bowler who relied on metronomic accuracy rather than express pace, **Shaun Pollock** (South Africa's most capped one-day international player of all time, with 294 appearances between 1996 and 2008) has taken more four-wicket-plus hauls for his country (17) and more wickets (387) than any other player in history. His best performance came when he took 6 for 35 against the West Indies at East London on 24 January 1999.

Highest and lowest

Highest score: 438 for 9 against Australia at Johannesburg on 12 March 2006.

Lowest score: 69 all out against Australia at Sydney on 14 December 1993.

Biggest victories

By runs: by 272 runs against Zimbabwe at Benoni on 22 October 2010.

By wickets: by ten wickets on six occasions.

By balls remaining (in the second innings): with 228 balls remaining against Bangladesh at Bloemfontein on 22 February 2003.

Smallest victories

By runs: by one run on three occasions.

By wickets: by one wicket on three occasions.

By balls remaining (in the second innings): off the last ball of the match on six occasions.

Most successful captain

History will remember him as the man at the centre of the most damaging scandal in the game's history – he was banned for life after admitting to his role in several match-fixing episodes – but no one led South Africa with greater success in one-day international cricket than Hansie Cronje. The Free State batsman led his side to 99 wins in 138 matches as captain between 1994 and 2000.

MOST RUNS: TOP 5

Pos	Runs	Player	Mat	Inns	NO	HS	Ave	100	50	0
1	11,469	J.H. Kallis (1996–2012)	316	302	53	139	46.06	17	85	16
2	8,094	H.H. Gibbs (1996–2010)	248	240	16	175	36.13	21	37	22
3	6,798	G. Kirsten (1993–2003)	185	185	19	188*	40.95	13	45	11
4	6,598	G.C. Smith (2002–12)	180	178	10	141	39.27	9	45	7
5	5,935	J.N. Rhodes (1992–2003)	245	220	51	121	35.11	2	33	12

MOST WICKETS: TOP 5

Pos	Wkts	Player	Mat	Overs	Runs	BBI	Ave	Econ	SR	4	5
1	387	S.M. Pollock (1996–2008)	294	2,571.4	9,409	6/35	24.31	3.65	39.8	12	5
2	272	A.A. Donald (1991–2003)	164	1,426.5	5,926	6/23	21.78	4.15	31.4	11	2
3	265	M. Ntini (1998–2009)	172	1,440.5	6,501	6/22	24.53	4.51	32.6	8	4
4	266	J.H. Kallis (1996–2012)	316	1,754.0	8,446	5/30	31.75	4.81	39.5	2	2
5	192	L. Klusener (1996–2004)	171	1,222.4	5,751	6/49	29.95	4.70	38.2	1	6

SRI LANKA

Following their elevation to Test status in 1982, for many years Sri Lanka were considered to be the minnows of world cricket, but they used the one-day international arena to propel themselves into the world's elite. In 1996, spectacularly, they shocked Australia in the final to capture the ICC World Cup and have been treated with the greatest respect ever since.

RESULT SUMMARY

Opposition	Span	Mat	Won	Lost	Tied	NR	%
Australia	1975–2012	84	28	53	0	3	34.56
Bangladesh	1986–2012	30	27	3	0	0	90.00
Bermuda	2007	1	1	0	0	0	100.00
Canada	2003–11	2	2	0	0	0	100.00
England	1982–2011	50	24	26	0	0	48.00
India	1979–2012	134	51	71	1	11	41.86
Ireland	2007	1	1	0	0	0	100.00
Kenya	1996–2011	6	5	1	0	0	83.33
Netherlands	2002–06	3	3	0	0	0	100.00
New Zealand	1979–2011	74	34	35	1	4	49.28
Pakistan	1975–2012	127	47	76	1	3	38.30
Scotland	2011	1	1	0	0	0	100.00
South Africa	1992–2012	51	24	25	1	1	49.00
UAE	2004–08	2	2	0	0	0	100.00
West Indies	1975–2011	49	20	26	0	3	43.47
Zimbabwe	1992–2011	47	39	7	0	1	84.78

Jayawardene's all-round contributions

Not only a prolific performer with the bat (he has scored 10,327 runs in 368 ODIs for Sri Lanka between 1998 and 2012), **Mahela Jayawardene** has also made a huge contribution in the field for Sri Lanka over the years. He holds the national record for the most catches in the 50-over game with 184.

Spectacular for more than 20 years

Behind Sachin Tendulkar the second-most capped ODI player of all time (appearing in a staggering 441 matches between 1989 and 2011), **Sanath Jayasuriya** started the trend of modern pinch-hitters at the top of the batting order and did much to help Sri Lanka towards the most glorious moment of their cricket history – winning the ICC World Cup in 1996. Over a decade and a half later he is still one of the most destructive hitters in the modern game, and has set numerous all-time records for his country: he has scored the most runs (13,364), holds the record for the highest score (189 against India at Sharjah on 29 October 2000), has hit the most centuries (28) and has the best strike-rate (91.27 runs per 100 balls).

Highest partnership

A spectacular performance by Upal Tharanga (109) and Sanath Jayasuriya (152) at the top of the order at Headingley on 1 July 2006 laid the foundations for Sri Lanka overhauling England's mighty total of 321 with a staggering 75 balls to spare. The pair put on 286 runs for the opening wicket – the highest partnership for any wicket for Sri Lanka in one-day international history.

Slick Sangakkara heads dismissals list

A highly influential performer for his country from the moment he made his debut against Pakistan at Galle in July 2000, **Kumar Sangakkara** is one of the best wicketkeeper-batsmen in world cricket. In 318 matches for Sri Lanka he has scored 10,213 runs (with a highest score of 138 not out against India at Jaipur on 31 October 2005) at an average of 38.10 – a Sri Lanka record – and also holds the national ODI wicketkeeping record of 367 dismissals behind the stumps (with 290 catches and 77 stumpings).

Highest and lowest

Highest score: 443 for 9 against the Netherlands at Amstelveen on 4 July 2006.

Lowest score: 43 all out against South Africa at Paark on 11 January 2012.

Biggest victories

By runs: by 245 runs against India at Sharjah on 29 October 2000.

By wickets: by ten wickets on five occasions.

By balls remaining (in the second innings): with 274 balls remaining against Zimbabwe at Colombo on 8 December 2001.

Smallest victories

By runs: by one run against Australia at Dambulla on 22 February 2004.

By wickets: by one wicket on two occasions; against England at Adelaide on 23 January 1999; and against Australia at Melbourne on 3 November 2010.

By balls remaining (in the second innings): with one ball remaining on three occasions.

Vaas tears into Zimbabwe

Chaminda Vaas ripped through Zimbabwe's batting line-up at Colombo on 8 December 2001 and stormed into the record books as the first bowler in one-day international cricket history to take eight wickets in an innings. The left-arm pace bowler finished with figures of 8 for 19 as Zimbabwe slumped to a miserable 38 all out.

Murali silenced detractors in record-breaking fashion

The first and only Tamil of Indian origin to play for Sri Lanka, **Muttiah Muralitharan** brushed aside the repeated controversies regarding his action that have remained throughout his career (the ICC has investigated the mechanics of his action twice) – by taking wicket after wicket. An integral part of Sri Lanka's 1996 ICC World Cup-winning outfit, the history-making spin bowler set numerous all-time records for his country. In 343 matches between 1993 and 2011 he took the most wickets (523) and had the most four-wicket-plus innings hauls (25, with a best return of 7 for 30 against India at Sharjah on 27 October 2000).

Four in a row for lethal Malinga

Lasith Malinga secured his reputation as one of the deadliest death bowlers in the business at Sri Lanka's Super Eight Match against South Africa in Guyana at the 2007 ICC World Cup. With two balls left in the 45th over, South Africa, needing 210 for victory, were cruising to the target on 206 for 5: Malinga dismissed Shaun Pollock (bowled) and Andrew Hall (caught) ... 206 for 7. He started his following over (the 47th) by dismissing Jacques Kallis (caught) to complete his hat-trick and then bowled Makhaya Ntini to make it four wickets in four balls – the only time this has happened in ODI history ... South Africa were 206 for 9. Unfortunately for Malinga and Sri Lanka, South Africa limped to the target to win by one wicket.

Ranatunga leads from the front

An innovative, forceful captain who led Sri Lanka to the greatest triumph in their history with victory in the 1996 ICC World Cup, Arjuna Ranatunga is the most successful leader in one-day international matches for Sri Lanka, having collected 89 wins in 193 matches as captain between 1988 and 1999.

MOST RUNS: TOP 5

Pos	Runs	Player	Mat	Inns	NO	HS	Ave	100	50	0
1	13,364	S.T. Jayasuriya (1989–2009)	441	429	18	189	32.51	28	68	34
2	10,327	D.P.M.D. Jayawardene (1998–2012)	368	346	34	144	33.09	14	64	25
3	10,213	K.C. Sangakkara (2000–12)	318	299	31	138*	38.10	13	68	10
4	9,284	P.A. de Silva (1984–2003)	308	296	30	145	34.90	11	64	17
5	8,529	M.S. Atapattu (1990–2007)	268	259	32	132*	37.57	11	59	13

MOST WICKETS: TOP 5

Pos	Wkts	Player	Mat	Overs	Runs	BBI	Ave	Econ	SR	4	5
1	523	M. Muralitharan (1993–2011)	343	3,072.1	12,066	7/30	23.07	3.92	35.2	15	10
2	399	W.P.U.J.C. Vaas (1994–2008)	321	2,620.1	10,955	8/19	27.45	4.18	39.4	9	4
3	319	S.T. Jayasuriya (1989–2009)	440	2,452.0	11,691	6/29	36.64	4.76	46.1	8	4
4	185	L.S. Malinga (2004–12)	117	960.4	4,876	6/38	26.35	5.07	31.1	6	5
5	183	C.R.D. Fernando (2001–12)	146	1,074.3	5,612	6/27	30.66	5.22	35.2	2	1

WEST INDIES

They were the kings of Test and one-day cricket in the 1970s and early '80s, years which saw them rule the roost in the five-day game and appear in three successive ICC World Cup finals (winning two of them). Since then the cricket gods have been less kind to the West Indies in the Test arena, but the men from the Caribbean have more than held their own in one-day cricket.

King of the big hitters

Kieron Pollard has quickly earned a reputation as one of the hardest hitters in world cricket. He caught the eye with 126 off only 71 balls in his first first-class innings, for Trinidad and Tobago against Barbados in January 2007, and made his one-day international debut for the West Indies (against South Africa) three months later. Pollard has gone on to score 1,288 runs (with a best of 119 off 110 balls against India in Chennai on 11 December 2011) in 56 matches at a strike-rate of 101.57 runs per 100 balls faced – the highest by any West Indies player to have scored 1,000 runs or more in one-day internationals.

The meanest sight in modern cricket

An ability to propel the ball with searing pace from a 6ft 7in frame made Curtly Ambrose the most feared sight for batsmen for over a decade. He was a magnificent performer both in Test matches (where he took 405 wickets in 98 matches) and in one-day internationals, with 225 wickets in 176 matches between 1988 and 2000, including ten four-wicket-plus hauls – a West Indies record – and a best return of 5 for 17 against Australia at Melbourne on 15 December 1988.

Gayle forces his way into the record books

When **Chris Gayle** is on his A game, there are few finer sights in world cricket. A bully at the crease in the Viv Richards mould, he has the ability to destroy the opposition's attack, off both the front foot and the back. In 225 one-day internationals for the West Indies between 1999 and 2011 he has scored 8,032 runs (at an average of 39.37) including a West Indies joint-record 19 centuries (with a highest score of 153 not out, against Zimbabwe at Bulawayo on 22 November 2003).

RESULT SUMMARY

Opposition	Span	Mat	Won	Lost	Tied	NR	%
Australia	1975–2012	130	59	65	3	3	47.63
Bangladesh	1999–2011	20	14	4	0	2	77.77
Bermuda	2008	1	1	0	0	0	100.00
Canada	2003–10	4	4	0	0	0	100.00
England	1973–2011	83	41	38	0	4	51.89
India	1979–2011	106	57	46	1	2	55.28
Ireland	2007–11	4	3	0	0	1	100.00
Kenya	1996–2003	6	5	1	0	0	83.33
Netherlands	2007–11	2	2	0	0	0	100.00
New Zealand	1975–2009	51	24	20	0	7	54.54
Pakistan	1975–2011	120	66	52	2	0	55.83
Scotland	1999–2007	2	2	0	0	0	100.00
South Africa	1992–2011	51	12	38	0	1	24.00
Sri Lanka	1975–2011	49	26	20	0	3	56.52
Zimbabwe	1983–2010	41	31	9	0	1	77.50

Davis demolishes Australia

Winston Davis produced a devastating spell of fast bowling on an unpredictable Headingley pitch to catapult the West Indies to a 101-run victory over Australia in the two sides' 1983 ICC World Cup Group B encounter. The St Vincent-born paceman took 7 for 51 – the best bowling figures by a West Indies player in one-day international cricket.

Born to play one-day cricket

Viv Richards was perhaps the most destructive batsman ever to play one-day international cricket. Displaying an ability to bully bowling attacks from the moment he made his debut against Sri Lanka at Old Trafford in June 1975, he became the fastest player in history to reach 1,000 one-day international runs (in 21 matches, a record since equalled by England's Kevin Pietersen) and went on to set numerous West Indian all-time records in the one-day game: he recorded the highest score (189 not out against England at Old Trafford on 31 May 1984); holds the record for the best average (47.00); and, despite never lifting the ICC World Cup (unlike Clive Lloyd, who lifted it twice), was the most successful West Indian captain in one-day history, leading his side to 67 wins in 125 matches as captain between 1980 and 1991).

MOST RUNS: TOP 5

Pos	Runs	Player	Mat	Inns	NO	HS	Ave	100	50	0
1	10,348	B.C. Lara (1990–2007)	295	285	32	169	40.90	19	62	14
2	8,778	S. Chanderpaul (1994–2011)	268	251	40	150	41.60	11	59	6
3	8,648	D.L. Haynes (1978–94)	238	237	28	152*	41.37	17	57	13
4	8,032	C.H. Gayle (1999–2011)	225	220	16	153*	39.37	19	42	20
5	6,721	I.V.A. Richards (1975–91)	187	167	24	189*	47.00	11	45	7

MOST WICKETS: TOP 5

Pos	Wkts	Player	Mat	Balls	Runs	BBI	Ave	Econ	SR	4	5
1	227	C.A. Walsh (1985–2000)	205	10,822	6,918	5/1	30.47	3.83	47.6	6	1
2	225	C.E.L. Ambrose (1988–2000)	176	9,353	5,429	5/17	24.12	3.48	41.5	6	4
3	193	C.L. Hooper (1987–2003)	227	9,573	6,958	4/34	36.05	4.36	49.6	3	0
4	157	M.D. Marshall (1980–92)	136	7,175	4,233	4/18	26.96	3.53	45.7	6	0
5	156	C.H. Gayle (1999–2011)	225	6,889	5,415	5/46	34.71	4.71	44.1	3	1

Most dismissals

Jeff Dujon is the most successful wicketkeeper in one-day international cricket. The Jamaican gloveman snared 204 victims (183 catches and 21 stumpings) in 169 matches between 1981 and 1991.

Most catches

No West Indian player has taken more catches in one-day international cricket than Carl Hooper. The Guyana-born batsman was no slouch in the field, taking 120 catches in 227 matches between 1987 and 2003.

Big Bird swoops into record books

A shoo-in for any all-time one-day international XI, Joel Garner has the best bowling average in the shortened format of the game of any player to have bowled 2,000 balls or more in one-day international cricket. The giant, 6ft 8in fast bowler, nicknamed "Big Bird", took 146 wickets in 98 matches between 1977 and 1987 at an average of 18.84.

Chanderpaul and Hooper's rescue act

Shavnarine Chanderpaul (150) and Carl Hooper (108) produced a remarkable two-man show to drag the West Indies to a 43-run victory over South Africa at East London on 24 January 1999. The only two batsmen in their team to reach double figures, the pair added 226 runs for the fourth wicket – the best partnership by a West Indian pair in one-day international cricket – to haul their side to 292 for 9. South Africa were 249 all out in reply.

Highest and lowest

Highest score: 360 for 4 against Sri Lanka at Karachi on 13 October 1987.

Lowest score: 54 all out against South Africa at Cape Town on 25 January 2004.

Biggest victories

By runs: by 215 runs against Netherlands at Delhi on 28 February 2011.

By wickets: by ten wickets on ten occasions.

By balls remaining (in the second innings): with 239 balls remaining against Scotland at Leicester on 27 May 1999.

Smallest victories

By runs: by one run on three occasions.

By wickets: by one wicket on nine occasions.

By balls remaining (in the second innings): off the last ball of the match on six occasions.

Most matches

Brian Lara has played in more one-day internationals than any other West Indies player. The West Indies' all-time leading run-scorer (he scored 10,348 runs at an average of 40.90) played in 295 one-day internationals between 1990 and 2007.

BANGLADESH

Considered the best of the rest following their victory in the ICC Trophy in Malaysia in 1997, Bangladesh were granted Test status in 2000 and soon found life with cricket's big boys a harsher proposition in all formats of the game. Having won just 67 of 244 one-day internationals, Bangladesh have the worst record of any of the current Test-playing nations.

OVERALL ONE-DAY INTERNATIONAL RECORD

Opposition	Span	Mat	Won	Lost	Tied	NR	%
All opponents	1986–2012	262	72	188	0	2	27.69

Highest and lowest

Highest score: 320 for 8 against Zimbabwe at Bulawayo on 11 August 2009.

Lowest score: 58 all out against West Indies at Dhaka on 4 March 2011.

Biggest victories

By runs: by 146 runs against Scotland at Dhaka on 17 December 2006.

By wickets: by nine wickets on two occasions: against Kenya at Khulna on 20 March 2006; and against Zimbabwe at Khulna on 30 November 2006.

By balls remaining (in the second innings): with 229 balls remaining against Zimbabwe at Chittagong on 3 November 2009.

Smallest victories

By runs: by three runs against New Zealand at Dhaka on 17 October 2010.

By wickets: by one wicket on two occasions: against Zimbabwe at Harare on 10 February 2007; and against Zimbabwe at Chittagong on 5 November 2009.

By balls remaining (in the second innings): with four balls remaining on two occasions: against Australia at Cardiff on 18 June 2005; and against India at Dhaka on 16 March 2012.

Tamim Iqbal secures unlikely victory

Having watched Charles Coventry compile a world record 194 not out to lead Zimbabwe to a massive total of 312 for 8 in the fourth one-day international at Bulawayo on 16 August 2009, Bangladesh could easily have slid to a despondent defeat. To their great credit, however, they chased down the total with relish. **Tamim Iqbal's** 154 off 138 balls – the highest-ever score by a Bangladesh player in a one-day international – was the foundation as Bangladesh reached the victory target with four wickets and 3.1 overs to spare.

A bright light for Bangladesh

One of Bangladesh's most impressive performers in all formats of the game in recent times, Shakib Al Hasan made his one-day international debut against Zimbabwe aged 19 in August 2006 and scored an unbeaten 30 to guide his side to a comfortable eight-wicket victory. It was a sign of things to come: in 108 one-day internationals to date, the classy left-hander has scored 3,939 runs at an average of 28.75 with five centuries, a record for a Bangladesh player in one-day international cricket.

Razzak defies doubters to set the pace

A left-arm spinner who has often fallen foul of referees for a suspect action – ICC tests subsequently found his bowling arm was bent up to 28 degrees (13 more than the permissible amount), **Abdur Razzak** has endured a stop-start international career. When he has played, however, he has been effective, taking 169 wickets in 117 matches – a record haul for a Bangladesh player in the 50-over format of the game.

Magic Mortaza too good for Kenya

Mashrafe Mortaza was the chief architect of Bangladesh's six-wicket victory over Kenya at the Gymkhana Club Ground in Nairobi on 15 August 2006 – Bangladesh's 20th victory in one-day international cricket. The medium-fast bowler ripped the heart out of the home side's batting line-up, taking 6 for 26 – the best figures by a Bangladesh bowler in one-day international history – to reduce Kenya to 118 all out. Bangladesh reached the victory target for the loss of four wickets with 138 balls to spare.

Highest partnership

Rajin Saleh (108 not out) and captain Habibul Bashar (64 not out) combined to great effect against Kenya at Fatullah on 25 March 2006, putting on an unbroken stand of 175 for the fourth wicket – a national record in ODI cricket – to secure a seven-wicket victory.

IRELAND

Granted one-day international status in 2005, Ireland have gone on to earn a reputation as the giant-killers of world cricket. At the 2007 ICC World Cup they produced some headline-grabbing results – a tie with Zimbabwe and a sensational three-wicket victory over Pakistan – to reach the Super Eights. And they did it again at the 2011 ICC World Cup when they beat England.

OVERALL ONE-DAY INTERNATIONAL RECORD

Opposition	Span	Mat	Won	Lost	Tied	NR	%
All opponents	2006–12	72	33	35	1	3	48.55

Most four-wicket-plus hauls

The Ireland record for the most four-wicket-plus hauls in one-day international cricket is two, a feat achieved by four players: Trent Johnston (in 59 matches between 2006 and 2012); Andre Botha (42 matches, 2006–11); Kyle McCallan (39 matches, 2006–09); and John Mooney (43 matches, 2006–12).

Mr Consistency

Paul Stirling has been Ireland's most consistent run-scorer in one-day international cricket. In 36 matches between 2008 and 2012 he has scored 1,418 runs (with a highest of 177 – Ireland's ODI best – against Canada at Toronto on 7 September 2010) with two centuries – his average (40.51) is an all-time record for Ireland in the 50-over format.

Highest and lowest

Highest score: 329 for 7 against England at Bangalore on 2 March 2011.

Lowest score: 77 all out against Sri Lanka at St George's, Grenada, on 18 April 2007.

Biggest victories

By runs: by 133 runs against Canada at Dublin on 19 September 2011.

By wickets: by nine wickets on two occasions.

By balls remaining (in the second innings): with 177 balls remaining against the Netherlands at Dublin on 18 August 2010.

Smallest victories

By runs: by one run against the Netherlands at Belfast on 11 July 2007.

By wickets: by three wickets on three occasions.

By balls remaining (in the second innings): with five balls remaining against England at Bangalore on 2 March 2011.

Records fall in losing cause

Kevin O'Brien, with 142 – the second-highest individual score by an Ireland player in a one-day international – and William Porterfield, with 104 not out, produced the best partnership in Ireland's history (227) to haul their side to a challenging 284 for 4 against Kenya in the two sides' ICC World Cricket League encounter at Nairobi on 2 February 2007. But their record-breaking performances were not enough to win Ireland the game; Kenya just reached their target with one wicket and six balls in hand.

O'Brien guns down England

Ireland's match against England at the 2011 ICC World Cup seemed to be heading to the pre-game script: England had posted 327 for 8 and Ireland, in reply, were floundering on 111 for 5 in the 25th over and heading for defeat. But Kevin O'Brien had other ideas: he smashed a 63-ball 113 – reaching his century off a mere 50 balls (the fastest in ODI history) – to help Ireland to a three-wicket victory.

Age no barrier for Johnston

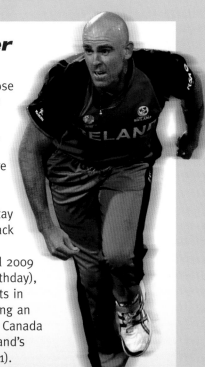

An Australian by birth, whose career developed at New South Wales alongside the likes of Brett Lee, Mark Taylor and Michael Slater before he switched his allegiance to Ireland, **Trent Johnston** has been a mainstay of his country's bowling attack in ODI cricket despite his advancing years. On 19 April 2009 (10 days before his 35th birthday), he enjoyed his best moments in the international arena, taking an Irish record 5 for 14 against Canada at Centurion. He is also Ireland's leading wicket-taker (with 61).

KENYA

Kenya caused one of the greatest shocks in ODI cricket history when they reached the semi-finals of the 2003 ICC World Cup, but that performance remains the exception in the Africans' encounters at the top table of international cricket. They remain very much among the second tier of world cricket.

OVERALL ONE-DAY INTERNATIONAL RECORD

Opposition	Span	Mat	Won	Lost	Tied	NR	%
All opponents	1996–2012	146	39	102	0	5	27.65

Highest and lowest

Highest score: 347 for 3 against Bangladesh at Nairobi on 10 October 1997.

Lowest score: 69 all out against New Zealand at Chennai on 20 February 2011.

Biggest victories

By runs: by 190 runs against Scotland at Mombasa on 17 January 2007.

By wickets: by ten wickets against Bermuda at Nairobi on 29 January 2007.

By balls remaining (in the second innings): with 191 balls remaining against Bermuda on 29 January 2007.

Smallest victories

By runs: by six runs against Scotland at Mombasa on 21 January 2007.

By wickets: by one wicket on two occasions: against Ireland at Nairobi on 2 February 2007; and against Bermuda at Nairobi on 28 October 2007.

By balls remaining (in the second innings): with six balls remaining against Ireland at Nairobi on 2 February 2007.

Kenya's finest

Steve Tikolo is regarded as the finest player in history to emerge from the non-Test-playing nations. He holds numerous all-time records for Kenya in one-day international cricket: he has played in the most matches (130 between 1996 and 2011); he has scored the most runs (3,362 at the respectable average of 29.49); and he has recorded the most centuries (three – with a highest score of 111 against Bermuda at Mombasa on 14 November 2006).

All-round asset

Thomas Odoyo's wholehearted all-round performances have made him a key member of Kenya's side from the moment he made his debut as a 17-year-old at the 1996 ICC World Cup. The first non-Test player to achieve the 1,500-run, 100-wicket double in one-day international cricket, he has scored 2,364 runs with the bat (with a highest score of 111 not out against Canada at Nairobi on 18 October 2007) in 129 matches, but it is his performances with the ball that are more noteworthy: he holds his country's all-time records for the most wickets (137) and for the most four-wicket-plus hauls (five – with a best of 4 for 25 against Bermuda at Mombasa on 12 November 2006).

Obuya heroics with the ball cause a stir

It was one of the finest days in Kenya's cricket history, and a sensational spell of bowling from Collins Obuya lay at the heart of it. The leg-spin bowler took 5 for 24 – the best-ever figures by a Kenyan bowler in a one-day international – to help his side to a headline-grabbing 53-run victory over Sri Lanka in the two countries' Pool B encounter at Nairobi in the 2003 ICC World Cup.

Kenya shock Bangladesh with record-breaking display

Dipak Chudasama (122) and Kennedy Otieno (144 – the highest-ever score by a Kenyan batsman in one-day cricket) recorded not only the highest partnership in their country's history but also the highest opening partnership in all 1,239 one-day internationals (their 225 surpassed Australian pair Geoff Marsh and David Boon's 212 in Jaipur in 1986–87) as Kenya cantered to a comfortable 150-run win over Bangladesh at Nairobi on 1 March 1997 – this was the first match for both countries after being granted one-day international status.

NETHERLANDS

Winners of the ICC Trophy in 2001, the Netherlands have never been able to make the transition from second-tier standouts to minor members of world cricket's elite. Regular qualifiers for the ICC World Cup (they appeared in 1996, 2003, 2007 and 2011), they have not yet won a one-day international match against a Test-playing nation in 15 attempts.

OVERALL ONE-DAY INTERNATIONAL RECORD

Opposition	Span	Mat	Won	Lost	Tied	NR	%
All opponents	1996–2012	69	26	41	0	2	38.80

A serious talent

The Netherlands' big-name player – and fast developing a reputation as being the best player outside the Test game – South African-born, but of Dutch descent, **Ryan ten Doeschate** has produced some outstanding performances for his country with both bat and ball since making his debut in July 2006. In 33 one-day internationals he has set Netherlands records for the most runs scored (1,541, at a hefty average of 67.00), for the most centuries (five, with a highest score of 119 against England at Nagpur on 22 February 2011), and also for the most wickets (55, at an average of 24.12).

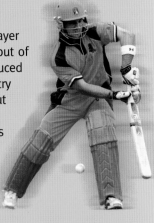

Breaking the World Cup duck

Revelling in the chance to play against opponents of whom they had the measure on the one-day game's greatest stage, Feiko Kloppenburg (121) and Klaas-Jan von Noortwijk (134 not out – the highest individual score by a Netherlands player in one-day international cricket) produced a performance of the highest class to propel their side to a first-ever victory in the ICC World Cup. The pair put on a record 228 for the second wicket to lead the Netherlands' charge to 314 for 4 against Namibia at Bloemfontein on 3 March 2003; they then bowled out Namibia for 250 to win the match by 64 runs.

Most successful captain

A steady performer behind the stumps, and an inspirational figure in the Netherlands squad, **Jeroen Smits** is the most successful Netherlands captain in one-day international cricket, leading his side to 11 wins in 17 matches as captain between 2007 and 2009.

Schiferli's strikes secure victory

Edgar Schiferli ripped through the heart of Kenya's batting line-up with a great spell of bowling to lay the foundations for the Netherlands' six-wicket victory over Kenya in the two sides' third-place play-off match at the 2009 ICC World Cup qualifying tournament, played at Potchefstroom on 19 April 2009. The medium-pacer took 4 for 23 – the best bowling performance by a Netherlands player in a one-day international.

Most matches

Bas Zuiderent first came to prominence when he hit 54 against England as an 18-year-old at the 1996 ICC World Cup and holds the unusual distinction of having played in every one of his country's World Cup matches. He is the most capped Netherlands player of all time in one-day international cricket, having made 57 appearances between 1996 and 2011.

Highest and lowest

Highest score: 315 for 8 against Bermuda at Rotterdam on 18 August 2007.

Lowest score: 80 all out against the West Indies at Dublin on 10 July 2007.

Biggest victories

By runs: by 172 runs against Bermuda at Rotterdam on 18 August 2007.

By wickets: by nine wickets against Afghanistan at Sharjah on 29 March 2012.

By balls remaining (in the second innings): with 183 balls remaining against Bermuda at Rotterdam on 18 August 2007.

Smallest victories

By runs: by six runs against Ireland at Nairobi on 5 February 2007.

By wickets: by one wicket against Canada at Benoni on 1 December 2006.

By balls remaining (in the second innings): with two balls remaining against Canada at Benoni on 1 December 2006.

SCOTLAND

Scotland have been a standout team in world cricket's second tier in recent years, but have failed to find the ingredients required to move to the next level. ICC Trophy winners for the first time in 2005, they have qualified for two of the last three ICC World Cups, but have still to record their first victory in the tournament and have never beaten a Test-status side in a one-day international.

OVERALL ONE-DAY INTERNATIONAL RECORD

Opposition	Span	Mat	Won	Lost	Tied	NR	%
All opponents	1999–2011	54	18	33	0	3	35.29

Highest and lowest

Highest score: 323 for 5 against Ireland at Edinburgh on 12 July 2011.

Lowest score: 68 all out against the West Indies at Leicester on 27 May 1999.

Biggest victories

By runs: by 77 runs against Kenya at Nairobi on 4 February 2007.

By wickets: by six wickets on two occasions: against the Netherlands at Dublin on 29 July 2008; and against Afghanistan at Ayr on 17 August 2010.

By balls remaining (in the second innings): with 166 balls remaining against the Netherlands at Dublin on 29 July 2008.

Smallest victories

By runs: by two runs against the Netherlands at Nairobi on 2 February 2007.

By wickets: by one wicket against the Netherlands at Amstelveen oin 1 July 2010.

By balls remaining (in the second innings): off the last ball of the match against Ireland at Nairobi on 30 January 2007.

Most centuries

The Scotland record for the most career centuries in one-day internationals is two, a feat achieved by two players: **Neil McCallum** (in 41 matches between 2006 and 2010, with a highest score of 121 not out against Ireland at Benoni on 1 April 2009); and Gavin Hamilton (in 38 matches between 1999 and 2011, with a highest score of 119 against Canada at Aberdeen on 7 July 2009).

Career change leads to national success

John Blain, who, in his youth, switched from life as a footballer with Falkirk FC to that of a professional cricketer, has been a key member of the Scotland bowling attack for over a decade. After playing in 33 matches between 1999 and 2009, he holds the Scotland records in one-day international cricket for: most wickets (41); and most four-wicket-plus innings hauls (two – a record he shares with Majid Haq).

Second time lucky

Gavin Hamilton put the disappointment of a solitary, non-run-scoring, non-wicket-taking Test appearance for England (against South Africa at Johannesburg in November 1999) behind him to forge a long and successful career with Scotland. The West Lothian-born all-rounder has appeared in 38 ODIs for his country since 1999 and has scored a Scottish record 1,231 runs.

One-man show from Watson secures victory

Ryan Watson produced a measured innings of considerable quality to single-handedly haul Scotland to a two-wicket victory over Canada at Mombasa on 18 January 2007. The Scotland No. 3 crafted an unbeaten 123 off 120 balls – the highest-ever score by a Scotland player in a one-day international – and guided his side to the 293-run victory target with one ball to spare.

Record tumbles in a losing cause

Gavin Hamilton (119) and Fraser Watts (101) put on a record-breaking display against Canada at Aberdeen on 7 July 2009, but Scotland's day still ended in disappointment. The pair added 203 for the opening wicket – a record partnership for Scotland in one-day internationals – to lead their side to a seemingly formidable 286 for 4; Canada, however, reached the target with six wickets in hand and eight balls to spare.

ZIMBABWE

Zimbabwe was a cricket nation on the up. They appeared in nine successive ICC World Cups between 1983 and 2007, causing several upsets along the way, and by the turn of the 21st century could call upon a core of players of real international class. But as the country crumbled politically, so did its cricket team and, once again, Zimbabwe stands among the second tier of world cricket.

OVERALL ONE-DAY INTERNATIONAL RECORD

Opposition	Span	Mat	Won	Lost	Tied	NR	%
All opponents	1983–2012	407	107	286	5	9	27.51

Leader of the bowling pack

The finest fast bowler Zimbabwe has produced, lion-hearted Heath Streak shone in both Test cricket (the first and only Zimbabwe bowler to take 100 Test wickets, he ended up with 216 scalps in a 65-Test career) and in one-day international cricket (in 187 matches between 1993 and 2005 he took 237 wickets, with a Zimbabwe record eight four-wicket-plus hauls and a best bowling performance of 5 for 32 against India at Bulawayo on 15 February 1997).

Olonga outclasses England

Henry Olonga produced the best bowling figures by a Zimbabwe bowler in a one-day international at Cape Town on 28 January 2000 – and the best by any bowler on African soil – to send England crashing to their sixth defeat in eight meetings against Zimbabwe. The paceman took 6 for 19 to send England (chasing 212) tumbling to 107 all out and a 104-run defeat.

Heroics by Coventry but defeat for Zimbabwe

It says much for the current state of Zimbabwe cricket that a match in which one of their players produced a world record-equalling performance in ODI cricket could end in defeat. **Charles Coventry** smashed an unbeaten 194 against Bangladesh at Bulawayo on 16 August 2009 – equalling Saeed Anwar's record in 50-over matches (but since broken by Sachin Tendulkar) – to lead Zimbabwe to 312 for 8; yet Bangladesh eased to the target with four wickets in hand and 2.1 overs to spare.

Highest and lowest

Highest score: 351 for 7 against Kenya at Mombasa on 29 January 2009.

Lowest score: 35 all out against Sri Lanka at Harare on 25 April 2004.

Biggest victories

By runs: by 202 runs against Kenya at Dhaka on 27 March 1999.

By wickets: by nine wickets against Kenya at Bulawayo on 15 December 2002.

By balls remaining (in the second innings): with 204 balls remaining against Kenya at Bulawayo on 15 December 2002.

Smallest victories

By runs: by one run against New Zealand at Christchurch on 4 March 1998.

By wickets: by one wicket on four occasions.

By balls remaining (in the second innings): off the last ball of the match on three occasions.

Most matches

A top-order batsman capable of churning out big scores and a slow left-arm bowler with wicket-taking capabilities, Grant Flower has played in more one-day internationals for Zimbabwe than any other player: 221 between 1992 and 2011.

Highest partnership

While those around them crumbled, Stuart Carlisle and Sean Ervine produced a determined performance to take Zimbabwe to within a whisker of pulling off a memorable victory over India at Adelaide on 24 January 2004. Chasing 281 for victory, the pair came together at 46 for 3 and added 202 runs in 34.2 overs – a record for Zimbabwe in one-day international cricket – before Ervine fell for 100. Carlisle was out for 109 just 12 balls later, and Zimbabwe finished their innings an agonizing three runs short.

OTHER TEAMS

The ICC's decision in recent years to allocate one-day international status to matches between world cricket's second-tier nations has led to a surge in the number of matches: in 1990, 61 one-day internationals were played throughout the world; by 2009, that number had risen to 150. Here are some of the outstanding performances from the best of the rest.

OVERALL RESULTS SUMMARY (AGAINST ALL OPPONENTS)

Opposition	Span	Mat	Won	Lost	Tied	NR	%
Afghanistan	2009–12	21	12	9	0	0	57.14
Africa XI	2005–07	6	1	4	0	1	16.67
Asia XI	2005–07	7	4	2	0	1	57.14
Bermuda	2006–09	35	7	28	0	0	20.00
Canada	1979–2011	70	17	52	0	1	24.63
East Africa	1975	3	0	3	0	0	0.00
Hong Kong	2004–08	4	0	4	0	0	0.00
ICC World XI	2005	4	1	3	0	0	25.00
Namibia	2003	6	0	6	0	0	0.00
UAE	1994–2008	11	1	10	0	0	9.09
USA	2004	2	0	2	0	0	0.00

[Hong Kong, Israel, Wales and others appeared in 1970s/80s World Cups or qualifiers]

Crowd-pleasing performance

In a match hastily arranged to raise funds for victims of the 2004 Boxing Day tsunami, the ICC World XI put on a blistering batting display against an Asia XI at Melbourne on 10 January 2005. Propelled by a 102-ball 115 from Ricky Ponting and a belligerent 47-ball 69 from Chris Cairns, they reached 344 for 8 off their 50 overs. The Asia XI slipped to 232 all out in reply to lose the match by 112 runs.

Canada put in their place

Having recorded a shock 60-run victory over Bangladesh in their first-ever ICC World Cup match in 2003, Canada had their hopes dented when they lost to Kenya by four wickets and then came crashing down to earth with a humiliating thump as Sri Lanka outclassed them in devastating fashion. Inserted on a lively pitch at Paarl, Canada were reduced to 36 all out in 18.4 overs – the lowest score in World Cup history. Sri Lanka then eased to the target in just 4.4 overs for the loss of one wicket.

Bagai the pick of the batsmen

Alongside the Netherlands' Ryan ten Doeschate, Canada's **Ashish Bagai** is the only player from one of cricket's minor nations to have scored 1,000 runs in ODIs. The Delhi-born wicketkeeper-batsman has scored 1,961 runs in 60 matches between 2003 and 2011, with a highest score of 137 not out against Scotland at Nairobi on 31 January 2007.

LEADING BATSMEN (BY TEAM)

Team	Player	Mat	Inns	NO	Runs	HS	Ave	100	50	0
Afghanistan	Mohammad Shahzad (2009–12)	19	19	1	721	118	40.05	3	3	1
Africa XI	S.M. Pollock (2005–07)	6	6	2	298	130	74.50	1	1	0
Asia XI	D.P.M.D. Jayawardene (2005–07)	5	5	1	269	107	67.25	1	2	0
Bermuda	I.H. Romaine (2006–09)	35	34	3	783	101	25.25	1	4	5
Canada	A. Bagai (2003–11)	60	59	8	1,961	137*	38.45	2	16	2
East Africa	Frasat Ali (1975)	3	3	0	57	45	19.00	0	0	1
Hong Kong	Tabarak Dar (2004–08)	4	4	0	101	36	25.25	0	0	0
ICC World XI	K.C. Sangakkara (2005)	3	3	0	138	64	46.00	0	2	0
Namibia	A.J. Burger (2003)	6	6	0	199	85	33.16	0	1	0
UAE	Mazhar Hussain (1994–96)	7	7	0	179	70	25.57	0	1	0
USA	C.B. Lambert (2004)	1	1	0	39	39	39.00	0	0	0

LEADING BOWLERS (BY TEAM)

Team	Player	Mat	Overs	Runs	Wkts	BBI	Ave	Econ	SR	4	5
Afghanistan	Samiulla Shenwari (2009–12)	21	167.3	720	27	4/31	26.66	4.29	37.2	1	0
Africa XI	M. Morkel (2007)	3	30.0	166	8	3/50	20.75	5.53	22.5	0	0
Asia XI	Z. Khan (2005–07)	6	47.0	199	13	3/21	15.30	4.23	21.6	0	0
Bermuda	R.D.M. Leverock (2006–09)	32	280.4	1,123	34	5/53	33.02	4.00	49.5	0	1
Canada	H.S. Baidwan (2008–11)	28	235.3	1,221	43	3/19	28.39	5.18	32.8	0	0
East Africa	Zulfiqar Ali (1975)	3	35.0	166	4	3/63	41.50	4.74	52.5	0	0
Hong Kong	Ilyas Gull (2004)	2	19.0	113	4	3/46	28.25	5.94	28.5	0	0
ICC World XI	D.L. Vettori (2005)	4	40.0	179	8	4/33	22.37	4.47	30.0	1	0
Namibia	R.J. van Vuuren (2003)	5	50.0	298	8	5/43	37.25	5.96	37.5	0	1
UAE	Khurram Khan (2004–08)	4	40.0	213	7	4/32	30.42	5.32	34.2	1	0
USA	R.W. Staple (2007)	2	10.0	76	2	2/76	38.00	7.60	30.0	0	0

Out of his depth

Weighing in at approximately 20 stones, Bermuda's **Dwayne Leverock** (the leading wicket-taker for Bermuda in one-day internationals) was probably the armchair fan's favourite player during the 2007 ICC World Cup, but he found himself on the wrong end of a good old-fashioned pummelling when Bermuda met India in a Group B encounter at Port of Spain, Trinidad, on 19 March 2007. The slow left-armer went for 96 runs off his ten overs, although he did take the wicket of Yuvraj Singh) – the second most expensive spell of bowling in World Cup history. India scored for 413 for 5 and went on to win the match by 257 runs – the largest margin of victory in one-day international cricket history.

Notable partnership

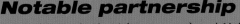

Mahendra Singh Dhoni (139 not out) and Mahela Jayawardene (107) proved the difference between the two sides as the Asia XI completed a 3–0 series sweep over the Africa XI at Chennai on 10 June 2007. Coming together in the 17th over with their side struggling on 72 for 5, the pair added 218 for the sixth wicket to lead the Asia XI to a mighty 331 for 8. In a spirited reply, the Africa XI were all out for 318.

Dhaniram enjoys second career with Canada

Having endured a brief and relatively unsuccessful first-class career as a lower-middle-order batsman with Guyana, the country of his birth, in the early 1990s, **Sunil Dhaniram** moved to Canada, added slow left-arm bowling to his armoury and revitalized his career as a solid all-rounder in the second tier of international cricket. In 44 one-day internationals for Canada between 2006 and 2010 he took a notable 41 wickets, with best figures of 5 for 32 against Bermuda at Ontario on 29 June 2008.

Codrington makes history for Canada

Canada's first-ever ICC World Cup campaign got off to a headline-grabbing start when they beat Bangladesh by 60 runs at Durban on 11 February 2003 to become the only "minor" cricket nation to record a victory over a Test-playing nation. The star of the show was Austin Codrington, a 27-year-old, Jamaican-born apprentice plumber who took 5 for 27 with his medium-pace bowling to help reduce Bangladesh (chasing 181) to 120 all out.

First forfeit of ODI

Canada forfeited their one-day international at Mombasa on 20 January 2007 owing to player illness; Kenya thus won the match without a ball being bowled – the only instance of such a case in the history of one-day international cricket.

PART III:
TWENTY20 CRICKET

Given the staggering manner in which Twenty20 cricket has been received by fans around the world, it seems strange to think the first Twenty20 international was staged as recently as 17 February 2005 and that it was taken less than seriously, with New Zealand players adorned with retro 1970s wigs and moustaches. It took a hastily arranged World Cup in South Africa in 2007 to change all that.

The 2007 ICC World Twenty20 was a spectacular success. When India faced off against Pakistan in the final, the match was beamed across 100 countries worldwide and became the tenth most-watched sports event of the year. India's five-run victory, and the ecstatic manner in which it was received, led to the subsequent establishment of the Indian Premier League and assured Twenty20 cricket's status on the domestic scene. The success of the 2009 and 2010 ICC World Twenty20 tournaments in England and the West Indies respectively has ensured international Twenty20 cricket is here to stay. For now, it may have been sidelined by existing television contracts committed to showing one-day internationals, but do not be too surprised if the 20-over game starts to form an increasing part of the cricket calendar in the years to come.

Paul Collingwood and his **England** team-mates celebrate after winning the ICC World Twenty20 tournament in May 2010.

ICC WORLD TWENTY20

It took some time, but the ICC finally realized that Twenty20 cricket not only provided great entertainment, but could also be a considerable money-spinner. The first three ICC World Twenty20s, held in South Africa, England and the West Indies respectively, have all been a spectacular success and the tournament looks set to become a permanent fixture on the international cricket calendar.

Smallest victory (by wickets)

The smallest margin of victory (by wickets) in ICC World Twenty20 competition is a win by two wickets, which occurred when New Zealand beat Sri Lanka by two wickets at Providence, Guyana, on 30 April 2010.

Indiscipline with ball costs West Indies

When the West Indies looked back to see how they failed to defend a target of 205 against South Africa in the opening match of the 2007 ICC World Twenty20 at Johannesburg, they would have looked no further than the extras column. The men from the Caribbean delivered an astonishing 23 wides (a tournament record) as South Africa cruised to an eight-wicket victory with 14 balls to spare.

Australia cruise into final four

With both sides needing to win to progress to the semi-finals of the 2007 ICC World Twenty20, the match between Australia and Sri Lanka at Cape Town on 20 September 2007 was rightly billed as a high-stakes, winner-takes-all encounter. It certainly wasn't a nail-biting one, however. Australia dismissed Sri Lanka for 101 and reached the victory target without losing a wicket – **Matthew Hayden** (58 not out) and Adam Gilchrist (31 not out) in 10.2 overs to record the first, and to date only, ten-wicket victory in ICC World Twenty20 history.

ICC WORLD TWENTY20 WINNERS

Year	Winner	(Host)
2007	India	(South Africa)
2009	Pakistan	(England)
2010	England	(West Indies)

Minnow-bashing at its best

Sri Lanka pulverized Kenya in the two sides' Group C meeting at Johannesburg in the 2007 ICC World Twenty20. Batting first, they blitzed the Kenyan bowling attack to all parts of the ground in amassing a gargantuan 260 for 6 off their 20 overs – the highest score by any team in any Twenty20 match – with **Sanath Jayasuriya** top-scoring with 88. Overwhelmed, Kenya crept to 88 for 9. Sri Lanka's 172-run margin of victory is the highest (by runs) in international Twenty20 history.

Kenya slump to record defeat

Kenya got their 2007 ICC World Twenty20 campaign off to the worst possible start against New Zealand at Durban on 12 September 2007. Put in to bat on a lively surface, they lost their first three batsmen in the first seven balls of the match without registering a run, slipped to 1 for 4 by the end of the second over and scrambled to 73 all out. New Zealand cantered to a nine-wicket victory with 74 balls remaining – the largest margin (by balls remaining) in international Twenty20 cricket history.

Most defeats

The record for the most defeats in ICC World Twenty20 matches is eight, a feat achieved by three teams: Bangladesh (in nine matches), England (in 17 matches) and New Zealand (in 16 matches).

Most victories

The record for the most victories recorded in ICC World Twenty20 matches is 12, recorded by two teams: Pakistan (champions in 2009, runners-up in 2007 and semi-finalists in 2010) and Sri Lanka (runners-up in 2009 and semi-finalists in 2010).

ICC WORLD TWENTY20 LEAGUE TABLE (RANKED BY WIN PERCENTAGE)

Pos	Team (Span)	Mat	Won	Lost	Tied	NR	%
1	South Africa (2007–10)	16	11	5	0	0	68.75
2	Sri Lanka (2007–10)	18	12	6	0	0	66.66
3	Pakistan (2007–10)	20	12	7	0	0	62.50
4	Australia (2007–10)	15	9	6	1	0	60.00
5	India (2007–10)	17	8	7	0	1	53.12
6	England (2007–10)	17	8	8	1	1	50.00
=	Netherlands (2009)	2	1	1	0	0	50.00
=	New Zealand (2007–10)	16	8	8	0	0	50.00
9	West Indies (2007–10)	13	6	7	0	0	46.15
10	Zimbabwe (2007–10)	4	1	3	0	0	25.00
11	Ireland (2009–10)	7	1	5	0	1	16.66
12	Bangladesh (2007–10)	9	1	8	0	0	11.11
13	Afghanistan (2010)	2	0	2	0	0	0.00
=	Kenya (2007)	2	0	2	0	0	0.00
=	Scotland (2007–09)	4	0	3	0	1	0.00

BELOW: *South Africa celebrate their slender one-run victory over New Zealand in their Group D encounter at the 2009 ICC World Twenty20 at Lord's.*

Last-ball successes

It was the most spectacular upset in the tournament's history as the Netherlands, making their first-ever appearance, shocked hosts England at the home of cricket, Lord's, in the two sides' opening Group B encounter at the 2009 ICC World Twenty20. Chasing 163 for victory, the men in orange squeaked over the winning line off the last ball of the match to record a memorable four-wicket victory. There has only been one other last-ball success in ICC World Twenty20 history: Sri Lanka beat India (by five wickets) off the final ball of the match at Gros Inlet on 11 May 2010.

ABOVE: *The Netherlands celebrate their unlikely last-ball victory over England at Lord's at the 2009 ICC World Twenty20.*

Fine line between victory and defeat

New Zealand have made a habit of being involved in ICC World Twenty20 games that have been resolved by the slenderest of margins. In their Group D encounter against South Africa at Lord's in 2009, they fell to defeat by one run; eleven months later, in their Super Eight match against Pakistan at Bridgetown, Barbados, they won by one run.
They are the only two instances of one-run victories in ICC World Twenty20 history.

Runs galore at Durban

India and England's Group E encounter at Durban in the 2007 ICC World Twenty20 captured the very essence of all that is good about the shortest format of the game – hard hitting and plenty of runs. India, boosted by six sixes in a Stuart Broad over from **Yuvraj Singh** – reached 218 for 4. England reached a spirited 200 for 6 in reply to lose the match by 18 runs. The match aggregate of 418 runs is the highest in the tournament's history.

BATTING RECORDS

MOST RUNS: TOP 10

Pos	Runs	Player	Mat	Inns	NO	HS	Ave	100	50	0
1	615	**D.P.M.D. Jayawardene** (SL, 2007–10)	18	18	3	100	41.00	1	4	0
2	580	K.P. Pietersen (Eng, 2007–10)	15	15	2	79	44.61	0	4	0
3	453	T.M. Dilshan (SL, 2007–10)	18	17	3	96*	32.35	0	3	2
4	444	G. Gambhir (Ind, 2007–10)	16	15	0	75	29.60	0	4	1
5	442	C.H. Gayle (WI, 2007–09)	11	11	1	117	44.20	1	3	1
6	420	K.C. Sangakkare (SL, 2007–10)	18	18	2	68	26.25	0	3	1
7	412	Kamran Akmal (Pak, 2007–10)	20	18	2	73	25.75	0	3	2
8	409	J.H. Kallis (SA, 2009–10)	10	10	1	73	45.44	0	3	0
9	389	A.B. de Villiers (SA, 2007–10)	16	16	3	79*	29.92	0	3	0
10	375	Yuvraj Singh (Ind, 2007–10)	16	15	2	70	28.84	0	3	0

Most ducks

It seems to be boom or bust for Sanath Jayasuriya as he reaches the twilight of his international career. The veteran opener may have recorded three half-centuries for Sri Lanka in 18 ICC World Twenty20 matches, but he has also recorded four ducks – the most by any individual player in the tournament's history.

Gambhir comes of age

He is now widely regarded as one of the best openers in world cricket, but when he looks back, Gautam Gambhir will see the 2007 ICC World Twenty20 as the moment when his career took off. Handed yet another chance to establish himself in a much-changed India side following the country's poor showing at the 2007 ICC World Cup, Gambhir grabbed it with both hands, hitting three half-centuries in the tournament, including a high-class knock of 75 in the pressure-cooker atmosphere of the final against Pakistan, which India won by five runs. Gambhir's effort remains the highest score yet recorded in an ICC World Twenty20 final.

Getting off to a record-breaking start

The 2007 ICC World Twenty20 got off to an explosive start from the moment the West Indies started their innings against hosts South Africa at Johannesburg on 11 September 2007. **Chris Gayle**, playing at his destructive best, smashed a sensational 57-ball 117 – the first century in international Twenty20 cricket. The left-hander blazed 88 of his runs in boundaries (a staggering 75.2 per cent), with a tournament record ten sixes and seven fours, to lead his side to 205 for 6. The fireworks did not end there. South Africa, inspired by an unbeaten 90 from Herschelle Gibbs, reached the victory target for the loss of two wickets with 14 balls to spare. Gayle may have experienced disappointment on that occasion, but his hard-hitting exploits did not end there: he holds the all-time ICC World Twenty20 record for the most career sixes hit (27) and for the highest career batting strike-rate (153.47).

Talk of the town

Tillakaratne Dilshan was the talk of world cricket during the 2009 ICC World Twenty20. Not only did he bring a new shot to the game (an audacious paddle scoop over his left shoulder, described in various quarters as the "flick shot", the "genuflector" or simply the "Dilshan"), he also kept on piling up the big scores. His tournament record 317 runs (with a highest score of 96 not out against the West Indies at The Oval) played a pivotal role in Sri Lanka's progress to the final, where they lost to Pakistan, and were enough to earn him the player of the tournament award.

HIGHEST SCORES BY BATTING POSITION

Pos	Score	Player	For	Against	Venue	Date
1/2	117	C.H. Gayle	West Indies	SA	Johannesburg	11 Sep 2007
1/2	100	D.P.M.D. Jayawardene	Sri Lanka	Zim	Providence	3 May 2010
3	101	**S.K. Raina**	India	SA	Gros Inlet	2 May 2010
4	89*	J.M. Kemp	South Africa	NZ	Durban	19 Sep 2007
5	59	D.J. Hussey	Australia	Eng	Bridgetown	16 May 2010
6	85*	C.L. White	Australia	SL	Bridgetown	9 May 2010
7	60*	M.E.K. Hussey	Australia	Pak	Gros Inlet	14 May 2010
8	35*	A.D. Mathews	Sri Lanka	Pak	Lord's	21 Jun 2009
9	28	Naeem Islam	Bangladesh	Ind	Trent Bridge	6 Jun 2009
10	22	Hamid Hassan	Afghanistan	SA	Bridgetown	5 May 2010
11	13*	J.D. Nel	Scotland	Pak	Durban	12 Sep 2007

Six sixes in an over

Yuvraj Singh is rightly regarded as one of the cleanest and most destructive strikers of the ball in world cricket, as Stuart Broad found out. In the 18th over of India's Group E match against England at Durban on 19 September 2007, the left-hander smashed the hapless English bowler for six consecutive sixes to become the first player in Twenty20 cricket (and the fourth in senior cricket) to achieve the feat.

Smith's end-of-innings blitz

Dwayne Smith provided some late-order fireworks to haul the West Indies to a respectable 164 for 8 in their must-win Group A encounter with Bangladesh at Johannesburg in the 2007 ICC World Twenty20. Batting at No. 7, the Barbados all-rounder smashed 29 off seven balls – his innings strike-rate of 414.28 runs scored per 100 balls is the highest in the tournament's history. Not that it was a match-winning performance: Bangladesh reached the target for the loss of four wickets with two overs to spare to send the West Indies crashing out of the tournament.

Super Sharma shines for India

Rohit Sharma is a classy performer with the bat who possesses that rare talent of being able to find gaps in the field at will. He was handed a place in his country's squad for the inaugural ICC World Twenty20 in South Africa in 2007 and, aged only 20, took his chance with both hands, hitting an unbeaten 50 (against South Africa) in his first innings in international cricket and an unbeaten 30 in India's sensational final win over Pakistan. An ever-present in India's limited-overs teams ever since (although he is yet to make his Test debut), he has performed with distinction in all three ICC World Twenty20 tournaments, hitting 303 runs in 12 innings (with a highest score of 79 not out) at an average of 60.00 – the highest by any player to complete 10 innings or more in the tournament's history.

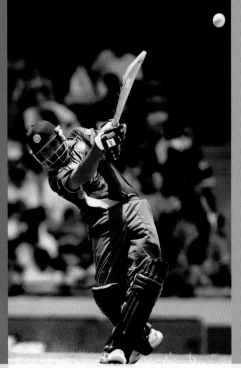

Akmal sets a tournament best

Defending champions Pakistan got their 2010 ICC World Twenty20 campaign off to the best of starts when they won their opening match against Bangladesh by 21 runs at Gros Inlet, St Lucia, on 1 May 2010. And for that, they had their openers to thank: Salman Butt scored 73 off 46 balls (with eight fours and two sixes) and Kamran Akmal scored 73 off 55 balls (with eight fours and one six) – the highest score by a designated wicketkeeper in the tournament's history.

Most scores of 50 or over

Mahela Jayawardene holds the all-time record for the most scores of 50-plus in ICC World Twenty20 matches. The Sri Lankan stroke player, the leading run-scorer in the competition's history (with 615 runs), has reached a half-century on five occasions (in 18 innings between 2007 and 2010), with a best score of 100 against Zimbabwe at Providence, Guyana, on 3 May 2010.

BOWLING RECORDS

MOST WICKETS: TOP 10

Pos	Wkts	Player	Mat	O	M	R	BBI	Ave	Econ	SR	4	5
1	27	**Shahid Afridi** (Pak, 2007–10)	20	80.0	1	519	4/11	19.22	6.48	17.7	2	0
2	26	Umar Gul (Pak, 2007–09)	14	52.1	0	313	5/6	12.03	6.00	12.0	1	1
3	25	S.L. Malinga (SL, 2007–10)	18	60.1	0	446	3/17	17.84	7.41	14.4	0	0
4	23	Saeed Ajmal (Pak, 2009–10)	13	50.2	0	332	4/19	14.43	6.59	13.1	2	0
5	20	M.G. Johnson (Aus, 2007–10)	14	52.1	0	351	3/15	17.55	6.72	15.6	0	0
6	19	S.C.J. Broad (Eng, 2007–10)	17	55.5	0	428	3/17	22.52	7.66	17.6	0	0
7	18	D.L. Vettori (NZ, 2007–10)	13	51.1	0	289	4/20	16.05	5.64	17.0	1	0
8	17	M. Morkel (SA, 2007–10)	10	39.0	0	262	4/17	15.41	6.71	13.7	2	0
9	16	B.A.W. Mendis (SL, 2009–10)	12	44.0	0	271	3/9	16.93	6.15	16.5	0	0
10	15	D.P. Nannes (Aus/Neth, 2009–10)	9	34.0	1	239	4/18	15.93	7.02	13.6	1	0

Afridi's records with the ball

Renowned more perhaps for his explosive performances with the bat, Shahid Afridi has developed into a highly effective leg-break bowler, particularly in the limited-over forms of the game, and he holds numerous all-time ICC World Twenty20 bowling records: he has taken more wickets (27), bowled more overs (80.0) and conceded more runs (519) than any other bowler in the tournament's history.

Keeping it tight

There has been no more miserly bowler in ICC World Twenty20 matches than Nikita Miller. The Jamaican slow left-arm bowler has bowled 12.0 overs for 63 runs in three matches at an economy rate of 5.25 runs per over – the lowest by any bowler to have delivered ten overs or more in the tournament's history.

Most maidens bowled

Given the nature of the game, a maiden over is a particularly rare feat in international Twenty20 cricket. The record for the most career maidens bowled in ICC World Twenty20 matches is three, set by Dilhara Fernando. The Sri Lankan paceman achieved the feat in 17 overs in five matches in the 2007 edition of the tournament held in South Africa.

Standout performer with the ball

A mainstay of Pakistan's bowling attack since making his international debut as a 19-year-old in 2003 (having made just nine prior first-class appearances), **Umar Gul** is the perfect death bowler, capable of bowling high-speed reverse-swinging yorkers in the closing overs of an innings. He played a pivotal role in Pakistan's success in the 2009 competition and holds the all-time tournament records for: the best bowling figures in an innings (5 for 6 against New Zealand at The Oval on 13 June 2009, a performance that saw him break the record for the best economy rate in an innings – 2.00); and for the most four-wicket-plus hauls in an innings (two, a record he shares with Pakistan team-mates Shahid Afridi and Saeed Amjal and South Africa's Morne Morkel).

PACE OR SPIN?

Twenty20 cricket has confounded the critics who predicted a crash-bang-wallop game in which spin bowlers were little more than lambs to the slaughter. As statistics for ICC World Twenty20 matches show, spin bowlers not only play an integral part in games, they can be equally as effective as pace bowlers, with both a better average and economy rate:

Type	Overs	Mdns	Runs	Wkts	BBI	Ave	Econ	SR	4	5
Pace	1862.4	24	14,467	607	5/6	23.83	7.76	18.4	15	1
Spin	1018.4	7	7,259	314	4/11	23.11	7.12	19.4	7	0

Better late than never for Charl Langeveldt

A left-arm bowler of genuine pace, **Charl Langeveldt** made his one-day international debut for South Africa (against Kenya) in 2000–01 and, a handful of Test appearances apart, seemed to reserve his best performances for the ODI arena. As such, it came as a surprise when he did not feature in either of the first two editions of the ICC World Twenty20 and, as he approached his 36th year, it seemed the opportunity to perform on Twenty20 cricket's biggest stage had passed him by. However, benefiting from injuries to others, he was named in South Africa's squad for the 2010 edition of the tournament and grabbed his chance with both hands, taking 11 wickets in the tournament at an average of 9.45 runs per wicket at a strike-rate of one wicket every 8.7 deliveries. Both his average and strike-rate marks are all-time records for any bowler to bowl ten overs or more in ICC World Twenty20 matches.

Cusack spell hands Ireland a chance

A great spell of bowling from **Alex Cusack** dragged Ireland back into contention against Sri Lanka in the two sides' Group F encounter at Lord's in the 2009 ICC World Twenty20. The Australian-born medium-fast bowler took 4 for 18 to help restrict Sri Lanka to 144 for 9 – but in vain, as Ireland reached 135 for 7 in reply to lose by nine runs. Cusack's effort is the best bowling performance in a losing cause in the tournament's history.

No ordinary cricketer

A globe-trotter, a Japanese speaker and a saxophone player who represented Australia in World Cup skiing events, **Dirk Nannes** is not your run-of-the-mill cricketer, but he is certainly a talented one. Of Dutch parentage, he played for the Netherlands at the 2009 ICC World Twenty20, after missing out on a place in Australia's squad, and performed with such distinction that he caught the Australian selectors' eyes and was rapidly drafted into Australia's squad for the 2010 edition of the tournament. Bowling with precision and raw pace, his 14 wickets in the tournament, which did much to propel Australia to the final, are the most by any bowler at a single ICC World Twenty20.

Pathan piles on the pressure

Where Gautam Gambhir (75) starred with the bat during India's five-run victory over Pakistan in the 2007 ICC World Twenty20 final, Irfan Pathan was the hero with the ball: the left-arm medium-fast bowler took 3 for 16 in the middle of the innings to pile on the pressure under which the Pakistan batsmen would ultimately crack. They remain the best bowling figures recorded in an ICC World Twenty20 final.

Most runs conceded in an innings

The ICC World Twenty20 record for the most runs conceded by a bowler in an innings is 64. Sri Lanka's **Sanath Jayasuriya** recorded figures of 4.0-0-64-0 against Pakistan at Johannesburg on 17 September 2007. Pakistan went on to win the match by 33 runs.

OTHER RECORDS

HIGHEST PARTNERSHIPS: TOP 10

Pos	Runs	Partners	Wkt	Team	Against	Venue	Date
1	166	D.P.M.D. Jayawardene, K.C. Sangakkara	2nd	Sri Lanka	WI	Bridgetown	7 May 2010
2	145	C.H. Gayle, D.S. Smith	1st	West Indies	SA	Johannesburg	11 Sep 2007
3	142	Kamran Akmal, Salman Butt	1st	Pakistan	Bang	Gros Islet	1 May 2010
4	136	G. Gambhir, V. Sehwag	1st	India	Eng	Durban	19 Sep 2007
5	133	C.H. Gayle, A.D.S. Fletcher	1st	West Indies	Aus	The Oval	6 Jun 2009
6	124	T.M. Dilshan, S.T. Jayasuriya	1st	Sri Lanka	WI	Nottingham	10 Jun 2009
7	120*	H.H. Gibbs, J.M. Kemp	3rd	South Africa	WI	Johannesburg	11 Sep 2007
8	119*	Shoaib Malik, Misbah-ul-Haq	5th	Pakistan	Aus	Johannesburg	18 Sep 2007
9	111	C. Kieswetter, K.P. Pietersen	2nd	England	Aus	Bridgetown	16 May 2010
10	109	Aftab Ahmed, Mohammad Ashraful	3rd	Bangladesh	WI	Johannesburg	13 Sep 2007

Sri Lankan stars put West Indies to the sword

Two sublime innings from the team's two best batsmen helped Sri Lanka ease to a comfortable victory over hosts West Indies in the two sides' Super Eight encounter at Bridgetown, Barbados, on 7 May 2010. Mahela Jayawardene (98 not out) and Kumar Sangakkara (68) added 166 runs off 16.3 overs for the second wicket – the highest partnership in the tournament's history – to lead Sri Lanka to an imposing 195 for 3. In response, the West Indies slipped to 138 for 8 and defeat by 57 runs.

Most wicketkeeping dismissals

Kumar Sangakkara is the most successful wicketkeeper to appear in the ICC World Twenty20. Sri Lanka's wicketkeeper-batsman and (up to the end of the 2011 ICC World Cup) captain has bagged 13 victims in 12 matches in the tournament (seven catches and six stumpings). He also holds the record for the most dismissals in a single tournament with nine in 2009 – a record he shares with Australia's Adam Gilchrist, who achieved the feat in 2007.

Most catches in an innings by a fielder

The record for the most catches in an innings by a fielder is four, by Darren Sammy, for the West Indies against Ireland at Providence, Guyana, on 30 April 2010.

De Villiers leads the way in the field

South Africa's **A.B. de Villiers** is fast developing a reputation as the best fielder in world cricket. Positioned for the most part at backward point or short midwicket – regular spots for many of the 20-over game's best fielders – he has taken more catches in ICC World Twenty20 matches than any other player (16 in 16 matches between 2007 and 2009).

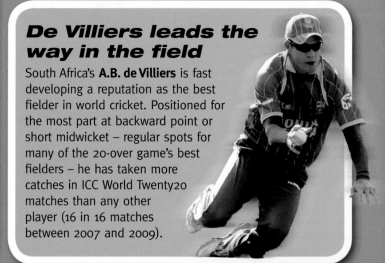

HIGHEST PARTNERSHIPS: BY WICKET

Wkt	Runs	Partners	Team	Opposition	Venue	Date
1st	145	C.H. Gayle, D.S. Smith	West Indies	SA	Johannesburg	11 Sep 2007
2nd	166	D.P.M.D. Jayawardene, K.C. Sangakkara	Sri Lanka	WI	Bridgetown	7 May 2007
3rd	120*	H.H. Gibbs, J.M. Kemp	South Africa	WI	Johannesburg	11 Sep 2007
4th	101	Younis Khan, Shoaib Malik	Pakistan	SL	Johannesburg	17 Sep 2007
5th	119*	Shoaib Malik, Misbah-ul-Haq	Pakistan	Aus	Johannesburg	18 Sep 2007
6th	101*	C.L. White, M.E.K. Hussey	Australia	SL	Bridgetown	9 May 2010
7th	74	M.E.K. Hussey, S.P.D. Smith	Australia	Ban	Bridgetown	5 May 2010
8th	53	M.E.K. Hussey, M.G. Johnson	Australia	Pak	Gros Inlet	14 May 2010
9th	36	R.G. Sharma, Z Khan	India	Aus	Bridgetown	7 May 2010
10th	20	N.O. Miller, S.J. Benn	West Indies	Aus	Gros Inlet	11 May 2010

Most catches in a tournament

The record for the most catches in a single tournament is eight, a feat achieved by two players: Mike Hussey and Dave Warner, both for Australia at the 2010 ICC World Twenty20.

Most successful captain

Tournament success may not have come his way, but in matches **Graeme Smith** is the most successful captain in ICC World Twenty20 history, leading South Africa to 11 wins in 16 matches between 2007 and 2010.

Most wicketkeeping dismissals in an innings

The ICC World Twenty20 record for the most dismissals in an innings by a keeper is four, a feat achieved by five players: Adam Gilchrist, for Australia against Zimbabwe at Cape Town on 12 September 2007 (4ct); Matt Prior, for England against South Africa at Cape Town on 16 September 2007 (4ct); Kamran Akmal, for Pakistan against the Netherlands at Lord's on 9 June 2009 (4st); Niall O'Brien, for Ireland against Sri Lanka at Lord's on 14 June 2009 (3ct, 1st); and **Mahendra Singh Dhoni**, for India against Afghanistan at Gros Inlet on 1 May 2010 (4ct).

ICC WORLD TWENTY20 PLAYER OF THE TOURNAMENT WINNERS

2007   Shahid Afridi (Pakistan)
2009   Tillakaratne Dilshan (Sri Lanka)
2010   **Kevin Pietersen** (England)

INTERNATIONAL TWENTY20

It took a comprehensive 100-run victory for England over Australia at the Rose Bowl in June 2005 before international Twenty20 cricket was taken seriously. Since then, as the ICC has tried to work out how best to integrate the new format into the international cricket calendar, matches – with the exception of ICC World Twenty20 tournaments – have been few and far between.

RESULT SUMMARY

Team	Span	Mat	Won	Lost	Tied	NR	%
Afghanistan	2010–12	11	6	5	0	0	54.54
Australia	2005–12	49	25	22	1	1	53.12
Bangladesh	2006–11	18	4	14	0	0	22.22
Bermuda	2008	3	0	3	0	0	0.00
Canada	2008–12	15	3	11	1	0	23.33
England	2005–12	44	23	19	0	2	54.76
India	2006–12	34	17	15	1	1	53.03
Ireland	2008–12	25	15	8	0	2	65.21
Kenya	2007–12	17	4	13	0	0	23.52
Netherlands	2008–12	14	8	5	0	1	61.53
New Zealand	2005–12	50	24	23	3	0	51.00
Pakistan	2006–12	53	32	20	1	0	61.32
Scotland	2007–12	16	4	11	0	1	26.66
South Africa	2005–112	44	29	15	0	0	65.90
Sri Lanka	2006–11	38	23	15	0	0	60.52
West Indies	2006–12	35	14	19	2	0	42.85
Zimbabwe	2006–12	20	3	16	1	0	17.50

Highest and lowest

Highest score: 260 for 6 – Sri Lanka v Kenya at Johannesburg on 14 September 2007.

Lowest score: 67 all out – Kenya v Ireland at Belfast on 4 August 2008.

Biggest victories

By runs: by 172 runs – Sri Lanka v Kenya at Johannesburg on 14 September 2007.

By wickets: by ten wickets on nine occasions.

By balls remaining: with 74 balls remaining – New Zealand v Kenya at Durban on 12 September 2007.

Smallest victories

By runs: by one run – on four occasions.

By wickets: by one wicket – England v Australia at Adelaide on 12 January 2011.

By balls remaining: off the last ball of the match on five occasions.

High scores

Chris Gayle's 117 for the West Indies in the opening game of the 2007 ICC World Twenty20 against South Africa at Johannesburg is the joint-highest score in international Twenty20 matches. It was equalled by Richard Levi of South Africa (117 not out of 51 balls) against New Zealand at Hamilton on 19 February 2012.

Made for the game

Andrew Symonds was a big-hitting batsman with a simple approach to the game – his mantra often seemed to be "see ball, hit ball". Indiscretions both on and off the pitch saw him in and out of the Australia side in all forms of cricket after his international debut in 1998 but, on his day, there was no finer batsman in Twenty20. In 14 Twenty20 internationals for Australia between 2004 and 2009 he scored 337 runs (with a highest score of 85 not out against New Zealand at Perth on 11 December 2007) at an average of 48.14 – the highest by any batsman to have completed ten innings or more – at a strike-rate of 169.34 runs per 100 balls faced – an all-time high in international Twenty20 cricket by any batsman with ten or more completed innings.

McCullum a big hit in Twenty20

There have been many examples of Twenty20 cricket enhancing a player's reputation, but perhaps the best is that of New Zealand's wicketkeeper-batsman **Brendon McCullum**. He ensured the Indian Premier League got off to a blistering start when he smashed 158 not out in the tournament's first-ever game – still the highest score in a Twenty20 match. He carried that form into international matches: he was the first batsman (of two – England's Kevin Pietersen is the other) to have scored more than 1,000 runs in Twenty20 internationals (1,352 runs, in 47 matches, with a highest score of 116 not out against Australia at Christchurch on 28 February 2010).

MOST RUNS: TOP 5

Pos	Runs	Player	M	I	NO	HS	Ave	BF	SR	100	50	0	4s	6s
1	1,352	B.B. McCullum (NZ, 2005–12)	47	47	8	116*	34.66	1,032	131.00	1	8	2	128	54
2	1.176	K.P. Pietersen (Eng, 2005–12)	36	36	5	79	37.93	831	141.51	0	7	1	119	32
3	982	G.C. Smith (SA, 2005–12)	33	33	2	89*	31.67	770	127.53	0	5	1	123	26
4	953	D.P.M.D. Jayawardene (SL, 2006–11)	35	35	5	100	31.76	684	139.32	1	6	3	105	23
5	894	T.M. Dilshan (SL, 2006–11)	35	34	6	104*	31.92	706	126.62	1	5	3	104	17

MOST WICKETS: TOP 5

Pos	Wkts	Player	Mat	Overs	Mdns	Runs	BBI	Ave	Econ	SR	4w	5w
1	56	**Shahid Afridi** (Pak, 2006–10)	48	180.5	3	1,115	4/11	19.91	6.16	19.3	3	0
2	55	Umar Gul (Pak, 2007–10)	39	132.4	2	863	5/6	15.69	6.50	14.4	3	1
3	51	Saeed Ajmal (Pak, 2009–10)	37	134.0	0	837	4/19	16.41	6.24	15.2	3	0
4	40	S.C.J. Broad (Eng, 2006–10)	34	120.3	0	876	3/17	21.90	7.26	18.0	0	0
=	40	B.A.W. Mendis (SL, 2008–11)	21	79.0	2	445	6/16	11.12	5.63	11.8	2	1
=	40	G.P. Swann (Eng, 2008–12)	30	103.0	2	659	3/13	16.47	6.39	15.4	0	0

Most career maidens

Zimbabwe's Ray Price is fast developing a reputation as being one of the most miserly bowlers on the international circuit. The slow left-armer has delivered a record four maidens in nine matches in T20 internationals – a feat equalled by Ireland's Trent Johnson in 2012.

Most catches

The record for the most catches by a fielder in Twenty20 international matches is 26, a feat achieved by Ross Taylor (in 39 matches for New Zealand between 2006 and 2012).

Off to a galloping start

A forthright opening stand from Graeme Smith (88) and Loots Bosman (94) placed South Africa in a match-winning position in their international Twenty20 match against England at Centurion on 15 November 2009. The pair added 170 runs for the opening wicket – a record partnership in international Twenty20 cricket – to lead South Africa to an impressive 241 for 6. England wilted to a distant 157 for 8 in reply.

Hat-tricks

There have been three hat-tricks in international Twenty20 cricket: by Australia's Brett Lee, against Bangladesh at Cape Town on 16 September 2007 – Shakib Al Hasan (caught), Mashrafe Mortaza (bowled) and Alok Kapali (lbw); by New Zealand's Jacob Oram, against Sri Lanka at Colombo on 2 September 2009 – Angelo Mathews (caught and bowled), Malinga Bandara (caught) and Nuwan Kulasekara (caught); and by New Zealand's **Tim Southee**, against Pakistan at Auckland on 26 December 2010 – Younis Khan (caught), Mohammad Hafeez (caught) and Umar Akmal (lbw).

PART IV: DOMESTIC CRICKET RECORDS

Domestic cricket is the lifeblood of the game, the breeding ground where cricket's future stars will learn their trade and the format through whose ranks every one of the game's greatest names has passed. It includes first-class cricket (timed matches), limited-overs cricket (matches of 40 to 60 overs per side) and Twenty20 cricket.

The term "first-class" dates back to May 1894, but records of matches between two representative sides go back much further than that. In 1709, Kent and Surrey staged the first-known inter-county match; in 1825, Kent and Sussex contested home-and-away fixtures (a forerunner to the county championship, which was constituted in 1890); in Australia, the first first-class match (between Tasmania and Victoria) took place in 1850–51; and by the early years of the 20th century, first-class cricket competitions were being contested throughout the world.

The majority of cumulative first-class records (most career runs/wickets etc.) belong to English cricketers of the game's Golden Age, directly as a result of the sheer volume of games in which they played: Wilfred Rhodes, for example, played 1,110 first-class matches in a 32-year career; in contrast, Graeme Hick, who retired in 2008 after 25 years in the county game, played just 526.

Limited-overs cricket in the domestic game is a more modern phenomenon that kicked off in England with the launch of the Sunday League in 1969. Twenty20 cricket has been played domestically since 2003, first in England, then South Africa, and now throughout the world, including the Indian Premier League – the richest tournament in the game.

Chennai Super Kings celebrate retaining their Indian Premier League crown in 2011 after beating Royal Challengers Bangalore in the final.

TEAM RECORDS

HIGHEST INNINGS TOTALS: TOP 10

Pos	Total	For	Against	Venue	Season
1	1,107	Victoria	New South Wales	Melbourne	1926–27
2	1,059	Victoria	Tasmania	Melbourne	1922–23
3	952–6d	Sri Lanka	India	Colombo	1997–98
4	951–7d	Sind	Baluchistan	Karachi	1973–74
5	944–6d	Hyderabad	Andhra Pradesh	Hyderabad	1993–94
6	918	New South Wales	South Australia	Sydney	1900–01
7	912–8d	Holkar	Mysore	Indore	1945–46
=	912–6d	Tamil Nadu	Goa	Panjim	1988–89
9	910–6d	Railways	Dera Ismail Khan	Lahore	1964–65
10	903–7d	England	Australia	The Oval	1938

Pakistan Railways steam to victory

It was the most one-sided game in first-class history. In Pakistan's 1964–65 domestic season, Pakistan Railways won the toss, batted and, thanks to centuries from Ijaz Hussain (124), Javed Babar (200), Pervez Akhtar (337 not out) and Mohammad Sharif (106 not out), reached a massive 910 for 6 declared. They then dismissed Dera Ismail Khan for 32 and 27 to win the match by an innings and 851 runs – the largest victory (by an innings) in first-class cricket history.

Essex peak too soon

When they were finally dismissed for 642 on the second day of their County Championship Division Two match against Glamorgan at Chelmsford in September 2004, Essex would no doubt have thought they had done enough, at the very least, to avoid defeat. But how fortunes can change: Glamorgan made 587 in reply; bowled out Essex for 165 second time around; and chased down the 221 runs required for victory for the loss of six wickets. Essex's first-innings total is the highest by a losing side in first-class cricket history.

Highest fourth-innings total to win a match

When Southern Province declared their second innings closed on 292 for 2 to set Central Province 513 runs to win the match at Kandy in 2003–04, they would have thought victory would soon be theirs. But Central Province had other ideas: led by centuries from Sajith Fernando (111) and Kumar Sangakkara (101) they reached the target for the loss of nine wickets. It is the highest successful run-chase in first-class cricket history.

Thriller at Taunton

Set 454 runs to win the game, Somerset fell agonizingly short in a thrilling encounter against West Indies A at Taunton in July 2002. Bolstered by a fine innings of 140 from **Peter Trego**, they finally fell for 453 to tie the game. It is the highest fourth-innings score by a team that has gone on to tie a game in first-class cricket history.

Highest fourth-innings total

The highest fourth-innings total in first-class cricket history was achieved during the England v South Africa Test match at Durban in 1938–39 – the last of the timeless Tests. Set 696 runs for victory, England had reached 654 for 5 when, at tea on the tenth day, following repeated interruptions for rain, the two sides agreed to call the match a draw – principally to allow the England players time to travel to Cape Town to catch the mail boat home.

Lowest completed first-class innings total to include a double-century

282 – Namibia against Kenya at Sharjah in January 2008, of which Gerrie Snyman made 230 (81.56 per cent of his team's total); his team-mates contributing 43 runs, with nine extras.

LOWEST INNINGS TOTALS: TOP 10

Pos	Total	For	Against	Venue	Season
1	12	Oxford University	MCC	Oxford	1877
=	12	Northamptonshire	Gloucestershire	Gloucester	1907
3	13	Auckland	Canterbury	Auckland	1877–78
=	13	Nottinghamshire	Yorkshire	Nottingham	1901
5	14	Surrey	Essex	Chelmsford	1983
6	15	MCC	Surrey	Lord's	1839
=	15	Victoria	MCC	Melbourne	1903–04
=	15	Northamptonshire	Yorkshire	Northampton	1908
=	15	Hampshire	Warwickshire	Birmingham	1922
10	16	MCC	Surrey	Lord's	1872
=	16	Derbyshire	Nottinghamshire	Nottingham	1879
=	16	Surrey	Nottinghamshire	The Oval	1880
=	16	Warwickshire	Kent	Tonbridge	1913
=	16	Trinidad	Barbados	Bridgetown	1942–43

NSW boosted by Bradman towards record-breaking victory

By the time both sides had completed the first innings of the Sheffield Shield Match at Sydney in 1929–30, New South Wales held a slender eight-run lead over Queensland. Then **Donald Bradman** came to the party, hitting a then world record 452 not out to lead his side to 761 for 8 declared. Bewildered by the prospect of chasing 770 to win the match, Queensland folded to 84 all out. New South Wales's victory – by 675 runs – is the largest (by runs) in first-class cricket history.

Donald Bradman is held aloft by his NSW team-mates after completing his then first-class cricket record score of 452 not out against Queensland in 1929–30.

Defiance in a losing cause

Although defeat was inevitable, Marahastra produced a defiant performance in their unlikely assault on the 959 runs required for victory against Bombay at Pune in 1948–49. Madhusudan Rege (100) and Sharad Deodhar (146) both scored centuries before Marahastra finally slipped to 604 all out – it remains the highest fourth-innings total in first-class cricket history by a side that has gone on to lose the match.

Lowest completed first-class innings total to include a half-century

66 all out – scored by the Indians against Yorkshire at Harrogate in 1932, of which Nazir Ali made 52 (78.79 per cent of his team's total); his team-mates contributing a further nine runs, with five extras.

Lowest completed first-class innings total to include a century

143 all out – Nottinghamshire against Hampshire at Bournemouth in 1981, of which Clive Rice made 105 not out (73.40 per cent of his team's total); his team-mates contributing 35 runs, with three extras.

Lowest completed first-class innings total to include a score of 350

500 all out – Otago against Canterbury at Christchurch in 1952–53, of which Bert Sutcliffe made 385 (77.00 per cent of the total); his team-mates contributing 86 runs, with 29 extras.

Lowest completed first-class innings total to include a triple-century

387 all out – The Rest against The Hindus at Bombay in 1943–44, of which **Vijay Hazare** made 309 (79.84 per cent of his team's total); his team-mates contributing 59 runs, with 19 extras.

BATTING RECORDS

HIGHEST INDIVIDUAL SCORE: TOP 10

Pos	Total	Player	For	Against	Venue	Season
1	501*	B.C. Lara	Warwicks	Durham	Edgbaston	1994
2	499	Hanif Mohammad	Karachi	Bahawalpur	Karachi	1958–59
3	452*	D.G. Bradman	New South Wales	Queensland	Sydney	1929–30
4	443*	B.B. Nimbalkar	Maharashtra	Kathiawar	Poona	1948–49
5	437	W.H. Ponsford	Victoria	Queensland	Melbourne	1927–28
6	429	W.H. Ponsford	Victoria	Tasmania	Melbourne	1922–23
7	428	Aftab Baloch	Sind	Baluchistan	Karachi	1973–74
8	424	A.C. MacLaren	Lancashire	Somerset	Taunton	1895
9	405*	G.A. Hick	Worcestershire	Somerset	Taunton	1988
10	400*	B.C. Lara	West Indies	England	Antigua	2003–04

Most hundreds in consecutive innings

The record for the most hundreds in consecutive innings in first-class cricket is six, a feat achieved by three players: Donald Bradman (in 1938–39), C.B. Fry (in 1901) and Mike Procter (in 1970–71).

Turner plays lone hand in survival

A magnificent performance from overseas player **Glenn Turner** single-handedly ensured that Worcestershire emerged from their 1977 County Championship encounter with Glamorgan at Swansea having suffered nothing worse than a draw. After the home side hit 309 for 4 in their first innings, only the New Zealand Test star stood tall for the visitors, hitting an unbeaten 141 out of a team total of 169 all out, a remarkable 83.43 per cent of his team's runs. It remains the highest percentage of runs scored in a completed innings in first-class cricket history.

Compton's year of years

1947 was the year in which Denis Compton's star shone at its brightest. He scored six centuries for England (including two in a failed Ashes campaign) and ended the year with 1,159 Test runs to his name (at an average of 82.78) to break Clem Hill's record for the most Test runs in a calendar year (1,060) that had stood since 1902. Compton was equally prolific in county cricket that year: in 50 innings for Middlesex and England during the 1947 English domestic season he hit 3,816 runs (at an average of 90.85) – an all-time record in first-class cricket.

Six sixes in an over for Sobers

It was a true milestone in the game and it was achieved, fittingly, by the best player of his generation. Playing for Nottinghamshire against Glamorgan at Swansea in the final match of the 1968 County Championship season, **Garfield Sobers** became the first player in almost a century of first-class cricket to hit six sixes in an over (the unfortunate bowler was Malcolm Nash). The feat has only been repeated once in first-class cricket: by Ravi Shastri (Mumbai v. Baroda at Mumbai in 1984–85, off the bowling of Tilak Rak).

White's one-man show for Somerset at Derby

Set an unlikely 579 runs to win their County Championship Division Two match against Derbyshire at Derby in August 2006, Somerset owed it to their overseas player Cameron White that their eventual margin of defeat (by 80 runs) was not even larger. The Victoria batsman, captaining the side, led from the front, hitting an unbeaten 260 (off 246 balls) as his team-mates capitulated to 498 all out around him. His effort is the highest-ever score by a batsman in the fourth innings of a match in first-class cricket history.

Lara's record-breaking run continues

Brian Lara was on the hottest batting streak in cricket history. Less than two months after breaking Garfield Sobers's world record Test score (Lara hit 375 not out against England at St John's in Antigua on 18 April 1994), he was at it again, this time for Warwickshire in their County Championship match against Durham at Edgbaston. The left-hander hit 501 not out to break Hanif Mohammad's record for the highest score in first-class cricket. His 427-ball innings contained ten sixes and 62 fours – a record number of boundaries by a batsman in a first-class innings.

Brilliant Bradman leads the way

The most prolific batsman to play the game, **Donald Bradman** not only holds the all-time record for the highest career average in Tests (99.94), but also in first-class cricket: in 234 first-class matches for New South Wales, South Australia and Australia between 1927 and 1949 he scored 28,067 runs with 117 centuries, 69 fifties, and a highest score of 452 not out, at an average of 95.14.

Muzumdar's dynamic debut

Amol Muzumdar's introduction to first-class cricket was the most eye-catching in history. Making his debut for Mumbai, against Haryana at Faridabad in the 1993–94 Ranji Trophy, the India Under-19 batsman, a school-mate of India Test legend Sachin Tendulkar, hit 260 – the highest score by any batsman on debut in first-class history (and one of only 12 players in history to score a double-century on debut). Although Muzumdar went on to enjoy a lengthy first-class career, he never hit such heady heights with the bat again – 260 remains his highest first-class score to this day.

For Surrey, read Ramprakash

One man and one man alone was the reason for Surrey's fourth-place finish in the 2007 County Championship. **Mark Ramprakash**, in his 38th year, was in the form of his life, hitting a staggering 30.02 per cent of his team's runs (excluding extras) during the course of the season. The classy right-hander hit 2,026 runs in 16 matches (at an average of 101.30), while his team-mates managed 4,721 runs between them (at an average of 26.08).

MOST CAREER RUNS: TOP 10

Pos	Runs	Player	Mat	Inns	NO	HS	Ave	100	50
1	61,760	J.B. Hobbs (1905–34)	834	1,325	107	316*	50.70	199	273
2	58,959	F.E. Woolley (1906–38)	978	1,530	84	305*	40.77	145	295
3	57,611	E.H. Hendren (1907–37)	833	1,300	166	301*	50.80	170	272
4	55,061	C.P. Mead (1905–36)	814	1,340	185	280*	47.67	153	258
5	54,211	W.G. Grace (1865–1908)	870	1,478	104	344	39.45	124	251
6	50,670	H. Sutcliffe (1919–45)	754	1,098	124	313	52.02	151	230
7	50,551	W.R. Hammond (1920–51)	634	1,005	104	336*	56.10	167	185
8	48,426	G. Boycott (1962–86)	609	1,014	162	261*	56.83	151	238
9	47,793	T.W. Graveney (1948–72)	732	1,223	159	258	44.91	122	233
10	44,846	G.A. Gooch (1973–2000)	581	990	75	333	49.01	128	217

HIGHEST CAREER AVERAGE: TOP 10

Pos	Ave	Player	Mat	Inns	NO	Runs	HS	100	50
1	95.14	D.G. Bradman (1927–49)	234	338	43	28,067	452*	117	69
2	71.64	V.M. Merchant (1929–51)	150	234	46	13,470	359*	45	52
3	69.86	G.A. Headley (1927–54)	103	164	22	9,921	344*	33	44
4	68.47	A.M. Rahane (2007–11)	50	82	11	4,862	265*	18	18
5	67.46	A.K. Sharma (1984–2001)	129	166	16	10,120	259*	38	36
6	65.18	W.H. Ponsford (1920–34)	162	235	23	13,819	437	47	43
7	64.99	W.M. Woodfull (1921–34)	174	245	39	13,388	284	49	58
8	63.52	R.G. Sharma (2006–11)	46	67	8	3,648	309*	12	16
9	63.10	S.S. Sugwekar (1987–2002)	85	122	18	6,563	299*	19	26
10	61.24	K.C. Ibrahim (1938–50)	60	89	12	4,716	250	14	22

MOST CENTURIES IN A CAREER: TOP 10

Pos	100s	Player	Mat	Inns	NO	Runs	HS	Ave
1	199	J.B. Hobbs (1905–34)	834	1,325	107	61,760	316*	50.70
2	170	E.H. Hendren (1907–37)	833	1,300	166	57,611	301*	50.80
3	167	W.R. Hammond (1920–51)	634	1,005	104	50,551	336*	56.10
4	153	C.P. Mead (1905–36)	814	1,340	185	55,061	280*	47.67
5	151	G. Boycott (1962–86)	609	1,014	162	48,426	261*	56.83
=	151	H. Sutcliffe (1919–45)	754	1,098	124	50,670	313	52.02
7	145	F.E. Woolley (1906–38)	978	1,530	84	58,959	305*	40.77
8	136	G.A. Hick (1983–2008)	526	871	84	41,112	405*	52.23
9	129	L. Hutton (1934–55)	513	814	91	40,140	364	55.51
10	128	G.A. Gooch (1973–2000)	581	990	75	44,846	333	49.01

Most centuries for one team

The most prolific run-scorer in the history of the first-class game (with an astonishing 61,760 career runs), **Jack Hobbs** also holds the all-time record for the most centuries scored for a single team: he hit 144 centuries for Surrey in a career that stretched from 1905 to 1934.

Most ducks in a career

A regular behind the stumps for Worcestershire for two decades between the mid-1930s and the mid-1950s, Reg Perks (who played in two Tests for England in 1939) holds the all-time record for the most ducks ever scored in first-class cricket. The keeper failed to trouble the scorers in 156 innings in a 595-match career.

Most innings in a scoreless career

Many cricketers with short first-class careers fail to score a single run, and finish with a batting average of 0.00. Seymour Clark, a wicketkeeper for Somerset in the 1930 season, is believed to hold the record for the most innings in a scoreless career, having played nine innings in his five matches, and finished with seven ducks and two scores of 0 not out. His highest-ever score in club cricket, incidentally, was 3.

Curiosity: the highest 11th-wicket partnership

In 1947 the ICC formally decreed that a first-class match should be between teams of 11 per side and of at least three days' duration. This was not retrospective, and several earlier matches featured teams of more than 11. In such matches the record highest 11th-wicket stand in first-class cricket is 89, by the Nawab of Pataudi and Phiroze Palia for India against the Rest of India at Lahore in 1931–32.

Deadly Derek loses his bite with the bat

The best spin bowler England has ever produced (he took 297 wickets in 86 Tests for his country between 1966 and 1982), "Deadly" **Derek Underwood** was far less lethal with the bat. In a 24-year first-class career (between 1963 and 1987), he registered just one century – 111, for Kent against Sussex at Hastings in 1984. The 591 matches it took him to reach the landmark is an all-time record in first-class cricket.

Longest sequence of consecutive scoreless innings

In 1990, Northamptonshire's Mark Robinson found himself in the record books for all the wrong reasons. Between 16 May (and an innings of 1 against Warwickshire at Northampton) and 15 September (1 not out against Leicestershire at Leicester), he went 12 innings without scoring a single run – a record in first-class cricket. He ended the season with a miserable three runs to his name; but he did altogether better with the ball, taking 40 wickets.

Prolific Ponsford at his best

In 1927, **Bill Ponsford**, a prolific accumulator of runs at the top of the order (he is the only player in history to have recorded two scores of 400-plus in first-class cricket), had a year to remember in 1927, hitting ten centuries in consecutive matches for Victoria (in the Sheffield Shield) and Australia – it is an all-time record for the most consecutive matches in which a batsman has scored a century in first-class cricket history.

Ramprakash in rollicking form

A legend in county cricket whose talent, to the bemused frustration of his many admirers, failed to shine through in Test matches (he averaged 27.32 in 52 Tests for England and made only two centuries – as opposed to 114 centuries in first-class cricket for Middlesex and Surrey), Mark Ramprakash has put any disappointments he may have suffered in the international arena behind him; and in 2010, in his 40th year, he is still one of the most prolific batsmen on the domestic circuit. For a while between June and August 2006 he was in scintillating form for Surrey, stringing together, in five successive matches, knocks of 156, 51 and 155, 167, 301 not out and 30, and 196, to break the all-time first-class cricket record for the most scores of 150-plus in successive matches. The magical run came to an end when he could "only" muster scores of 77 and 31 against Glamorgan at The Oval between 30 August and 1 September 2006.

Holkar's batsmen hit heady heights in Indore

The first Ranji Trophy semi-final between Holkar and Mysore at Indore in March 1946 was as one-sided an affair as could exist in the game. Batting first, Holkar raced to a mighty 912 for 8 declared, with centuries from Kamal Chandarkar (142), Chandu Sarwate (101), Madhavsinh Jagdale (164), C.K. Nayudu (101), Bhausaheb Nimbalkar (172) and Ramesh Singh (100). The six centuries scored in an innings is an all-time record in first-class cricket. For the record, Holkar proceeded to win the match by an innings and 213 runs (and went on to beat Baroda in the Ranji Trophy final).

Ending the long wait

Renowned as a tall off-spinner who used his height and unerring accuracy, rather than any great amount of spin imparted on the ball, to forge a successful 16-year career with Lancashire (between 1948 and 1964) and also play in 16 Tests for England, **Roy Tattersall** was resolute in defence with the bat, but not a prolific run-scorer. He holds the all-time first-class record for the most matches played before scoring a maiden half-century (306). The magic moment came when he scored 58 against Leicestershire at Old Trafford in 1958.

HIGHEST PARTNERSHIPS: BY WICKET

Wkt	Runs	Partners	For	Against	Venue	Season
1st	561	Waheed Mirza/Mansoor Akhtar	Karachi Whites	Quetta	Karachi	1976–77
2nd	580	Rafatullah Mohmand/Aamer Sajjad	WPDA	Sui SGC	Sheikhupura	2009–10
3rd	624	K.C. Sangakkara/D.P.M.D. Jayawardene	Sri Lanka	South Africa	Colombo	2006
4th	577	V.S. Hazare/Gul Mohammad	Baroda	Holkar	Baroda	1946–47
5th	520*	C.A. Pujara/R.A. Jadeja	Saurashtra	Orissa	Rajkot	2008–09
6th	487*	G.A. Headley/C.C. Passailaigue	Jamaica	Lord Tennyson's XI	Kingston	1931–32
7th	460	Bhupinder Singh/P. Dharmani	Punjab	Delhi	Delhi	1994–95
8th	433	A. Sims/V.T. Trumper	Australians	Canterbury	Christchurch	1913–14
9th	283	A. Warren/J. Chapman	Derbyshire	Warwickshire	Blackwell	1910
10th	307	A.F. Kippax/J.E.H. Hooker	New South Wales	Victoria	Melbourne	1928–29

BOWLING RECORDS

MOST CAREER WICKETS: TOP 10

Pos	Wkts	Player	Mat	Balls	Runs	BBI	Ave	Econ	SR	5wi	10wm
1	4,204	**W. Rhodes** (1898–1930)	1,110	185,799	70,322	9/24	16.72	2.27	44.1	287	68
2	3,776	A.P. Freeman (1914–36)	592	154,658	69,577	10/53	18.42	2.69	40.9	386	140
3	3,278	C.W.L. Parker (1903–35)	635	157,059	63,817	10/79	19.46	2.43	47.9	277	91
4	3,061	J.T. Hearne (1888–1923)	639	144,470	54,351	9/32	17.75	2.25	47.1	255	66
5	2,979	T.W.J. Goddard (1922–52)	593	142,211	59,116	10/113	19.84	2.49	47.7	251	86
6	2,874	A.S. Kennedy (1907–36)	677	150,851	61,035	10/37	21.23	2.42	52.4	225	45
7	2,857	D. Shackleton (1948–69)	647	159,043	53,303	9/30	18.65	2.01	55.6	194	38
8	2,844	G.A.R. Lock (1946–71)	654	150,168	54,709	10/54	19.23	2.18	52.8	196	50
9	2,830	F.J. Titmus (1949–82)	792	173,489	63,315	9/52	22.37	2.18	61.3	168	26
10	2,809	W.G. Grace (1865–1908)	870	124,831	50,980	10/49	18.14	2.45	44.4	240	64

A day to remember

The second, and ultimately final, day of Kent's County Championship match against Northamptonshire at Northampton, on 31 May 1907, has gone down as one of the most unusual in first-class cricket history and, for Kent slow left-arm bowler Colin "Charlie" Blythe, as the most remarkable of his career. Batting first, Kent made a below-par 254. Enter Blythe: on the second day he took 10 for 30 as the home side fell to 60 all out in their first innings; in the second innings he took 7 for 18 as Northamptonshire, following on, folded to a miserable 31 all out and an innings-and-155-run defeat. Blythe's morning efforts had yielded figures of 17 for 48 – the best in a single day in first-class cricket history.

Lethal Lillywhite marches into history books

William Lillywhite, one of the early exponents of round-arm bowling, enjoyed a remarkable 28-year first-class career for Cambridge Town Club, Hampshire, Middlesex, Surrey and Sussex. In 237 matches between 1825 and 1853, the 5ft 4in fast bowler took 1,576 wickets at an astonishing average of 1.54 runs per wicket – the best average of any bowler in the history of first-class cricket.

Master of his trade

With his smooth, well-balanced run-up, high action and controlled, almost calculated variation, slow left-arm bowler **Hedley Verity** was a true master of his trade. In 378 matches for Yorkshire in the 1930s (he also played in 40 Tests for England) he took an astonishing 1,956 wickets, including a best of 10 for 10 against Nottinghamshire at Headingley in 1932 – the best figures ever recorded in first-class cricket.

Best figures in a match

No bowler has ever managed to better Jim Laker's Ashes-winning feat for England against Australia at Old Trafford in 1956. The Yorkshire off-spin bowler took 9 for 37 in the first innings and a Test-best 10 for 53 in the second to record the best match figures in the history of the game – 19 for 90.

Ten wickets in an innings – all bowled

The best all-round cricketer of his day, who would go on to lend his name to the world's most famous cricket annual, the Wisden Cricketers' Almanack, John Wisden made history playing for the South against the North at Lord's in 1850. In the second innings of the match he became the first, and to date only, bowler in first-class cricket to take all ten wickets clean bowled.

BEST CAREER AVERAGE: TOP 10

Pos	Ave	Player	Mat	Balls	Runs	Wts	BBI	Econ	SR	5	10
1	1.54	F.W. Lillywhite (1825–53)	237	15,265	2,435	1,576	10/?	0.95	9.6	155	55
2	5.43	W. Clarke (1826–55)	143	14,027	4,319	795	9/29	1.84	17.6	82	25
3	6.19	J. Dean Sr (1835–61)	305	23,770	7,084	1,144	9/34	1.78	20.7	86	18
4	6.66	J. Wisden (1845–63)	186	24,208	7,390	1,109	10/58	1.83	21.8	111	39
5	7.73	T. Sherman (1846–70)	82	7,643	2,662	344	8/?	2.08	22.2	29	8
6	9.71	G. Freeman (1865–80)	44	10,075	2,797	288	8/11	1.66	34.9	32	10
7	11.43	J. Jackson (1855–67)	115	20,828	7,491	655	9/27	2.15	31.7	59	20
8	11.69	A. Rylott (1870–88)	85	16,928	5,333	456	9/30	1.89	37.1	39	14
9	11.82	S. Draai (1973–87)	48	7,873	2,506	212	6/21	1.90	37.1	14	3
10	11.95	V.A. Barnes (1978–95)	68	11,481	3,862	323	9/46	2.01	35.5	24	6

Tich stands tall with the ball in his hand

Standing at a mere 5ft 2in, leg-break bowler **Alfred Percy "Tich" Freeman** was one of the greatest and most prolific slow bowlers the game has ever seen. A remarkable performer for Kent, for whom he played 592 matches between 1914 and 1936 (although he failed to replicate his county form for England, playing in only 12 Tests between 1924 and 1929), he set all-time first-class records for the most five-wicket hauls in a career (386); the most ten-wicket hauls in matches (140); and the most wickets in a season (a remarkable 304 in 1928).

Lawrence registers an all-time low

A slow left-arm bowler for Oxford University between 1982 and 1986, Mark Lawrence holds the unusual distinction of having the worst career average of any bowler to have bowled 5,000 balls or more in first-class cricket. In 30 matches for the varsity side he took 42 wickets at an average of 70.92 runs per wicket.

Most runs conceded in an innings

The main victim of Victoria's savage response to New South Wales's first-innings total of 221 in the two states' Sheffield Shield encounter at Melbourne in December 1926 was **Arthur Mailey**. As the home side compiled a world-record total of 1,107 all out, the leg-break bowler bowled 64 (eight-ball) overs, with no maidens, and finished with figures of 4 for 362 – it is the highest number of runs conceded by a bowler in an innings in first-class cricket history. After the match Mailey joked that his figures would have been better had it not been for three dropped catches, "two of them by a man in the pavilion wearing a bowler hat".

OUTSTANDING ANALYSIS (QUALIFICATION: SEVEN WICKETS FOR TEN RUNS OR FEWER)

Figures	Player	For	Against	O-M-R-W	Venue	Season
10 for 10	H. Verity	Yorkshire	Nottinghamshire	19.4-16-10-10	Headingley	1932
9 for 2	G. Elliott	Victoria	Tasmania	19-17-2-9	Launceston	1857–58
9 for 7	Ahad Khan	Railways	Dera Ismail Khan	6.3-4-7-9	Lahore	1964–65
8 for 2	J.C. Laker	England	The Rest	14-12-2-8	Bradford	1950
8 for 4	D. Shackleton	Hampshire	Somerset	11.1-7-4-8	Weston-s-Mare	1955
8 for 5	E. Peate	Yorkshire	Surrey	16-11-5-8	Holbeck	1883
7 for 3	F.R. Spofforth	Australians	England XI	8.3-6-3-7	Edgbaston	1884
7 for 4	W.A. Henderson	NE Transvaal	Orange Free State	9.3-7-4-7	Bloemfontein	1937–38
7 for 4	Rajinder Goel	Haryana	Jammu and Kashmir	7-4-4-7	Chandigarh	1977–78

100 WICKETS IN A SEASON OUTSIDE ENGLAND

Wkts	Player	Season	Country	Runs	Ave
116	M.W. Tate	1926–27	India, Ceylon	1,599	13.78
107	Ijaz Faqih	1985–86	Pakistan	1,719	16.06
106	C.T.B. Turner	1887–88	Australia	1,441	13.59
106	R. Benaud	1957–58	South Africa	2,056	19.39
105	Murtaza Hussain	1995–96	Pakistan	1,882	17.92
104	S.F. Barnes	1913–14	South Africa	1,117	10.74
104	Sajjad Akbar	1989–90	Pakistan	2,328	22.38
103	Abdul Qadir	1982–83	Pakistan	2,367	22.98

250 WICKETS IN A SEASON

Wkts	Player	Season	Overs	Mdns	Runs	Ave
304	A.P. Freeman	1928	1,976.1	423	5,489	18.05
298	A.P. Freeman	1933	2,039	651	4,549	15.26
290	T. Richardson	1895	1,690.1*	463	4,170	14.37
283	C.T.B. Turner	1888	2,427.2**	1,127	3,307	11.68
276	A.P. Freeman	1931	1618	360	4,307	15.60
275	A.P. Freeman	1930	1,914.3	472	4,632	16.84
273	T. Richardson	1897	1,603.4*	495	3,945	14.45
267	A.P. Freeman	1929	1,670.5	381	4,879	18.27
261	W. Rhodes	1900	1,553	455	3,606	13.81

* five-ball overs; ** four-ball overs

Mr Wickets

The most prolific wicket-taker the game of cricket has ever seen, **Wilfred Rhodes** took 4,204 wickets in a 1,110-match first-class career for Yorkshire and England between 1898 and 1930. The slow left-arm bowler also holds the all-time first-class record for registering the most instances of 100 wickets in a season, with 23.

Another oddity

In their match against England at The Oval in 1863, Surrey lost four wickets in the course of a four-ball over from George Bennett. It is the only instance in first-class history of a bowler succeeding with every delivery of an over, albeit an abbreviated one.

Getting off to the best of starts

A top-order batsman and an occasional leg-break bowler, Ricey Phillips had to wait until the fifth match of his first-class career (for Border against Eastern Province at Port Elizabeth in the final match of the 1939–40 South African domestic season) before his captain finally threw him the ball. And what an impact he made: becoming the first, and to date only, bowler in first-class cricket history to take a hat-trick in the first over of his career.

Four wickets in four balls

There have been 31 instances in first-class cricket of bowlers taking four wickets in four balls, but only one instance in which the feat was split over two innings. Nottinghamshire's A.K. Walker dismissed Leicestershire's Firth with the last ball of the first innings and then dismissed Lester, Tompkin and Smithson with his first three balls of the second in the match at Leicester in 1956.

Five wickets in six balls

Five wickets in six balls has been achieved four times: by Bill Copson for Derbyshire against Warwickshire in 1937; by William Henderson for North East Transvaal against Orange Free State at Bloemfontein in 1937–38; by Pat Pocock for Surrey against Sussex at Eastbourne in 1972; and by **Yasir Arafat** for Rawalpindi against Faisalabad at Rawalpindi in 2004–05. Pocock's spell also included six wickets in nine balls and seven wickets in 11 balls, both records.

Seven wickets in 11 balls

Sussex lost five wickets in the course of the final (six-ball) over of their match with Surrey at Eastbourne in 1972. **Pat Pocock,** who had taken three wickets in his previous over, captured four more, taking in all seven wickets in 11 balls, a feat unique in first-class cricket.

Most first-class hat-tricks

England's premier spin bowler in both the pre- and post-Second World War years, Doug Wright was a highly effective leg-break bowler, who delivered the ball at medium pace or faster and, on his day, was unplayable, particularly on the uncovered wickets of the time. In 497 first-class matches for Kent and England (he appeared in 34 Tests taking 108 wickets) between 1932 and 1957, he took 2,056 wickets, with a best return of 9 for 47, and took seven hat-tricks – still a record in first-class cricket.

Underwood spins his way into record books

The record for the most instances of 100 wickets in a season since the reduction of the number of games played in the County Championship in 1969 is five, held by Kent and England's Derek Underwood, who achieved the feat in 1969 (101), 1971 (102), 1978 (110), 1979 (106) and 1983 (106).

Two hat-tricks in a match

There have been seven instances in first-class cricket of a bowler taking two hat-tricks in a match: Alfred Shaw (for Nottinghamshire against Gloucestershire at Nottingham in 1884); Albert Trott (for Middlesex against Somerset at Lord's in 1907); Jimmy Matthews (for Australia against South Africa at Old Trafford in 1912); Charlie Parker (for Gloucestershire against Middlesex at Bristol in 1924); Roly Jenkins (for Worcestershire against Surrey at Worcester in 1949); Joginder Rao (for Services against Northern Punjab at Amritsar in 1963–64); and Amin Lakhani (for the Combined XI against the Indians at Multan in 1978–79). Remarkably, both Trott and Rao's efforts both came in the same innings.

Hearne off to a flier

Only three bowlers in the game's history – Wilfred Rhodes (with 4,207), Tich Freeman (3,776) and Charlie Parker (3,276) – have taken more wickets than Jack Hearne, a fast-medium bowler with a textbook action, who finished his 593-match first-class career for Middlesex and England in 1923 with 3,278 wickets to his name. His best year came in the early part of his career, in 1896, when he became the fastest person in history to take 100 wickets in a season (reaching the milestone on 12 June) and ended the year with a haul of 257 wickets. Charlie Parker equalled Hearne's 12 June feat in 1931.

HAT-TRICK ON DEBUT

Player	Team	Opposition	Venue	Season
H. Hay	South Australia	Lord Hawke's XI	Adelaide	1902–03
H.A. Sedgwick	Yorkshire	Worcestershire	Hull	1906
V.B. Ranjane	Maharashtra	Saurashtra	Poona	1956–57
J.S. Rao	Services	Jammu & Kashmir	Delhi	1963–64
R.O. Estwick	Barbados	Guyana	Bridgetown	1982–83
S.A. Ankola	Maharashtra	Gujarat	Poona	1988–89
J. Srinath	Karnataka	Hyderabad	Secunderabad	1989–90
S.P. Mukherjee	Bengal	Hyderabad	Secunderabad	1989–90
S.M. Harwood	Victoria	Tasmania	Melbourne	2002–03
P. Connell	Ireland	Netherlands	Rotterdam	2008
A. Mithun	Karnataka	Uttar Pradesh	Meerat	2009–10

OTHER RECORDS

Record-breaking wicketkeeper

A fine performer behind the stumps who was forced to play second fiddle to Alan Knott in the England set-up for over half a decade before finally getting, and then seizing, his chance (he made just one Test appearance between February 1971 and December 1977 before going on to enjoy a 57-match international career), **Bob Taylor** was a record-breaker in first-class cricket. In 639 matches for Derbyshire and England between 1960 and 1988 he set the all-time first-class record for the most dismissals – 1,649, with a record 1,473 catches and 176 stumpings.

A safe pair of hands

The second-highest run-scorer in first-class cricket history (he scored 58,959 runs in his career at an average of 40.77), **Frank Woolley** also possessed the safest pair of hands the game has ever seen. In 979 matches for Kent and England between 1906 and 1938 he took an unbelievable 1,018 catches – and remains the only player in history to have surpassed the milestone of 1,000 catches.

Most catches in an innings by a fielder

The record for the most catches in an innings by a fielder is seven, a feat achieved by two players: Mickey Stewart, for Surrey against Northamptonshire at Northampton in 1957; and Tony Brown, for Gloucestershire against Nottinghamshire at Nottingham in 1966.

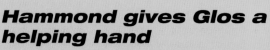

Hammond gives Glos a helping hand

Walter Hammond was the outstanding performer for Gloucestershire in their County Championship match against Surrey at Cheltenham in August 1928. Not only did the England star shine with the bat (hitting 139 in the first innings and 143 in the second), he also played a major role in the field, taking four catches in Surrey's first innings and a sensational six in their second – his ten catches in the match is an all-time record for a fielder in first-class cricket. Gloucestershire went on to win the match by 189 runs.

The fastest hands in world cricket

The first genuine wicketkeeper-batsman in world cricket (he scored 2,434 runs at an average of 40.56 and made 97 dismissals in 47 Tests for England between 1929 and 1939), **Les Ames** was the sharpest gloveman first-class cricket has ever seen. In a career spanning 25 years and 593 matches for Kent and England between 1925 and 1951 he made an all-time record 418 career stumpings.

James stars in bore draw

Hampshire's rain-affected three-day match against the touring Indians at Southampton in June–July 1996 may have meandered into a futile draw, but for **Kevan James** it was a match to remember. In India's first innings, the veteran all-rounder became one of only 31 players in history to take four wickets in four balls. His heroics did not end there: he went on to compile a studied, three-and-a-half-hour 103 to become the only player in first-class cricket history to take four wickets in successive deliveries with the ball and score a century with the bat.

Most matches in career

No player in history has played in more first-class matches than Wilfred Rhodes, the man who personified Yorkshire when the White Rose county was enjoying its heyday (Yorkshire won 12 County Championships during his time there, including four in a row between 1922 and 1925). He appeared in a mighty 1,110 first-class matches for Europeans (India), Maharaja of Patiala's XI, Yorkshire and England between 1898 and 1930.

Giffen's one-man show

A solid right-hand batsman and a slow-medium bowler, George Giffen produced perhaps the finest display in first-class cricket history to help South Australia to an innings-and-164-run victory over Victoria at Adelaide in November 1891. The South Australia captain hit 271 with the bat and proceeded to take 9 for 96 and 7 for 70 with the ball to lead his side to a comfortable victory. He is the only player in history to score 200-plus runs in an innings and take 15-plus wickets in a match in first-class cricket.

James is the undisputed star of the show

Wicketkeeper Wayne James (who would represent Zimbabwe in four Test matches and 11 one-day internationals between 1992 and 1996) enjoyed the best match of his career playing for Matabeleland against Mashonaland at Bulawayo in April 1996. In Mashonaland's first innings (265 all out) he claimed a remarkable nine victims (seven catches and two stumpings) to equal the all-time record for the most dismissals in an innings (set by Tahir Rashid – eight catches and one stumping – playing for Habib Bank against PACO at Gujranwala in 1992–93); he was then dismissed for 99 as Matabeleland made 220 all out in reply. In Mashonaland's second innings (128 all out) he bagged a further four victims (all catches) to break the all-time record for the most dismissals in a match (13). But he was not finished there: in Matabeleland's second innings he hit an unbeaten 99 to guide them to a six-wicket victory.

Vintage year for Parks

Fifth-placed Sussex may have finished a disappointing and distant 55 points adrift of champions Yorkshire in the 1937 County Championship, but for Jim Parks the year signalled the zenith of a 23-year career. Entering his 34th year, the right-hand batsman and slow-medium bowler scored 3,003 runs and took 101 wickets. Unless there is a radical overhaul of the structure of county cricket, the record will never be broken.

All-round perfection for Hirst

Yorkshire had George Hirst to thank for their comfortable 389-run County Championship victory over Somerset at Bath in August 1906. Described by Lord Hawke as "the greatest county cricketer of all time", Hirst scored 111 and 117 not out with the bat and took 6 for 70 and 5 for 45 with the ball to become the first, and to date only, player in first-class cricket history to score a century and take five wickets in both innings of a match. He ended the 1906 season with 2,385 runs and 208 wickets to his name to become the only man in cricket history to score 2,000 runs and take 200 wickets in a season.

20,000 RUNS AND 2,000 WICKETS IN A CAREER

Player	Runs	Ave	Wkts	Ave
W.E. Astill (1906–39)	22,731	22.55	2,431	23.76
T.E. Bailey (1945–67)	28,641	33.42	2,082	23.13
W.G. Grace (1865–1908)	54,896	39.55	2,876	17.92
G.H. Hirst (1891–1929)	36,323	34.13	2,739	18.72
R. Illingworth (1951–83)	24,134	28.06	2,072	20.28
W. Rhodes (1898–1930)	39,802	30.83	4,187	16.71
M.W. Tate (1912–37)	21,717	25.01	2,784	18.16
F.J. Titmus (1949–82)	21,588	23.11	2,830	22.37
F.E. Woolley (1906–38)	58,969	40.75	2,068	19.85

LIST A MATCHES

According to the ICC's Classification of Official Cricket released in 2006, matches that fall under the List A category are all limited-overs matches that are either one-day internationals, other international limited-over matches, limited-overs matches from premier one-day tournaments in domestic cricket or official one-day matches between touring teams and first-class teams.

HIGHEST INNINGS TOTALS: TOP 5

Pos	Total	Overs	For	Against	Venue	Season
1	496–4	50	Surrey	Gloucestershire	The Oval	2007
2	443–9	50	Sri Lanka	Netherlands	Amstelveen	2006
3	438–5	50	Surrey	Glamorgan	The Oval	2002
4	438–9	49.5	South Africa	Australia	Johannesburg	2005–06
5	434–4	50	Australia	South Africa	Johannesburg	2005–06

LOWEST INNINGS TOTALS: TOP 5

Pos	Total	Overs	For	Against	Venue	Season
1	18	14.3	West Indies U19	Barbados	Guyana	2007–08
2	23	19.4	Middlesex	Yorkshire	Leeds	1974
3	30	20.4	Chittagong B	Sylhet Division	Dhaka	2002-03
4	31	13.5	Border	South Western Districts	East London	2007–08
5	34	21.1	Saurashtra	Mumbai	Mumbai	1999–2000

Indiscipline costs Durham dear

Durham's slip-shod performance in the field was the principal reason for their four-wicket defeat by Derbyshire in the two sides' NatWest Trophy second-round encounter at Darlington played over 6 and 7 July 1994. Defending 278, Durham conceded a staggering and all-time List A record 62 extras (20 leg-byes, 21 wides and 21 no-balls) as Derbyshire eased to victory with 11 balls to spare.

The Jo'burg run-fest

South Africa's rollicking run-chase at Johannesburg on 12 March 2006, which saw them successfully chase down Australia's mighty total of 434 for 4 with one wicket and one ball to spare to clinch the five-match series 3–2, not only provided the scene for perhaps the most highly entertaining one-day international match in history, but also ensured the game entered the record books. The 872 runs scored in the match (for the loss of 13 wickets) is an all-time aggregate record in List A cricket.

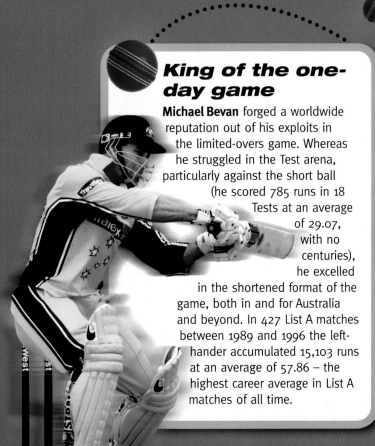

King of the one-day game

Michael Bevan forged a worldwide reputation out of his exploits in the limited-overs game. Whereas he struggled in the Test arena, particularly against the short ball (he scored 785 runs in 18 Tests at an average of 29.07, with no centuries), he excelled in the shortened format of the game, both in and for Australia and beyond. In 427 List A matches between 1989 and 1996 the left-hander accumulated 15,103 runs at an average of 57.86 – the highest career average in List A matches of all time.

Herschelle hits the heights

In the 30th over of South Africa's ICC World Cup Group A match against the Netherlands at St Kitts on 16 March 2007, **Herschelle Gibbs** showed exactly why he is regarded as one of the most exciting batsmen of modern times. He became only the third man in the game's history (alongside Garfield Sobers and Ravi Shastri) – and the only player in a List A match – to hit six sixes in an over.

MOST RUNS IN A CAREER: TOP 10

Pos	Runs	Player	Mat	Inns	NO	HS	Ave	50	100
1	22,211	**G.A. Gooch** (1973–97)	613	601	48	198*	40.16	139	44
2	22,059	G.A. Hick (1983–2008)	651	630	96	172*	41.30	139	40
3	21,999	S.R. Tendulkar (1989–2012)	551	538	55	200*	45.54	114	60
4	16,995	I.V.A. Richards (1973–93)	500	466	61	189*	41.96	109	26
5	16,349	C.G. Greenidge (1970–92)	440	436	33	186*	40.56	94	33
6	16,135	R.T. Ponting (1992–2012)	448	438	53	164	41.90	94	34
7	16,128	S.T. Jayasuriya (1989–2011)	557	542	25	189	31.19	82	31
8	15,658	A.J. Lamb (1972–95)	484	463	63	132*	39.14	98	19
9	15,651	D.L. Haynes (1977–97)	419	416	44	152*	42.07	110	28
10	15,622	S.C. Ganguly (1989–2012)	437	421	43	183	41.32	97	31

MOST RUNS IN AN INNINGS: TOP 10

Pos	Runs	Player	For	Against	Venue	Season
1	268	A.D. Brown	Surrey	Glamorgan	The Oval	2002
2	222*	R.G. Pollock	Eastern Province	Border	East London	1974–75
3	219	V. Sehwag	India	West Indies	Indore	2011–12
4	207	Mohammad Ali	Pakistan Customs	Defence Housing Authority	Sialkot	2004–05
5	206	A.I. Kallicharran	Warwickshire	Oxfordshire	Birmingham	1984
6	204*	Khalid Latif	Karachi Dolphins	Quetta Bears	Karachi	2008–09
7	203	A.D. Brown	Surrey	Hampshire	Guildford	1997
8	202*	A. Barrow	Natal	South Africa African XI	Durban	1975–76
9	201	V.J. Wells	Leicestershire	Berkshire	Leicester	1996
=	201*	R.S. Bopara	Essex	Leicestershire	Leicester	2008

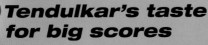

Tendulkar's taste for big scores

Fast closing in on **Graham Gooch**'s all-time record for the most runs scored in List A matches (22,211 runs), **Sachin Tendulkar** (21,999 in April 2012) has had a greater taste for making three-figure scores than any other batsman in List A cricket history. India's batting maestro has compiled 60 innings of a hundred or more in 551 List A matches between 1989 and 2012, with a highest score of 200 not out for India against South Africa at Gwalior on 24 February 2010.

On a hot streak

All-rounder Mike Procter was one of the most naturally talented cricketers ever to play the game. Sadly, owing to South Africa's exclusion from international cricket during the Apartheid years, the world was denied the opportunity of seeing Procter perform in his prime on the international stage. When he was at his best, he was simply brilliant: playing for Rhodesia in the 1970–71 South African domestic season, he became the first, and to date only, player in history to hit six consecutive hundreds in List A matches.

Somerset class too much for minnows Devon

The gulf in class verged on becoming painful to watch as Somerset cruised past Devon in their NatWest Trophy first-round encounter at Torquay on 27 June 1990. Batting first, Somerset, thanks to centuries from **Chris Tavaré** (162 not out) and Graham Rose (110), reached 413 for 4 off their 60 overs. They then dismissed Devon for 67 (with Roland Lefebvre taking 7 for 15) to secure a 346-run victory – the largest margin of victory (by runs) in any List A match.

MOST WiCKETS: TOP 10

Pos	Wkts	Player	Mat	Balls	Runs	BBI	Ave	Econ	SR	4w	5w
1	881	**Wasim Akram** (1984–2003)	594	29,719	19,303	5/10	21.91	3.89	33.7	34	12
2	684	A.A. Donald (1985–2004)	458	22,856	14,941	6/15	21.84	3.92	33.4	27	11
3	682	M. Muralitharan (1991–2011)	453	23,734	15,270	7/30	22.39	3.85	35.1	17	12
4	674	J.K. Lever (1968–90)	481	23,208	13,278	5/8	19.70	3.43	34.4	26	8
=	674	Waqar Younis (1988–2004)	411	19,811	15,083	7/36	22.37	4.56	29.3	27	17
6	647	J.E. Emburey (1975–2000)	536	26,399	16,811	5/23	25398	3.82	40.8	23	3
7	612	I.T. Botham (1973–93)	470	22,899	15,264	5/27	24.94	3.99	37.4	15	3
8	598	D. Gough (1990–2008)	420	20,665	14,457	7/27	24.17	4.19	34.5	21	7
9	573	S.M. Pollock (1992–2008)	435	21,588	13,141	6/21	22.93	3.65	37.6	18	7
10	572	D.L. Underwood (1963–87)	411	19,825	11,099	8/31	19.40	3.35	34.6	25	8

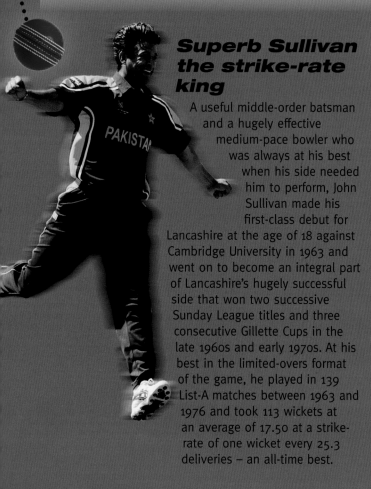

Superb Sullivan the strike-rate king

A useful middle-order batsman and a hugely effective medium-pace bowler who was always at his best when his side needed him to perform, John Sullivan made his first-class debut for Lancashire at the age of 18 against Cambridge University in 1963 and went on to become an integral part of Lancashire's hugely successful side that won two successive Sunday League titles and three consecutive Gillette Cups in the late 1960s and early 1970s. At his best in the limited-overs format of the game, he played in 139 List-A matches between 1963 and 1976 and took 113 wickets at an average of 17.50 at a strike-rate of one wicket every 25.3 deliveries – an all-time best.

Most five-wicket hauls

One of only five bowlers in history to have taken more than 650 wickets in List matches (he took 674), **Waqar Younis** was not the most prolific of wicket-takers in the shortened format of the game (that honour falls to his new-ball partner in crime Wasim Akram) but, with an ability to reverse-swing the ball at extreme pace, he was one of the deadliest. He holds the all-time record for the most five-wicket hauls in List A matches with 17 in 411 matches for Glamorgan, Karachi, Lahore, Multan, National Bank of Pakistan, Rawalpindi, Redco Pakistan Ltd, Surrey, United Bank Limited and Pakistan between 1988 and 2004.

The leanest spell in history

The wicket may well have suited him, but, nevertheless, Brian Langford produced an unplayable spell of bowling for Somerset in their Sunday League encounter with Essex at Yeovil on 27 July 1979. Bowling off-spin, the Somerset captain took 0 for 0 off his eight overs – setting an all-time record low economy rate in an innings in List A matches that cannot be beaten (0.00). Somerset went on to win the match by two wickets.

Fred Rumsey: the ultimate one-day bowler

A left-arm fast-medium bowler who, at the peak of his powers, was good enough to play five Test matches for England between 1964 and 1965 (taking 17 wickets), Fred Rumsey was at his best in the one-day arena, so much so that in the final five years of his career it was the only form of the game he played. In 95 List A matches for Derbyshire, Somerset, Worcestershire and England between 1963 and 1973 his career economy rate was 2.73 runs per over – an all-time record in List A cricket for any bowler who has bowled 2,500 balls or more.

Lacking a cutting edge

A steady line-and-length bowler who relied on seam and swing movement to trouble opposition batsmen, Pommie Mbangwa was good enough to play 15 Tests and 29 one-day internationals for Zimbabwe between 1996 and 2002, but his lack of pace left him without that vital cutting edge. He holds two unwanted all-time records: of all bowlers to have bowled 2,500 balls or more in List A matches (of which Mbangwa played 64, for Mashonaland, Matabeleland and Zimbabwe between 1995 and 2004) he has the worst career bowling average (54.39) and the worst career strike-rate (taking a wicket every 75.5 deliveries).

BEST FIGURES IN AN INNINGS: TOP 10

Pos	Figures	Player	For	Against	Venue	Season
1	8–15	R.L. Sanghvi	Delhi	Himachal Pradesh	Una	1997–98
2	8–19	W.P.U.J.C. Vaas	Sri Lanka	Zimbabwe	Colombo	2001–02
3	8–20	D.T. Kottehewa	Nondescripts CC	Ragama CC	Colombo	2007–08
4	8–21	M.A. Holding	Derbyshire	Sussex	Hove	1988
5	8–26	K.D. Boyce	Essex	Lancashire	Old Trafford	1971
6	8–30	G.D.R. Eranga	Burgher RC	Sri Lanka Army SC	Colombo	2007–08
7	8–31	D.L. Underwood	Kent	Scotland	Edinburgh	1987
8	8–43	S.W. Tait	South Australia	Tasmania	Adelaide	2003–04
9	8–52	K.A. Stoute	West Indies A	Lancashire	Old Trafford	2010
10	8–66	S.R.G. Francis	Somerset	Derbyshire	Derby	2004

Rhodes the record-breaker

A consistent performer behind the stumps (and good enough to play in 11 Tests for England between 1994 and 1995), **Steve Rhodes** bagged more victims in List A matches than any other wicket-keeper in history. One of Wisden's five Cricketers of the Year in 1994, he claimed 661 dismissals in 477 matches for Yorkshire, Worcestershire and England between 1984 and 2004.

Highest partnership

An all-time record in one-day international cricket, the second-wicket partnership of 331 between Sachin Tendulkar (186 not out) and Rahul Dravid (153) for India against New Zealand at Hyderabad on 8 November 1999 is also the highest-ever partnership in List A matches and one of only three 300-plus partnerships in history – the others being: Ghulam Ali and Sohail Jaffar's unbeaten partnership of 326 for PIA against ADBP at Sialkot in 2000–01; and Tim Curtis and Tom Moody's unbeaten partnership of 309 for Worcestershire against Surrey at The Oval in 1994.

Room to improve

A former England Under-19 bowler who made his first-class debut for Somerset in 2000, Gareth Andrew switched to Worcestershire in 2007 but, despite the move, has still failed to fulfil his early potential on a regular basis. In 93-match List-A career, he has taken a respectable 94 wickets at an average of 34.41, but he has also gone for 6.30 runs per over – the worst economy rate in history of any bowler to have bowled 2,500 balls or more in List-A matches.

Most matches

No cricketer has played more List A matches in a career than **Graeme Hick,** who played in 651 matches for Zimbabwe, Chandigarh Lions, Northern Districts, Queensland, Worcestershire and England between 1984 and 2008.

5,000 RUNS AND 500 WICKETS

Player	Mat	Runs	HS	Ave	100	Wkts	BBI	Ave	5w	Ct	St
C.E.B. Rice (1970–94)	479	13,474	169	37.32	11	517	6/18	22.64	6	174	0
I.T. Botham (1973–93)	470	10,474	175*	29.50	7	612	5/27	24.94	3	196	0
Imran Khan (1973–92)	425	10,100	114*	33.22	5	507	6/14	22.31	6	84	0
Wasim Akram (1984–2003)	594	6,993	89*	18.90	0	881	5/10	21.91	12	147	0
P.A.J. DeFreitas (1985–2004)	479	5,181	90	18.56	0	539	5/13	27.92	7	101	0
S.M. Pollock (1992–2008)	435	5,494	134*	26.66	3	573	6/21	22.93	7	153	0

TWENTY20 CRICKET

Introduced first in England in 2003 to arrest the decline in the number of spectators attending domestic cricket, Twenty20 cricket proved enormously popular and soon spread to all parts of the world, providing fans with some scintillating cricket along the way.

HIGHEST TOTALS: TOP 5

Score	For	Overs	RR	Inns	Against	Venue	Date
260–6	Sri Lanka	20.0	13.00	1	Kenya	Johannesburg	14 Sep 2007
254–3	Gloucestershire	20.0	12.70	1	Middlesex	Uxbridge	26 Jun 2011
250–3	Somerset	20.0	12.50	1	Gloucs	Taunton	27 Jun 2006
246–5	Chennai	20.0	12.30	1	Rajasthan	Chennai	3 Apr 2010
245–4	Nondescripts	20.0	12.25	1	SL Air SC	Colombo	16 Oct 2005

LOWEST TOTALS: TOP 5

Score	Team	Overs	RR	Inns	Opposition	Venue	Date
30	Tripura	11.1	2.68	1	Jharkhand	Dhanbad	20 Oct 2009
44	Leeward Isl.	12.5	3.42	2	Trinidad & T	North Sound	11 Jan 2012
47	Titans	14.3	3.24	1	Eagles	Centurion	28 Apr 2004
47	Northants	12.5	3.66	2	Durham	Chester-le-S.	14 Jul 2011
55	Namibia	10.4	5.15	2	Scotland	Windhoek	5 Oct 2011

One for the future

A standout performer for Namibia at the 2006 Under-19 World Cup in Sri Lanka (at which he topped his country's bowling averages), Louis van der Westhuizen has made a seamless transition from youth to senior cricket and has put in some eye-catching performances, particularly with the bat. In 15 Twenty20 matches to date he has scored 402 runs (with a highest score of 145) at a strike-rate of 183.56 runs per 100 deliveries – an all-time record in the 20-over format of the game.

Most consecutive wins

The power team of domestic Twenty20 cricket in Pakistan, the Sialkot Stallions have produced the longest winning streak in Twenty20 history, stringing together 25 successive victories between 24 February 2006 and 10 October 2010.

Cobras shock the Titans

When the Titans, led by a 27-ball 71 from Albie Morkel, posted 220 for 4 off their 20-over allocation in the second leg of the Standard Bank Pro20 Series semi-final against Cape Cobras at Centurion on 9 March 2011, they would have had every reason to be confident of victory. But the Cobras had other ideas: opener Richard Levi hit a 31-ball 60 and Owais Shah a 34-ball 64 to help the visitors over the winning line with five wickets and two balls to spare. Their score of 224 for 5 is the highest by any team batting second in Twenty20 history.

Harris's record-breaking swansong

A stalwart for New Zealand in limited-overs cricket for over a decade between 1992 and 2004 (he was the first New Zealand player to appear in 250 one-day internationals), **Chris Harris** was in the twilight of his career when Twenty20 cricket arrived, but, in the few matches he has played, he has made a considerable impact. In 25 innings for Canterbury between 2006 and 2011 he scored 636 runs at an average of 70.66 – the highest career average of any player to have completed ten innings or more in Twenty20 cricket.

Most sixes in a career

There is no bigger hitter in Twenty20 cricket than Chris Gayle. In 92 matches for Barisal Burners, Jamaica, Kolkata Knight Riders, Matabeleland Tuskers, PCA Masters XI, Royal Challengers Bangalore, Stanford Superstars, Sydney Thunder, West Indians, West Indies and Western Australia between 2005 and 2012 the hard-hitting left-hander has struck 222 sixes – an all-time record in the 20-over format of the game.

MOST RUNS: TOP 10

Pos	Runs	Player	Mat	Inns	NO	HS	Ave	BF	SR	100	50	0
1	4,251	**D.J. Hussey (2004–11)**	169	164	31	100*	31.96	3115	136.46	1	24	13
2	4,226	B.J. Hodge (2003–11)	144	140	23	106	36.11	3319	127.32	2	29	10
3	3,744	B.B. McCullum (2005–12)	131	130	15	158*	32.55	2728	137.24	4	18	6
4	3,520	O.A. Shah (2003–12)	136	129	29	80	35.20	2698	130.46	0	20	7
5	3,368	D.A. Warner (2007–12)	117	117	8	135*	30.89	2356	142.95	4	19	9
6	3,237	C.H. Gayle (2005–12)	92	91	12	117	40.97	2090	154.88	7	19	10
7	3,227	H.H. Gibbs (2004–12)	137	134	9	101*	25.81	2562	125.95	1	23	19
8	3,002	L.R.P.L. Taylor (2006–12)	123	115	23	111*	32.63	2043	146.94	1	15	6
9	2,800	S.B. Styris (2005–12)	137	127	18	106*	25.68	2089	134.03	1	9	2
10	2,775	K.C. Sangakkara (2004–11)	101	97	8	94	31.17	2151	129.00	0	18	8

Most consecutive defeats

The Quetta Bears, who play in Pakistan's domestic Twenty20 cricket competition, hold the all-time record for the most consecutive defeats in the T20 format of the game. Between 25 April 2005 and 27 September 2011 they slumped to 22 consecutive defeats.

Big-hitting Napier puts Sussex to the sword

By 2008, after a couple of injury-blighted seasons, Graham Napier, a useful hard-hitting batsman and medium-pace bowler (particularly in limited-overs cricket) found himself some way down the pecking order with his county side, Essex. Then, on 24 June 2008, he produced an innings that sent shockwaves around the world. Batting at No. 3 for Essex in their South Division Twenty20 match against Sussex at Chelmsford, he bludgeoned a spectacular 58-ball 152 not out, an innings that contained 16 sixes – the most by a player in a single innings in Twenty20 history. Essex went on to win the match by 128 runs.

Harvey's century-making heroics

A hard-hitting lower-order batsman and a medium-pace bowler with one of the deadliest slower balls in the business, **Ian Harvey** may have struggled to establish himself in international cricket with Australia (playing 73 one-day internationals over a seven-year period), but he has achieved almost legendary status in county cricket in England (playing for Gloucestershire, Hampshire, Northamptonshire and Yorkshire), particularly for his exploits in Twenty20 cricket. He was the first player in history to reach three figures in the 20-over game (100 not out for Gloucestershire against Warwickshire at Edgbaston on 23 June 2003) and has passed 100 on a further two occasions.

HIGHEST SCORES: TOP 5

Pos	Runs	Player	Balls	4s	6s	SR	For	Against	Venue	Date
1	158*	B.B. McCullum	73	10	13	216.43	Kolkata	Bangalore	Bangalore	18 Apr 2008
2	152*	G.R. Napier	58	10	16	262.06	Essex	Sussex	Chelmsford	24 Jun 2008
3	145	LP vd Westhuizen	50	14	12	290.00	Namibia	Kenya	Windhoek	7 Nov 2011
3	141*	C.L. White	70	14	6	201.42	Somerset	Worcs	Worcester	9 Jul 2006
5	135*	D.A. Warner	69	11	8	195.65	NSW	Super Kings	Chennai	4 Oct 2011

MOST WICKETS: TOP 10

Pos	Wkts	Player	Mat	Overs	Mdns	Runs	BBI	Ave	Econ	SR	4	5
1	175	**D.P. Nannes** (2007–12)	139	509.5	7	3664	5/40	20.93	7.18	17.4	5	1
2	149	A.C. Thomas (2004–12)	129	429.3	9	3093	4/27	20.75	7.20	17.2	1	0
3	145	Yasir Arafat (2006–12)	123	415.4	5	3297	4/17	22.73	7.93	17.2	5	0
4	137	Shahid Afridi (2004–12)	108	393.4	4	2513	5/20	18.34	6.38	17.2	4	1
5	132	J.A. Morkel (2004–12)	163	456.0	7	3652	4/30	27.66	8.00	20.7	2	0
6	125	S.L. Malinga (2004–11)	95	337.4	5	2260	5/13	18.08	6.69	16.2	2	1
7	124	M. Muralitharan (2005–12)	108	405.0	5	2598	4/16	20.95	6.41	19.5	3	0
8	121	Saeed Ajmal (2005–12)	83	299.5	6	1905	4/14	15.74	6.35	14.8	5	0
=	121	C.K. Langeveldt (2004–12)	93	327.3	4	2470	5/16	20.41	7.54	16.2	4	1
10	120	Azhar Mahmood (2003–12)	117	394.5	4	2991	4/20	24.92	7.57	19.7	2	0

A keen eye for a wicket

A pugnacious all-rounder who played in four Tests and 35 one-day internationals for England, Adam Hollioake's medium-pace bowling – and his "knuckle" ball in particular – proved enormously effective in Twenty20 cricket. In 22 matches for Surrey and Essex between 2003 and 2007 he took 40 wickets in 64.1 overs at a strike-rate of one wicket every 9.6 deliveries – the best in history by any player to have bowled 300 balls or more in Twenty20 matches.

Most dismissals

The leading wicketkeeper in Twenty20 cricket is Kamran Akmal. The Lahore-born keeper, an outstanding performer for Pakistan in all three ICC World Twenty20 tournaments and in the Indian Premier League (for Rajasthan Royals), has claimed 102 dismissals (with 50 catches and 52 stumpings) in 86 matches for Lahore Eagles, Lahore Lions, Rajasthan Royals and Pakistan between 2005 and 2012.

From obscurity to the record books

A left-arm medium pace bowler and a former West Indies Under-15 bowler who made his List A debut in 2007, Krishmar Santokie's career seemed to be spiralling towards anonymity, but an injury to Jerome Taylor offered him a chance of redemption for Jamaica in the inaugural Caribbean Twenty20 in 2010 and he grasped the opportunity with both hands, taking ten wickets in the tournament and going for only 5.50 runs per over. His international T20 debut came the following season and by 2012 he had taken 48 wickets in 22 T20 matches at an incredible average of 9.43 – the best ever by any bowler to have bowled 300 balls or more in Twenty20.

Mr Twenty20

David Hussey's exploits in international cricket may have been overshadowed by those of his elder brother Mike, but he has always been a standout performer in domestic cricket over the years and has produced the goods in Twenty20 cricket. No one has scored more runs (4,251 at an average of 31.96), played in more matches (169 for Australia, Australia A, Kings XI Punjab, Kolkata Knight Riders, Melbourne Stars, Northern Districts, Nottinghamshire and Victoria between 2004 and 2012) or taken more catches (96 – at an average of 0.568 catches per match).

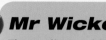

Badree shows his mean streak

A leg-spin bowler of early promise who made his first-class debut for Trinidad and Tobago in the 2001–02 season but then failed to nail down a regular place in the side, Samuel Badree has redefined himself as an extremely effective bowler in the limited-overs formats of the game, particularly Twenty20 cricket. He has played in 39 matches, bowled 436 deliveries and conceded just 589 runs. His economy rate of 4.40 runs conceded per over, is the best by any bowler in Twenty20 history.

Mr Wickets

The undisputed king of bowling in Twenty20 cricket (he was a star for Pakistan in both the 2007 and 2009 ICC World Twenty20 tournaments), **Umar Gul** holds the record for the most four-wicket-plus hauls in Twenty20 cricket, with seven in 78 matches for Peshawar Panthers, Kolkata Knight Riders, Western Australia and Pakistan between 2005 and 2012.

Aussie duo in prime form for Punjab

A swashbuckling second-wicket partnership of 206 runs – the highest partnership for any wicket in Twenty20 history – between Australian overseas players **Adam Gilchrist** (106 off 55 balls) and Shaun Marsh (79 off 49 balls) propelled Kings XI Punjab to a massive total of 232 for 2 against Bangalore in the two sides' group match in the 2011 Indian Premier League at Dharamsala on 17 May 2011. The visitors did not come close to reaching the target, crashing to 121 all out in 17 overs to lose the match by 111 runs.

Most man of the match awards

The all-time record for the most Man of the Match awards received by a player in Twenty20 matches is 16, a feat achieved by three players: **Brad Hodge** (below, for Durham, Kolkata Knight Riders, Lancashire, Leicestershire, Victoria and Australia); Chris Gayle (for Barisal Burners, Kolkata Knight Riders, PCA XI, Royal Challengers Bangalore, Stanford Superstars, Sydney Thunders, Western Australia and the West Indies; and Azhar Mahmood (for Auckland, Dhaka Gladiators, Kent Leopards, Surrey and Pakistan).

Best figures in an innings when on a losing side

The best-ever figures recorded in Twenty20 cricket by a bowler who has ended up on the losing side are 6 for 25, achieved by two players: Irfanuddin (4.0-0-25-6 for Karachi Dolphins against Sialkot Stallions at Karachi on 3 March 2006 – a match Sialkot won by 29 runs); and Michael Dighton (3.0-0-25-6 for Tasmania against Queensland at Toowoomba on 1 January 2007 – a match Queensland won by 38 runs).

Most maidens

No bowler has bowled more maidens in Twenty20 cricket than Praveen Kumar. The medium-pacer, fast developing a reputation as one of the most effective line-and-length bowlers in the game, has delivered a record ten maidens in 74 matches (for India, Indians, Kings XI Punjab, Royal Challengers Bangalore and Uttar Pradesh) between 2007 and 2012.

Mascarenhas makes his mark

It did not take Dmitri Mascarenhas long to prove his immense value as a Twenty20 bowler. On 9 July 2004, playing for Hampshire against Sussex at Hove, he dismissed Mark Davis (caught), Mushtaq Ahmed (bowled) and Jason Lewry (caught) in successive deliveries to record the first hat-trick (of 49) in T20 history.

BEST FIGURES IN AN INNINGS: TOP 5

Pos	Player	O	M	R	W	Econ	For	Against	Venue	Date
1	A.V. Suppiah	3.4	0	5	6	1.36	Somerset	Glamorgan	Cardiff	5 Jul 2011
2	Sohail Tanvir	4.0	0	14	6	3.50	Rajasthan	Chennai	Jaipur	4 May 2008
3	S.R. Abeywardene	4.0	0	15	6	3.75	Panadura	SL Air SC	Colombo	30 Oct 2005
4	T.G. Southee	4.0	0	16	6	4.00	Essex	Glamorgan	Chelmsford	8 Jul 2011
=	B.A.W. Mendis	4.0	1	16	6	4.40	Sri Lanka	Australia	Pallekele	8 Aug 2011

INDIAN PREMIER LEAGUE

First contested in 2008, principally off the back of the surge of enthusiasm in India for the new format of the game following the country's 2007 ICC World Twenty20 triumph, the Indian Premier League (IPL), featuring eight franchises, has been a huge success, attracting vast crowds and the best players from around the world.

Cashing in in Chennai

Chennai hit their stride in spectacular and record-breaking fashion against Rajasthan at Chennai on 3 April 2010. Having won the toss and elected to bat they put the Royals' bowlers to the sword, with Murali Vijay hitting a 56-ball 127 and Albie Morkel swatting a 34-ball 62 to take them to 246 for 5 – the highest team total in IPL history. The Royals made a creditable 223 for 5 in reply as Chennai went on to win the match by 23 runs.

INDIAN PREMIER LEAGUE WINNERS

2008	Rajasthan Royals
2009	Deccan Chargers
2010	**Chennai Super Kings**
2011	Chennai Super Kings

McCullum takes centre stage

As the entire world looked on with reserved anticipation, a Hollywood scriptwriter could not have come up with a better first act for the first-ever match in the IPL – Kolkata against Bangalore at Bangalore on 18 April 2008. And if the script was sensational, Brendon McCullum's performance with the bat was the star turn. The Kolkata opener bludgeoned the highest individual score in Twenty20 history, 158 not out off 73 deliveries – an innings that contained a tournament record 13 sixes, to lead his side to a mighty 222 for 3 and an eventual 140-run victory.

RESULT SUMMARY

Team (Span)	Mat	Won	Lost	Tied	NR	%
Chennai Super Kings (2008–11)	62	37	24	1	0	60.48
Deccan Chargers (2008–11)	60	25	35	0	0	41.66
Delhi Daredevils (2008–11)	57	28	28	0	1	50.00
Kings XI Punjab (2008–11)	57	27	29	1	0	48.24
Kochi Tuskers Kerala (2011)	14	6	8	0	0	42.85
Kolkata Knight Riders (2008–11)	55	24	30	1	0	44.54
Mumbai Indians (2008–11)	59	33	26	0	0	55.93
Pune Warriors (2011)	14	4	9	0	1	30.76
Rajasthan Royals (2008–11)	56	30	25	1	0	54.46
Royal Challengers Bangalore (2008–11)	62	31	31	0	0	50.00

Rajasthan Royals lose grip of IPL crown

Rajasthan's defence of the IPL crown they won in spectacular style in 2007 got off to the worst of starts against Bangalore at Cape Town in 18 April 2009. Having restricted their opponents to an under-par 133 for 8, the Royals' batsmen slumped in less than regal fashion to 58 all out – the lowest team total in all IPL matches – and a 75-run defeat.

MOST RUNS: TOP 10

Pos	Runs	Player	Mat	Inns	NO	HS	Ave	BF	SR	100	50	0	4s	6s
1	1,813	**S.K. Raina** (2008–11)	62	60	10	98	36.26	1292	140.32	0	13	1	153	78
2	1,723	S.R. Tendulkar (2008–11)	51	51	8	100*	40.06	1434	120.15	1	10	2	218	20
3	1,603	A.C. Gilchrist (2008–11)	60	60	1	109*	27.16	1123	142.74	2	9	6	177	82
4	1,556	J.H. Kallis (2008–11)	57	56	8	89*	32.41	1387	112.18	0	14	5	173	27
5	1,542	R.G. Sharma (2008–11)	61	58	9	87	31.46	1187	129.90	0	11	3	128	64
6	1,475	G. Gambhir (2008–11)	55	54	8	86	32.06	1191	123.84	0	10	3	176	15
7	1,425	M.S. Dhoni (2008–11)	59	51	15	70*	39.58	1028	138.61	0	8	2	111	55
8	1,384	V. Sehwag (2008–11)	50	50	3	119	29.44	816	169.60	1	9	4	168	60
9	1,367	K.C. Sangakkara (2008–11)	50	47	2	94	30.37	1072	127.51	0	9	4	161	23
10	1,294	Y.K. Pathan (2008–11)	58	53	5	100	26.95	828	156.28	1	6	1	113	74

Star of the show

He may have come with a hefty price tag, but Adam Gilchrist has been a standout performer for both the Deccan Chargers (who he led to the title in 2009) and Kings XI Punjab during his stint in the Indian Premier League and no batsman has hit more sixes: 82 in 60 matches between 2008 and 2011.

Largest victories

By runs: by 140 runs – Kolkata v Bangalore at Bangalore on 18 April 2008.

By wickets: by ten wickets on four occasions.

By balls remaining: with 87 balls remaining – Mumbai v Kolkata at Mumbai on 16 May 2008.

Smallest victories

By runs: by one run on two occasions – Punjab v Mumbai at Mumbai on 21 May 2008; and Punjab v Deccan at Johannesburg on 17 May 2009.

By wickets: by two wickets – Bangalore v Chennai at Durban on 14 May 2009.

By balls remaining: off the last ball of the match on eight occasions.

Most scores of 50 or over

Controversially left out of South Africa's side for the inaugural ICC World Twenty20 because the selectors questioned his worth in the 20-over game, Jacques Kallis has shone for Bangalore and Kolkata in the IPL. He has made 14 half-centuries in 57 matches – an all-time record in the IPL.

Tendulkar shines for the Indians

Sachin Tendulkar had memorable IPL season for the Mumbai Indians in 2010. The legendary batsman compiled a single-season record of 618 runs, at an average of 47.53, and a strike-rate of 132.61 runs per 100 deliveries.

HIGHEST INDIVIDUAL SCORE: TOP 10

Pos	Runs	Player	Balls	4s	6s	SR	Team	Opposition	Ground	Date
1	158*	B.B. McCullum	73	10	13	216.43	Kolkata	Bangalore	Bangalore	18 Apr 2008
2	127	M. Vijay	56	8	11	226.78	Kings	Rajasthan	Chennai	3 Apr 2010
3	120*	P.C. Valthaty	63	19	2	190.47	Punjab	Kings	Mohali	13 Apr 2011
4	119	V. Sehwag	56	13	6	212.50	Delhi	Deccan	Hyderabad	5 May 2011
5	117*	A. Symonds	53	11	7	220.75	Deccan	Rajasthan	Hyderabad	24 Apr 2008
6	116*	M.E.K. Hussey	54	8	9	214.81	Kings	Punjab	Mohali	19 Apr 2008
7	115	S.E. Marsh	69	11	7	166.66	Punjab	Rajasthan	Mohali	28 May 2008
8	114*	S.T. Jayasuriya	48	9	11	237.50	Mumbai	Kings	Mumbai	14 May 2008
=	114*	M.K. Pandey	73	10	4	156.16	Bangalore	Deccan	Centurion	21 May 2009
10	110*	D.P.M.D. Jayawardene	59	14	3	186.44	Punjab	Kolkata	Kolkata	4 Apr 2010

MOST WICKETS: TOP 10

Pos	Wkts	Player	Mat	Inns	Overs	Mdns	Runs	BBI	Ave	Econ	SR	4	5
1	64	**R.P. Singh** (2008–11)	56	56	203.0	2	1,574	4/22	24.09	7.75	19.0	2	0
2	61	S.L. Malinga (2009–11)	42	42	161.3	4	1,031	5/13	16.90	6.38	15.8	1	1
=	61	A. Mishra (2008–11)	45	45	168.2	3	1,153	5/17	18.90	6.84	16.5	1	1
4	60	P.P. Ojha (2008–11)	54	53	186.1	0	1,328	3/21	22.13	7.13	18.6	0	0
5	58	I.K. Pathan (2008–11)	56	55	195.3	5	1,510	3/24	26.03	7.72	20.2	0	0
6	57	P.P. Chawla (2008–11)	55	55	182.0	1	1,400	4/17	24.56	7.69	19.1	1	0
=	57	S.K. Warne (2008–11)	55	54	199.0	1	1,447	4/21	25.38	7.27	20.9	1	0
8	56	J.A. Morkel (2008–11)	54	53	180.4	3	1,514	4/32	27.03	8.38	19.3	1	0
9	55	M.M. Patel (2008–11)	45	45	157.1	3	1,137	5/21	20.67	7.23	17.1	0	1
10	48	Harbhajan Singh (2008–11)	46	45	160.3	2	1,085	5/18	22.60	6.76	20.0	1	1
=	48	Z. Khan (2008–11)	46	46	170.2	2	1,330	3/21	27.70	7.80	21.2	0	0

Record-breaking road to recovery

Some players have used the Indian Premier League as a platform to launch themselves out of relative obscurity, and one such example is Goa-born Shadab Jakati. After ten relatively unsuccessful seasons in domestic cricket for Goa, the left-arm spinner joined Chennai in 2009 and has shone, taking 26 wickets in 20 matches at a strike-rate of a wicket every 15.4 deliveries – the best in IPL history. He played a major role in Chennai's march to the IPL crown in 2010.

Terrific Tanvir tames the Super Kings

A scintillating spell of bowling from Sohail Tanvir saw Rajasthan cruise to victory over the Chennai Super Kings at Jaipur on 4 May 2008. The left-arm Pakistan paceman, who cost the Royals US$100,000 at auction, took 6 for 14 off his four-over stint – the best bowling figures in Twenty20 history (and the competition's only six-wicket haul) – to send Chennai spinning to 109 all out. Rajasthan cantered to victory for the loss of two wickets with 34 balls to spare.

Chennai's Ashwin the economy rate king

A tall off-spinner whose performances for Chennai in the Indian Premier League have propelled him into the fringes of India's Twenty20 squad, Ravichandran Ashwin is the most miserly bowler in IPL history. Often bowling with the new ball at the start of the innings, he has gone for 694runs in 115.0 overs bowled – an economy rate of 56.03 runs per over (the best in IPL history).

Highest partnership

Kings XI Punjab's Australian duo of Adam Gilchrist (106 off 55 balls) and Shaun Marsh (79 off 49 balls) put Bangalore's bowlers to the sword in an Indian Premier League group match at Dharamsala on 17 May 2011. The pair put on 206 runs for the second wicket – the highest partnership in the tournament's history – to lead their side to a mighty total of 232 for 2 off their 20-over allocation and an eventual 111-run victory.

Most dismissals

Not merely a belligerent performer with the bat (only Suresh Raina and Sachin Tendulkar have scored more runs in the IPL), **Adam Gilchrist** has also shone behind the stumps for the Deccan Chargers: he has claimed 50 dismissals (34 catches, 16 stumpings) in 60 matches – an all-time tournament record.

Malinga prospers for Mumbai

Arguably the best fast bowler Sri Lanka has ever produced, Lasith Malinga's decision to retire from Test cricket in April 2011 to concentrate on the shorter (and more lucrative) formats of the game may have sent ripples of disappointment flooding through the game (more through fear that such a decision may become the norm rather than the exception), but Test cricket's loss has certainly been the Mumbai Indians' gain. The paceman was in electric form for the Indian Premier League franchise in 2011, taking an all-time tournament high 28 wickets at an average of 13.39 at a strike-rate of one wicket every 13.5 deliveries.

Keeping it tight

Wickets are not the be all and end all in Twenty20 cricket; a four-over stint that goes for anything less than six runs per over is a success. Two bowlers have done far better than that, each going for a miserly, tournament-record six runs off his four-over allocation (an economy rate of 1.50): Fidel Edwards (4.0-1-6-0 for Deccan against Kolkata at Cape Town on 19 April 2009); and **Ashish Nehra** (4.0-1-6-1 for Delhi against Punjab at Bloemfontein on 15 May 2009).

Most successful captain

A revelation for India since he took over the captaincy from Rahul Dravid in all forms of the game after leading his side to the ICC World Twenty20 crown in South Africa in 2007, **Mahendra Singh Dhoni** has proved equally inspirational for the Chennai Super Kings. He has guided his side to 36 wins in 59 matches – the most by any captain in the tournament's history – and led his side (the most expensive franchise in the competition) to the IPL crown in 2010 and 2011.

Regal Raina

Suresh Raina has made quite an impact on the Indian Premier League. The Chennai Super Kings left-hander has scored more runs than any other batsman in the competition's history (1,813 in 62 matches at an average of 36.26), has taken the most catches (31 – at an average of 0.500 catches per innings) and has also made his mark with the ball: his spell of 2 for 0 off 0.3 overs against Rajasthan Royals at Jaipur on 9 May 2011 set the Indian Premier League record for the best strike-rate in an innings – one wicket every 1.5 deliveries.

Most matches as umpire

No one has officiated in more Indian Premier League matches than Rudi Koertzen. The South African, who has stood in 108 Test matches and a record 209 one-day internationals (both since 1992), has umpired 42 matches in the competition between 2008 and 2011.

HIGHEST PARTNERSHIP BY WICKET

Wkt	Runs	Partners	Team	Opposition	Venue	Date
1st	159	M.E.K. Hussey, M. Vijay	Chennai	Bangalore	Chennai	28 May 2011
2nd	206	A.C. Gilchrist, S.E. Marsh	Punjab	Bangalore	Dhuramsala	17 May 2011
3rd	152	M. Vijay, J.A. Morkel	Chennai	Rajasthan	Chennai	3 Apr 2010
4th	128	D.A. Warner, P.D. Collingwood	Delhi	Kolkata	Delhi	29 Mar 2010
5th	130*	O.A. Shah, A.D. Mathews	Kolkata	Deccan	Mumbai	12 Mar 2010
6th	104	D.J. Hussey, W.P. Saha	Kolkata	Punjab	Mohali	3 May 2008
7th	60	R.A. Jadeja, S.K. Warne	Rajasthan	Punjab	Cape Town	26 Apr 2009
8th	53*	R. McLaren, Harbhajan Singh	Mumbai	Deccan	Mumbai	28 Mar 2010
9th	36	Harbhajan Singh, A.N. Ahmed	Mumbai	Chennai	Chennai	6 Apr 2010
10th	29*	S.K. Trivedi, M.M. Patel	Rajasthan	Delhi	Bloemfontein	17 May 2009

PART V: OTHER CRICKET

The first women's cricket club – the White Heather Club in Yorkshire – was established in 1887, but it was a further 47 years before the first women's Test match was played (Australia playing England in December 1934). Despite its rich history, women's cricket has never achieved the same status as the men's game, even though it has been more innovative. The first women's World Cup, for example, was contested in 1973, two years before the men's equivalent; they also staged the first Twenty20 international, in August 2004, six months before the men. When the ICC Women's World Twenty20 in England was staged in conjunction with the men's tournament it showed that, even though it has some distance to go, the women's game is making great strides.

The importance of international youth cricket often gets lost amid the sheer weight of games played at a higher level, but many of those who go on to perform with distinction in the upper echelons of the game have passed through its ranks: 17 of the 29 players who took part in the 2009 Ashes series had played in youth Test cricket. The first youth Tests and one-day internationals were played in 1974 and, since 1998, there has been an ICC Under-19 World Cup every two years.

Australia's women celebrate their three-run victory over New Zealand in the final of the 2010 ICC Women's World Twenty20 on 16 May 2010.

WOMEN'S TEST CRICKET

Anyone who thought that the first-ever women's Test match, played between Australia and England at Brisbane in December 1934, heralded the dawn of a proliferation of women's cricket around the world, has been proved sadly wrong. Since that milestone match (which England won by nine wickets), only 133 further women's Test matches have been played – compared to the 2,035 men's Test matches.

RESULTS SUMMARY

Team (Span)	Mat	Won	Lost	Tied	Draw	W/L	%W	%L	%D
Australia (1934–2011)	69	19	9	0	41	2.11	27.53	13.04	59.42
England (1934–2011)	89	19	12	0	58	1.58	21.34	13.48	65.16
India (1976–2006)	34	3	6	0	25	0.50	8.82	17.64	73.52
Ireland (2000)	1	1	0	0	0	–	100.00	0.00	0.00
Netherlands (2007)	1	0	1	0	0	0.00	0.00	100.00	0.00
New Zealand (1935–2004)	45	2	10	0	33	0.20	4.44	22.22	73.33
Pakistan (1998–2004)	3	0	2	0	1	0.00	0.00	66.66	33.33
South Africa (1960–2007)	11	1	4	0	6	0.25	9.09	36.36	54.54
Sri Lanka (1998)	1	1	0	0	0	–	100.00	0.00	0.00
West Indies (1976–2004)	12	1	3	0	8	0.33	8.33	25.00	66.66

Greenwood shines in brief career

In her six Tests for England between 1976 and 1979, Yorkshire-born Julia Greenwood made a massive impact with the ball. The opening bowler took 29 wickets, including English record match figures of 11 for 63 against the West Indies at Canterbury in June 1979, at a strike-rate of one wicket every 38.7 deliveries – an all-time record in women's Test cricket for any player to have bowled 1,000 deliveries or more.

Consistency the key for Annetts

Denise Annetts announced her arrival on the Test stage for Australia, against England at Wetherby in August 1987, in spectacular style. Making her debut in the drawn Second Test, she scored 193 not out and shared a record women's Test partnership of 309 with Lindsay Reeler (110 not out). Although she failed to hit such heady heights again, the Sydney-born right-hander remained a consistent run-gatherer throughout her career: in ten Tests between 1987 and 1992 she scored 819 runs (with two centuries and six half-centuries) at an average of 81.90 – the highest by any player to have completed ten innings or more in women's Test cricket history.

Most dismissals in a career

The current head of the selection panel for the Australian women's team, Christina Matthews, was an outstanding performer as a wicketkeeper for the Test team. In 20 matches between 1984 and 1995 she claimed 58 dismissals (with 46 catches and 12 stumpings) – an all-time record in women's Test cricket.

Most catches

Carole Hodges was a stalwart with the bat for England in 18 Tests between 1984 and 1992 – she scored 1,164 runs (fifth on the all-time list) at an average of 40.13, with a highest score of 158 not out against New Zealand at Canterbury in July 1984. Hodges also proved her worth in the field, taking 25 catches in her career – an all-time record in women's Test cricket.

The queen of batting

The most capped women's Test cricketer of all time (she played in 27 Tests for England between 1979 and 1998), **Jan Brittin** was the most prolific run-scorer women's cricket has ever seen, scoring 1,935 runs at an average of 49.61. She set all-time women's Test records for the most centuries (five, with a highest score of 167 against Australia at Harrogate in August 1998) and for the most runs scored in a calendar year (with 531 runs in five innings in 1994).

MOST RUNS: TOP 5

Pos	Runs	Player	Mat	Inns	NO	HS	Ave	100	50	0
1	1,935	J.A. Brittin (Eng, 1979–98)	27	44	5	167	49.61	5	11	2
2	1,594	**R. Heyhoe-Flint** (Eng, 1960–79)	22	38	3	179	45.54	3	10	1
3	1,522	C.M. Edwards (Eng, 1996–2011)	19	35	4	117	49.09	4	8	0
4	1,301	D.A. Hockley (NZ, 1979–96)	19	29	4	126*	52.04	4	7	1
5	1,164	C.A. Hodges (Eng, 1984–92)	18	31	2	158*	40.13	2	6	3

Shaiza leads from the front

Kiran Baluch (with her massive contribution of 242 not out) wasn't the only Pakistan player to forge a place for herself in the all-time record books in the only Test against the West Indies at Karachi in March 2004. For where Baluch shone with the bat, captain Shaiza Khan wreaked devastation with the ball. The leg-spinner took 7 for 59 in the first innings and 6 for 167 during the West Indies' match-saving effort in the second to record match figures of 13 for 226 – the best in women's Test cricket history.

Highest and lowest

Highest team total: 569 for 6 declared – Australia v England at Guildford in August 1998.

Lowest team total: 35 all out – England v Australia at Melbourne in February 1958.

Biggest victories

By an innings: by an innings and 337 runs – England v New Zealand at Christchurch in February 1935.

By runs: by 309 runs – Sri Lanka v Pakistan at Colombo in April 1998.

Smallest victories

By runs: by two runs – England v India at Jamshedpur in November 1995.

By wickets: by two wickets – Australia v England at Worcester in June–July 1951.

Brilliant Baluch hits all-time high

Kiran Baluch was an ever-present at the top of the batting order for Pakistan from the moment they played in their first-ever Test match, against Sri Lanka, in April 1998, but the highlight of her career came in her final match, against the West Indies at Karachi in March 2004. After Pakistan lost the toss and were put in to bat, she batted for nine hours 44 minutes, faced 488 balls, hit 38 fours and compiled a massive score of 242 – the highest individual score in women's Test cricket. The match, however, meandered into a disappointing draw.

MOST WICKETS: TOP 5

Pos	Wkts	Player	Mat	Balls	Runs	BBI	BBM	Ave	Econ	SR	5	10
1	77	M.B. Duggan (Eng, 1949–63)	17	3,734	1,039	7/6	9/58	13.49	1.66	48.4	5	0
2	68	E.R. Wilson (Aus, 1948–58)	11	2,885	803	7/7	11/16	11.80	1.67	42.4	4	2
3	63	D.F. Edulji (Ind, 1976–91)	20	5,098	1,624	6/64	6/64	25.77	1.85	83.5	1	0
4	60	M.E. Maclagan (Eng, 1934–51)	14	3,432	935	7/10	7/41	15.58	1.63	57.2	3	0
=	60	C.L. Fitzpatrick (Aus, 1991–2006)	13	3,603	1,147	5/29	9/112	19.11	1.91	60.0	2	0
=	60	S. Kulkarni (Ind, 1976–91)	19	3,320	1,647	6/99	7/57	27.45	2.88	59.2	5	0

WOMEN'S ODI CRICKET

It was women, not men, who contested cricket's first-ever World Cup. The 1973 ICC Women's World Cup, held in England (and won by the hosts), heralded the start of one-day international cricket in the women's game, and the format has proved more popular than the Test game: 46 women's one-day internationals were staged around the world in 2009 alone, a year which saw just a single Test.

RESULTS SUMMARY

Team (Span)	Mat	Won	Lost	Tied	NR	%
Australia (1973–2012)	254	196	51	1	6	79.23
Bangladesh (2011)	1	1	0	0	0	100.00
Denmark (1989–99)	33	6	27	0	0	18.18
England (1973–2012)	264	148	105	2	9	58.43
India (1978–2012)	193	98	90	1	4	52.11
International XI (1973–82)	18	3	14	0	1	17.64
Ireland (1987–2012)	120	37	79	0	4	31.89
Jamaica (1973)	5	1	4	0	0	20.00
Japan (2003)	5	0	5	0	0	0.00
Netherlands (1984–2011)	101	19	81	0	1	19.00
New Zealand (1973–2012)	257	128	121	2	6	51.39
Pakistan (1997–2011)	89	22	65	0	2	25.28
Scotland (2001–03)	8	1	7	0	0	12.50
South Africa (1997–2011)	90	40	45	1	4	47.09
Sri Lanka (1997–2012)	92	44	45	0	3	49.43
Trinidad & Tobago (1973)	6	2	4	0	0	33.33
West Indies (1979–2012)	96	47	46	1	2	50.53
Young England (1973)	6	1	5	0	0	16.66

WORLD CUP WINNERS

Year	Winners	(Host)
1973	England	(England)
1978	Australia	(India)
1982	Australia	(New Zealand)
1988	Australia	(Australia)
1993	England	(England)
1997	Australia	(India)
2000	New Zealand	(New Zealand)
2005	Australia	(South Africa)
2009	England	(Australia)

Most dismissals

A player very much in the Adam Gilchrist mould, Rebecca Rolls was a hard-hitting opening batsman (scoring 2,201 runs in 104 matches between 1997 and 2007 at an average of 25.01) and an able performer behind the stumps, claiming 133 dismissals (89 catches and 44 stumpings) – an all-time record in women's one-day international cricket.

Most hundreds

Two players share the record for the most hundreds scored in women's one-day internationals (eight): **Claire Taylor** (in 114 matches for England between 1998 and 2009, with a highest score of 156 not out against India at Lord's on 14 August 2006); and Karen Rolton (in 141 matches for Australia between 1995 and 2009, with a highest score of 154 not out against Sri Lanka at Christchurch on 1 December 2000).

Sensational Shah sets tongues wagging

Ever since she caused a sensation by making her international debut at the age of 12, against Ireland at Dublin on 23 July 2000, **Sajjida Shah** has been a regular and successful member of the Pakistan side. And her headline-grabbing feats have not been solely restricted to her debut: in Pakistan's ICC Women's Trophy match against Japan at Amsterdam on 21 July 2003 she took 7 for 4 off eight overs of off-spin (as Japan slumped to 28 all out) to record the best bowling figures in women's one-day international cricket history.

MOST CAREER RUNS: TOP 5

Pos	Runs	Player	Mat	Inns	NO	HS	Ave	100	50	0
1	4,844	B.J. Clark (Aus, 1991–2005)	118	114	12	229*	47.49	5	30	3
2	4,814	K.L. Rolton (Aus, 1995–2009)	141	132	32	154*	48.14	8	33	4
3	4,755	**C.M. Edwards** (Eng, 1997–2012)	155	145	19	173*	37.73	6	37	13
4	4,196	M. Raj (Ind, 1999–2012)	135	122	32	114*	46.62	3	33	4
5	4,101	S.C. Taylor (Eng, 1998–2011)	126	120	18	156*	40.20	8	23	6

MOST CAREER WICKETS: TOP 5

Pos	Wkts	Player	Mat	Overs	Mdns	Runs	BBI	Ave	Econ	SR	4	5
1	180	C.L. Fitzpatrick (Aus, 1993–2007)	109	1,002.5	188	3,023	5/14	16.79	3.01	33.4	7	4
2	141	N. David (Ind, 1995–2008)	97	815.2	189	2,305	5/20	16.34	2.82	34.6	4	2
3	138	J. Goswami (Ind, 2002–12)	118	936.1	174	2,942	6/31	21.31	3.14	40.7	3	2
4	135	L.C. Sthalekar (Aus, 2001–12)	114	887.0	89	3,289	5/35	24.36	3.70	39.4	1	1
5	102	C.E. Taylor (Eng, 1988–2005)	105	856.4	205	2,443	4/13	23.95	2.85	50.3	2	0

Pioneer of the women's game

Rachel Heyhoe-Flint, an integral figure in English women's cricket for over a generation, had done so much to get the ICC Women's World Cup tournament off the ground in the first place, that it seemed more than appropriate when, on 28 July 1973, she became the first woman in history to lift the trophy. A fine all-round batsman, capable of blunting an attack with her defence or destroying it with cavalier strokeplay, she enjoyed a long and successful career: in 23 matches between 1973 and 1982 she scored 643 runs (with a highest score of 114 against Young England at Ilford on 18 July 1973) at an average of 58.45 – the highest in women's one-day international history.

Clark puts Denmark to the sword

The gulf in class between Australia and Denmark in the two countries' Group A encounter at the 1997 ICC Women's World Cup, at Mumbai, was palpable and painful, and Australian captain **Belinda Clark** exploited it with surgical ruthlessness. The right-handed opener (who is the all-time leading scorer in women's one-day international cricket with 4,844 runs in 118 matches and has also taken the most catches – 45) smashed an unbeaten 155-ball 229 – the first and only 200-plus innings in women's one-day international cricket – to lead her side to a monstrous 412 for 3 off their 50 overs. In reply, the hapless Denmark were all out for 49.

Highest and lowest

Highest team total: 455 for 5 (50 overs) – New Zealand v Pakistan at Christchurch on 29 January 1997.

Lowest team total: 22 all out (23.4 overs) – Netherlands v West Indies at Deventer on 9 July 2008.

Biggest victories

By runs: by 408 runs – New Zealand v Pakistan at Christchurch on 29 January 1997.

By wickets: by ten wickets – on 33 occasions.

By balls remaining: with 307 balls remaining – Australia v Denmark at Dulwich on 28 July 1993.

Smallest victories

By runs: by one run – on five occasions.

By wickets: by one wicket – on eight occasions.

By balls remaining: off the last ball of the match – on 12 occasions.

WOMEN'S TWENTY20

As was the case with the 50-over World Cup, the women stole a march on the men in Twenty20 cricket. The first-ever Twenty20 international match was played between England Women and New Zealand Women at Hove on 6 August 2004 – a match New Zealand won by nine runs. Since then, cricket's newest format has become a staple of the women's game.

RESULTS SUMMARY

Team	Span	Mat	Won	Lost	Tied	NR	%
Australia	2005–12	48	27	19	2	0	58.33
England	2004–12	48	33	13	1	1	71.27
India	2006–12	30	12	18	0	0	40.00
Ireland	2008–11	13	6	7	0	0	46.15
Netherlands	2008–11	11	0	10	0	1	0.00
New Zealand	2004–12	47	24	22	1	0	52.12
Pakistan	2009–11	18	6	11	1	0	36.11
South Africa	2007–11	21	3	17	1	0	15.00
Sri Lanka	2009–11	16	4	11	0	1	26.66
West Indies	2008–12	34	23	10	1	0	69.11

Tied matches

There have been three tied matches in women's Twenty20 internationals: Australia v New Zealand at Allan Border Field, Brisbane, on 18 October 2006; Australia v England at Warner Park, Basseterre, St Kitts, on 5 May 2010; and West Indies v Pakistan at Providence Stadium, Guyana, on 11 September 2011.

Most career catches

England's Jenny Gunn holds the record for the most catches in women's Twenty20 internationals. She has taken 32 catches in 46 matches between 2004 and 2012.

Unlikely bowling heroine

A specialist top-order batsman she may be, but it was Amy Satterthwaite's performance with the ball that grabbed the headlines following the third Twenty20 international between England and New Zealand at Taunton on 16 August 2007. Bowling right-arm medium pace, the 20-year-old New Zealander tore through England's batting line-up, taking 6 for 17 – the best bowling figures ever recorded in women's Twenty20 international cricket – to lead her side to a 38-run victory.

All-round excellence

A latecomer to women's international cricket, she made her Test debut for Australia at the age of 28, Shelley Nitschke has been a standout performer in women's Twenty20 cricket. An incisive slow left-arm bowler and hard-hitting left-handed batsman, she stands third (behind the West Indies' Anisa Mohammed and compatriot Lisa Sthaliker) on the all-time wicket-taker's list (with 43). She is also fourth on the all-time run-scorer's list (with 776 runs in 36 matches at an average of 23.51). She was voted the international women's player of the year in 2010.

The English run-machine

Charlotte Edwards, a stylish right-hand batsman, has starred for England from the moment she made her Test debut at the age of 16 against New Zealand in July 1996. A heavy scorer in all forms of the game (1,522 runs, average 49.09 in Tests and 4,755 runs, average 37.73 in one-day internationals), she has shone in international Twenty20 cricket. No woman has scored more runs (1,214). She was also, following England's success in the inaugural tournament held in England in 2009, the first woman in history to lift the ICC Women's World Twenty20 cup.

Hitting new heights

Shandre Fritz was the star of the show as South Africa compiled 205 for 1 (the highest score in women's Twenty20 international cricket) against Netherlands at Potchefstroom on 14 October 2010. The Cape Town-born right-hander smashed an unbeaten 116 – the highest score by a woman in the 20-over format of the game.

MOST CAREER RUNS: TOP 5

Pos	Runs	Player	Mat	Inns	NO	HS	Ave	100	50	0
1	1,214	C.M. Edwards (Eng, 2004–12)	46	45	6	76*	31.12	0	4	2
2	887	S.W. Bates (NZ, 2007–12)	43	43	2	68	21.63	0	4	4
3	784	L.J. Poulton (Aus, 2006–12)	40	40	2	61	20.63	0	2	2
4	776	S. Nitschke (Aus, 2005–11)	36	35	2	56	23.51	0	3	2
5	774	S.J. McGlashan (NZ, 2004–11)	46	45	3	84	18.42	0	2	1

MOST CAREER WICKETS: TOP 5

Pos	Wkts	Player	Mat	Inns	Overs	Mdns	Runs	BBI	Ave	Econ	SR	4	5
1	56	L.C. Sthalekar (Aus, 2005–12)	42	42	158.2	1	949	4/18	18.60	5.99	18.6	1	0
2	52	A. Mohammed (WI, 2008–12)	32	31	107.4	1	564	5/10	10.84	5.23	12.4	4	1
3	43	S. Nitschke (Aus, 2005–12)	36	35	128.0	4	705	4/21	16.39	5.50	17.8	1	0
4	39	H.L. Colvin (Eng, 2007–12)	28	28	106.1	2	568	3/17	14.56	5.35	16.3	0	0
5	38	L.A. Marsh (Eng, 2007–12)	41	40	153.1	2	816	3/17	21.47	5.32	24.1	0	0

WORLD CUP WINNERS

Year	Winners	Host
2009	England	England
2010	**Australia**	West Indies

Captain Fantastic

The eldest of a trio of siblings (along with brother Roger and sister Jill) to play cricket for Ireland, Heather Whelan, captain of the side since 2005, has led from the front in all forms of the game, particularly in Twenty20 cricket. In four matches she has taken six wickets with her right-arm medium-fast bowling at an average of 6.66 and an economy rate of 3.07 runs per over – both are records by any bowler to have bowled 30 balls or more in women's Twenty20 international matches.

Most scores of 50-plus

Aged just 17 when she made her debut for the West Indies against Ireland in Dublin in June 2008, Stafanie Taylor got her international Twenty20 career off to an explosive start, smashing 90 off 49 balls in her side's comfortable 75-run victory (the fourth-highest score in women's Twenty20 history). And the hard-hitting right-hander has continued to catch the eye: in 29 innings for her country she has passed 50 on eight occasions – the most by any woman.

Highest and lowest

Highest team total: 205 for 1 – South Africa v Netherlands at Potchefstroom on 14 October 2010.

Lowest team total: 60 all out – Pakistan v England at Taunton on 16 June 2009.

Biggest victories

By runs: by 115 runs – South Africa v Netherlands at Potchefstroom on 14 October 2010.

By wickets: by ten wickets – England v India at Taunton on 11 June 2009.

By balls remaining: with 70 balls remaining – New Zealand v Pakistan at Basseterre, St Kitts, on 10 May 2010.

Smallest victories

By runs: by one run on three occasions.

By wickets: by two wickets – England v India at Mumbai on 4 March 2010.

By balls remaining: off the last ball of the match – England v India at Mumbai on 4 March 2010.

Most dismissals

An explosive talent with the bat, considered by many to be the finest player England has produced in recent years, **Sarah Taylor** has also made her mark as a wicketkeeper in international Twenty20 cricket. She has taken 29 dismissals (10 catches and 19 stumpings) in 31 matches between 2006 and 2012. No woman has claimed more in international Twenty20 cricket.

YOUTH TEST CRICKET

Representative youth cricket around the world plays a vital role as the nursery for international cricketers of the future. The vast majority of players who have gone on to enjoy a first-class career and beyond have, at some stage, passed through youth Test cricket's doors.

RESULT SUMMARY

Team (Span)	Mat	Won	Lost	Tied	Draw	W/L	%W	%L	%D
Australia U19 (1979–2009)	69	27	15	0	27	1.80	39.13	21.73	39.13
Bangladesh U19 (2004–09)	12	1	4	0	7	0.25	8.33	33.33	58.33
England U19 (1974–2011)	133	33	38	0	62	0.86	24.81	28.57	46.61
India U19 (1979–2009)	67	20	12	0	35	1.66	29.85	17.91	52.23
New Zealand U19 (1986–2008)	43	11	10	0	22	1.10	25.58	23.25	51.16
Pakistan U19 (1979–2007)	64	10	13	0	41	0.76	15.62	20.31	64.06
South Africa U19 (1995–2008)	23	3	9	0	11	0.33	13.04	39.13	47.82
Sri Lanka U19 (1984–2011)	43	6	14	0	23	0.42	13.95	32.55	53.48
West Indies U19 (1974–2011)	36	12	5	0	18	2.60	36.11	13.88	50.00
Zimbabwe U19 (1996–97)	6	0	4	0	2	0.00	0.00	66.66	33.33

Highest and lowest

Highest team total: 646 for 9 declared – South Africa U19 v England U19 at Chelmsford in August 2003.

Lowest team total: 47 all out – Zimbabwe U19 v England U19 at Harare in January 1996.

Record-breaker with the ball

Ashish Zaidi's record-breaking efforts with the ball did much to land India Under-19 a 1–0 series success in their four-Test series against arch-rivals Pakistan in 1990. The right-arm fast-medium bowler took a Youth Test record 33 wickets in the series, including a haul of 9 for 57 in the Second Test at Kanpur – the best single-innings bowling figures in Youth Test cricket history. Although Zaidi did not go on to represent India at senior level, he enjoyed a 14-year, 110-match first-class career with Uttar Pradesh.

Highest individual score

Clinton Peake was the undoubted star for Australia in their drawn Second Youth Test match against India at Melbourne in March 1995. With India having amassed 426 all out in their first innings, Peake, a pint-sized, Geelong-born left-hander, led Australia's response in style, hitting an unbeaten 304 – the highest-ever score in Youth Test cricket – to take his side to a result-killing 565 for 8. Peake failed to fulfil his potential in senior cricket, going on to play only nine first-class matches for Victoria.

Most matches

Although the validity of his recorded date of birth remains in doubt, **Hasan Raza** caused a sensation when he made his Test debut for Pakistan (against Zimbabwe at Faisalabad in October 1996) unofficially aged 14 years 227 days. His subsequent Test career remained a stuttering one (he appeared in a total of seven Tests, with the last one coming against England at Lahore starting on 29 November 2005), but he did go on to enjoy a successful Youth Test career, hitting four centuries in 18 matches (the most games by any player in Youth Test cricket), before settling into a first-class career in Pakistan domestic cricket.

Most runs in a series

At an early age **Marcus Trescothick** displayed the sublime natural talent that would see him go on to score over 10,000 runs for England in all forms of the game between 2000 and 2006. A prolific run-scorer in youth cricket, the left-hander's performances hit heady heights during England's three-Test home series against India in 1994. Opening the batting with future England captain Michael Vaughan, Trescothick scored a Youth Test record 467 runs in the series, with a highest score of 206 in the Third Test at Edgbaston. His exploits did not save England, however; India won the series 1–0.

YOUTH ODI CRICKET

Limited-overs matches have been a regular feature on the youth-international circuit since the first match between the West Indies and England at Trinidad in August 1976. A biennial ICC Youth World Cup was launched in 1998 (although a one-off tournament had previously been held in Australia in 1988). Australia have been the most successful team with three victories (1988, 2002 and 2010).

YOUTH WORLD CUP WINNERS

Year	Winner	(Host)
1988	Australia	(Australia)
1998	England	(South Africa)
2000	India	(Sri Lanka)
2002	Australia	(New Zealand)
2004	Pakistan	(Bangladesh)
2006	Pakistan	(Sri Lanka)
2008	India	(Malaysia)
2010	**Australia**	(New Zealand)

Highest and lowest

Highest team total: 480 for 6 – Australia U19 v Kenya U19 at Dunedin on 20 January 2002.

Lowest team total: 22 all out – Scotland U19 v Australia U19 at Chittagong on 22 February 2004.

Doropoulos puts England to the sword

An innings of high class from Theo Doropoulos propelled Australia to a comprehensive 84-run victory over England in the fifth one-day international at Sydney on 13 February 2003 to secure a 4–1 series win. The Western Australia right-hander hit an unbeaten 179 off 155 balls – the highest individual score in youth one-day international cricket – to steer his side to 270 for 6. In reply, England were all out for 186.

Most dismissals

Wicketkeeper-batsman Dinesh Chandimal has been the most prolific wicketkeeper in youth one-day international cricket, claiming 51 dismissals (with 30 catches and 21 stumpings) in 23 matches for Sri Lanka between 2007 and 2009.

MOST RUNS: TOP 5

Pos	Runs	Player	Mat	Inns	NO	HS	Ave	100	50	0
1	1,318	Ahmed Shehzad (Pak, 2007–10)	40	39	4	115	37.65	1	8	2
2	1,316	T.M. Srivastava (Ind U19, 2005–08)	34	31	4	110	48.74	2	11	1
3	1,168	Mahmudul Hasan (Bang U19, 2007–10)	57	54	4	82*	23.36	0	7	7
4	1,125	Q. de Kock (SA U19, 2010–12)	24	24	1	146	48.91	3	5	2
5	1,040	P.B.B. Rajapaksa (SL U19, 2009–11)	34	33	4	154*	35.86	2	3	2

MOST WICKETS: TOP 5

Pos	Wkts	Player	Mat	Overs	Mdns	Runs	BBI	Ave	Econ	SR	4	5
1	73	Imad Wasim (Pak U19, 2005–08)	49	364.4	24	1,547	5/38	21.19	4.24	29.9	3	1
2	71	P.P. Chawla (Ind U19, 2003–07)	37	295.4	29	1,169	5/24	16.46	3.95	24.9	3	1
3	66	Mahmudul Hasan (Bang U19, 2007–10)	57	380.1	30	1,465	4/17	22.19	3.85	34.5	1	0
4	64	S.S. Pathirana (SL U19, 2005–08)	39	355.3	23	1,514	5/52	23.65	4.25	33.3	4	1
5	59	K.P.C.M. Peiris (SL U19, 2007–10)	38	283.5	29	1,278	5/25	21.66	4.50	28.8	2	1

INDEX

A

Abbas, Zaheer 69, 71, 113, 115, 121, 167, 188
Abedin, Minhajul 177
Abeywardene, Sanjeewa 237
Adams, Jimmy 110
Adams, Paul 74, 147
Adcock, Neil 74, 101
Afghanistan
    one-day international 162, 202
    Twenty20 207, 214
Africa XI
    one-day international 162, 202
Afridi, Shahid 18, 33, 157, 167, 168, 170, 188, 189, 210, 213, 215, 236, 237
Agarkar, Ajit 185
Ahmed, Aftab 212, 241
Ahmed, Ijaz 121, 154, 165
Ahmed, Mushtaq 48, 70, 117, 121, 137
Ahmed, Shabbir 144
Ahsan, Haseeb 40
Ajmal, Saeed 115, 125, 210, 215, 236
Akbar, Sajjad 226
Akhtar, Mansoor 223
Akhtar, Pervez 218
Akhtar, Shoaib 70, 144
Akmal, Kamran 68, 71, 208, 209, 212, 213, 236
Akmal, Umar 215
Akram, Wasim 32, 33, 34, 39, 48, 70, 71, 113, 115, 117, 121, 123, 124, 125, 138, 156, 166, 170, 171, 172, 173, 189, 232, 233
Alam, Intikhab 71, 115, 117
Alexander, Gerry 42, 83, 122, 123
Ali, Abid 40
Ali, Ashraf 174
Ali, Frasat 202
Ali, Mohammad 231
Ali, Nazir 219
Ali, Zulfiqar 203
all-round records 46–7
Allom, Maurice 40
Amarnath, Lala 63
Amarnath, Mohinder 113
Ambrose, Curtly 31, 39, 82, 95, 99, 123, 135, 194, 195
Ames, Les 20, 228
Amiss, Dennis 167, 168
Amla, Hashim 73, 100, 101, 133, 167, 169, 190
Anderson, Jimmy 58, 103, 115, 140, 183
Andhra Pradesh 218
Andrew, Gareth 233
Ankola, Salil 227
Annetts, Denise 244
Anurasiri, Don 78
Anwar, Saeed 19, 69, 125, 167, 172, 188, 189
Ao, Tau 176
Arafat, Yasir 226, 236
Archer, Ron 19, 52, 168, 169
Armstrong, Warwick 44
Ashes series
    1886–87 56
    1894–95 13, 18
    1902 52
    1920–21 13
    1928–29 13
    1930 25
    1934 20
    1938 12, 36, 56, 88
    1948 19
    1984–85 88
    records 88, 89
Ashraful, Mohammad 28, 84, 143, 146, 212
Ashwin, Ravichandran 240
Asia XI
    one-day international 162, 202
Asif, Mohammad 137
Astill, Ewart 229
Astle, Nathan 64, 67, 105, 111, 132, 154, 160, 186, 187
Atapattu, Marvan 33, 77, 79, 136, 193
Atherton, Michael 31, 39, 57, 59, 96, 97, 140
Atkinson, Denis 48
Attewell, William 36
Auckland 219
Australia
    v Bangladesh 52, 84, 148, 180
    v Canada 180
    domestic team records 218, 219
    v England 10, 12, 17, 19, 20, 21, 36, 52, 55, 56, 88–9, 180, 218
    ICC Champions Trophy 160, 161
    v ICC World XI 52, 180
    ICC World Cup 152, 153
    v India 18, 20, 52, 60, 61, 106–7, 165, 180
    v Ireland 180
    v Kenya 180
    v Namibia 180
    v Netherlands 180
    v New Zealand 52, 64, 104–5, 180
    one-day international 162, 163, 165, 180–1
    v Pakistan 16, 52, 68, 120–1, 165, 180
    v Scotland 180
    v South Africa 16, 24, 52, 72, 92–3, 180, 230
    v Sri Lanka 52, 76, 129, 180, 237
    Test records 12, 52–5, 88, 89, 104–5, 106–7, 120–1, 129, 141, 148
    Twenty20 206, 207, 214, 215
    v United States of America 180
    v West Indies 12, 15, 19, 20, 21, 52, 80, 98–9, 180
    women's one-day international 246, 247
    women's Test 244
    women's Twenty20 248
    youth Test 250
    youth World Cup 251
    v Zimbabwe 52, 85, 141, 180
Azharuddin, Mohammad 15, 29, 44, 61, 63, 103, 119, 174, 175, 185

B

Baber, Javed 218
Badree, Samuel 236
Bagai, Ashish 202
Baidwan, Harvir 203
Bailey, Trevor 31, 229
Baloch, Aftab 220
Baluch, Kiran 245
Baluchistan 218
Bandara, Malinga 215
Bangladesh
    v Australia 52, 84, 148
    v England 56, 84, 149
    ICC Champions Trophy 160, 161
    ICC Trophy 176
    ICC World Cup 153
    v India 60, 84, 143
    v New Zealand 64, 84, 145
    one-day international 162, 163, 196
    v Pakistan 19, 68, 84, 144
    v South Africa 72, 84, 147
    v Sri Lanka 28, 76, 84, 146
    Test records 12, 16, 84, 85, 143, 144, 145, 146, 147, 148, 149
    Twenty20 206–7, 214, 215
    v West Indies 18, 80, 84, 148
    women's ODI 246
    youth Test 250
    v Zimbabwe 13, 84, 85
Bannerman, Charles 10, 27
Barbados 219, 230
Bardsley, Warren 27
Bari, Wasim 42, 71, 112, 114
Barlow, Eddie 93
Barnes, Sydney 35, 40, 41, 48, 58, 89, 90, 91, 226
Barnes, Vincent 225
Barrington, Ken 26, 57, 96, 103
Barrow, Alan 231
Bashar, Habibul 84, 144, 147, 148, 196
Bates, Billy 41
Bates, Suzie 249
batting records
    Australian 52, 53, 89, 93, 99, 105, 107, 121, 129, 140, 148, 181
    Bangladeshi 143, 144, 145, 146, 147, 148, 149
    domestic 220–3, 229, 234, 235, 239
    English 57, 89, 91, 95, 97, 103, 127, 149, 183
    ICC Champions Trophy 161
    ICC Trophy 177
    ICC World Cup 154–5
    Indian 61, 103, 107, 109, 113, 119, 126, 131, 133, 143, 185
    Indian Premier League 239
    List A matches 233
    New Zealand 64, 97, 101, 105, 111, 117, 119, 128, 132, 145, 187
    one-day international 165, 166–9, 175, 181, 183, 185, 187, 189, 191, 193, 195, 202
    Pakistani 69, 113, 117, 121, 123, 125, 137, 138, 144, 189, 191
    South African 73, 91, 93, 101, 130, 133, 134, 137, 139, 147
    Sri Lankan 77, 125, 126, 127, 128, 129, 134, 135, 136, 146, 193
    Twenty20 208–9, 234, 235
    West Indian 81, 95, 99, 109, 110, 111, 123, 130, 135, 142, 148, 195
    women's one-day international 247
    women's Test 245
    women's Twenty20 249
    youth one-day international 251
    Zimbabwean 85, 131, 132, 136, 138, 139, 140, 141, 142
Bedi, Bishan 62, 63, 103, 107, 109, 119
Bedser, Alec 14, 39, 41, 58
Bell, Ian 102, 127, 149
Benaud, Richie 13, 19, 52, 54, 93, 107, 226
Benn, Sulieman 213
Bennett, George 226
Bermuda
    ICC World Cup 152, 153
    International Twenty20 214
    Twenty20 214
Bevan, Michael 167, 230
Bichel, Andy 141
Bishop, Ian 82
Blain, John 200
Bland, Colin 45
Blewett, Greg 31, 93
Blignaut, Andy 142
Blythe, Colin 224
Boje, Nicky 134
Bond, Shane 66, 111, 156, 186
Boock, Stephen 66
Boon, David 53, 105, 165
Bopara, Ravi 231
Border 230
Border, Allan 24, 44, 53, 55, 89, 99, 104, 105, 107, 121, 159
Bosman, Loots 215
Botha, Andre 197
Botham, Ian 38, 41, 46, 47, 58, 59, 89, 97, 102, 103, 115, 183, 232, 233
Boucher, Mark 42, 48, 73, 75, 91, 92, 173
bowling records
    Australian 54, 89, 93, 99, 105, 107, 121, 129, 140, 148, 181
    Bangladeshi 84, 143, 144, 145, 146, 147
    domestic 224–7, 229, 236, 237, 240
    English 58, 89, 91, 95, 97, 103, 127, 149, 183
    ICC Champions Trophy 161
    ICC Trophy 177
    ICC World Cup 156–7
    Indian 62, 103, 107, 109, 113, 131, 133, 143, 185
    Indian Premier League 240
    List A matches 232
    New Zealand 66, 97, 101, 105, 111, 117, 128, 132, 145, 187
    one-day international 165, 170–3, 181, 183, 185, 187, 189, 191, 193, 195, 203
    Pakistani 70, 113, 117, 121, 123, 125, 137, 138, 189
    South African 74, 91, 93, 101, 130, 133, 134, 137, 139, 147, 191
    Sri Lankan 77, 125, 126, 127, 128, 129, 134, 135, 136, 146, 193
Twenty20 208–9, 234, 235
West Indian 81, 95, 99, 109, 110, 111, 123, 130, 135, 142, 148, 195
    women's one-day international 247
    women's Test 245
    women's Twenty20 249
    youth one-day international 251
    Zimbabwean 85, 131, 132, 136, 138, 139, 140, 141, 142
Boyce, Keith 233
Boycott, Geoffrey 30, 32, 57, 89, 95, 169, 221, 222
Bracewell, John 66, 105
Bradman, Donald 13, 19, 20, 25, 26, 27, 28, 30, 48, 49, 53, 55, 89, 93, 106, 219, 220, 221
Bravo, Dwayne 19, 130
Brearley, Mike 59
Bresnan, Tim 182
Briggs, Johnny 35, 41
Brittin, Jan 244, 245
Broad, Stuart 48, 115, 183, 210, 215
Brown, Tony 228, 231
Burger, Jan-Berrie 202
Burgess, Mark 117, 119
Burke, Jim 36, 54
Butchart, Ian 158
Butcher, Mark 140
Butt, Salman 212

C

Caddick, Andy 58, 97
Cairns, Chris 46, 64, 66, 97, 105, 110, 132, 145, 158, 187, 202
Cairns, Lance 66, 187
Cameron, Frank 101
Cameron, Jock 75
Campbell, Alistair 138
Campbell, Sherwin 111
Canada
    ICC Trophy 176
    ICC World Cup 153
    International Twenty20 214
    one-day international 162, 163, 202, 203
    Twenty20 214
Canterbury 219
Carlisle, Stuart 201
Central Province 218
century see hundreds
Chanderpaul, Shivnarine 15, 19, 24, 81, 95, 109, 111, 123, 130, 195
Chandrasekhar, Bhagwath 62, 103, 109, 119
Chapman, John 223
Chappell, Greg 27, 28, 44, 53, 55, 89, 104, 105, 121, 164
Chappell, Ian 55, 104
Chatfield, Ewan 66, 111
Chawla, Piyush 240, 251
Cheetham, Jack 75, 100
Chennai Super Kings 217, 234, 237, 238, 239
Chittagong B 230
Chudasama, Dipak 198
Clark, Belinda 247
Clark, Seymour 222
Clarke, Michael 32, 107, 121, 158, 181
Clarke, Nolan 177
Clarke, William 225
Codrington, Austin 203
Collinge, Richard 48, 66, 97
Collingwood, Paul 183, 241
Collins, Pedro 148
Collymore, Corey 135
Colvin, Heather 249
Compton, Denis 90, 91, 114, 220
Coney, Jeremy 67
Congdon, Bevan 64, 66, 67, 97, 111, 119
Connell, Peter 227
Cook, Alastair 102, 127, 149
Copson, Bill 226
Cosier, Gary 164
Coventry, Charles 168, 196, 201
Cowdrey, Colin 39, 57, 59, 95, 97
Cowie, Jack 66
Croft, Colin 123
Cronje, Hansie 73, 75, 159, 174, 191
Crowe, Martin 64, 65, 67, 97, 105, 117, 187
Cullinan, Daryll 73, 101, 134
Cusack, Alex 158, 211

D

Dar, Tabarak 202
Das, Shiv Sunder 131
David, Neetu 247
Davidson, Alan 13, 46, 99
Davis, Winston 194
de Kock, Quinton 251
de Silva, Asoka 36
de Silva, Aravinda 77, 79, 125, 126, 128, 154, 193
de Villiers, A.B. 19, 30, 33, 73, 75, 130, , 167, 208, 212
Dean, Jemmy 225
Deccan Chargers 238, 240
DeFreitas, Phil 233
Delhi Daredevils 217, 238
Denmark
    ICC Trophy 177
    women's one-day international 246, 247
Depeiaza, Clairmonte 48
Derbyshire 219
Dev, Kapil 14, 33, 34, 35, 38, 41, 46, 47, 61, 62, 63, 103, 107, 109, 113, 126, 158, 159, 168, 185
Devon 231
Dexter, Ted 59, 114
Dhaniram, Sunil 172
Dharmani, Pankaj 223
Dharmasena, Kumar 78, 168
Dhoni, Mahendra Singh 42, 61, 63, 130, 166, 167, 175, 184, 203, 213, 239
Dighton, Michael 237
Dillon, Merv 31
Dilshan, Tillakaratne 77, 79, 127, 146, 158, 208, 212, 213, 215
dismissals records 33, 42
    Ashes 88
    Australian 55, 104, 106, 121
    English 59
    ICC Champions Trophy 160

ICC World Cup 158
Indian 63
New Zealand 67
Pakistani 71, 117, 124, 189
South African 75, 91
Twenty20 212, 213
West Indian 83, 99, 122, 195
youth one-day
    international 251
Doeschate, Ryan ten 167,
    199
domestic cricket
    batting records 220–3,
        229, 234, 235, 239
    bowling records 224–7,
        229, 236, 237, 240
    fielding records 228, 237
    Indian Premier League
        238–41
    List A matches 230–3
    team records 218
    Twenty20 234–7
    wicketkeeping records 228
Donald, Allan 74, 91, 93,
    133, 134, 137, 139, 156,
    191, 232
Doropoulos, Theo 251
Dottin, Deandra 248
Dowling, Graham 67, 118,
    119
Draai, Stephen 225
Dravid, Rahul 24, 27, 31,
    44, 49, 61, 63, 102, 103,
    107, 109, 113, 118, 119,
    126, 131, 133, 143, 158,
    161, 166, 175, 184, 185,
    233, 241
ducks records 18, 31, 57, 73,
    164, 208
Duff, Reggie 31
Duggan, Mary 245
Dujon, Jeff 42, 43, 83, 99,
    108, 111, 195
Durham 230, 234

E
East Africa
    ICC World Cup 153
    one-day international 162,
        202
Edrich, John 32, 89, 90, 91,
    96, 168
Edulji, Diana 245
Edwards, Anthony 177
Edwards, Charlotte 245, 247,
    248, 249
Edwards, Fidel 171, 241
Elahi, Saleem 167
Elferink, Ronnie 176
Elliott, Gideon 225
Emburey, John 232
Endean, Russell 33
Engineer, Farok 63
England
    v Australia 10, 12, 17, 19,
        20, 21, 36, 51, 52, 56,
        87, 88–9, 182, 218
    v Bangladesh 56, 84, 149,
        182
    v Canada 182
    domestic team records
        218, 219
    v East Africa 182
    ICC Champions Trophy 161
    ICC World Cup 153, 159
    v India 14, 56, 60, 102–3,
        182
    v Ireland 182
    v Kenya 182
    v Namibia 182
    v Netherlands 182
    v New Zealand 56, 64, 65,
        96–7, 182
    one-day international 162,
        164, 182–3
    v Pakistan 56, 68, 114–15,
        182
    v Scotland 182
    v South Africa 14, 15, 18, 20,
        21, 56, 72, 90–1, 182, 218

v Sri Lanka 56, 76, 127,
    182
Test records 12, 56–9,
    88–9, 94–5, 96–7, 102–3,
    114–15, 127, 149
Twenty20 206, 207, 214,
    215
v United Arab Emirates 182
v West Indies 15, 56, 80,
    94–5, 182
women's one-day
    international 246
women's Test 244
women's Twenty20 248
youth Test 250
youth World Cup 251
v Zimbabwe 13, 56, 85,
    182
Ervine, Sean 201
Essex 218, 219, 237
Estwick, Roddy 227
Evans, Edwin 41
Evans, Godfrey 42, 43, 59

F
Faqih, Ijaz 226
Faulkner, Aubrey 73, 91
Fernando, Dilhara 78, 146,
    193, 210
Fernando, Salith 218
Ferris, J.J. 20, 54
fielding records 44–5
    Australian 55, 89, 99, 120
    domestic 228, 237
    English 59
    ICC Champions Trophy 160
    Indian 63, 107, 113
    New Zealand 67, 119
    one-day international 174
    Pakistani 71
    South African 75, 91, 101
    Sri Lankan 79, 124
    Twenty20 212, 213, 215,
        237
    West Indian 83
Finn, Stephen 149
Fitzpatrick, Cathryn 245, 247
Fleetwood-Smith, Chuck 36
Fleming, Damien 40, 110
Fleming, Stephen 27, 44, 64,
    65, 67, 96, 97, 101, 111,
    119, 128, 132, 145, 154,
    159, 172, 174, 187
Fletcher, Andre 212
Flintoff, Andrew 32, 46, 183
Flower, Andy 25, 30, 85, 131,
    132, 136, 138, 139, 140,
    167, 175
Flower, Grant 40, 85, 131,
    132, 136, 138, 169, 201
Foster, Tip 26
Francis, Simon 233
Fredericks, Roy 168
Freeman, Alfred 224, 225,
    226, 227
Freeman, George 225
Fritz, Shandre 248
Fry, C.B. 220

G
Gambhir, Gautam 28, 30,
    143, 208, 208, 210,
    212, 239
Ganguly, Sourav 31, 61, 63,
    143, 154, 158, 161, 166,
    175, 185, 231
Garner, Joel 82, 95, 99, 111,
    123, 158, 170, 171, 195
Gavaskar, Sunil 14, 24, 26,
    27, 28, 32, 60, 61, 63,
    102, 103, 107, 109, 113
Gayle, Chris 19, 28, 32, 81,
    83, 111, 130, 142, 148,
    161, 194, 195, 195, 208,
    208, 209, 212, 213, 214,
    234, 235, 237
Ghani, Nasim-ul 37
Gibbons, Noel 177
Gibbs, Herschelle 25, 73, 75,
    101, 130, 137, 139, 154,

155, 163, 167, 169, 190,
    191, 212, 213, 230, 235
Gibbs, Lance 41, 82, 95, 109
Gibraltar
    ICC Trophy 176, 177
Giffen, George 47, 229
Gilchrist, Adam 18, 32, 42,
    43, 55, 105, 106, 154,
    158, 165, 172, 174, 181,
    206, 213, 237, 239,
    240, 241
Giles, Ashley 127
Gillespie, Jason 24, 54, 148
Gilmour, Gary 157
Glamorgan 218, 230, 237
Gloucestershire 219, 230,
    234, 235
Goa 218
Goddard, John 83
Goddard, Trevor 20, 24, 74,
    75, 91, 93, 224
Goel, Rajinder 225
Gomes, Rupert 177
Gomez, Gerry 82
Gooch, Graham 24, 27, 33,
    39, 57, 59, 95, 97, 103,
    183, 221, 222, 231
Goodwin, Murray 140
Goswami, Jhulan 247
Gough, Darren 58, 183, 232
Gower, David 28, 30, 39, 40,
    57, 59, 89, 97, 103, 115
Grace, E.M. 49
Grace, W.G. 49, 221, 224, 229
Graveney, Tom 115, 221
Greenidge, Gordon 49, 81,
    83, 95, 98, 99, 108, 109,
    111, 123, 231
Greenwood, Julia 244
Gregory, Jack 44
Griffin, Gerry 40
Griffith, Adrian 32
Grimmett, Clarrie 35, 41, 54,
    89, 92, 93, 99
Gripper, Trevor 141
ground records 22–3
Grout, Wally 55
Gul, Umar 125, 144, 210,
    215, 236
Gull, Ilyas 203
Gunn, Jenny 248
Gupte, Subhash 113, 119
Guptill, Martin 167

H
Haddin, Brad 55
Hadlee, Richard 34, 41, 46,
    64, 66, 97, 105, 111, 117,
    119, 128
Hafeez, Mohammad 144, 215
Hall, Andrew 30, 175, 193,
    237
Hall, Wes 82, 109
Hameed, Yasir 69
Hamilton, Gavin 200
Hammond, Walter 17, 26,
    28, 47, 57, 59, 89, 91,
    221, 222, 228
Hampshire 219, 237
Haq, Inzamam-ul 19, 69, 71,
    114, 116, 117, 123, 125,
    138, 166, 189, 212, 213
Haq, Majid 200
Haq, Misbah-ul 71
Harmison, Steve 80, 149
Harper, Roger 45
Harris, Chris 187, 234
Harris, Ryan 170
Harvey, Ian 235
Harvey, Neil 19, 52, 93
Harwood, Shane 227
Hasan, Mahmudul 251
Hasan, Shakib Al 84, 145,
    148, 149, 196, 215
Hassan, Hamid 209
Hastings, Brian 48
Hay, Henry 227
Hayden, Matthew 18, 25, 27,
    32, 48, 52, 53, 55, 93,
    104, 107, 141, 154, 206

Haynes, Desmond 17, 33, 49,
    81, 95, 98, 99, 108, 111,
    123, 167, 172, 195, 231
Hayward, Tom 19, 39
Hazare, Vijay 219, 223
Headley, George 26, 81,
    221, 223
Healy, Ian 39, 42, 55
Hearne, Jack 224, 227
Henderson, Claude 139
Henderson, Tyron 236
Henderson, William 225, 226
Hendren, Patsy 13, 221, 222
Herath, Rangana 78, 125
Heyhoe-Flint, Rachel 245,
    247
Hick, Graeme 220, 222,
    231, 233
Hilditch, Andrew 33
Hill, Clem 31, 89
Hinds, Wavell 142
Hirst, George 229
Hirwani, Narendra 37, 62, 108
Hobbs, Jack 26, 28, 29, 49,
    57, 89, 91, 221, 222
Hockley, Debbie 245
Hodge, Brad 158, 235, 237
Hodges, Carole 244, 245
Hogg, Brad 156
Hoggard, Matthew 58, 127,
    149
Holding, Michael 82, 95, 99,
    175, 233
Holkar 218, 223
Hollioake, Adam 236
Hong Kong
    one-day international 162,
        203
Hooker, Hal 223
Hooper, Carl 83, 123, 195
Hossain, Shahadat 37, 143,
    146, 147
Houghton, Dave 85, 158
Howarth, Geoff 67
Howell, Adam 132
Hughes, Kim 32, 55, 121
Hughes, Merv 40, 41, 99
hundreds records 19, 26,
    28–9, 120, 139, 154, 165,
    222, 246
Hunte, Conrad 123
Hurst, Alan 31
Hussain, Ijaz 218
Hussain, Murtaza 113, 202,
    226
Hussain, Nasser 59, 140
Hussey, David 209, 235,
    237, 241
Hussey, Mike 129, 180, 209,
    213, 239, 241
Hutton, Len 12, 29, 32, 33,
    56, 57, 88, 91, 95, 222
Hyderabad 218, 234

I
Ibadulla, Khalid 69
Ibrahim, K.C. 221
ICC Champions Trophy 160–1
ICC Trophy 176–7
ICC World XI
    v Australia 52
    one-day international 162,
        202
ICC World Cup
    batting records 153, 154–5
    best attended 159
    bowling records 156–7
    dismissals records 158
    partnership records 158
    team records 12, 152–3
    wicketkeeping records 158
    winners 152
Illingworth, Ray 59, 229
India
    v Australia 18, 20, 52, 60,
        106–7, 165, 184
    v Bangladesh 60, 84, 143,
        184
    v Bermuda 184
    v East Africa 184

v England 14, 56, 60,
    102–3, 184
v Hong Kong 184
ICC Champions Trophy 160,
    161
ICC World Cup 151, 152,
    153, 159
v Ireland 184
v Kenya 184
v Namibia 184
v Netherlands 184
v New Zealand 60, 61, 64,
    118–19, 184
one-day international 162,
    163, 164, 165, 184–5
v Pakistan 21, 60, 68,
    122–3, 184
v Scotland 184
v South Africa 18, 60, 72,
    133, 184
v Sri Lanka 19, 60, 61, 76,
    126, 184, 218
Test records 12, 60–3,
    102–3, 106–7, 108–9,
    112–13, 118–19, 126, 131,
    133, 143
Twenty20 206, 207, 214
v United Arab Emirates 184
v West Indies 13, 60, 80,
    108–9, 184
women's one-day
    international 246
women's Test 244
women's Twenty20 248
youth Test 250
youth World Cup 251
v Zimbabwe 60, 85, 131,
    184
Indian Premier League 217,
    238–41
Ingram, Colin 167
International XI
    women's one-day
        international 246
International Twenty20
    214–15
Iqbal, Asif 117
Iqbal, Tamim 145, 148,
    149, 196
Ireland
    v England 153
    ICC Trophy 176
    ICC World Cup 153
    one-day international 162,
        197
    Twenty20 207, 214
    women's one-day
        international 246
    women's Test 244
    women's Twenty20 248
Irfanuddin 237
Ironmonger, Bert 37
Islam, Naeem 209

J
Jackson, John 225
Jackson, Stanley 19
Jacobs, Ridley 42, 83, 158,
    169
Jacques, Phil 20
Jadeja, Ajay 175
Jadeja, Ravindra 223, 241
Jaffer, Wasim 143
Jaisimha, Motganhalli 32
Jakati, Shadab 240
Jamaica
    women's one-day
        international 246
James, Kevan 229
James, Wayne 229
Japan
    women's one-day
        international 246
Jarvis, Terry 110
Jayasuriya, Sanath 32, 48,
    76, 77, 78, 79, 125, 126,
    127, 134, 136, 154, 164,
    166, 167, 168, 170, 172,
    175, 192, 193, 206, 208,
    211, 212, 223, 231, 239

Jayawardene, Mahela 19,
    24, 27, 32, 33, 44, 45,
    48, 49, 77, 79, 124, 125,
    126, 127, 128, 129, 134,
    135, 146, 154, 160, 166,
    174, 175, 192, 193, 202,
    203, 208, 209, 212, 213,
    215, 239
Jayawardene, Prasanna 43,
    79, 146
Jenkins, Roly 227
John, Vinothen 128
Johnson, Mitchell 93, 210,
    213
Johnson, Richard 140
Johnston, Trent 197, 215
Jones, Andrew 128
Jones, Ernie 40

K
Kaif, Mohammad 158
Kallicharran, Alvin 231
Kallis, Jacques 19, 24, 27,
    28, 31, 44, 46, 73, 74,
    75, 91, 93, 100, 101, 130,
    133, 134, 137, 139, 147,
    154, 161, 166, 191, 193,
    208, 239
Kaluwitharana, Romesh 79
Kaneria, Danish 31, 69, 70,
    113, 121, 125, 137, 144
Kanhai, Rohan 81, 95, 108,
    109
Karachi Dolphins 237
Kapali, Alok 215
Kardar, Abdul 71
Karim, Aasif 177
Karthik, Dinesh 143
Kasprowicz, Michael 129
Katich, Simon 20, 105, 141
Kemp, Justin 175, 209,
    212, 213
Kendall, Tom 41
Kennedy, Alex 224
Kent 219, 224
Kenya
    ICC Champions Trophy 161
    ICC Trophy 177
    ICC World Cup 153, 159
    v Namibia 218
    one-day international 162,
        198
    Twenty20 206, 207, 214,
        234
Khan, Ahad 225
Khan, Arshad 48
Khan, Asim 177
Khan, Imran 46, 70, 71, 113,
    115, 117, 121, 123, 125,
    159, 170, 189, 233
Khan, Khurram 203
Khan, Majid 28, 36, 69,
    71, 117
Khan, Mohsin 33, 120
Khan, Moin 71, 124, 189
Khan, Younis 45, 48, 68, 69,
    71, 113, 114, 125, 137,
    144, 213, 216
Khan, Zaheer 31, 32, 61, 62,
    107, 119, 131, 143, 156,
    157, 185, 203, 213, 240
Kieswetter, Craig 212
King, Reon 142
Kings XI Punjab 237, 238,
    239, 240, 241
Kippax, Alan 223
Kirmani, Syed 40, 63, 158
Kirsten, Gary 73, 75, 91, 93,
    101, 137, 139, 147, 155,
    190, 191
Kloppenburg, Feiko 199
Klusener, Lance 133, 154, 191
Knight, Nick 13, 169
Knott, Alan 42, 59, 102
Kochi Tuskers Kerala 238
Koertzen, Rudi 175, 241
Kohli, Virat 167
Kolkata Knight Riders 238,
    239
Kottehewa, Tharaka 233

Kulasekara, Nuwan 215
Kulkarni, Shubhangi 245
Kumar, Praveen 237
Kumble, Anil 34, 38, 62, 103, 107, 109, 112, 113, 119, 126, 131, 133, 143, 170, 185
Kuruppu, Brendon 26

L

Laker, Jim 34, 36, 41, 58, 224, 225
Lakhani, Amin 227
Lamb, Allan 32, 231
Lambert, Clayton 202
Langer, Justin 53, 104, 105, 121
Langeveldt, Charl 211, 236
Langford, Brian 232
Lara, Brian 24, 25, 27, 28, 32, 33, 39, 44, 81, 83, 94, 95, 99, 110, 111, 123, 130, 135, 142, 154, 166, 195, 220, 221
Latif, Khalid 231
Latif, Rashid 71
Lawrence, Godfrey 100
Lawrence, Mark 225
Lawry, Bill 49, 98
Lawson, Geoff 39
Lawson, Jermaine 82, 148
Laxman, V.V.S. 30, 44, 61, 63, 106, 107, 109, 119, 133, 240
lbws records 21
Lee, Brett 54, 93, 99, 105, 107, 141, 148, 156, 157, 161, 170, 173, 181, 215
Lees, Warren 67
Leeward Islands 234
Lefebvre, Roland 176, 177
Lehmann, Darren 18, 148
Lever, John 103, 232
Leverock, Dwayne 203
Levi, Richard 214
Lewis, Mike 172
Lifmann, R.E. 177
Lillee, Dennis 40, 41, 43, 54, 89, 105, 121, 180
Lilley, Dick 39
Lillywhite, William 224, 225
Lindsay, Denis 24, 43, 75
Lindwall, Ray 54, 89
List A matches 230–3
Lloyd, Clive 81, 83, 95, 98, 99, 108, 109, 154, 159
Lloyd, David 168
Lock, Tony 14, 40, 96, 97, 224
Logan, Richard 233
Lohmann, George 34, 36, 41, 90

M

Macartney, Charlie 28
McCallan, Kyle 197
McCallum, Neil 200
McCullum, Brendon 64, 67, 145, 155, 187, 214, 215, 235, 238, 239
McDermott, Craig 12, 54, 105, 129, 181
McDonald, Colin 19, 52
McGarrell, Neil 142
MacGill, Stuart 148
McGlashan, Sara 249
McGlew, Jackie 75, 101
McGrath, Glenn 31, 34, 38, 39, 53, 54, 89, 93, 99, 105, 107, 121, 129, 141, 156, 159, 161, 162, 170, 171, 181
McKenzie, Garth 39, 54, 99
McKenzie, Neil 48, 147
Maclagan, Myrtle 245
MacLaren, Archie 220
MacLaren, Ryan 241
MacMillan, Craig 160, 187
Mahanama, Roshan 48, 126
Maharoof, Farveez 160
Mahmood, Azhar 48, 236, 237

Mahmood, Fazal 16, 70, 113, 120, 123
Mailey, Arthur 44, 54, 225
Malaysia
  ICC Trophy 176
Malik, Saleem 69, 71, 115, 117, 121, 189, 212, 213
Malik, Shoaib 213
Malinga, Lasith 78, 146, 157, 171, 172, 175, 193, 210, 236, 240, 241
Mankad, Vinoo 61, 62, 103, 113, 118
Marahastra 219
Marsh, Geoff 165
Marsh, Laura 249
Marsh, Rod 42, 55, 88, 121
Marsh, Shaun 237, 239, 240, 241
Marshall, Hamish 187
Marshall, Malcolm 39, 82, 95, 99, 108, 109, 111, 123, 195
Martin, Chris 31, 65, 66, 100, 101, 117, 145
Martyn, Damien 169
Masakadza, Hamilton 139, 142
Mascarenhas, Dmitri 237
Mashud, Khaled 84
Massie, Bob 54
Mathews, Angelo 175, 209, 215, 241
Matthews, Christina 244
Matthews, Jimmy 39, 227
May, Peter 39, 59, 95
May, Tim 12
Mbangwa, Pommie 171, 232
MCC 219
Mead, Phil 221, 222
Meckiff, Ian 40
Mendis, Ajantha 126, 171, 173, 210, 215, 237
Mendis, Duleep 79
Merchant, Vijay 221
Miandad, Javed 29, 48, 69, 71, 113, 115, 116, 117, 120, 121, 154, 189
Middlesex 223, 230, 234
Miller, Keith 19, 52
Miller, Nikita 213
Mills, Kyle 161, 187
Mithun, Abhimanyu 227
Mirza, Waheed 223
Mishra, Amit 240
Mitchell, Bruce 75, 91
Mohammad, Anisa 248, 249
Mohammad, Gul 223
Mohammad, Hanif 14, 69, 115, 220
Mohammad, Khan 70
Mohammad, Mushtaq 71, 115, 116, 117
Mohammad, Sadiq 117
Mohammad, Shoaib 48, 117
Mohmand, Rafatullah 223
Mongia, Nayan 63
Mooney, John 197
More, Kiran 43, 63
Morgan, Eoin 102
Morkel, Albie 240, 241
Morkel, Morne 74, 147, 190, 203, 210, 236
Morris, Arthur 19, 39
Morrison, Danny 31, 66, 105, 117
Mortaza, Mashrafe 145, 196, 215
Mortensen, Ole 177
Mukherjee, Saradindu 227
Mumbai 230
Mumbai Indians 238, 239
Muralitharan, Muttiah 31, 34, 38, 40, 41, 45, 76, 78, 79, 124, 125, 126, 127, 128, 129, 134, 135, 136, 146, 156, 157, 161, 170, 173, 193, 232, 236
Murdoch, Billy 27

Murray, David 83
Murray, Deryck 94
Murray, Junior 12, 83, 110
Mushtaq, Saqlain 70, 125, 138, 157, 170, 173, 189
Muzumdar, Amol 221
Myles, Simon 176
Mysore 218, 223

N

Nadkarni, Bapu 36, 62
Nafees, Shahriar 148
Namibia
  ICC World Cup 153
  v Kenya 218
  one-day international 162, 202
  v Scotland 234
Nannes, Dirk 210, 211, 236
Napier, Graham 235
Nash, Dion 101
Nawab of Pataudi 63, 118
Nawaz, Sarfraz 70, 113, 115, 120, 121
Nazar, Mudassar 29, 68, 69, 113
Nel, Andre 74, 130, 139
Nel, Dewald 209
Netherlands
  ICC Champions Trophy 161
  ICC Trophy 176, 177
  ICC World Cup 153
  International Twenty20 214
  one-day international 162, 164, 199
  v Sri Lanka 230
  Twenty20 207, 214
  women's one-day international 246
  women's Test 244
  women's Twenty20 248
New South Wales 218, 219
New Zealand
  v Australia 52, 64, 104–5, 186
  v Bangladesh 64, 84, 186
  v Canada 186
  domestic team records 219
  v East Africa 186
  v England 56, 64, 65, 96–7, 186
  ICC Champions Trophy 160, 161
  ICC World Cup 153
  v India 60, 64, 118–19, 186
  v Ireland 186
  v Kenya 186
  v Netherlands 186
  one-day international 162, 164, 186–7
  v Pakistan 12, 64, 68, 116–17, 186
  v Scotland 186
  v South Africa 64, 72, 100–1, 186
  v Sri Lanka 64, 65, 76, 128, 186
  Test records 12, 64–7, 96–7, 100–1, 104–5, 110–11, 116–17, 118–19, 128, 132
  Twenty20 206, 207, 214, 215
  v United Arab Emirates 186
  v United States of America 186
  v West Indies 42, 64, 80, 110–11, 164, 186
  women's one-day international 246
  women's Test 244
  women's Twenty20 248, 249
  youth Test 250
  v Zimbabwe 64, 85, 132, 186
Nicol, Rob 167
Nimbalkar, Bhausaheb 220
Nitschke, Shelley 248, 249
Noble, Monty 21, 39, 89
Nondescripts 234

Noreiga, Jack 82
Northamptonshire 219, 224, 234
Nottinghamshire 219
Nourse, Dudley 75, 91
Ntini, Makhaya 38, 73, 74, 91, 93, 101, 130, 134, 137, 147, 173, 191, 193

O

O'Brien, Iain 145
O'Brien, Kevin 153, 156, 197
O'Brien, Niall 213
Obuya, Collins 198
Odoyo, Thomas 198
Odumbe, Maurice 177
Ojha, Pragyan 240
Old, Chris 39
Oldfield, Bert 43
Olonga, Henry 40, 201
Omar, Javed 169
one-day international cricket
  Afghanistan 162, 202
  Africa XI 162, 202
  Asia XI 162, 202
  Australia 180–1
  Bangladesh 196
  batting records 153, 165, 166–9, 175, 181, 183, 185, 187, 189, 191, 193, 195, 202
  Bermuda 162, 202
  bowling records 165, 170–3, 181, 183, 185, 187, 189, 191, 193, 195, 203
  Canada 162, 163, 202, 203
  East Africa 162, 202
  England 182–3
  fielding records 174
  Hong Kong 162, 202
  ICC World XI 162, 202
  India 184–5
  Ireland 197
  Kenya 198
  Namibia 162, 202
  Netherlands 199
  New Zealand 186–7
  Scotland 200
  South Africa 190–1
  Sri Lanka 192–3
  United Arab Emirates 162, 202
  United States of America 162, 202
  West Indies 194–5
  wicketkeeping records 174
  women's 246–7
  youth 251
  Zimbabwe 201
Oram, Jacob 156, 187, 215
Otieno, Kennedy 198
Oxford University 219

P

Pakistan
  v Afghanistan 189
  v Australia 16, 52, 68, 120–1, 165, 188
  v Bangladesh 19, 68, 84, 144, 188
  v Canada 188
  domestic team records 218, 219
  v England 56, 68, 114–15, 188
  v Hong Kong 188
  ICC Champions Trophy 161
  ICC World Cup 152, 153, 159
  v India 21, 60, 68, 112–13, 188
  v Ireland 188
  v Kenya 188
  v Namibia 188
  v Netherlands 188
  v New Zealand 12, 64, 68, 116–17, 188
  one-day international 162, 163, 165, 188–9
  v Scotland 188

v South Africa 68, 72, 137, 188
v Sri Lanka 68, 76, 124–5, 188
Test records 12, 68–71, 112–13, 114–15, 116–17, 120–1, 122–3, 124–5, 137, 138
Twenty20 206, 207, 214, 215
v United Arab Emirates 188
v West Indies 14, 18, 21, 68, 80, 122–3, 188
women's one-day international 246
women's Test 244
women's Twenty20 248
youth Test 250
youth World Cup 251
v Zimbabwe 68, 85, 138, 188
Pakistan Railways 218
Palmer, Joey 41
Pandey, Manish 239
Papua New Guinea
  ICC Trophy 176, 177
Parker, Charlie 224, 227
Parks, Jim 229
Parore, Adam 67, 97
partnership records 48–9, 55, 158, 212, 213, 223, 233, 241
Pascoe, Len 171
Passailaigue, Charles 223
Patel, Dipak 132
Patel, Jasubhai 106
Patel, Munaf 240, 241
Pathan, Irfan 131, 143, 211, 240
Pathan, Yusuf 237, 239
Pathirana, Sachith 251
Paynter, Eddie 26
Peake, Clinton 250
Peate, Ted 225
Peel, Bobby 13
Peiris, Chathura 251
Perks, Reg 222
Peterson, Robin 25
Petherick, Peter 40
Phillips, Ricey 226
Pietersen, Kevin 102, 149, 169, 208, 212, 213, 214, 215
Pocock, Pat 226, 227
Pollard, Kieron 194, 239
Pollock, Graeme 24, 73, 93, 231
Pollock, Peter 74, 93, 101
Pollock, Shaun 30, 34, 46, 73, 74, 75, 91, 101, 130, 134, 137, 139, 170, 172, 191, 193, 202, 232, 233
Ponsford, Bill 48, 55, 89, 220, 221, 223
Ponting, Ricky 24, 26, 27, 44, 48, 53, 55, 92, 93, 99, 104, 105, 107, 121, 129, 141, 148, 154, 155, 158, 159, 160, 161, 165, 166, 174, 180, 181, 202, 231
Porterfield, William 197
Powell, Daren 135
Prasanna, Erpalli 62, 107, 119
Prashad, Paul 177
Price, Ray 141, 142, 215
Prince, Ashwell 19
Pringle, Chris 117
Prior, Matt 43, 213
Procter, Mike 220, 231
Pujara, Cheteshwar 223
Pune Warriors 238
Pushpakumara, Ravindra 136

Q

Qadir, Abdul 70, 115, 121, 123, 226
Qasim, Iqbal 70, 113, 121
Queensland 237
Quetta Bears 235

R

Rae, Allan 49
Rafique, Mohammad 143, 144, 148
Rahane, Ajinkya 221
Raina, Suresh 209, 239, 241
Raj, Mithali 247
Raja, Wasim 123
Rajapaksa, Bhanuka 251
Rajasthan Royals 234, 237, 238, 239
Ramadhin, Sonny 39, 95, 111
Ramdin, Denesh 83
Ramprakash, Mark 220, 223
Ranatunga, Arjuna 77, 79, 125, 128, 193
Ranjane, Vasant 227
Rao, Joginder 227
Ratnayake, Rumesh 78
Rawalpindi Rams 234
Raza, Hasan 250
Razzaq, Abdul 19, 189
Razzaq, Abdur 196
Read, Walter 32
Reeve, Dermot 157
Reid, Bruce 181
Reid, John F. 65
Reid, John R. 64, 65, 67, 101
Rhodes, Jonty 45, 174, 191
Rhodes, Steve 233
Rhodes, Wilfred 47, 89, 224, 226, 227, 229
Rice, Clive 219, 233
Richards, Viv 17, 28, 30, 81, 83, 94, 95, 99, 108, 109, 122, 123, 154, 164, 168, 169, 175, 194, 195, 231
Richardson, Dave 75
Richardson, Richie 28, 31, 81, 83, 99
Richardson, Tom 226
Richardson, Vic 44, 55
Roach, Kemar 148, 157
Roberts, Andy 82, 109, 157, 158, 171
Robinson, Mark 222
Rolls, Rebecca 246
Rolton, Karen 246, 247
Romaine, Irving 202
Rowe, Lawrence 26, 27, 69, 111
Roy, Pankaj 61, 118
Royal Challengers Bangalore 237, 238, 239
Rudolph, Jacques 26
Rumsey, Fred 232
runs see batting
Russell, Jack 42, 59
Rutherford, Ken 67
Rylott, Arnold 225

S

Saha, Wriddhiman 241
Sajjad, Aamer 223
Sajjad, Pervez 36, 70, 117
Saleh, Rajin 196
Samaraweera, Thilan 48, 77, 125, 135, 146
Sammy, Darren 148, 212
Sandham, Andy 26
Sangakkara, Kumar 19, 48, 49, 77, 79, 124, 125, 126, 127, 129, 134, 135, 136, 146, 160, 166, 192, 193, 202, 208, 212, 213, 218, 223, 235, 239
Sanghvi, Rahul 233
Santokie, Krishmar 236
Sarkar, Hannan 32
Sarwan, Ramnaresh 15, 19, 32, 130, 135, 142, 148, 158
Satterthwaite, Amy 248
Saurashtra 230
Schiferli, Edgar 199
Schoonheim, Rene 177
scores records 14, 127
Scotland
  ICC Trophy 176

ICC World Cup 153, 159
v Namibia 234
one-day international 162, 200
Twenty20 207, 214
women's one-day international 246
Sedgwick, Herbert 227
Sehwag, Virender 30, 43, 45, 60, 61, 107, 112, 113, 117, 126, 133, 167, 178, 184, 212, 231, 239
Shackleton, Derek 224, 225
Shah, Owais 235, 241
Shah, Sajjida 246
Shahzad, Ahmed 251
Shahzad, Mohammad 202
Sharif, Mohammad 218
Sharma, Ajay 221
Sharma, Chetan 157
Sharma, Rohit 209, 213, 221, 239
Shastri, Ravi 25, 32
Shaw, Alfred 227
Shaw, Arthur 10
Shehzad, Ahmed 251
Shenwari, Samiullah 203
Shepherd, David 159
Sherman, Thomas 225
Sherwell, Percy 43, 75
Sialkot Stallions 234, 237
Sidebottom, Ryan 97
Silva, Amal 43, 79
Simmons, Phil 171
Simpson, Bobby 45, 49, 55, 98, 107
Sims, A. 223
Sinclair, Matthew 46
Sinclair, Mathew 26
Sind 218
Singh, Bhupinder 223
Singh, Gursharan 45
Singh, Harbhajan 34, 38, 62, 107, 119, 126, 131, 133, 185, 240, 241
Singh, R.P. 240
Singh, Yajuvindra 44, 63
Singh, Yuvraj 25, 185, 208, 209
Smith, Dwayne 209, 212, 213
Smith, Graeme 19, 21, 48, 73, 75, 90, 91, 100, 101, 130, 137, 147, 159, 191, 213, 215
Smith, Ian 32, 42, 43, 67, 118
Smith, Robin 182
Smith, Steven 213
Smits, Jeroen 199
Snedden, Martin 156
Snow, John 95
Sobers, Garfield 25, 26, 27, 29, 36, 46, 47, 80, 81, 82, 83, 95, 109, 122, 123, 220
Sohail, Aamer 188
Somerset 218, 231, 234, 237
South Africa
v Australia 16, 24, 52, 72, 92–3, 190, 191, 230
v Bangladesh 72, 84, 147, 190, 191
v Canada 190
v England 14, 15, 18, 20, 21, 56, 72, 90–1, 190, 218
ICC Champions Trophy 160, 161
ICC World Cup 152, 153, 159
v India 18, 60, 72, 133, 190
v Ireland 190
v Kenya 190
v Netherlands 190, 191
v New Zealand 64, 72, 100–1, 190
one-day international 162, 163, 164, 190–1
v Pakistan 68, 72, 73, 137, 190
v Scotland 190
v Sri Lanka 72, 76, 134, 190

Test records 12, 72–5, 100–1, 130, 133, 134, 137, 139, 147
Twenty20 206, 207, 214, 215
v United Arab Emirates 190
v West Indies 19, 72, 80, 130, 190
women's one-day international 246
women's Test 244
women's Twenty20 248, 249
youth Test 250
v Zimbabwe 72, 85, 139, 190
South Australia 218
South Western Districts 230
Southee, Tim 215, 237
Southern Province 218
Spofforth, Fred 38, 41, 225
Sri Lanka
v Australia 52, 76, 192, 193, 237
v Bangladesh 28, 76, 84, 146, 192
v Bermuda 192
v Canada 192
v England 56, 76, 127, 192, 193
ICC Champions Trophy 160, 161
ICC Trophy 176
ICC World Cup 152, 153
v India 19, 43, 60, 76, 126, 192, 193, 218
v Ireland 192
v Kenya 192
v Netherlands 192, 193, 230
v New Zealand 64, 65, 76, 128, 192
one-day international 162, 163, 192–3
v Pakistan 68, 76, 124–5, 192
v Scotland 192
v South Africa 72, 76, 135, 192, 193
Test records 12, 76–9, 124–5, 126, 127, 128, 129, 134, 135, 136, 146
Twenty20 206, 207, 214, 215, 234
v United Arab Emirates 192
v West Indies 25, 76, 80, 135, 192, 193
women's one-day international 246
women's Test 244
women's Twenty20 248
youth Test 250
v Zimbabwe 76, 85, 136, 192, 193, 230
Sri Lanka Air 234, 237
Srikkanth, Kris 44, 165
Srinath, Javagal 34, 62, 131, 133, 156, 185, 227
Srivastava, Tanmay 251
Staple, Richard 203
Statham, Brian 41, 58, 91
Stewart, Alec 39, 42, 57, 59, 96, 97, 115, 140, 169, 182, 183
Stewart, Mickey 228
Steyn, Dale 74, 101, 133, 147
Sthalekar, Lisa 247, 249
Stirling, Paul 197
Stollmeyer, Jeffrey 49
Stoute, Kevin 233
Strang, Bryan 139
Strang, Paul 85, 132, 140
Strauss, Andrew 59, 103, 115, 153, 183
Streak, Heath 13, 85, 131, 132, 136, 138, 140, 141, 142, 175, 201
Stuart, Anthony 81
Stuart, Colin 142
Styris, Scott 160, 235

Sugwekar, Shantanu 221
Sullivan, John 232
Suppiah, Arul 237
Surrey 219, 226, 227, 230
Sussex 227, 237
Sutcliffe, Bert 119
Sutcliffe, Herbert 26, 49, 57, 89, 97, 119, 221, 222
Swann, Graeme 115, 149, 215
Symcox, Pat 48
Symonds, Andrew 214, 239

T
Tait, Shaun 233
Tamhane, Naren 63
Tamil Nadu 218
Tanvir, Sohail 237, 240
Tasmania 218, 237
Tate, Maurice 226, 229
Tattersall, Roy 223
Tayfield, Hugh 74, 91, 93, 101
Taylor, Bob 42, 59, 228
Taylor, Bruce 66, 111
Taylor, Claire 246, 247
Taylor, Herbie 75, 91
Taylor, Jerome 135, 236
Taylor, Mark 44, 53, 55, 121
Taylor, Ross 67, 132, 215, 234, 235
Taylor, Sarah 249
Taylor, Stefanie 249
Tendulkar, Sachin 24, 27, 28, 31, 33, 49, 61, 63, 102, 103, 106, 107, 118, 119, 126, 131, 133, 143, 153, 154, 155, 158, 166, 167, 168, 169, 174, 175, 184, 185, 231, 233, 239, 240
Tennyson, Lionel 13
Test cricket
all-round records 46–7
Australian records 12, 52–5, 88, 89, 104–5, 106–7, 120–1, 129, 141, 148
Bangladeshi records 12, 16, 84, 85, 143, 144, 145, 146, 147, 148, 149
batting records 24–33
bowling records 34–41
English records 12, 56–9, 88–9, 94–5, 96–7, 102–3, 114–15, 127, 149
fielding records 44–5
ground records 22–3
Indian records 12, 60–3, 102–3, 106–7, 108–9, 112–13, 118–19, 126, 131, 133, 143
New Zealand records 12, 64–7, 96–7, 100–1, 104–5, 110–11, 116–17, 118–19, 128, 132
Pakistani records 12, 68–71, 112–13, 114–15, 116–17, 120–1, 122–3, 124–5, 137, 138
partnership records 48–9
South African 12, 72–5, 100–1, 130, 133, 134, 137, 139, 147
Sri Lankan 12, 76–9, 124–5, 126, 127, 128, 129, 134, 135, 136, 146
team records 12–21
West Indian records 12, 13, 16, 17, 80–3, 94–5, 108–9, 110–11, 122–3, 130, 135, 142, 148
wicketkeeping records 42–3
women's 244–5
youth 250
Zimbabwean records 12, 85, 131, 132, 136, 139, 140, 141, 142
Tharanga, Upal 158, 175, 192

Thomas, Alfonso 236
Thomson, Jeff 99
Thorpe, Graham 57, 59
Tikolo, Steve 198
Tillakaratne, Hashan 44, 77, 79, 125, 135
Titans 234
Titmus, Fred 224, 229
Toshack, Ernie 36
Trescothick, Marcus 127, 149, 183, 250
Trinidad 219
Trinidad and Tobago 234
women's one-day international 246
Tripura 234
Trivedi, Siddharth 241
Trott, Albert 37, 227
Trott, Jonathan 48, 149, 167, 169, 182
Troup, Gary 111
Trueman, Fred 14, 35, 41, 58, 95, 103
Trumble, Hugh 21, 39, 41, 89
Trumper, Victor 28, 52, 223
Tsotsobe, Lonwabo 171
Tudor, Alex 30
Tuffey, Daryl 117
Turner, Charlie 20, 36, 40, 226
Turner, Glenn 64, 110, 111, 168, 169, 186, 220
Twenty20 cricket
batting records 208–9, 234, 235
bowling records 210–11, 236, 237
dismissals records 212, 213
domestic 234–7
fielding records 212, 213, 215, 237
India Premier League 217, 234, 236, 237, 238–41
International 214–15
partnership records 212, 213
team records 206–7
wicketkeeping records 212, 213, 236
women's 248–9
Twose, Roger 158

U
Umar, Qasim 120
Umar, Taufeeq 19, 71, 137, 144
Underwood, Derek 58, 97, 103, 115, 222, 227, 232, 233
United Arab Emirates
ICC Trophy 176
ICC World Cup 153
one-day international 162, 202
United States of America
ICC Champions Trophy 160, 161
one-day international 162, 202

V
Vaas, Chaminda 46, 77, 78, 125, 127, 128, 129, 135,136, 146, 156, 157, 170, 171, 172, 193, 233
Valentine, Alf 111
Valthaty, Paul 239
van der Westhuizen, Louis 234, 235
van Vuuren, Rudi 203
Vaughan, Michael 21, 33, 59, 96, 127, 149, 183
Vengsarkar, Dilip 61, 103, 109, 113
Venkataraghavan, Srinivas 62, 109, 118, 119
Verity, Hedley 36, 58, 224, 225
Vermeulen, Mark 141
Vettori, Daniel 38, 46, 64,

66, 67, 97, 105, 111, 119, 128, 132, 145, 187, 203, 210
Victoria 218, 219
Vijay, Murali 239, 241
Vincent, Lou 91, 186
Viswanath, Gundappa 61, 103, 107
Vogler, Bert 75, 91
von Noortwijk, Klaas-Jan 199

W
Wadekar, Ajit 63
Wadsworth, Ken 67
Waite, Johnny 75, 101
Walcott, Clyde 29, 98
Walker, Alan 223
Walsh, Courtney 12, 31, 34, 38, 39, 41, 80, 82, 83, 99, 109, 111, 123, 130, 173, 195
Walters, Doug 27, 32, 98, 105
Warnapura, Bandula 79
Warne, Shane 17, 24, 31, 34, 35, 38, 39, 41, 46, 54, 55, 89, 93, 99, 105, 120, 121, 129, 141, 148, 157, 181, 240, 241
Warner, David 213, 235, 241
Warren, Arnold 223
Warwickshire 219, 235
Washbrook, Cyril 91
Wasim, Imad 251
Watkins, Alan 249
Watling, Bradley-John 132
Watson, Ryan 200
Watson, Shane 160, 169, 180, 181
Watts, Fraser 200
Waugh, Mark 39, 44, 53, 55, 93, 99, 154, 181
Waugh, Steve 16, 18, 27, 28, 30, 31, 33, 53, 89, 93, 99, 104, 105, 129, 141, 148, 181
Weekes, Everton 26, 29, 109
Wells, Vince 231
Wessels, Kepler 75
West Indies
v Australia 12, 15, 19, 20, 21, 52, 80, 98–9, 194
v Bangladesh 18, 80, 84, 148, 194
v Bermuda 194
v Canada 194, 195
v England 15, 56, 80, 94–5, 194
ICC Champions Trophy 160, 161
ICC World Cup 152, 153
v India 60, 80, 108–9, 194
v Ireland 194
v Kenya 194
v Netherlands 194
v New Zealand 42, 64, 80, 110–11, 164, 194
one-day international 162, 164, 194–5
v Pakistan 14, 18, 21, 68, 80, 122–3, 194
v Scotland 194, 195
v South Africa 19, 72, 80, 130, 194, 195
v Sri Lanka 25, 76, 80, 135, 194, 195
Test records 12, 13, 16, 17, 80–3, 94–5, 108–9, 110–11, 122–3, 130, 135, 142, 148
Twenty20 206, 207, 214
women's one-day international 246
women's Test 244
women's Twenty20 248, 249
youth Test 230, 250
v Zimbabwe 80, 85, 142, 194
Whelan, Heather 249

White, Cameron 209, 213, 220, 235
Whittall, Guy 132, 138, 140
Whitty, Bill 93
wicketkeeping records
Australian 55
domestic 228
English 59, 102
ICC Champions Trophy 160
ICC World Cup 158
Indian 63
New Zealand 67, 100
one-day international 174
Pakistani 71, 117, 189
South African 75
Sri Lankan 79
Test 42–3
Twenty20 212, 213, 236
West Indian 83, 99
youth one-day international 251
Wickramasinghe, Pramodya 78, 125
wides records 20
Wijesuriya, Roger 37
Willis, Bob 58, 89, 97, 103
Wilson, Betty 245
Wisden, John 224, 225
Wishart, Craig 142
women's one-day international 246–7
women's Test 244–5
women's Twenty20 248–9
Women's World Cup 246
Woodfull, Bill 55, 221
Woolley, Frank 20, 221, 222, 228, 229
Worcestershire 234
Wright, Doug 227
Wright, John 31, 64, 67, 97, 105, 119
Wyatt, Bob 36, 58

Y
Yadav, Shivlal 107
Yorkshire 219, 230
Youhana, Yousuf 165
Younis, Waqar 32, 70, 71, 115, 117, 123, 125, 138, 144, 170, 172, 173, 189, 232
Yousuf, Mohammad 19, 25, 28, 48, 69, 71, 113, 114, 115, 117, 122, 123, 138, 144, 189
Yousuf, Saleem 71
youth one-day international 251
youth Test 250
youth World Cup 251

Z
Zaidi, Ashish 250
Zimbabwe
v Australia 52, 85, 141
v Bangladesh 13, 84, 85
v England 13, 56, 85, 140
ICC Champions Trophy 161
ICC Trophy 176
ICC World Cup 152, 153, 159
v India 60, 85, 131
v New Zealand 64, 85, 132
one-day international 162, 163, 201
v Pakistan 68, 85, 138
v South Africa 72, 85, 139
v Sri Lanka 76, 85, 136
Test records 12, 85, 131, 132, 136, 139, 140, 141, 142
Twenty20 207, 214, 215
v West Indies 80, 85, 142
youth Test 250
Zondeki, Monde 139
Zoysa, Nuwan 78
Zuiderent, Bas 199

CREDITS

The publishers would like to thank the following sources for their kind permission to reproduce the pictures in this book. The page numbers for each of the photographs are listed below, giving the page on which they appear in the book.

Location indicator: (T-top, B-bottom, L-left, R-right).

Action Images: /Zahid Hussein/Reuters: 245C; /Reuters 132BL

Getty Images: 12R, 28L, 99TR, 105TL, 117BR, 185T; /Arif Ali/AFP: 116BR; /Scott Barbour: 112B; /Daniel Berehulak/IPL2010: 240BR; /Hamish Blair: 5BL, 15R, 18B, 39BR, 63L, 79BL, 99BR, 107BL, 121R, 135L, 141L, 152BR, 156BR, 158BR, 159R, 161, 162, 163BL, 165, 174TR, 191TL, 234BR; /Shaun Botterill: 6-7, 102L, 102BR, 164TR, 192BL, 200B; /Gordon Brooks/AFP: 94R; /Simon Bruty: 37R, 119BR; /Ron Case: 122BL; /Central Press: 12L, 20TL, 29TL, 35TL, 56, 88BR, 90BL, 103B, 104BR, 111T, 114BR, 119BL, 245TL; / Robert Cianflone: 55L; /Chris Cole: 58C, 71BR, 109L; /Graham Crouch: 197BR; /Lucas Dawson: 171C; /Kristian Dowling: 22, Back Endpaper; /Emmanuel Dunand/AFP: 20BL; /Duif du Toit/Gallo Images: 133BL, 143C, 147C; /Patrick Eagar: 61C; /Evening Standard: 26BL, 94BL; /Stu Forster: 67TR, 72, 84TR, 249BR; /Fox Photos: 29TR, 219BL; /Michael Fresco: 32R; /Gallo Images: 133C, 175L, 176C, 202, 212BR; /Paul Gilham: 149B; /Stefan Gosatti: 246BL; /Laurence Griffiths: 171TL, 183C; /J. A. Hampton: 16B; /Asif Hassan/AFP: 123TR; /Julian Herbert: 15L, 67L, 149L, 160BR, 170BL, 206R, 209B, 211C; /Mike Hewitt: 10-11, 23, 32L, 65TR, 79R, 93T, 140BR, 158L, 160BL, 173TL; /Hulton Archive: 17TR, 19BL, 36L, 157T, 169C; /Martin Hunter: 251; /Sajjad Hussain/AFP: 187B, 213BR, 214; /Alexander Joe/AFP: 27BR, 173B; /Hannah Johnston: 66C; /Bradley Kanaris: 17BL; /Paul Kane: 141B; /Keystone: 104BC; / Matt King: 167C, 247C; /Ross Kinnaird: 163R; /Glyn Kirk/AFP: 48TR; /Saeed Khan/AFP: 124L; /Mark Kolbe: 129C; /Christopher Lee: 211TR; /Matthew Lewis: 4BR, 92BR, 239R; /Joe Mann: 189C; /Clive Mason: 153R, 155BR, 157BL, 163BR, 176BL, 232L; /Marty Melville: 84BL, 144C, 145L; /Sandra Mu: 234BL; /Indranil Mukherjee/AFP: 83R; /David Munden/Popperfoto: 24R, 31L, 59BR, 89B, 95BR, 99BL, 107TR, 112BR, 124BR, 138B, 159TR, 189BR, 250BL, 250BR; /Adrian Murrell: 14TR, 17BR, 28R, 29BL, 39TR, 40TR, 41, 43TR, 47L, 55BR, 65C, 69BL, 70L, 71L, 83BR, 97R, 103TR, 115BL, 123BL, 127R, 168R, 170R, 172BL, 187C, 188BL, 228BL; / Mark Nolan: 142C; /Punit Paranjpe/AFP: 178-179, 209TR; /John Parkin: 190BL; /Pal Pillai/AFP: 43BL,126B, 241TR; /Popperfoto: 9, 13TL, 13BL, 21BC, 21BR, 26TL, 46, 57BL, 218BL, 228R; /Craig Prentis: 247BR; /Adam Pretty: 106BL; /Aamir Qureshi/AFP: 212BR; /Ben Radford: 47C, 66BL, 82, 88BL, 121L, 177T, 182BL, 221TL; /Mark Ralston/AFP: 31TR; /Raveendran/AFP: 237T; /Rischgitz: 38C; /Quinn Rooney: 78R, 129B, 211BR; /Clive Rose: 2, 25BR, 35BR, 78B, 130B, 140BL, 175BR, 185BR, 199B, 211L, 213BL; /STR/ AFP: 152BL; /Jewel Samad/AFP: 63TR; /Dibyangshu Sarkar/AFP: 50-51, 118BR, 241L; /Ross Setford: 101BR, 174BR; /Tom Shaw: Front Endpaper, 86-87, 90BR, 135B, 142BL, 153C, 153BR, 156BL, 169L, 203R, 206BL; /Michael Steele: 150-151, 154TL, 154B, 157R, 249L; /Rizwan Tabassum/AFP: 246BR; /Bob Thomas: 97L, 105BR, 113BL, 115T; /Bob Thomas/Popperfoto: 13BR, 20R, 27T; / Titmuss: 47B; /Topical Press Agency: 49L, 222TL; /Touchline: 65BR, 92BL, 100R, 130L, 134C, 248B; /Munir Uz Zaman/AFP: 169BR, 180BL, 196C, 196B; /Sena Vidanagama/AFP: 134BL, 146BL; /Phil Walter: 26BR, 27BL, 85, 132C, 186C; /Lakruwan Wanniarachchi/ AFP: 5B, 146C, 208TR, 210TR; /Lee Warren/Gallo Images: 4R, 145C; /William West/AFP: 96BL, 201B

Press Association Images: 33R, 40BR, 43TL, 47T, 58BR, 59TL, 81B, 91L, 97BL, 116BL, 117TL, 125BR, 219BR, 220TR, 221TR, 224BL, 226TR, 229; /AP: 108BL, 136C, 136B, 237R; /Shakil Adil/AP: 42, 68, 122BR; /Gemunu Amarasinghe/AP: 44T, 76, 120BR; / Matthew Ashton: 177BR, 200R, 233L; /Sayyid Azim/AP: 198R; /Mark Baker/AP: 174BL; /Kate Blatchford: 128B; /Jon Buckle: 38L, 62R, 63BR, 93BR; /Graham Chadwick: 30R, 231TR; /K. M. Chaudary/AP: 138TR, 144BR; /Thalia Codrington/AP: 183BL; /Gareth Copley: 48BL, 73L, 74C, 159BL; /Sherwin Crasto/AP: 131R; /Bikas Das/AP: 60, 147B, 191BR; /Saurabh Das/AP: 216-217; /David Davies: 191C, 192R; /Anthony Devlin: 207BL, 210BL, 236BR; /Matthew Fearn: 75BR; /Anna Gowthorpe: 30L; /Rob Griffith/AP: 55TR, 195BR; /Laurence Griffiths: 38R, 227BR; /Themba Hadebe/AP: 131B, 139C, 155T, 172R, 181BR, 186BL, 186BR, 190B, 208BL, 230BR, 238, 239L; /Tom Hevezi/AP: 25TL, 75L; /Steve Holland/AP: 180BR; /Owen Humphreys: 189T; /Eranga Jayawardena/AP: 19TL, 24L, 49BR, 126C, 168B, 192BR, 193C; /Rajanish Kakade/AP: 77BR; /Mark Kolbe: 167BR; /Andres Leighton/AP: 19BR, 37L, 204-205, 215C; /Claire Mackintosh: 83TL; /Tony Marshall: 166BR, 183B, 207R, 221BR, 232R, 248BR; /Brendan Monks: 44B; /Peter Morrison/AP: 199C; /Rebecca Naden: 33L, 45T, 65BL, 110BL, 194BL, 201L, 233R; /Anjum Naveed/AP: 226BL; /Phil Noble: 230BL; / Phil O'Brien: 233C; /Gurinder Osan/AP: 79TR, 125TL, 184B, 184BR, 188BR; /Aijaz Rahi/AP: 4TR, 5L, 21TR, 77B, 182B, 197B, 236L, 242-243; /Rick Rycroft/AP: 235R; /S&G and Barratts: 14BL, 14BR, 25BL, 26TR, 29BR, 35BR, 36R, 39TL, 40BL, 45B, 49TR, 52, 54BL, 57R, 58BL, 61BR, 62B, 70R, 71TR, 73R, 80, 81R, 98, 100B, 101T, 106R, 109R, 113TR, 114BL, 118BL, 120BL, 164B, 194BR, 195L, 220BL, 222B, 223TL, 223R, 224R, 225L, 225R, 227TL, 228BR, 231BR, 244BR; /Ross Setford/AP: 81BL, 110BR, 111BR, 128C, 215B; /Aman Sharma/AP: 18T, 69BR, 155BL, 166BL, 181TR, 207BR, 231BL, 235L, 240L; /Eric Shaw: 95BL; /Neal Simpson: 54R, 74BL, 137L, 137B, 244BL; /Gautam Singh/AP: 53BR, 61R, 143BR; /Lynne Sladky/AP: 203C; /Michael Steele: 67BR, 127B, 198BL; / Paul Thomas/AP: 187TR; /Topham Picturepoint: 53R, 89T; /Grant Treeby/World Sports Pictures: 75TR; /Rui Vieira: 91T; /Matthew Vincent: 218R; /Phil Walter/AP: 16T, 104BL; /Peter Wilcock: 139B

Topfoto.co.uk: 34, 37BL

Every effort has been made to acknowledge correctly and contact the source and/copyright holder of each picture, and Carlton Books Limited apologises for any unintentional errors or omissions, which will be corrected in further editions of this book.

ABOUT THE AUTHOR

Chris Hawkes is a former youth international cricketer who spent three seasons as a full-time professional with Leicestershire CCC (1990–92). Since retiring as a player, he has worked as a sports writer and editor as well as making several appearances on radio and television as a cricket analyst. He has written several books, including *Cricket World Cup Guide 2007*, The *Official ITV Sport Rugby World Cup Guide 2007, Twenty20 Cricket Guide 2009, World Rugby Records and Winter Sports Records.* He lives in Normandy in north-western France.